Homebrew™

The Festering Season

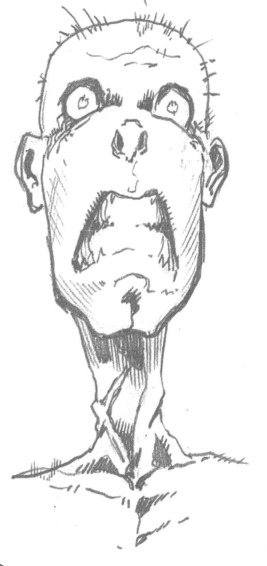

STICKMAN GRAPHICS, New York, NY

The Festering Season

Kevin Tinsley
words & colors

Tim Smith 3
art

Deborah S. Creighton
editor

Sharpfont™ & Homebrew logo
designed by Dave Sharpe

The Festering Season is entirely fictional, created solely for the purpose of entertainment. Although inspired by actual incidents, it is in no way intended to be an accurate representation of Vodou, Palo, Santeria, Catholicism, the New York City Police Department, or the world as we know it. The opinions expressed in this book are the opinions of the fictional characters alone, and are not necessarily shared by the creators, editor, or publisher. We apologize up front to those overly sensitive or rabidly politically correct individuals whom we may offend. Please keep this in mind before you harass, arrest, surveille, cast spells upon, curse, stick pins in small fetishes made in our likenesses, or otherwise violate our constitutional and civil rights.

Library of Congress Control Number: 2002093129
Hardcover ISBN: 0-9675423-1-6
Softcover ISBN: 0-9675423-2-4

Published by: Stickman Graphics
141 16th Street
Brooklyn, NY 11215-5302
www.stickmangraphics.com
stickmangraphics@stickmangraphics.com

Printed in the Canada.
10 9 8 7 6 5 4 3 2 1

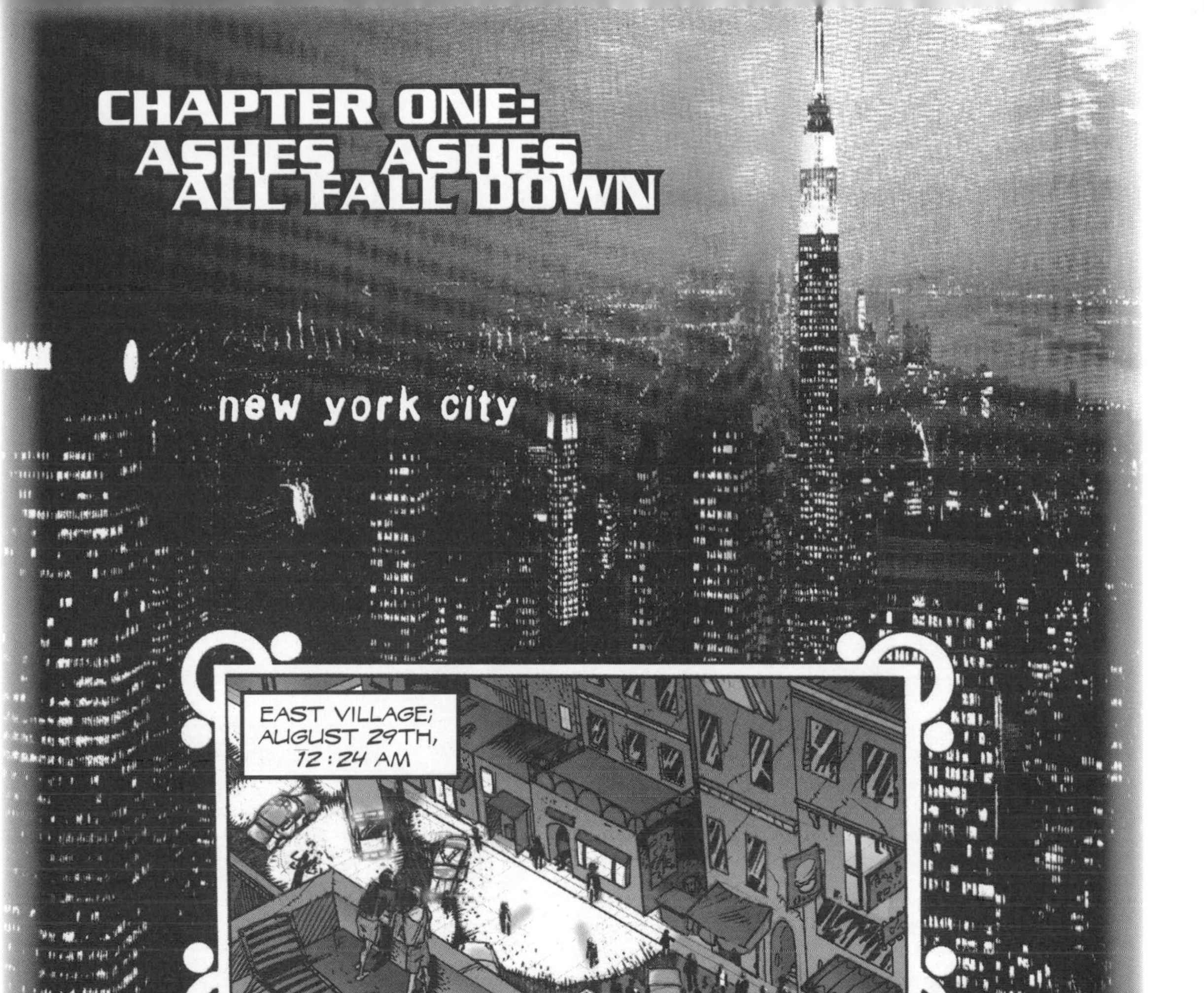

CHAPTER ONE:
ASHES ASHES
ALL FALL DOWN

new york city

EAST VILLAGE;
AUGUST 29TH,
12:24 AM

WHAT'S THE
WORD, BENSON?

THE *RAT SQUAD*
IS GONNA BE ALL
OVER *THIS* ONE,
DETECTIVE!

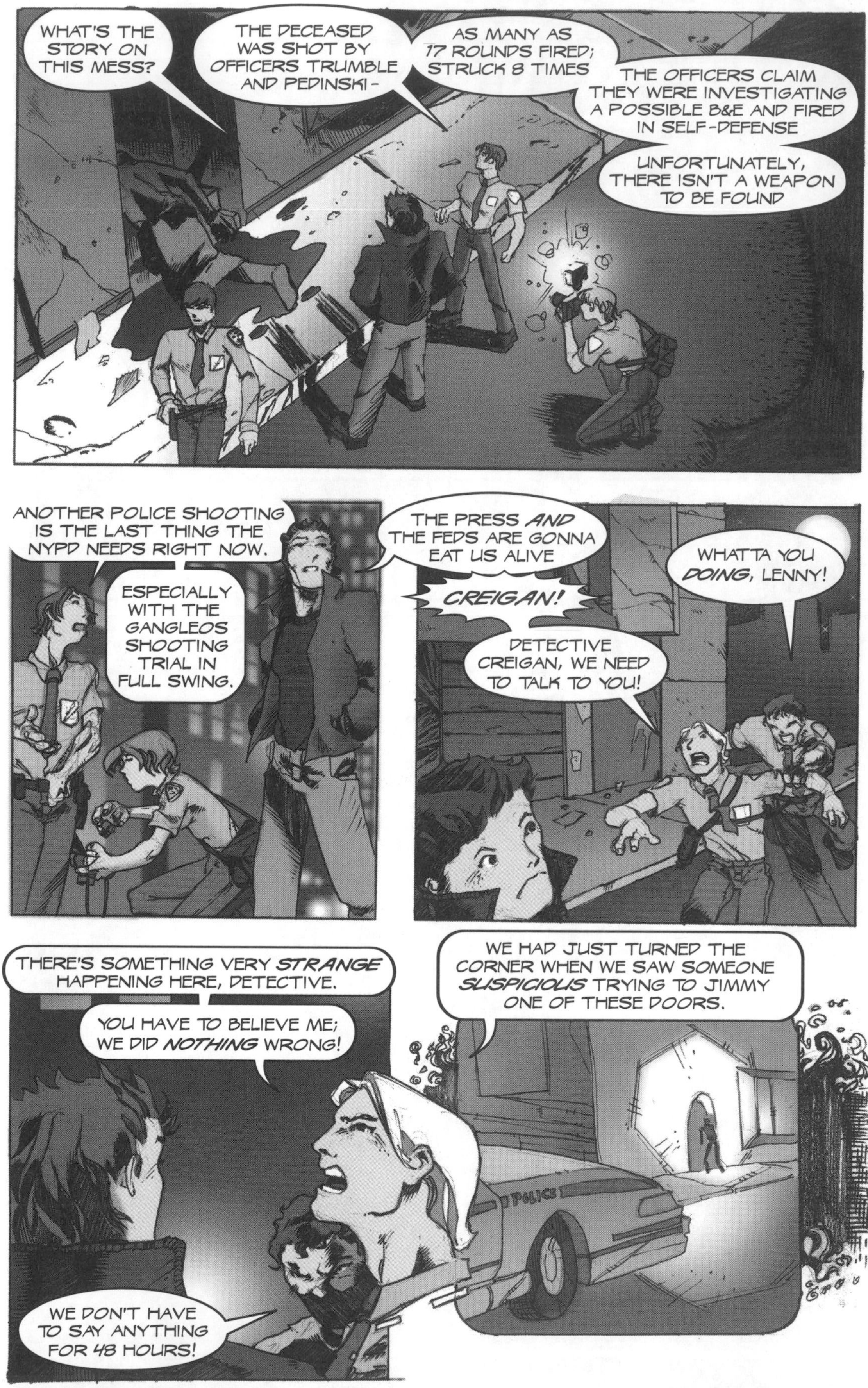
WHAT'S THE STORY ON THIS MESS?
THE DECEASED WAS SHOT BY OFFICERS TRUMBLE AND PEDINSKI -
AS MANY AS 17 ROUNDS FIRED; STRUCK 8 TIMES
THE OFFICERS CLAIM THEY WERE INVESTIGATING A POSSIBLE B&E AND FIRED IN SELF-DEFENSE
UNFORTUNATELY, THERE ISN'T A WEAPON TO BE FOUND
ANOTHER POLICE SHOOTING IS THE LAST THING THE NYPD NEEDS RIGHT NOW.
ESPECIALLY WITH THE GANGLEOS SHOOTING TRIAL IN FULL SWING.
THE PRESS *AND* THE FEDS ARE GONNA EAT US ALIVE
CREIGAN!
WHATTA YOU *DOING*, LENNY!
DETECTIVE CREIGAN, WE NEED TO TALK TO YOU!
THERE'S SOMETHING VERY *STRANGE* HAPPENING HERE, DETECTIVE.
YOU HAVE TO BELIEVE ME; WE DID *NOTHING* WRONG!
WE HAD JUST TURNED THE CORNER WHEN WE SAW SOMEONE *SUSPICIOUS* TRYING TO JIMMY ONE OF THESE DOORS.
POLICE
WE DON'T HAVE TO SAY ANYTHING FOR 48 HOURS!

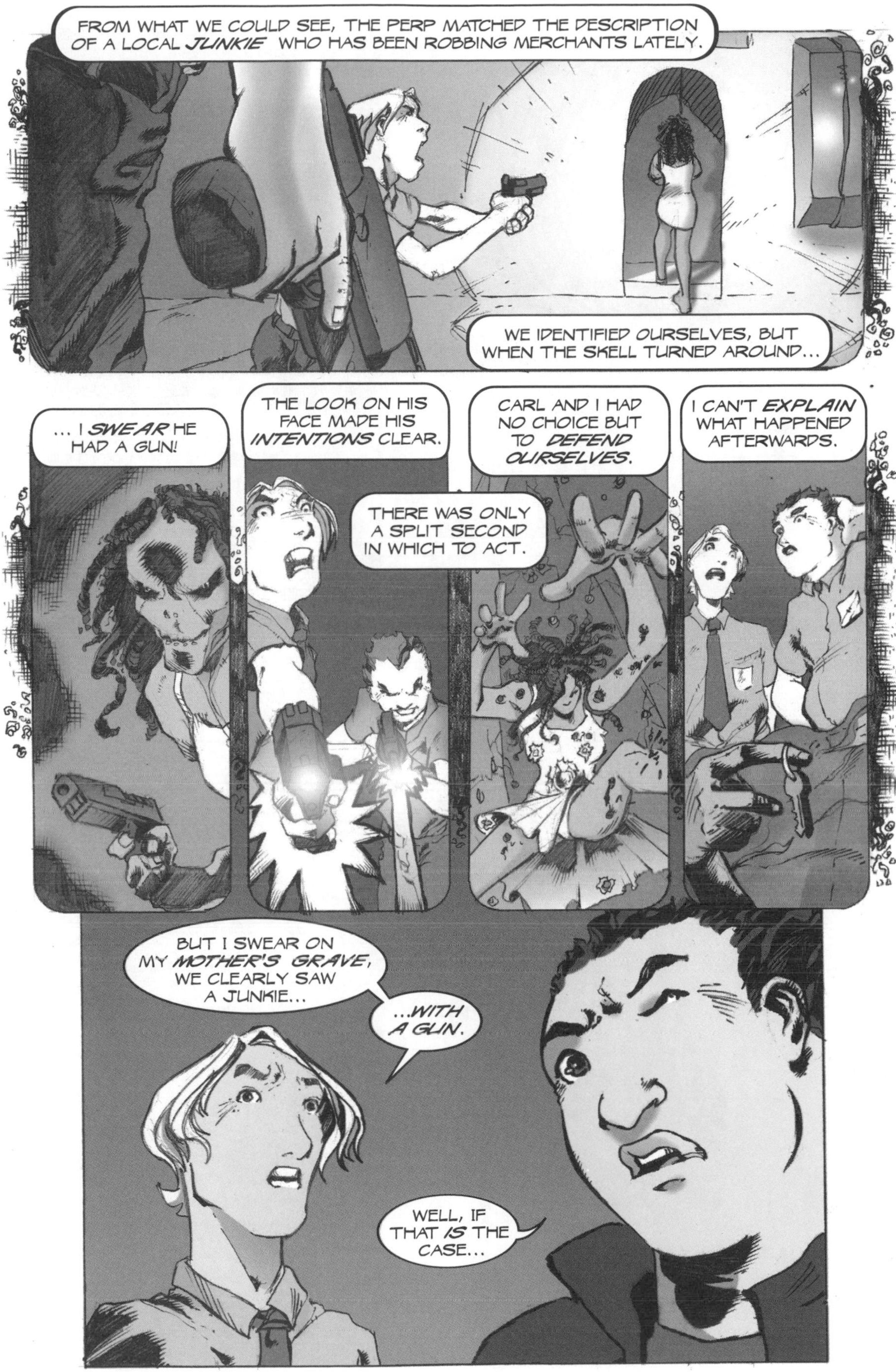
FROM WHAT WE COULD SEE, THE PERP MATCHED THE DESCRIPTION OF A LOCAL JUNKIE WHO HAS BEEN ROBBING MERCHANTS LATELY.
WE IDENTIFIED OURSELVES, BUT WHEN THE SKELL TURNED AROUND...
... I SWEAR HE HAD A GUN!
THE LOOK ON HIS FACE MADE HIS INTENTIONS CLEAR.
THERE WAS ONLY A SPLIT SECOND IN WHICH TO ACT.
CARL AND I HAD NO CHOICE BUT TO DEFEND OURSELVES.
I CAN'T EXPLAIN WHAT HAPPENED AFTERWARDS.
BUT I SWEAR ON MY MOTHER'S GRAVE, WE CLEARLY SAW A JUNKIE...
...WITH A GUN.
WELL, IF THAT IS THE CASE...

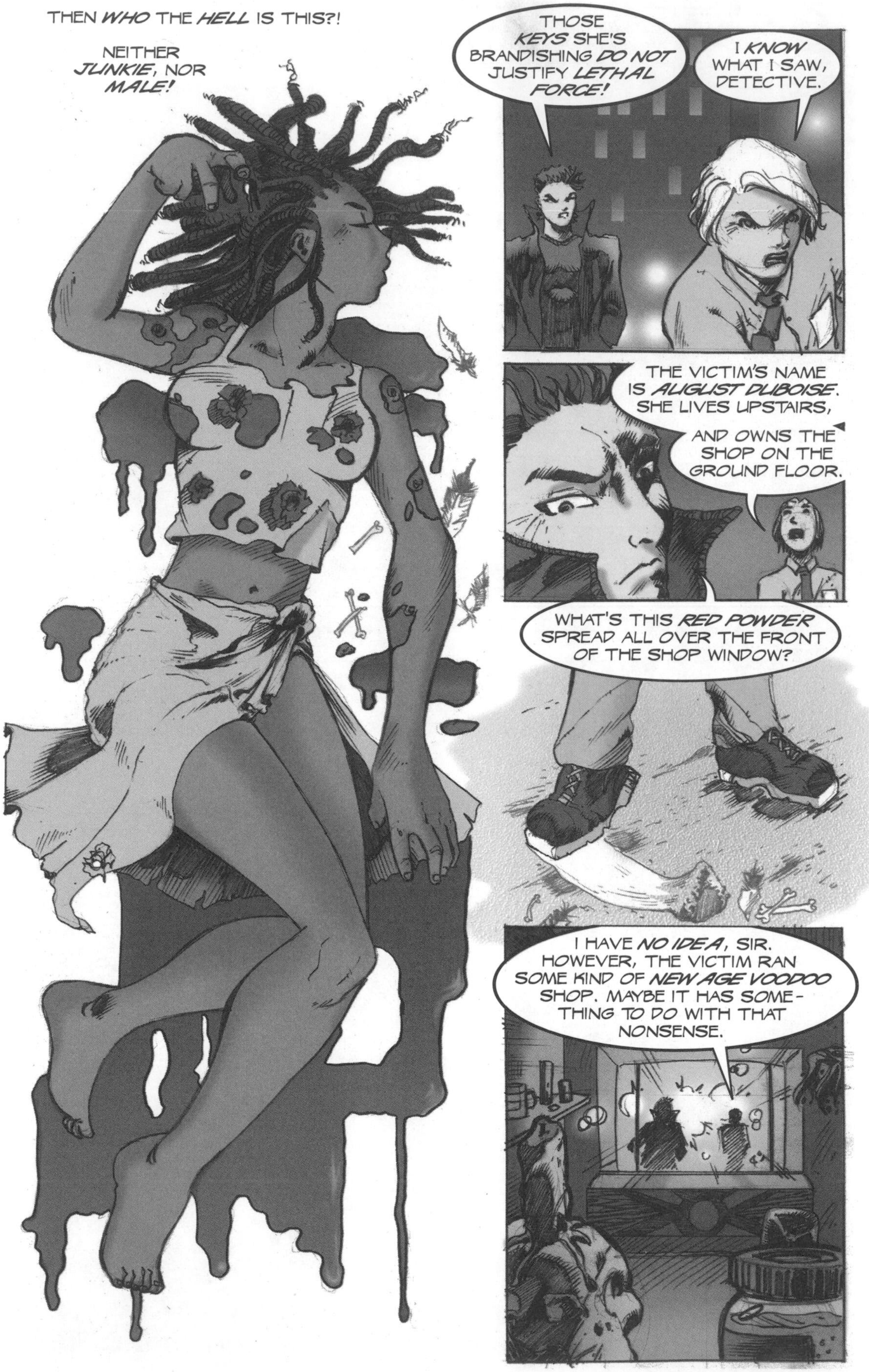

THEN *WHO* THE *HELL* IS THIS?!
NEITHER *JUNKIE*, NOR *MALE!*
THOSE *KEYS* SHE'S BRANDISHING *DO NOT* JUSTIFY *LETHAL FORCE!*
I *KNOW* WHAT I SAW, DETECTIVE.
THE VICTIM'S NAME IS *AUGUST DUBOISE*. SHE LIVES UPSTAIRS,
AND OWNS THE SHOP ON THE GROUND FLOOR.
WHAT'S THIS *RED POWDER* SPREAD ALL OVER THE FRONT OF THE SHOP WINDOW?
I HAVE *NO IDEA*, SIR. HOWEVER, THE VICTIM RAN SOME KIND OF *NEW AGE VOODOO* SHOP. MAYBE IT HAS SOMETHING TO DO WITH THAT NONSENSE.

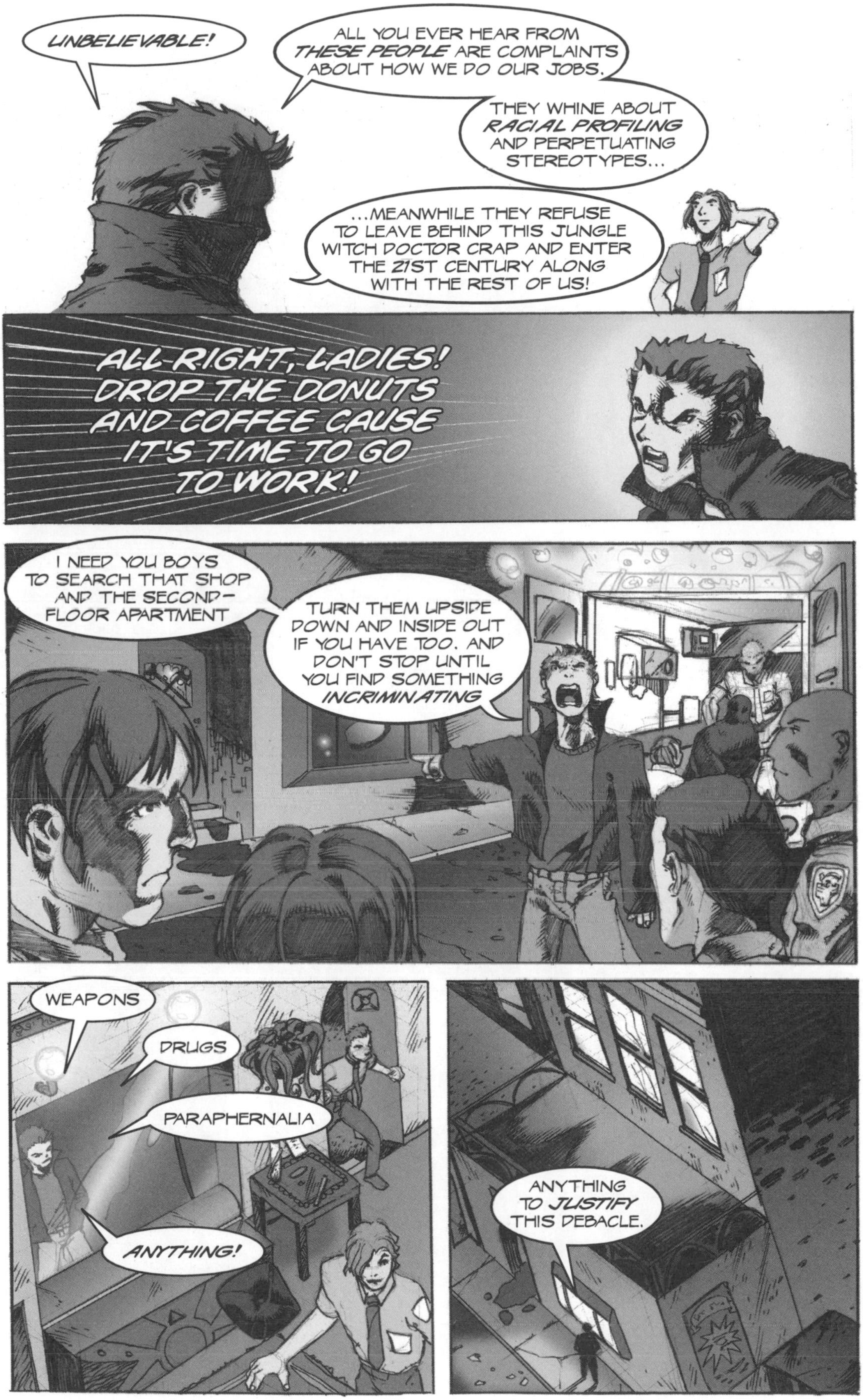
UNBELIEVABLE!
ALL YOU EVER HEAR FROM THESE PEOPLE ARE COMPLAINTS ABOUT HOW WE DO OUR JOBS.
THEY WHINE ABOUT RACIAL PROFILING AND PERPETUATING STEREOTYPES...
...MEANWHILE THEY REFUSE TO LEAVE BEHIND THIS JUNGLE WITCH DOCTOR CRAP AND ENTER THE 21ST CENTURY ALONG WITH THE REST OF US!
ALL RIGHT, LADIES! DROP THE DONUTS AND COFFEE CAUSE IT'S TIME TO GO TO WORK!
I NEED YOU BOYS TO SEARCH THAT SHOP AND THE SECOND-FLOOR APARTMENT
TURN THEM UPSIDE DOWN AND INSIDE OUT IF YOU HAVE TOO. AND DON'T STOP UNTIL YOU FIND SOMETHING INCRIMINATING
WEAPONS
DRUGS
PARAPHERNALIA
ANYTHING!
ANYTHING TO JUSTIFY THIS DEBACLE.

Haiti

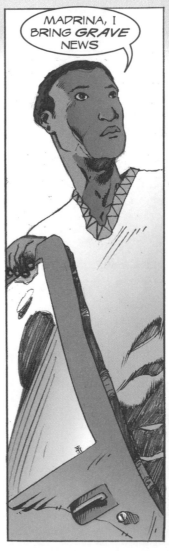

MADRINA, I BRING *GRAVE* NEWS

AS I SUSPECTED! A VEIL OF *APPREHENSION* FELL OVER US ALL LAST NIGHT

RENE'S MOTHER HAS BEEN KILLED IN SOME KIND OF *ACCIDENT!*

HER AUNT, *LUCILLE*, DEMANDS THAT SHE RETURN TO *NEW YORK* AT ONCE

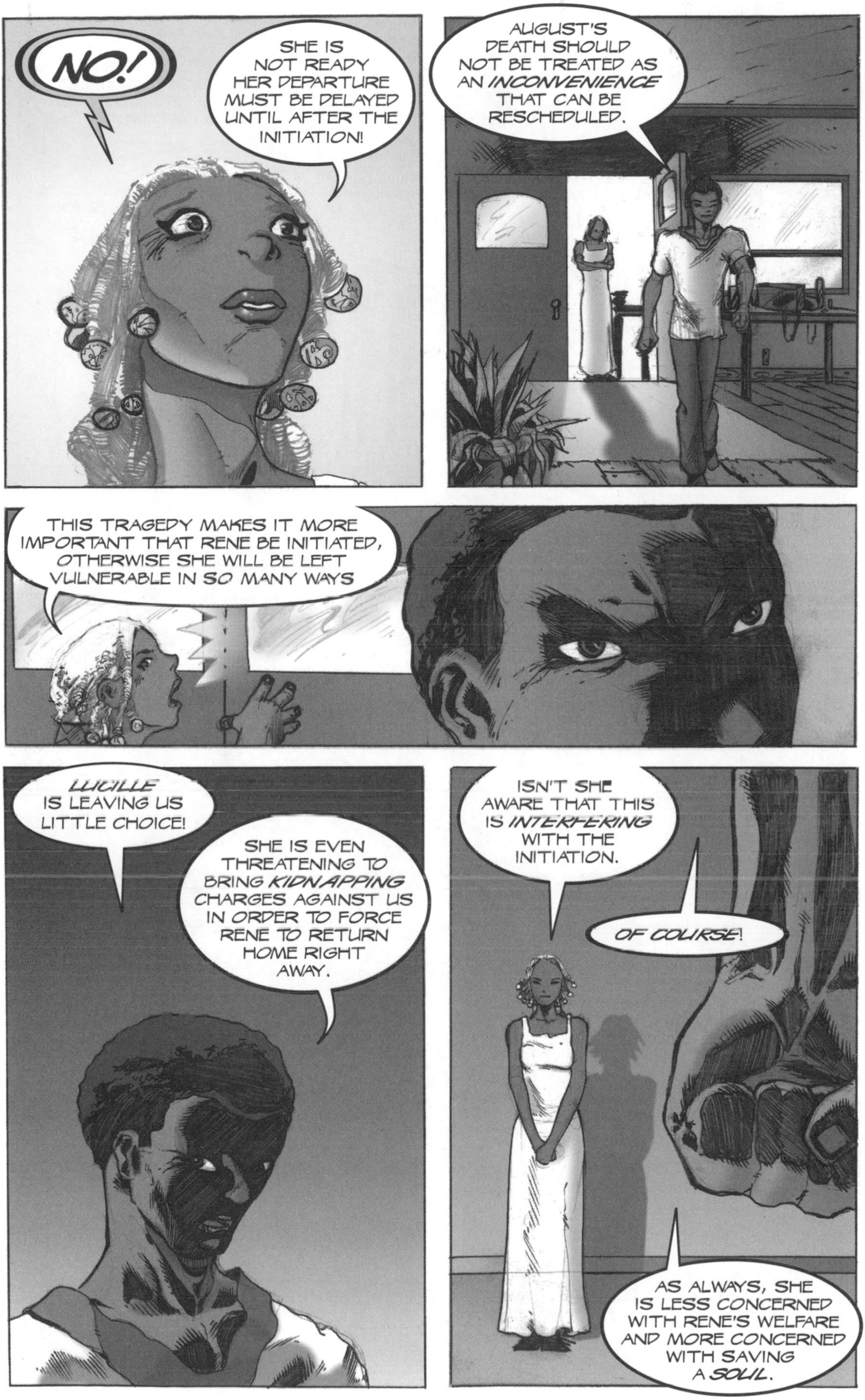
NO!
SHE IS NOT READY HER DEPARTURE MUST BE DELAYED UNTIL AFTER THE INITIATION!
AUGUST'S DEATH SHOULD NOT BE TREATED AS AN *INCONVENIENCE* THAT CAN BE RESCHEDULED.
THIS TRAGEDY MAKES IT MORE IMPORTANT THAT RENE BE INITIATED, OTHERWISE SHE WILL BE LEFT VULNERABLE IN SO MANY WAYS
LUCILLE IS LEAVING US LITTLE CHOICE!
SHE IS EVEN THREATENING TO BRING *KIDNAPPING* CHARGES AGAINST US IN ORDER TO FORCE RENE TO RETURN HOME RIGHT AWAY.
ISN'T SHE AWARE THAT THIS IS *INTERFERING* WITH THE INITIATION.
OF COURSE!
AS ALWAYS, SHE IS LESS CONCERNED WITH RENE'S WELFARE AND MORE CONCERNED WITH SAVING A *SOUL*.

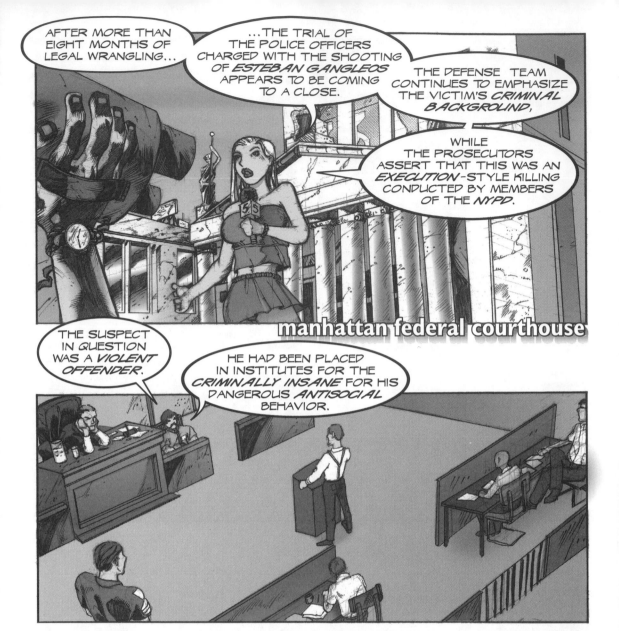

AFTER MORE THAN EIGHT MONTHS OF LEGAL WRANGLING...

...THE TRIAL OF THE POLICE OFFICERS CHARGED WITH THE SHOOTING OF *ESTEBAN GANGLEOS* APPEARS TO BE COMING TO A CLOSE.

THE DEFENSE TEAM CONTINUES TO EMPHASIZE THE VICTIM'S *CRIMINAL BACKGROUND,*

WHILE THE PROSECUTORS ASSERT THAT THIS WAS AN *EXECUTION*-STYLE KILLING CONDUCTED BY MEMBERS OF THE *NYPD.*

manhattan federal courthouse

THE SUSPECT IN QUESTION WAS A *VIOLENT OFFENDER.*

HE HAD BEEN PLACED IN INSTITUTES FOR THE *CRIMINALLY INSANE* FOR HIS DANGEROUS *ANTISOCIAL* BEHAVIOR.

HE WAS A SUSPECT IN NUMEROUS *HEINOUS* CRIMES, INCLUDING MURDER AND RAPE.

SO THAT MAKES HIS *EXECUTION* ALL RIGHT THEN, CAPTAIN?

OBJECTION!

8

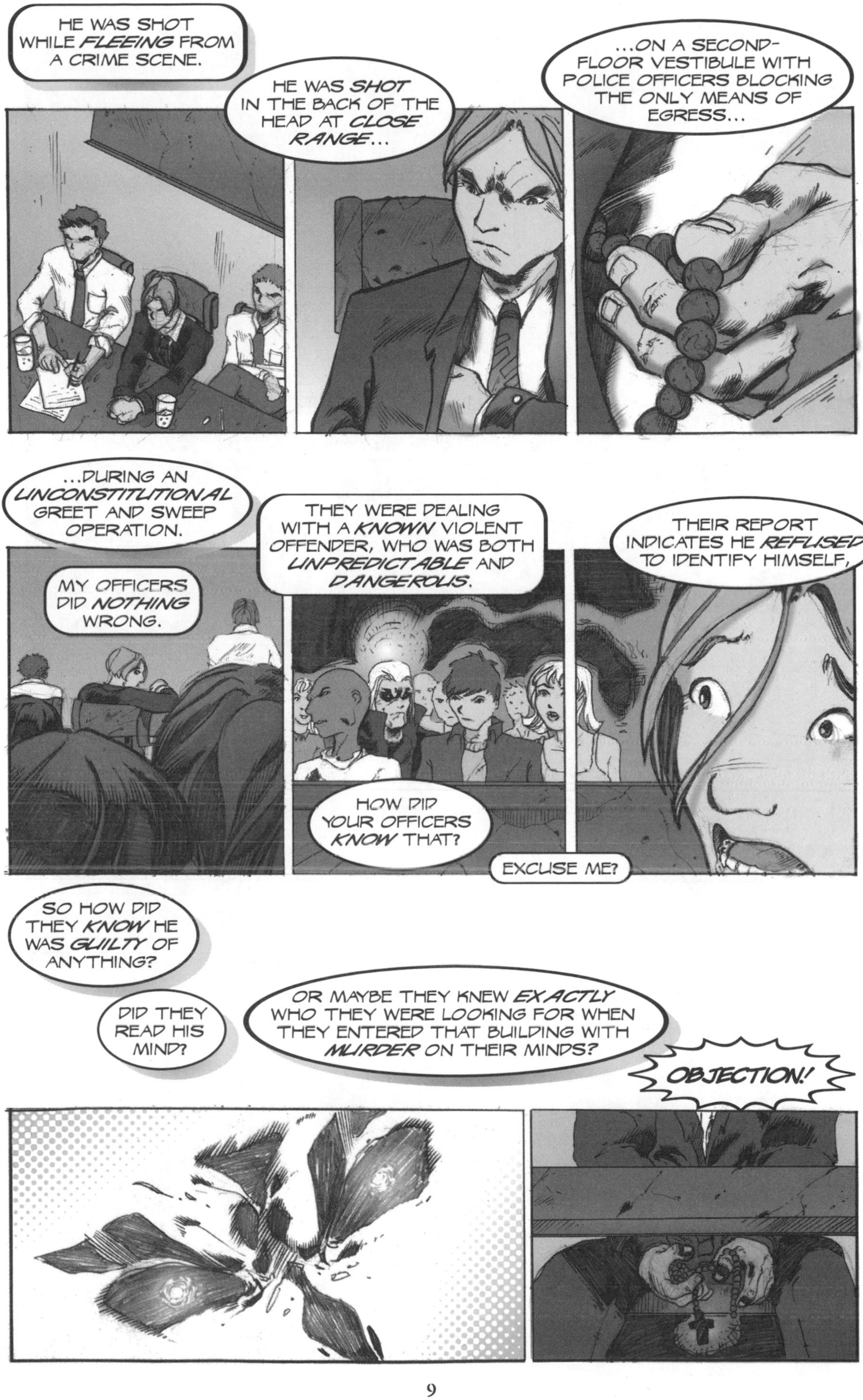
HE WAS SHOT WHILE FLEEING FROM A CRIME SCENE.
HE WAS SHOT IN THE BACK OF THE HEAD AT CLOSE RANGE...
...ON A SECOND-FLOOR VESTIBULE WITH POLICE OFFICERS BLOCKING THE ONLY MEANS OF EGRESS...
...DURING AN UNCONSTITUTIONAL GREET AND SWEEP OPERATION.
MY OFFICERS DID NOTHING WRONG.
THEY WERE DEALING WITH A KNOWN VIOLENT OFFENDER, WHO WAS BOTH UNPREDICTABLE AND DANGEROUS.
HOW DID YOUR OFFICERS KNOW THAT?
THEIR REPORT INDICATES HE REFUSED TO IDENTIFY HIMSELF,
EXCUSE ME?
SO HOW DID THEY KNOW HE WAS GUILTY OF ANYTHING?
DID THEY READ HIS MIND?
OR MAYBE THEY KNEW EXACTLY WHO THEY WERE LOOKING FOR WHEN THEY ENTERED THAT BUILDING WITH MURDER ON THEIR MINDS?
OBJECTION!

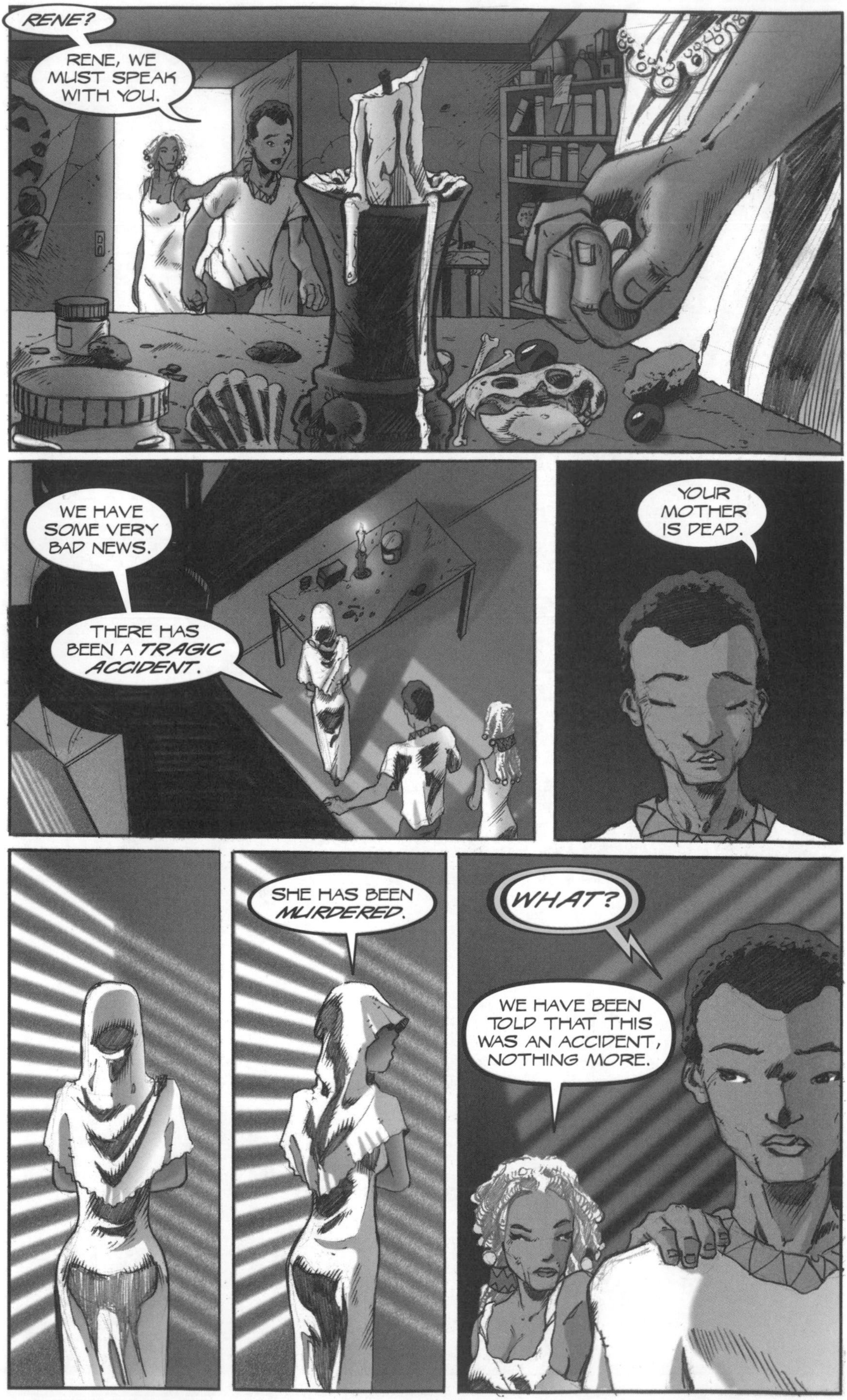
RENE?
RENE, WE MUST SPEAK WITH YOU.
WE HAVE SOME VERY BAD NEWS.
THERE HAS BEEN A *TRAGIC ACCIDENT*.
YOUR MOTHER IS DEAD.
SHE HAS BEEN *MURDERED*.
WHAT?
WE HAVE BEEN TOLD THAT THIS WAS AN ACCIDENT, NOTHING MORE.

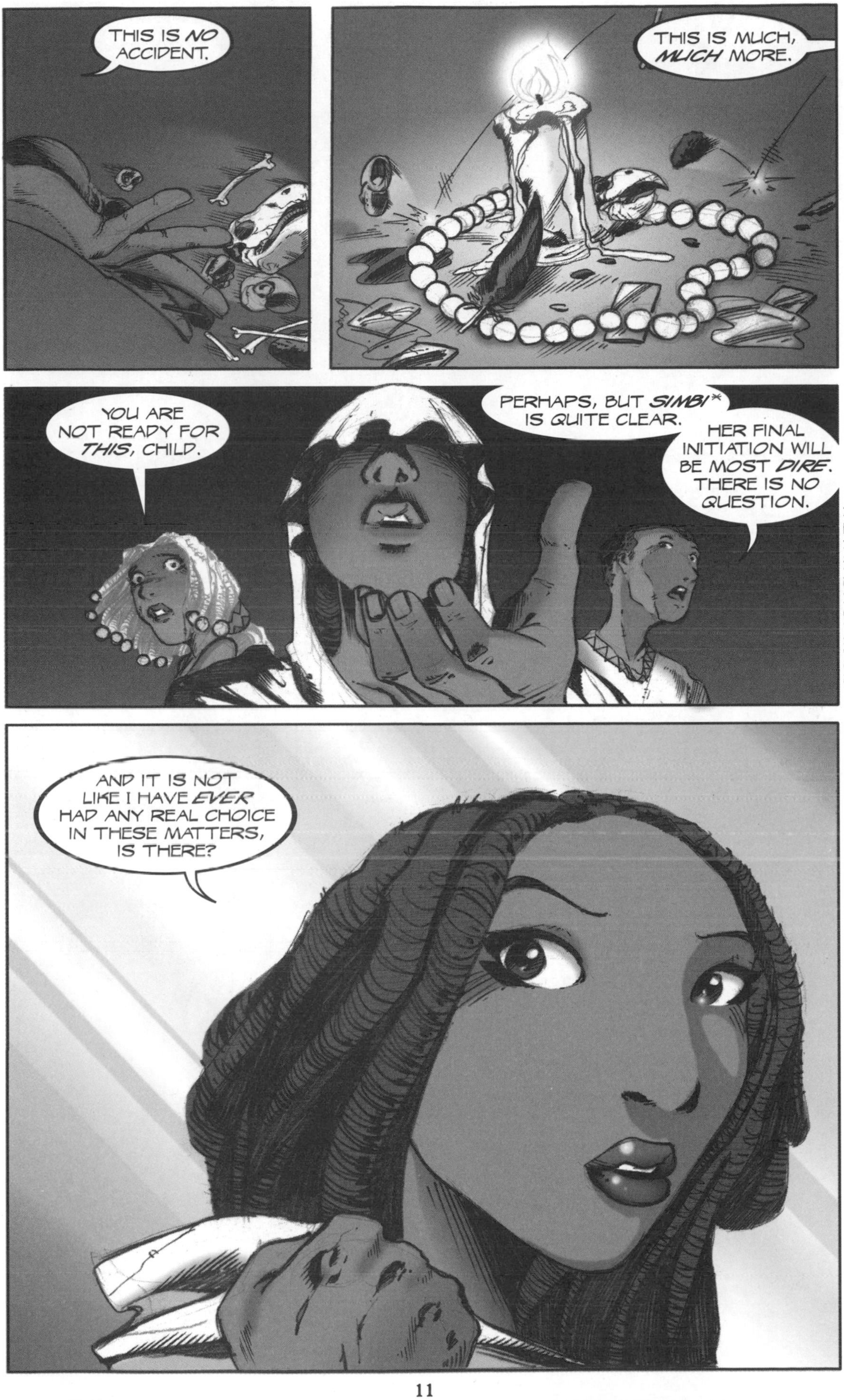
THIS IS *NO* ACCIDENT.
THIS IS MUCH, *MUCH* MORE.
YOU ARE NOT READY FOR *THIS*, CHILD.
PERHAPS, BUT *SIMBI** IS QUITE CLEAR.
HER FINAL INITIATION WILL BE MOST *DIRE*. THERE IS NO QUESTION.
AND IT IS NOT LIKE I HAVE *EVER* HAD ANY REAL CHOICE IN THESE MATTERS, IS THERE?

*THE PATRON OF MAGIC

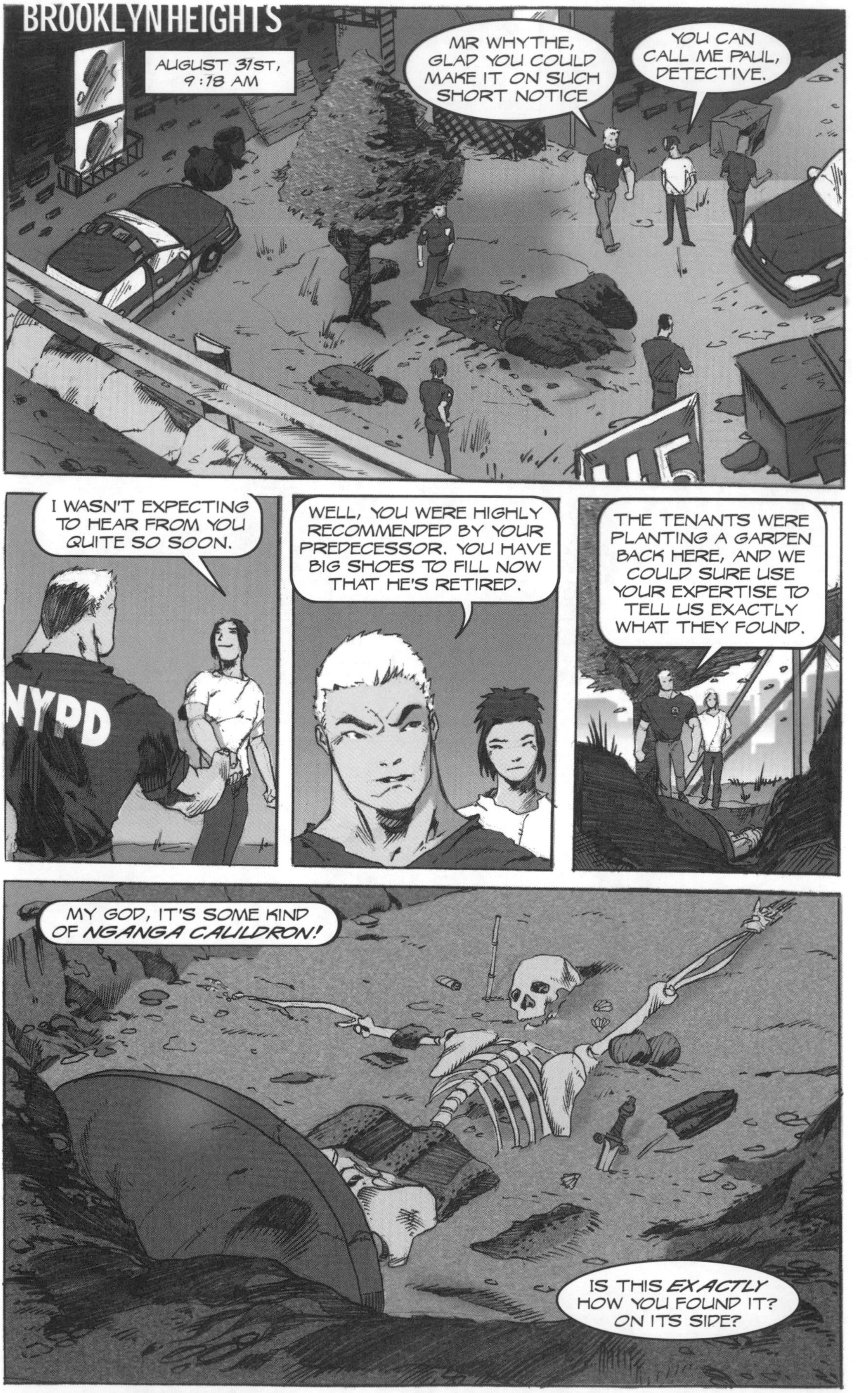
BROOKLYN HEIGHTS
AUGUST 31ST, 9:18 AM
MR WHYTHE, GLAD YOU COULD MAKE IT ON SUCH SHORT NOTICE
YOU CAN CALL ME PAUL, DETECTIVE.
I WASN'T EXPECTING TO HEAR FROM YOU QUITE SO SOON.
NYPD
WELL, YOU WERE HIGHLY RECOMMENDED BY YOUR PREDECESSOR. YOU HAVE BIG SHOES TO FILL NOW THAT HE'S RETIRED.
THE TENANTS WERE PLANTING A GARDEN BACK HERE, AND WE COULD SURE USE YOUR EXPERTISE TO TELL US EXACTLY WHAT THEY FOUND.
MY GOD, IT'S SOME KIND OF *NGANGA CAULDRON!*
IS THIS *EXACTLY* HOW YOU FOUND IT? ON ITS SIDE?

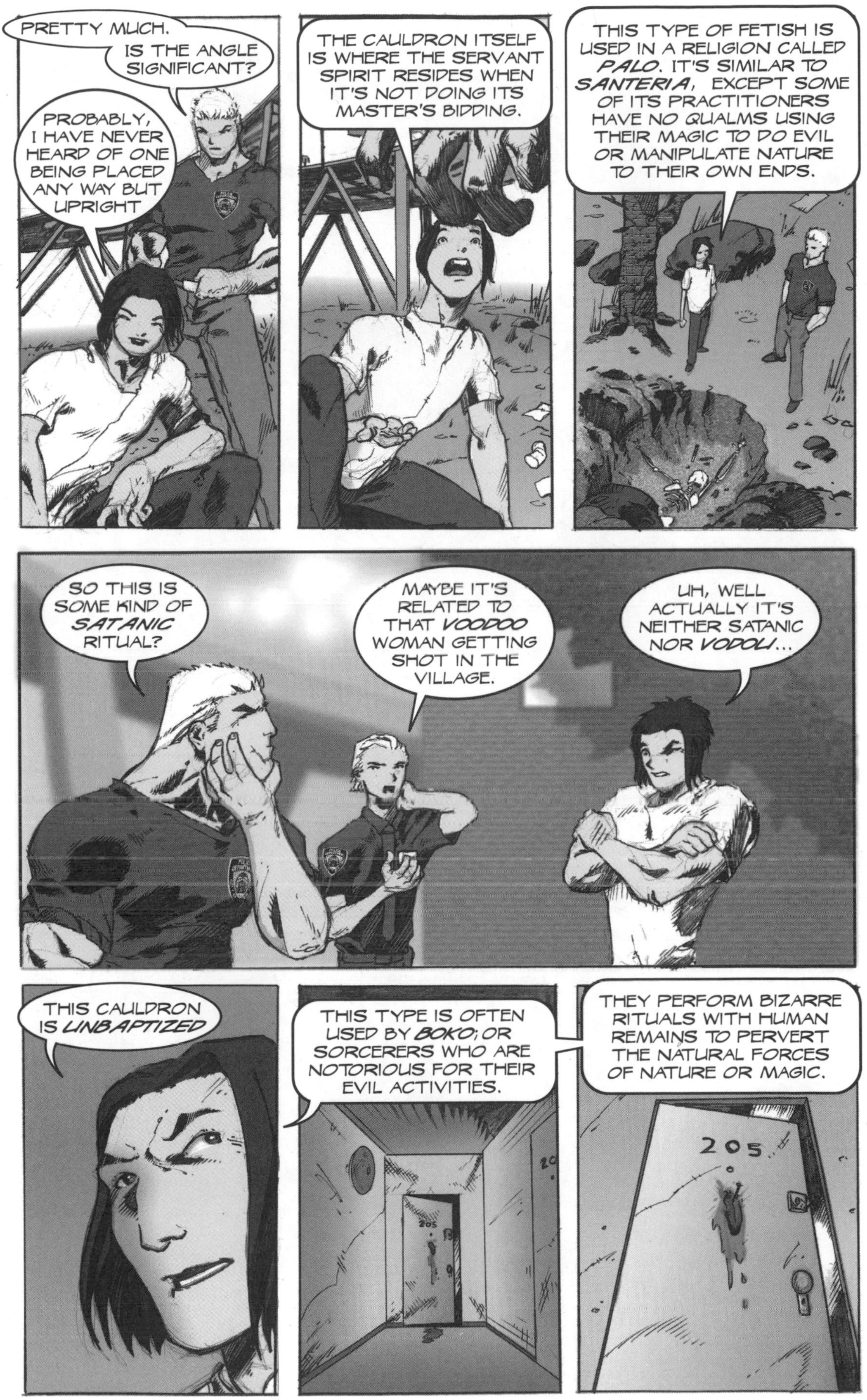
PRETTY MUCH.
IS THE ANGLE SIGNIFICANT?
PROBABLY, I HAVE NEVER HEARD OF ONE BEING PLACED ANY WAY BUT UPRIGHT
THE CAULDRON ITSELF IS WHERE THE SERVANT SPIRIT RESIDES WHEN IT'S NOT DOING ITS MASTER'S BIDDING.
THIS TYPE OF FETISH IS USED IN A RELIGION CALLED PALO. IT'S SIMILAR TO SANTERIA, EXCEPT SOME OF ITS PRACTITIONERS HAVE NO QUALMS USING THEIR MAGIC TO DO EVIL OR MANIPULATE NATURE TO THEIR OWN ENDS.
SO THIS IS SOME KIND OF SATANIC RITUAL?
MAYBE IT'S RELATED TO THAT VOODOO WOMAN GETTING SHOT IN THE VILLAGE.
UH, WELL ACTUALLY IT'S NEITHER SATANIC NOR VODOU...
THIS CAULDRON IS UNBAPTIZED
THIS TYPE IS OFTEN USED BY BOKO; OR SORCERERS WHO ARE NOTORIOUS FOR THEIR EVIL ACTIVITIES.
THEY PERFORM BIZARRE RITUALS WITH HUMAN REMAINS TO PERVERT THE NATURAL FORCES OF NATURE OR MAGIC.
205

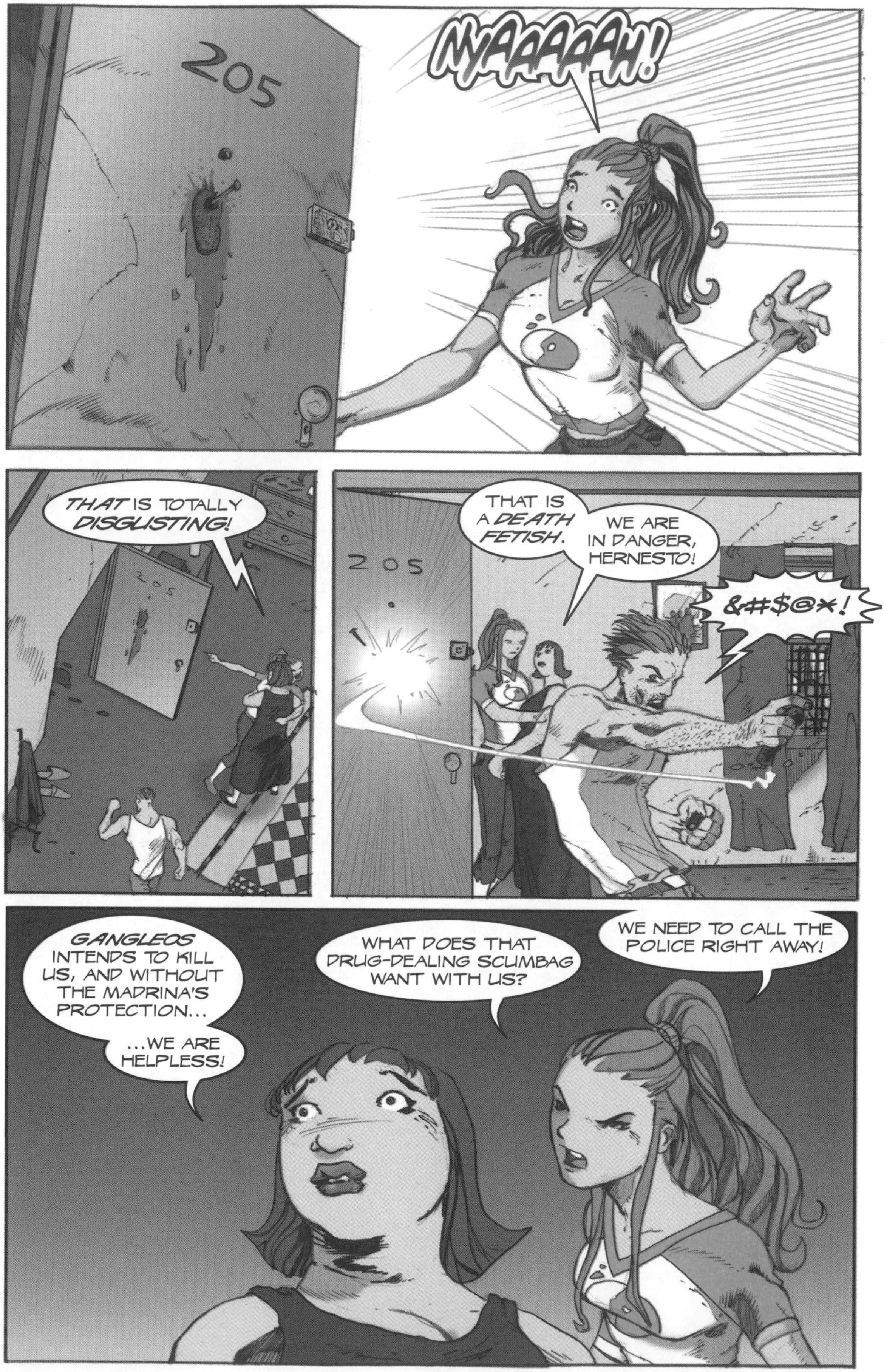
NYAAAAAH!
THAT IS TOTALLY DISGUSTING!
205
THAT IS A DEATH FETISH.
WE ARE IN DANGER, HERNESTO!
&#$@*!
GANGLEOS INTENDS TO KILL US, AND WITHOUT THE MADRINA'S PROTECTION...
...WE ARE HELPLESS!
WHAT DOES THAT DRUG-DEALING SCUMBAG WANT WITH US?
WE NEED TO CALL THE POLICE RIGHT AWAY!

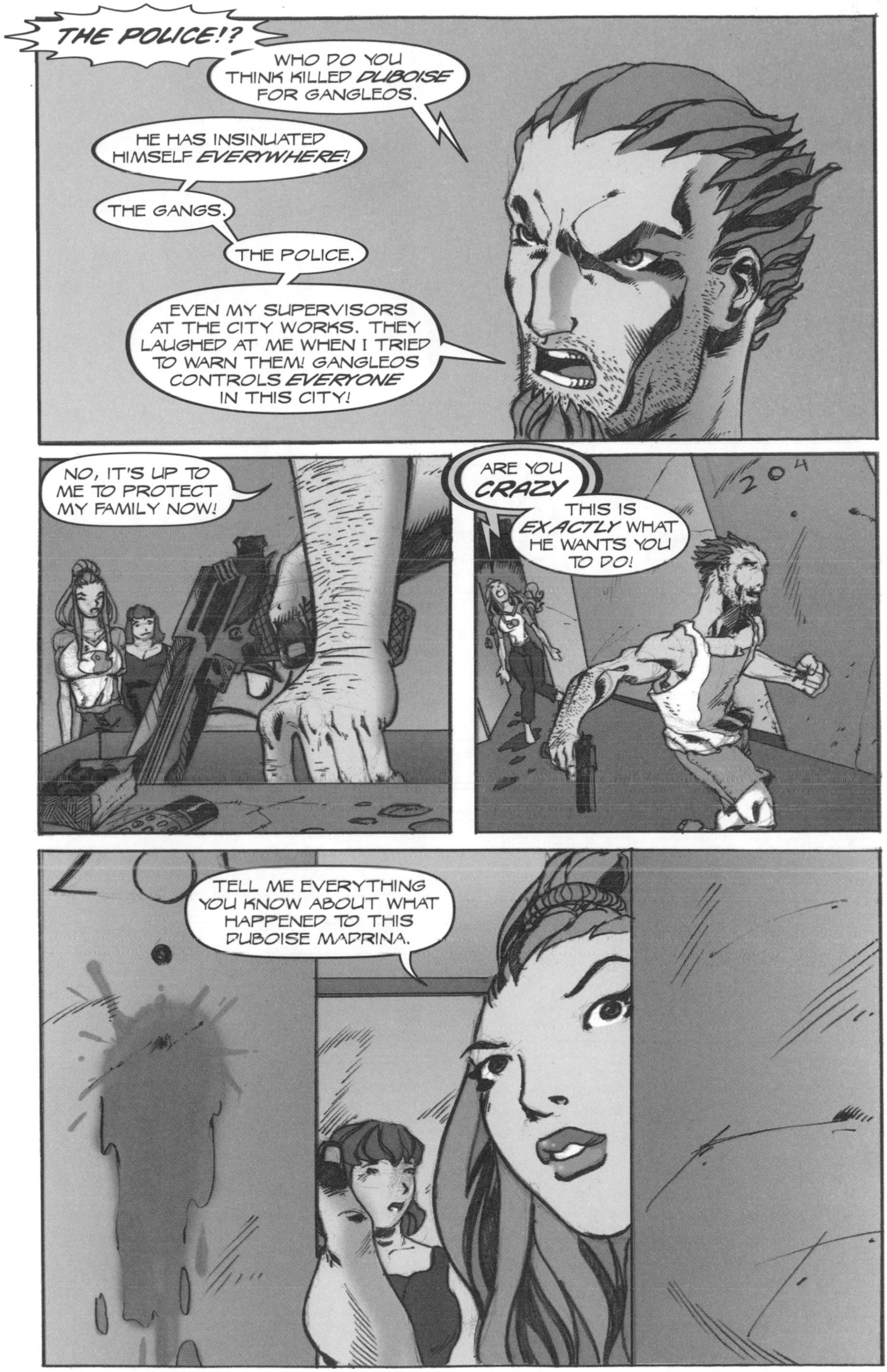
THE POLICE!?
WHO DO YOU THINK KILLED DUBOISE FOR GANGLEOS.
HE HAS INSINUATED HIMSELF EVERYWHERE!
THE GANGS.
THE POLICE.
EVEN MY SUPERVISORS AT THE CITY WORKS. THEY LAUGHED AT ME WHEN I TRIED TO WARN THEM! GANGLEOS CONTROLS EVERYONE IN THIS CITY!
NO, IT'S UP TO ME TO PROTECT MY FAMILY NOW!
ARE YOU CRAZY
THIS IS EXACTLY WHAT HE WANTS YOU TO DO!
TELL ME EVERYTHING YOU KNOW ABOUT WHAT HAPPENED TO THIS DUBOISE MADRINA.

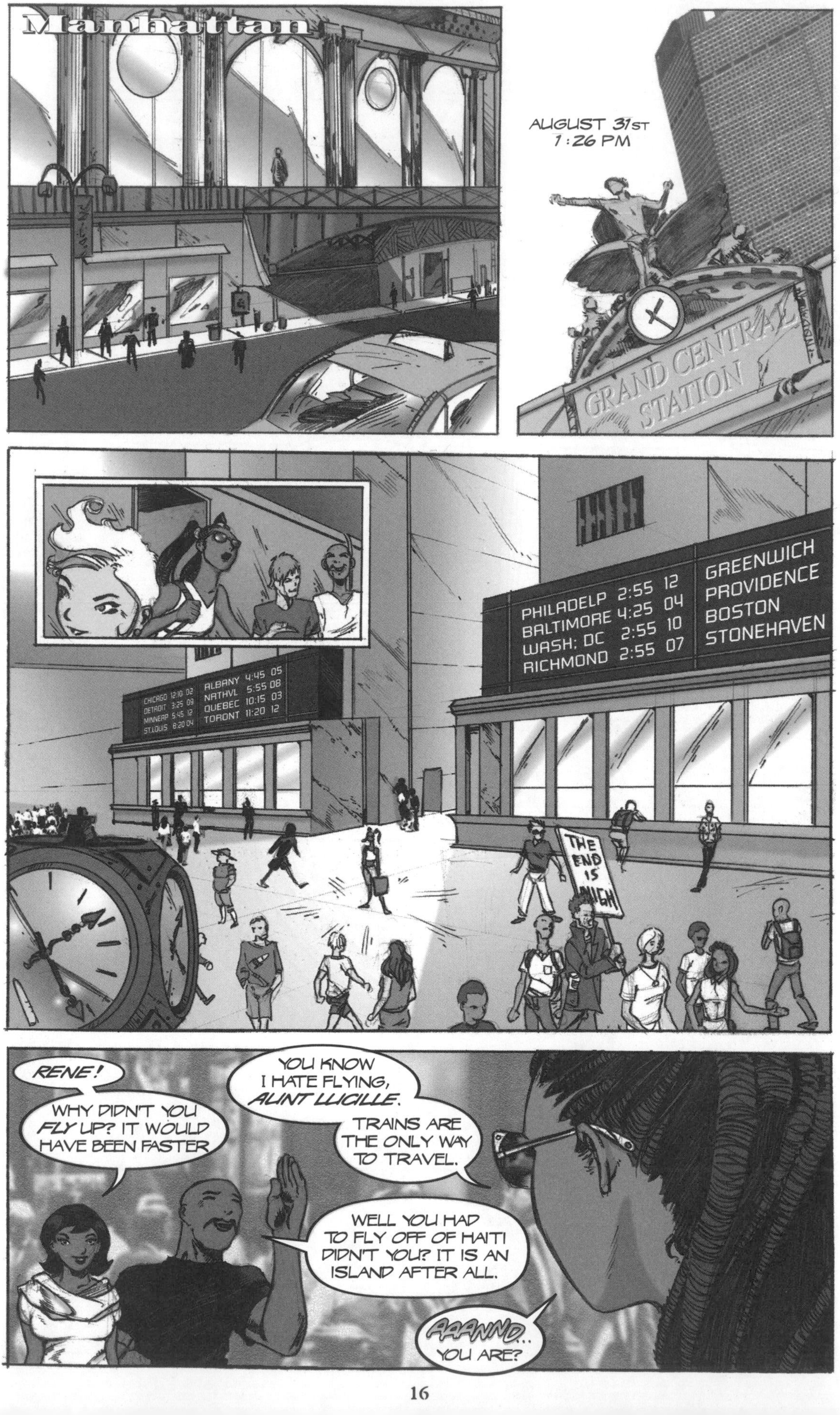
Manhattan
AUGUST 31st
7:26 PM
GRAND CENTRAL STATION
CHICAGO 12:10 02
DETROIT 3:25 09
MINNEAP 5:45 12
ST.LOUIS 8:20 04
ALBANY 4:45 05
NATHVL 5:55 08
QUEBEC 10:15 03
TORONT 11:20 12
PHILADELP 2:55 12
BALTIMORE 4:25 04
WASH: DC 2:55 10
RICHMOND 2:55 07
GREENWICH
PROVIDENCE
BOSTON
STONEHAVEN
THE END IS NIGH
RENE!
WHY DIDN'T YOU FLY UP? IT WOULD HAVE BEEN FASTER
YOU KNOW I HATE FLYING, AUNT LUCILLE.
TRAINS ARE THE ONLY WAY TO TRAVEL.
WELL YOU HAD TO FLY OFF OF HAITI DIDN'T YOU? IT IS AN ISLAND AFTER ALL.
AAANND... YOU ARE?

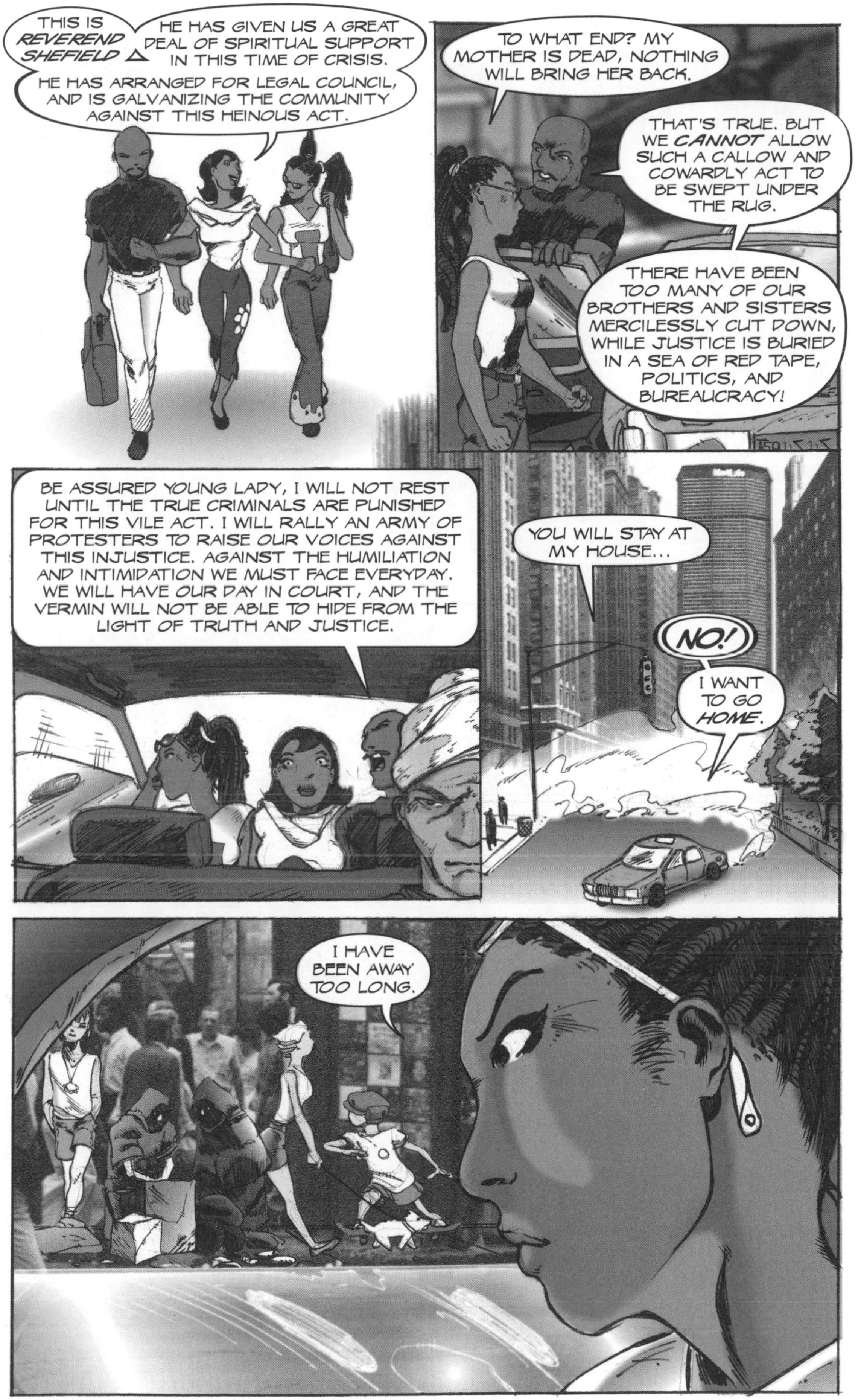
THIS IS REVEREND SHEFIELD
HE HAS GIVEN US A GREAT DEAL OF SPIRITUAL SUPPORT IN THIS TIME OF CRISIS.
HE HAS ARRANGED FOR LEGAL COUNCIL, AND IS GALVANIZING THE COMMUNITY AGAINST THIS HEINOUS ACT.
TO WHAT END? MY MOTHER IS DEAD, NOTHING WILL BRING HER BACK.
THAT'S TRUE. BUT WE CANNOT ALLOW SUCH A CALLOW AND COWARDLY ACT TO BE SWEPT UNDER THE RUG.
THERE HAVE BEEN TOO MANY OF OUR BROTHERS AND SISTERS MERCILESSLY CUT DOWN, WHILE JUSTICE IS BURIED IN A SEA OF RED TAPE, POLITICS, AND BUREAUCRACY!
BE ASSURED YOUNG LADY, I WILL NOT REST UNTIL THE TRUE CRIMINALS ARE PUNISHED FOR THIS VILE ACT. I WILL RALLY AN ARMY OF PROTESTERS TO RAISE OUR VOICES AGAINST THIS INJUSTICE. AGAINST THE HUMILIATION AND INTIMIDATION WE MUST FACE EVERYDAY. WE WILL HAVE OUR DAY IN COURT, AND THE VERMIN WILL NOT BE ABLE TO HIDE FROM THE LIGHT OF TRUTH AND JUSTICE.
YOU WILL STAY AT MY HOUSE...
NO!
I WANT TO GO HOME.
I HAVE BEEN AWAY TOO LONG.

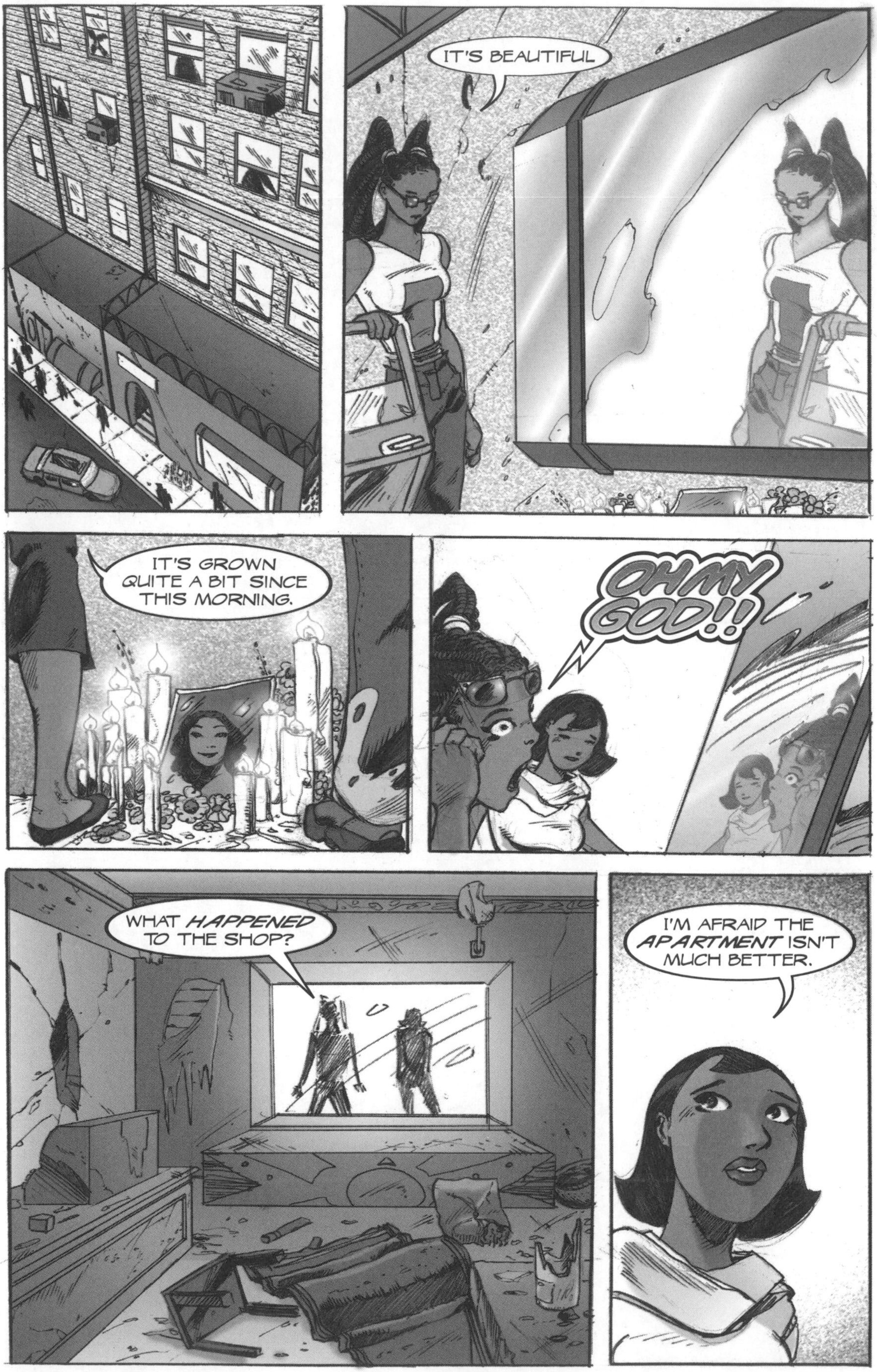
IT'S BEAUTIFUL
IT'S GROWN QUITE A BIT SINCE THIS MORNING.
OH MY GOD!!
WHAT *HAPPENED* TO THE SHOP?
I'M AFRAID THE *APARTMENT* ISN'T MUCH BETTER.

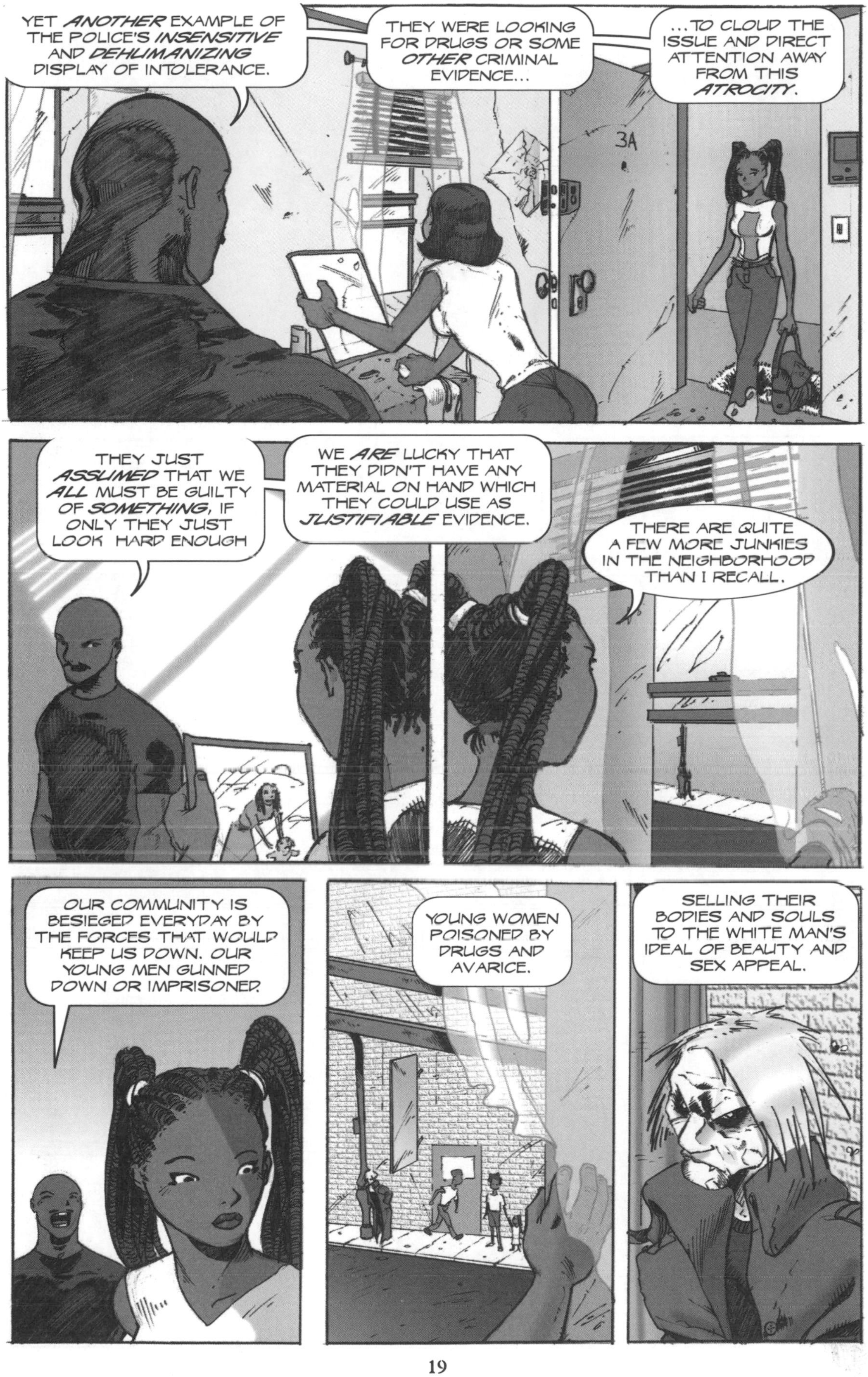

YET ANOTHER EXAMPLE OF THE POLICE'S INSENSITIVE AND DEHUMANIZING DISPLAY OF INTOLERANCE.
THEY WERE LOOKING FOR DRUGS OR SOME OTHER CRIMINAL EVIDENCE...
...TO CLOUD THE ISSUE AND DIRECT ATTENTION AWAY FROM THIS ATROCITY.
3A
THEY JUST ASSUMED THAT WE ALL MUST BE GUILTY OF SOMETHING, IF ONLY THEY JUST LOOK HARD ENOUGH
WE ARE LUCKY THAT THEY DIDN'T HAVE ANY MATERIAL ON HAND WHICH THEY COULD USE AS JUSTIFIABLE EVIDENCE.
THERE ARE QUITE A FEW MORE JUNKIES IN THE NEIGHBORHOOD THAN I RECALL.
OUR COMMUNITY IS BESIEGED EVERYDAY BY THE FORCES THAT WOULD KEEP US DOWN. OUR YOUNG MEN GUNNED DOWN OR IMPRISONED.
YOUNG WOMEN POISONED BY DRUGS AND AVARICE.
SELLING THEIR BODIES AND SOULS TO THE WHITE MAN'S IDEAL OF BEAUTY AND SEX APPEAL.

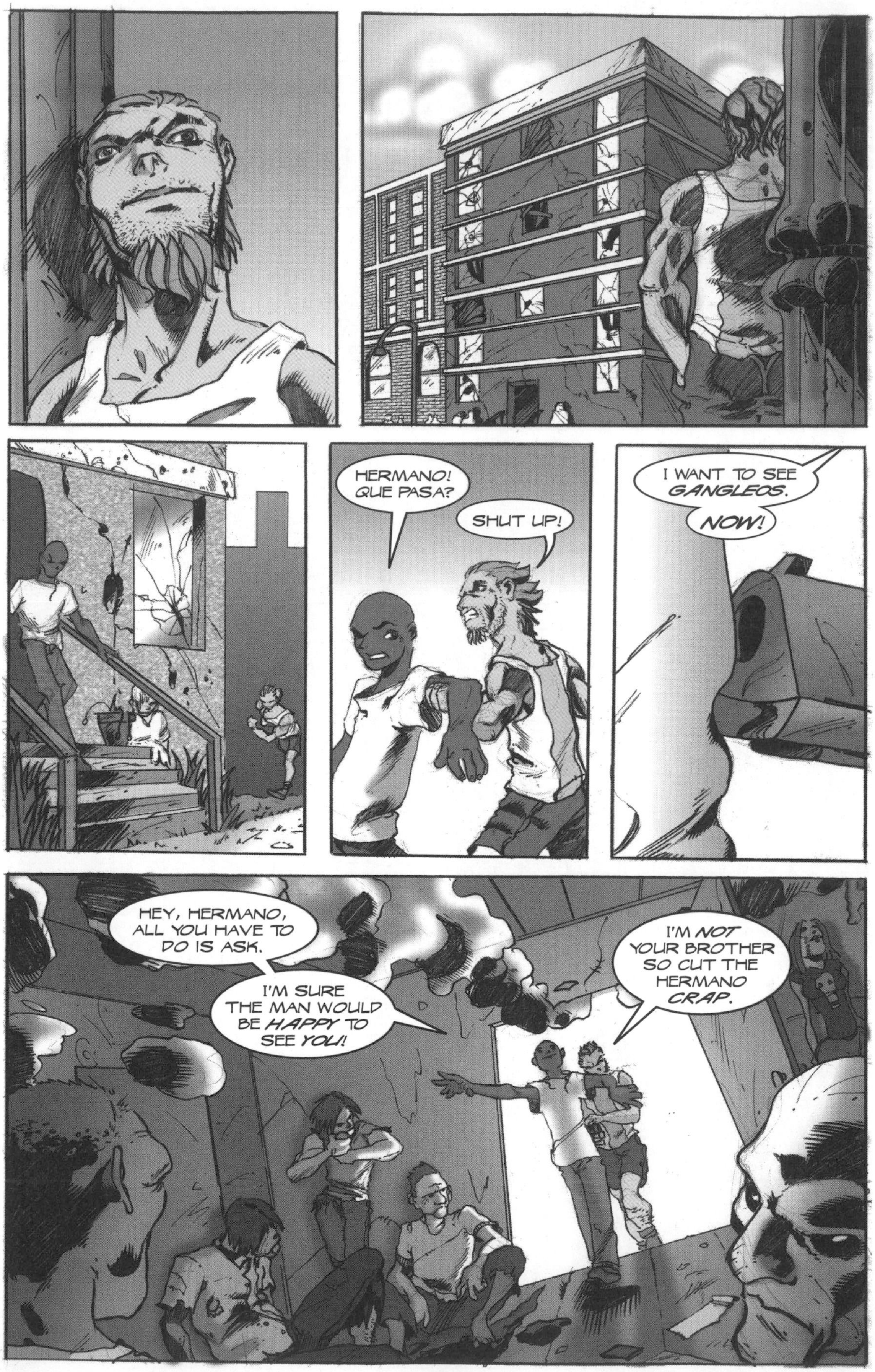
HERMANO! QUE PASA?
SHUT UP!
I WANT TO SEE GANGLEOS.
NOW!
HEY, HERMANO, ALL YOU HAVE TO DO IS ASK.
I'M SURE THE MAN WOULD BE HAPPY TO SEE YOU!
I'M NOT YOUR BROTHER SO CUT THE HERMANO CRAP.

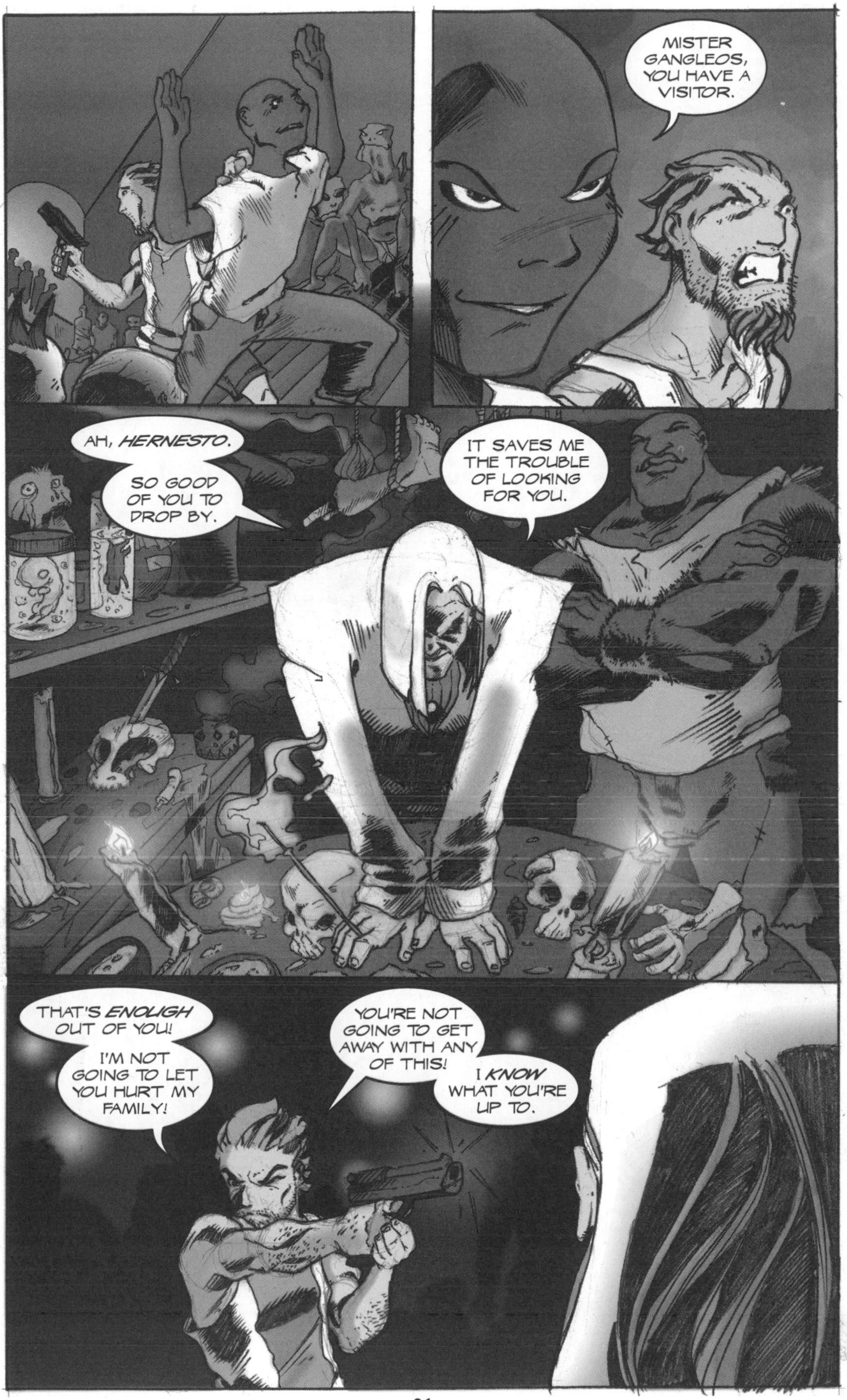
MISTER GANGLEOS, YOU HAVE A VISITOR.
AH, HERNESTO.
SO GOOD OF YOU TO DROP BY.
IT SAVES ME THE TROUBLE OF LOOKING FOR YOU.
THAT'S ENOUGH OUT OF YOU!
I'M NOT GOING TO LET YOU HURT MY FAMILY!
YOU'RE NOT GOING TO GET AWAY WITH ANY OF THIS!
I KNOW WHAT YOU'RE UP TO.

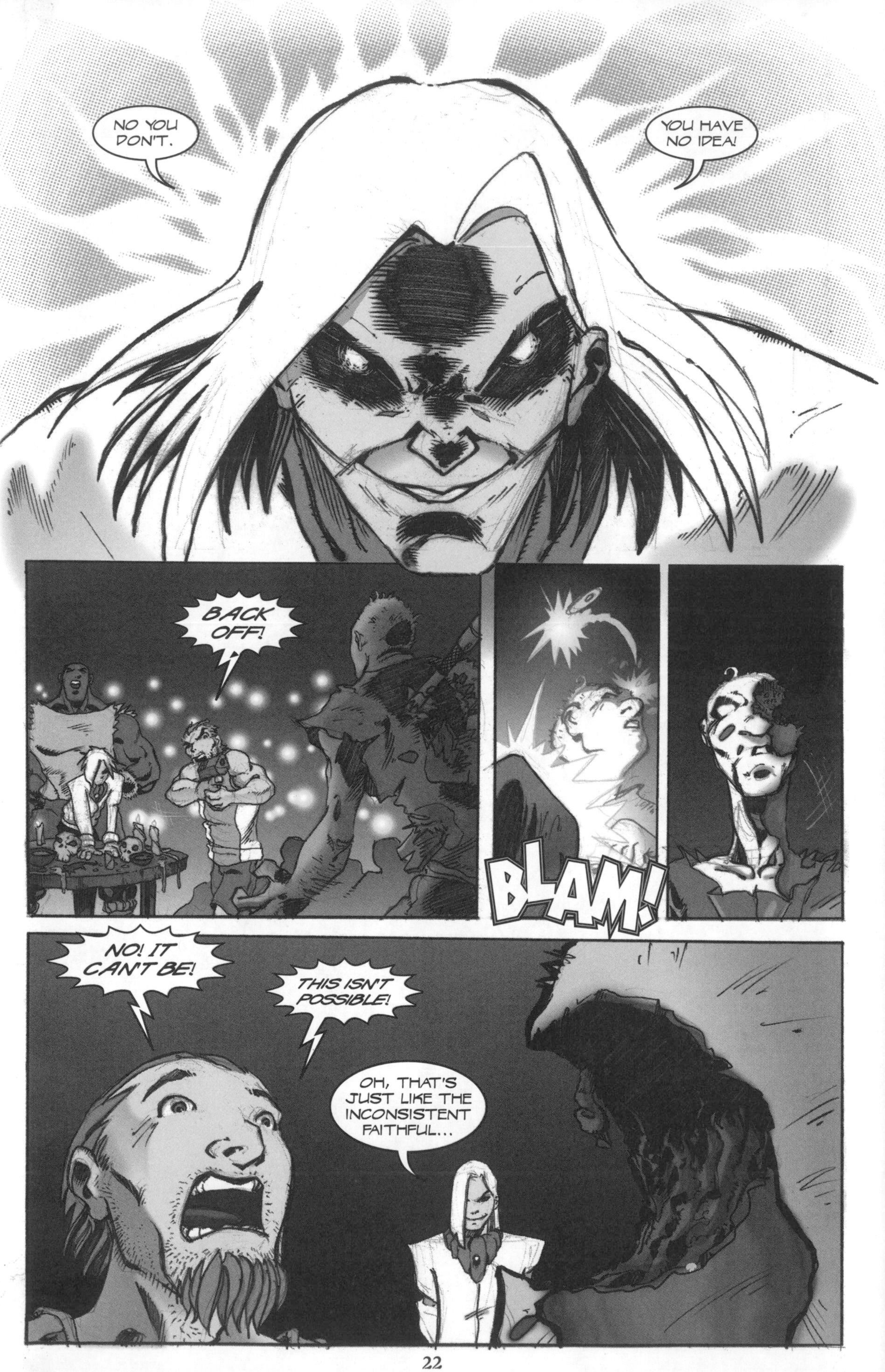
NO YOU DON'T.
YOU HAVE NO IDEA!
BACK OFF!
BLAM!
NO! IT CAN'T BE!
THIS ISN'T POSSIBLE!
OH, THAT'S JUST LIKE THE INCONSISTENT FAITHFUL...

BLAM!
BLAM!
BLAM!

...YOU HAVE NO PROBLEM BELIEVING IN MYTHS AND LEGENDS BASED SOLELY ON FAITH...

BUT ONCE YOU ARE SHOWN INCONTROVERTIBLE EVIDENCE AS TO THE REALITY OF YOUR MYTHS,

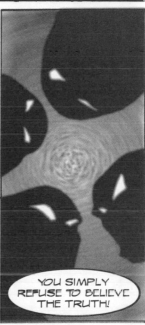

YOU SIMPLY REFUSE TO BELIEVE THE TRUTH!

DUMP THE BODY WHERE IT WILL BE FOUND.

HE WILL BE MORE USEFUL AS A MESSAGE TO THE LOCALS.

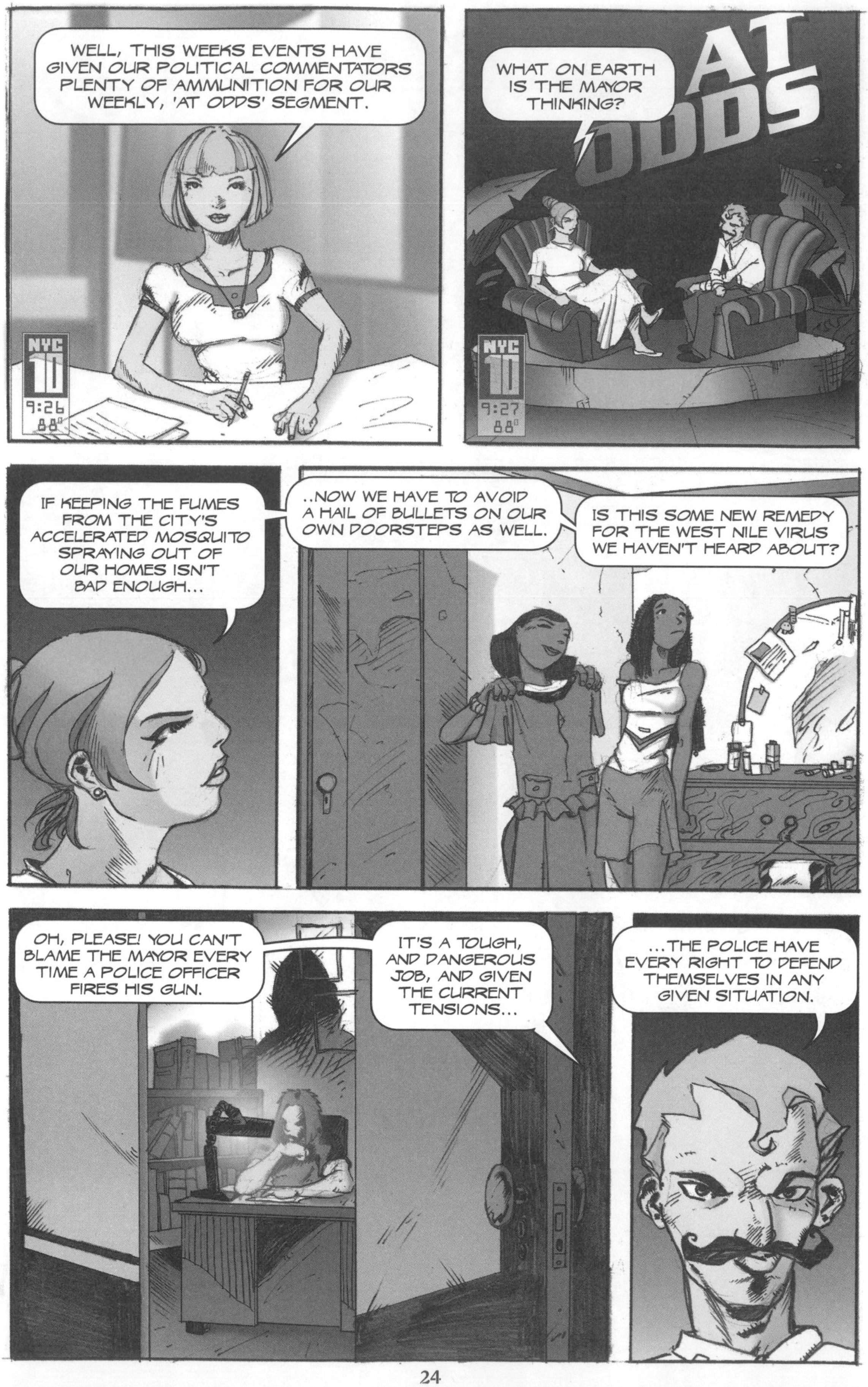
WELL, THIS WEEKS EVENTS HAVE GIVEN OUR POLITICAL COMMENTATORS PLENTY OF AMMUNITION FOR OUR WEEKLY, 'AT ODDS' SEGMENT.
NYC 10
9:26
88°
AT ODDS
WHAT ON EARTH IS THE MAYOR THINKING?
NYC 10
9:27
88°
IF KEEPING THE FUMES FROM THE CITY'S ACCELERATED MOSQUITO SPRAYING OUT OF OUR HOMES ISN'T BAD ENOUGH...
..NOW WE HAVE TO AVOID A HAIL OF BULLETS ON OUR OWN DOORSTEPS AS WELL.
IS THIS SOME NEW REMEDY FOR THE WEST NILE VIRUS WE HAVEN'T HEARD ABOUT?
OH, PLEASE! YOU CAN'T BLAME THE MAYOR EVERY TIME A POLICE OFFICER FIRES HIS GUN.
IT'S A TOUGH, AND DANGEROUS JOB, AND GIVEN THE CURRENT TENSIONS...
...THE POLICE HAVE EVERY RIGHT TO DEFEND THEMSELVES IN ANY GIVEN SITUATION.

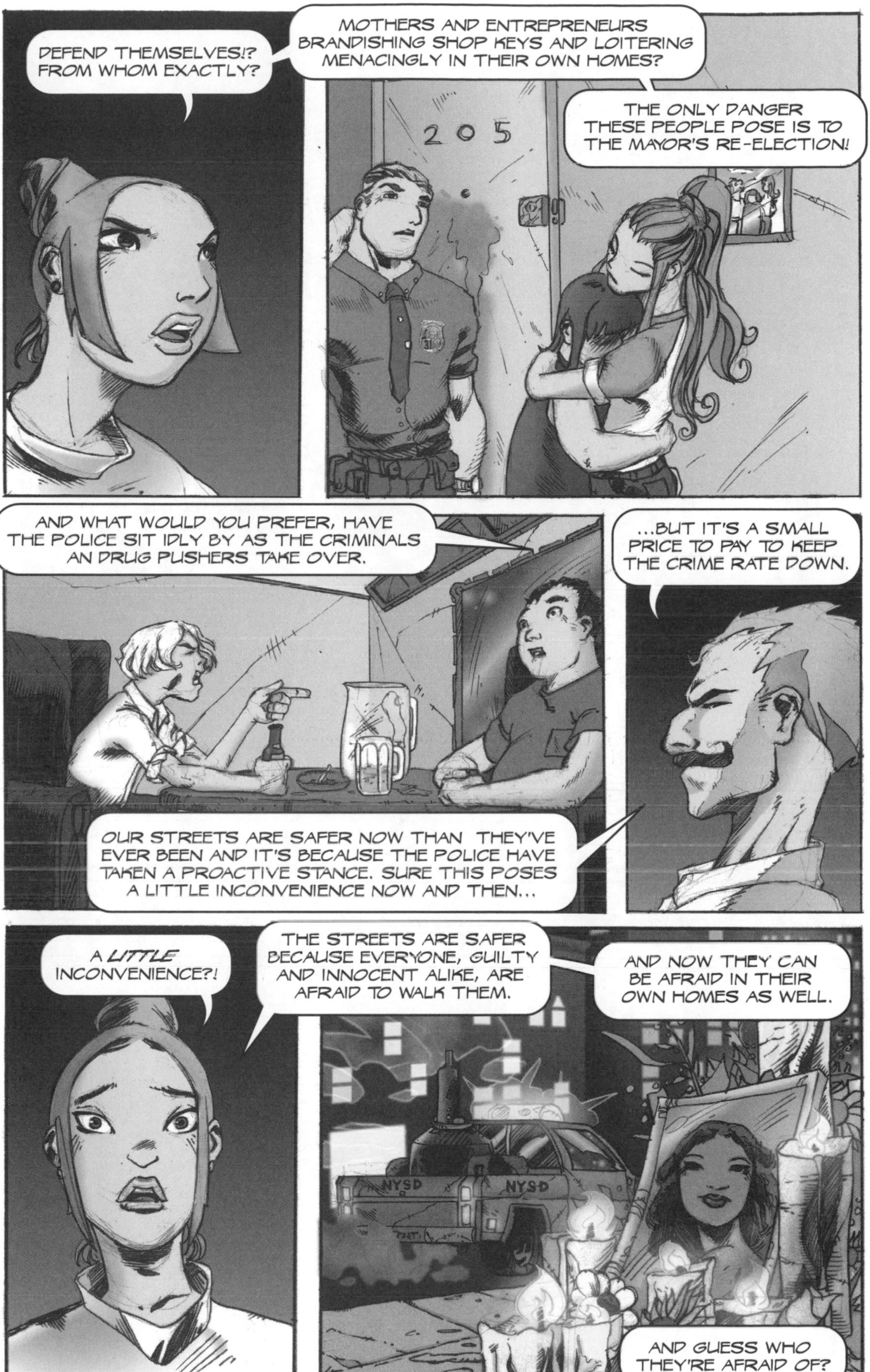
DEFEND THEMSELVES!? FROM WHOM EXACTLY?
MOTHERS AND ENTREPRENEURS BRANDISHING SHOP KEYS AND LOITERING MENACINGLY IN THEIR OWN HOMES?
THE ONLY DANGER THESE PEOPLE POSE IS TO THE MAYOR'S RE-ELECTION!
205
AND WHAT WOULD YOU PREFER, HAVE THE POLICE SIT IDLY BY AS THE CRIMINALS AN DRUG PUSHERS TAKE OVER.
OUR STREETS ARE SAFER NOW THAN THEY'VE EVER BEEN AND IT'S BECAUSE THE POLICE HAVE TAKEN A PROACTIVE STANCE. SURE THIS POSES A LITTLE INCONVENIENCE NOW AND THEN...
...BUT IT'S A SMALL PRICE TO PAY TO KEEP THE CRIME RATE DOWN.
A *LITTLE* INCONVENIENCE?!
THE STREETS ARE SAFER BECAUSE EVERYONE, GUILTY AND INNOCENT ALIKE, ARE AFRAID TO WALK THEM.
AND NOW THEY CAN BE AFRAID IN THEIR OWN HOMES AS WELL.
NYSD
NYSD
AND GUESS WHO THEY'RE AFRAID OF?

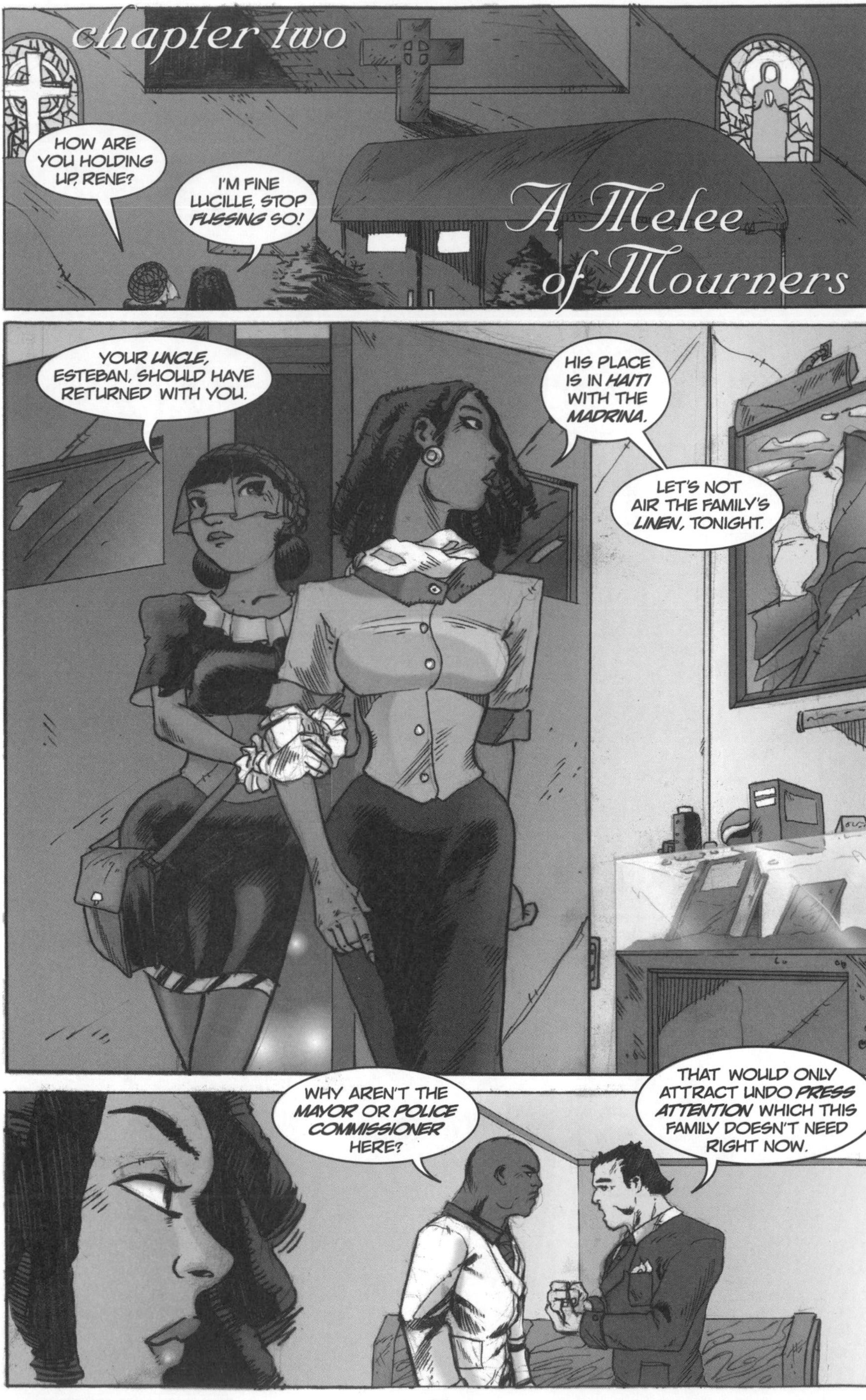
chapter two
HOW ARE YOU HOLDING UP, RENE?
I'M FINE LUCILLE, STOP FUSSING SO!
A Melee of Mourners
YOUR UNCLE, ESTEBAN, SHOULD HAVE RETURNED WITH YOU.
HIS PLACE IS IN HAITI WITH THE MADRINA.
LET'S NOT AIR THE FAMILY'S LINEN, TONIGHT.
WHY AREN'T THE MAYOR OR POLICE COMMISSIONER HERE?
THAT WOULD ONLY ATTRACT UNDO PRESS ATTENTION WHICH THIS FAMILY DOESN'T NEED RIGHT NOW.

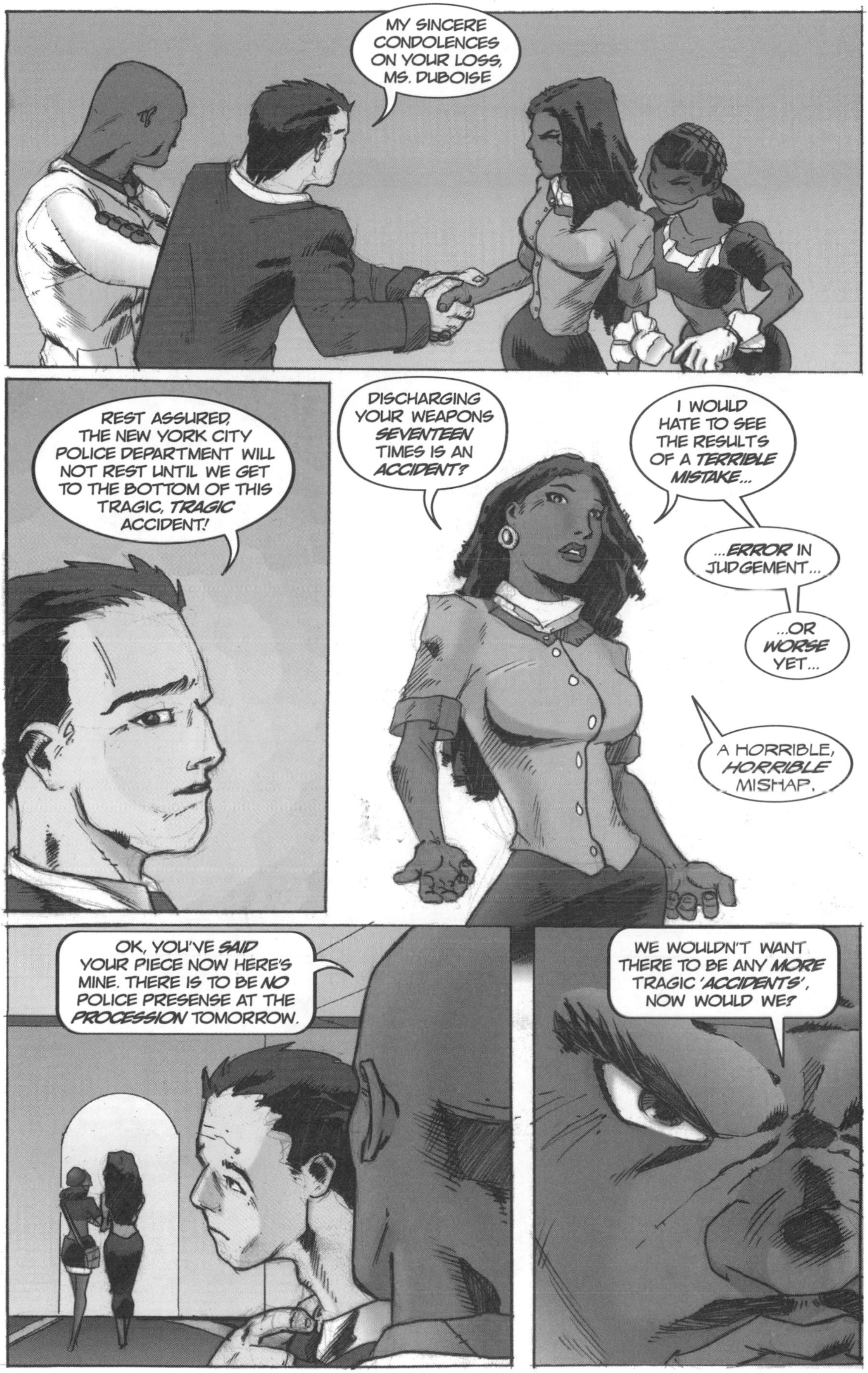
MY SINCERE CONDOLENCES ON YOUR LOSS, MS. DUBOISE
REST ASSURED, THE NEW YORK CITY POLICE DEPARTMENT WILL NOT REST UNTIL WE GET TO THE BOTTOM OF THIS TRAGIC, *TRAGIC* ACCIDENT!
DISCHARGING YOUR WEAPONS *SEVENTEEN* TIMES IS AN *ACCIDENT?*
I WOULD HATE TO SEE THE RESULTS OF A *TERRIBLE MISTAKE...*
...*ERROR* IN JUDGEMENT...
...OR *WORSE* YET...
A HORRIBLE, *HORRIBLE* MISHAP.
OK, YOU'VE *SAID* YOUR PIECE NOW HERE'S MINE. THERE IS TO BE *NO* POLICE PRESENSE AT THE *PROCESSION* TOMORROW.
WE WOULDN'T WANT THERE TO BE ANY *MORE* TRAGIC '*ACCIDENTS*', NOW WOULD WE?

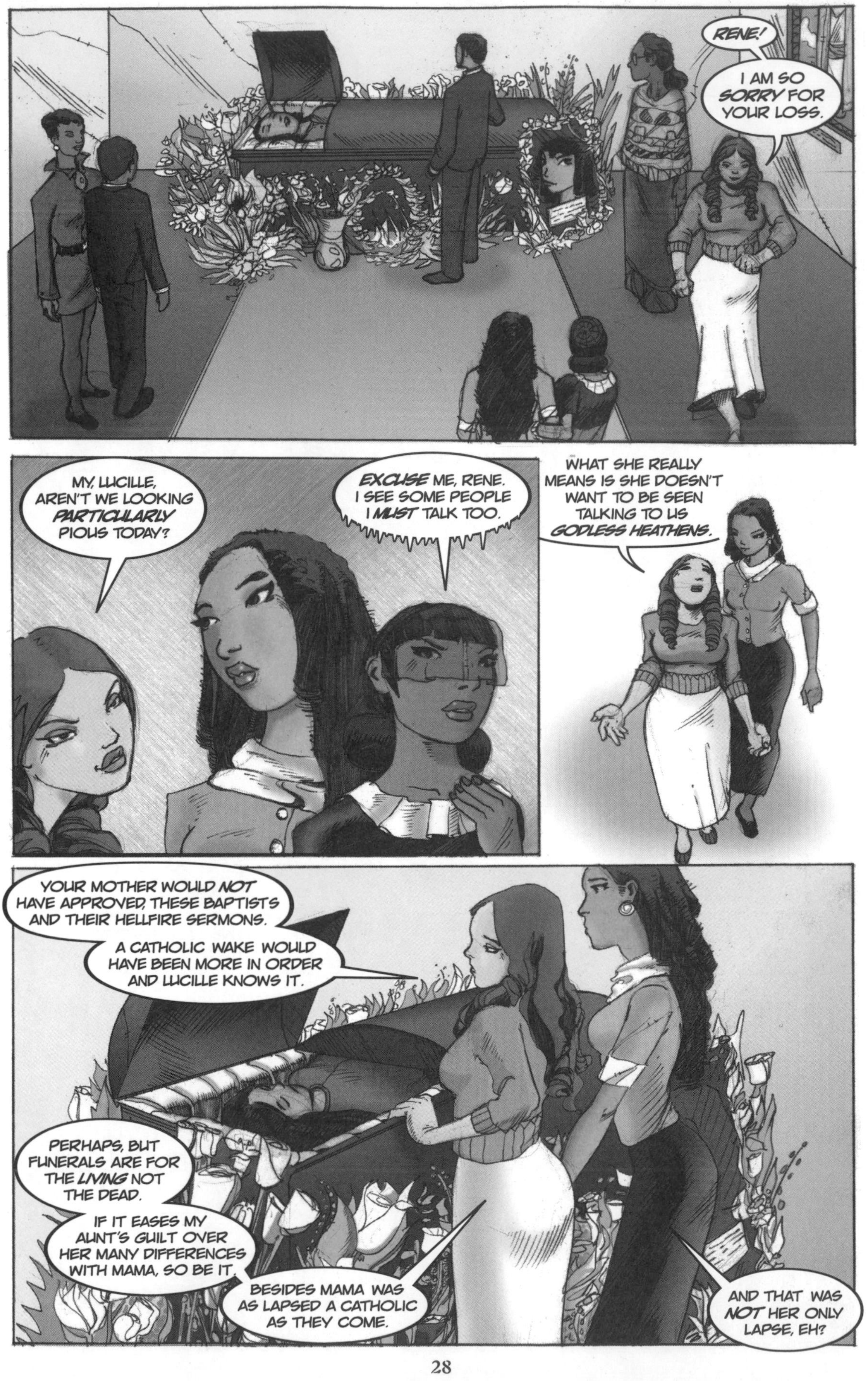
RENE!
I AM SO SORRY FOR YOUR LOSS.
MY, LUCILLE, AREN'T WE LOOKING PARTICULARLY PIOUS TODAY?
EXCUSE ME, RENE. I SEE SOME PEOPLE I MUST TALK TOO.
WHAT SHE REALLY MEANS IS SHE DOESN'T WANT TO BE SEEN TALKING TO US GODLESS HEATHENS.
YOUR MOTHER WOULD NOT HAVE APPROVED, THESE BAPTISTS AND THEIR HELLFIRE SERMONS.
A CATHOLIC WAKE WOULD HAVE BEEN MORE IN ORDER AND LUCILLE KNOWS IT.
PERHAPS, BUT FUNERALS ARE FOR THE LIVING NOT THE DEAD.
IF IT EASES MY AUNT'S GUILT OVER HER MANY DIFFERENCES WITH MAMA, SO BE IT.
BESIDES MAMA WAS AS LAPSED A CATHOLIC AS THEY COME.
AND THAT WAS NOT HER ONLY LAPSE, EH?

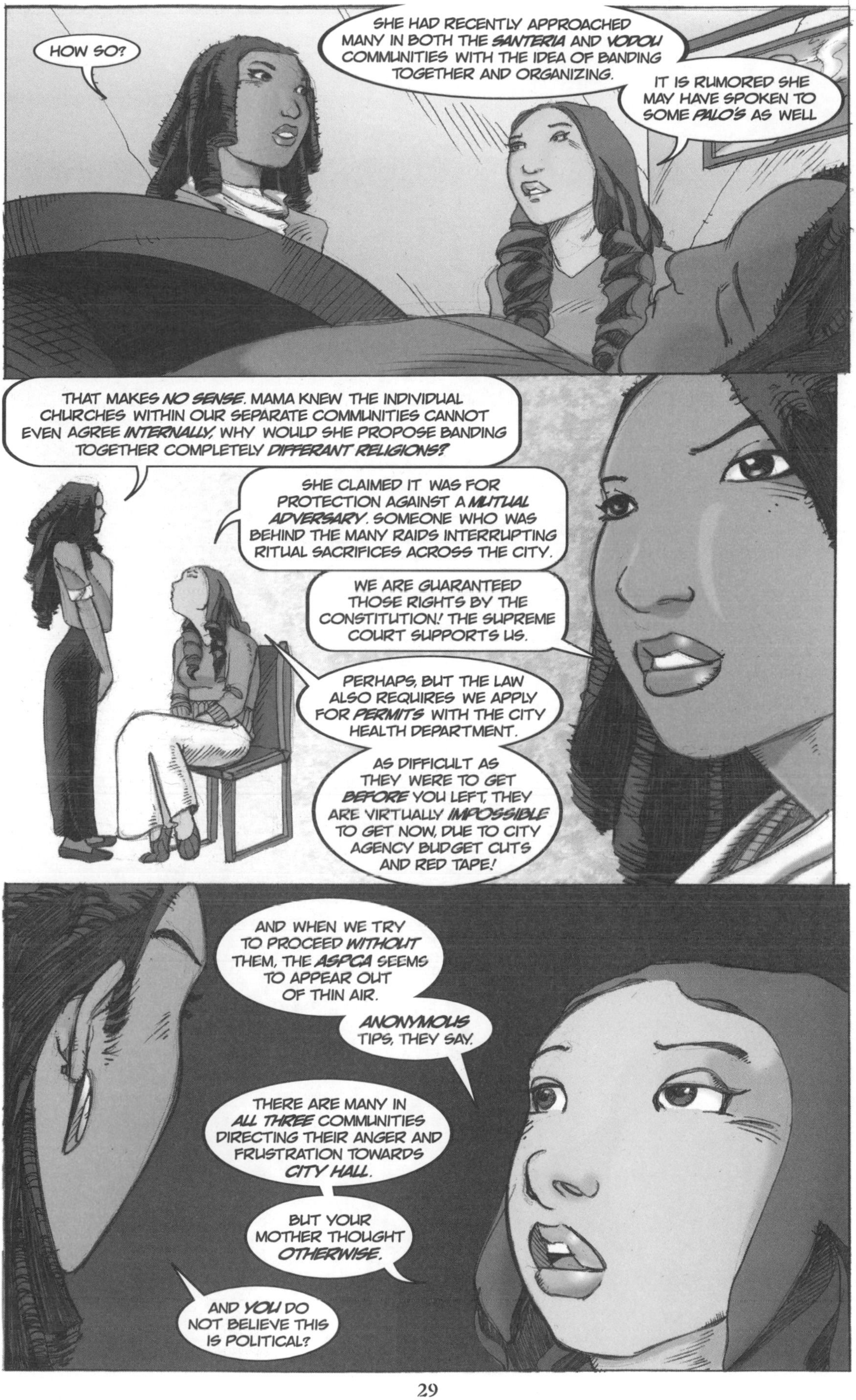
HOW SO?
SHE HAD RECENTLY APPROACHED MANY IN BOTH THE SANTERIA AND VODOU COMMUNITIES WITH THE IDEA OF BANDING TOGETHER AND ORGANIZING.
IT IS RUMORED SHE MAY HAVE SPOKEN TO SOME PALO'S AS WELL
THAT MAKES NO SENSE. MAMA KNEW THE INDIVIDUAL CHURCHES WITHIN OUR SEPARATE COMMUNITIES CANNOT EVEN AGREE INTERNALLY, WHY WOULD SHE PROPOSE BANDING TOGETHER COMPLETELY DIFFERANT RELIGIONS?
SHE CLAIMED IT WAS FOR PROTECTION AGAINST A MUTUAL ADVERSARY. SOMEONE WHO WAS BEHIND THE MANY RAIDS INTERRUPTING RITUAL SACRIFICES ACROSS THE CITY.
WE ARE GUARANTEED THOSE RIGHTS BY THE CONSTITUTION! THE SUPREME COURT SUPPORTS US.
PERHAPS, BUT THE LAW ALSO REQUIRES WE APPLY FOR PERMITS WITH THE CITY HEALTH DEPARTMENT.
AS DIFFICULT AS THEY WERE TO GET BEFORE YOU LEFT, THEY ARE VIRTUALLY IMPOSSIBLE TO GET NOW, DUE TO CITY AGENCY BUDGET CUTS AND RED TAPE!
AND WHEN WE TRY TO PROCEED WITHOUT THEM, THE ASPCA SEEMS TO APPEAR OUT OF THIN AIR.
ANONYMOUS TIPS, THEY SAY.
THERE ARE MANY IN ALL THREE COMMUNITIES DIRECTING THEIR ANGER AND FRUSTRATION TOWARDS CITY HALL.
BUT YOUR MOTHER THOUGHT OTHERWISE.
AND YOU DO NOT BELIEVE THIS IS POLITICAL?

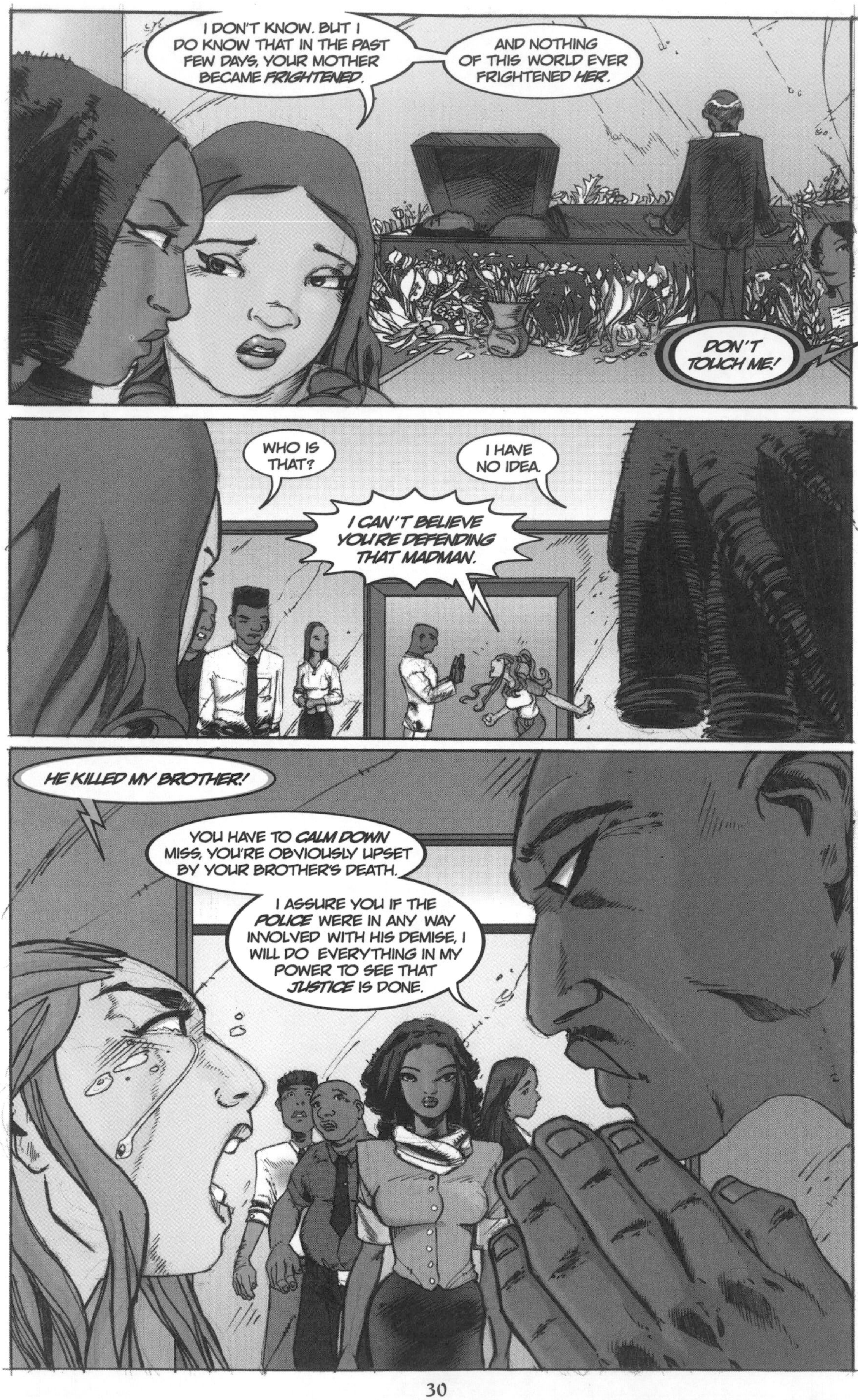
I DON'T KNOW. BUT I DO KNOW THAT IN THE PAST FEW DAYS, YOUR MOTHER BECAME FRIGHTENED.
AND NOTHING OF THIS WORLD EVER FRIGHTENED HER.
DON'T TOUCH ME!
WHO IS THAT?
I HAVE NO IDEA.
I CAN'T BELIEVE YOU'RE DEFENDING THAT MADMAN.
HE KILLED MY BROTHER!
YOU HAVE TO CALM DOWN MISS, YOU'RE OBVIOUSLY UPSET BY YOUR BROTHER'S DEATH.
I ASSURE YOU IF THE POLICE WERE IN ANY WAY INVOLVED WITH HIS DEMISE, I WILL DO EVERYTHING IN MY POWER TO SEE THAT JUSTICE IS DONE.

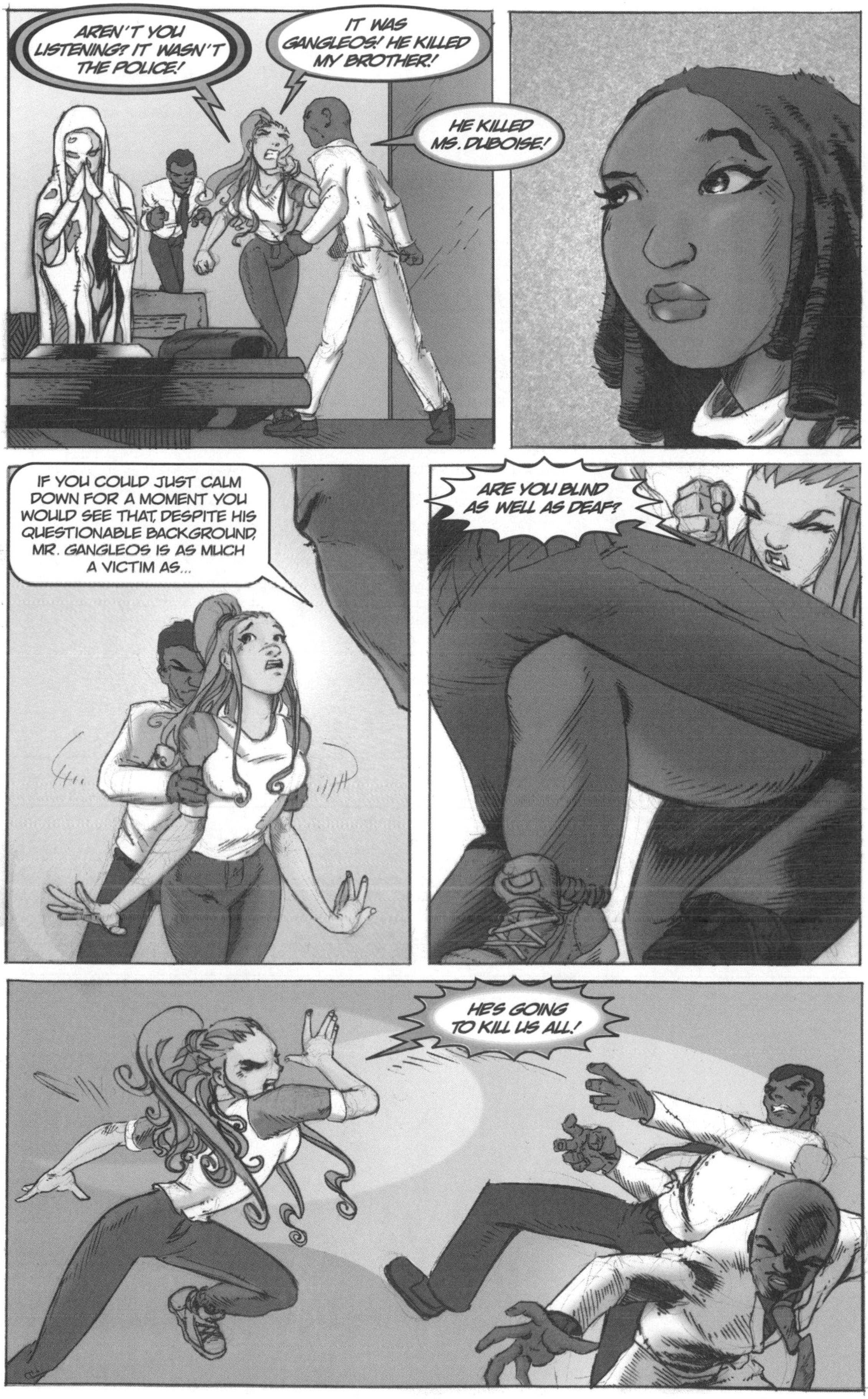
AREN'T YOU LISTENING? IT WASN'T THE POLICE!
IT WAS GANGLEOS! HE KILLED MY BROTHER!
HE KILLED MS. DUBOISE!
IF YOU COULD JUST CALM DOWN FOR A MOMENT YOU WOULD SEE THAT, DESPITE HIS QUESTIONABLE BACKGROUND, MR. GANGLEOS IS AS MUCH A VICTIM AS...
ARE YOU BLIND AS WELL AS DEAF?
HE'S GOING TO KILL US ALL!

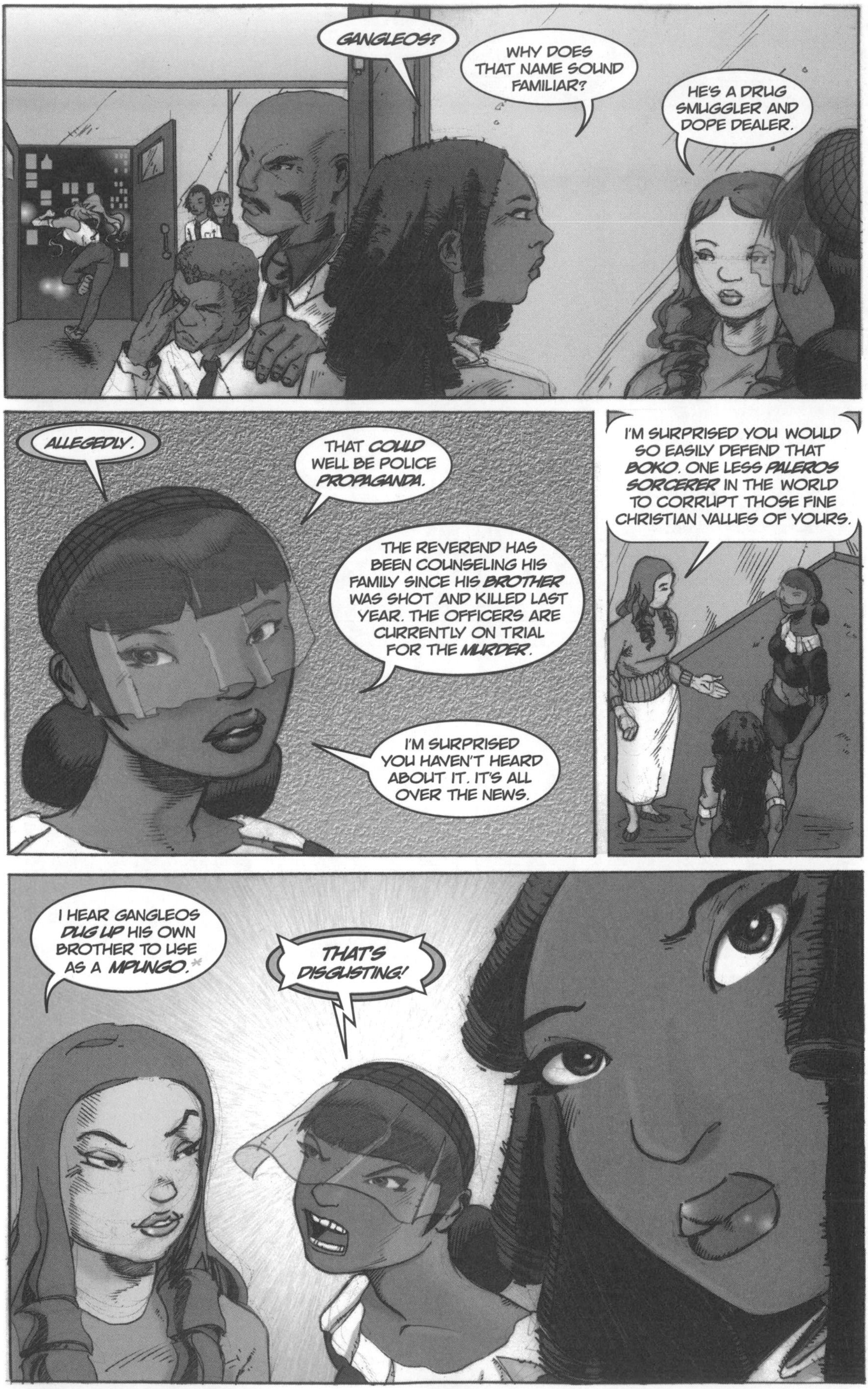
GANGLEOS?
WHY DOES THAT NAME SOUND FAMILIAR?
HE'S A DRUG SMUGGLER AND DOPE DEALER.
ALLEGEDLY.
THAT COULD WELL BE POLICE PROPAGANDA.
THE REVEREND HAS BEEN COUNSELING HIS FAMILY SINCE HIS BROTHER WAS SHOT AND KILLED LAST YEAR. THE OFFICERS ARE CURRENTLY ON TRIAL FOR THE MURDER.
I'M SURPRISED YOU HAVEN'T HEARD ABOUT IT. IT'S ALL OVER THE NEWS.
I'M SURPRISED YOU WOULD SO EASILY DEFEND THAT BOKO. ONE LESS PALEROS SORCERER IN THE WORLD TO CORRUPT THOSE FINE CHRISTIAN VALUES OF YOURS.
I HEAR GANGLEOS DUG UP HIS OWN BROTHER TO USE AS A MPUNGO.*
THAT'S DISGUSTING!

* DISEMBODIED SPIRIT SERVANT

SEPTEMBER 1st
12:45 PM

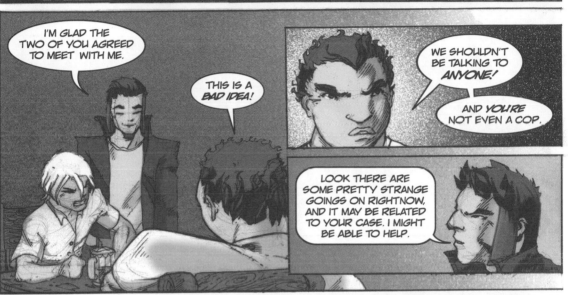

I'M GLAD THE TWO OF YOU AGREED TO MEET WITH ME.

THIS IS A *BAD IDEA!*

WE SHOULDN'T BE TALKING TO *ANYONE!*

AND *YOU'RE* NOT EVEN A COP.

LOOK THERE ARE SOME PRETTY STRANGE GOINGS ON RIGHTNOW, AND IT MAY BE RELATED TO YOUR CASE. I MIGHT BE ABLE TO HELP.

AHH, MAN! GET A LOAD OF THIS.

THEY'RE BROADCASTING THE *FUNERAL PROCESSION* ON LIVE TV! LIKE THIS WAS *PRINCESS DI* OR SOMETHIN!

THERE'S NO ESCAPING THIS *CRAP.* IT'S EVEN HAUNTING US IN OUR OWN BAR FOR CHRIST SAKE.

33

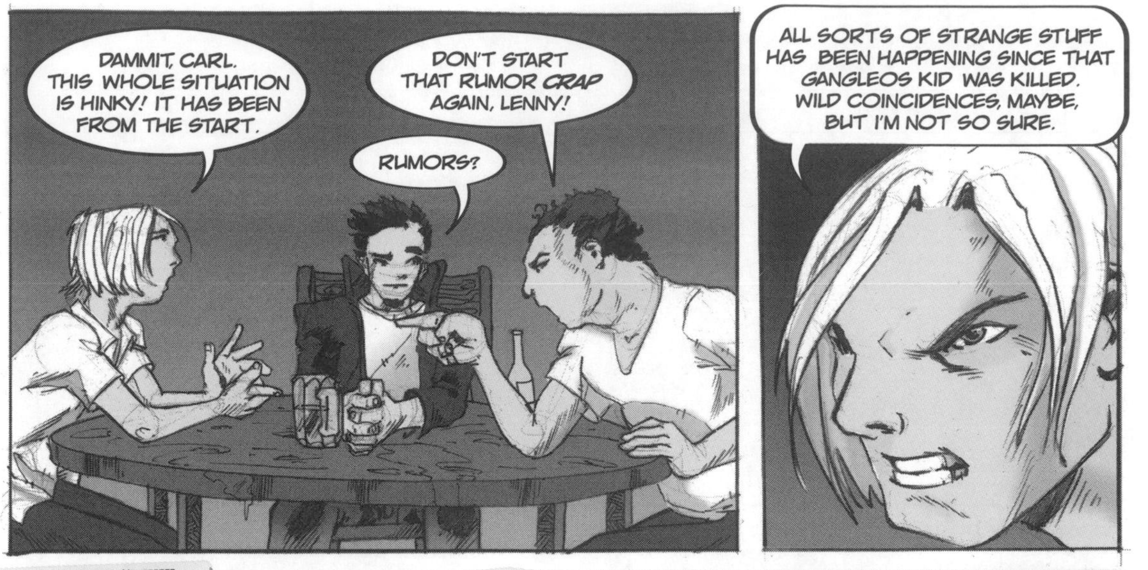
DAMMIT, CARL. THIS WHOLE SITUATION IS HINKY! IT HAS BEEN FROM THE START.
DON'T START THAT RUMOR CRAP AGAIN, LENNY!
RUMORS?
ALL SORTS OF STRANGE STUFF HAS BEEN HAPPENING SINCE THAT GANGLEOS KID WAS KILLED. WILD COINCIDENCES, MAYBE, BUT I'M NOT SO SURE.

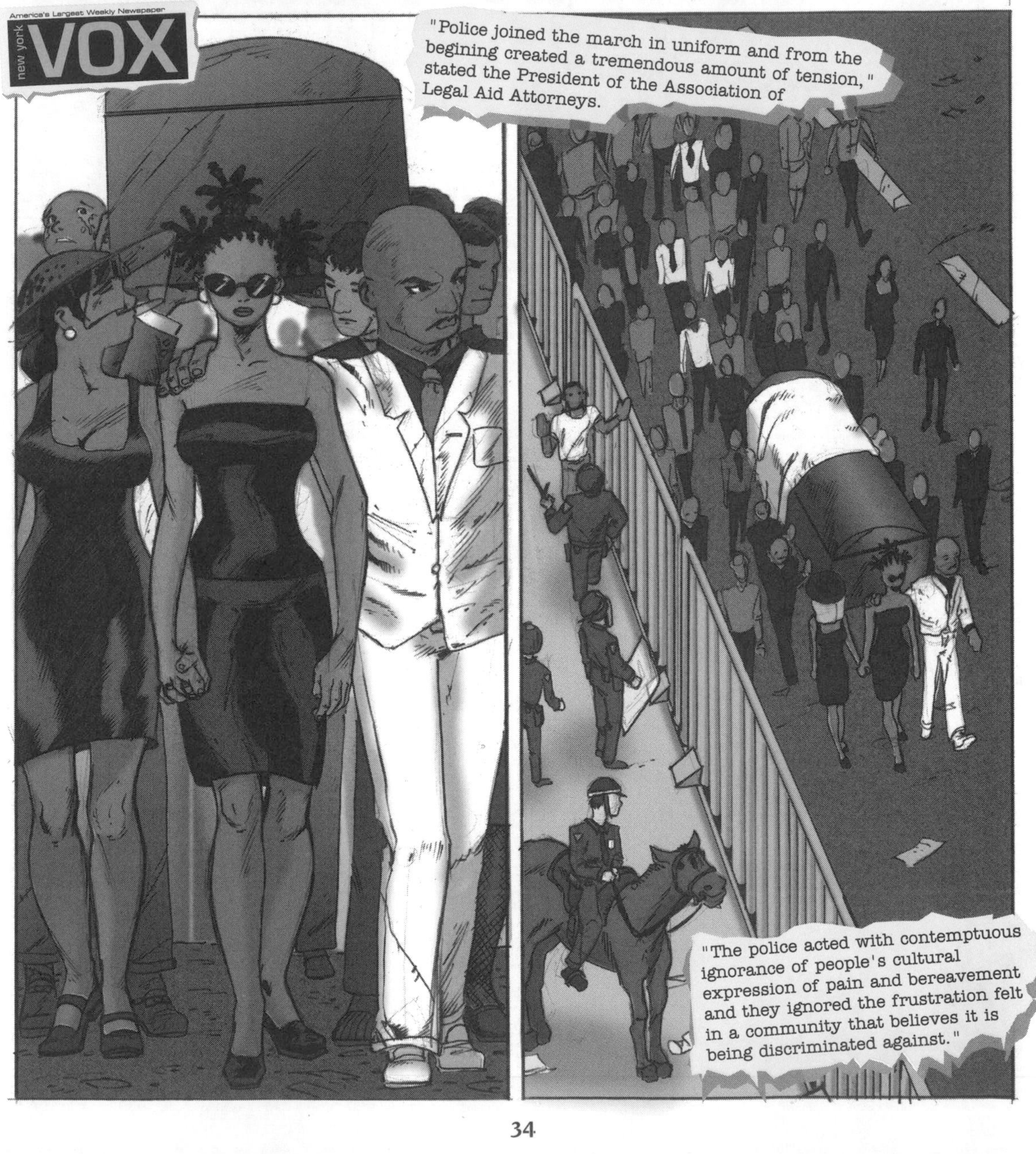
America's Largest Weekly Newspaper
new york VOX
"Police joined the march in uniform and from the begining created a tremendous amount of tension," stated the President of the Association of Legal Aid Attorneys.
"The police acted with contemptuous ignorance of people's cultural expression of pain and bereavement and they ignored the frustration felt in a community that believes it is being discriminated against."

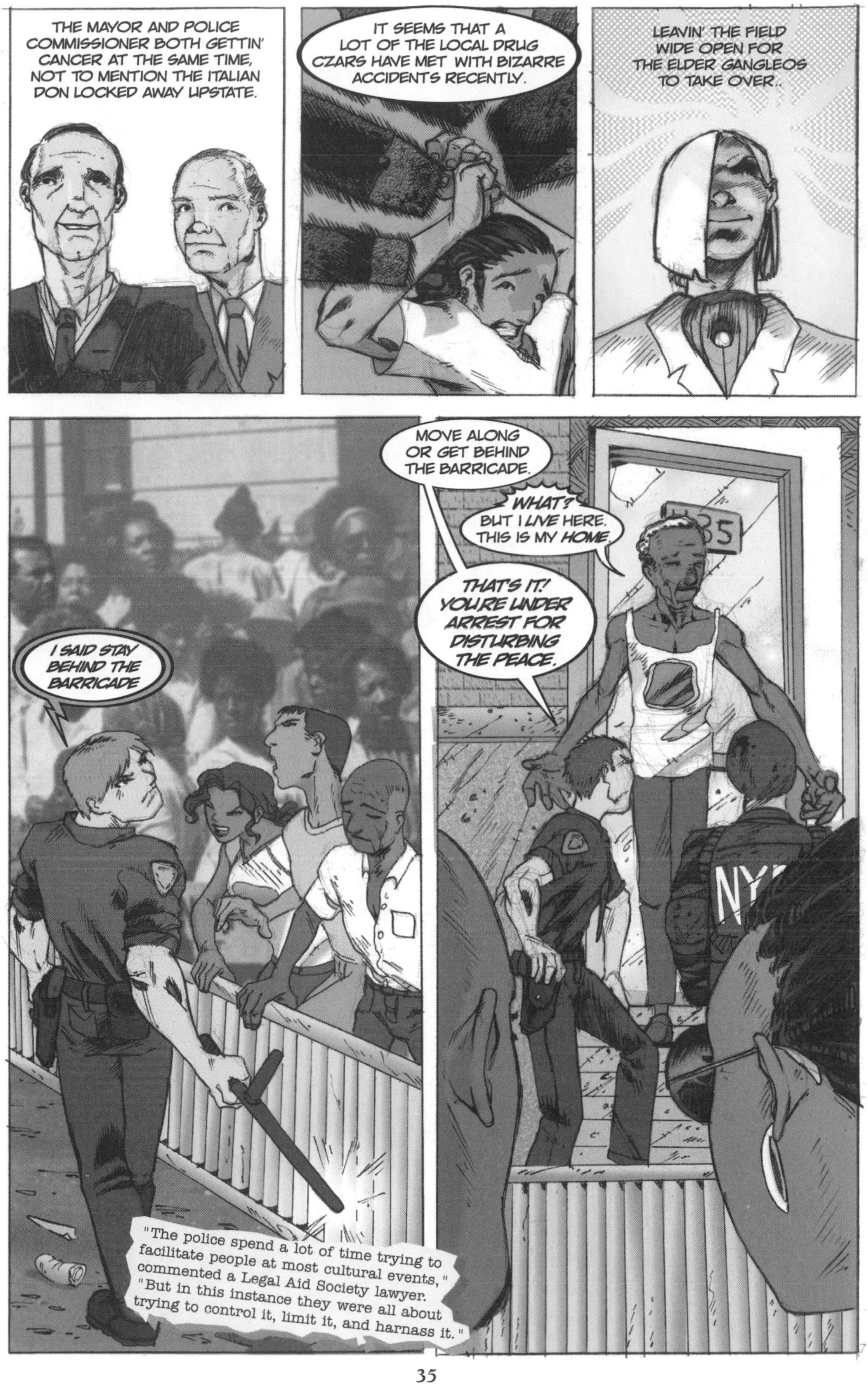
THE MAYOR AND POLICE COMMISSIONER BOTH GETTIN' CANCER AT THE SAME TIME, NOT TO MENTION THE ITALIAN DON LOCKED AWAY UPSTATE.
IT SEEMS THAT A LOT OF THE LOCAL DRUG CZARS HAVE MET WITH BIZARRE ACCIDENTS RECENTLY.
LEAVIN' THE FIELD WIDE OPEN FOR THE ELDER GANGLEOS TO TAKE OVER..
I SAID STAY BEHIND THE BARRICADE
MOVE ALONG OR GET BEHIND THE BARRICADE.
WHAT? BUT I LIVE HERE. THIS IS MY HOME.
THAT'S IT! YOU'RE UNDER ARREST FOR DISTURBING THE PEACE.
NY
"The police spend a lot of time trying to facilitate people at most cultural events," commented a Legal Aid Society lawyer. "But in this instance they were all about trying to control it, limit it, and harnass it."

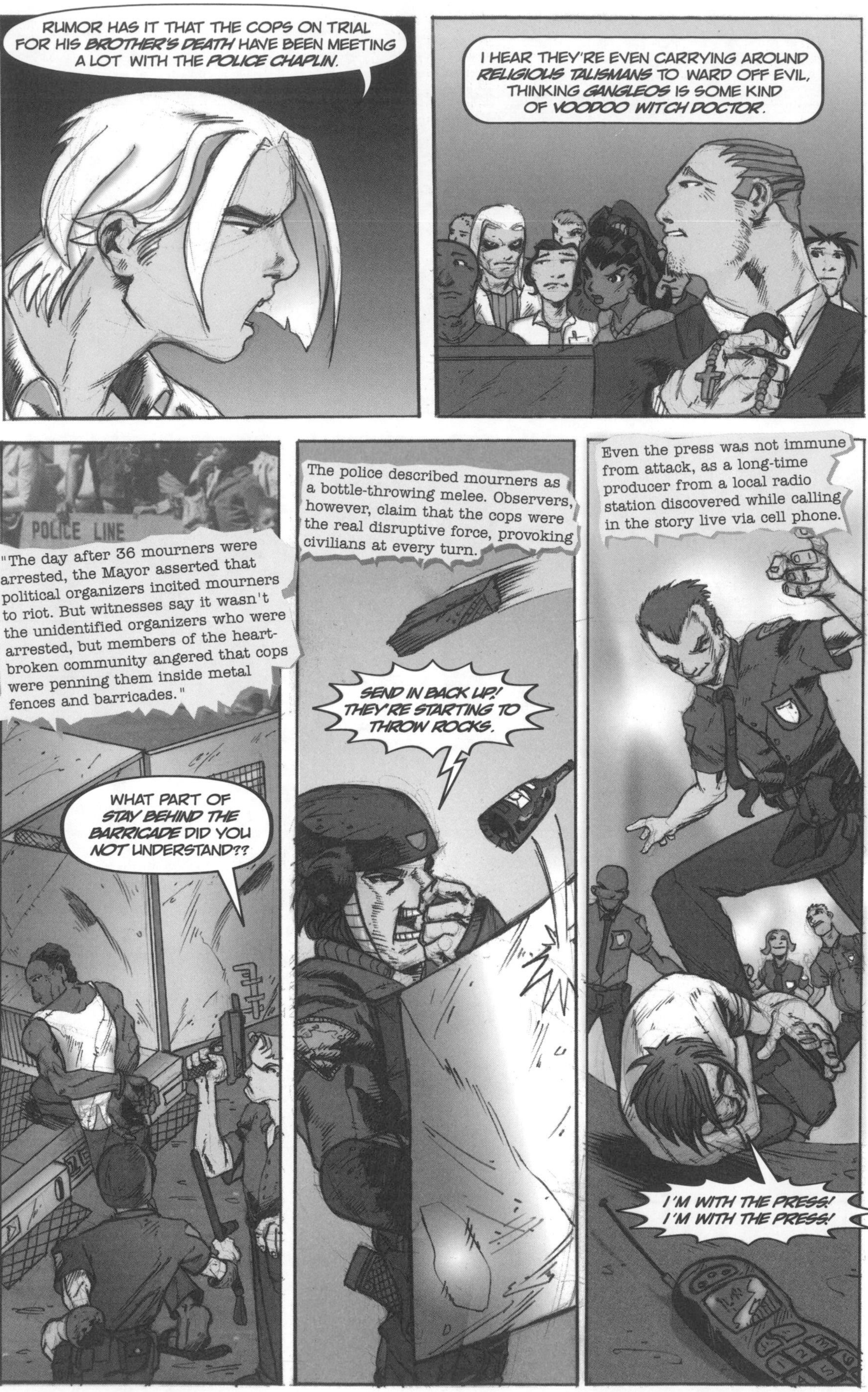
RUMOR HAS IT THAT THE COPS ON TRIAL FOR HIS BROTHER'S DEATH HAVE BEEN MEETING A LOT WITH THE POLICE CHAPLIN.
I HEAR THEY'RE EVEN CARRYING AROUND RELIGIOUS TALISMANS TO WARD OFF EVIL, THINKING GANGLEOS IS SOME KIND OF VOODOO WITCH DOCTOR.
POLICE LINE
"The day after 36 mourners were arrested, the Mayor asserted that political organizers incited mourners to riot. But witnesses say it wasn't the unidentified organizers who were arrested, but members of the heart-broken community angered that cops were penning them inside metal fences and barricades."
WHAT PART OF STAY BEHIND THE BARRICADE DID YOU NOT UNDERSTAND??
The police described mourners as a bottle-throwing melee. Observers, however, claim that the cops were the real disruptive force, provoking civilians at every turn.
SEND IN BACK UP! THEY'RE STARTING TO THROW ROCKS.
Even the press was not immune from attack, as a long-time producer from a local radio station discovered while calling in the story live via cell phone.
I'M WITH THE PRESS! I'M WITH THE PRESS!

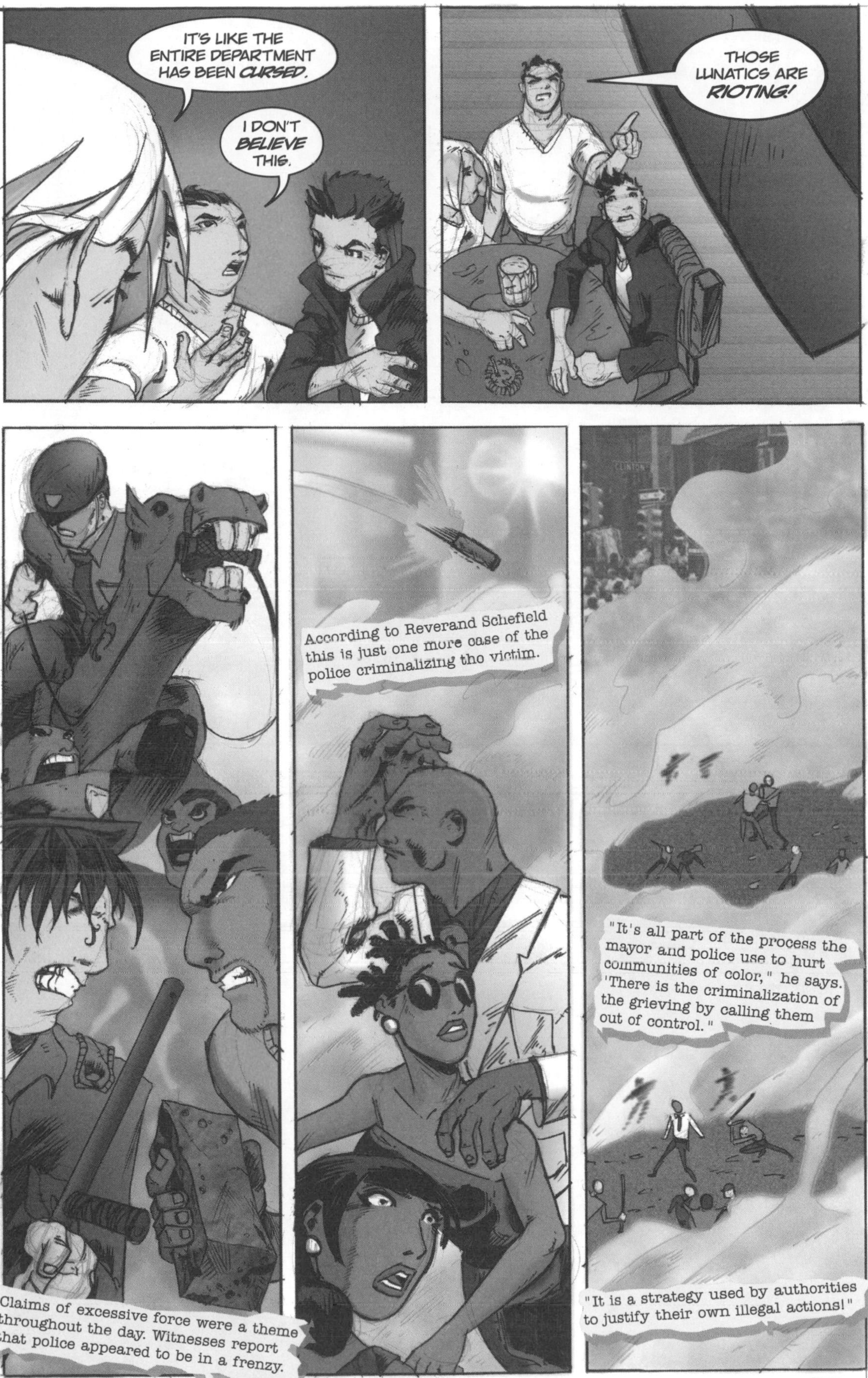
IT'S LIKE THE ENTIRE DEPARTMENT HAS BEEN CURSED.
I DON'T BELIEVE THIS.
THOSE LUNATICS ARE RIOTING!
Claims of excessive force were a theme throughout the day. Witnesses report that police appeared to be in a frenzy.
According to Reverand Schefield this is just one more case of the police criminalizing the victim.
CLINTON
"It's all part of the process the mayor and police use to hurt communities of color," he says. "There is the criminalization of the grieving by calling them out of control."
"It is a strategy used by authorities to justify their own illegal actions!"

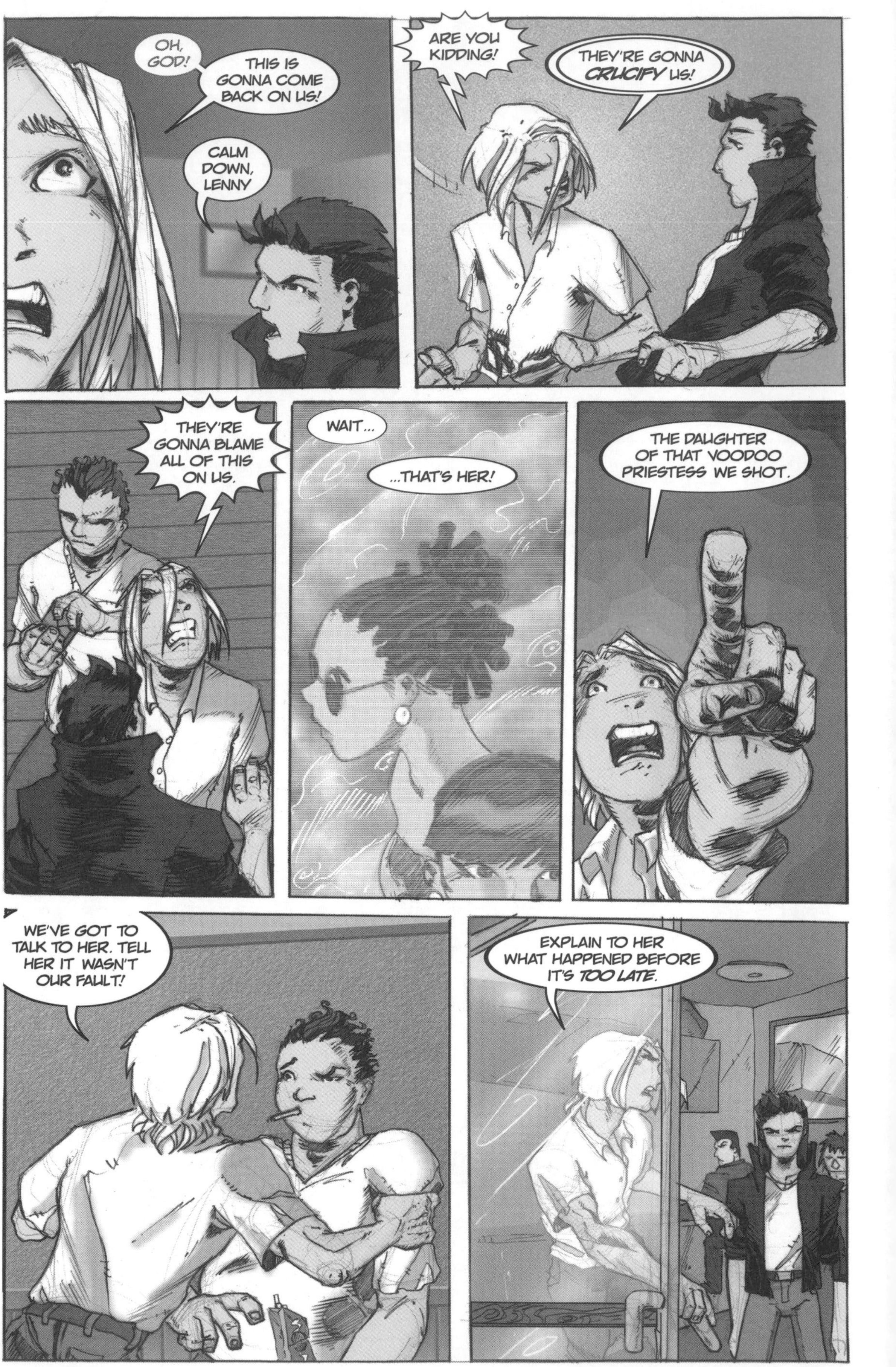
OH, GOD!
THIS IS GONNA COME BACK ON US!
CALM DOWN, LENNY
ARE YOU KIDDING!
THEY'RE GONNA CRUCIFY US!
THEY'RE GONNA BLAME ALL OF THIS ON US.
WAIT...
...THAT'S HER!
THE DAUGHTER OF THAT VOODOO PRIESTESS WE SHOT.
WE'VE GOT TO TALK TO HER. TELL HER IT WASN'T OUR FAULT!
EXPLAIN TO HER WHAT HAPPENED BEFORE IT'S TOO LATE.

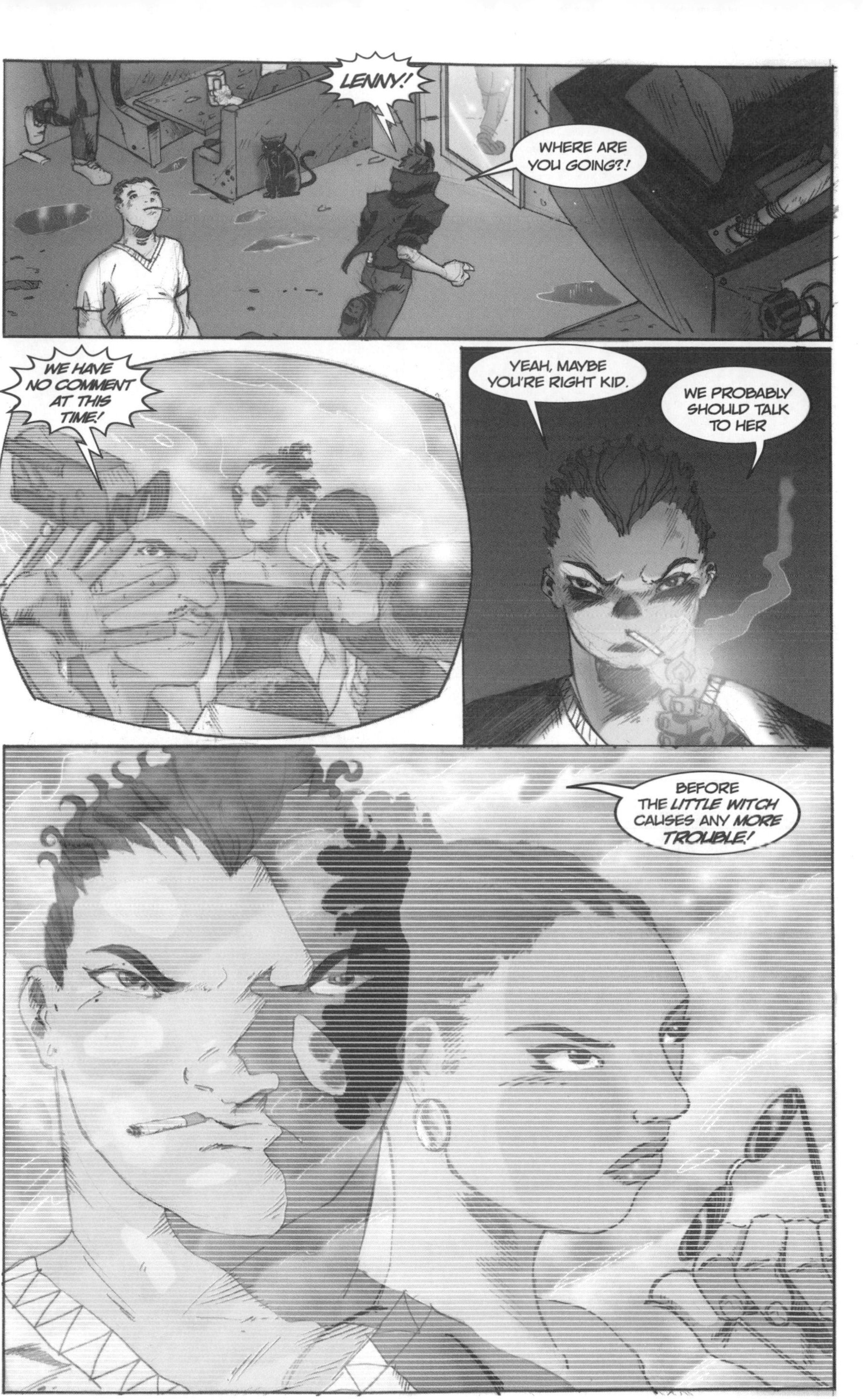
LENNY!!
WHERE ARE YOU GOING?!
WE HAVE NO COMMENT AT THIS TIME!
YEAH, MAYBE YOU'RE RIGHT KID.
WE PROBABLY SHOULD TALK TO HER
BEFORE THE *LITTLE WITCH* CAUSES ANY *MORE TROUBLE!*

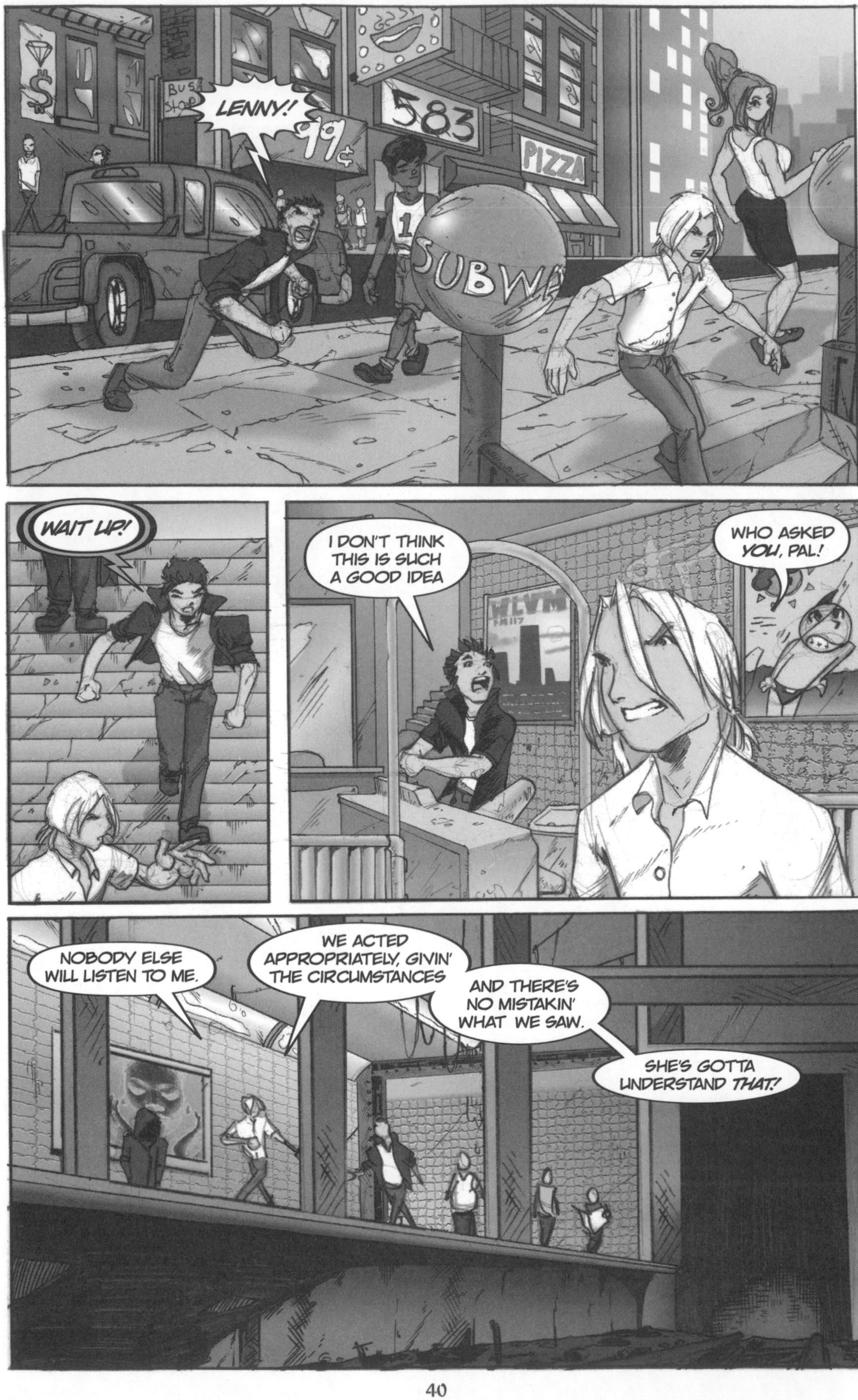
BUS STOP
LENNY!
99¢
583
PIZZA
SUBWA
WAIT UP!
I DON'T THINK THIS IS SUCH A GOOD IDEA
WHO ASKED *YOU*, PAL!
NOBODY ELSE WILL LISTEN TO ME.
WE ACTED APPROPRIATELY, GIVIN' THE CIRCUMSTANCES
AND THERE'S NO MISTAKIN' WHAT WE SAW.
SHE'S GOTTA UNDERSTAND *THAT!*

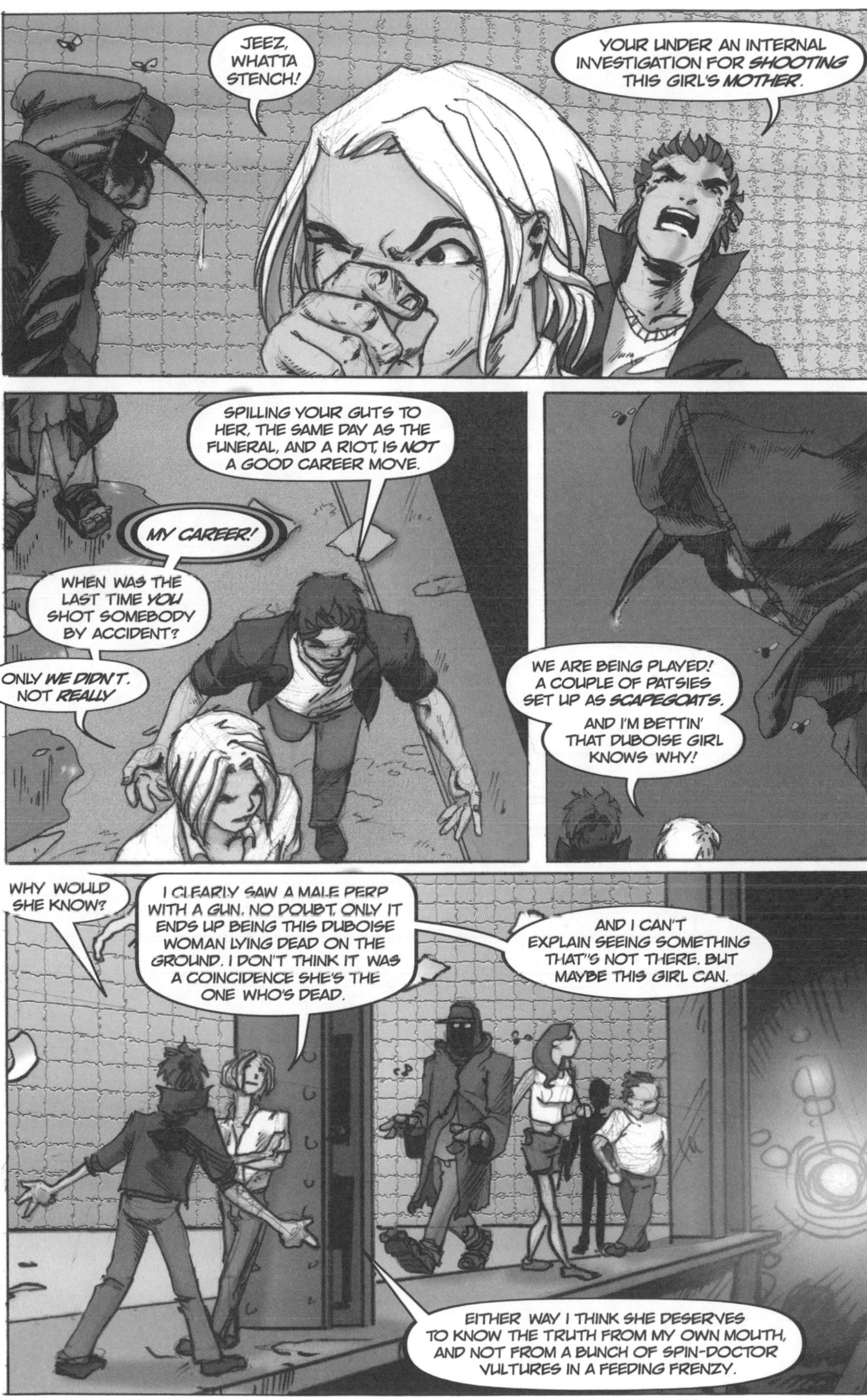
JEEZ, WHATTA STENCH!
YOUR UNDER AN INTERNAL INVESTIGATION FOR SHOOTING THIS GIRL'S MOTHER.
SPILLING YOUR GUTS TO HER, THE SAME DAY AS THE FUNERAL, AND A RIOT, IS NOT A GOOD CAREER MOVE.
MY CAREER!
WHEN WAS THE LAST TIME YOU SHOT SOMEBODY BY ACCIDENT?
ONLY WE DIDN'T. NOT REALLY
WE ARE BEING PLAYED! A COUPLE OF PATSIES SET UP AS SCAPEGOATS.
AND I'M BETTIN' THAT DUBOISE GIRL KNOWS WHY!
WHY WOULD SHE KNOW?
I CLEARLY SAW A MALE PERP WITH A GUN. NO DOUBT. ONLY IT ENDS UP BEING THIS DUBOISE WOMAN LYING DEAD ON THE GROUND. I DON'T THINK IT WAS A COINCIDENCE SHE'S THE ONE WHO'S DEAD.
AND I CAN'T EXPLAIN SEEING SOMETHING THAT'S NOT THERE. BUT MAYBE THIS GIRL CAN.
EITHER WAY I THINK SHE DESERVES TO KNOW THE TRUTH FROM MY OWN MOUTH, AND NOT FROM A BUNCH OF SPIN-DOCTOR VULTURES IN A FEEDING FRENZY.

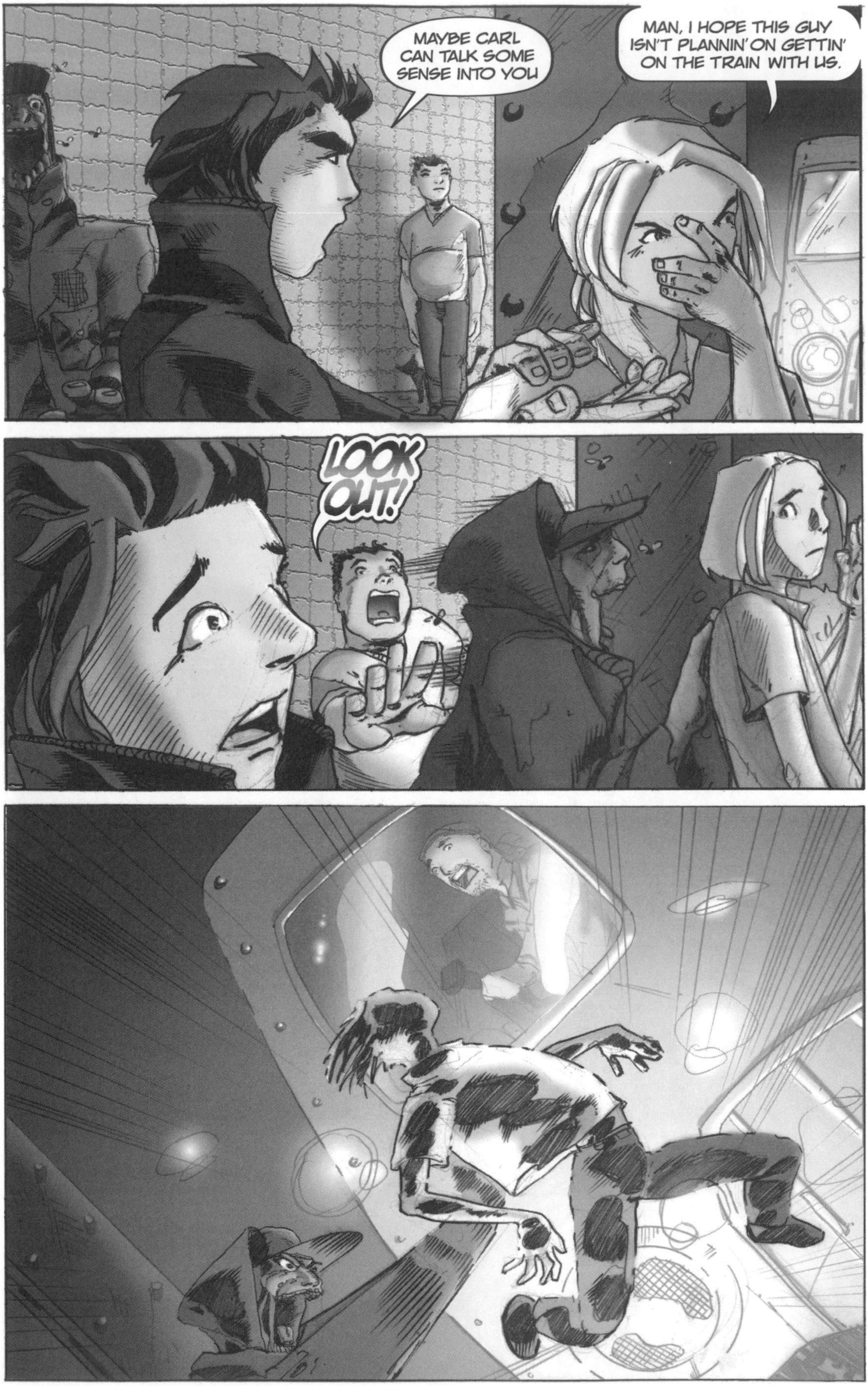
MAYBE CARL CAN TALK SOME SENSE INTO YOU
MAN, I HOPE THIS GUY ISN'T PLANNIN' ON GETTIN' ON THE TRAIN WITH US.
LOOK OUT!

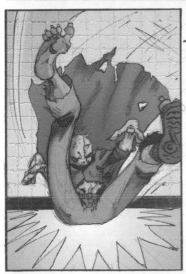

I'LL KILL YOU, YOU SON OF A ...

GOOD LORD!

CHOKE!

43

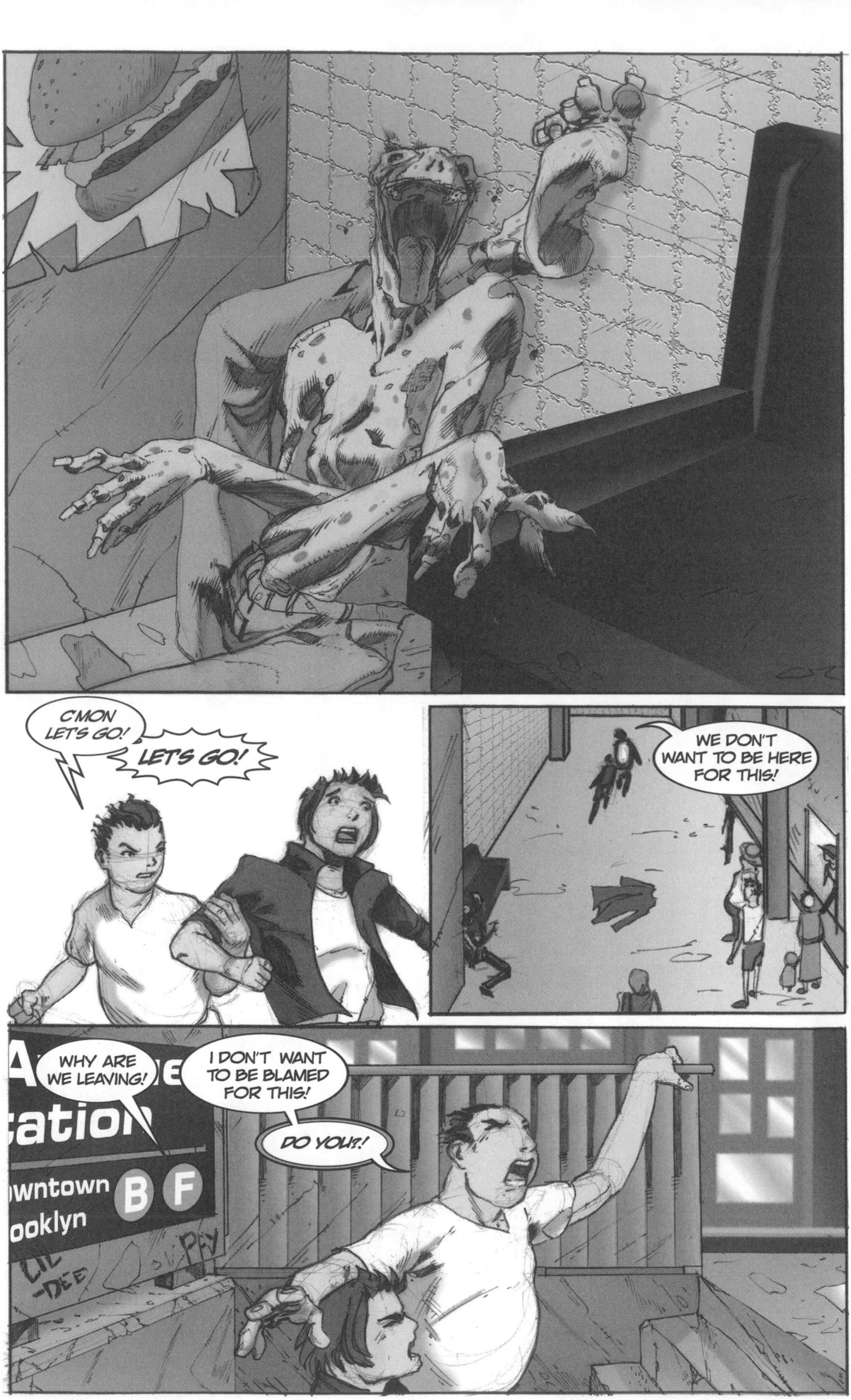
C'MON LET'S GO!
LET'S GO!
WE DON'T WANT TO BE HERE FOR THIS!
cation
ownntown
ooklyn
B
F
WHY ARE WE LEAVING!
I DON'T WANT TO BE BLAMED FOR THIS!
DO YOU?!

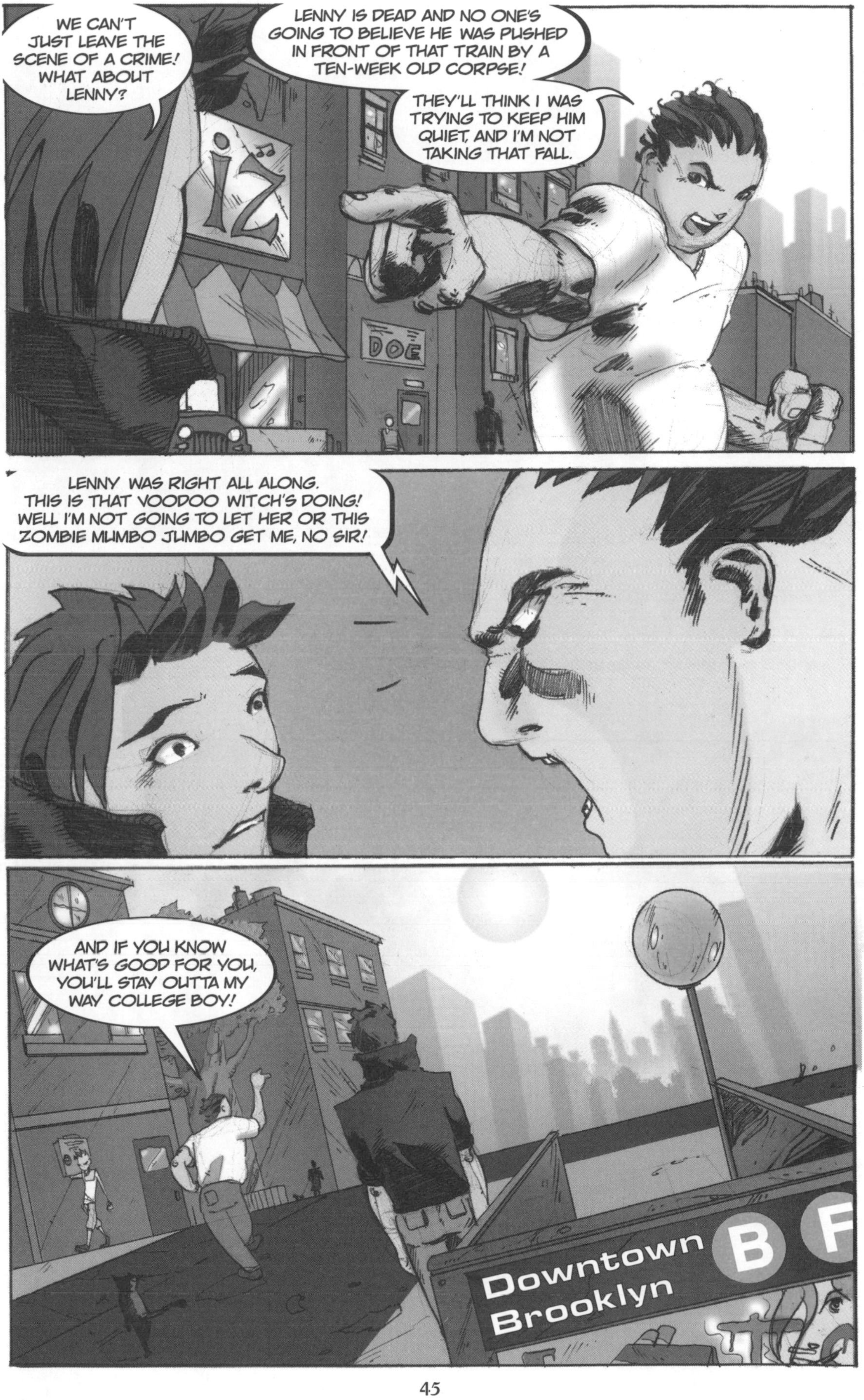
WE CAN'T JUST LEAVE THE SCENE OF A CRIME! WHAT ABOUT LENNY?
LENNY IS DEAD AND NO ONE'S GOING TO BELIEVE HE WAS PUSHED IN FRONT OF THAT TRAIN BY A TEN-WEEK OLD CORPSE!
THEY'LL THINK I WAS TRYING TO KEEP HIM QUIET, AND I'M NOT TAKING THAT FALL.
IZ
DOE
LENNY WAS RIGHT ALL ALONG. THIS IS THAT VOODOO WITCH'S DOING! WELL I'M NOT GOING TO LET HER OR THIS ZOMBIE MUMBO JUMBO GET ME, NO SIR!
AND IF YOU KNOW WHAT'S GOOD FOR YOU, YOU'LL STAY OUTTA MY WAY COLLEGE BOY!
Downtown Brooklyn
B F

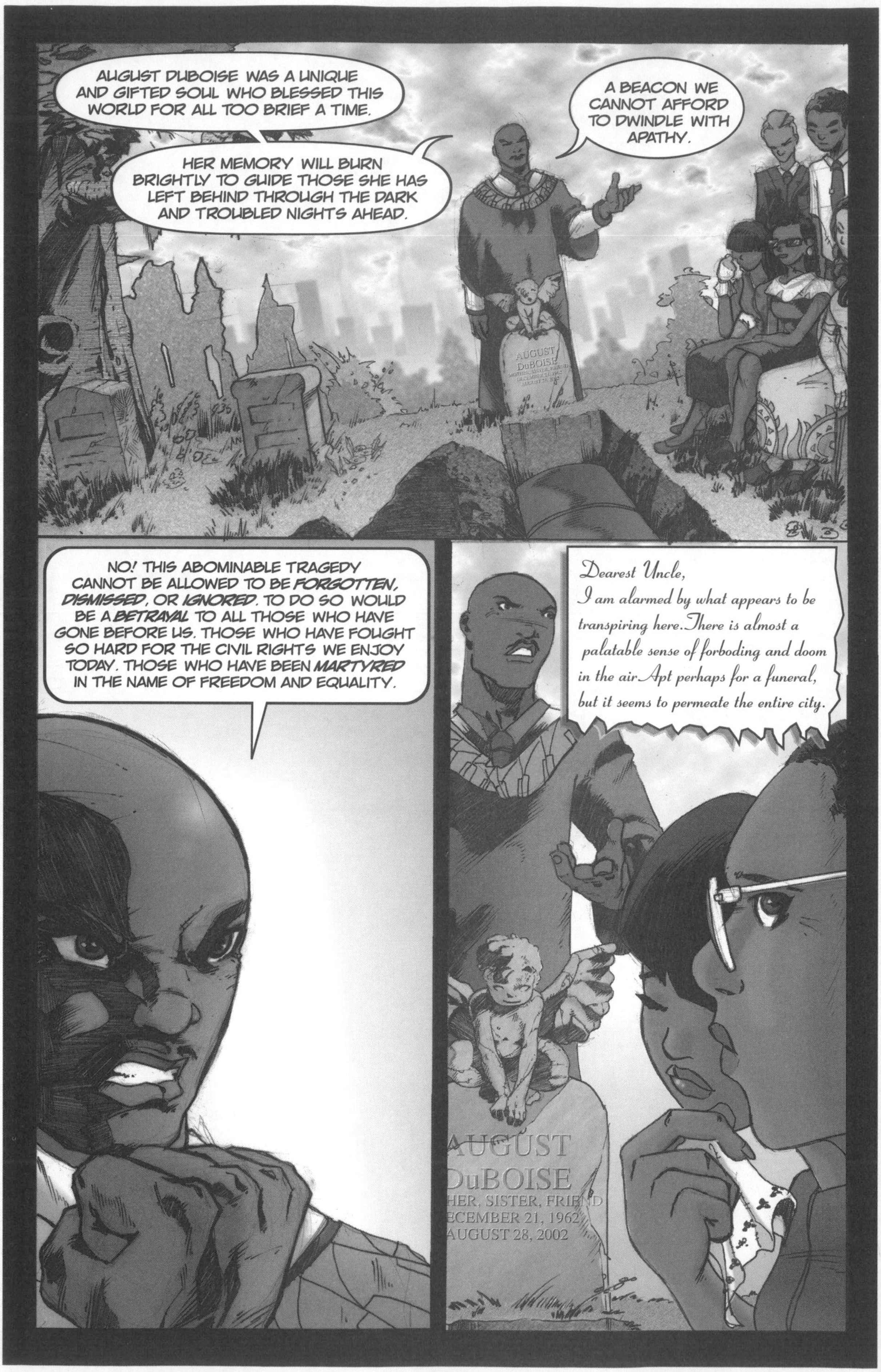
AUGUST DUBOISE WAS A UNIQUE AND GIFTED SOUL WHO BLESSED THIS WORLD FOR ALL TOO BRIEF A TIME.
HER MEMORY WILL BURN BRIGHTLY TO GUIDE THOSE SHE HAS LEFT BEHIND THROUGH THE DARK AND TROUBLED NIGHTS AHEAD.
A BEACON WE CANNOT AFFORD TO DWINDLE WITH APATHY.
NO! THIS ABOMINABLE TRAGEDY CANNOT BE ALLOWED TO BE FORGOTTEN, DISMISSED, OR IGNORED. TO DO SO WOULD BE A BETRAYAL TO ALL THOSE WHO HAVE GONE BEFORE US. THOSE WHO HAVE FOUGHT SO HARD FOR THE CIVIL RIGHTS WE ENJOY TODAY. THOSE WHO HAVE BEEN MARTYRED IN THE NAME OF FREEDOM AND EQUALITY.
Dearest Uncle,
I am alarmed by what appears to be transpiring here. There is almost a palatable sense of forboding and doom in the air. Apt perhaps for a funeral, but it seems to permeate the entire city.
AUGUST
DuBOISE
HER, SISTER, FRIEND
ECEMBER 21, 1962
AUGUST 28, 2002

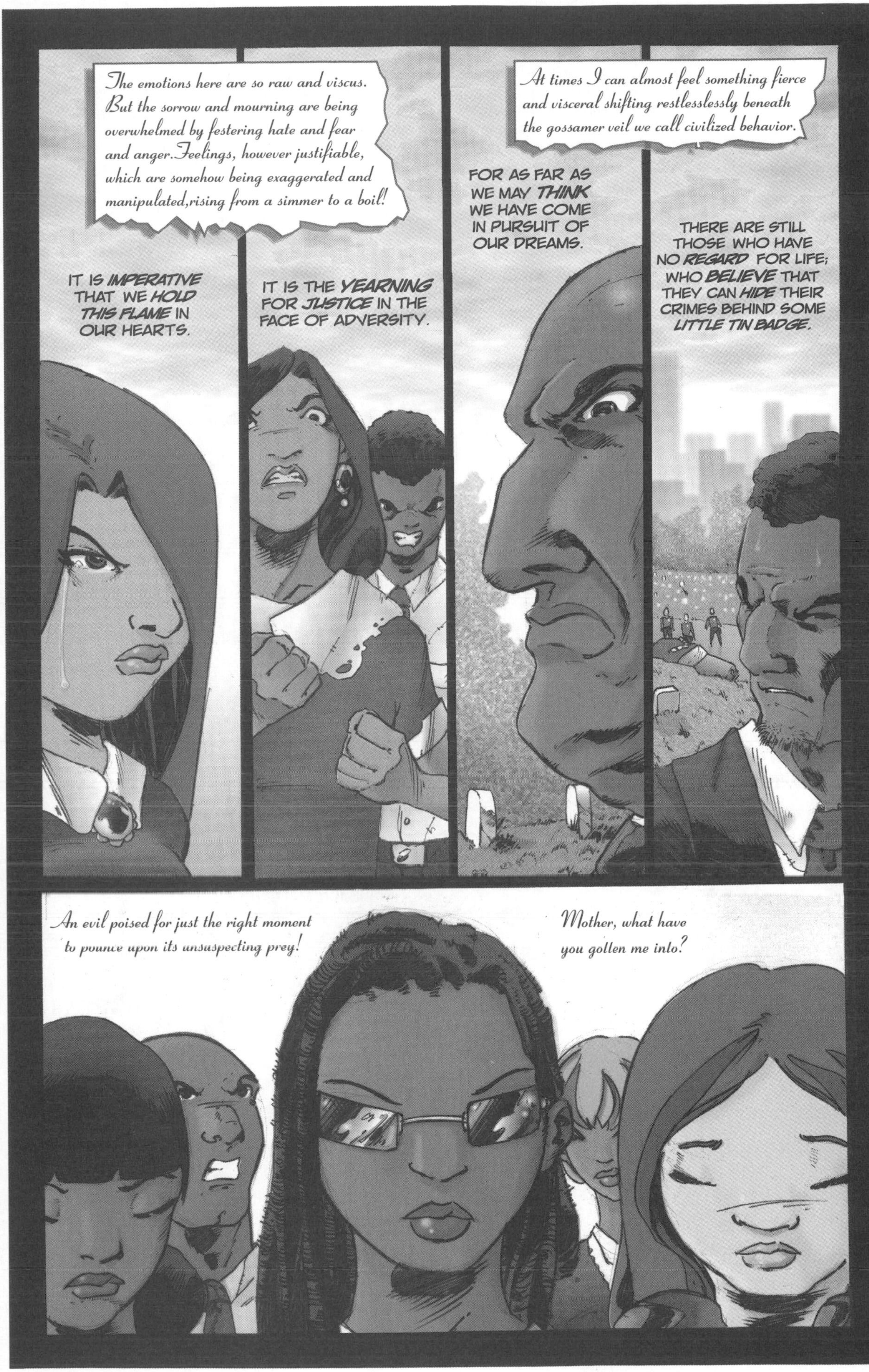
The emotions here are so raw and viscus. But the sorrow and mourning are being overwhelmed by festering hate and fear and anger. Feelings, however justifiable, which are somehow being exaggerated and manipulated, rising from a simmer to a boil!
IT IS IMPERATIVE THAT WE HOLD THIS FLAME IN OUR HEARTS.
IT IS THE YEARNING FOR JUSTICE IN THE FACE OF ADVERSITY.
At times I can almost feel something fierce and visceral shifting restlesslessly beneath the gossamer veil we call civilized behavior.
FOR AS FAR AS WE MAY THINK WE HAVE COME IN PURSUIT OF OUR DREAMS.
THERE ARE STILL THOSE WHO HAVE NO REGARD FOR LIFE; WHO BELIEVE THAT THEY CAN HIDE THEIR CRIMES BEHIND SOME LITTLE TIN BADGE.
An evil poised for just the right moment to pounce upon its unsuspecting prey!
Mother, what have you gotten me into?

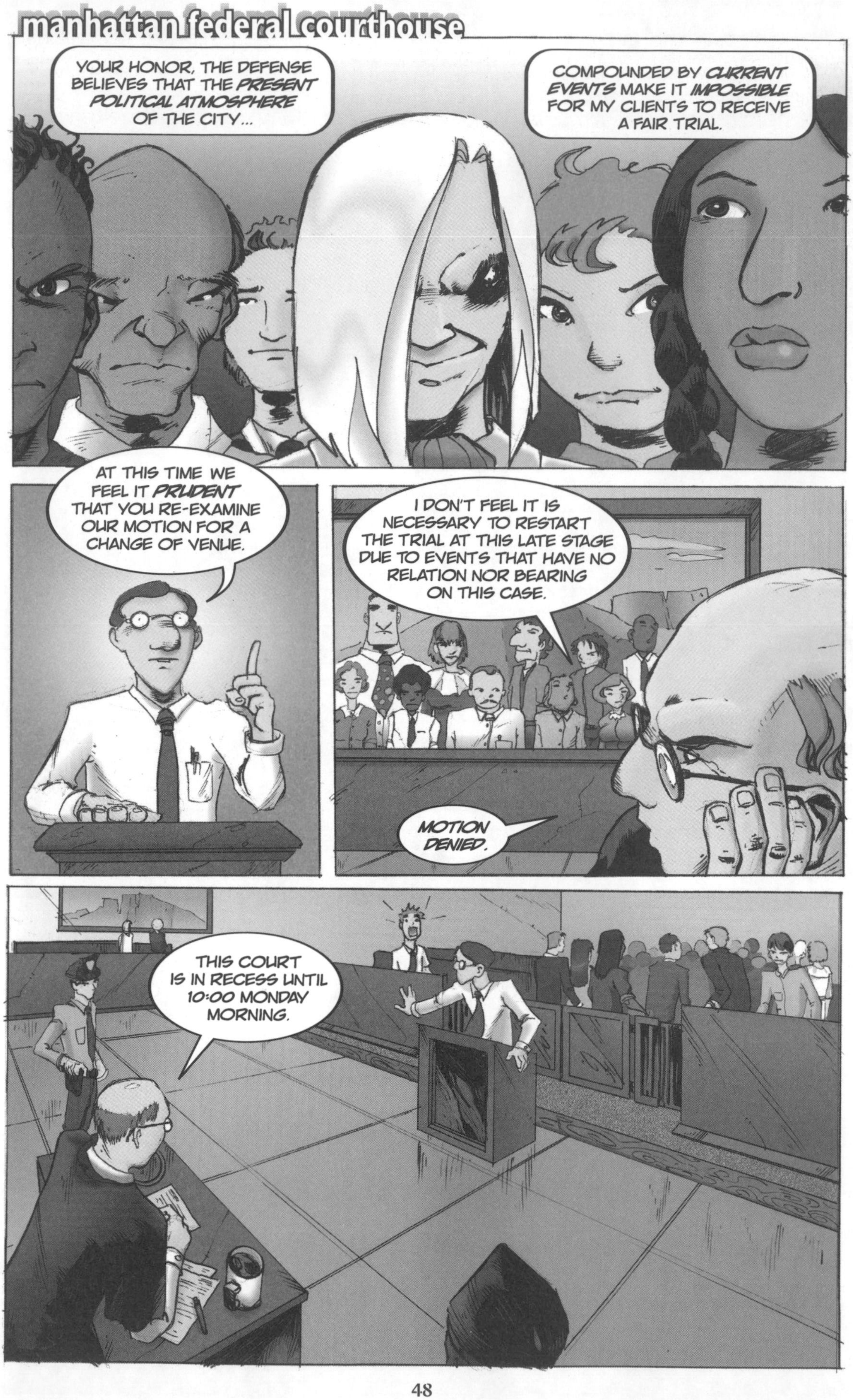
manhattan federal courthouse
YOUR HONOR, THE DEFENSE BELIEVES THAT THE PRESENT POLITICAL ATMOSPHERE OF THE CITY...
COMPOUNDED BY CURRENT EVENTS MAKE IT IMPOSSIBLE FOR MY CLIENTS TO RECEIVE A FAIR TRIAL.
AT THIS TIME WE FEEL IT PRUDENT THAT YOU RE-EXAMINE OUR MOTION FOR A CHANGE OF VENUE.
I DON'T FEEL IT IS NECESSARY TO RESTART THE TRIAL AT THIS LATE STAGE DUE TO EVENTS THAT HAVE NO RELATION NOR BEARING ON THIS CASE.
MOTION DENIED.
THIS COURT IS IN RECESS UNTIL 10:00 MONDAY MORNING.

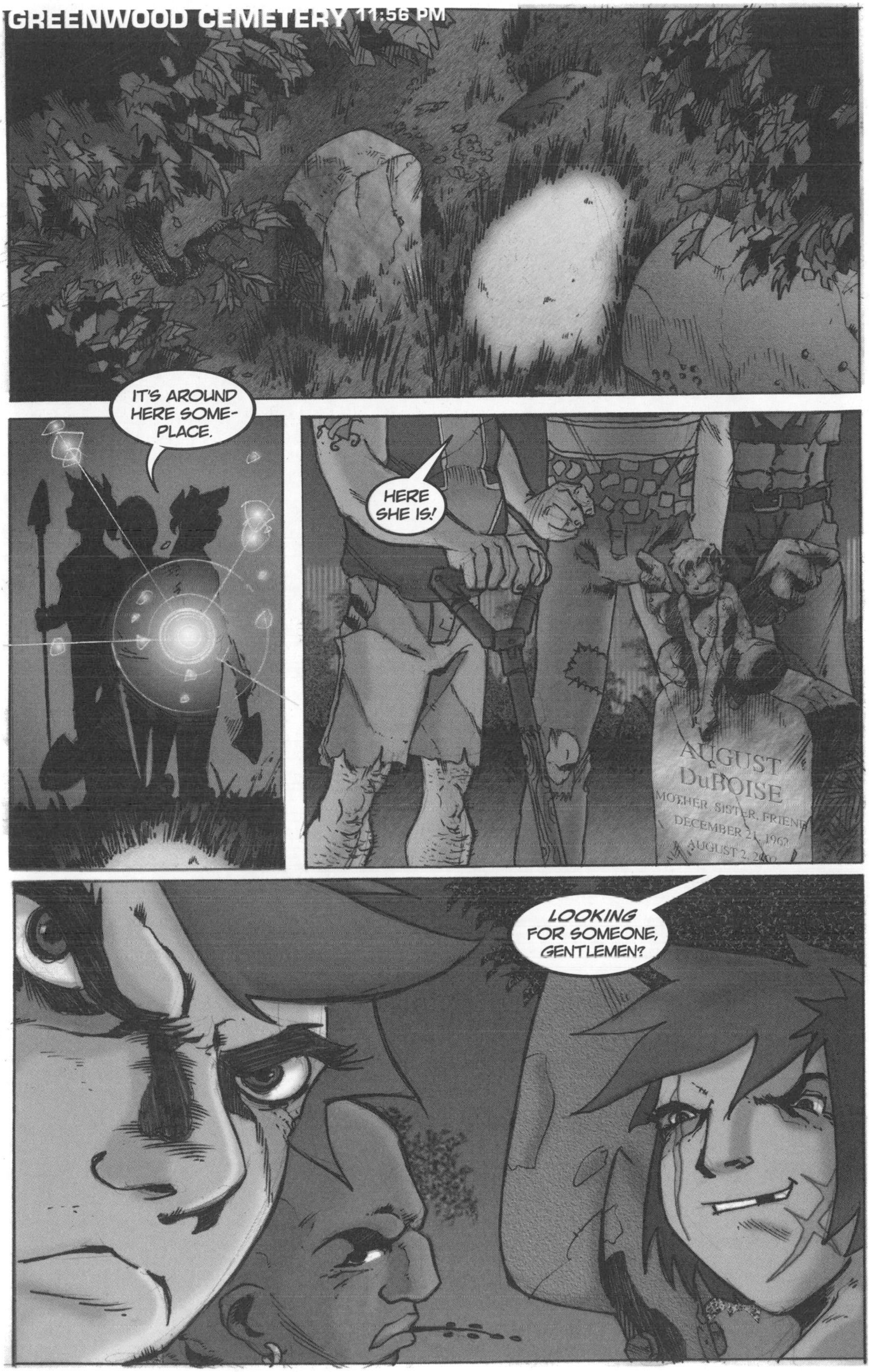
GREENWOOD CEMETERY 11:56 PM
IT'S AROUND HERE SOME-PLACE.
HERE SHE IS!
AUGUST DuBOISE
MOTHER, SISTER, FRIEND
LOOKING FOR SOMEONE, GENTLEMEN?

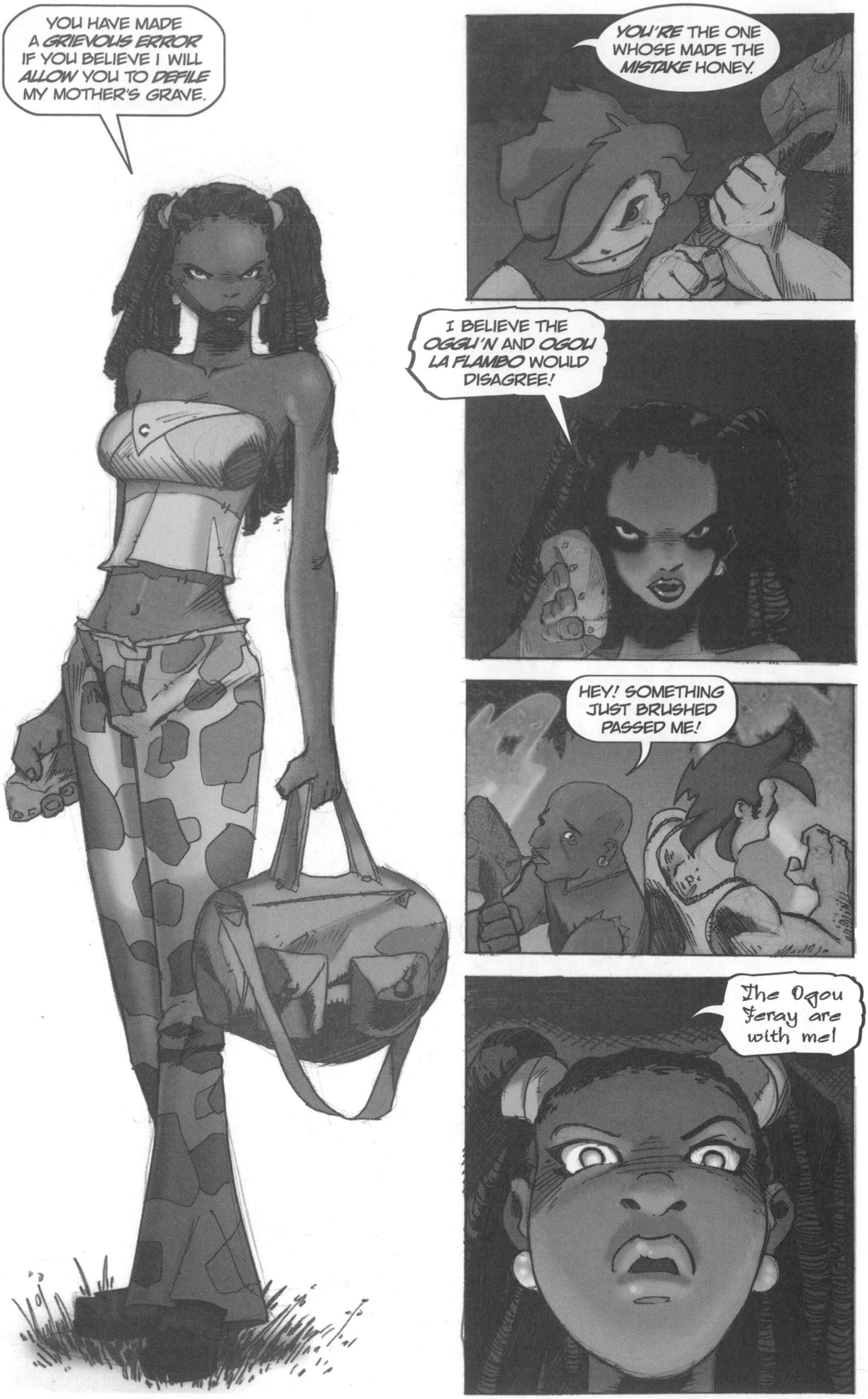
YOU HAVE MADE A GRIEVOUS ERROR IF YOU BELIEVE I WILL ALLOW YOU TO DEFILE MY MOTHER'S GRAVE.
YOU'RE THE ONE WHOSE MADE THE MISTAKE HONEY.
I BELIEVE THE OGGU'N AND OGOU LA FLAMBO WOULD DISAGREE!
HEY! SOMETHING JUST BRUSHED PASSED ME!
The Ogou Feray are with me!

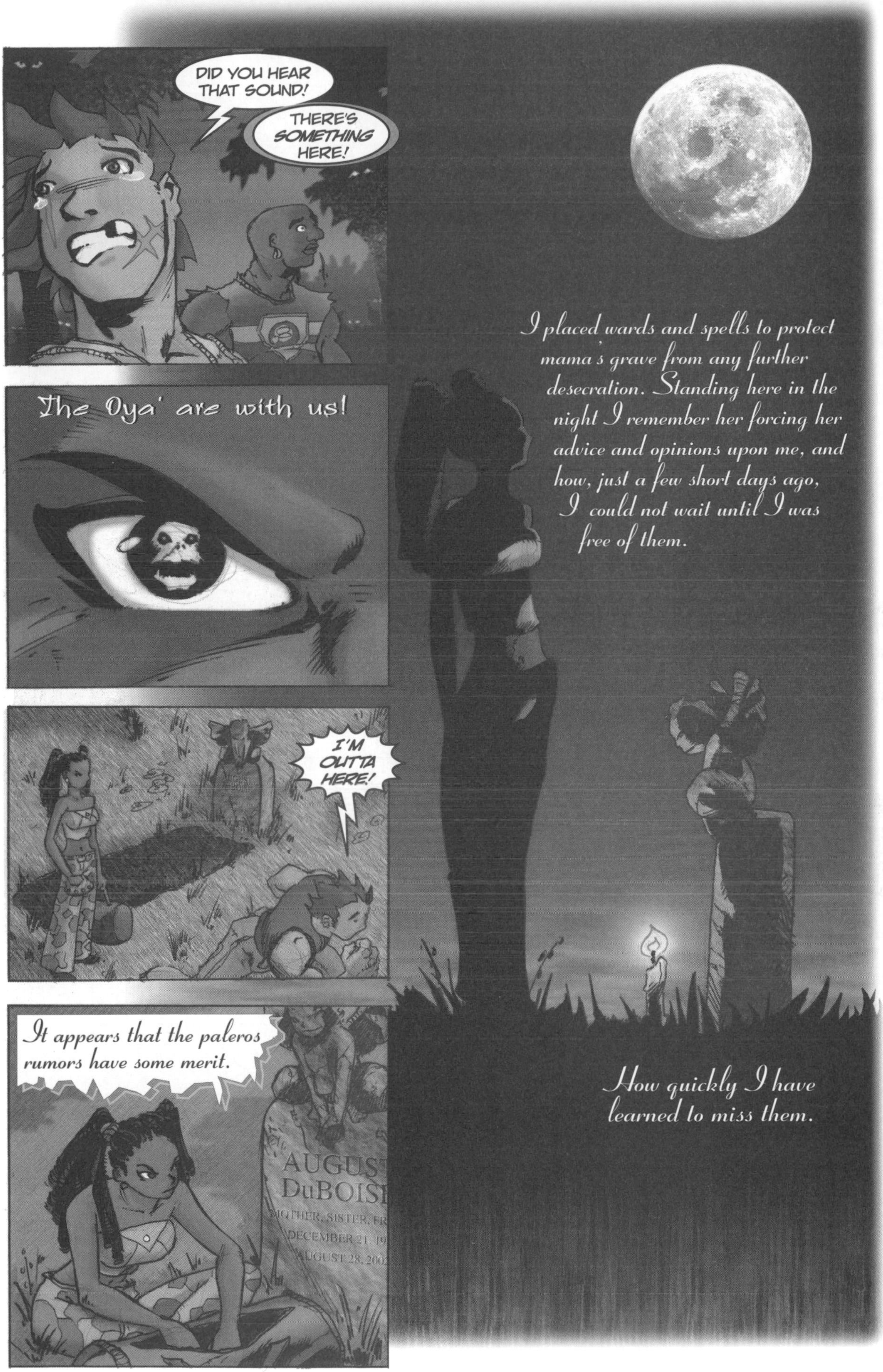

DID YOU HEAR THAT SOUND!
THERE'S SOMETHING HERE!
The Oya' are with us!
I'M OUTTA HERE!
It appears that the paleros rumors have some merit.
I placed wards and spells to protect mama's grave from any further desecration. Standing here in the night I remember her forcing her advice and opinions upon me, and how, just a few short days ago, I could not wait until I was free of them.
How quickly I have learned to miss them.

Chapter Three
The Rules of Deception

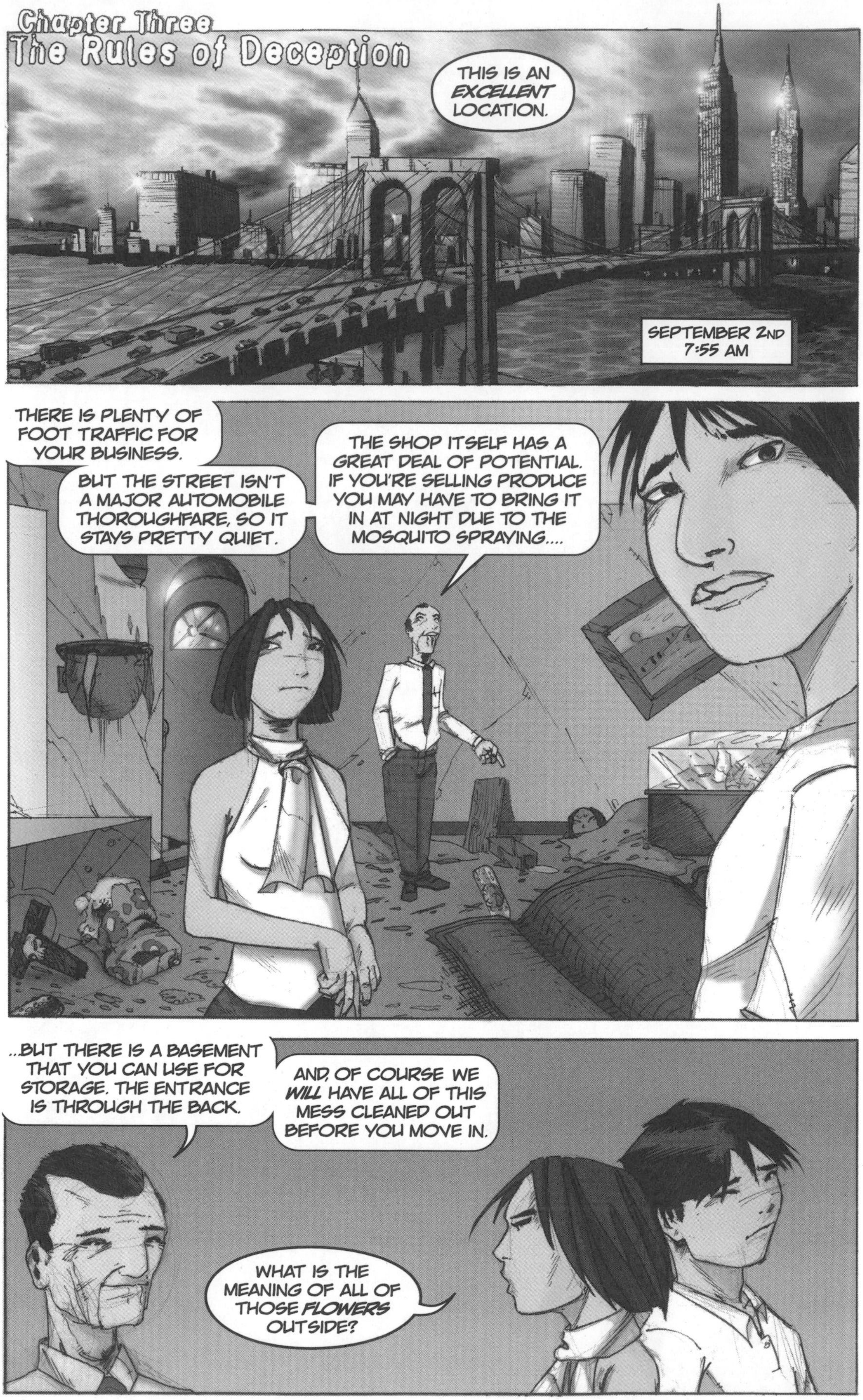
THIS IS AN *EXCELLENT* LOCATION.
SEPTEMBER 2ND 7:55 AM
THERE IS PLENTY OF FOOT TRAFFIC FOR YOUR BUSINESS.
BUT THE STREET ISN'T A MAJOR AUTOMOBILE THOROUGHFARE, SO IT STAYS PRETTY QUIET.
THE SHOP ITSELF HAS A GREAT DEAL OF POTENTIAL. IF YOU'RE SELLING PRODUCE YOU MAY HAVE TO BRING IT IN AT NIGHT DUE TO THE MOSQUITO SPRAYING....
...BUT THERE IS A BASEMENT THAT YOU CAN USE FOR STORAGE. THE ENTRANCE IS THROUGH THE BACK.
AND, OF COURSE WE *WILL* HAVE ALL OF THIS MESS CLEANED OUT BEFORE YOU MOVE IN.
WHAT IS THE MEANING OF ALL OF THOSE *FLOWERS* OUTSIDE?

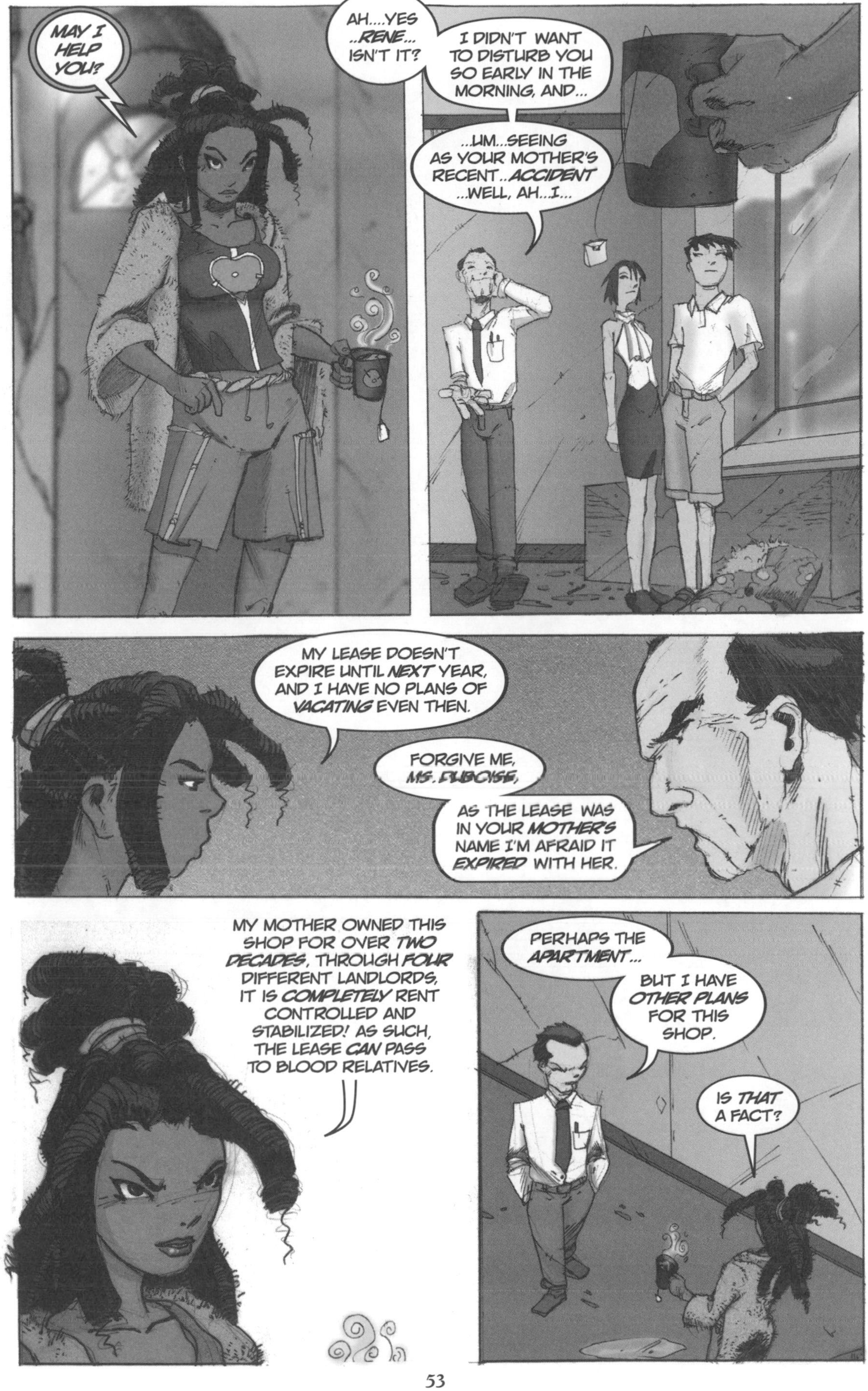
MAY I HELP YOU?
AH....YES ...RENE... ISN'T IT?
I DIDN'T WANT TO DISTURB YOU SO EARLY IN THE MORNING, AND...
...UM...SEEING AS YOUR MOTHER'S RECENT...ACCIDENT ...WELL, AH...I...
MY LEASE DOESN'T EXPIRE UNTIL NEXT YEAR, AND I HAVE NO PLANS OF VACATING EVEN THEN.
FORGIVE ME, MS. DUBOISE,
AS THE LEASE WAS IN YOUR MOTHER'S NAME I'M AFRAID IT EXPIRED WITH HER.
MY MOTHER OWNED THIS SHOP FOR OVER TWO DECADES, THROUGH FOUR DIFFERENT LANDLORDS, IT IS COMPLETELY RENT CONTROLLED AND STABILIZED! AS SUCH, THE LEASE CAN PASS TO BLOOD RELATIVES.
PERHAPS THE APARTMENT...
BUT I HAVE OTHER PLANS FOR THIS SHOP.
IS THAT A FACT?

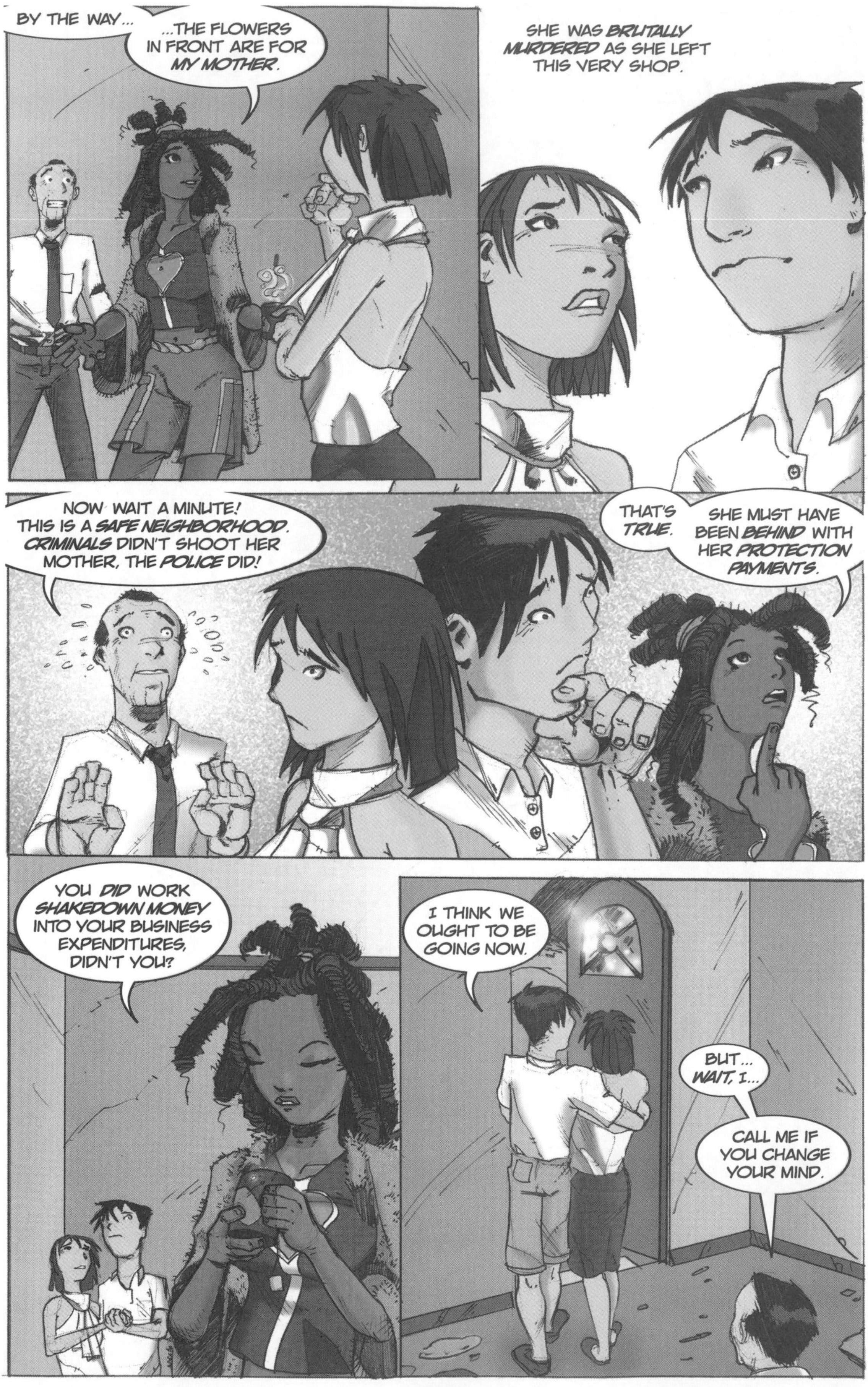
BY THE WAY...
...THE FLOWERS IN FRONT ARE FOR MY MOTHER.
SHE WAS BRUTALLY MURDERED AS SHE LEFT THIS VERY SHOP.
NOW WAIT A MINUTE! THIS IS A SAFE NEIGHBORHOOD. CRIMINALS DIDN'T SHOOT HER MOTHER, THE POLICE DID!
THAT'S TRUE.
SHE MUST HAVE BEEN BEHIND WITH HER PROTECTION PAYMENTS.
YOU DID WORK SHAKEDOWN MONEY INTO YOUR BUSINESS EXPENDITURES, DIDN'T YOU?
I THINK WE OUGHT TO BE GOING NOW.
BUT... WAIT, I...
CALL ME IF YOU CHANGE YOUR MIND.

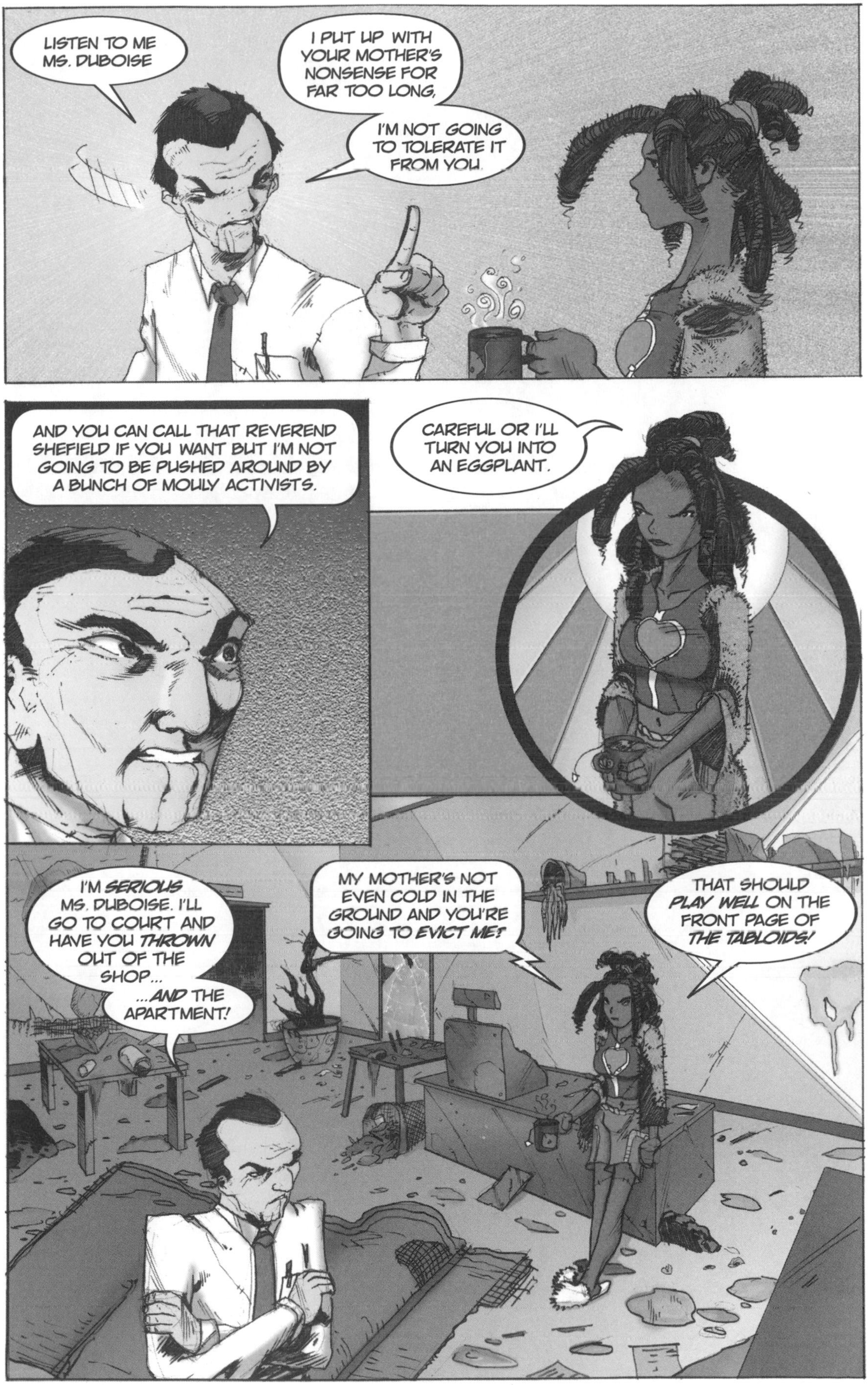
LISTEN TO ME MS. DUBOISE
I PUT UP WITH YOUR MOTHER'S NONSENSE FOR FAR TOO LONG,
I'M NOT GOING TO TOLERATE IT FROM YOU.
AND YOU CAN CALL THAT REVEREND SHEFIELD IF YOU WANT BUT I'M NOT GOING TO BE PUSHED AROUND BY A BUNCH OF MOULY ACTIVISTS.
CAREFUL OR I'LL TURN YOU INTO AN EGGPLANT.
I'M SERIOUS MS. DUBOISE. I'LL GO TO COURT AND HAVE YOU THROWN OUT OF THE SHOP...
...AND THE APARTMENT!
MY MOTHER'S NOT EVEN COLD IN THE GROUND AND YOU'RE GOING TO EVICT ME?
THAT SHOULD PLAY WELL ON THE FRONT PAGE OF THE TABLOIDS!

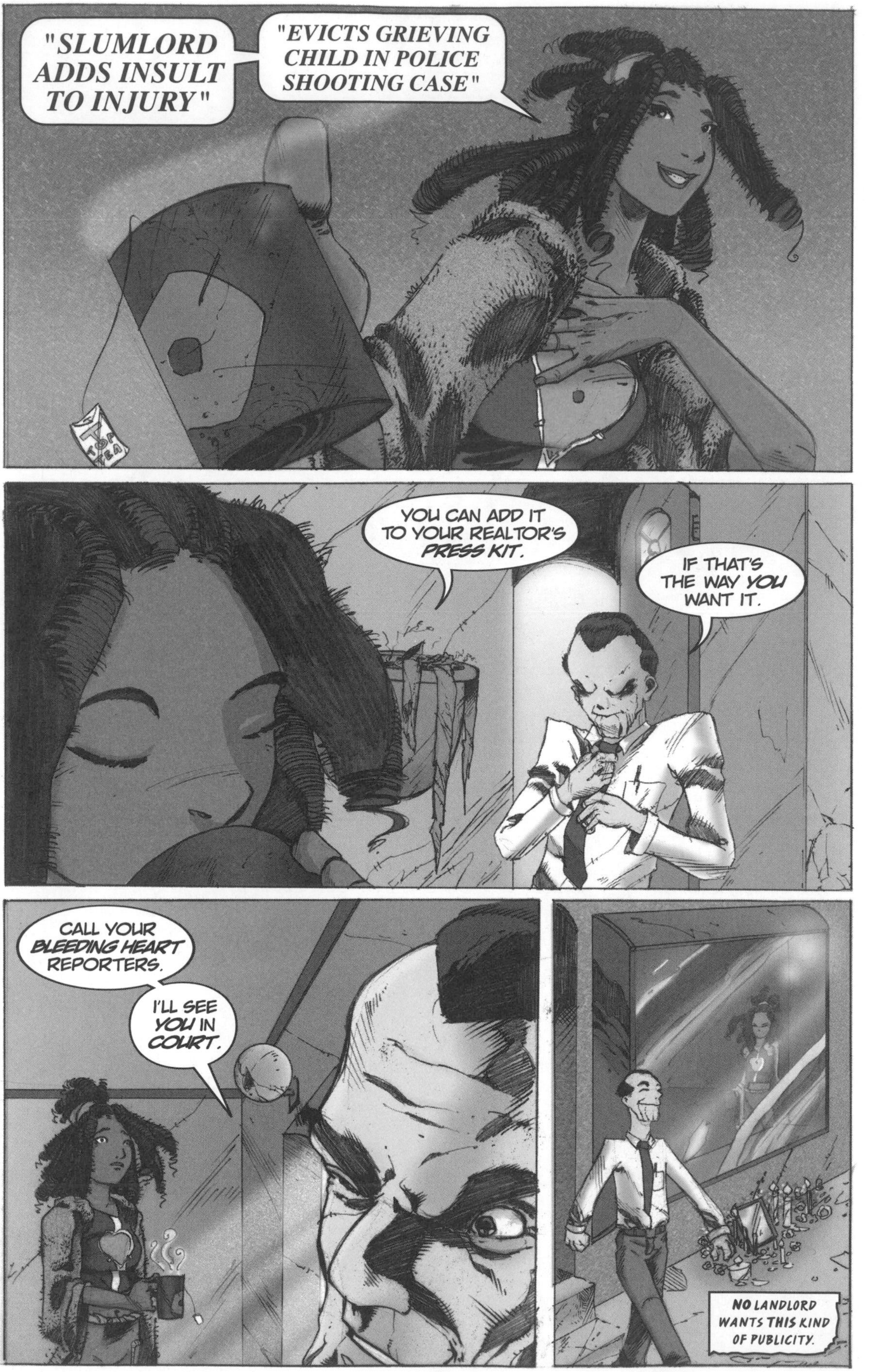
"SLUMLORD ADDS INSULT TO INJURY"
"EVICTS GRIEVING CHILD IN POLICE SHOOTING CASE"
YOU CAN ADD IT TO YOUR REALTOR'S PRESS KIT.
IF THAT'S THE WAY YOU WANT IT.
CALL YOUR BLEEDING HEART REPORTERS.
I'LL SEE YOU IN COURT.
NO LANDLORD WANTS THIS KIND OF PUBLICITY.

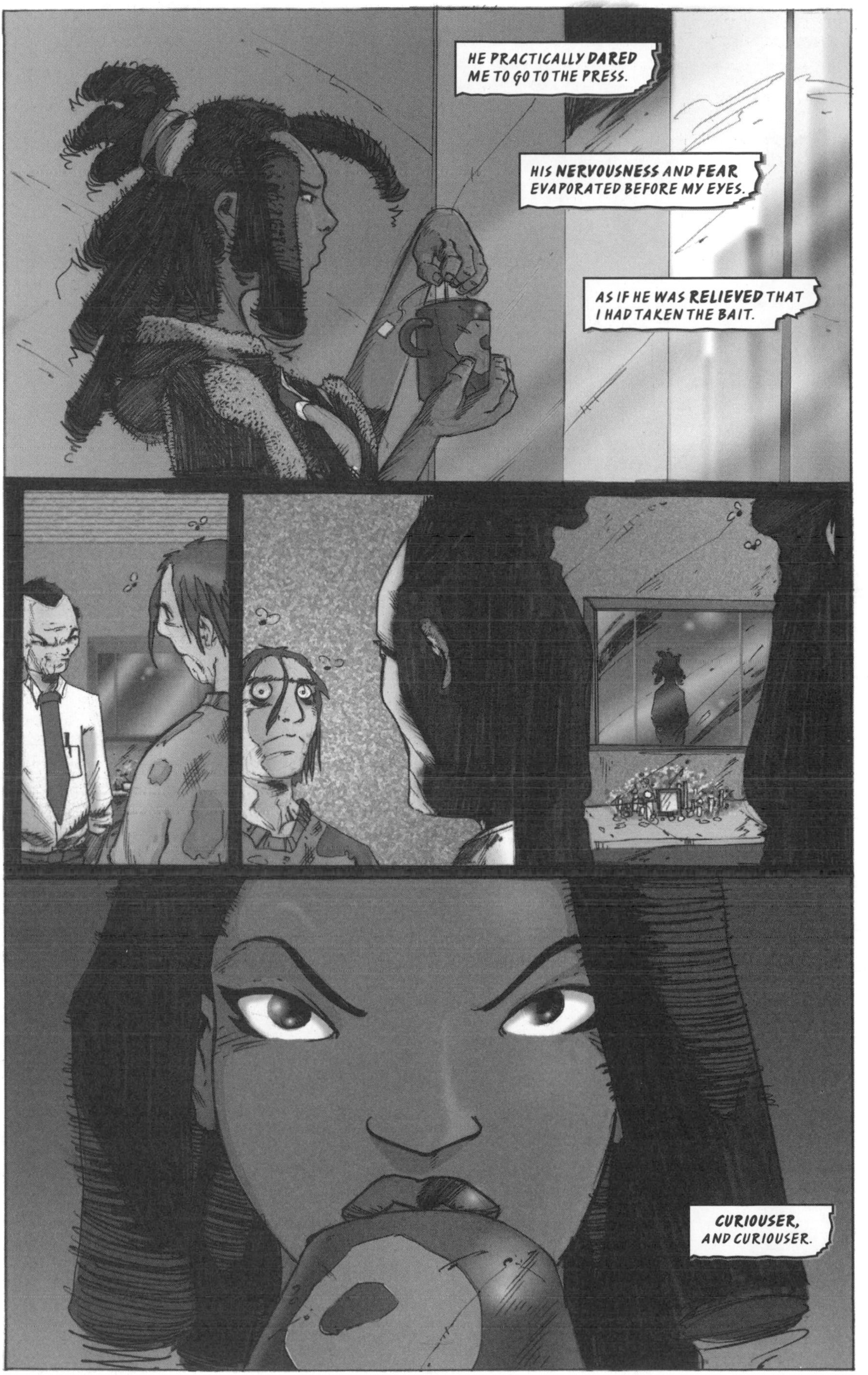
HE PRACTICALLY DARED ME TO GO TO THE PRESS.
HIS NERVOUSNESS AND FEAR EVAPORATED BEFORE MY EYES.
AS IF HE WAS RELIEVED THAT I HAD TAKEN THE BAIT.
CURIOUSER, AND CURIOUSER.

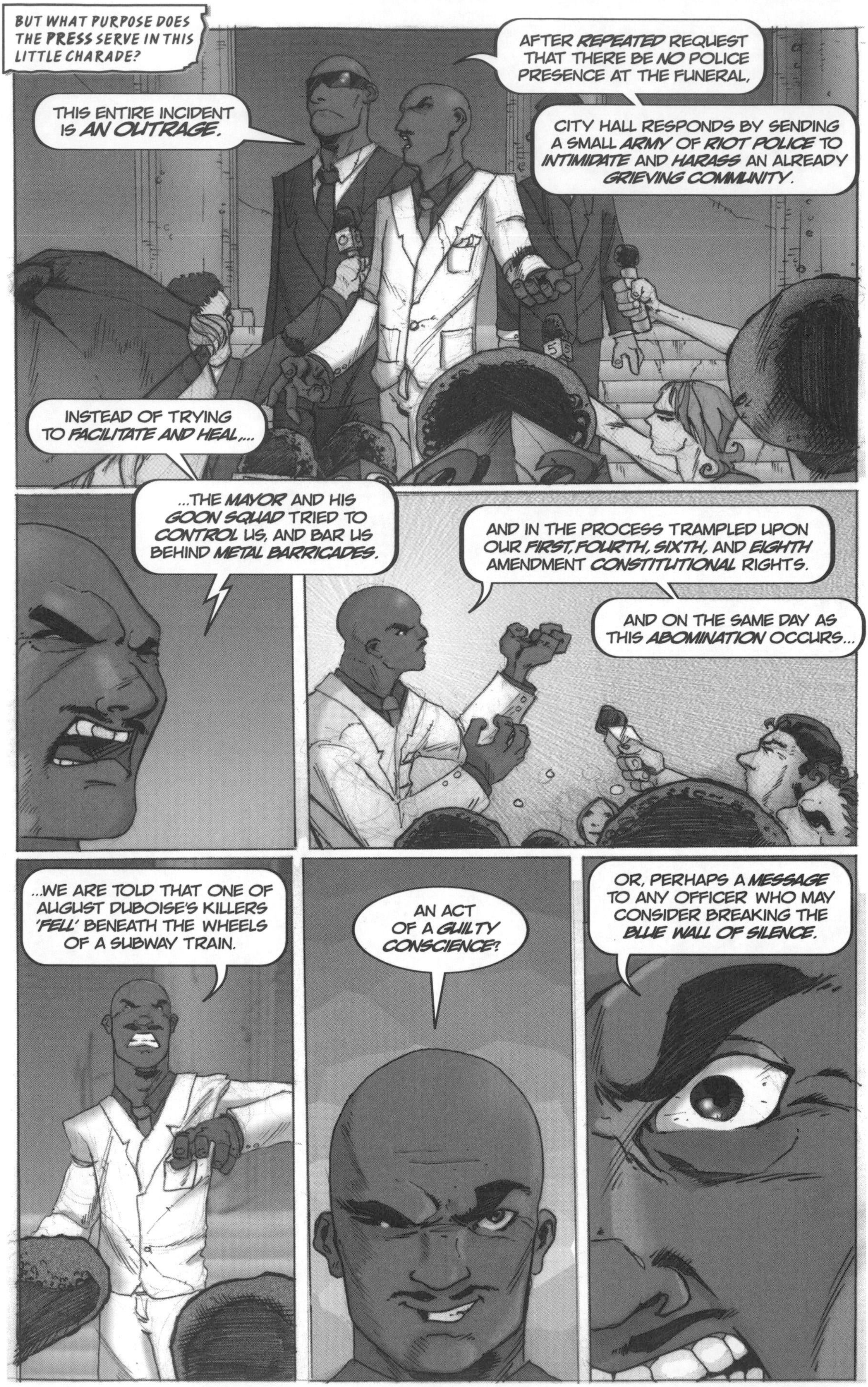
BUT WHAT PURPOSE DOES THE PRESS SERVE IN THIS LITTLE CHARADE?
THIS ENTIRE INCIDENT IS AN OUTRAGE.
AFTER REPEATED REQUEST THAT THERE BE NO POLICE PRESENCE AT THE FUNERAL,
CITY HALL RESPONDS BY SENDING A SMALL ARMY OF RIOT POLICE TO INTIMIDATE AND HARASS AN ALREADY GRIEVING COMMUNITY.
INSTEAD OF TRYING TO FACILITATE AND HEAL,...
...THE MAYOR AND HIS GOON SQUAD TRIED TO CONTROL US, AND BAR US BEHIND METAL BARRICADES.
AND IN THE PROCESS TRAMPLED UPON OUR FIRST, FOURTH, SIXTH, AND EIGHTH AMENDMENT CONSTITUTIONAL RIGHTS.
AND ON THE SAME DAY AS THIS ABOMINATION OCCURS...
...WE ARE TOLD THAT ONE OF AUGUST DUBOISE'S KILLERS 'FELL' BENEATH THE WHEELS OF A SUBWAY TRAIN.
AN ACT OF A GUILTY CONSCIENCE?
OR, PERHAPS A MESSAGE TO ANY OFFICER WHO MAY CONSIDER BREAKING THE BLUE WALL OF SILENCE.

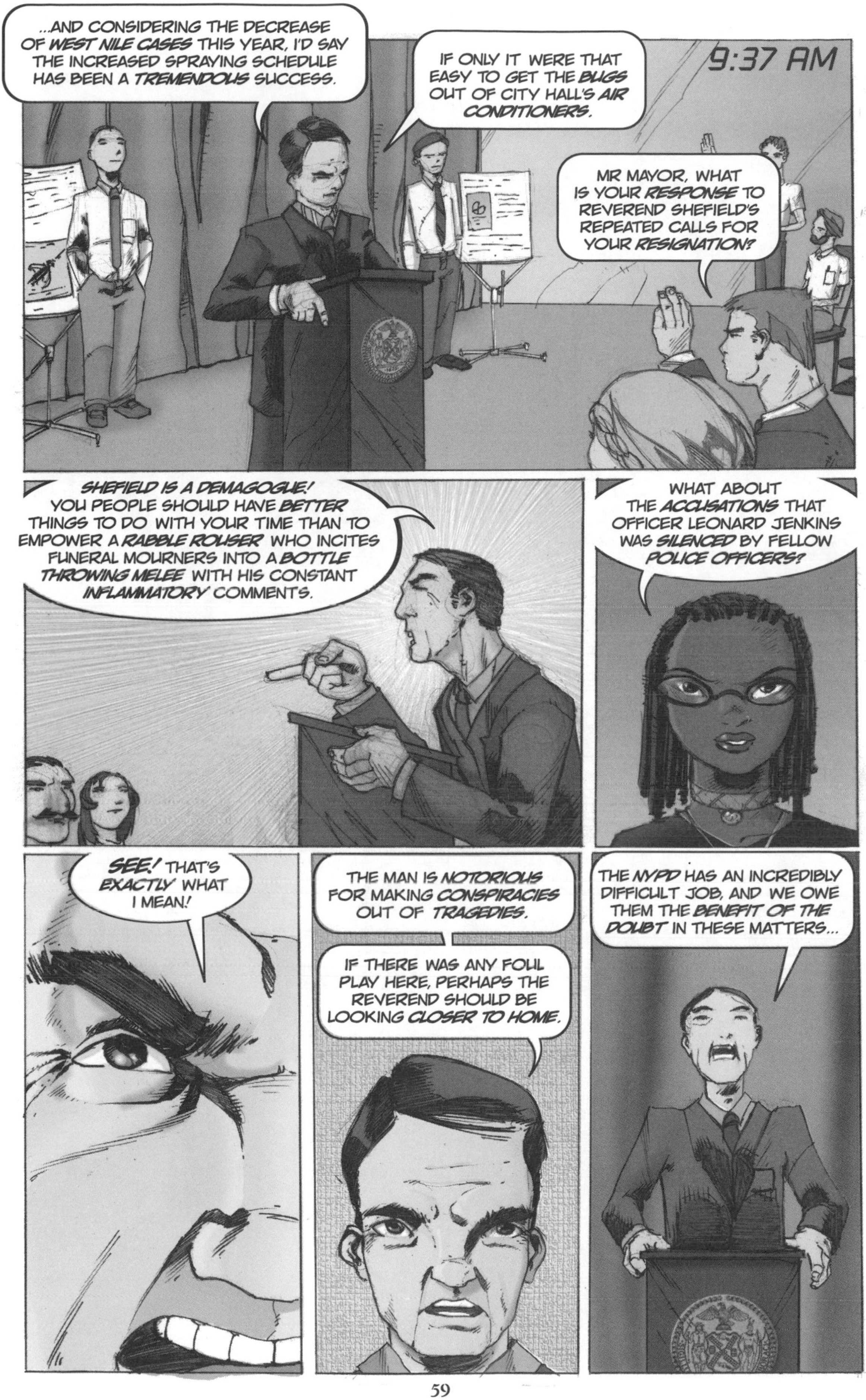
...AND CONSIDERING THE DECREASE OF WEST NILE CASES THIS YEAR, I'D SAY THE INCREASED SPRAYING SCHEDULE HAS BEEN A TREMENDOUS SUCCESS.
IF ONLY IT WERE THAT EASY TO GET THE BUGS OUT OF CITY HALL'S AIR CONDITIONERS.
9:37 AM
MR MAYOR, WHAT IS YOUR RESPONSE TO REVEREND SHEFIELD'S REPEATED CALLS FOR YOUR RESIGNATION?
SHEFIELD IS A DEMAGOGUE! YOU PEOPLE SHOULD HAVE BETTER THINGS TO DO WITH YOUR TIME THAN TO EMPOWER A RABBLE ROUSER WHO INCITES FUNERAL MOURNERS INTO A BOTTLE THROWING MELEE WITH HIS CONSTANT INFLAMMATORY COMMENTS.
WHAT ABOUT THE ACCUSATIONS THAT OFFICER LEONARD JENKINS WAS SILENCED BY FELLOW POLICE OFFICERS?
SEE! THAT'S EXACTLY WHAT I MEAN!
THE MAN IS NOTORIOUS FOR MAKING CONSPIRACIES OUT OF TRAGEDIES.
IF THERE WAS ANY FOUL PLAY HERE, PERHAPS THE REVEREND SHOULD BE LOOKING CLOSER TO HOME.
THE NYPD HAS AN INCREDIBLY DIFFICULT JOB, AND WE OWE THEM THE BENEFIT OF THE DOUBT IN THESE MATTERS...

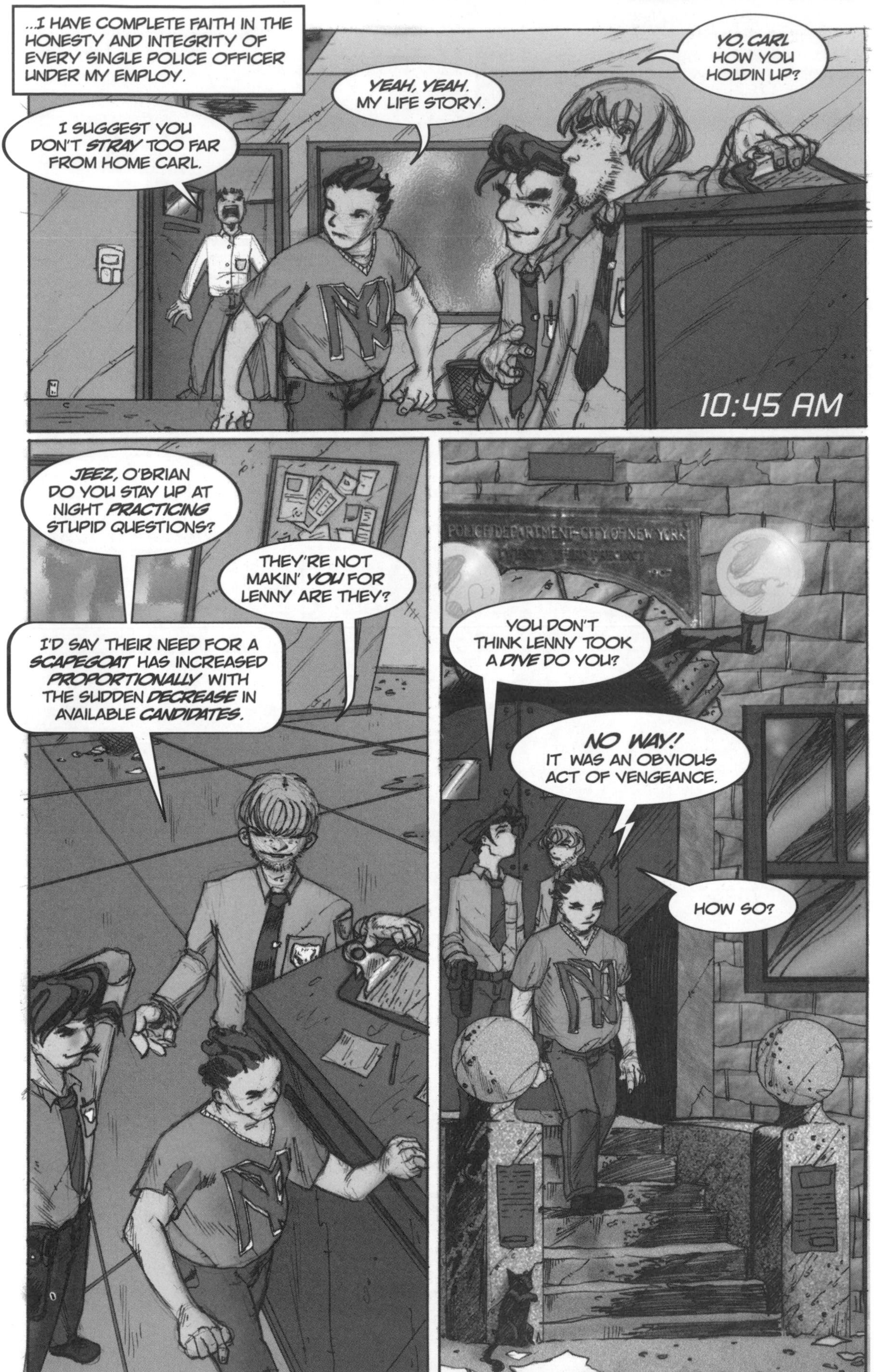
...I HAVE COMPLETE FAITH IN THE HONESTY AND INTEGRITY OF EVERY SINGLE POLICE OFFICER UNDER MY EMPLOY.
I SUGGEST YOU DON'T STRAY TOO FAR FROM HOME CARL.
YEAH, YEAH. MY LIFE STORY.
YO, CARL HOW YOU HOLDIN UP?
10:45 AM
JEEZ, O'BRIAN DO YOU STAY UP AT NIGHT PRACTICING STUPID QUESTIONS?
THEY'RE NOT MAKIN' YOU FOR LENNY ARE THEY?
I'D SAY THEIR NEED FOR A SCAPEGOAT HAS INCREASED PROPORTIONALLY WITH THE SUDDEN DECREASE IN AVAILABLE CANDIDATES.
POLICE DEPARTMENT-CITY OF NEW YORK
YOU DON'T THINK LENNY TOOK A DIVE DO YOU?
NO WAY! IT WAS AN OBVIOUS ACT OF VENGEANCE.
HOW SO?

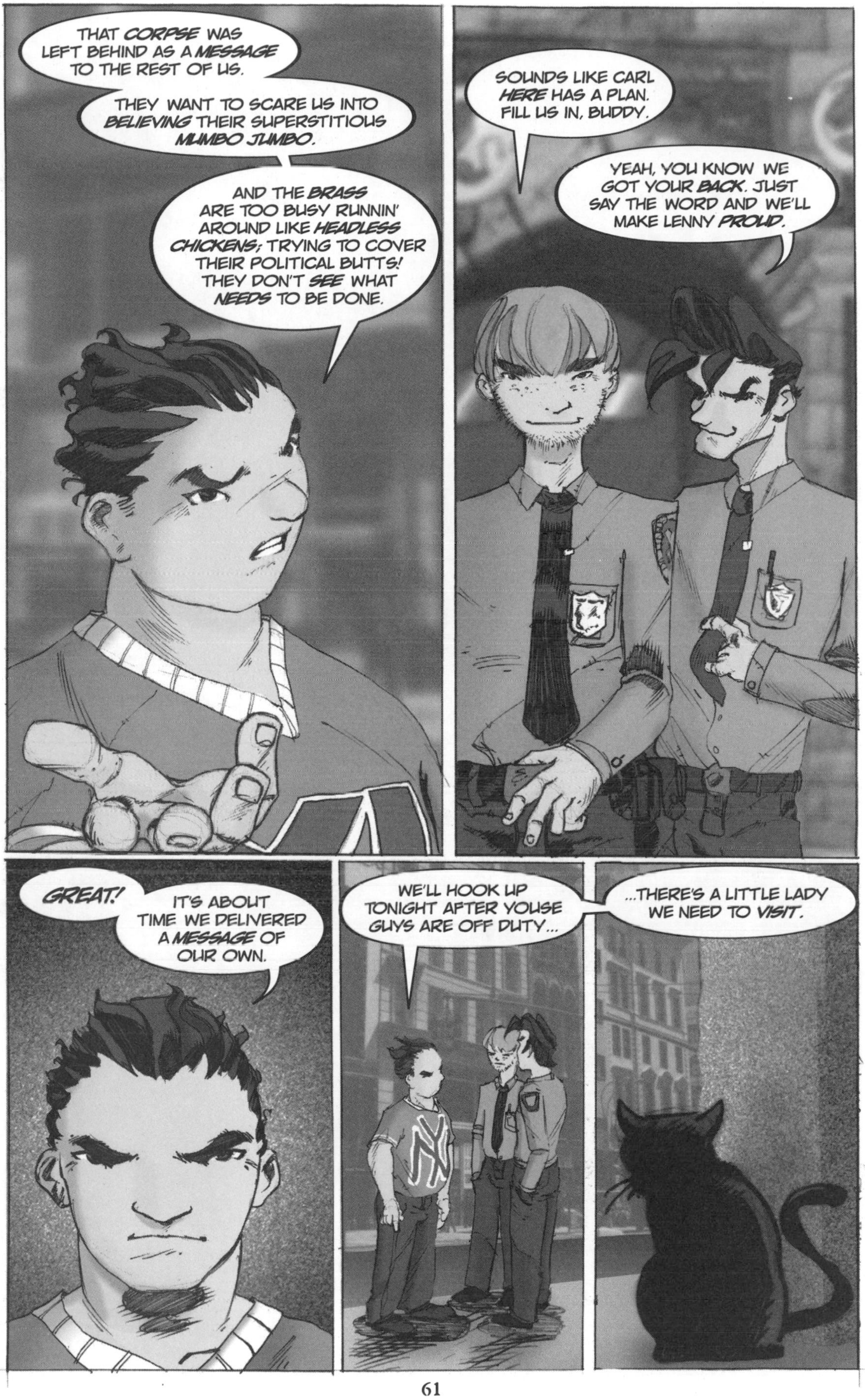
THAT CORPSE WAS LEFT BEHIND AS A MESSAGE TO THE REST OF US.
THEY WANT TO SCARE US INTO BELIEVING THEIR SUPERSTITIOUS MUMBO JUMBO.
AND THE BRASS ARE TOO BUSY RUNNIN' AROUND LIKE HEADLESS CHICKENS; TRYING TO COVER THEIR POLITICAL BUTTS! THEY DON'T SEE WHAT NEEDS TO BE DONE.
SOUNDS LIKE CARL HERE HAS A PLAN. FILL US IN, BUDDY.
YEAH, YOU KNOW WE GOT YOUR BACK. JUST SAY THE WORD AND WE'LL MAKE LENNY PROUD.
GREAT!
IT'S ABOUT TIME WE DELIVERED A MESSAGE OF OUR OWN.
WE'LL HOOK UP TONIGHT AFTER YOUSE GUYS ARE OFF DUTY...
...THERE'S A LITTLE LADY WE NEED TO VISIT.

SIGH

11:08 AM

...THEN, AFTER TAKING ALL THE CREDIT FOR SINGLE-HANDEDLY WIPING OUT THE MOSQUITO POPULATION,...

...THE MAYOR PROCEEDS TO PRAISE THE BOYS IN BLUE FOR DOING THE SAME TO A HAITIAN FUNERAL PROCESSION.

MAN, THE *STEROIDS* THEY'RE GIVING HIZHONER FOR HIS PROSTATE MUST BE SOME *MAJOR STUFF!*

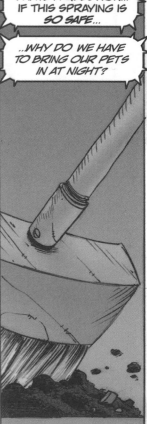

I HAVE A QUESTION... IF THIS SPRAYING IS *SO SAFE...*

...WHY DO WE HAVE TO BRING OUR PETS IN AT NIGHT?

62

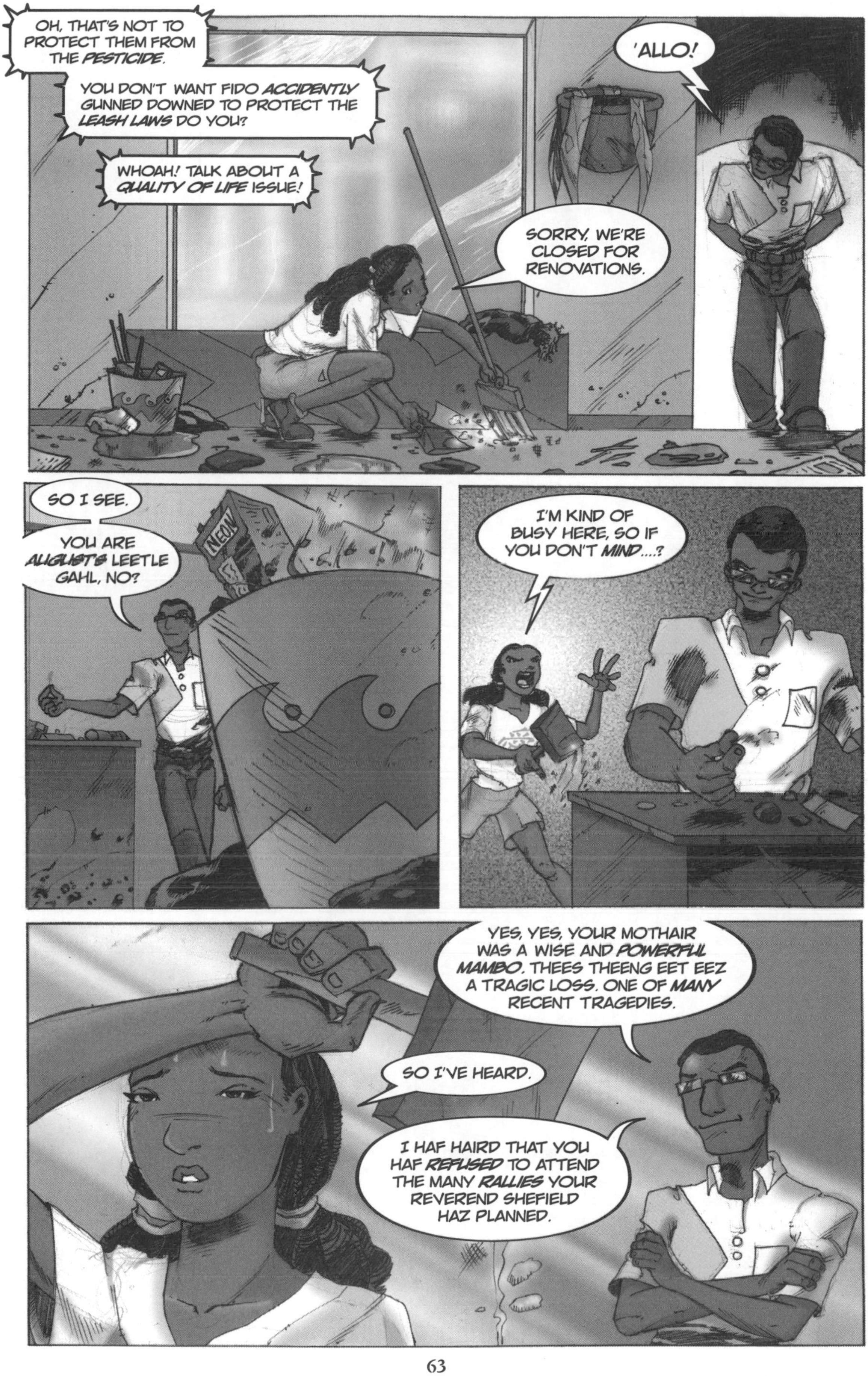
OH, THAT'S NOT TO PROTECT THEM FROM THE PESTICIDE.
YOU DON'T WANT FIDO ACCIDENTLY GUNNED DOWNED TO PROTECT THE LEASH LAWS DO YOU?
WHOAH! TALK ABOUT A QUALITY OF LIFE ISSUE!
'ALLO!
SORRY, WE'RE CLOSED FOR RENOVATIONS.
SO I SEE.
YOU ARE AUGUST'S LEETLE GAHL, NO?
NEON
I'M KIND OF BUSY HERE, SO IF YOU DON'T MIND....?
YES, YES, YOUR MOTHAIR WAS A WISE AND POWERFUL MAMBO. THEES THEENG EET EEZ A TRAGIC LOSS. ONE OF MANY RECENT TRAGEDIES.
SO I'VE HEARD.
I HAF HAIRD THAT YOU HAF REFUSED TO ATTEND THE MANY RALLIES YOUR REVEREND SHEFIELD HAZ PLANNED.

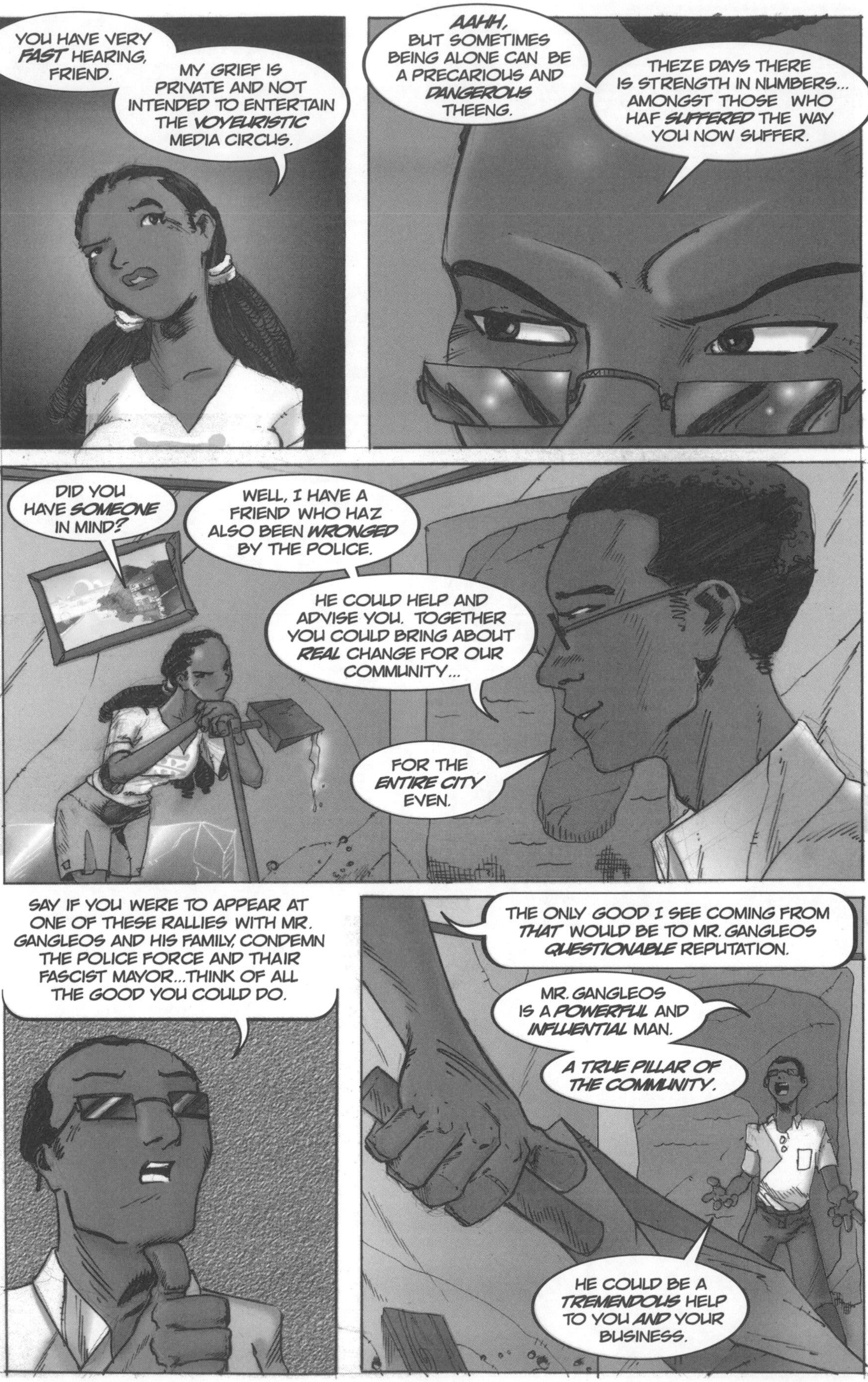

YOU HAVE VERY FAST HEARING, FRIEND.
MY GRIEF IS PRIVATE AND NOT INTENDED TO ENTERTAIN THE VOYEURISTIC MEDIA CIRCUS.
AAHH, BUT SOMETIMES BEING ALONE CAN BE A PRECARIOUS AND DANGEROUS THEENG.
THEZE DAYS THERE IS STRENGTH IN NUMBERS... AMONGST THOSE WHO HAF SUFFERED THE WAY YOU NOW SUFFER.
DID YOU HAVE SOMEONE IN MIND?
WELL, I HAVE A FRIEND WHO HAZ ALSO BEEN WRONGED BY THE POLICE.
HE COULD HELP AND ADVISE YOU. TOGETHER YOU COULD BRING ABOUT REAL CHANGE FOR OUR COMMUNITY...
FOR THE ENTIRE CITY EVEN.
SAY IF YOU WERE TO APPEAR AT ONE OF THESE RALLIES WITH MR. GANGLEOS AND HIS FAMILY, CONDEMN THE POLICE FORCE AND THAIR FASCIST MAYOR...THINK OF ALL THE GOOD YOU COULD DO.
THE ONLY GOOD I SEE COMING FROM THAT WOULD BE TO MR. GANGLEOS QUESTIONABLE REPUTATION.
MR. GANGLEOS IS A POWERFUL AND INFLUENTIAL MAN.
A TRUE PILLAR OF THE COMMUNITY.
HE COULD BE A TREMENDOUS HELP TO YOU AND YOUR BUSINESS.

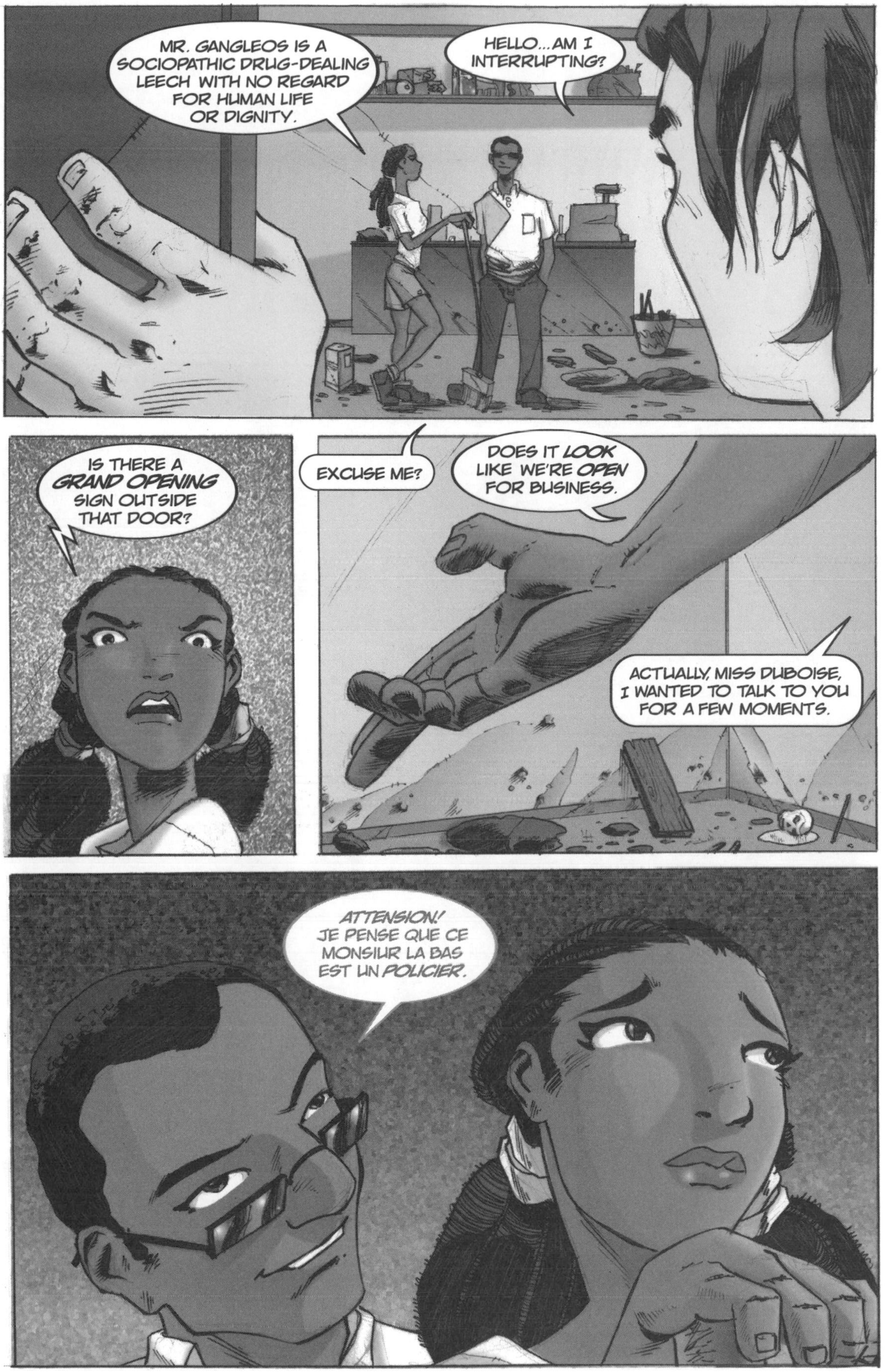
MR. GANGLEOS IS A SOCIOPATHIC DRUG-DEALING LEECH WITH NO REGARD FOR HUMAN LIFE OR DIGNITY.
HELLO...AM I INTERRUPTING?
IS THERE A GRAND OPENING SIGN OUTSIDE THAT DOOR?
EXCUSE ME?
DOES IT LOOK LIKE WE'RE OPEN FOR BUSINESS.
ACTUALLY, MISS DUBOISE, I WANTED TO TALK TO YOU FOR A FEW MOMENTS.
ATTENSION! JE PENSE QUE CE MONSIUR LA BAS EST UN POLICIER.

ACTUALLY I WORK AS A GRADUATE INSTRUCTOR AT NYU. MY NAME'S PAUL WHYTHE. I'M A CULTURAL ANTHROPOLOGIST.

LOOK...

TELL YOUR BOSS I'M SORRY FOR THE LOSS OF HIS BROTHER, BUT I PREFER TO GRIEVE ALONE.

GRIEF CAN BE A TERRIBLY LONELY THING FOR ONE SO YOUNG AND VULNERABLE. YOU SHOULD RECONSIDER WHAT I HAVE SAID.

PERHAPS GETTING OUT OF THIS MUSTY OLD SHOP AND HAVING SOME FUN IS JUST WHAT YOU NEED, EH?

MAYBE I COULD PERSUADE YOU TO JOIN ME AT SOME CLUBS WITH *VERY* EXCLUSIVE GUEST LISTS.

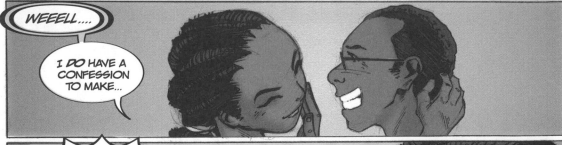

WEEELL....

I *DO* HAVE A CONFESSION TO MAKE...

I DON'T LIKE DRUG-DEALING FLUNKIES OR PLAYA WANNABE'S, AND I DAMN SURE DON'T LIKE TO BE TOUCHED BY THEM!

PLINK!

OWW!

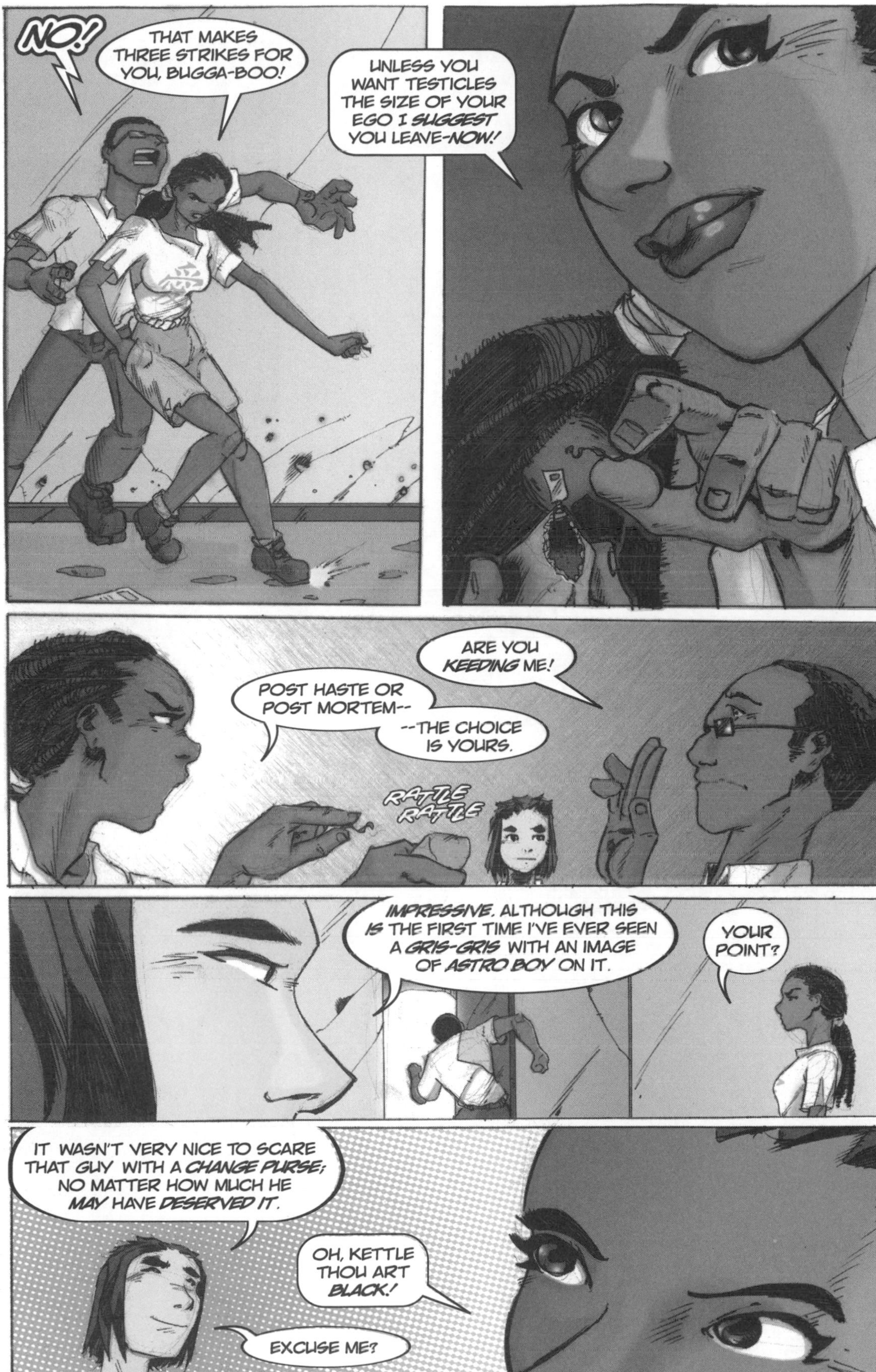
NO!
THAT MAKES THREE STRIKES FOR YOU, BUGGA-BOO!
UNLESS YOU WANT TESTICLES THE SIZE OF YOUR EGO I SUGGEST YOU LEAVE-NOW!
POST HASTE OR POST MORTEM--
ARE YOU KEEDING ME!
--THE CHOICE IS YOURS.
RATTLE RATTLE
IMPRESSIVE. ALTHOUGH THIS IS THE FIRST TIME I'VE EVER SEEN A GRIS-GRIS WITH AN IMAGE OF ASTRO BOY ON IT.
YOUR POINT?
IT WASN'T VERY NICE TO SCARE THAT GUY WITH A CHANGE PURSE; NO MATTER HOW MUCH HE MAY HAVE DESERVED IT.
OH, KETTLE THOU ART BLACK!
EXCUSE ME?

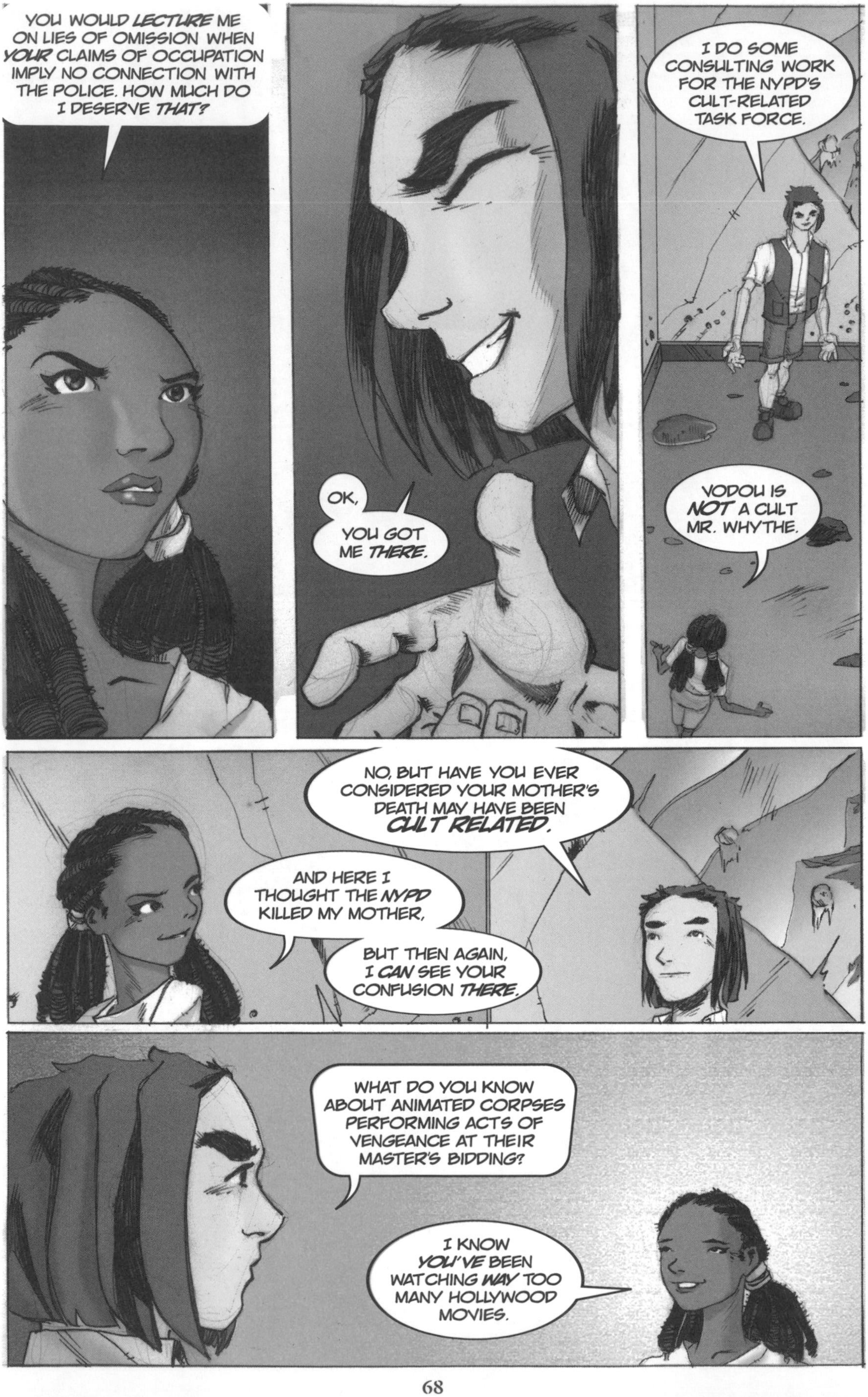
YOU WOULD LECTURE ME ON LIES OF OMISSION WHEN YOUR CLAIMS OF OCCUPATION IMPLY NO CONNECTION WITH THE POLICE. HOW MUCH DO I DESERVE THAT?
OK,
YOU GOT ME THERE.
I DO SOME CONSULTING WORK FOR THE NYPD'S CULT-RELATED TASK FORCE.
VODOU IS NOT A CULT MR. WHYTHE.
NO, BUT HAVE YOU EVER CONSIDERED YOUR MOTHER'S DEATH MAY HAVE BEEN CULT RELATED.
AND HERE I THOUGHT THE NYPD KILLED MY MOTHER,
BUT THEN AGAIN, I CAN SEE YOUR CONFUSION THERE.
WHAT DO YOU KNOW ABOUT ANIMATED CORPSES PERFORMING ACTS OF VENGEANCE AT THEIR MASTER'S BIDDING?
I KNOW YOU'VE BEEN WATCHING WAY TOO MANY HOLLYWOOD MOVIES.

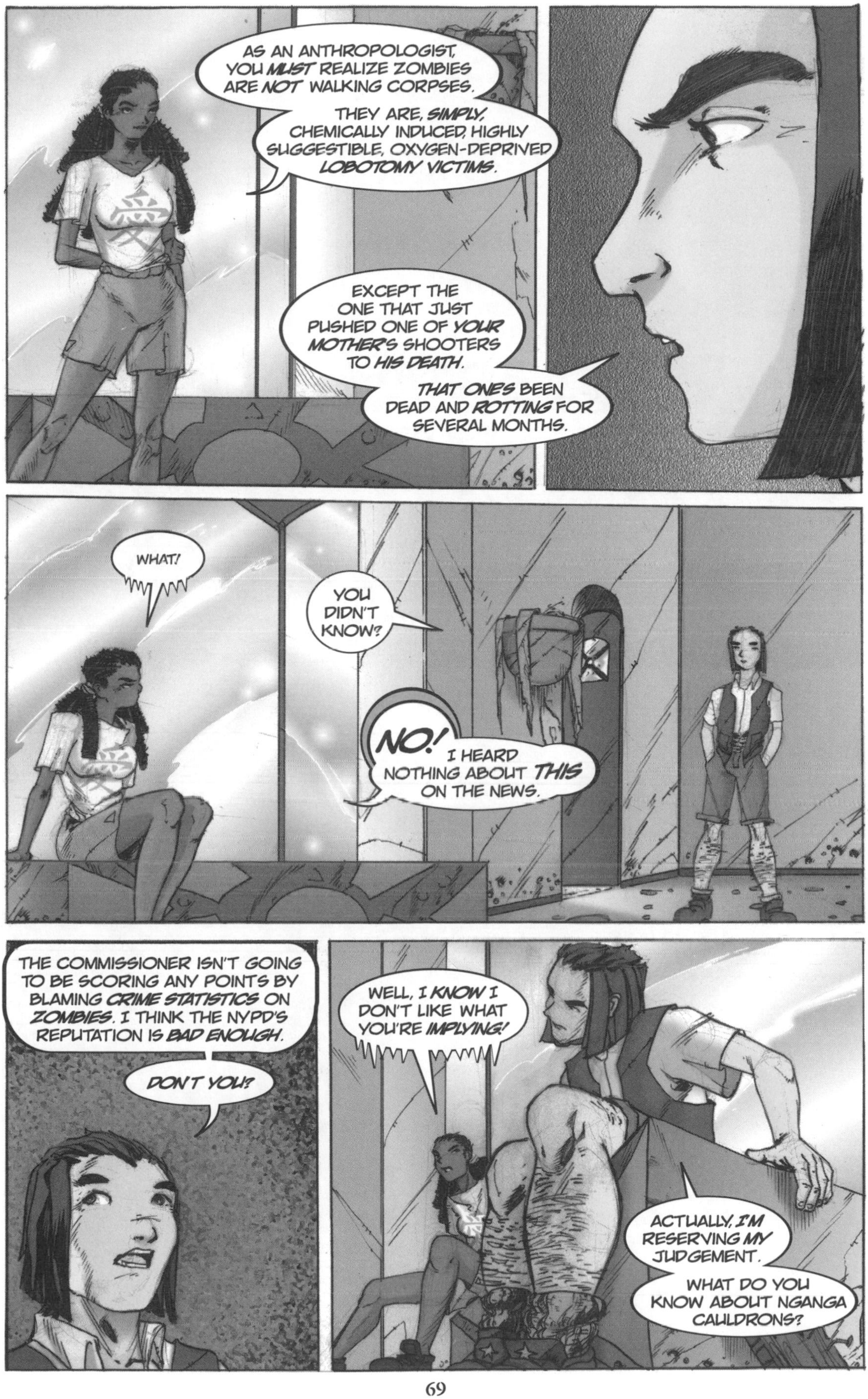
AS AN ANTHROPOLOGIST, YOU MUST REALIZE ZOMBIES ARE NOT WALKING CORPSES.
THEY ARE, SIMPLY, CHEMICALLY INDUCED, HIGHLY SUGGESTIBLE, OXYGEN-DEPRIVED LOBOTOMY VICTIMS.
EXCEPT THE ONE THAT JUST PUSHED ONE OF YOUR MOTHER'S SHOOTERS TO HIS DEATH.
THAT ONE'S BEEN DEAD AND ROTTING FOR SEVERAL MONTHS.
WHAT!
YOU DIDN'T KNOW?
NO! I HEARD NOTHING ABOUT THIS ON THE NEWS.
THE COMMISSIONER ISN'T GOING TO BE SCORING ANY POINTS BY BLAMING CRIME STATISTICS ON ZOMBIES. I THINK THE NYPD'S REPUTATION IS BAD ENOUGH.
DON'T YOU?
WELL, I KNOW I DON'T LIKE WHAT YOU'RE IMPLYING!
ACTUALLY, I'M RESERVING MY JUDGEMENT.
WHAT DO YOU KNOW ABOUT NGANGA CAULDRONS?

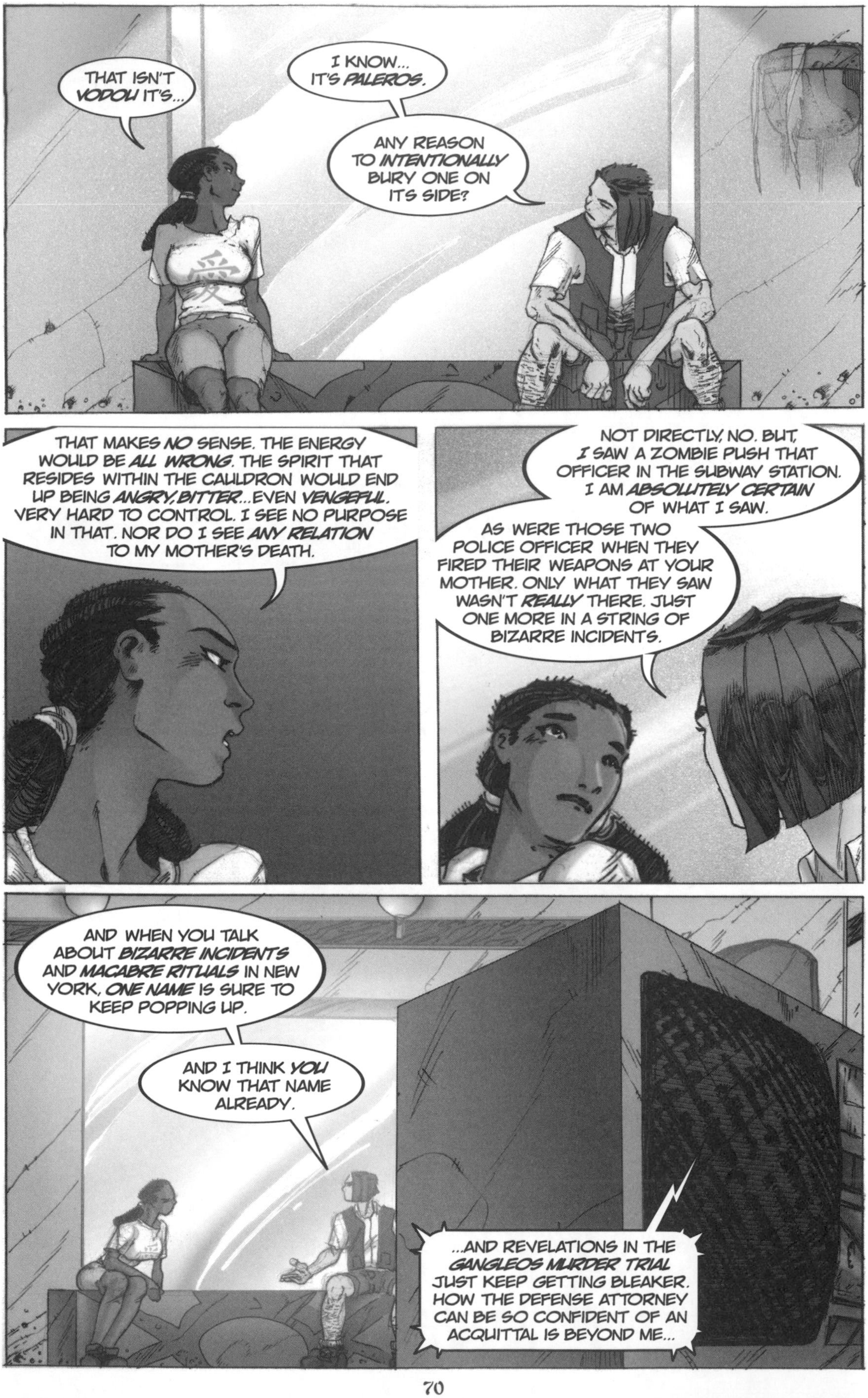
THAT ISN'T VODOU IT'S...
I KNOW... IT'S PALEROS.
ANY REASON TO INTENTIONALLY BURY ONE ON ITS SIDE?
THAT MAKES NO SENSE. THE ENERGY WOULD BE ALL WRONG. THE SPIRIT THAT RESIDES WITHIN THE CAULDRON WOULD END UP BEING ANGRY, BITTER...EVEN VENGEFUL. VERY HARD TO CONTROL. I SEE NO PURPOSE IN THAT. NOR DO I SEE ANY RELATION TO MY MOTHER'S DEATH.
NOT DIRECTLY, NO. BUT, I SAW A ZOMBIE PUSH THAT OFFICER IN THE SUBWAY STATION. I AM ABSOLUTELY CERTAIN OF WHAT I SAW.
AS WERE THOSE TWO POLICE OFFICER WHEN THEY FIRED THEIR WEAPONS AT YOUR MOTHER. ONLY WHAT THEY SAW WASN'T REALLY THERE. JUST ONE MORE IN A STRING OF BIZARRE INCIDENTS.
AND WHEN YOU TALK ABOUT BIZARRE INCIDENTS AND MACABRE RITUALS IN NEW YORK, ONE NAME IS SURE TO KEEP POPPING UP.
AND I THINK YOU KNOW THAT NAME ALREADY.
...AND REVELATIONS IN THE GANGLEOS MURDER TRIAL JUST KEEP GETTING BLEAKER. HOW THE DEFENSE ATTORNEY CAN BE SO CONFIDENT OF AN ACQUITTAL IS BEYOND ME...

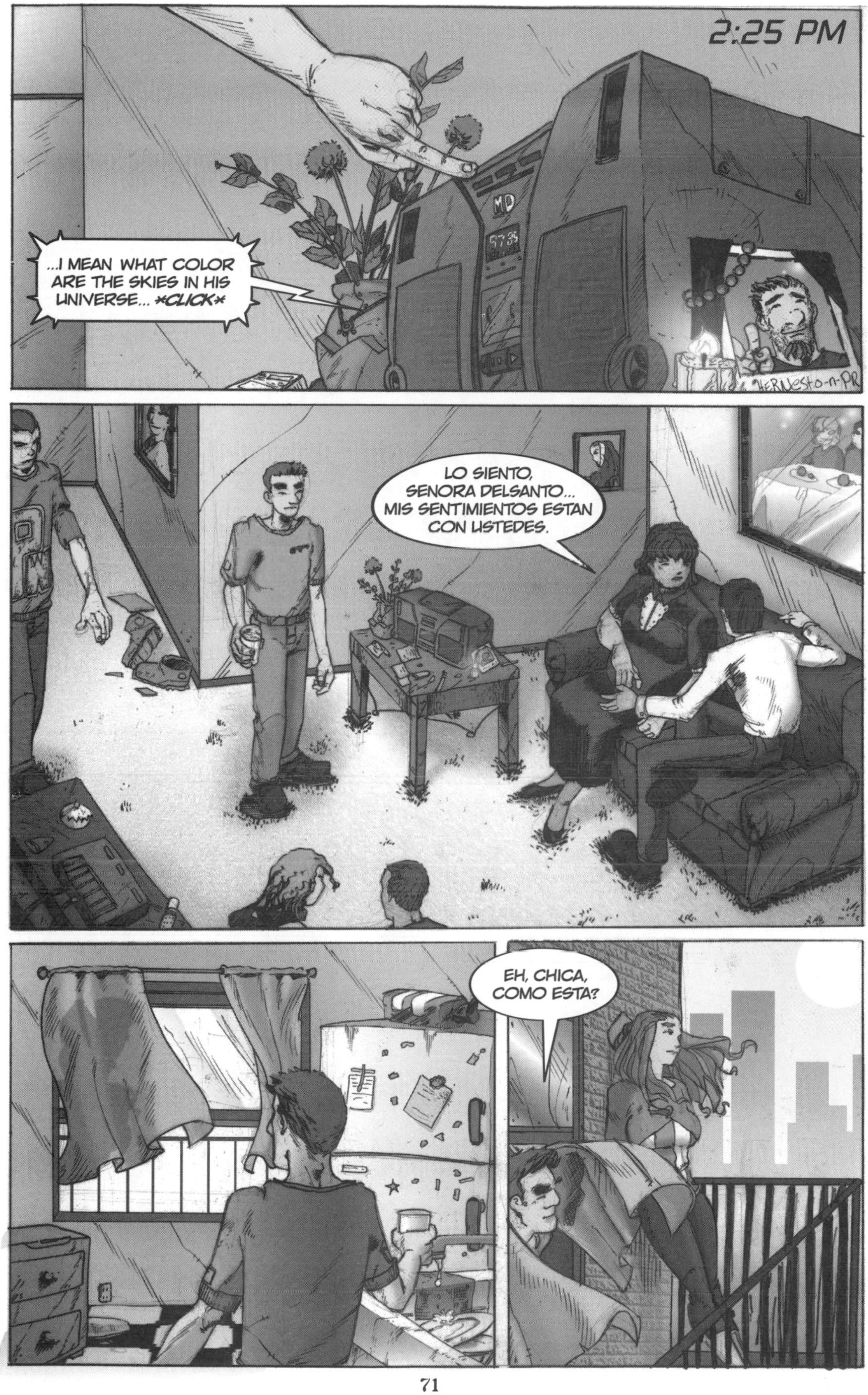
2:25 PM
...I MEAN WHAT COLOR ARE THE SKIES IN HIS UNIVERSE... *CLICK*
LO SIENTO, SENORA DELSANTO... MIS SENTIMIENTOS ESTAN CON USTEDES.
EH, CHICA, COMO ESTA?

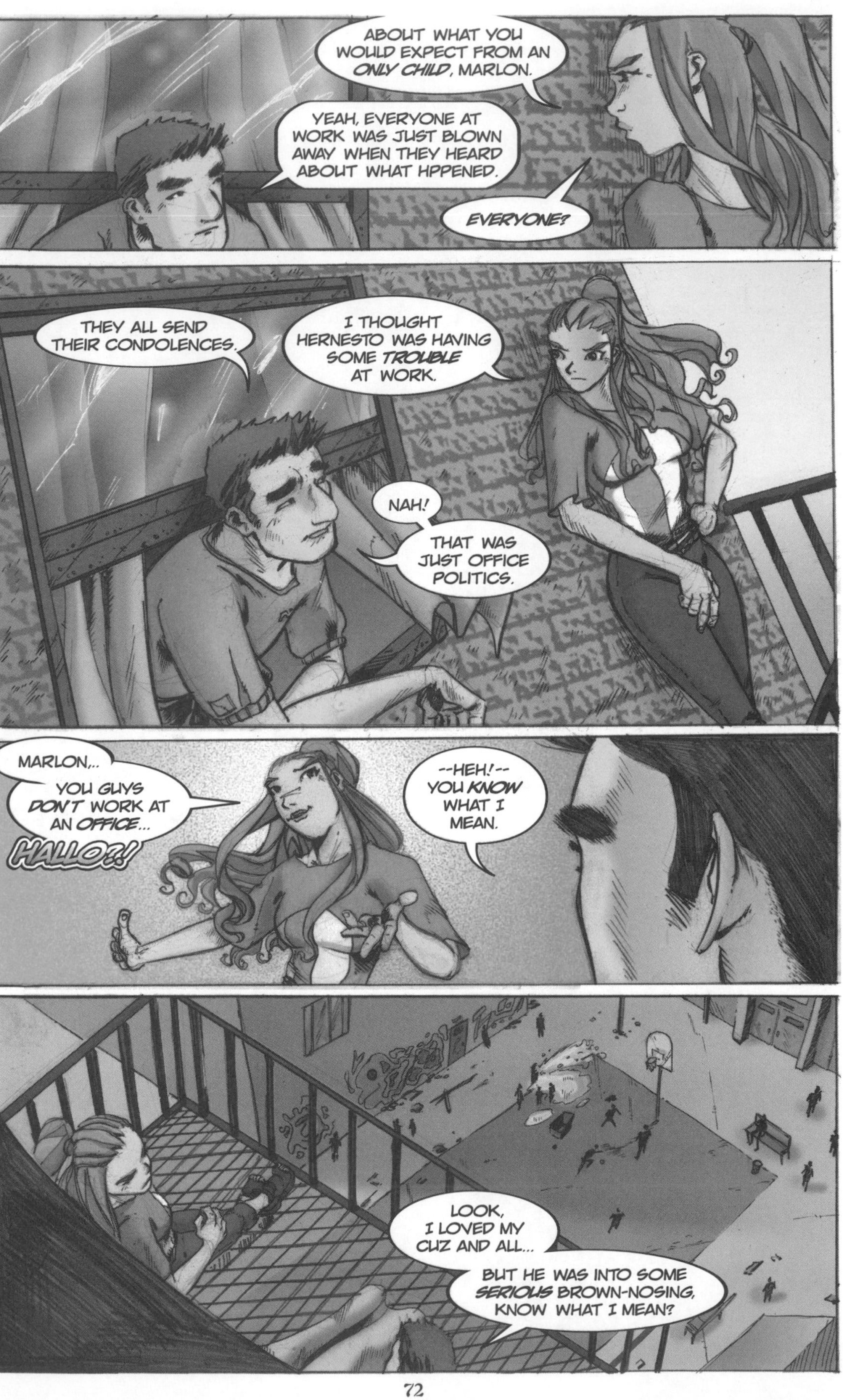

ABOUT WHAT YOU WOULD EXPECT FROM AN ONLY CHILD, MARLON.
YEAH, EVERYONE AT WORK WAS JUST BLOWN AWAY WHEN THEY HEARD ABOUT WHAT HPPENED.
EVERYONE?
THEY ALL SEND THEIR CONDOLENCES.
I THOUGHT HERNESTO WAS HAVING SOME TROUBLE AT WORK.
NAH!
THAT WAS JUST OFFICE POLITICS.
MARLON,..
YOU GUYS DON'T WORK AT AN OFFICE...
HALLO?!
--HEH!-- YOU KNOW WHAT I MEAN.
LOOK, I LOVED MY CUZ AND ALL...
BUT HE WAS INTO SOME SERIOUS BROWN-NOSING, KNOW WHAT I MEAN?

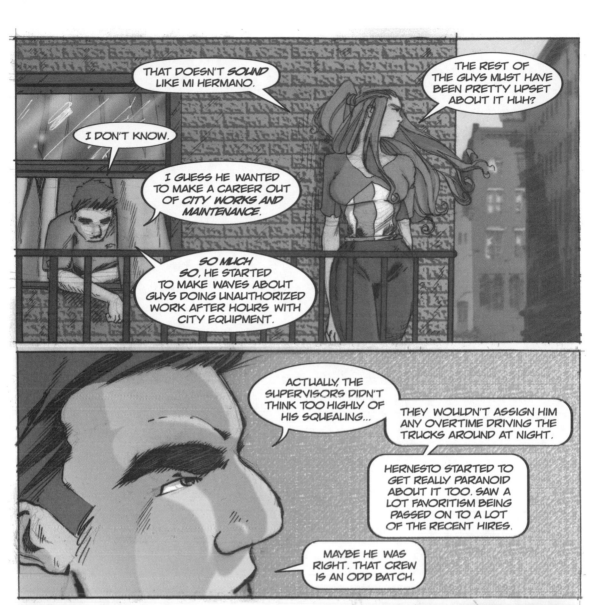

THAT DOESN'T *SOUND* LIKE MI HERMANO.

THE REST OF THE GUYS MUST HAVE BEEN PRETTY UPSET ABOUT IT HUH?

I DON'T KNOW.

I GUESS HE WANTED TO MAKE A CAREER OUT OF *CITY WORKS AND MAINTENANCE.*

SO MUCH SO, HE STARTED TO MAKE WAVES ABOUT GUYS DOING UNAUTHORIZED WORK AFTER HOURS WITH CITY EQUIPMENT.

ACTUALLY, THE SUPERVISORS DIDN'T THINK *TOO* HIGHLY OF HIS SQUEALING...

THEY WOULDN'T ASSIGN HIM ANY OVERTIME DRIVING THE TRUCKS AROUND AT NIGHT.

HERNESTO STARTED TO GET REALLY PARANOID ABOUT IT TOO. SAW A LOT FAVORITISM BEING PASSED ON TO A LOT OF THE RECENT HIRES.

MAYBE HE WAS RIGHT. THAT CREW IS AN ODD BATCH.

THE *RECENT* HIRES?

YEA, A LOT OF THEM *USED* TO BE PART OF A BUNCH OF *DIFFERENT* GANGS.

THAT *INCLUDE* GANGLEOS' OLD CREW?

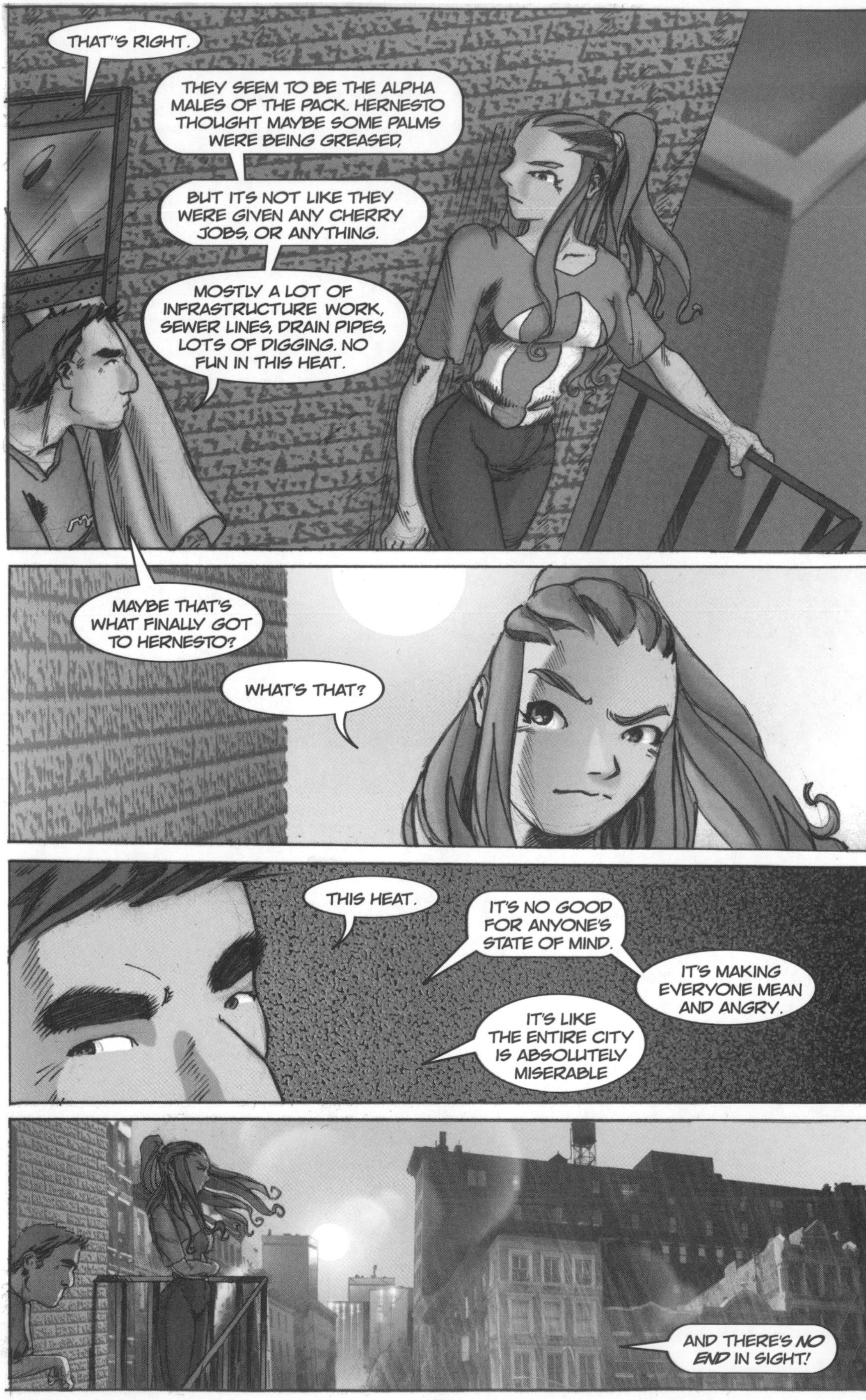

THAT'S RIGHT.
THEY SEEM TO BE THE ALPHA MALES OF THE PACK. HERNESTO THOUGHT MAYBE SOME PALMS WERE BEING GREASED,
BUT ITS NOT LIKE THEY WERE GIVEN ANY CHERRY JOBS, OR ANYTHING.
MOSTLY A LOT OF INFRASTRUCTURE WORK, SEWER LINES, DRAIN PIPES, LOTS OF DIGGING. NO FUN IN THIS HEAT.
MAYBE THAT'S WHAT FINALLY GOT TO HERNESTO?
WHAT'S THAT?
THIS HEAT.
IT'S NO GOOD FOR ANYONE'S STATE OF MIND.
IT'S MAKING EVERYONE MEAN AND ANGRY.
IT'S LIKE THE ENTIRE CITY IS ABSOLUTELY MISERABLE
AND THERE'S *NO END* IN SIGHT!

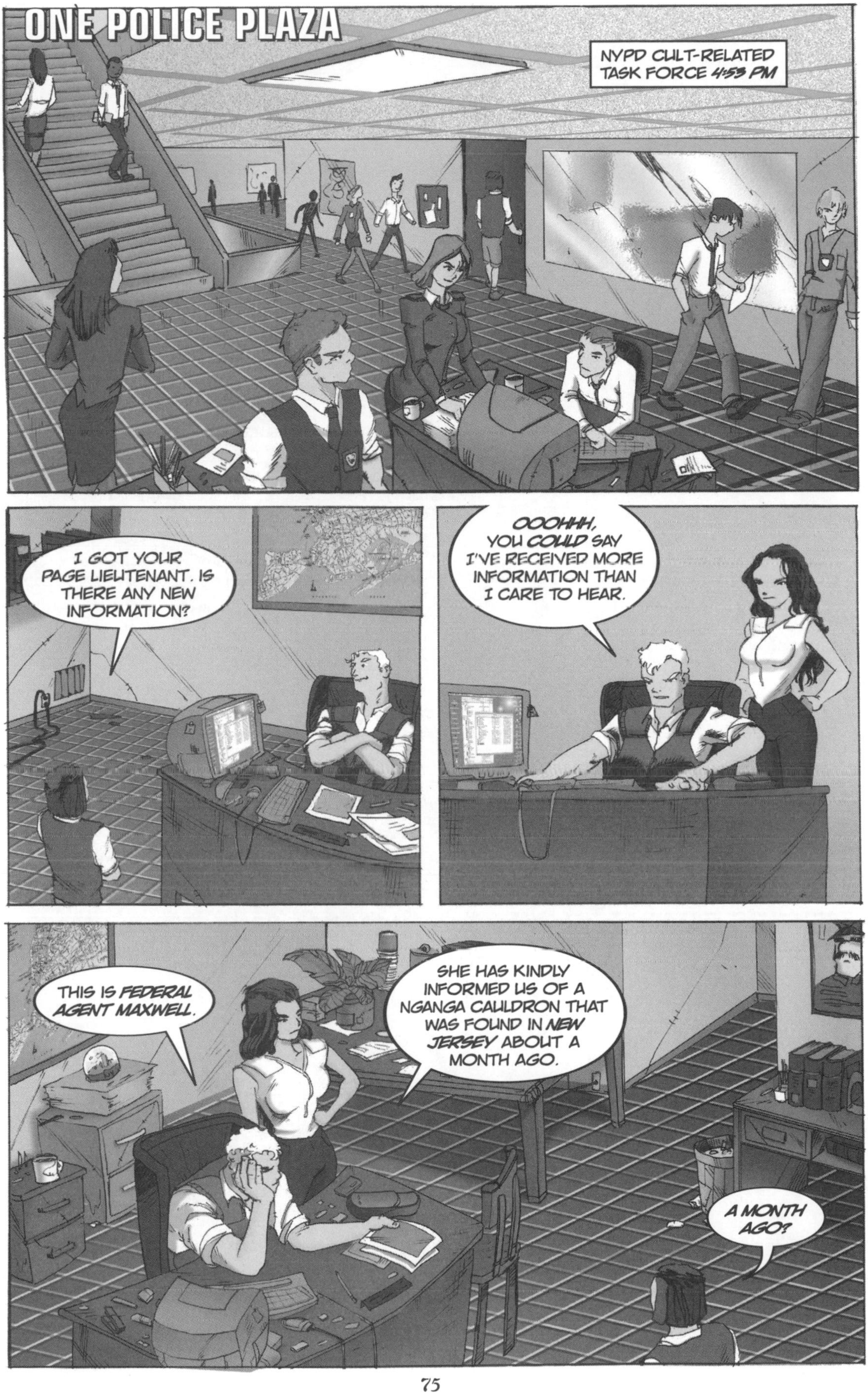
ONE POLICE PLAZA
NYPD CULT-RELATED TASK FORCE 4:53 PM
I GOT YOUR PAGE LIEUTENANT. IS THERE ANY NEW INFORMATION?
OOOHHH, YOU *COULD* SAY I'VE RECEIVED MORE INFORMATION THAN I CARE TO HEAR.
THIS IS *FEDERAL AGENT MAXWELL*.
SHE HAS KINDLY INFORMED US OF A NGANGA CAULDRON THAT WAS FOUND IN *NEW JERSEY* ABOUT A MONTH AGO.
A MONTH AGO?

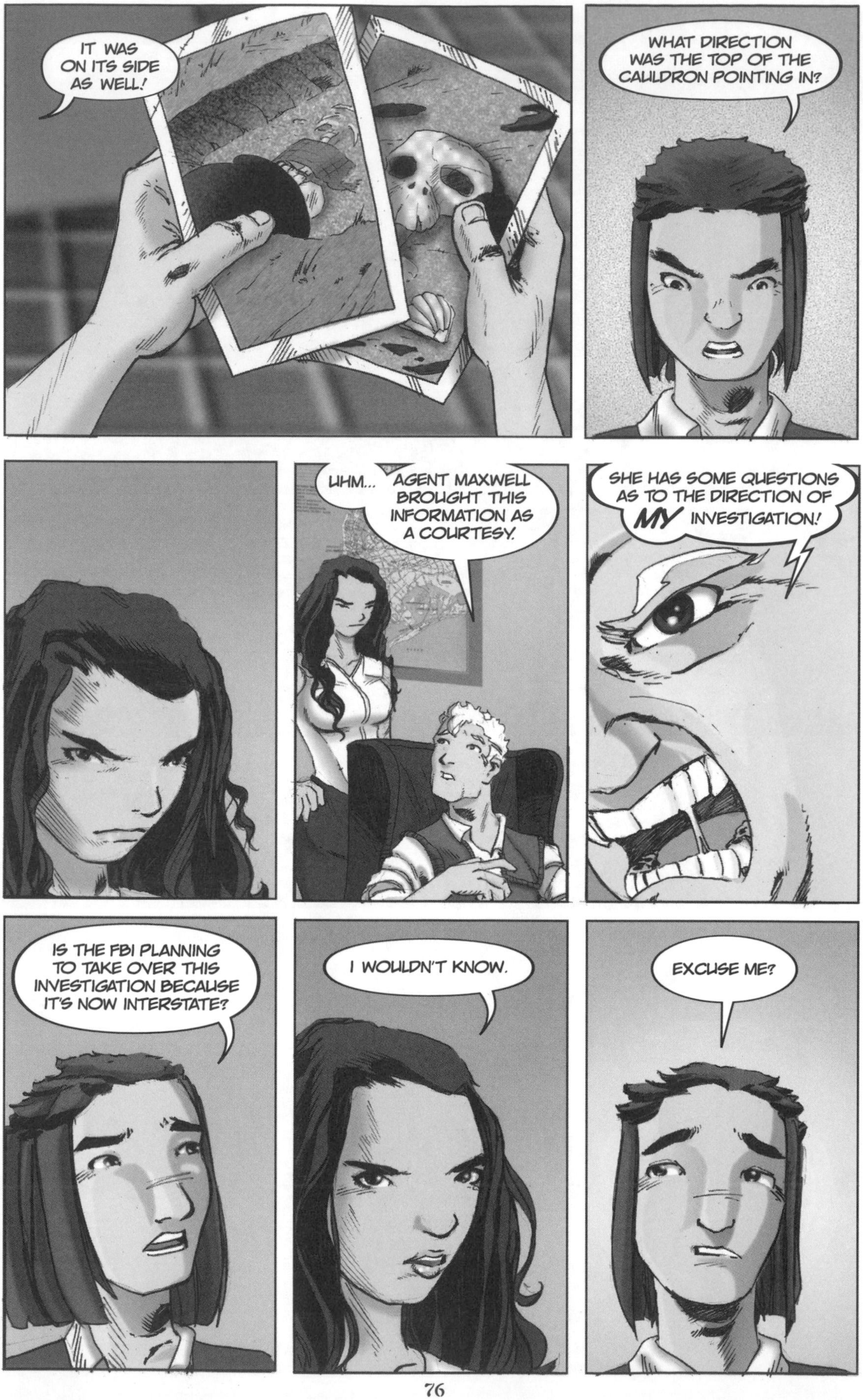
IT WAS ON ITS SIDE AS WELL!
WHAT DIRECTION WAS THE TOP OF THE CAULDRON POINTING IN?
UHM...
AGENT MAXWELL BROUGHT THIS INFORMATION AS A COURTESY.
SHE HAS SOME QUESTIONS AS TO THE DIRECTION OF MY INVESTIGATION!
IS THE FBI PLANNING TO TAKE OVER THIS INVESTIGATION BECAUSE IT'S NOW INTERSTATE?
I WOULDN'T KNOW.
EXCUSE ME?

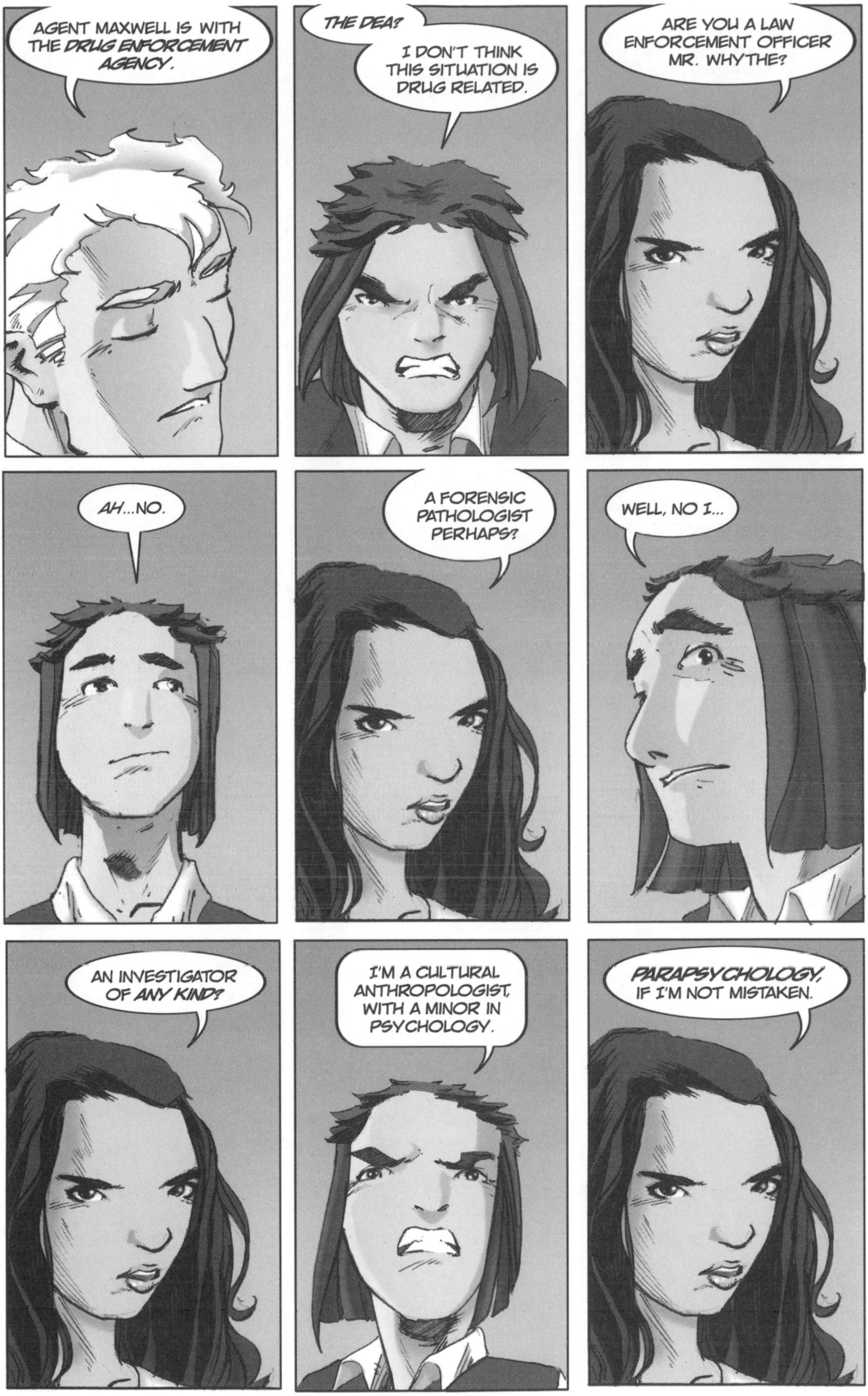
AGENT MAXWELL IS WITH THE *DRUG ENFORCEMENT AGENCY*.
THE DEA?
I DON'T THINK THIS SITUATION IS DRUG RELATED.
ARE YOU A LAW ENFORCEMENT OFFICER MR. WHYTHE?
AH...NO.
A FORENSIC PATHOLOGIST PERHAPS?
WELL, NO I...
AN INVESTIGATOR OF *ANY KIND?*
I'M A CULTURAL ANTHROPOLOGIST, WITH A MINOR IN PSYCHOLOGY.
PARAPSYCHOLOGY, IF I'M NOT MISTAKEN.

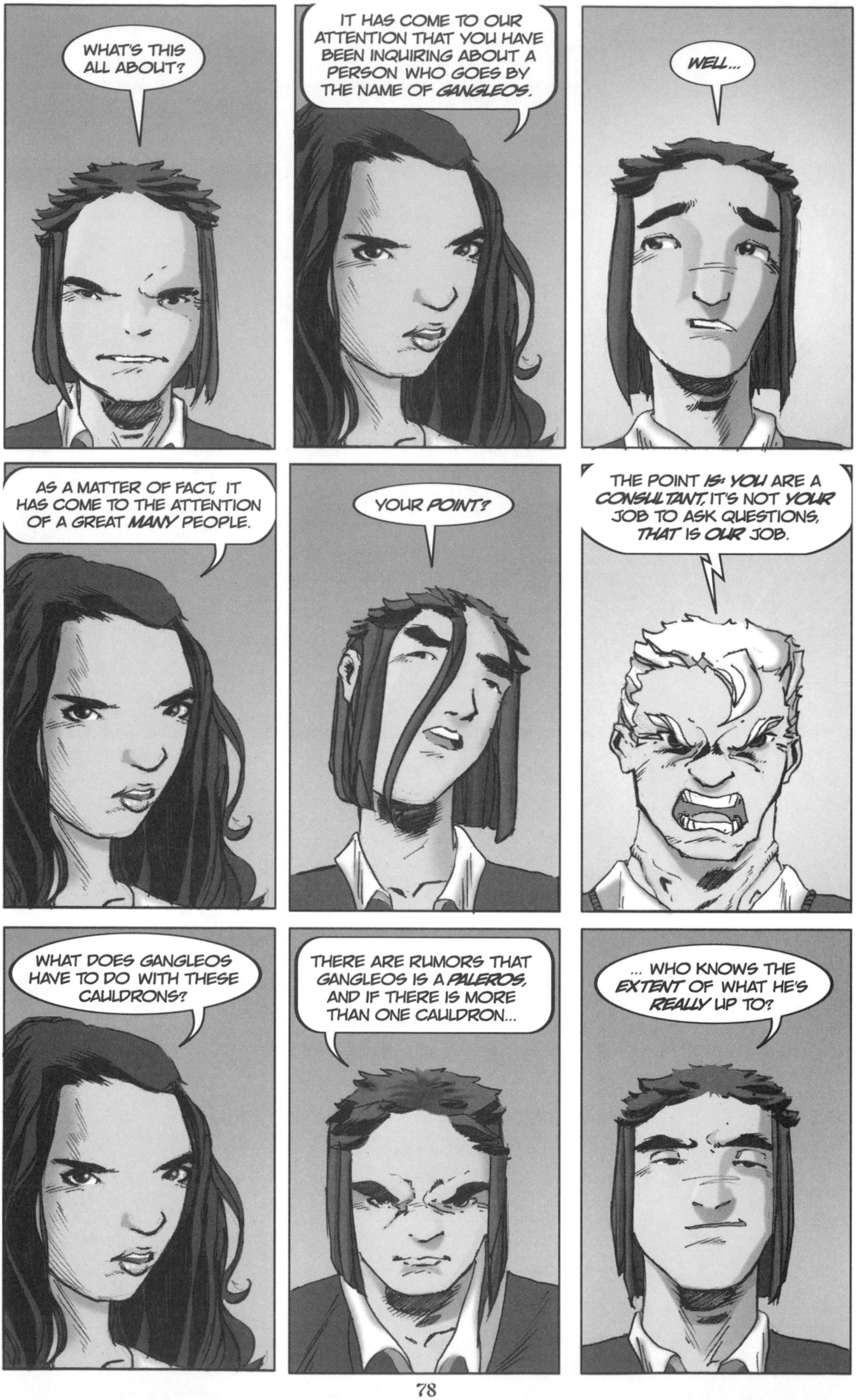
WHAT'S THIS ALL ABOUT?
IT HAS COME TO OUR ATTENTION THAT YOU HAVE BEEN INQUIRING ABOUT A PERSON WHO GOES BY THE NAME OF GANGLEOS.
WELL...
AS A MATTER OF FACT, IT HAS COME TO THE ATTENTION OF A GREAT MANY PEOPLE.
YOUR POINT?
THE POINT IS: YOU ARE A CONSULTANT, IT'S NOT YOUR JOB TO ASK QUESTIONS, THAT IS OUR JOB.
WHAT DOES GANGLEOS HAVE TO DO WITH THESE CAULDRONS?
THERE ARE RUMORS THAT GANGLEOS IS A PALEROS, AND IF THERE IS MORE THAN ONE CAULDRON...
... WHO KNOWS THE EXTENT OF WHAT HE'S REALLY UP TO?

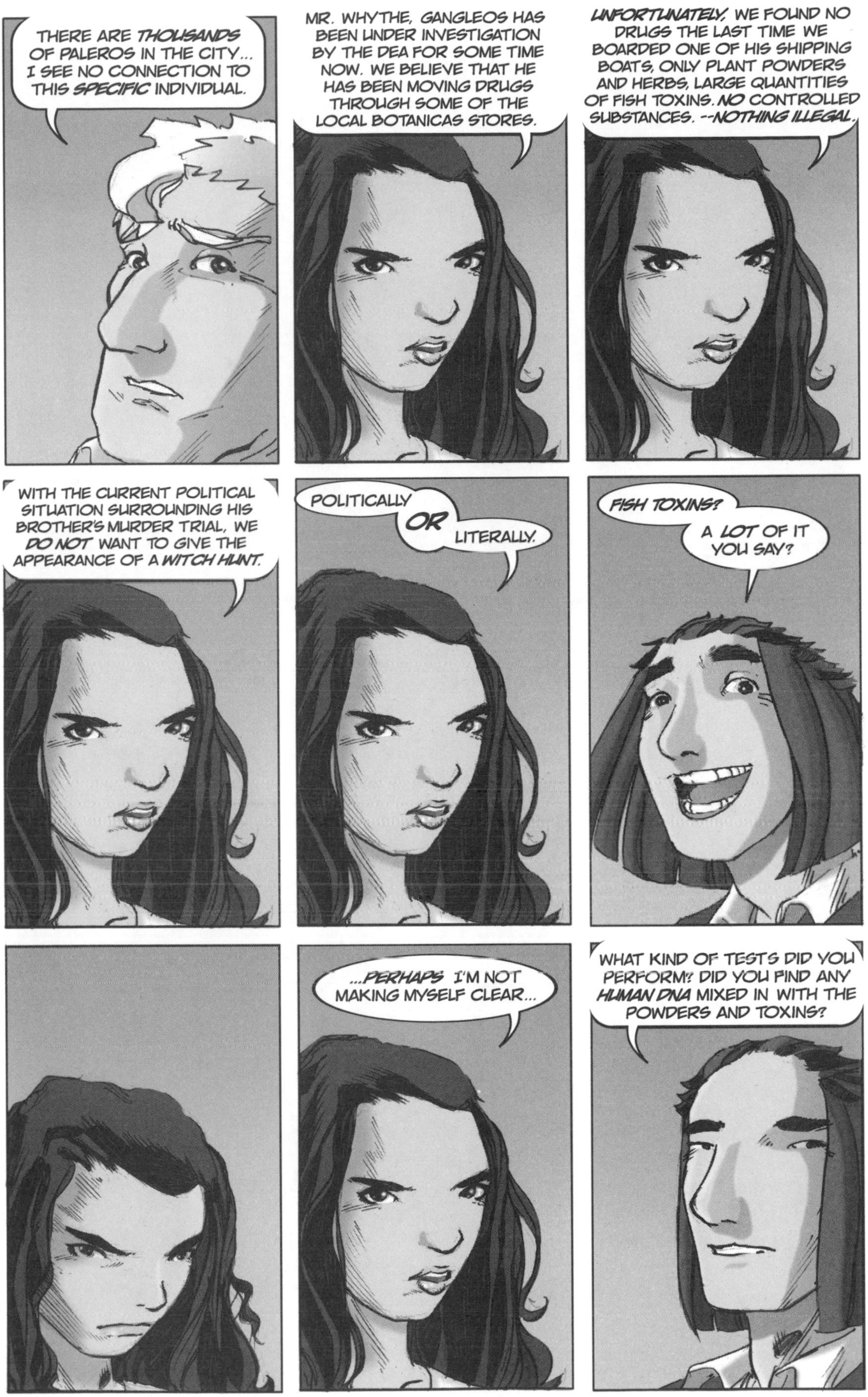
THERE ARE THOUSANDS OF PALEROS IN THE CITY... I SEE NO CONNECTION TO THIS SPECIFIC INDIVIDUAL.
MR. WHYTHE, GANGLEOS HAS BEEN UNDER INVESTIGATION BY THE DEA FOR SOME TIME NOW. WE BELIEVE THAT HE HAS BEEN MOVING DRUGS THROUGH SOME OF THE LOCAL BOTANICAS STORES.
UNFORTUNATELY, WE FOUND NO DRUGS THE LAST TIME WE BOARDED ONE OF HIS SHIPPING BOATS, ONLY PLANT POWDERS AND HERBS, LARGE QUANTITIES OF FISH TOXINS. NO CONTROLLED SUBSTANCES. --NOTHING ILLEGAL.
WITH THE CURRENT POLITICAL SITUATION SURROUNDING HIS BROTHER'S MURDER TRIAL, WE DO NOT WANT TO GIVE THE APPEARANCE OF A WITCH HUNT.
POLITICALLY
OR
LITERALLY.
FISH TOXINS?
A LOT OF IT YOU SAY?
...PERHAPS I'M NOT MAKING MYSELF CLEAR...
WHAT KIND OF TESTS DID YOU PERFORM? DID YOU FIND ANY HUMAN DNA MIXED IN WITH THE POWDERS AND TOXINS?

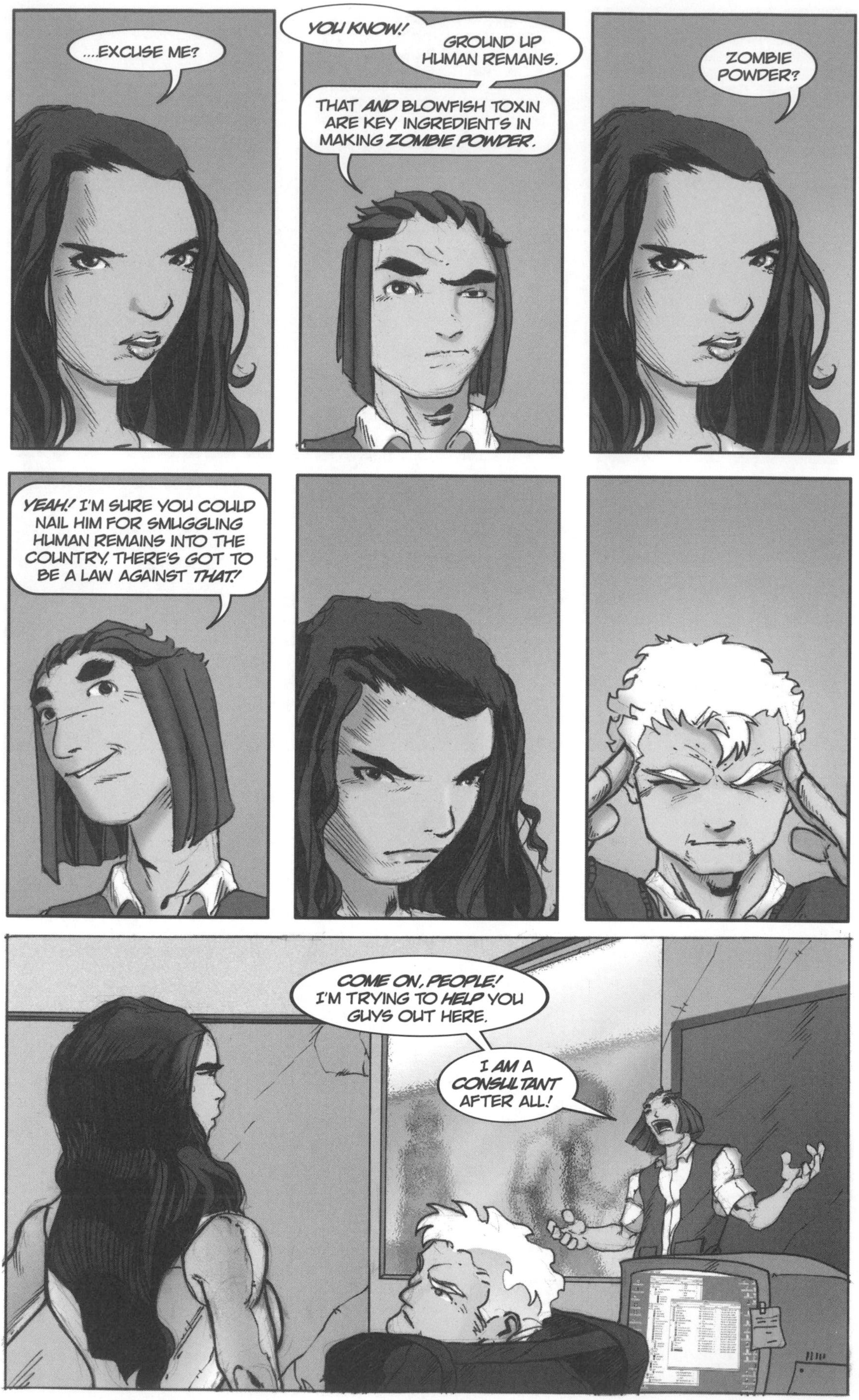
....EXCUSE ME?
YOU KNOW!
GROUND UP HUMAN REMAINS.
THAT AND BLOWFISH TOXIN ARE KEY INGREDIENTS IN MAKING ZOMBIE POWDER.
ZOMBIE POWDER?
YEAH! I'M SURE YOU COULD NAIL HIM FOR SMUGGLING HUMAN REMAINS INTO THE COUNTRY, THERE'S GOT TO BE A LAW AGAINST THAT!
COME ON, PEOPLE! I'M TRYING TO HELP YOU GUYS OUT HERE.
I AM A CONSULTANT AFTER ALL!

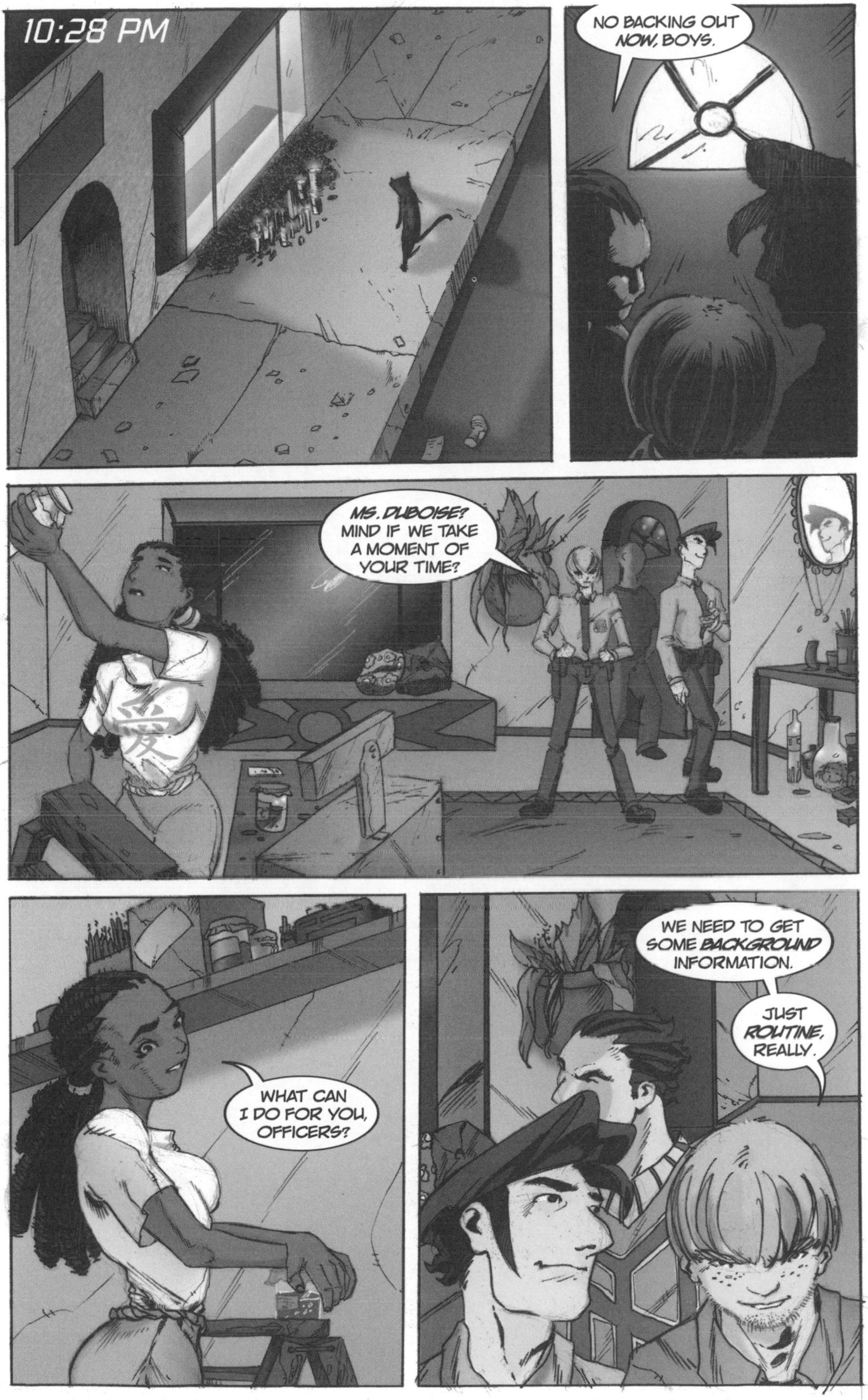
10:28 PM
NO BACKING OUT NOW, BOYS.
MS. DUBOISE? MIND IF WE TAKE A MOMENT OF YOUR TIME?
WHAT CAN I DO FOR YOU, OFFICERS?
WE NEED TO GET SOME BACKGROUND INFORMATION.
JUST ROUTINE, REALLY.

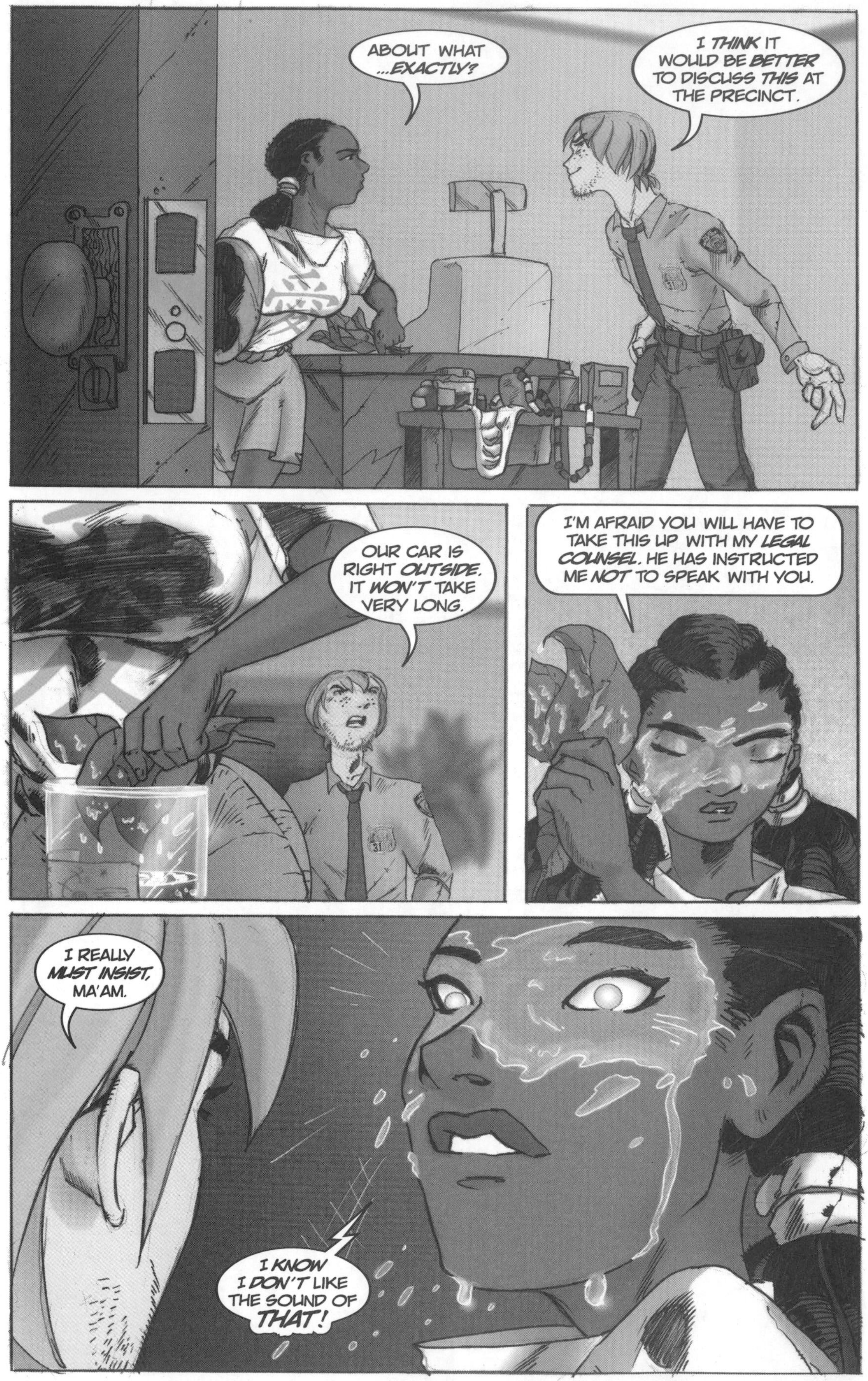
ABOUT WHAT ...EXACTLY?
I THINK IT WOULD BE BETTER TO DISCUSS THIS AT THE PRECINCT.
OUR CAR IS RIGHT OUTSIDE. IT WON'T TAKE VERY LONG.
I'M AFRAID YOU WILL HAVE TO TAKE THIS UP WITH MY LEGAL COUNSEL. HE HAS INSTRUCTED ME NOT TO SPEAK WITH YOU.
I REALLY MUST INSIST, MA'AM.
I KNOW I DON'T LIKE THE SOUND OF THAT!

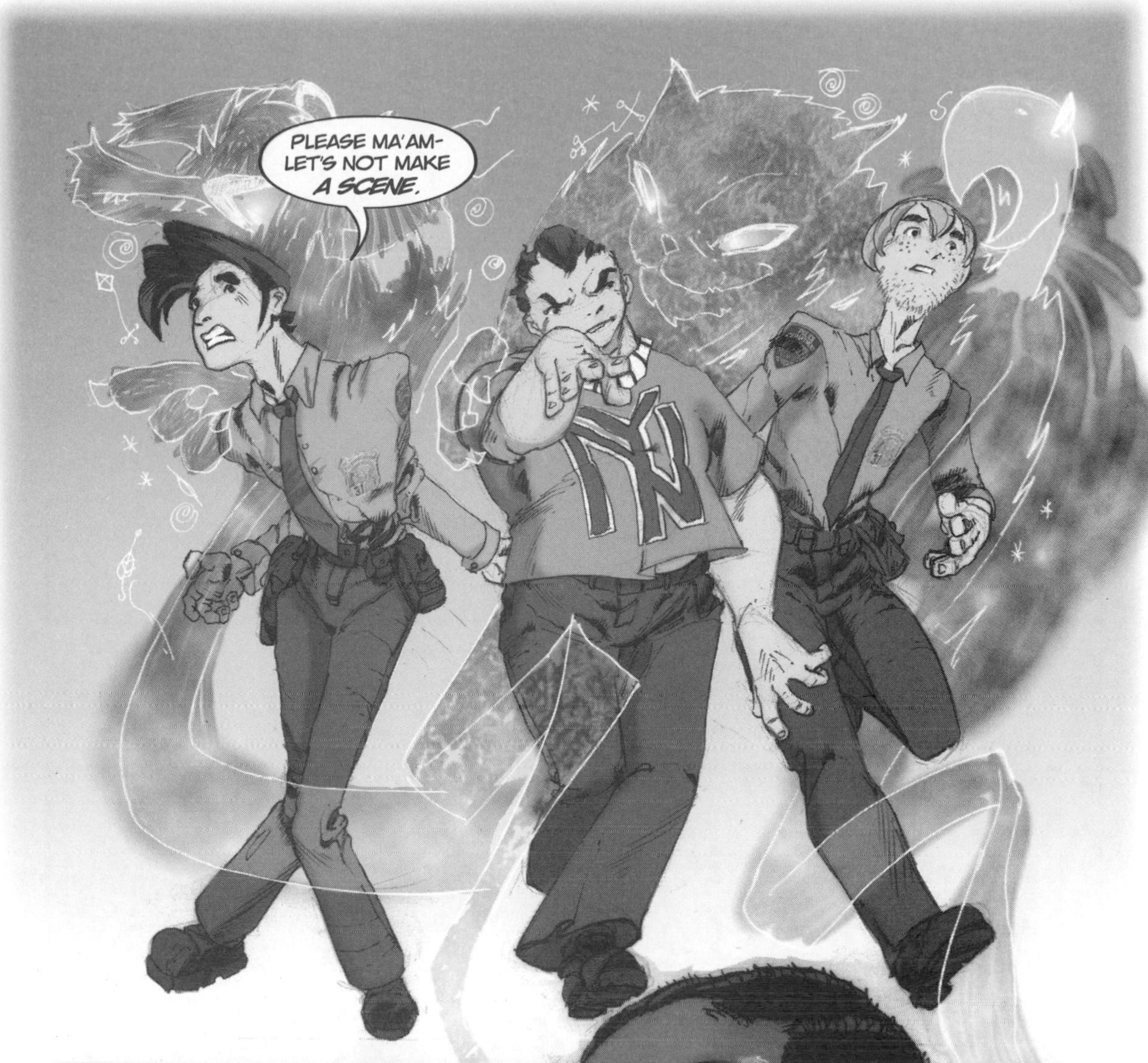
PLEASE MA'AM-
LET'S NOT MAKE
A SCENE.

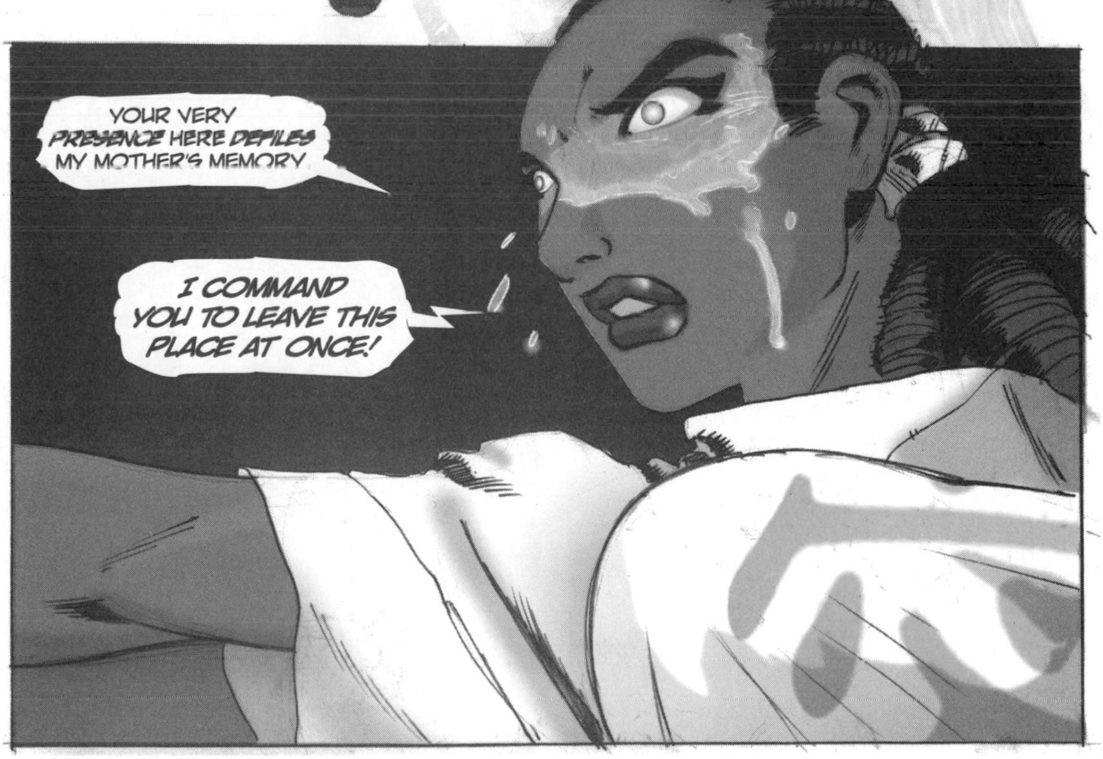
YOUR VERY
PRESENCE HERE DEFILES
MY MOTHER'S MEMORY.
I COMMAND
YOU TO LEAVE THIS
PLACE AT ONCE!

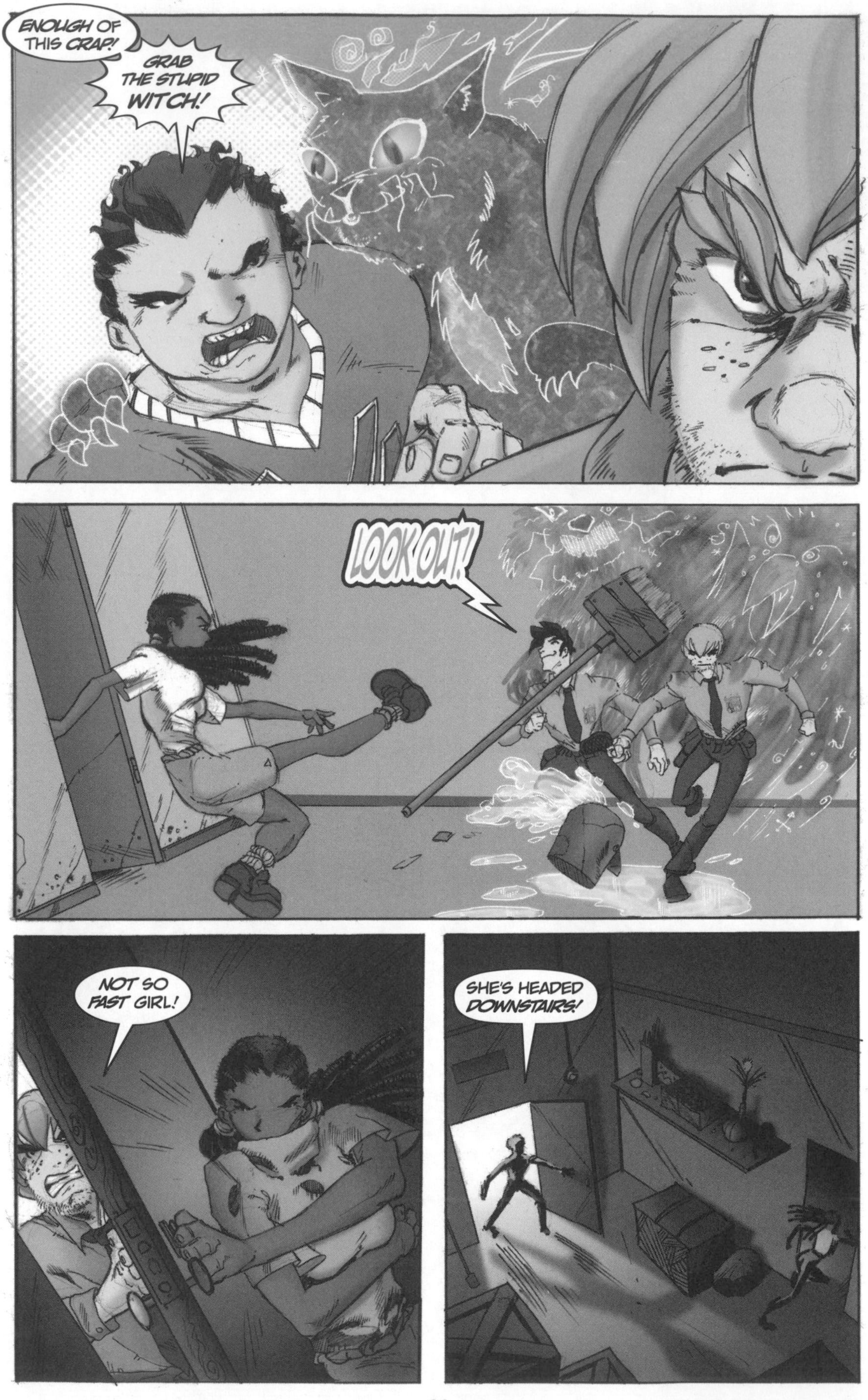
ENOUGH OF THIS CRAP!
GRAB THE STUPID WITCH!
LOOK OUT!
NOT SO FAST GIRL!
SHE'S HEADED DOWNSTAIRS!

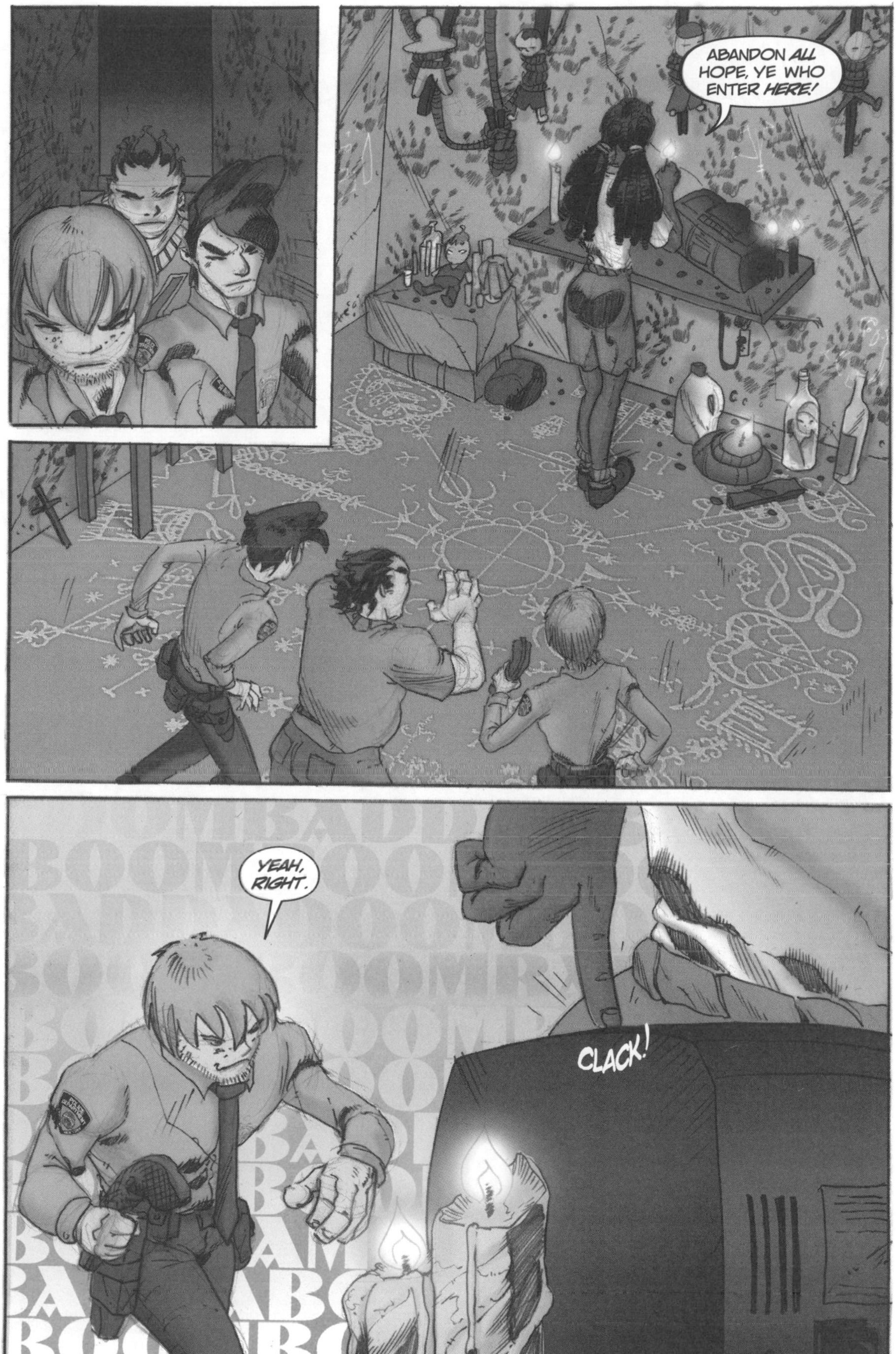
ABANDON ALL HOPE, YE WHO ENTER HERE!
YEAH, RIGHT.
CLACK!

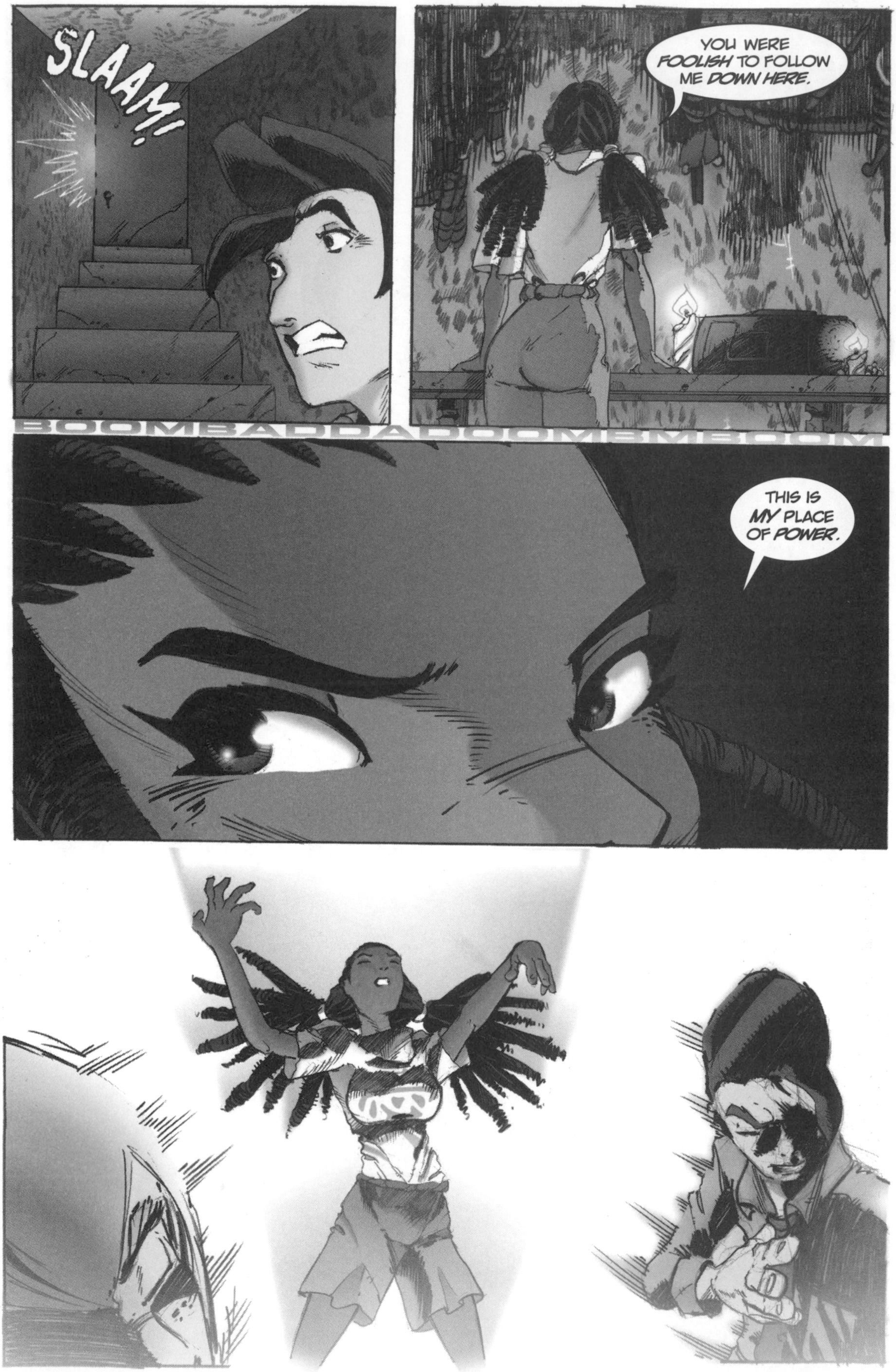
SLAAM!!
YOU WERE FOOLISH TO FOLLOW ME DOWN HERE.
BOOMBADDADOOMBMBOOM
THIS IS MY PLACE OF POWER.

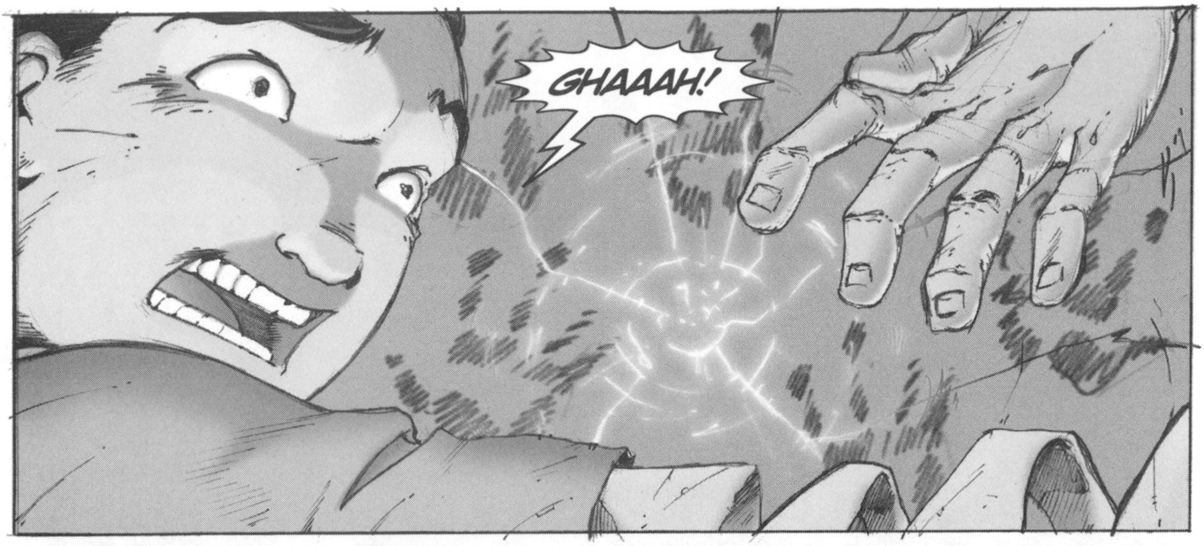
GHAAAH!

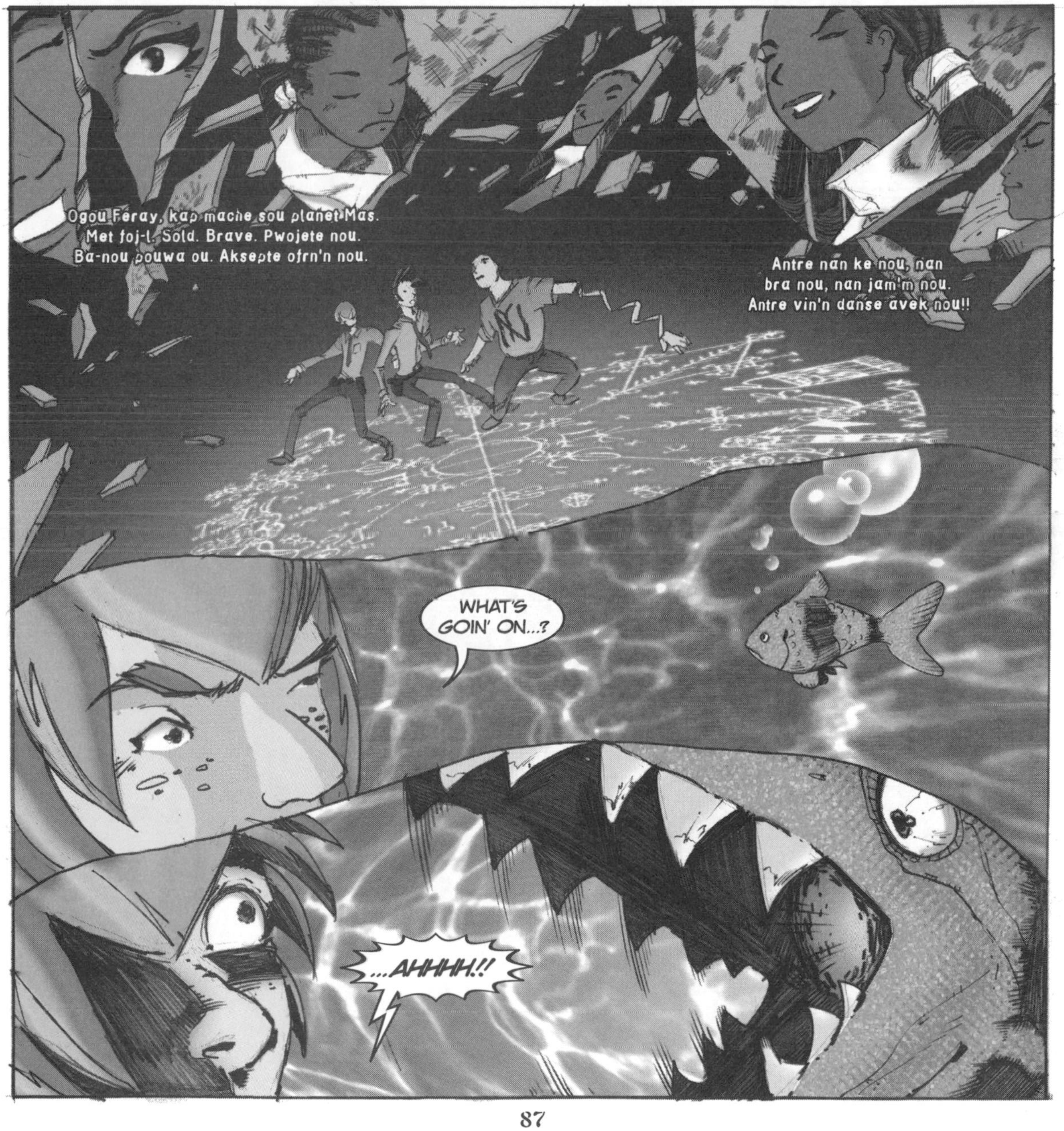
Ogou Feray, kap mache sou planet Mas. Met foj-l. Sold. Brave. Pwojete nou. Ba-nou pouwa ou. Aksepte ofrn'n nou.
Antre nan ke nou, nan bra nou, nan jam'm nou. Antre vin'n danse avek nou!!
WHAT'S GOIN' ON...?
...AHHHH!!

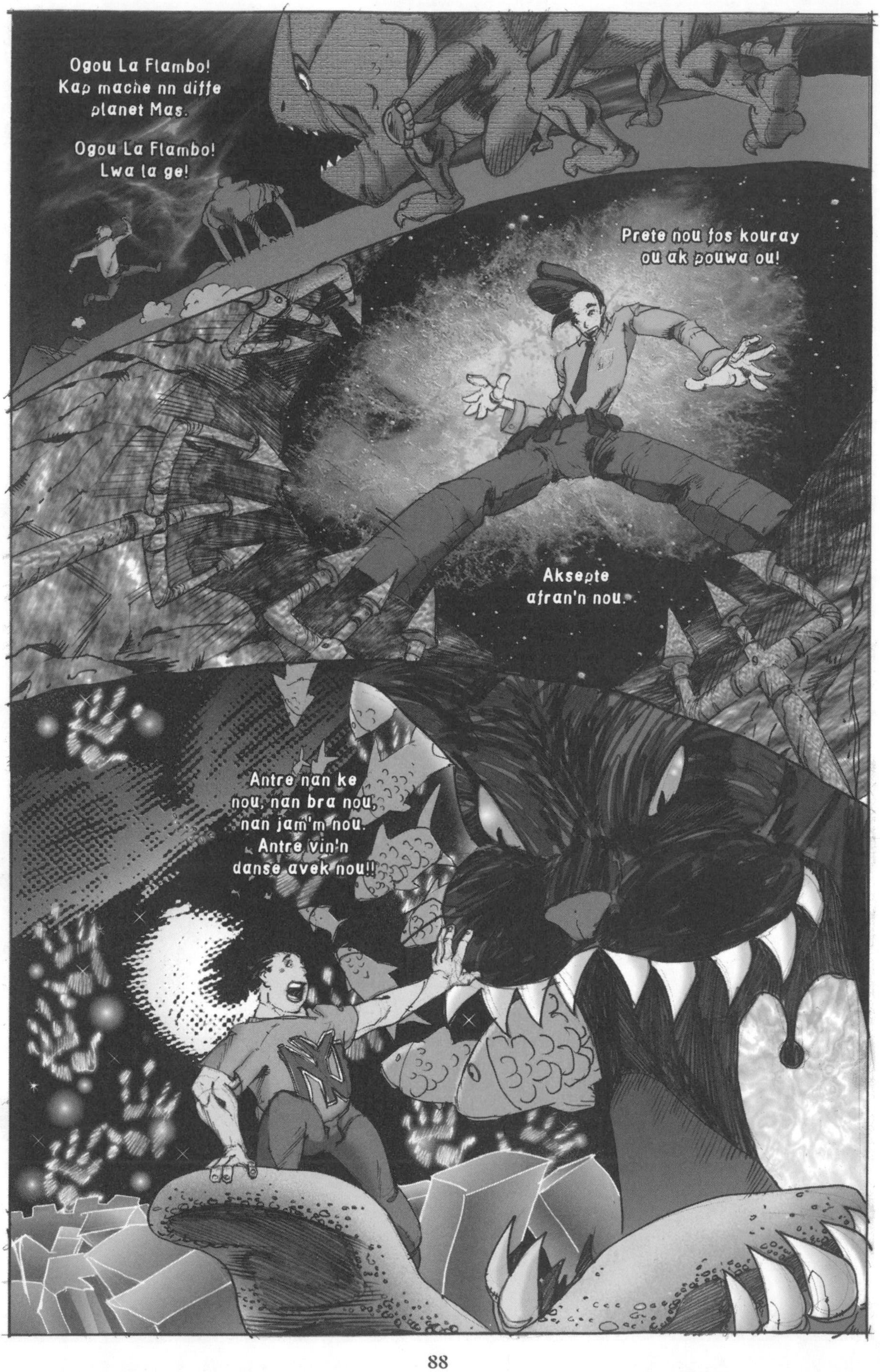
Ogou La Flambo!
Kap mache nn diffe
planet Mas.
Ogou La Flambo!
Lwa la ge!
Prete nou fos kouray
ou ak pouwa ou!
Aksepte
afran'n nou.
Antre nan ke
nou, nan bra nou,
nan jam'm nou.
Antre vin'n
danse avek nou!!

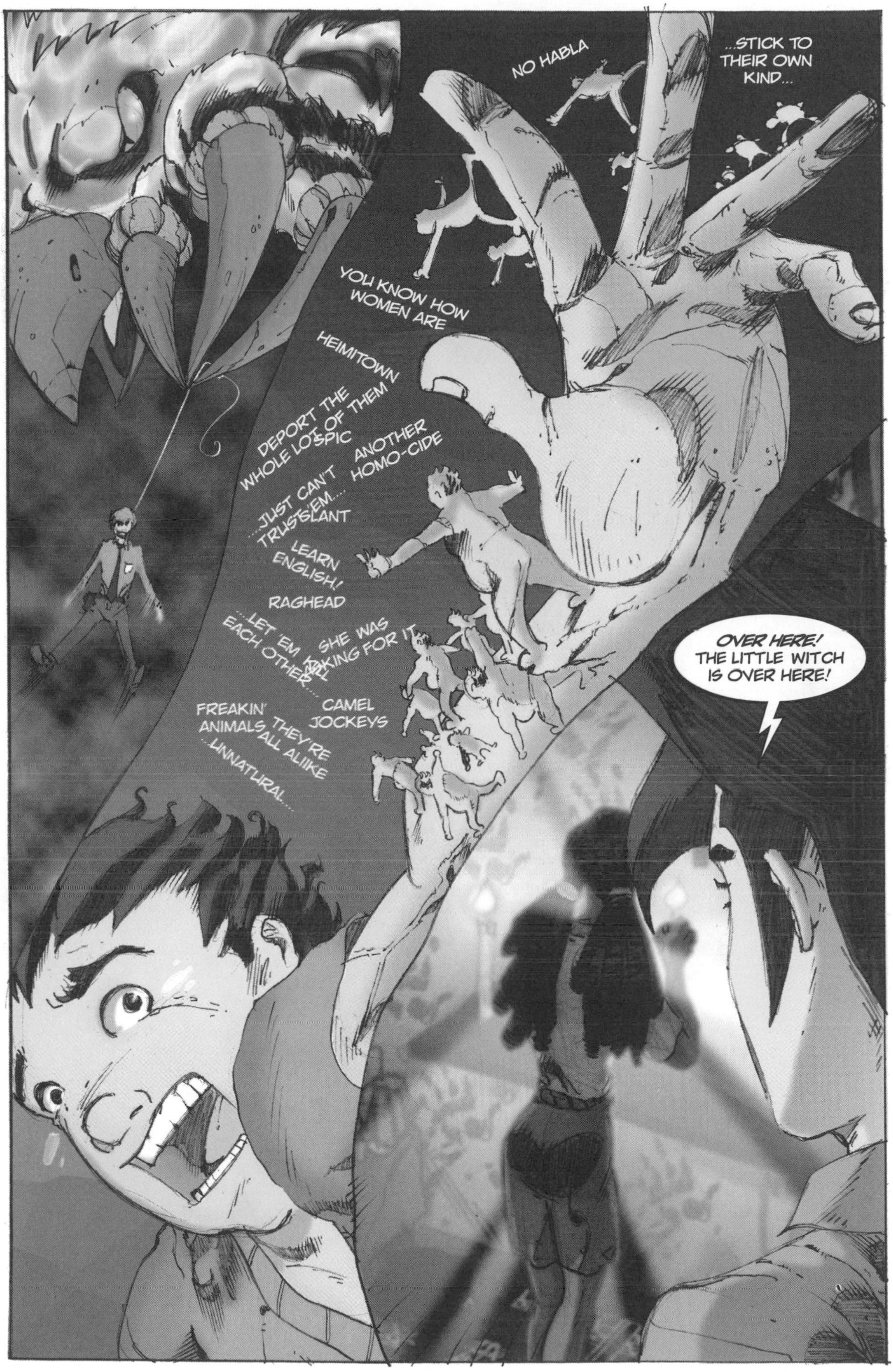
NO HABLA
...STICK TO THEIR OWN KIND...
YOU KNOW HOW WOMEN ARE
HEIMITOWN
DEPORT THE WHOLE LOT OF THEM
SPIC
...JUST CAN'T TRUST 'EM...
ANOTHER HOMO-CIDE
SLANT
LEARN ENGLISH!
RAGHEAD
...LET 'EM KILL EACH OTHER...
SHE WAS ASKING FOR IT
CAMEL JOCKEYS
FREAKIN' ANIMALS
THEY'RE ALL ALIKE
...UNNATURAL...
OVER HERE! THE LITTLE WITCH IS OVER HERE!

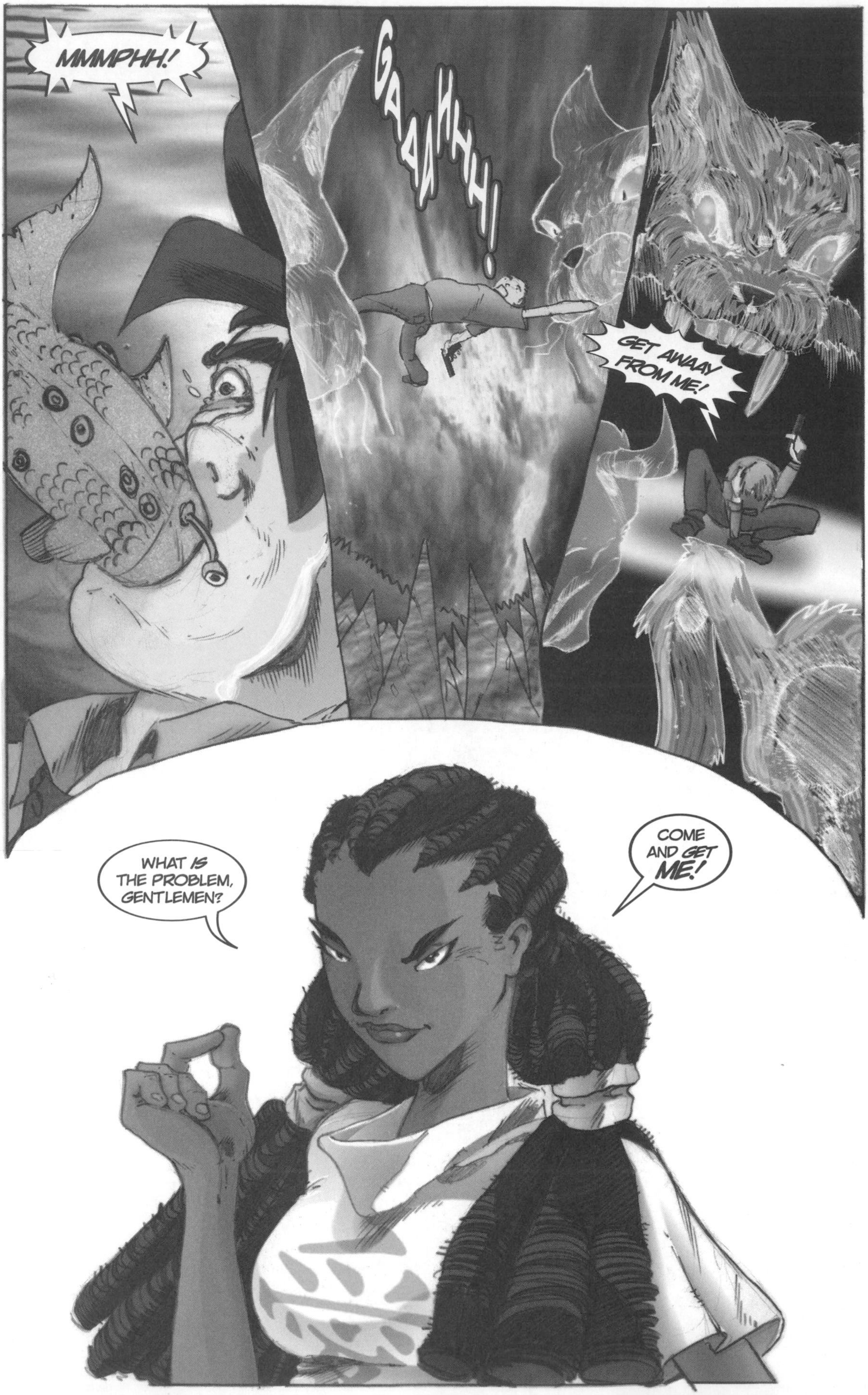
MMMPHH!
GAAAHHHH!
GET AWAAY FROM ME!
WHAT IS THE PROBLEM, GENTLEMEN?
COME AND GET ME!

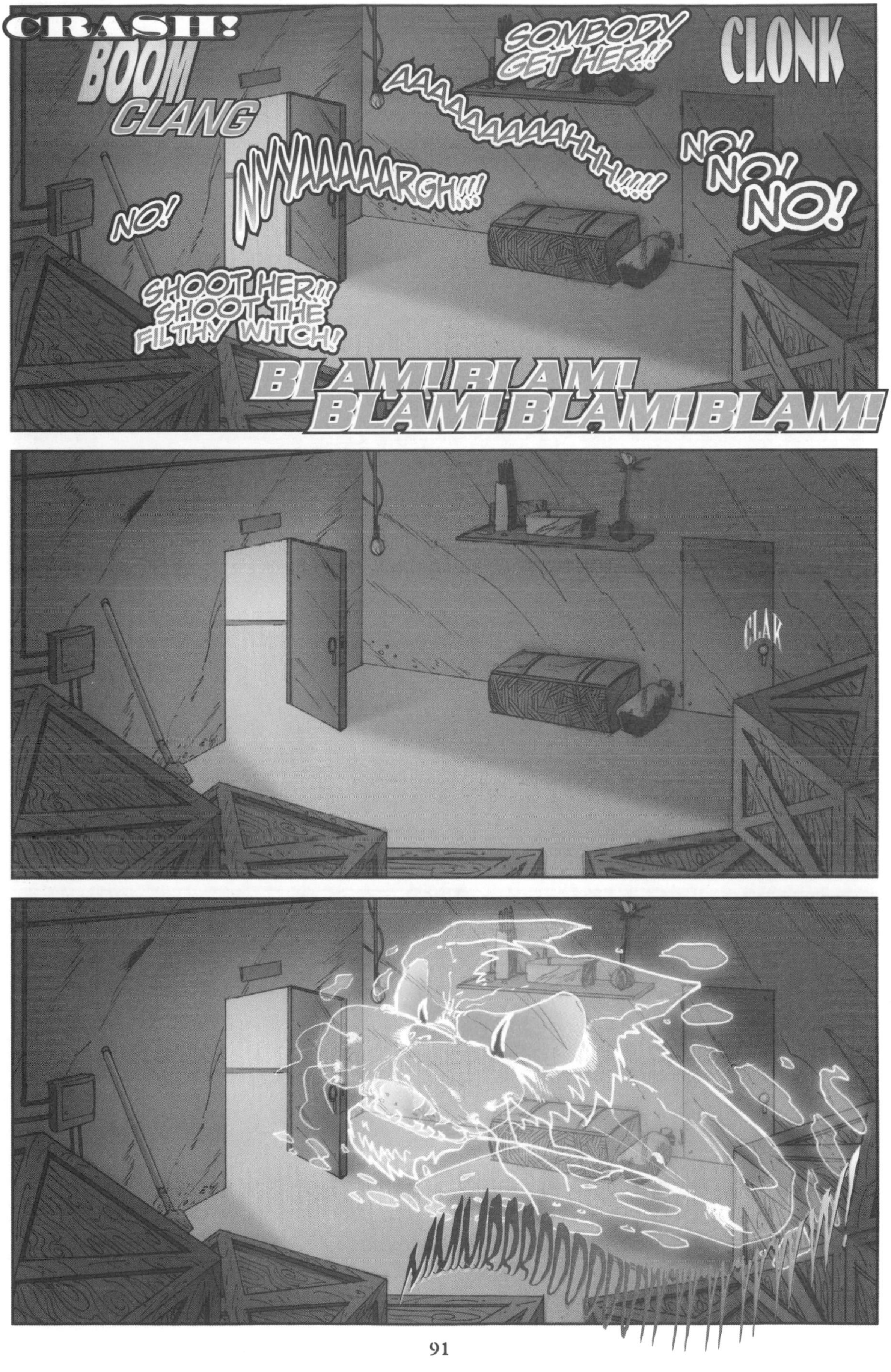
CRASH!
BOOM
CLANG
NO!
NYYAAAAAARGH!!!
AAAAAAAAAAHHH!!!!
SOMBODY GET HER!!
CLONK
NO! NO! NO!
SHOOT HER!! SHOOT THE FILTHY WITCH!
BLAM! BLAM! BLAM! BLAM! BLAM!
CLAK

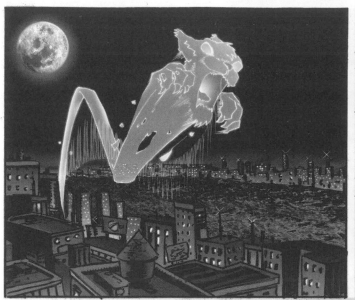

...AND SHE HAS MADE *NOH* EFFORT TO CONTACT THE PRESS ABOUT HAIR LOOMING *EVICTION.*

APPARENTLY SHE HASN'T EVEN *BOTHAIRD* TO TEL *SHEFEELD* OR HAIR *AUNT,* BUTT EENSTED SPEND ALL DAY CLEENING THEE SHOP.

NOT TO WORRY;

IF RENE DOESN'T *WANT* TO PLAY, I HAVE *TAKEN STEPS* TO ELIMINATE...

...*EH?*

WHAT *EEZ* THAT *NOISE?*

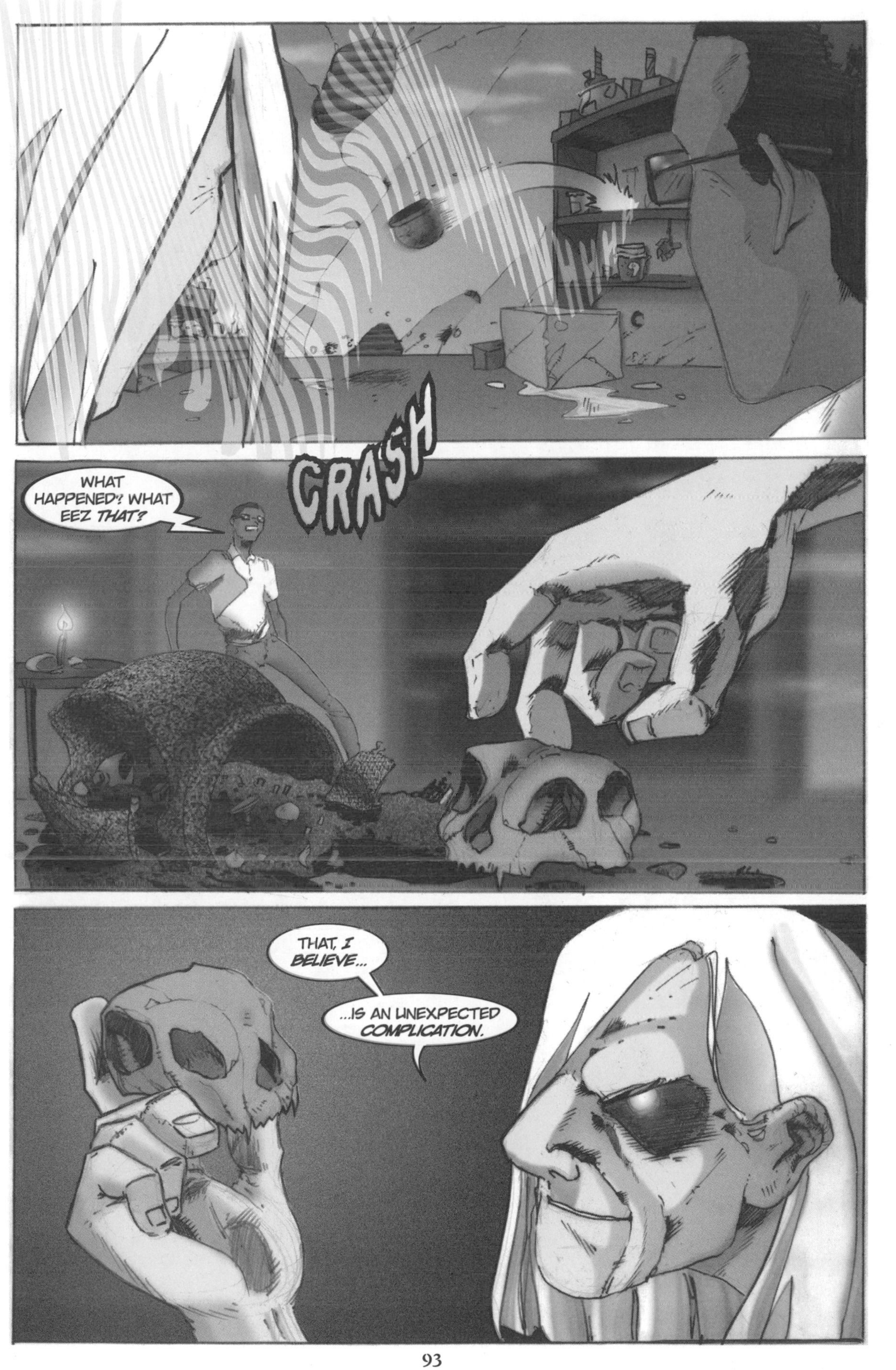
CRASH
WHAT HAPPENED? WHAT EEZ THAT?
THAT, I BELIEVE...
...IS AN UNEXPECTED COMPLICATION.

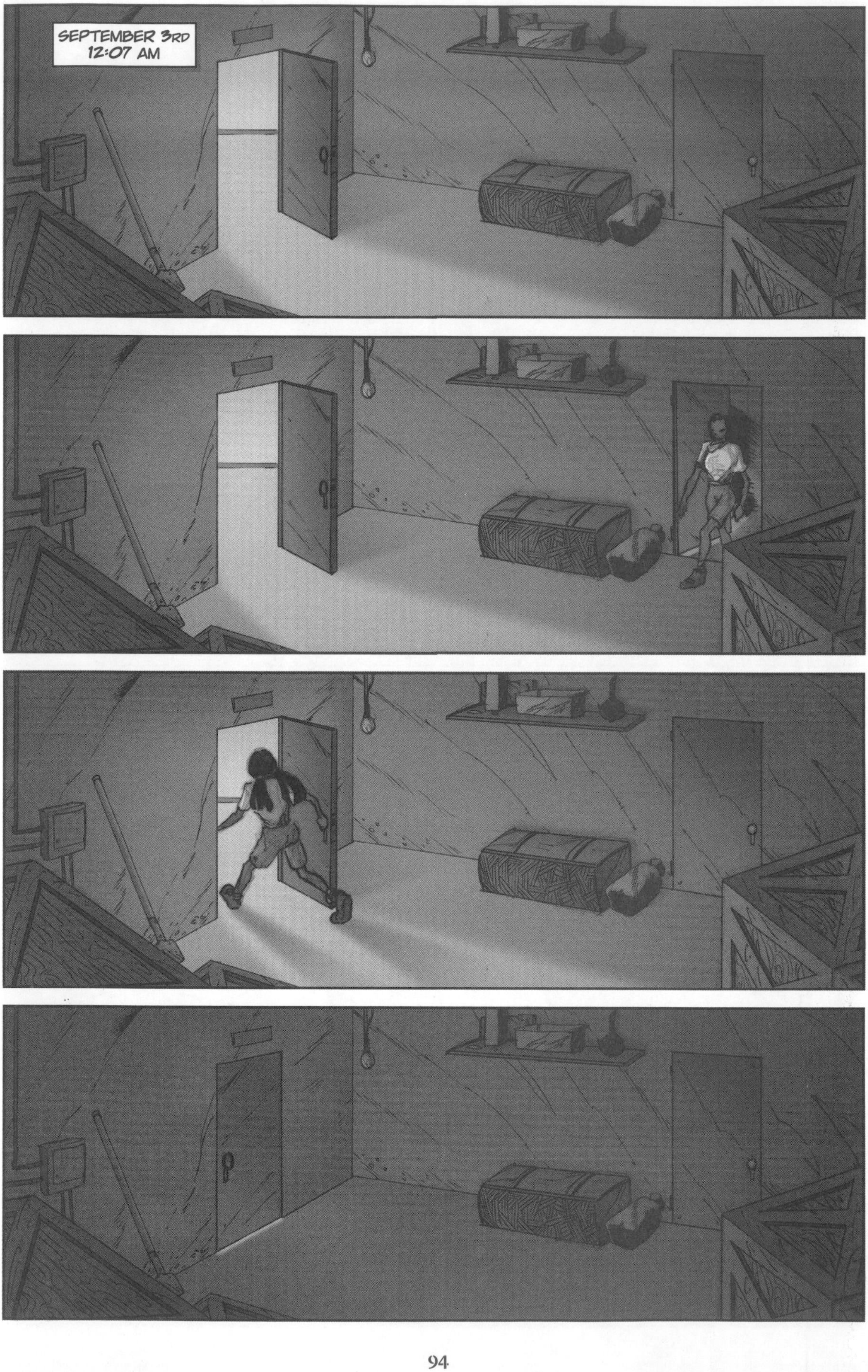
SEPTEMBER 3RD
12:07 AM

CHAPTER FOUR

PERSISTENCE OF VISION

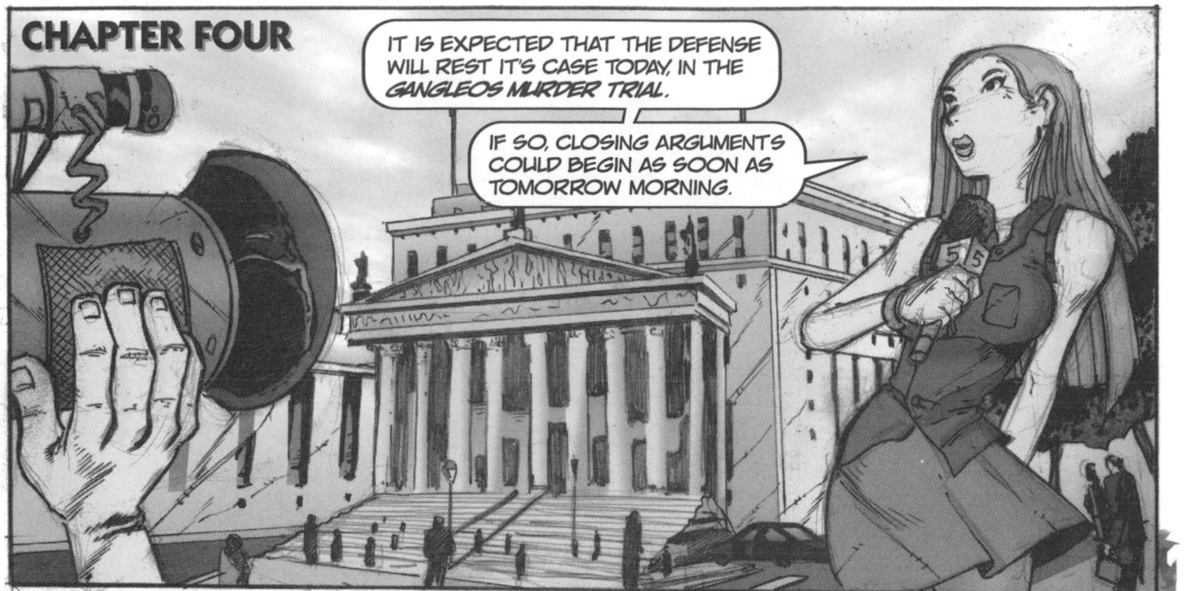
IT IS EXPECTED THAT THE DEFENSE WILL REST IT'S CASE TODAY, IN THE *GANGLEOS MURDER TRIAL.*
IF SO, CLOSING ARGUMENTS COULD BEGIN AS SOON AS TOMORROW MORNING.

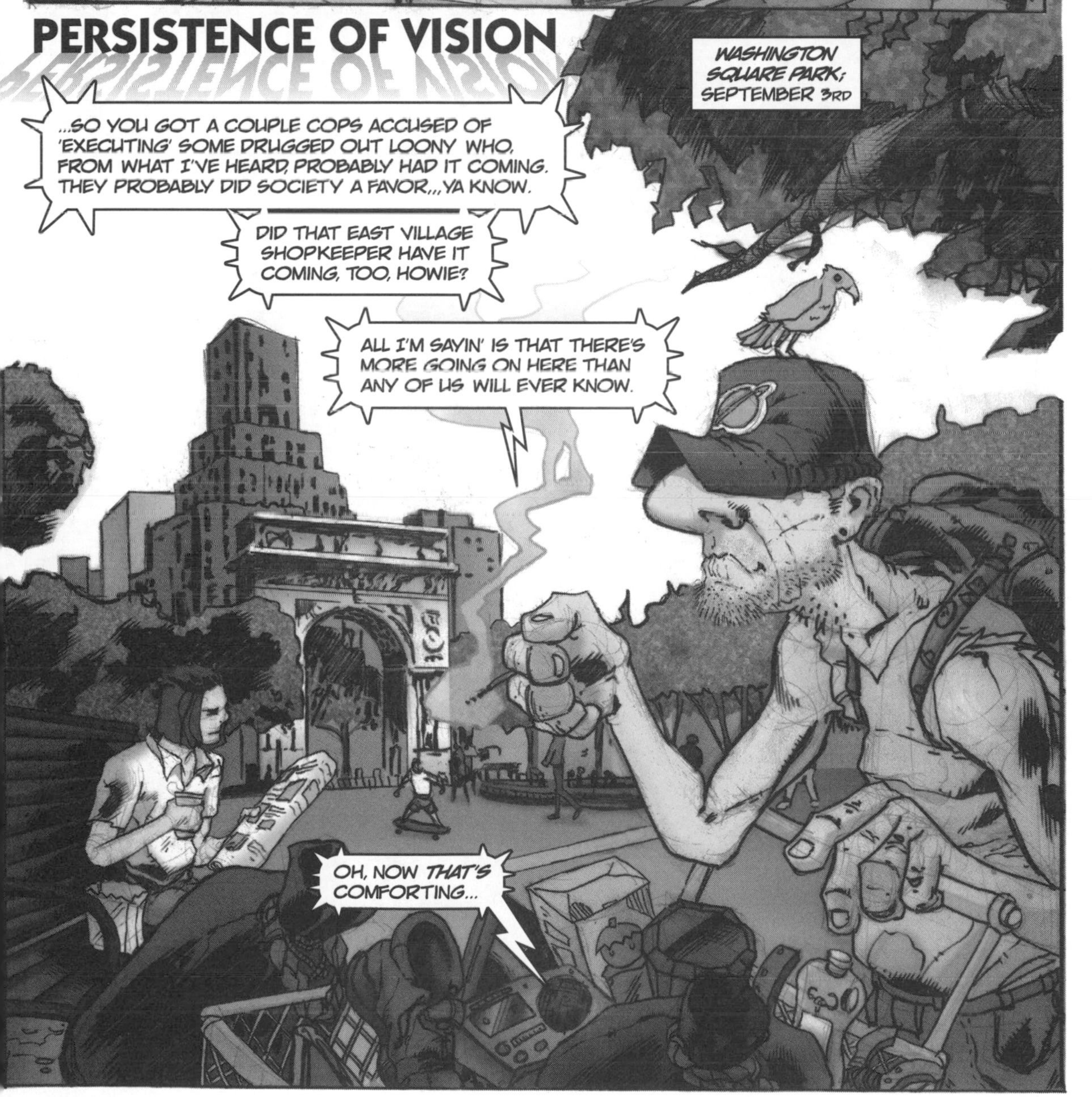
WASHINGTON SQUARE PARK; SEPTEMBER 3RD
...SO YOU GOT A COUPLE COPS ACCUSED OF 'EXECUTING' SOME DRUGGED OUT LOONY WHO, FROM WHAT I'VE HEARD, PROBABLY HAD IT COMING. THEY PROBABLY DID SOCIETY A FAVOR,,,YA KNOW.
DID THAT EAST VILLAGE SHOPKEEPER HAVE IT COMING, TOO, HOWIE?
ALL I'M SAYIN' IS THAT THERE'S MORE GOING ON HERE THAN ANY OF US WILL EVER KNOW.
OH, NOW *THAT'S* COMFORTING...

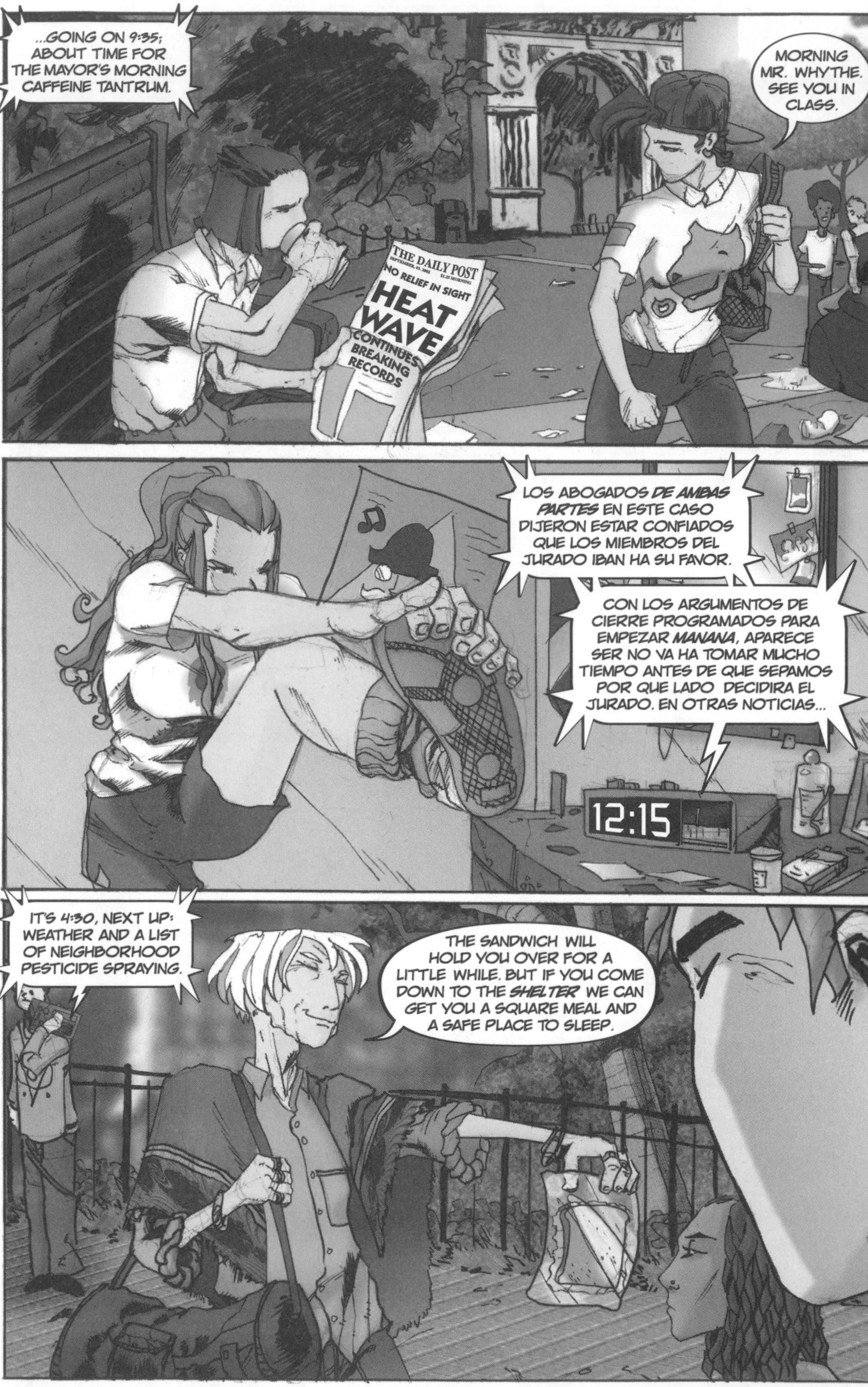
...GOING ON 9:35; ABOUT TIME FOR THE MAYOR'S MORNING CAFFEINE TANTRUM.
MORNING MR. WHYTHE. SEE YOU IN CLASS.
THE DAILY POST
NO RELIEF IN SIGHT
HEAT WAVE
CONTINUES BREAKING RECORDS
LOS ABOGADOS DE AMBAS PARTES EN ESTE CASO DIJERON ESTAR CONFIADOS QUE LOS MIEMBROS DEL JURADO IBAN HA SU FAVOR.
CON LOS ARGUMENTOS DE CIERRE PROGRAMADOS PARA EMPEZAR MANANA, APARECE SER NO VA HA TOMAR MUCHO TIEMPO ANTES DE QUE SEPAMOS POR QUE LADO DECIDIRA EL JURADO. EN OTRAS NOTICIAS...
12:15
IT'S 4:30, NEXT UP: WEATHER AND A LIST OF NEIGHBORHOOD PESTICIDE SPRAYING.
THE SANDWICH WILL HOLD YOU OVER FOR A LITTLE WHILE. BUT IF YOU COME DOWN TO THE SHELTER WE CAN GET YOU A SQUARE MEAL AND A SAFE PLACE TO SLEEP.

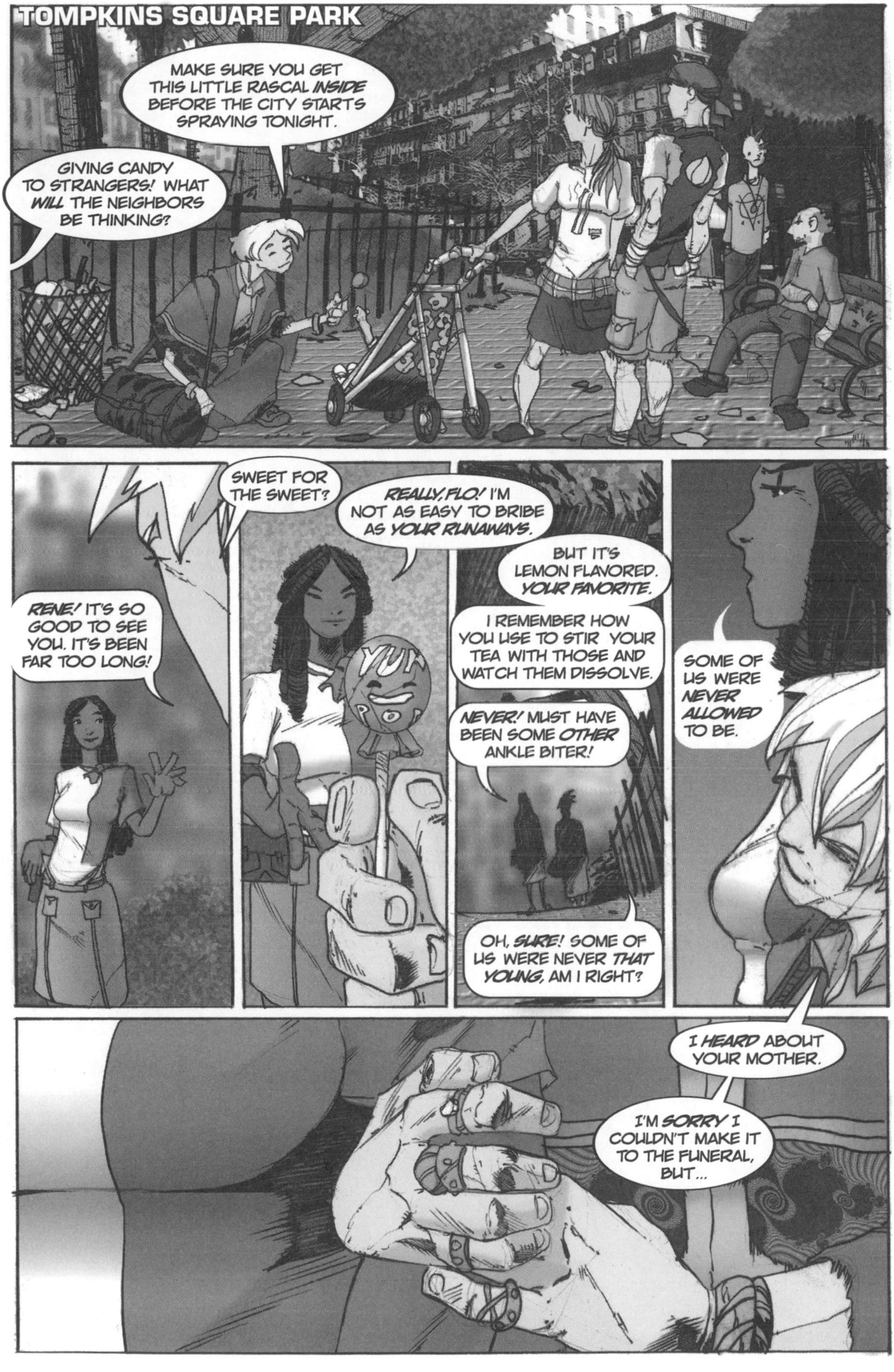
TOMPKINS SQUARE PARK
MAKE SURE YOU GET THIS LITTLE RASCAL *INSIDE* BEFORE THE CITY STARTS SPRAYING TONIGHT.
GIVING CANDY TO STRANGERS! WHAT *WILL* THE NEIGHBORS BE THINKING?
RENE! IT'S SO GOOD TO SEE YOU. IT'S BEEN FAR TOO LONG!
SWEET FOR THE SWEET?
REALLY, FLO! I'M NOT AS EASY TO BRIBE AS *YOUR RUNAWAYS*.
BUT IT'S LEMON FLAVORED. *YOUR FAVORITE*.
I REMEMBER HOW YOU USE TO STIR YOUR TEA WITH THOSE AND WATCH THEM DISSOLVE.
NEVER! MUST HAVE BEEN SOME *OTHER* ANKLE BITER!
OH, *SURE!* SOME OF US WERE NEVER *THAT YOUNG*, AM I RIGHT?
SOME OF US WERE *NEVER ALLOWED* TO BE.
I *HEARD* ABOUT YOUR MOTHER.
I'M *SORRY* I COULDN'T MAKE IT TO THE FUNERAL, BUT...

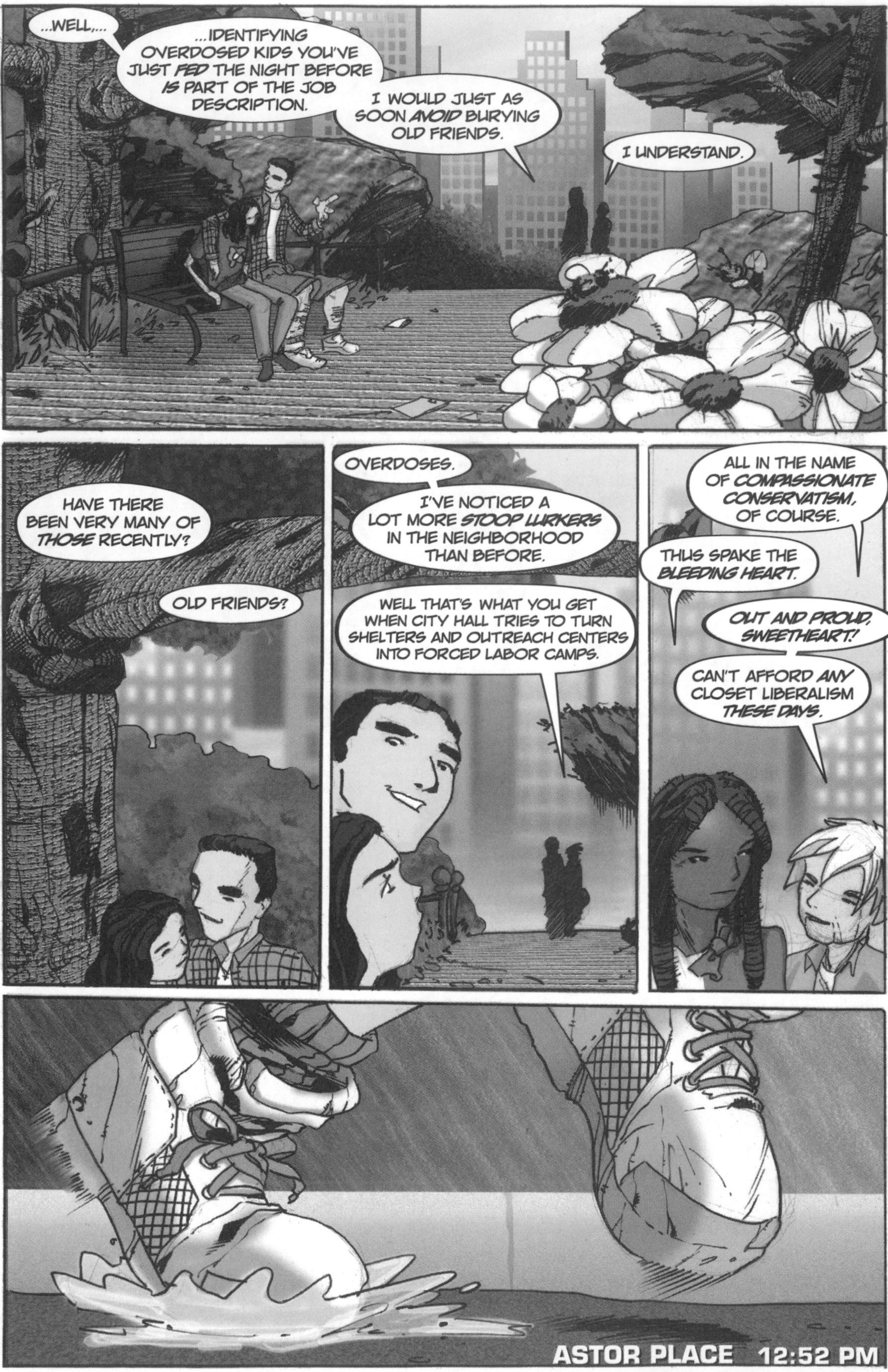
...WELL,...
...IDENTIFYING OVERDOSED KIDS YOU'VE JUST FED THE NIGHT BEFORE IS PART OF THE JOB DESCRIPTION.
I WOULD JUST AS SOON AVOID BURYING OLD FRIENDS.
I UNDERSTAND.
HAVE THERE BEEN VERY MANY OF THOSE RECENTLY?
OLD FRIENDS?
OVERDOSES.
I'VE NOTICED A LOT MORE STOOP LURKERS IN THE NEIGHBORHOOD THAN BEFORE.
WELL THAT'S WHAT YOU GET WHEN CITY HALL TRIES TO TURN SHELTERS AND OUTREACH CENTERS INTO FORCED LABOR CAMPS.
ALL IN THE NAME OF COMPASSIONATE CONSERVATISM, OF COURSE.
THUS SPAKE THE BLEEDING HEART.
OUT AND PROUD, SWEETHEART!
CAN'T AFFORD ANY CLOSET LIBERALISM THESE DAYS.
ASTOR PLACE 12:52 PM

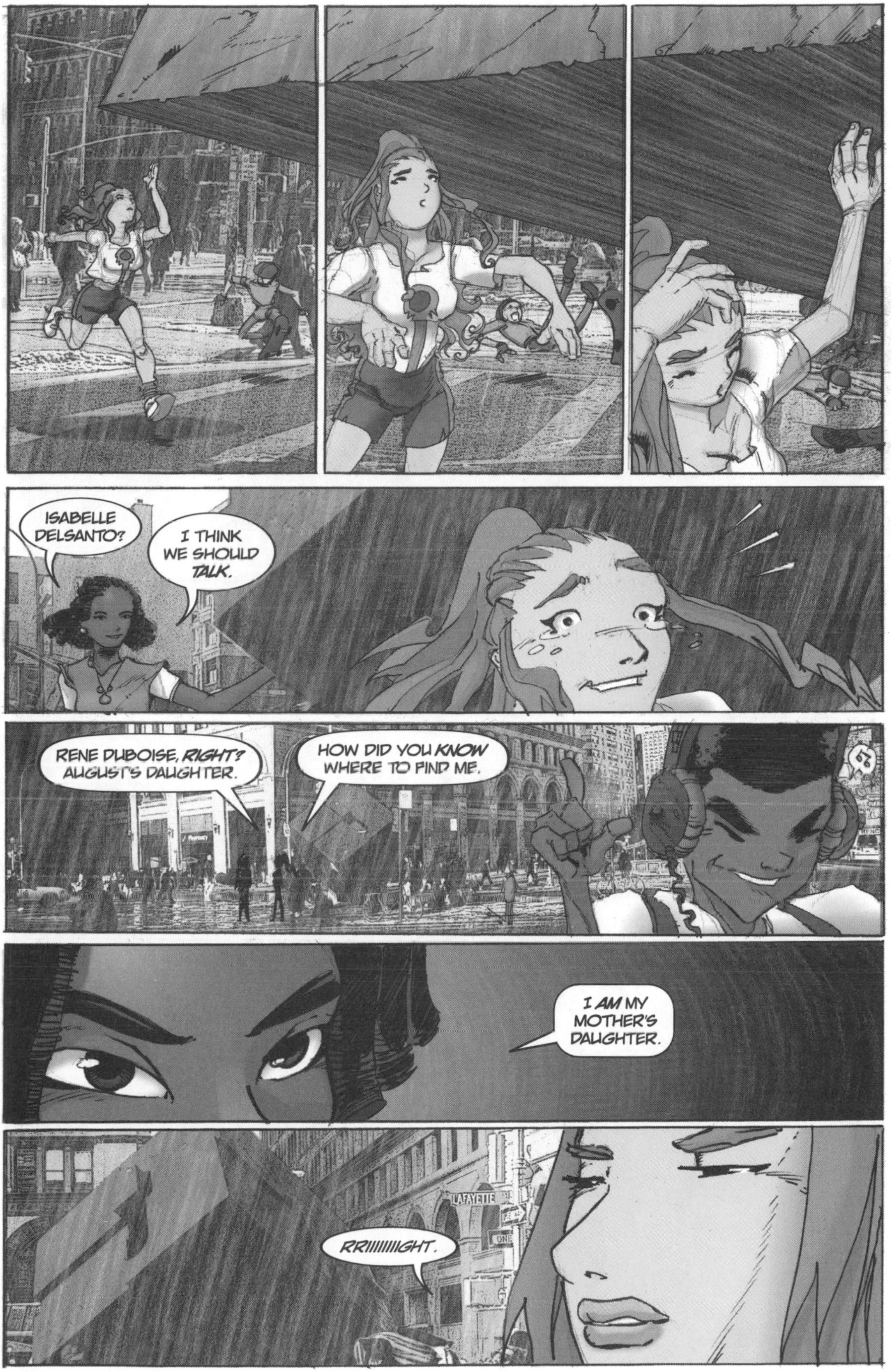

ISABELLE DELSANTO?
I THINK WE SHOULD TALK.
RENE DUBOISE, RIGHT? AUGUST'S DAUGHTER.
HOW DID YOU KNOW WHERE TO FIND ME.
I AM MY MOTHER'S DAUGHTER.
LAFAYETTE
ONE
RRIIIIIIIGHT.

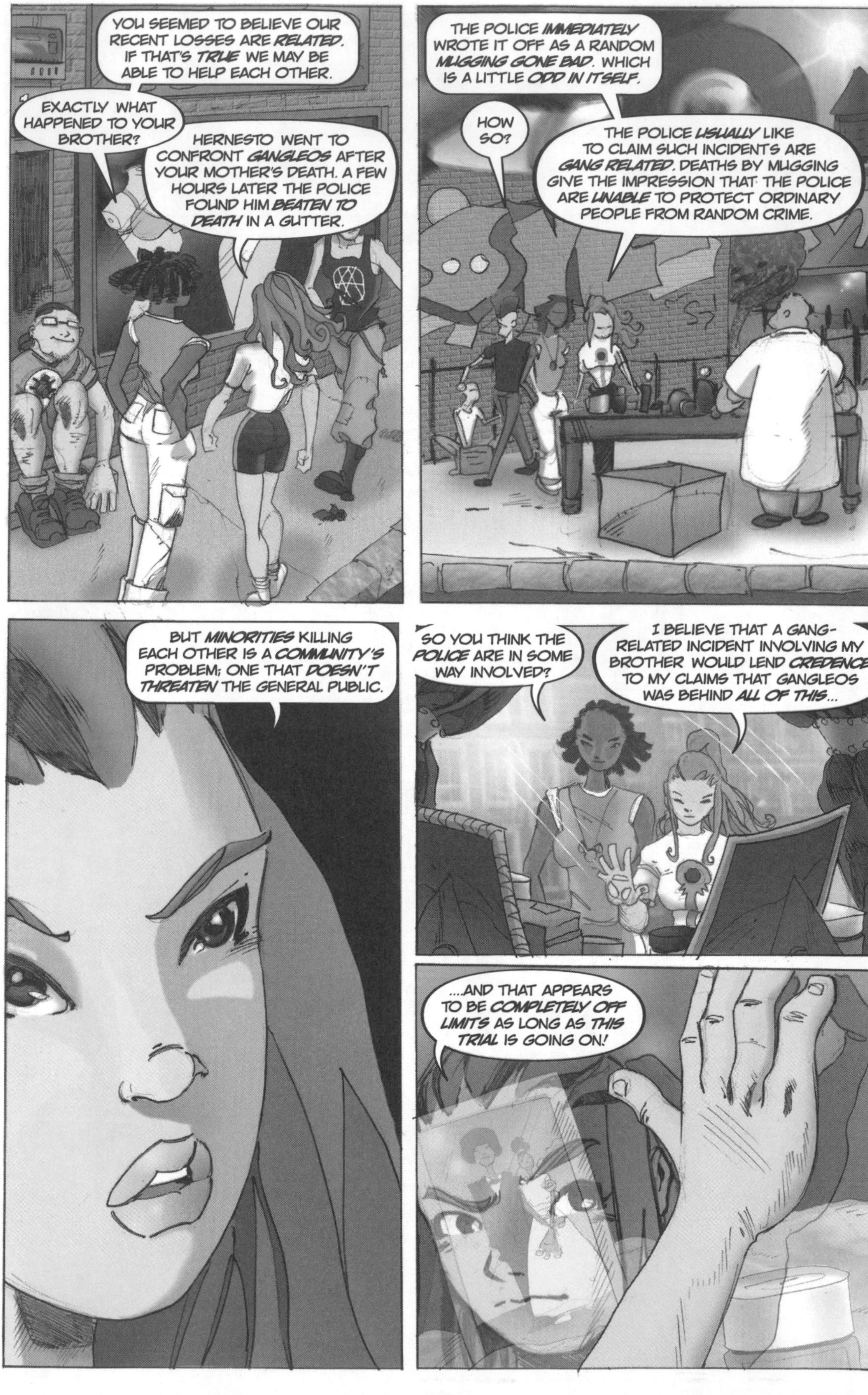
YOU SEEMED TO BELIEVE OUR RECENT LOSSES ARE RELATED. IF THAT'S TRUE WE MAY BE ABLE TO HELP EACH OTHER.
EXACTLY WHAT HAPPENED TO YOUR BROTHER?
HERNESTO WENT TO CONFRONT GANGLEOS AFTER YOUR MOTHER'S DEATH. A FEW HOURS LATER THE POLICE FOUND HIM BEATEN TO DEATH IN A GUTTER.
THE POLICE IMMEDIATELY WROTE IT OFF AS A RANDOM MUGGING GONE BAD. WHICH IS A LITTLE ODD IN ITSELF.
HOW SO?
THE POLICE USUALLY LIKE TO CLAIM SUCH INCIDENTS ARE GANG RELATED. DEATHS BY MUGGING GIVE THE IMPRESSION THAT THE POLICE ARE UNABLE TO PROTECT ORDINARY PEOPLE FROM RANDOM CRIME.
BUT MINORITIES KILLING EACH OTHER IS A COMMUNITY'S PROBLEM; ONE THAT DOESN'T THREATEN THE GENERAL PUBLIC.
SO YOU THINK THE POLICE ARE IN SOME WAY INVOLVED?
I BELIEVE THAT A GANG-RELATED INCIDENT INVOLVING MY BROTHER WOULD LEND CREDENCE TO MY CLAIMS THAT GANGLEOS WAS BEHIND ALL OF THIS...
...AND THAT APPEARS TO BE COMPLETELY OFF LIMITS AS LONG AS THIS TRIAL IS GOING ON!

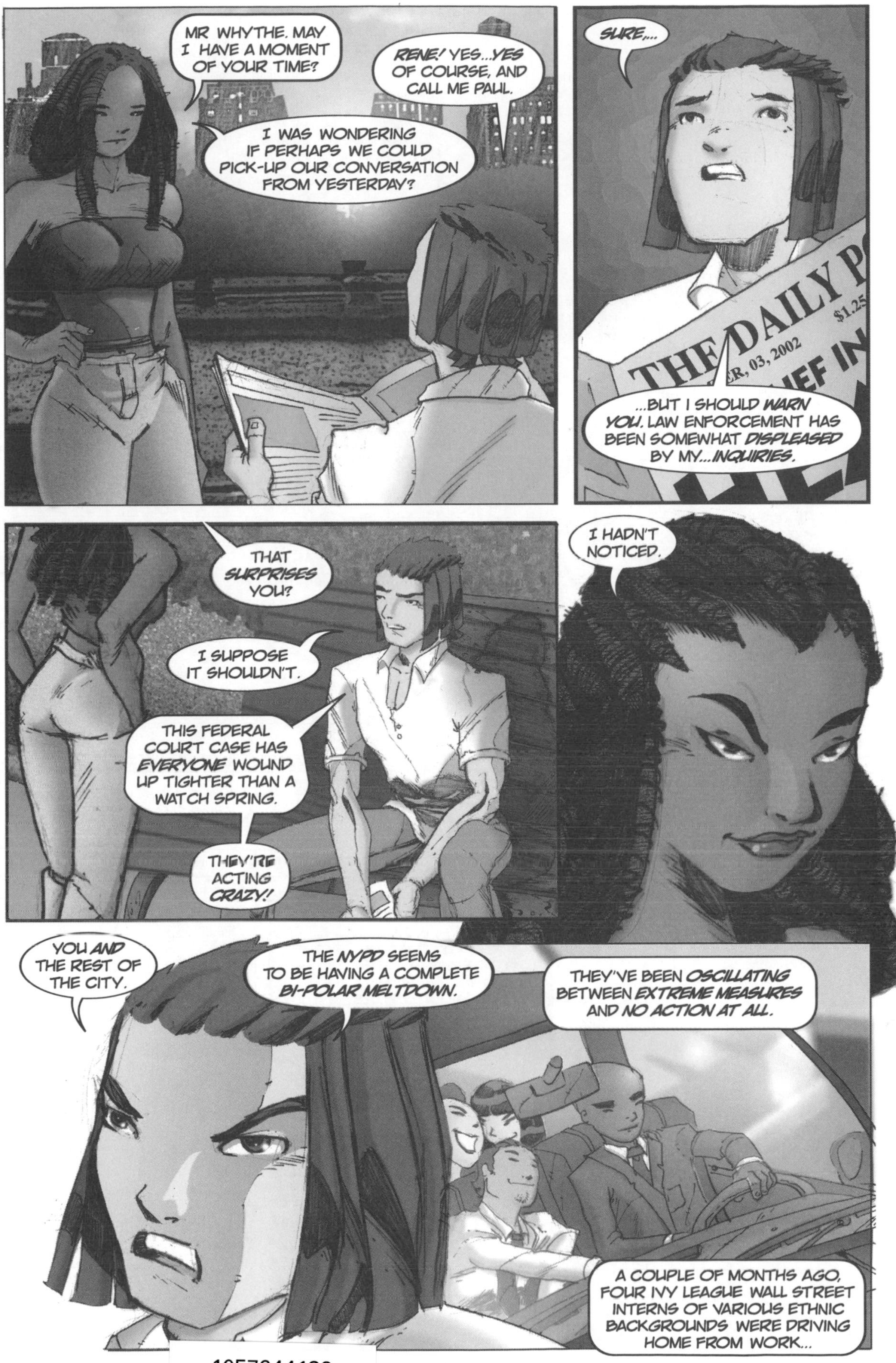
MR WHYTHE. MAY I HAVE A MOMENT OF YOUR TIME?
RENE! YES...YES OF COURSE, AND CALL ME PAUL.
I WAS WONDERING IF PERHAPS WE COULD PICK-UP OUR CONVERSATION FROM YESTERDAY?
SURE,...
THE DAILY P
ER, 03, 2002
$1.25
...BUT I SHOULD WARN YOU. LAW ENFORCEMENT HAS BEEN SOMEWHAT DISPLEASED BY MY...INQUIRIES.
THAT SURPRISES YOU?
I SUPPOSE IT SHOULDN'T.
THIS FEDERAL COURT CASE HAS EVERYONE WOUND UP TIGHTER THAN A WATCH SPRING.
THEY'RE ACTING CRAZY!
I HADN'T NOTICED.
YOU AND THE REST OF THE CITY.
THE NYPD SEEMS TO BE HAVING A COMPLETE BI-POLAR MELTDOWN.
THEY'VE BEEN OSCILLATING BETWEEN EXTREME MEASURES AND NO ACTION AT ALL.
A COUPLE OF MONTHS AGO, FOUR IVY LEAGUE WALL STREET INTERNS OF VARIOUS ETHNIC BACKGROUNDS WERE DRIVING HOME FROM WORK...

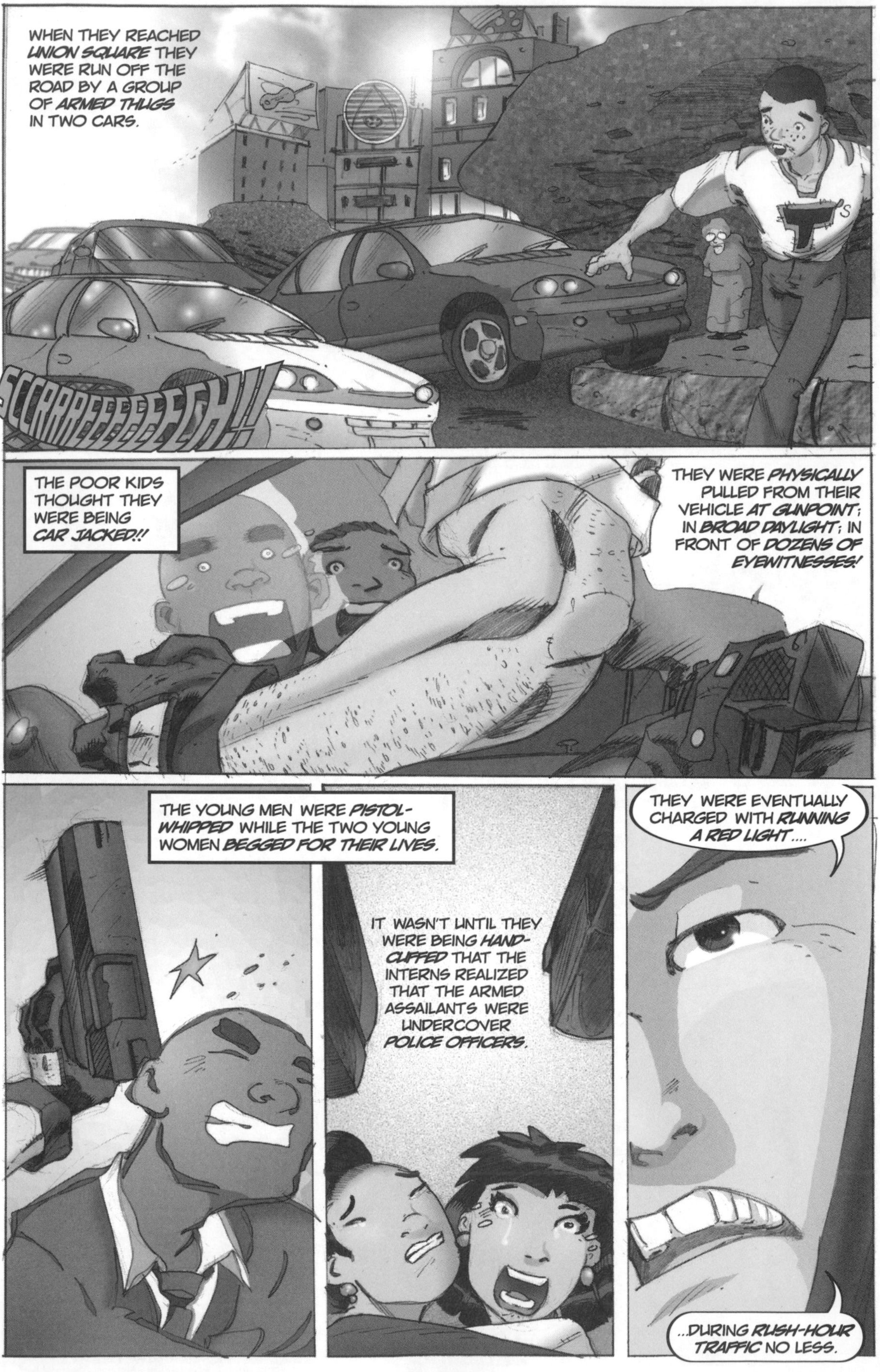
WHEN THEY REACHED UNION SQUARE THEY WERE RUN OFF THE ROAD BY A GROUP OF ARMED THUGS IN TWO CARS.
SCCRRREEEEEEECH!!
THE POOR KIDS THOUGHT THEY WERE BEING CAR JACKED!!
THEY WERE PHYSICALLY PULLED FROM THEIR VEHICLE AT GUNPOINT; IN BROAD DAYLIGHT; IN FRONT OF DOZENS OF EYEWITNESSES!
THE YOUNG MEN WERE PISTOL-WHIPPED WHILE THE TWO YOUNG WOMEN BEGGED FOR THEIR LIVES.
IT WASN'T UNTIL THEY WERE BEING HAND-CUFFED THAT THE INTERNS REALIZED THAT THE ARMED ASSAILANTS WERE UNDERCOVER POLICE OFFICERS.
THEY WERE EVENTUALLY CHARGED WITH RUNNING A RED LIGHT....
...DURING RUSH-HOUR TRAFFIC NO LESS.

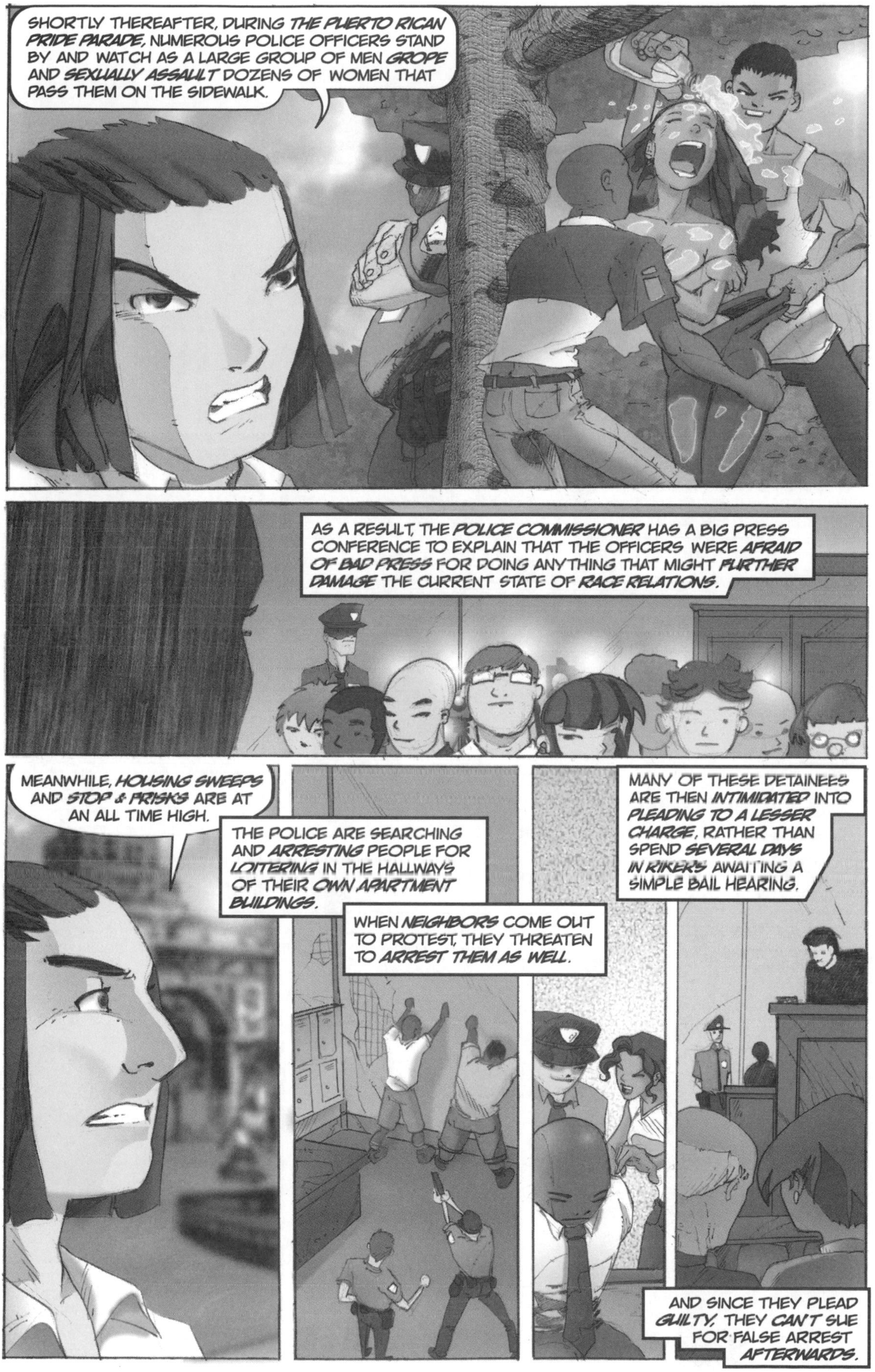
SHORTLY THEREAFTER, DURING THE PUERTO RICAN PRIDE PARADE, NUMEROUS POLICE OFFICERS STAND BY AND WATCH AS A LARGE GROUP OF MEN GROPE AND SEXUALLY ASSAULT DOZENS OF WOMEN THAT PASS THEM ON THE SIDEWALK.
AS A RESULT, THE POLICE COMMISSIONER HAS A BIG PRESS CONFERENCE TO EXPLAIN THAT THE OFFICERS WERE AFRAID OF BAD PRESS FOR DOING ANYTHING THAT MIGHT FURTHER DAMAGE THE CURRENT STATE OF RACE RELATIONS.
MEANWHILE, HOUSING SWEEPS AND STOP & FRISKS ARE AT AN ALL TIME HIGH.
THE POLICE ARE SEARCHING AND ARRESTING PEOPLE FOR LOITERING IN THE HALLWAYS OF THEIR OWN APARTMENT BUILDINGS.
WHEN NEIGHBORS COME OUT TO PROTEST, THEY THREATEN TO ARREST THEM AS WELL.
MANY OF THESE DETAINEES ARE THEN INTIMIDATED INTO PLEADING TO A LESSER CHARGE, RATHER THAN SPEND SEVERAL DAYS IN RIKER'S AWAITING A SIMPLE BAIL HEARING.
AND SINCE THEY PLEAD GUILTY, THEY CAN'T SUE FOR FALSE ARREST AFTERWARDS.

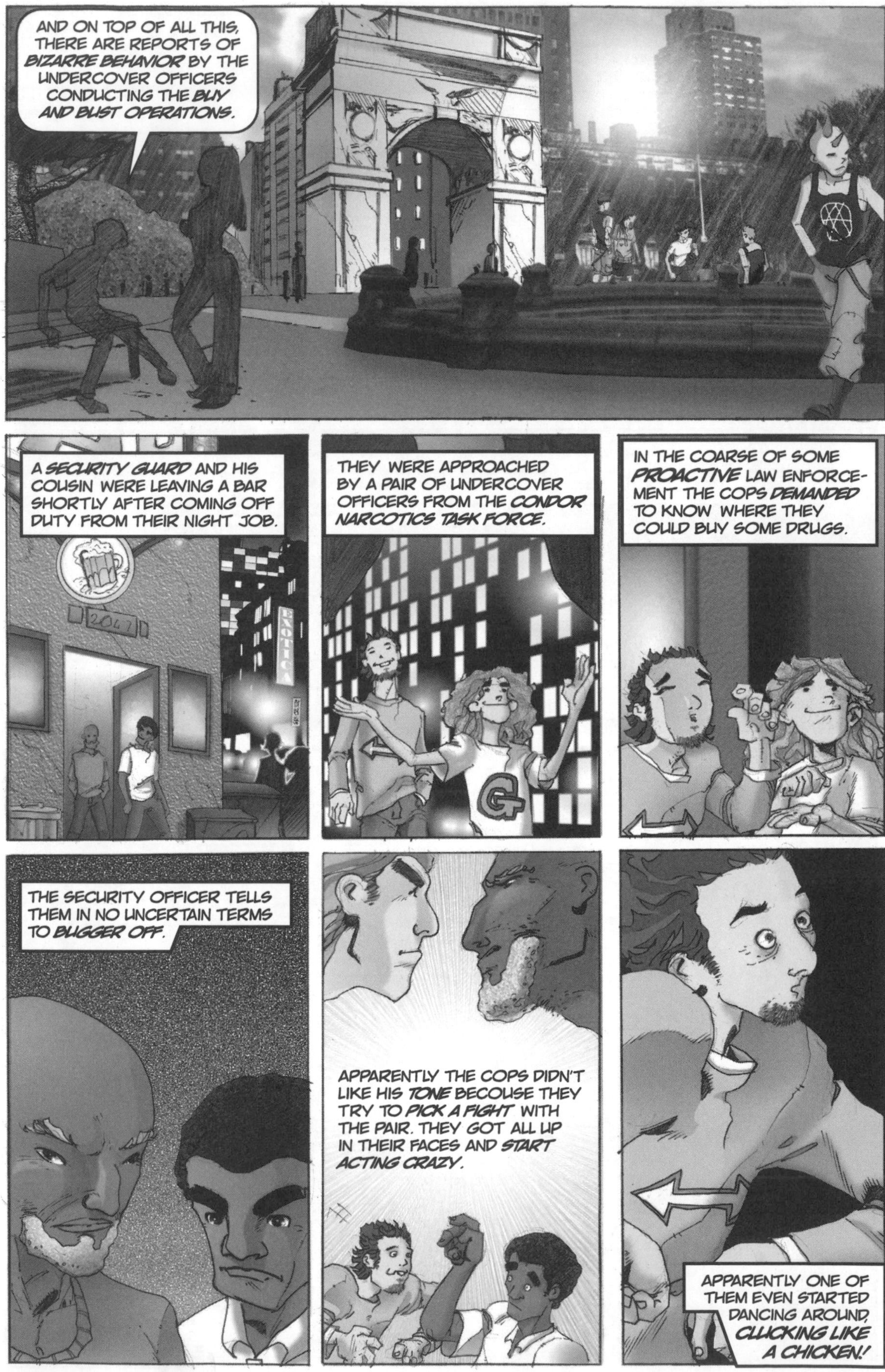
AND ON TOP OF ALL THIS, THERE ARE REPORTS OF BIZARRE BEHAVIOR BY THE UNDERCOVER OFFICERS CONDUCTING THE BUY AND BUST OPERATIONS.
A SECURITY GUARD AND HIS COUSIN WERE LEAVING A BAR SHORTLY AFTER COMING OFF DUTY FROM THEIR NIGHT JOB.
2047
EXOTICA
THEY WERE APPROACHED BY A PAIR OF UNDERCOVER OFFICERS FROM THE CONDOR NARCOTICS TASK FORCE.
IN THE COARSE OF SOME PROACTIVE LAW ENFORCEMENT THE COPS DEMANDED TO KNOW WHERE THEY COULD BUY SOME DRUGS.
THE SECURITY OFFICER TELLS THEM IN NO UNCERTAIN TERMS TO BUGGER OFF.
APPARENTLY THE COPS DIDN'T LIKE HIS TONE BECOUSE THEY TRY TO PICK A FIGHT WITH THE PAIR. THEY GOT ALL UP IN THEIR FACES AND START ACTING CRAZY.
APPARENTLY ONE OF THEM EVEN STARTED DANCING AROUND, CLUCKING LIKE A CHICKEN!

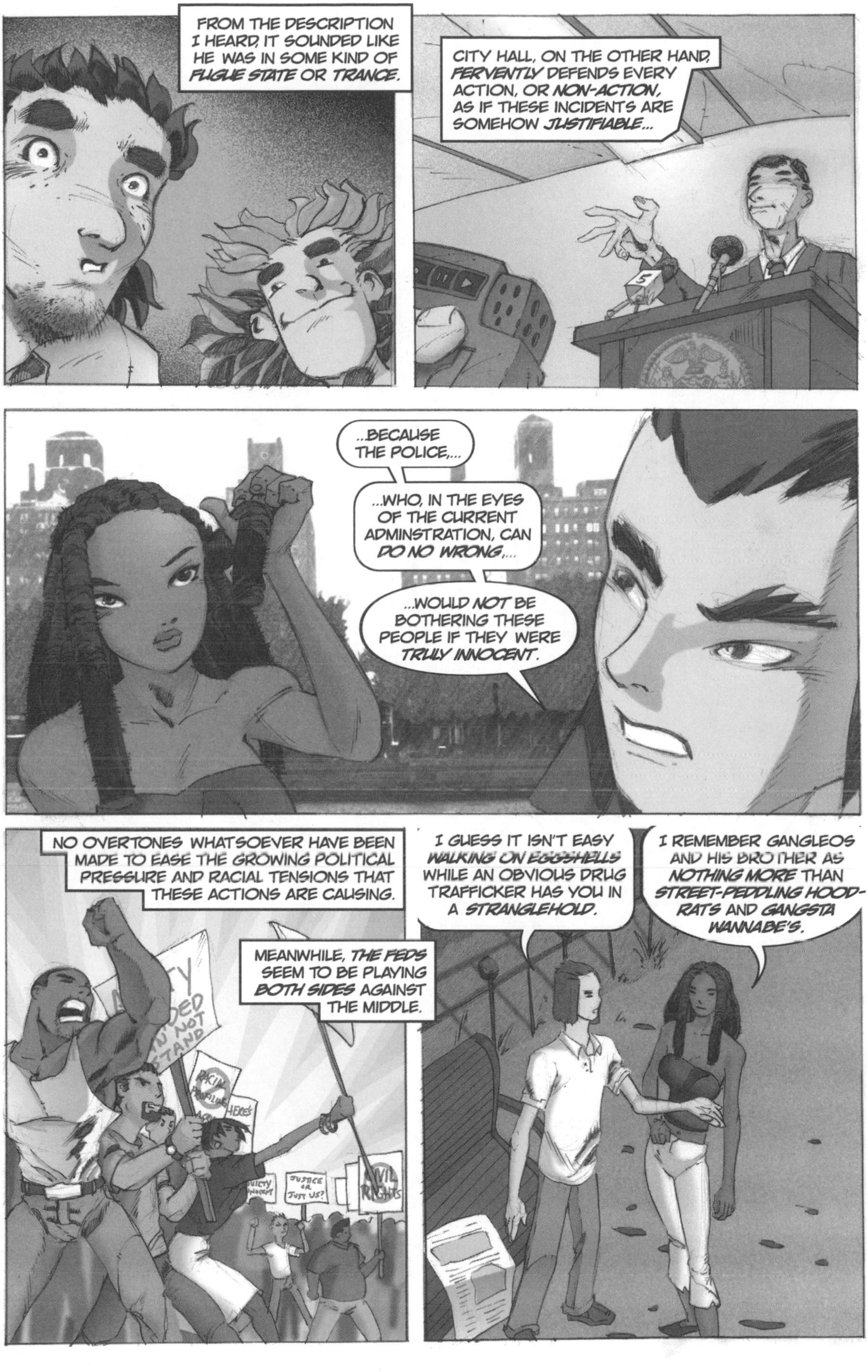
FROM THE DESCRIPTION I HEARD, IT SOUNDED LIKE HE WAS IN SOME KIND OF FUGUE STATE OR TRANCE.
CITY HALL, ON THE OTHER HAND, FERVENTLY DEFENDS EVERY ACTION, OR NON-ACTION, AS IF THESE INCIDENTS ARE SOMEHOW JUSTIFIABLE...
...BECAUSE THE POLICE,...
...WHO, IN THE EYES OF THE CURRENT ADMINSTRATION, CAN DO NO WRONG,...
...WOULD NOT BE BOTHERING THESE PEOPLE IF THEY WERE TRULY INNOCENT.
NO OVERTONES WHATSOEVER HAVE BEEN MADE TO EASE THE GROWING POLITICAL PRESSURE AND RACIAL TENSIONS THAT THESE ACTIONS ARE CAUSING.
MEANWHILE, THE FEDS SEEM TO BE PLAYING BOTH SIDES AGAINST THE MIDDLE.
JUSTICE OR JUST US?
CIVIL RIGHTS
I GUESS IT ISN'T EASY WALKING ON EGGSHELLS WHILE AN OBVIOUS DRUG TRAFFICKER HAS YOU IN A STRANGLEHOLD.
I REMEMBER GANGLEOS AND HIS BROTHER AS NOTHING MORE THAN STREET-PEDDLING HOOD-RATS AND GANGSTA WANNABE'S.

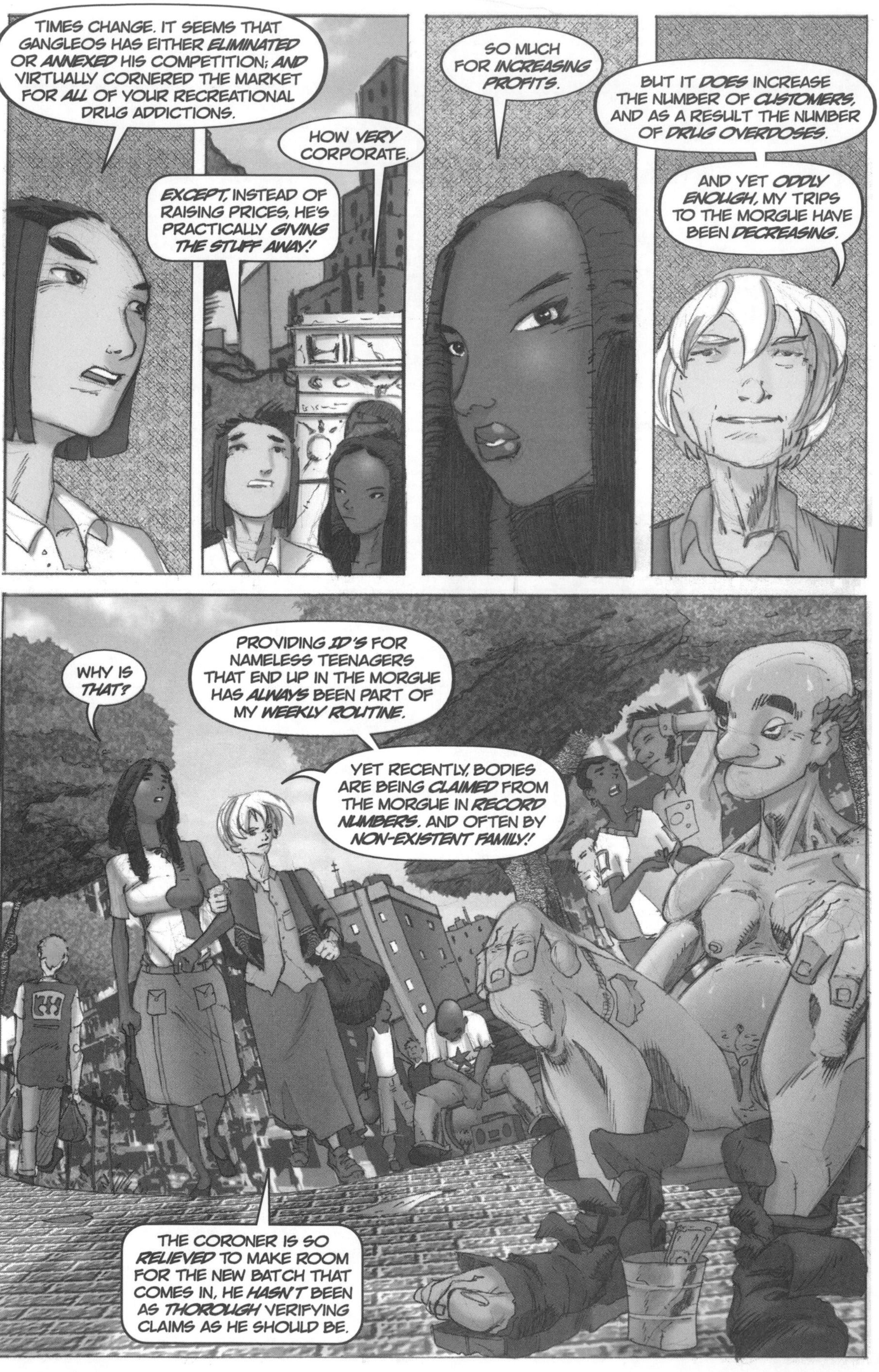
TIMES CHANGE. IT SEEMS THAT GANGLEOS HAS EITHER ELIMINATED OR ANNEXED HIS COMPETITION; AND VIRTUALLY CORNERED THE MARKET FOR ALL OF YOUR RECREATIONAL DRUG ADDICTIONS.
HOW VERY CORPORATE.
EXCEPT, INSTEAD OF RAISING PRICES, HE'S PRACTICALLY GIVING THE STUFF AWAY!
SO MUCH FOR INCREASING PROFITS.
BUT IT DOES INCREASE THE NUMBER OF CUSTOMERS, AND AS A RESULT THE NUMBER OF DRUG OVERDOSES.
AND YET ODDLY ENOUGH, MY TRIPS TO THE MORGUE HAVE BEEN DECREASING.
WHY IS THAT?
PROVIDING ID'S FOR NAMELESS TEENAGERS THAT END UP IN THE MORGUE HAS ALWAYS BEEN PART OF MY WEEKLY ROUTINE.
YET RECENTLY, BODIES ARE BEING CLAIMED FROM THE MORGUE IN RECORD NUMBERS. AND OFTEN BY NON-EXISTENT FAMILY!
THE CORONER IS SO RELIEVED TO MAKE ROOM FOR THE NEW BATCH THAT COMES IN, HE HASN'T BEEN AS THOROUGH VERIFYING CLAIMS AS HE SHOULD BE.

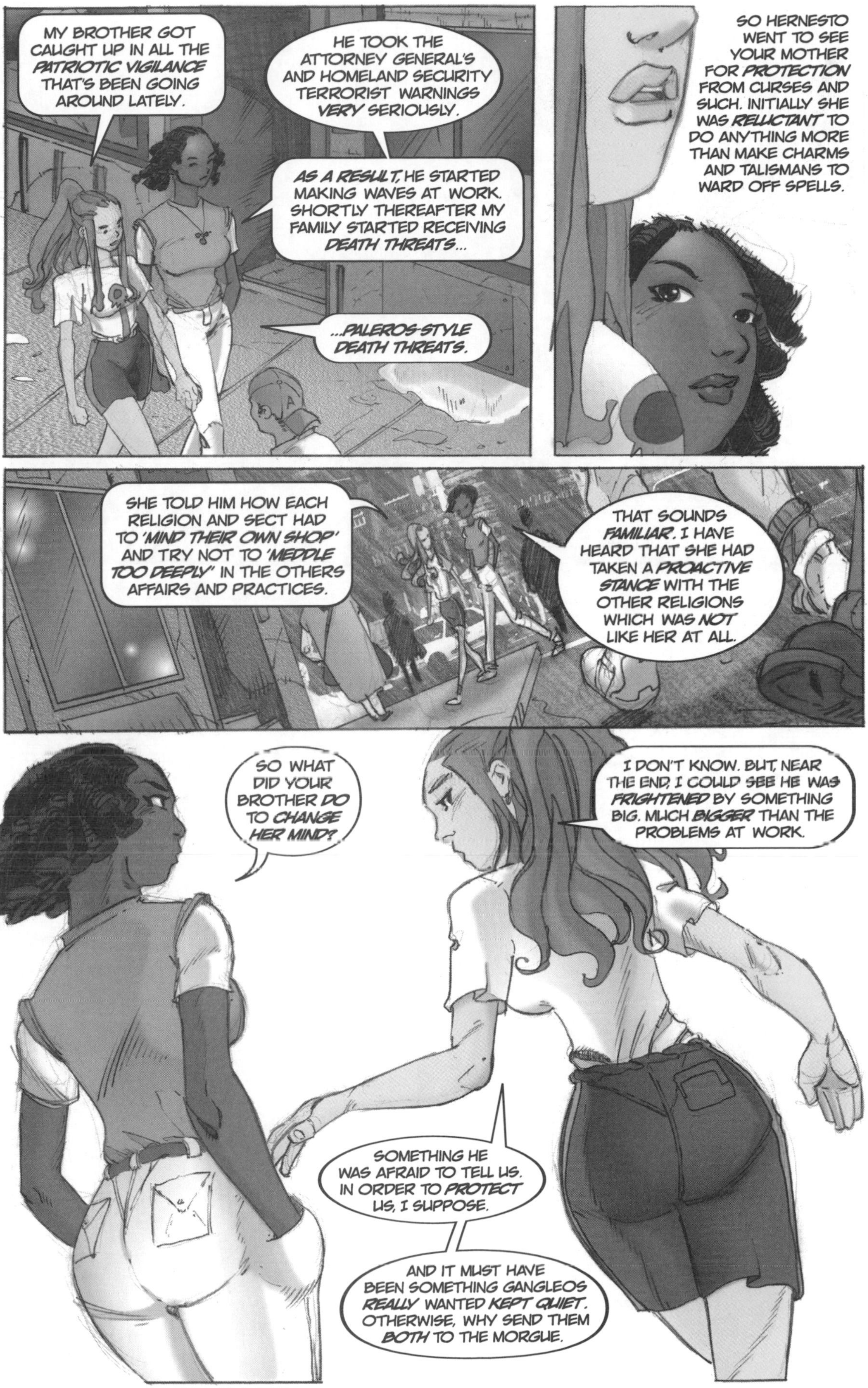
MY BROTHER GOT CAUGHT UP IN ALL THE PATRIOTIC VIGILANCE THAT'S BEEN GOING AROUND LATELY.
HE TOOK THE ATTORNEY GENERAL'S AND HOMELAND SECURITY TERRORIST WARNINGS VERY SERIOUSLY.
AS A RESULT, HE STARTED MAKING WAVES AT WORK. SHORTLY THEREAFTER MY FAMILY STARTED RECEIVING DEATH THREATS...
...PALEROS-STYLE DEATH THREATS.
SO HERNESTO WENT TO SEE YOUR MOTHER FOR PROTECTION FROM CURSES AND SUCH. INITIALLY SHE WAS RELUCTANT TO DO ANYTHING MORE THAN MAKE CHARMS AND TALISMANS TO WARD OFF SPELLS.
SHE TOLD HIM HOW EACH RELIGION AND SECT HAD TO 'MIND THEIR OWN SHOP' AND TRY NOT TO 'MEDDLE TOO DEEPLY' IN THE OTHERS AFFAIRS AND PRACTICES.
THAT SOUNDS FAMILIAR. I HAVE HEARD THAT SHE HAD TAKEN A PROACTIVE STANCE WITH THE OTHER RELIGIONS WHICH WAS NOT LIKE HER AT ALL.
SO WHAT DID YOUR BROTHER DO TO CHANGE HER MIND?
I DON'T KNOW. BUT, NEAR THE END, I COULD SEE HE WAS FRIGHTENED BY SOMETHING BIG. MUCH BIGGER THAN THE PROBLEMS AT WORK.
SOMETHING HE WAS AFRAID TO TELL US. IN ORDER TO PROTECT US, I SUPPOSE.
AND IT MUST HAVE BEEN SOMETHING GANGLEOS REALLY WANTED KEPT QUIET. OTHERWISE, WHY SEND THEM BOTH TO THE MORGUE.

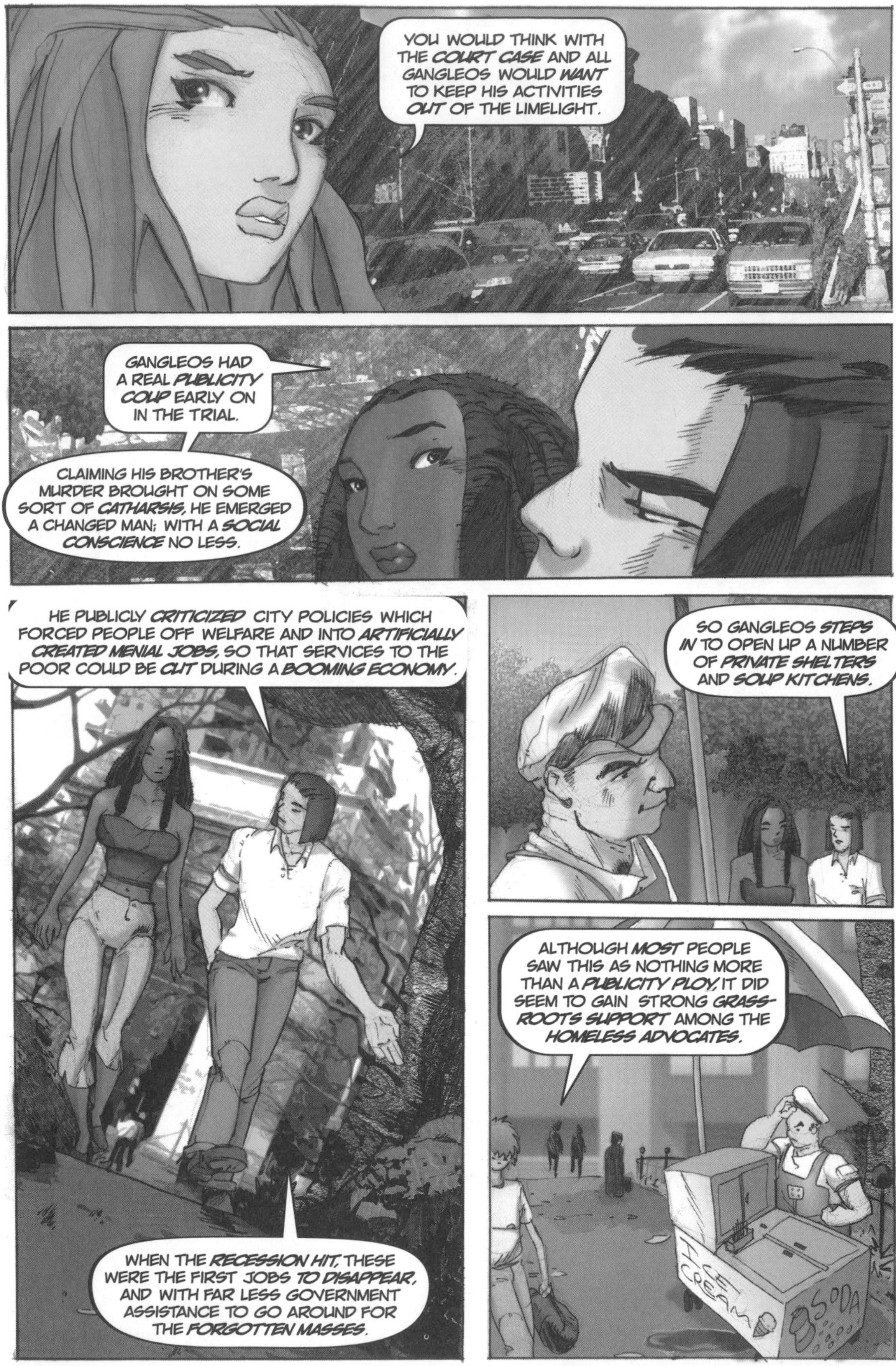
YOU WOULD THINK WITH THE COURT CASE AND ALL GANGLEOS WOULD WANT TO KEEP HIS ACTIVITIES OUT OF THE LIMELIGHT.
GANGLEOS HAD A REAL PUBLICITY COUP EARLY ON IN THE TRIAL.
CLAIMING HIS BROTHER'S MURDER BROUGHT ON SOME SORT OF CATHARSIS, HE EMERGED A CHANGED MAN; WITH A SOCIAL CONSCIENCE NO LESS.
HE PUBLICLY CRITICIZED CITY POLICIES WHICH FORCED PEOPLE OFF WELFARE AND INTO ARTIFICIALLY CREATED MENIAL JOBS, SO THAT SERVICES TO THE POOR COULD BE CUT DURING A BOOMING ECONOMY.
WHEN THE RECESSION HIT, THESE WERE THE FIRST JOBS TO DISAPPEAR, AND WITH FAR LESS GOVERNMENT ASSISTANCE TO GO AROUND FOR THE FORGOTTEN MASSES.
SO GANGLEOS STEPS IN TO OPEN UP A NUMBER OF PRIVATE SHELTERS AND SOUP KITCHENS.
ALTHOUGH MOST PEOPLE SAW THIS AS NOTHING MORE THAN A PUBLICITY PLOY, IT DID SEEM TO GAIN STRONG GRASS-ROOTS SUPPORT AMONG THE HOMELESS ADVOCATES.
ICE CREAM
SODA

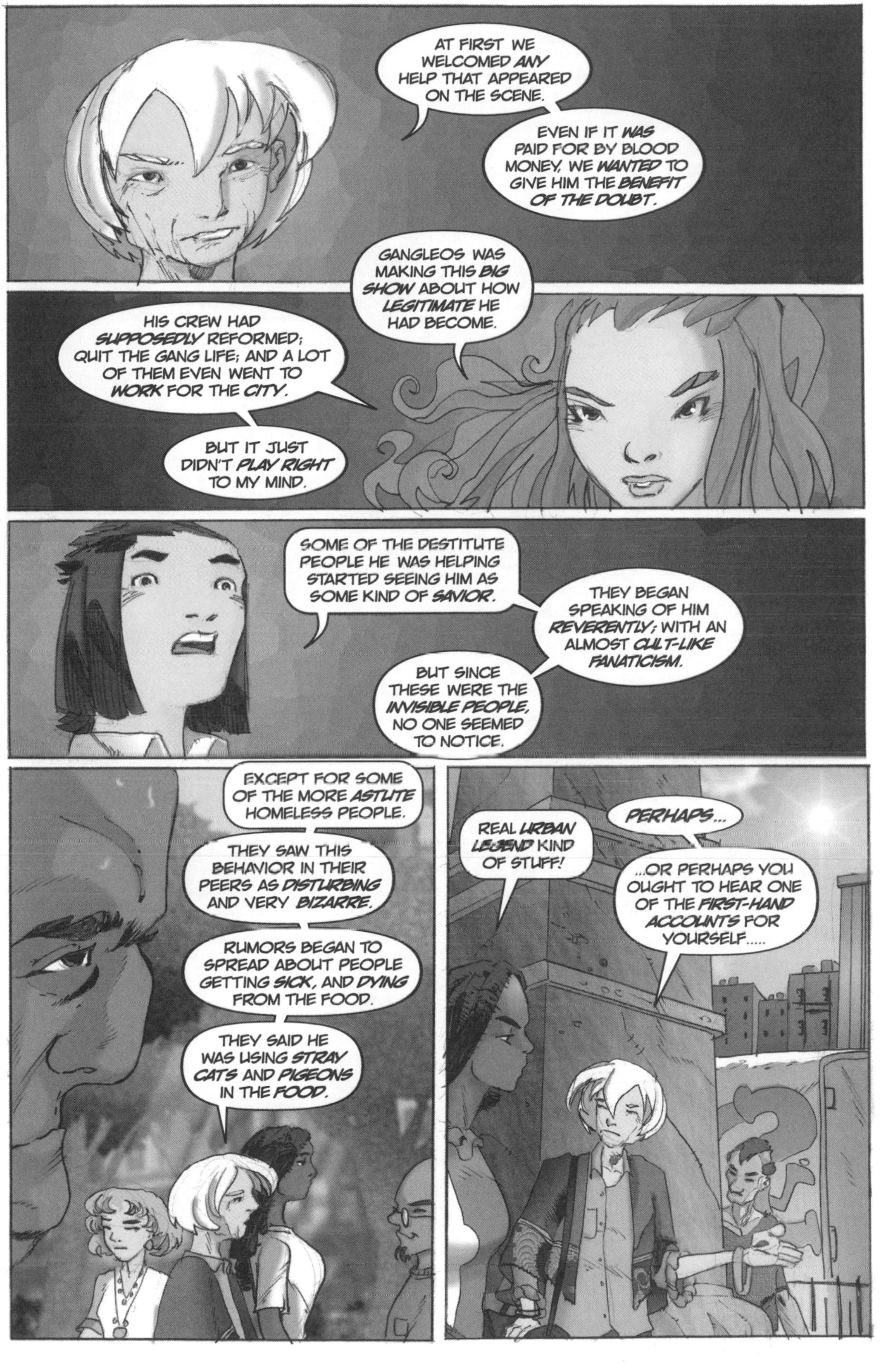
AT FIRST WE WELCOMED ANY HELP THAT APPEARED ON THE SCENE.
EVEN IF IT WAS PAID FOR BY BLOOD MONEY, WE WANTED TO GIVE HIM THE BENEFIT OF THE DOUBT.
GANGLEOS WAS MAKING THIS BIG SHOW ABOUT HOW LEGITIMATE HE HAD BECOME.
HIS CREW HAD SUPPOSEDLY REFORMED; QUIT THE GANG LIFE; AND A LOT OF THEM EVEN WENT TO WORK FOR THE CITY.
BUT IT JUST DIDN'T PLAY RIGHT TO MY MIND.
SOME OF THE DESTITUTE PEOPLE HE WAS HELPING STARTED SEEING HIM AS SOME KIND OF SAVIOR.
THEY BEGAN SPEAKING OF HIM REVERENTLY; WITH AN ALMOST CULT-LIKE FANATICISM.
BUT SINCE THESE WERE THE INVISIBLE PEOPLE, NO ONE SEEMED TO NOTICE.
EXCEPT FOR SOME OF THE MORE ASTUTE HOMELESS PEOPLE.
THEY SAW THIS BEHAVIOR IN THEIR PEERS AS DISTURBING AND VERY BIZARRE.
RUMORS BEGAN TO SPREAD ABOUT PEOPLE GETTING SICK, AND DYING FROM THE FOOD.
THEY SAID HE WAS USING STRAY CATS AND PIGEONS IN THE FOOD.
REAL URBAN LEGEND KIND OF STUFF!
PERHAPS...
...OR PERHAPS YOU OUGHT TO HEAR ONE OF THE FIRST-HAND ACCOUNTS FOR YOURSELF.....

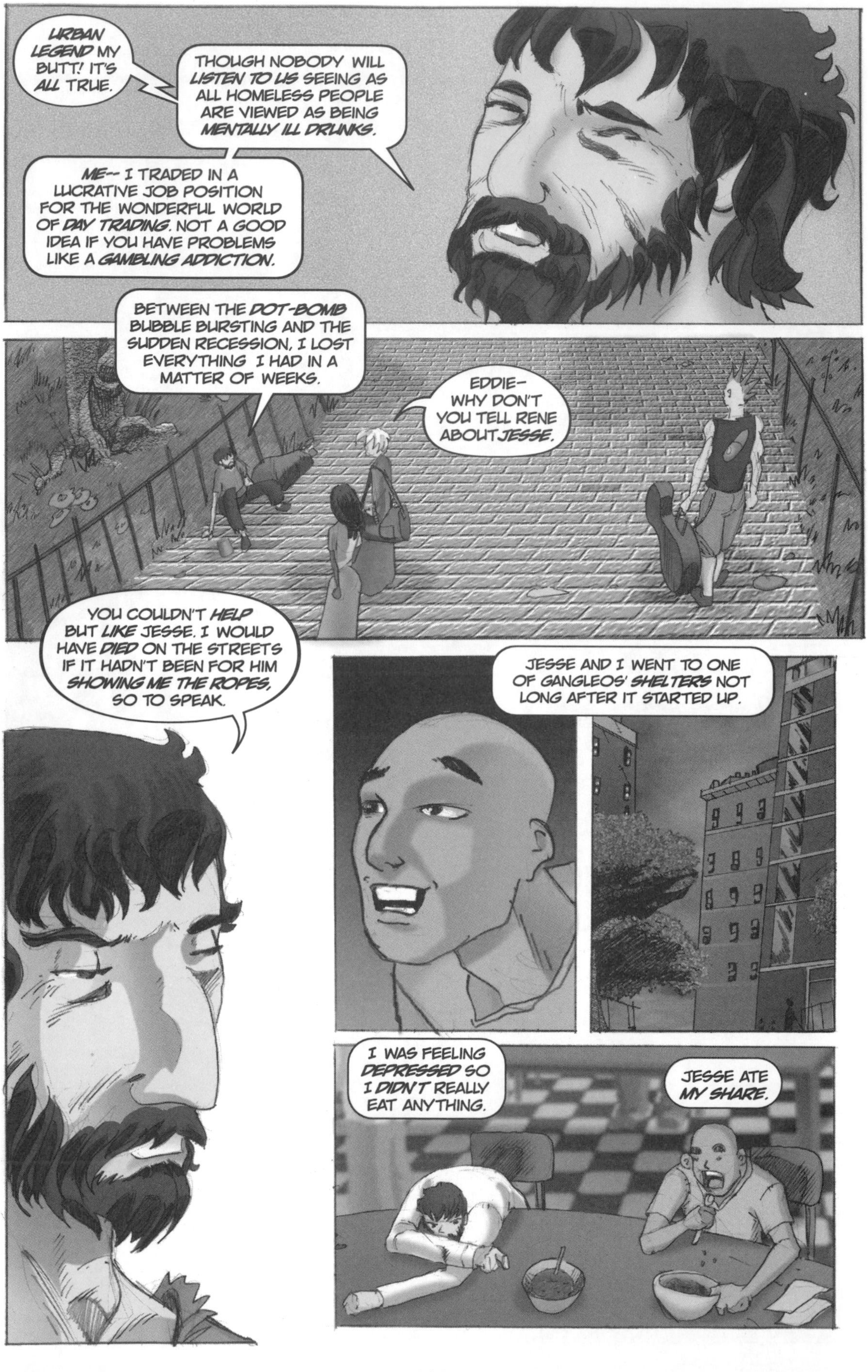
URBAN LEGEND MY BUTT! IT'S ALL TRUE.
THOUGH NOBODY WILL LISTEN TO US SEEING AS ALL HOMELESS PEOPLE ARE VIEWED AS BEING MENTALLY ILL DRUNKS.
ME-- I TRADED IN A LUCRATIVE JOB POSITION FOR THE WONDERFUL WORLD OF DAY TRADING. NOT A GOOD IDEA IF YOU HAVE PROBLEMS LIKE A GAMBLING ADDICTION.
BETWEEN THE DOT-BOMB BUBBLE BURSTING AND THE SUDDEN RECESSION, I LOST EVERYTHING I HAD IN A MATTER OF WEEKS.
EDDIE- WHY DON'T YOU TELL RENE ABOUT JESSE.
YOU COULDN'T HELP BUT LIKE JESSE. I WOULD HAVE DIED ON THE STREETS IF IT HADN'T BEEN FOR HIM SHOWING ME THE ROPES, SO TO SPEAK.
JESSE AND I WENT TO ONE OF GANGLEOS' SHELTERS NOT LONG AFTER IT STARTED UP.
I WAS FEELING DEPRESSED SO I DIDN'T REALLY EAT ANYTHING.
JESSE ATE MY SHARE.

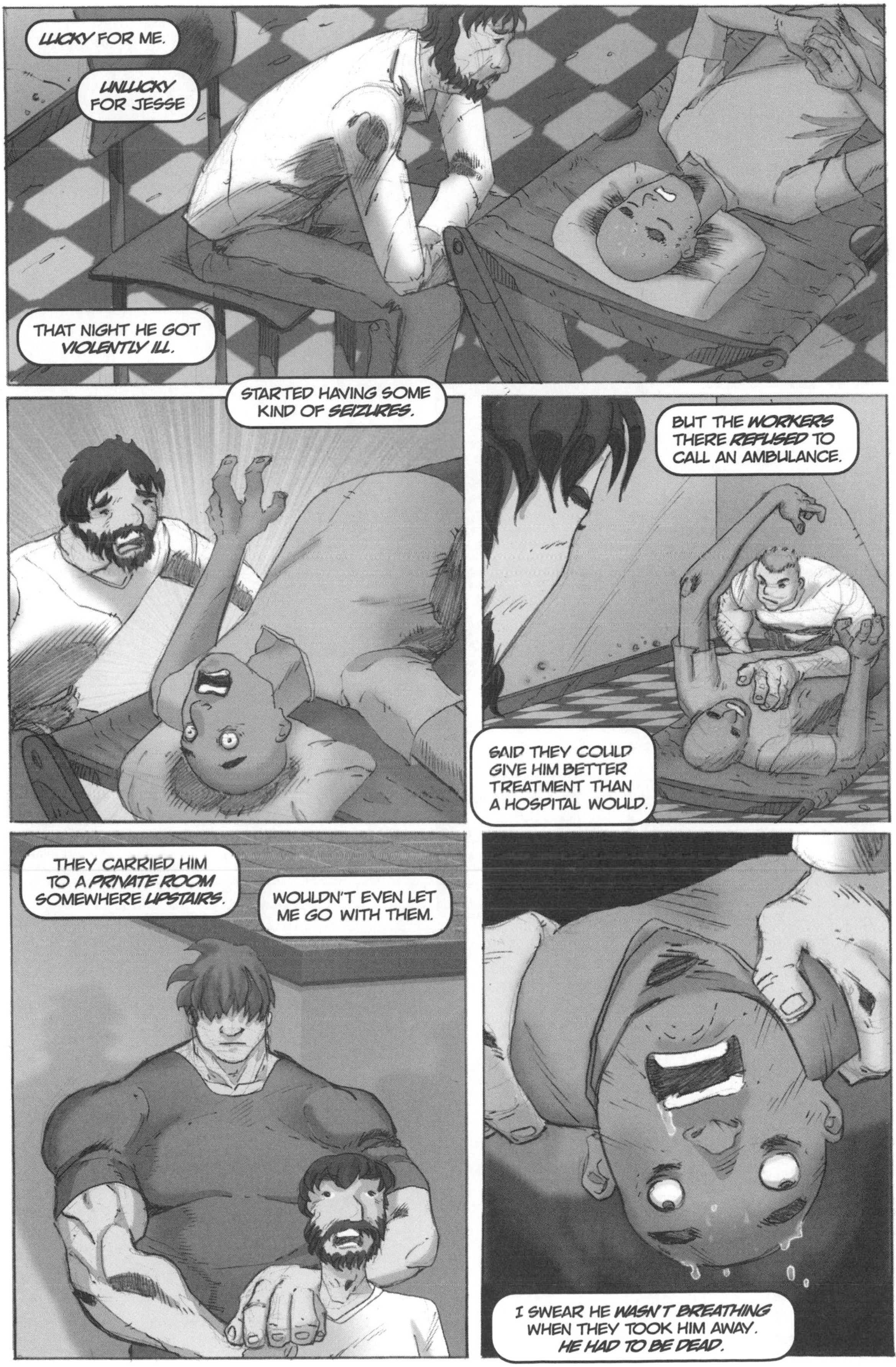
LUCKY FOR ME.
UNLUCKY FOR JESSE
THAT NIGHT HE GOT VIOLENTLY ILL.
STARTED HAVING SOME KIND OF SEIZURES.
BUT THE WORKERS THERE REFUSED TO CALL AN AMBULANCE.
SAID THEY COULD GIVE HIM BETTER TREATMENT THAN A HOSPITAL WOULD.
THEY CARRIED HIM TO A PRIVATE ROOM SOMEWHERE UPSTAIRS.
WOULDN'T EVEN LET ME GO WITH THEM.
I SWEAR HE WASN'T BREATHING WHEN THEY TOOK HIM AWAY. HE HAD TO BE DEAD.

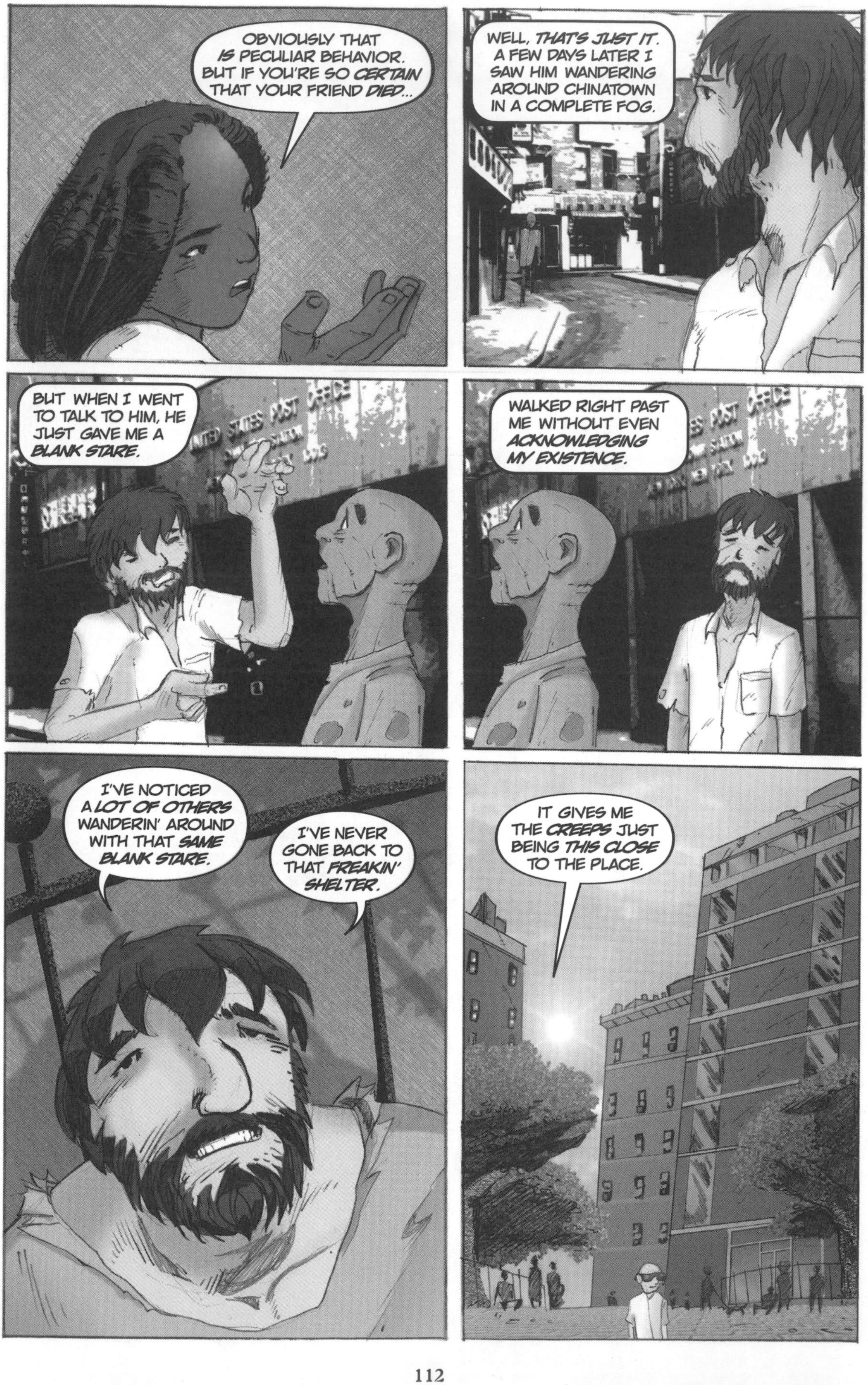
OBVIOUSLY THAT IS PECULIAR BEHAVIOR. BUT IF YOU'RE SO CERTAIN THAT YOUR FRIEND DIED...
WELL, THAT'S JUST IT. A FEW DAYS LATER I SAW HIM WANDERING AROUND CHINATOWN IN A COMPLETE FOG.
BUT WHEN I WENT TO TALK TO HIM, HE JUST GAVE ME A BLANK STARE.
UNITED STATES POST OFFICE
WALKED RIGHT PAST ME WITHOUT EVEN ACKNOWLEDGING MY EXISTENCE.
I'VE NOTICED A LOT OF OTHERS WANDERIN' AROUND WITH THAT SAME BLANK STARE.
I'VE NEVER GONE BACK TO THAT FREAKIN' SHELTER.
IT GIVES ME THE CREEPS JUST BEING THIS CLOSE TO THE PLACE.

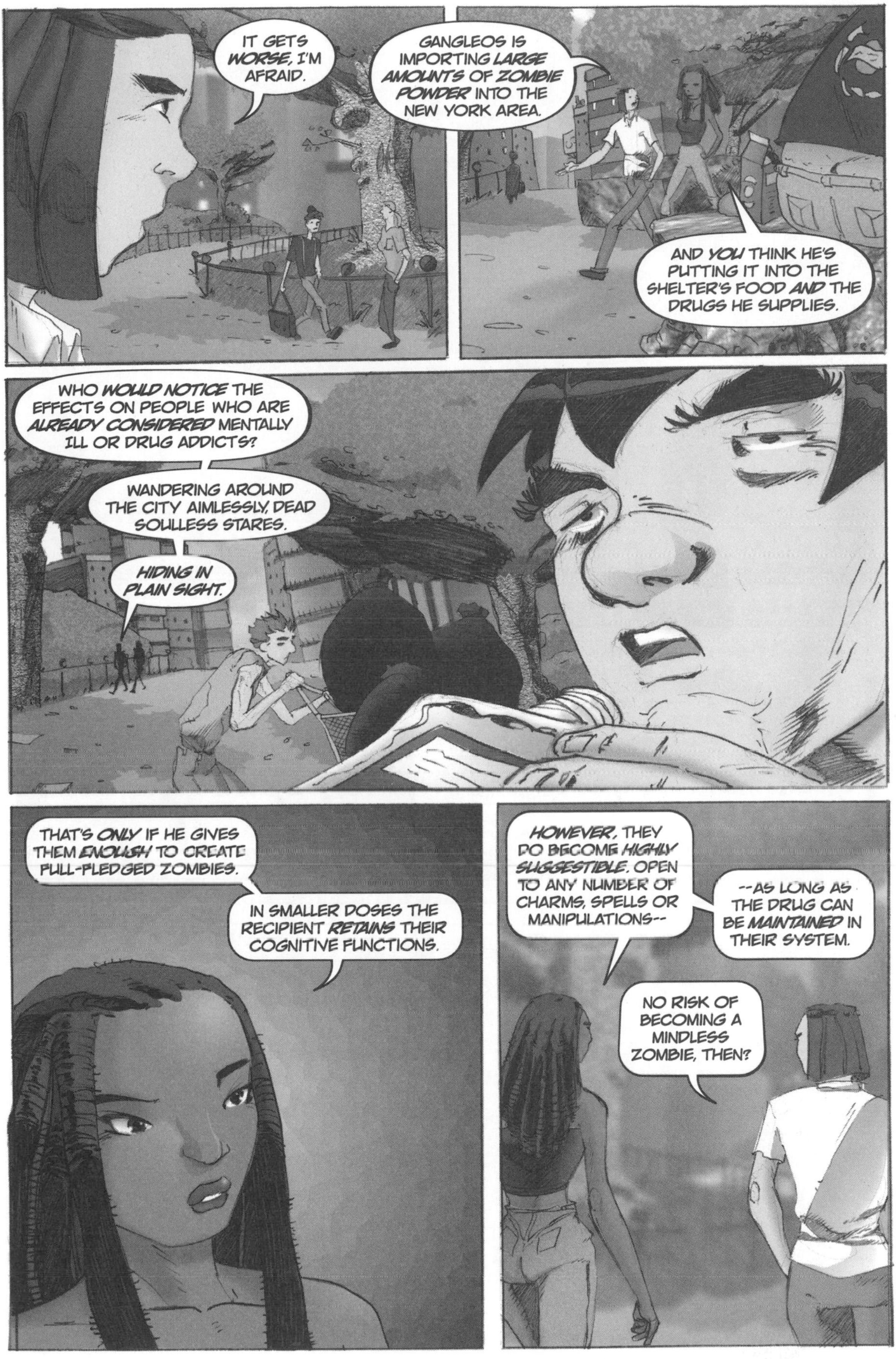
IT GETS WORSE, I'M AFRAID.
GANGLEOS IS IMPORTING LARGE AMOUNTS OF ZOMBIE POWDER INTO THE NEW YORK AREA.
AND YOU THINK HE'S PUTTING IT INTO THE SHELTER'S FOOD AND THE DRUGS HE SUPPLIES.
WHO WOULD NOTICE THE EFFECTS ON PEOPLE WHO ARE ALREADY CONSIDERED MENTALLY ILL OR DRUG ADDICTS?
WANDERING AROUND THE CITY AIMLESSLY, DEAD SOULLESS STARES.
HIDING IN PLAIN SIGHT.
THAT'S ONLY IF HE GIVES THEM ENOUGH TO CREATE FULL-FLEDGED ZOMBIES.
IN SMALLER DOSES THE RECIPIENT RETAINS THEIR COGNITIVE FUNCTIONS.
HOWEVER, THEY DO BECOME HIGHLY SUGGESTIBLE. OPEN TO ANY NUMBER OF CHARMS, SPELLS OR MANIPULATIONS--
--AS LONG AS THE DRUG CAN BE MAINTAINED IN THEIR SYSTEM.
NO RISK OF BECOMING A MINDLESS ZOMBIE, THEN?

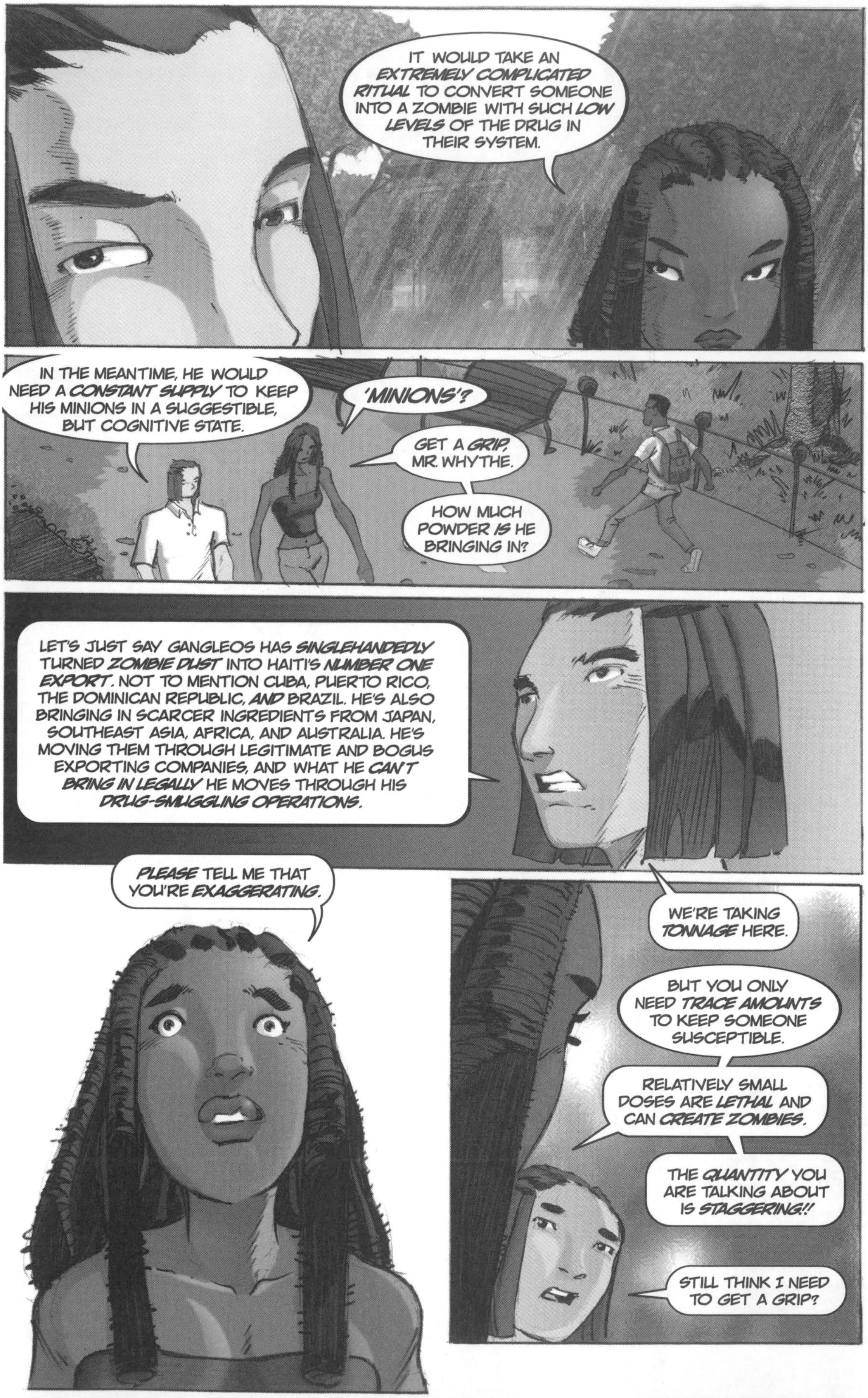
IT WOULD TAKE AN EXTREMELY COMPLICATED RITUAL TO CONVERT SOMEONE INTO A ZOMBIE WITH SUCH LOW LEVELS OF THE DRUG IN THEIR SYSTEM.
IN THE MEANTIME, HE WOULD NEED A CONSTANT SUPPLY TO KEEP HIS MINIONS IN A SUGGESTIBLE, BUT COGNITIVE STATE.
'MINIONS'?
GET A GRIP, MR. WHYTHE.
HOW MUCH POWDER IS HE BRINGING IN?
LET'S JUST SAY GANGLEOS HAS SINGLEHANDEDLY TURNED ZOMBIE DUST INTO HAITI'S NUMBER ONE EXPORT. NOT TO MENTION CUBA, PUERTO RICO, THE DOMINICAN REPUBLIC, AND BRAZIL. HE'S ALSO BRINGING IN SCARCER INGREDIENTS FROM JAPAN, SOUTHEAST ASIA, AFRICA, AND AUSTRALIA. HE'S MOVING THEM THROUGH LEGITIMATE AND BOGUS EXPORTING COMPANIES, AND WHAT HE CAN'T BRING IN LEGALLY HE MOVES THROUGH HIS DRUG-SMUGGLING OPERATIONS.
PLEASE TELL ME THAT YOU'RE EXAGGERATING.
WE'RE TAKING TONNAGE HERE.
BUT YOU ONLY NEED TRACE AMOUNTS TO KEEP SOMEONE SUSCEPTIBLE.
RELATIVELY SMALL DOSES ARE LETHAL AND CAN CREATE ZOMBIES.
THE QUANTITY YOU ARE TALKING ABOUT IS STAGGERING!!
STILL THINK I NEED TO GET A GRIP?

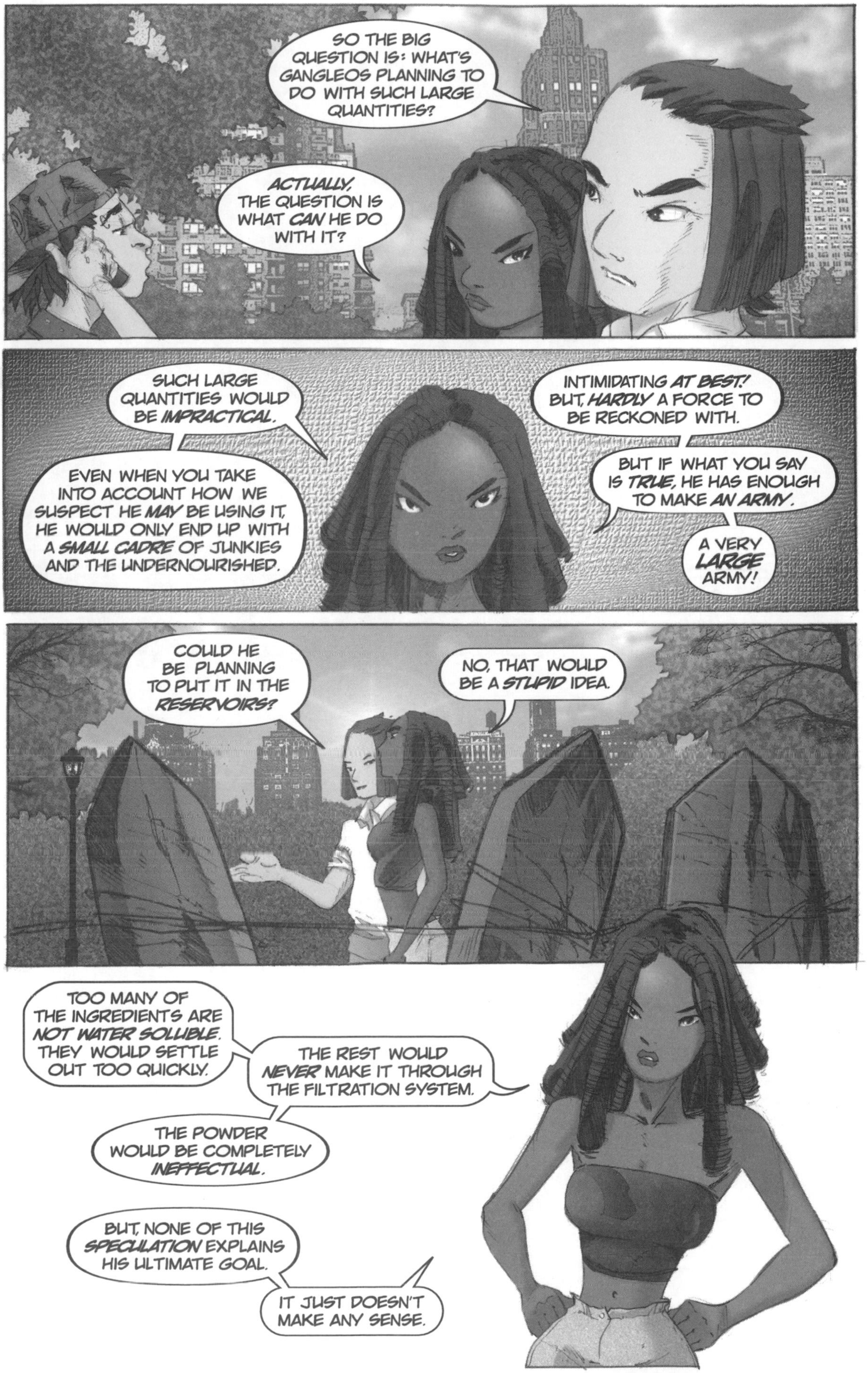
SO THE BIG QUESTION IS: WHAT'S GANGLEOS PLANNING TO DO WITH SUCH LARGE QUANTITIES?
ACTUALLY, THE QUESTION IS WHAT CAN HE DO WITH IT?
SUCH LARGE QUANTITIES WOULD BE IMPRACTICAL.
EVEN WHEN YOU TAKE INTO ACCOUNT HOW WE SUSPECT HE MAY BE USING IT, HE WOULD ONLY END UP WITH A SMALL CADRE OF JUNKIES AND THE UNDERNOURISHED.
INTIMIDATING AT BEST! BUT, HARDLY A FORCE TO BE RECKONED WITH.
BUT IF WHAT YOU SAY IS TRUE, HE HAS ENOUGH TO MAKE AN ARMY.
A VERY LARGE ARMY!
COULD HE BE PLANNING TO PUT IT IN THE RESERVOIRS?
NO, THAT WOULD BE A STUPID IDEA.
TOO MANY OF THE INGREDIENTS ARE NOT WATER SOLUBLE. THEY WOULD SETTLE OUT TOO QUICKLY.
THE REST WOULD NEVER MAKE IT THROUGH THE FILTRATION SYSTEM.
THE POWDER WOULD BE COMPLETELY INEFFECTUAL.
BUT, NONE OF THIS SPECULATION EXPLAINS HIS ULTIMATE GOAL.
IT JUST DOESN'T MAKE ANY SENSE.

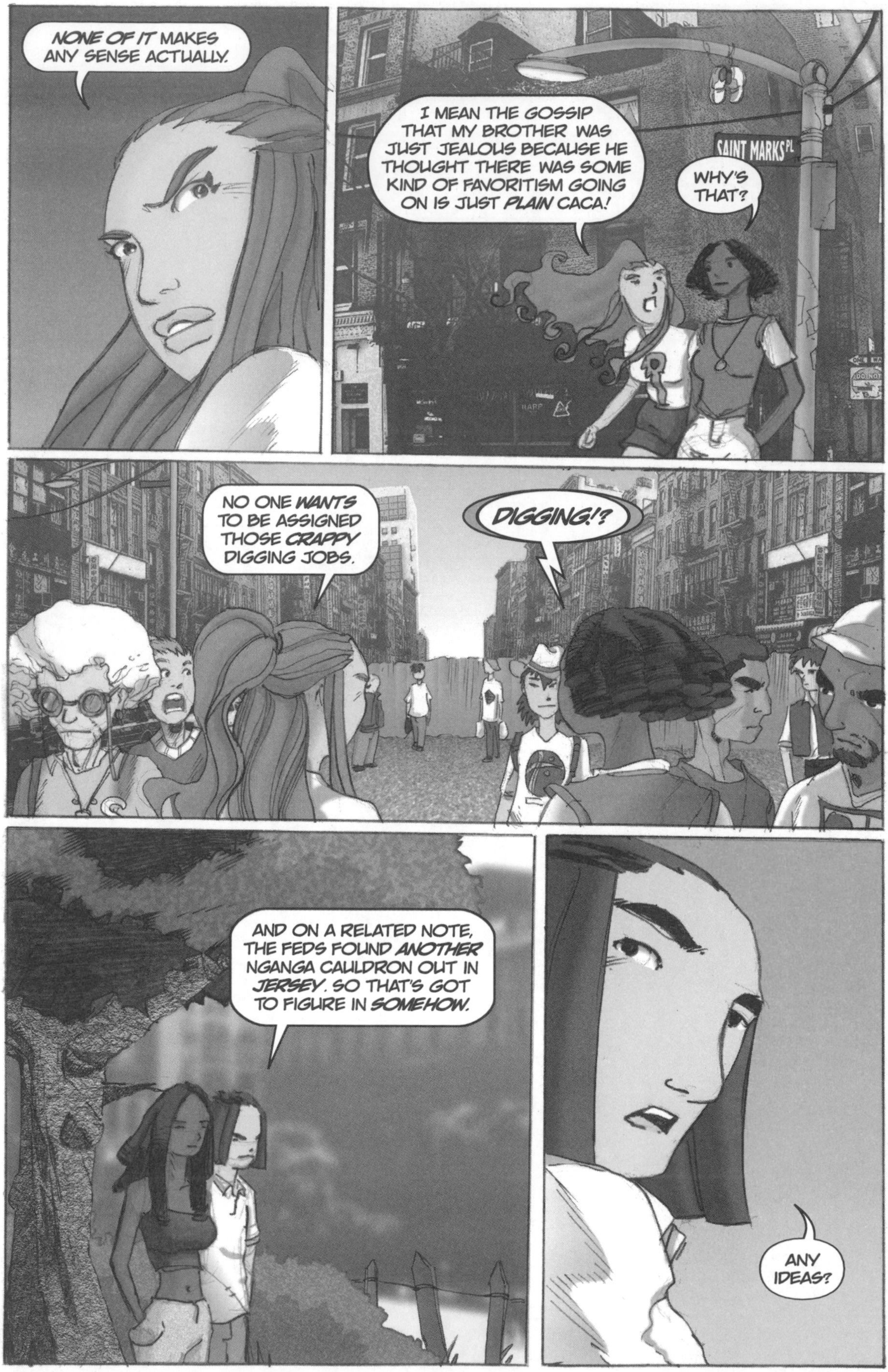
NONE OF IT MAKES ANY SENSE ACTUALLY.
I MEAN THE GOSSIP THAT MY BROTHER WAS JUST JEALOUS BECAUSE HE THOUGHT THERE WAS SOME KIND OF FAVORITISM GOING ON IS JUST PLAIN CACA!
SAINT MARKS PL
WHY'S THAT?
NO ONE WANTS TO BE ASSIGNED THOSE CRAPPY DIGGING JOBS.
DIGGING!?
AND ON A RELATED NOTE, THE FEDS FOUND ANOTHER NGANGA CAULDRON OUT IN JERSEY. SO THAT'S GOT TO FIGURE IN SOMEHOW.
ANY IDEAS?

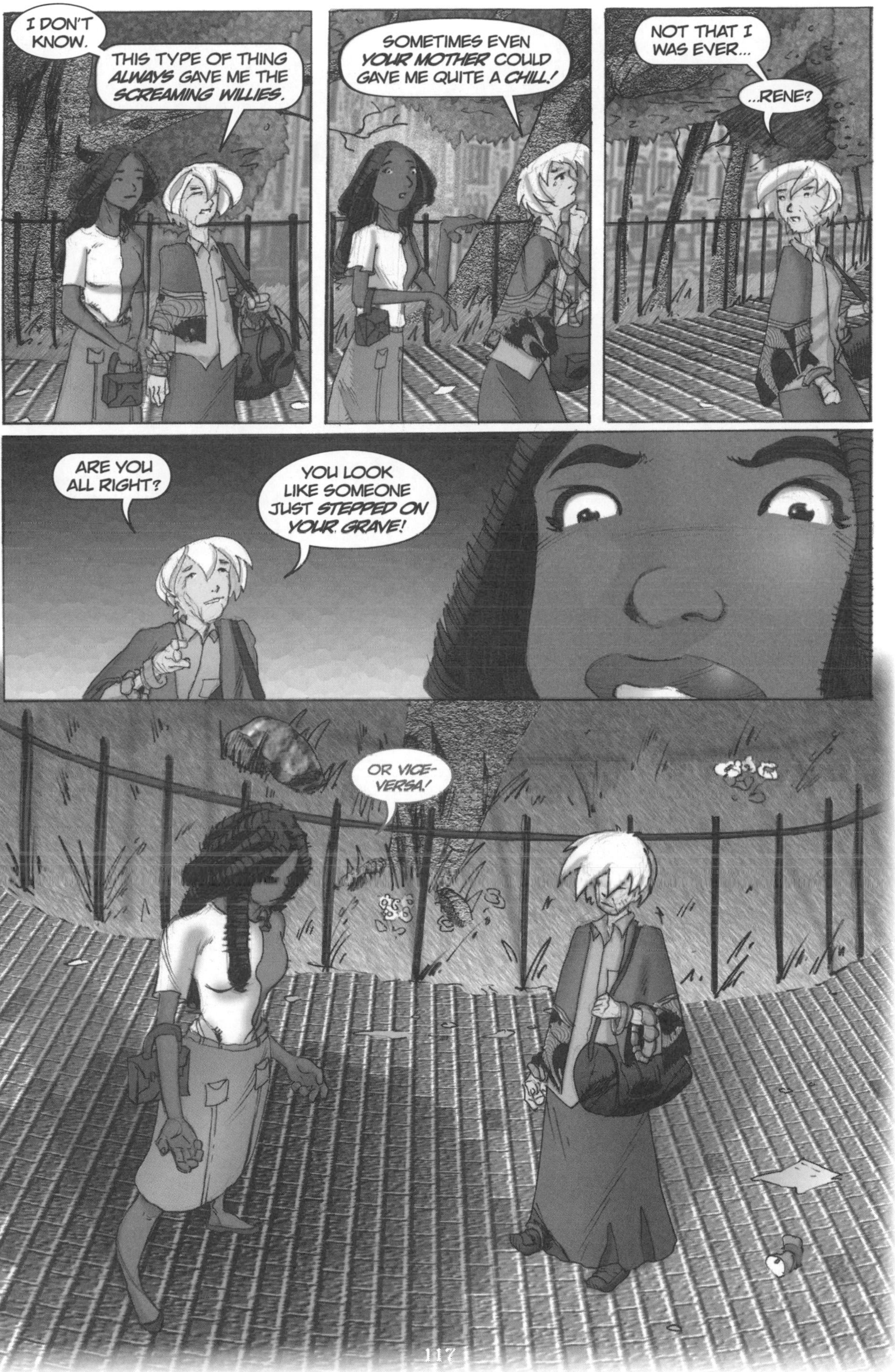
I DON'T KNOW.
THIS TYPE OF THING ALWAYS GAVE ME THE SCREAMING WILLIES.
SOMETIMES EVEN YOUR MOTHER COULD GAVE ME QUITE A CHILL!
NOT THAT I WAS EVER...
...RENE?
ARE YOU ALL RIGHT?
YOU LOOK LIKE SOMEONE JUST STEPPED ON YOUR GRAVE!
OR VICE-VERSA!

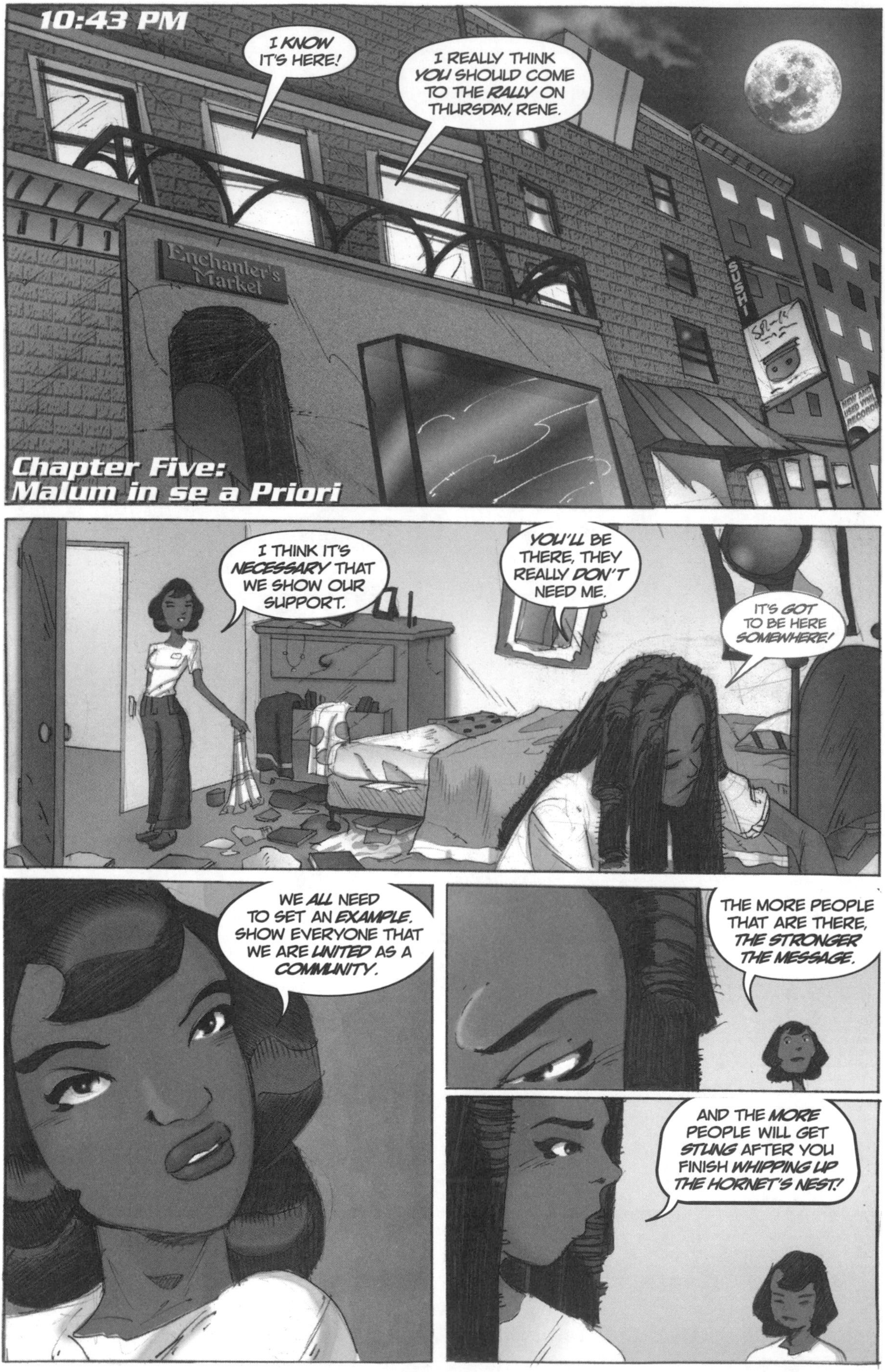
10:43 PM
I KNOW IT'S HERE!
I REALLY THINK YOU SHOULD COME TO THE RALLY ON THURSDAY, RENE.
Enchanter's Market
SUSHI
NEW AND USED VINYL RECORDS
Chapter Five: Malum in se a Priori
I THINK IT'S NECESSARY THAT WE SHOW OUR SUPPORT.
YOU'LL BE THERE, THEY REALLY DON'T NEED ME.
IT'S GOT TO BE HERE SOMEWHERE!
WE ALL NEED TO SET AN EXAMPLE. SHOW EVERYONE THAT WE ARE UNITED AS A COMMUNITY.
THE MORE PEOPLE THAT ARE THERE, THE STRONGER THE MESSAGE.
AND THE MORE PEOPLE WILL GET STUNG AFTER YOU FINISH WHIPPING UP THE HORNET'S NEST!

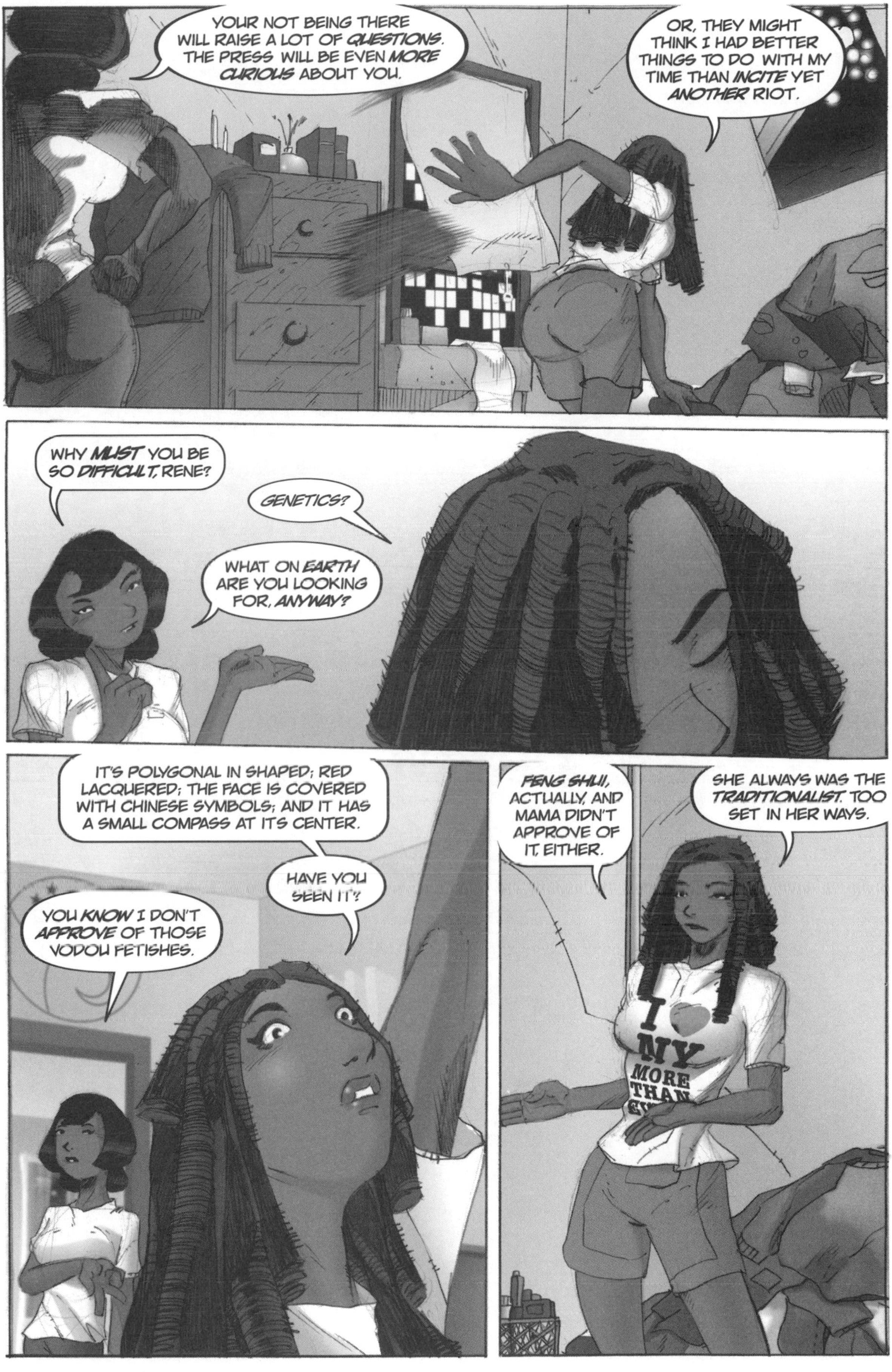
YOUR NOT BEING THERE WILL RAISE A LOT OF QUESTIONS. THE PRESS WILL BE EVEN MORE CURIOUS ABOUT YOU.
OR, THEY MIGHT THINK I HAD BETTER THINGS TO DO WITH MY TIME THAN INCITE YET ANOTHER RIOT.
WHY MUST YOU BE SO DIFFICULT, RENE?
GENETICS?
WHAT ON EARTH ARE YOU LOOKING FOR, ANYWAY?
IT'S POLYGONAL IN SHAPED; RED LACQUERED; THE FACE IS COVERED WITH CHINESE SYMBOLS; AND IT HAS A SMALL COMPASS AT ITS CENTER.
HAVE YOU SEEN IT?
YOU KNOW I DON'T APPROVE OF THOSE VODOU FETISHES.
FENG SHUI, ACTUALLY, AND MAMA DIDN'T APPROVE OF IT, EITHER.
SHE ALWAYS WAS THE TRADITIONALIST. TOO SET IN HER WAYS.
I NY MORE THAN

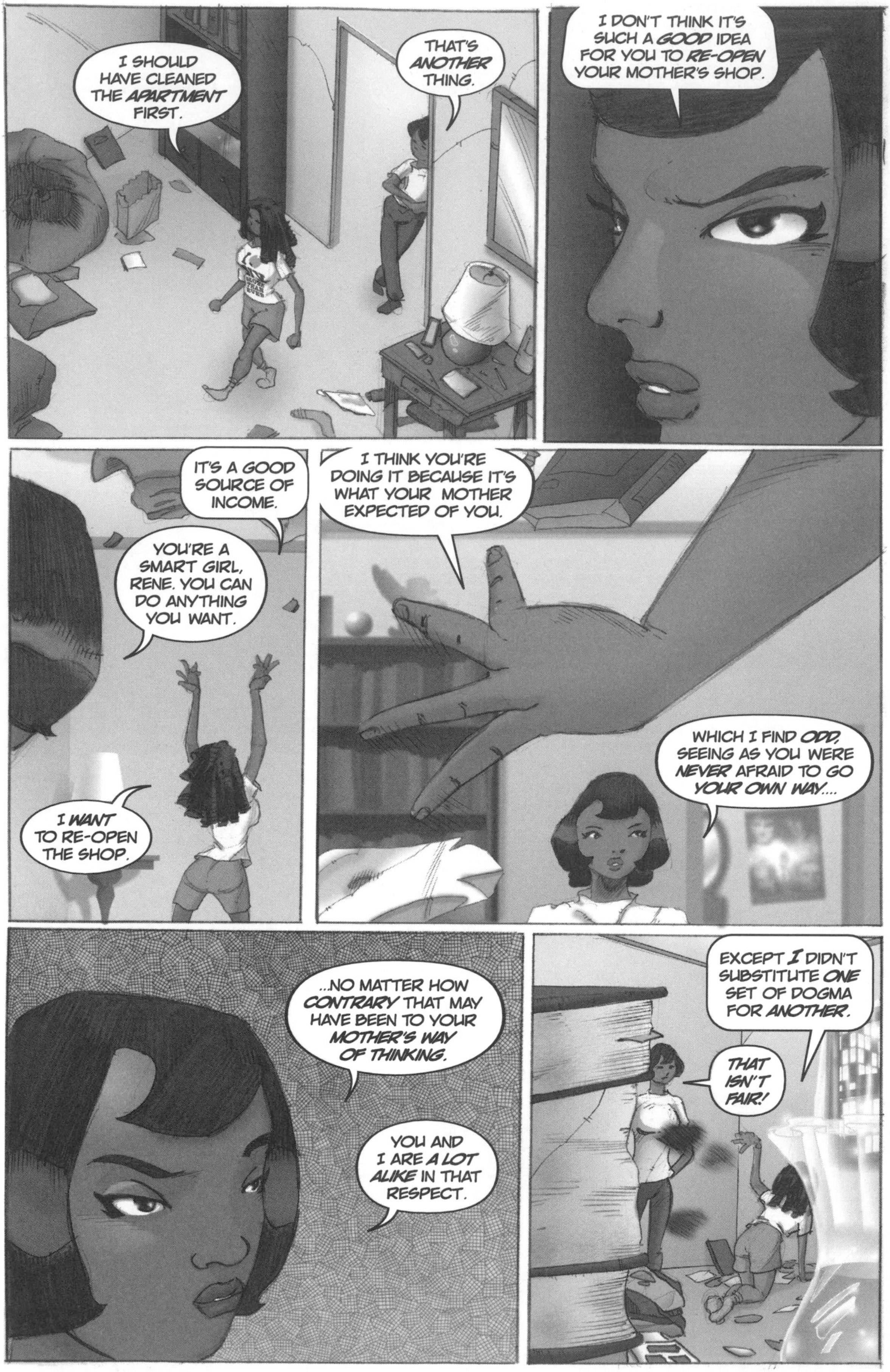
I SHOULD HAVE CLEANED THE APARTMENT FIRST.
THAT'S ANOTHER THING.
I DON'T THINK IT'S SUCH A GOOD IDEA FOR YOU TO RE-OPEN YOUR MOTHER'S SHOP.
IT'S A GOOD SOURCE OF INCOME.
YOU'RE A SMART GIRL, RENE. YOU CAN DO ANYTHING YOU WANT.
I WANT TO RE-OPEN THE SHOP.
I THINK YOU'RE DOING IT BECAUSE IT'S WHAT YOUR MOTHER EXPECTED OF YOU.
WHICH I FIND ODD, SEEING AS YOU WERE NEVER AFRAID TO GO YOUR OWN WAY....
...NO MATTER HOW CONTRARY THAT MAY HAVE BEEN TO YOUR MOTHER'S WAY OF THINKING.
YOU AND I ARE A LOT ALIKE IN THAT RESPECT.
THAT ISN'T FAIR!
EXCEPT I DIDN'T SUBSTITUTE ONE SET OF DOGMA FOR ANOTHER.

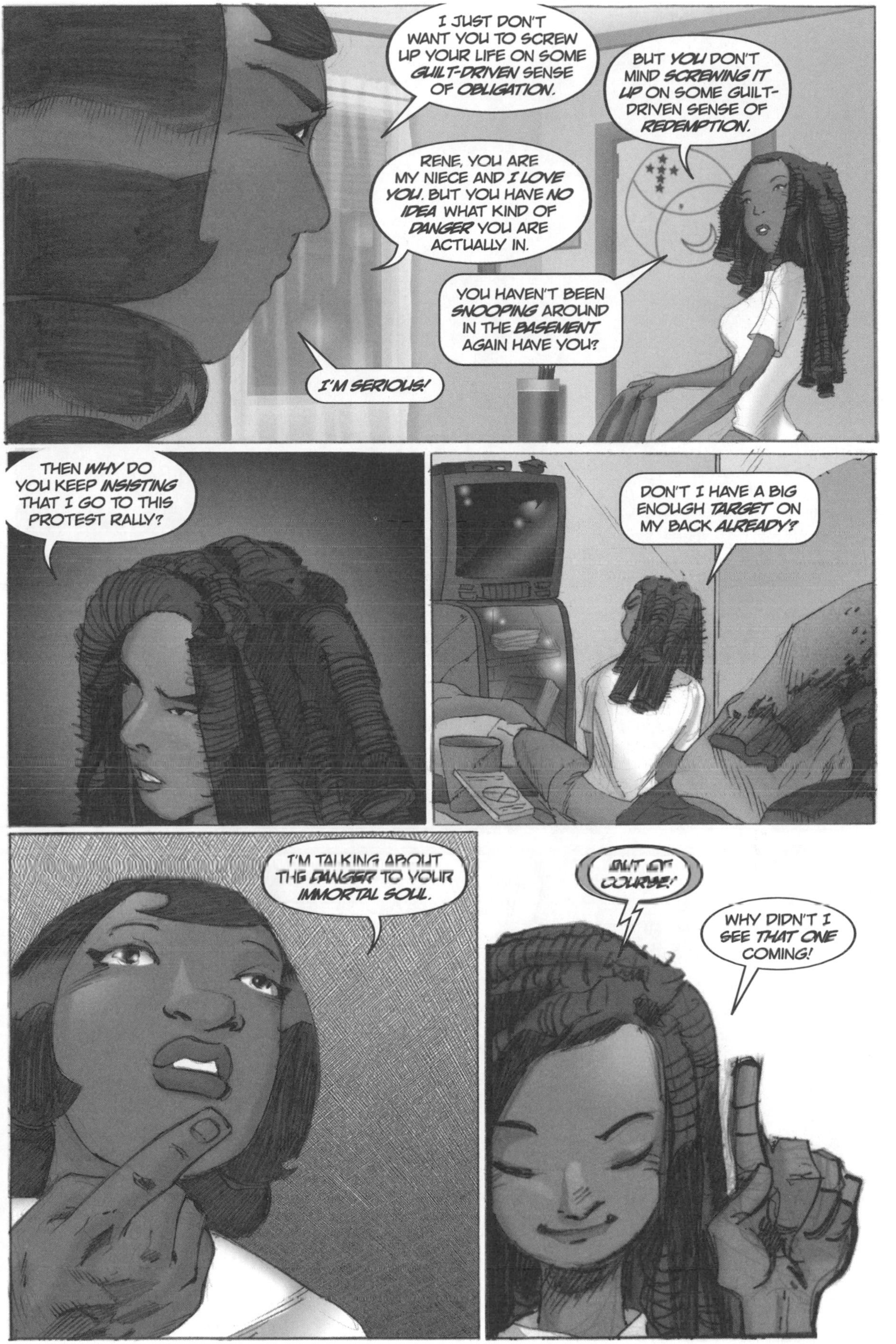
I JUST DON'T WANT YOU TO SCREW UP YOUR LIFE ON SOME *GUILT-DRIVEN* SENSE OF *OBLIGATION*.
BUT *YOU* DON'T MIND *SCREWING IT UP* ON SOME GUILT-DRIVEN SENSE OF *REDEMPTION*.
RENE, YOU ARE MY NIECE AND *I LOVE YOU*. BUT YOU HAVE *NO IDEA* WHAT KIND OF *DANGER* YOU ARE ACTUALLY IN.
YOU HAVEN'T BEEN *SNOOPING* AROUND IN THE *BASEMENT* AGAIN HAVE YOU?
I'M SERIOUS!
THEN *WHY* DO YOU KEEP *INSISTING* THAT I GO TO THIS PROTEST RALLY?
DON'T I HAVE A BIG ENOUGH *TARGET* ON MY BACK *ALREADY*?
I'M TALKING ABOUT THE *DANGER* TO YOUR *IMMORTAL SOUL*.
BUT OF COURSE!
WHY DIDN'T I SEE *THAT ONE* COMING!

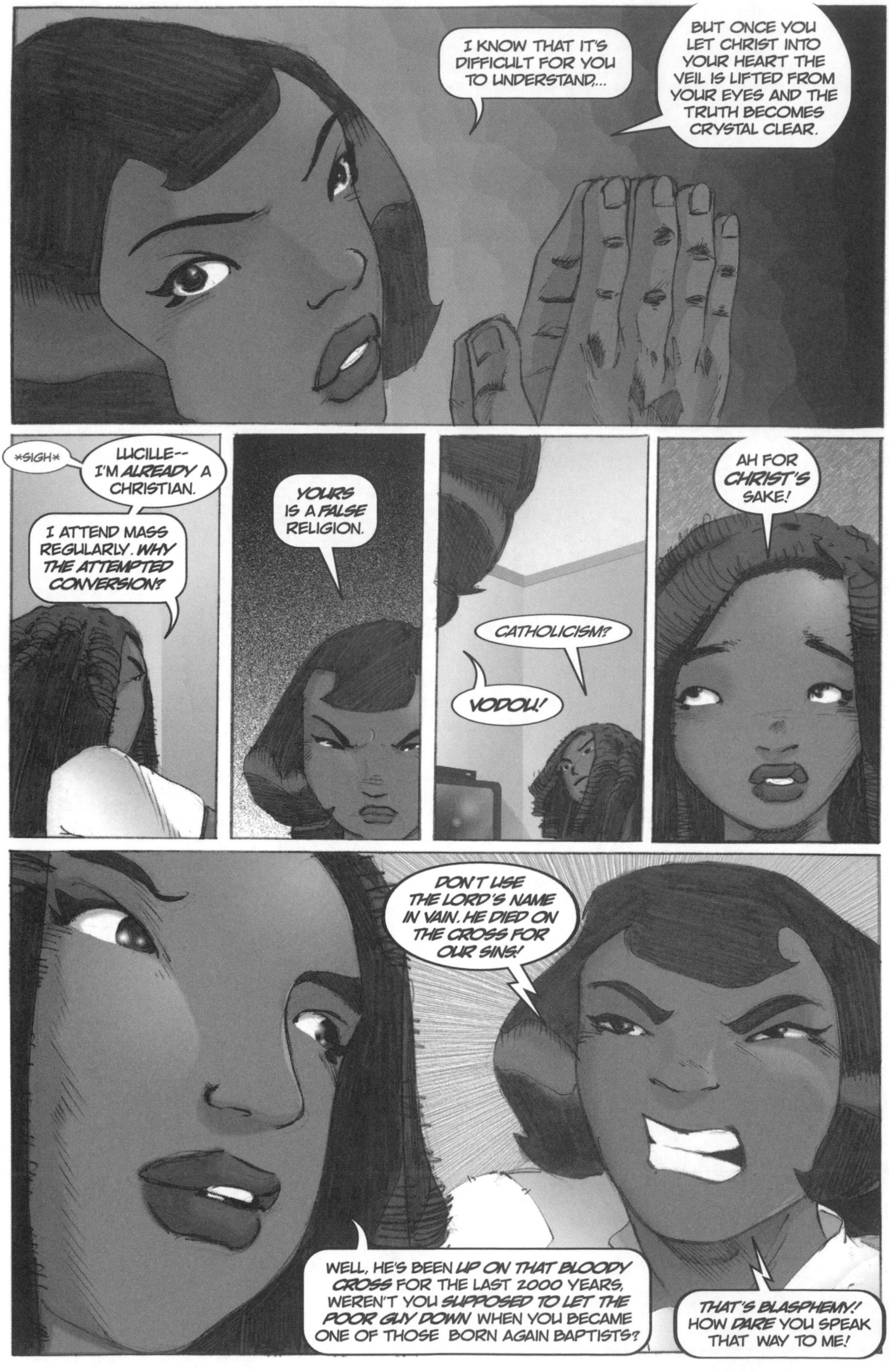
I KNOW THAT IT'S DIFFICULT FOR YOU TO UNDERSTAND,...
BUT ONCE YOU LET CHRIST INTO YOUR HEART THE VEIL IS LIFTED FROM YOUR EYES AND THE TRUTH BECOMES CRYSTAL CLEAR.
SIGH
LUCILLE-- I'M ALREADY A CHRISTIAN.
I ATTEND MASS REGULARLY. WHY THE ATTEMPTED CONVERSION?
YOURS IS A FALSE RELIGION.
CATHOLICISM?
VODOU!
AH FOR CHRIST'S SAKE!
DON'T USE THE LORD'S NAME IN VAIN. HE DIED ON THE CROSS FOR OUR SINS!
WELL, HE'S BEEN UP ON THAT BLOODY CROSS FOR THE LAST 2000 YEARS, WEREN'T YOU SUPPOSED TO LET THE POOR GUY DOWN WHEN YOU BECAME ONE OF THOSE BORN AGAIN BAPTISTS?
THAT'S BLASPHEMY! HOW DARE YOU SPEAK THAT WAY TO ME!

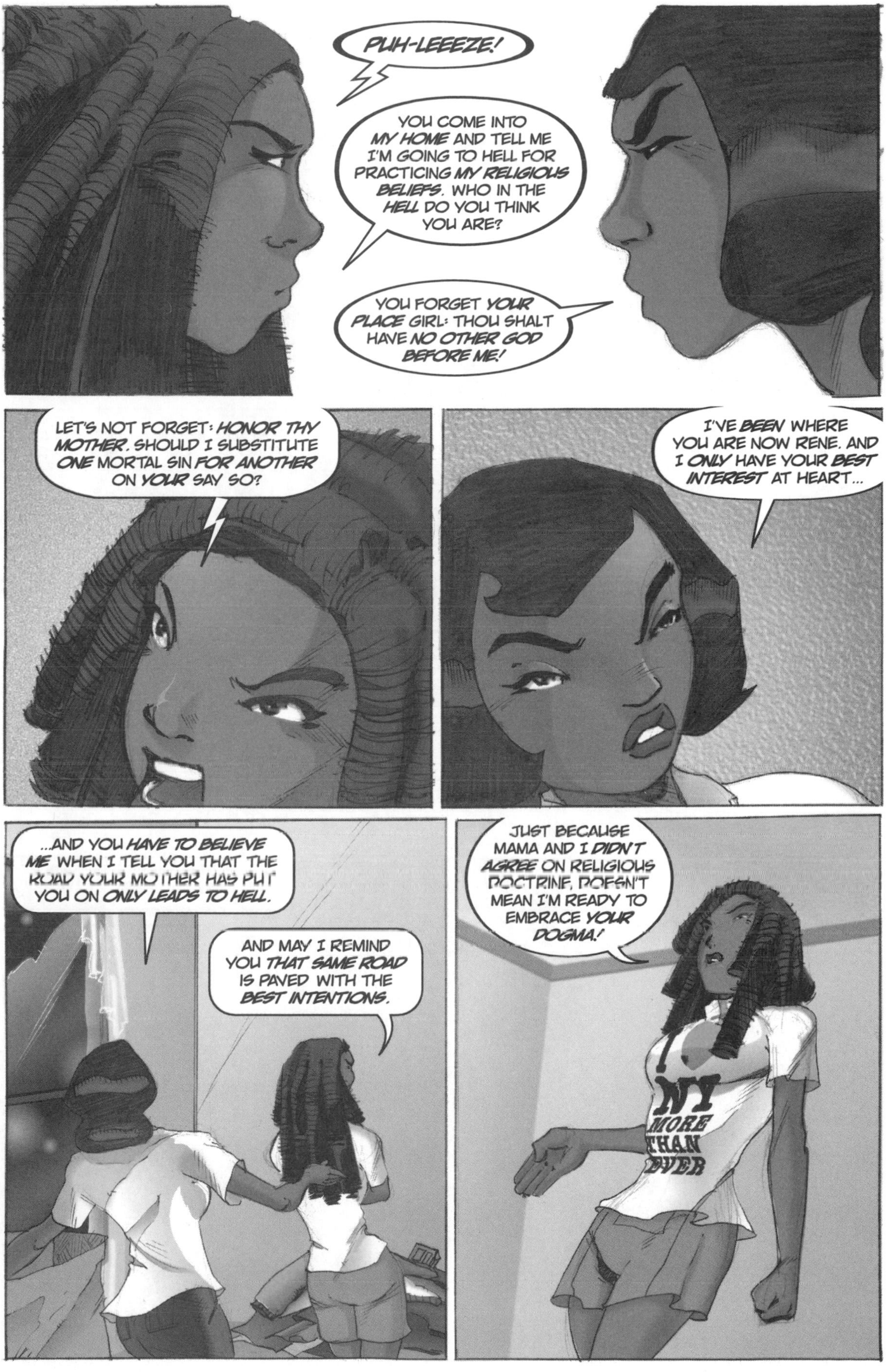
PUH-LEEEZE!
YOU COME INTO MY HOME AND TELL ME I'M GOING TO HELL FOR PRACTICING MY RELIGIOUS BELIEFS. WHO IN THE HELL DO YOU THINK YOU ARE?
YOU FORGET YOUR PLACE GIRL: THOU SHALT HAVE NO OTHER GOD BEFORE ME!
LET'S NOT FORGET: HONOR THY MOTHER. SHOULD I SUBSTITUTE ONE MORTAL SIN FOR ANOTHER ON YOUR SAY SO?
I'VE BEEN WHERE YOU ARE NOW RENE. AND I ONLY HAVE YOUR BEST INTEREST AT HEART...
...AND YOU HAVE TO BELIEVE ME WHEN I TELL YOU THAT THE ROAD YOUR MOTHER HAS PUT YOU ON ONLY LEADS TO HELL.
AND MAY I REMIND YOU THAT SAME ROAD IS PAVED WITH THE BEST INTENTIONS.
JUST BECAUSE MAMA AND I DIDN'T AGREE ON RELIGIOUS DOCTRINE, DOESN'T MEAN I'M READY TO EMBRACE YOUR DOGMA!
NY
MORE
THAN
EVER

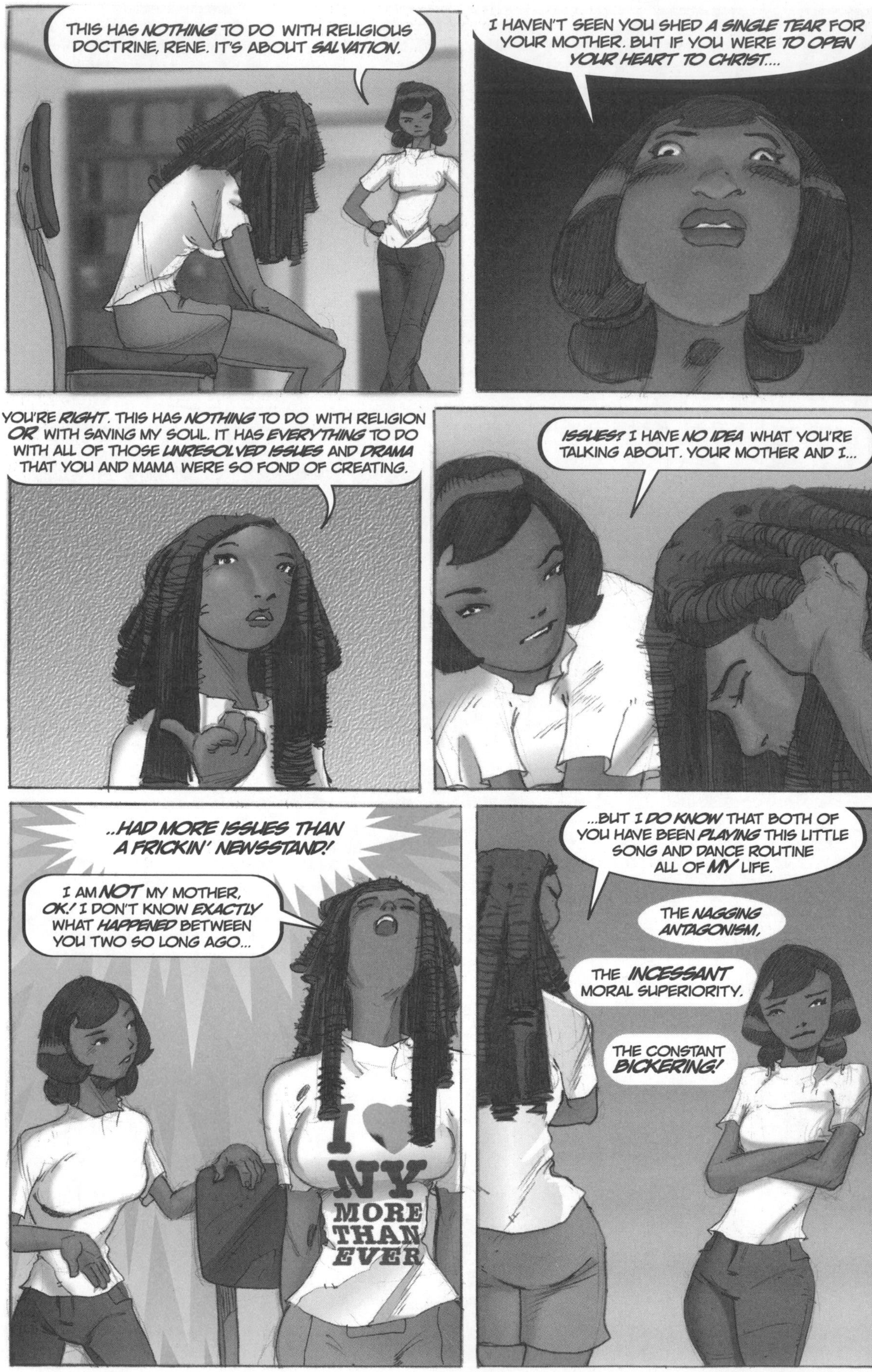
THIS HAS NOTHING TO DO WITH RELIGIOUS DOCTRINE, RENE. IT'S ABOUT SALVATION.
I HAVEN'T SEEN YOU SHED A SINGLE TEAR FOR YOUR MOTHER. BUT IF YOU WERE TO OPEN YOUR HEART TO CHRIST....
YOU'RE RIGHT. THIS HAS NOTHING TO DO WITH RELIGION OR WITH SAVING MY SOUL. IT HAS EVERYTHING TO DO WITH ALL OF THOSE UNRESOLVED ISSUES AND DRAMA THAT YOU AND MAMA WERE SO FOND OF CREATING.
ISSUES? I HAVE NO IDEA WHAT YOU'RE TALKING ABOUT. YOUR MOTHER AND I...
..HAD MORE ISSUES THAN A FRICKIN' NEWSSTAND!
I AM NOT MY MOTHER, OK.! I DON'T KNOW EXACTLY WHAT HAPPENED BETWEEN YOU TWO SO LONG AGO...
I ♥ NY MORE THAN EVER
...BUT I DO KNOW THAT BOTH OF YOU HAVE BEEN PLAYING THIS LITTLE SONG AND DANCE ROUTINE ALL OF MY LIFE.
THE NAGGING ANTAGONISM,
THE INCESSANT MORAL SUPERIORITY.
THE CONSTANT BICKERING!

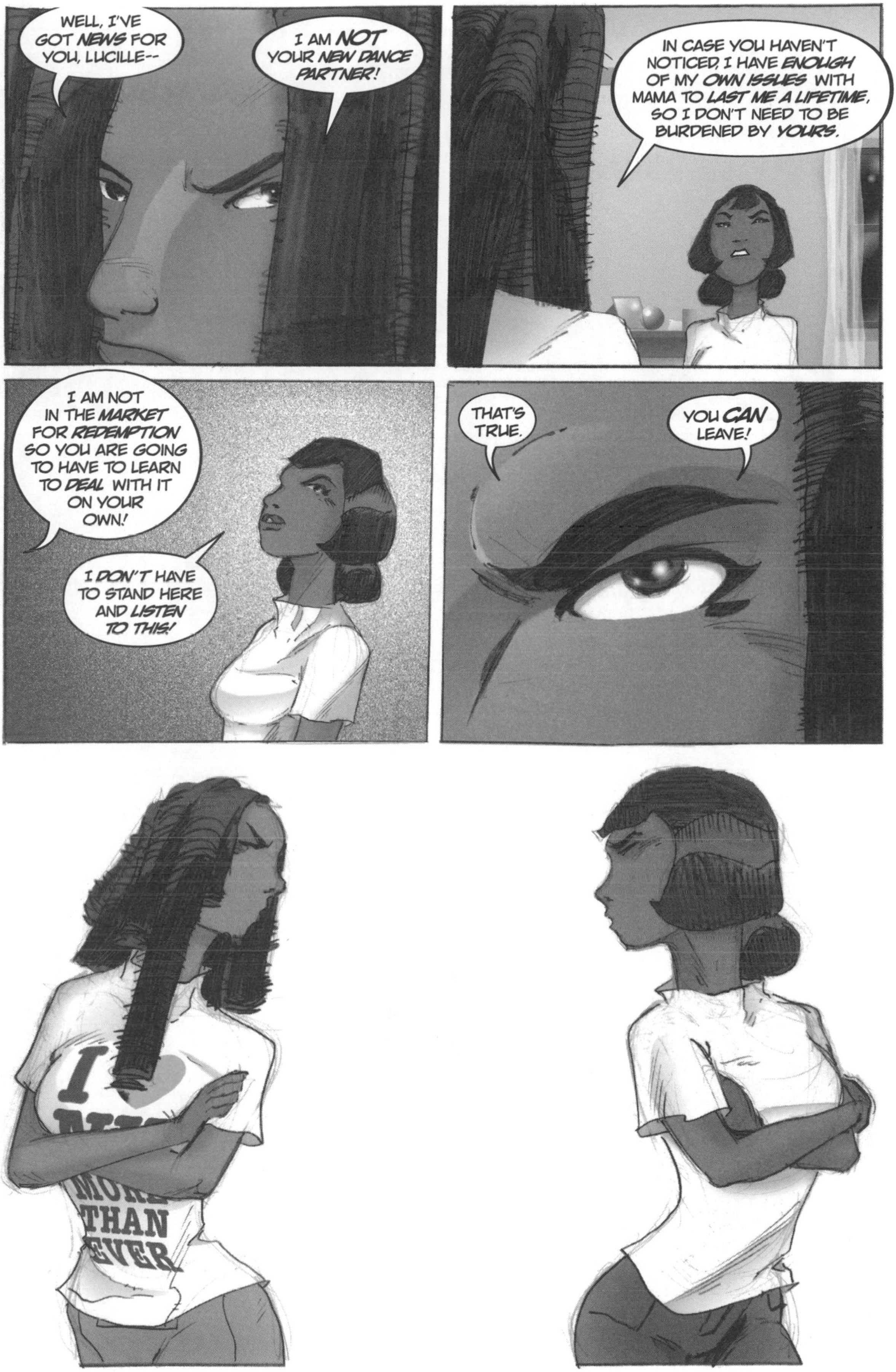
WELL, I'VE GOT NEWS FOR YOU, LUCILLE--
I AM NOT YOUR NEW DANCE PARTNER!
IN CASE YOU HAVEN'T NOTICED, I HAVE ENOUGH OF MY OWN ISSUES WITH MAMA TO LAST ME A LIFETIME, SO I DON'T NEED TO BE BURDENED BY YOURS.
I AM NOT IN THE MARKET FOR REDEMPTION SO YOU ARE GOING TO HAVE TO LEARN TO DEAL WITH IT ON YOUR OWN!
I DON'T HAVE TO STAND HERE AND LISTEN TO THIS!
THAT'S TRUE.
YOU CAN LEAVE!
MORE THAN EVER

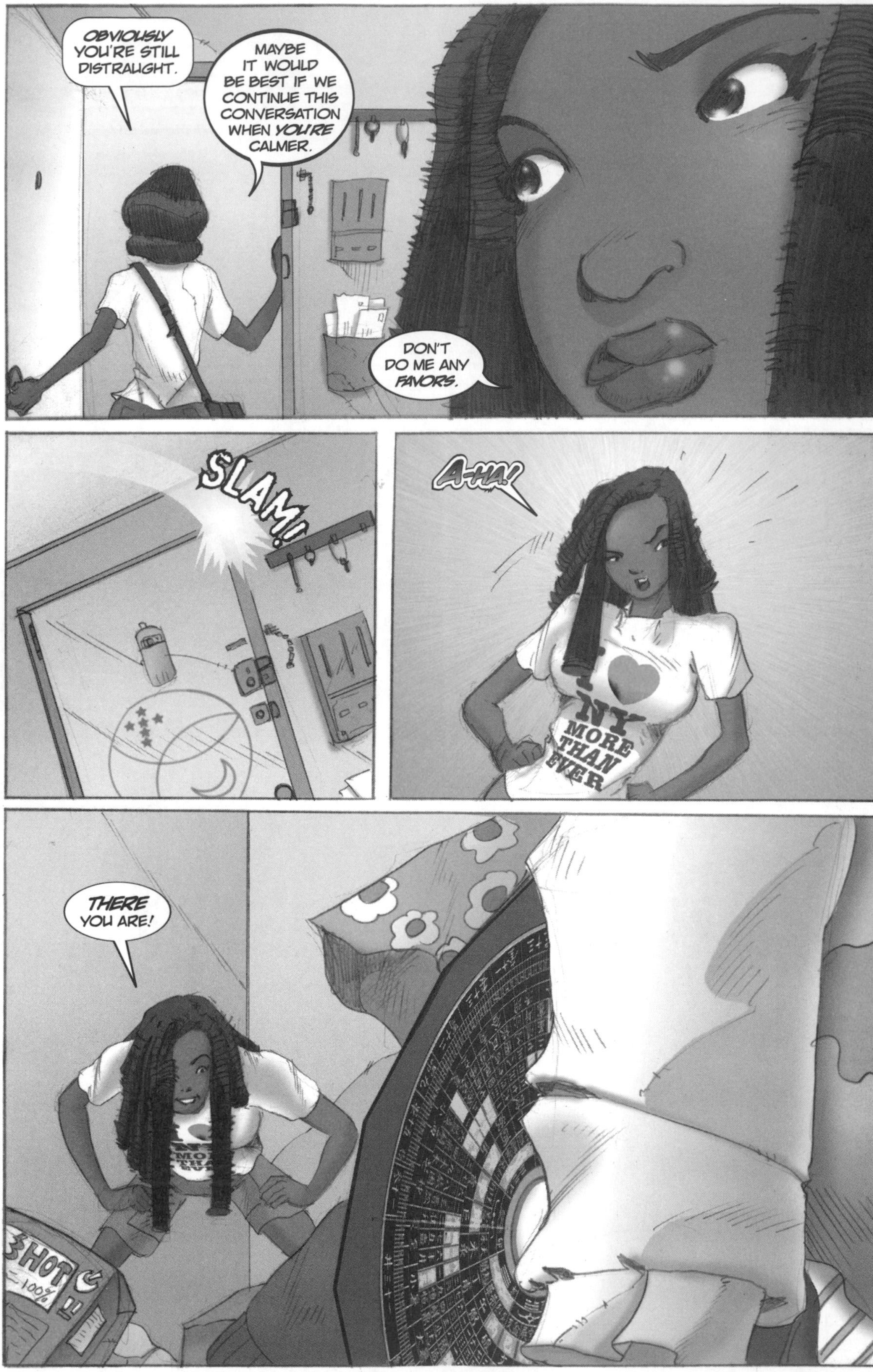
OBVIOUSLY YOU'RE STILL DISTRAUGHT.
MAYBE IT WOULD BE BEST IF WE CONTINUE THIS CONVERSATION WHEN YOU'RE CALMER.
DON'T DO ME ANY FAVORS.
SLAM!!
A-HA!
I ♥ NY MORE THAN EVER
THERE YOU ARE!
3HOT
100%

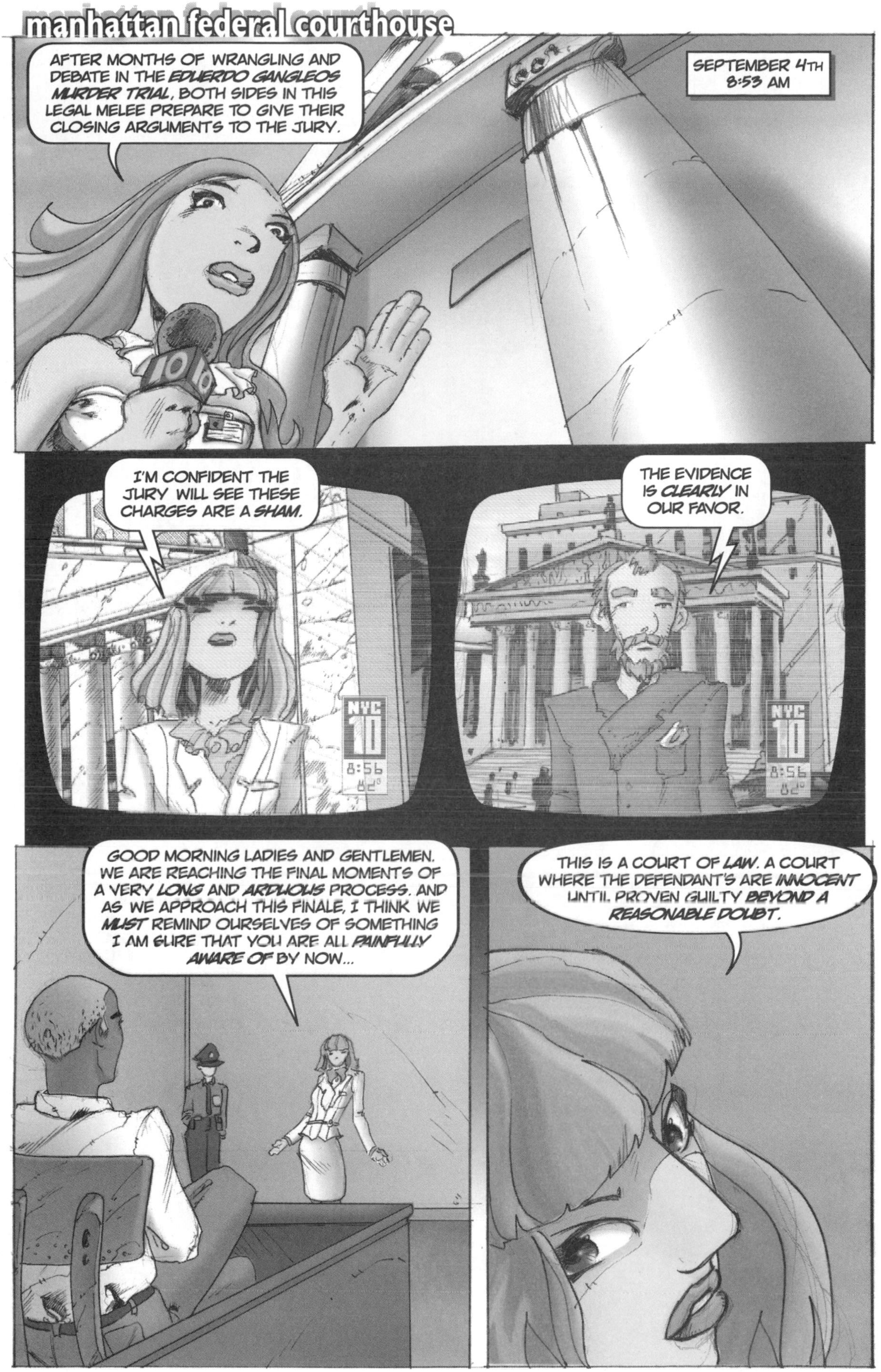
manhattan federal courthouse
AFTER MONTHS OF WRANGLING AND DEBATE IN THE EDUERDO GANGLEOS MURDER TRIAL, BOTH SIDES IN THIS LEGAL MELEE PREPARE TO GIVE THEIR CLOSING ARGUMENTS TO THE JURY.
SEPTEMBER 4TH 8:53 AM
I'M CONFIDENT THE JURY WILL SEE THESE CHARGES ARE A SHAM.
NYC 10
8:56
THE EVIDENCE IS CLEARLY IN OUR FAVOR.
NYC 10
8:56
GOOD MORNING LADIES AND GENTLEMEN. WE ARE REACHING THE FINAL MOMENTS OF A VERY LONG AND ARDUOUS PROCESS. AND AS WE APPROACH THIS FINALE, I THINK WE MUST REMIND OURSELVES OF SOMETHING I AM SURE THAT YOU ARE ALL PAINFULLY AWARE OF BY NOW...
THIS IS A COURT OF LAW. A COURT WHERE THE DEFENDANT'S ARE INNOCENT UNTIL PROVEN GUILTY BEYOND A REASONABLE DOUBT.

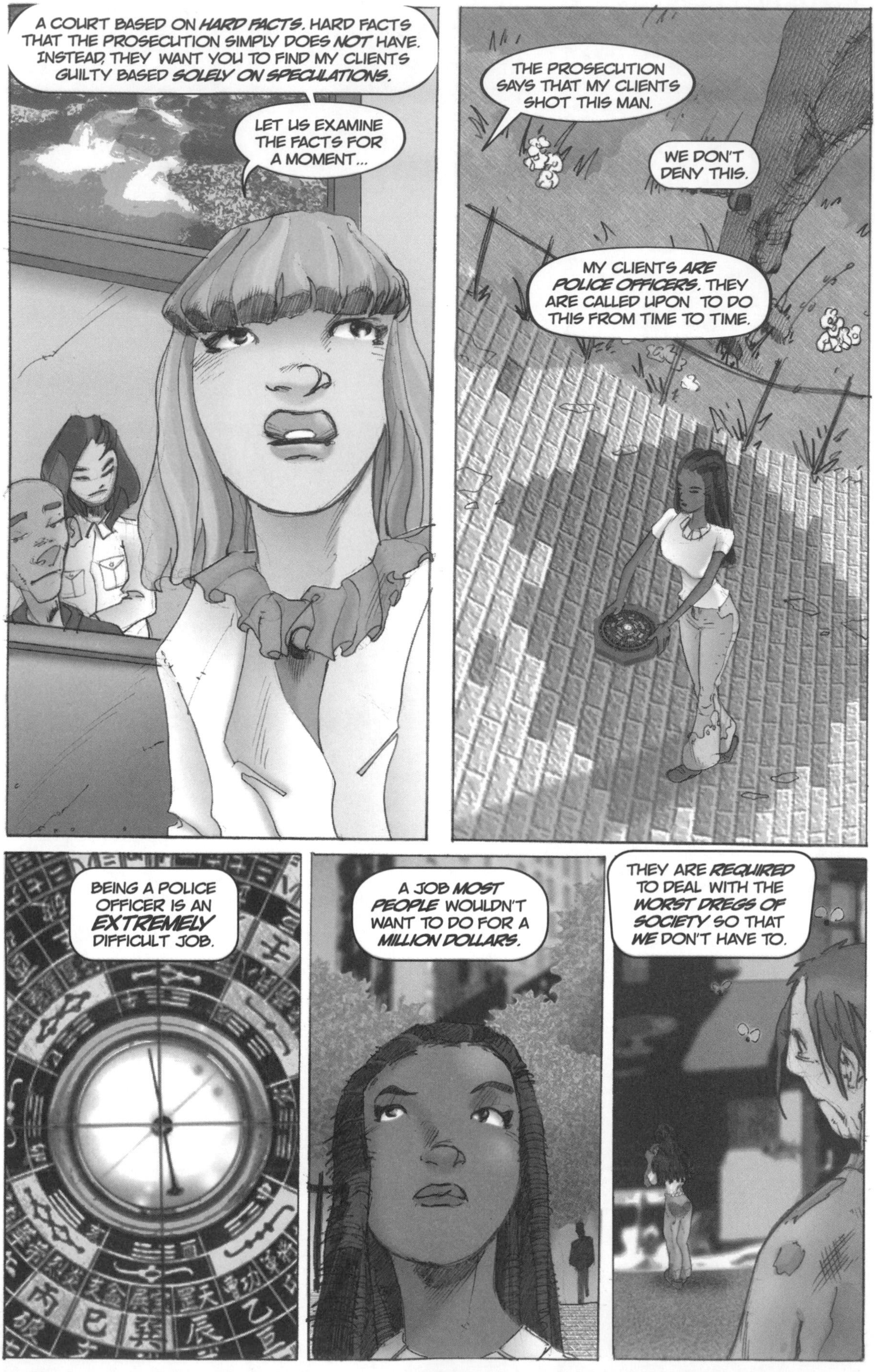
A COURT BASED ON HARD FACTS. HARD FACTS THAT THE PROSECUTION SIMPLY DOES NOT HAVE. INSTEAD, THEY WANT YOU TO FIND MY CLIENTS GUILTY BASED SOLELY ON SPECULATIONS.
LET US EXAMINE THE FACTS FOR A MOMENT...
THE PROSECUTION SAYS THAT MY CLIENTS SHOT THIS MAN.
WE DON'T DENY THIS.
MY CLIENTS ARE POLICE OFFICERS. THEY ARE CALLED UPON TO DO THIS FROM TIME TO TIME.
BEING A POLICE OFFICER IS AN EXTREMELY DIFFICULT JOB.
A JOB MOST PEOPLE WOULDN'T WANT TO DO FOR A MILLION DOLLARS.
THEY ARE REQUIRED TO DEAL WITH THE WORST DREGS OF SOCIETY SO THAT WE DON'T HAVE TO.

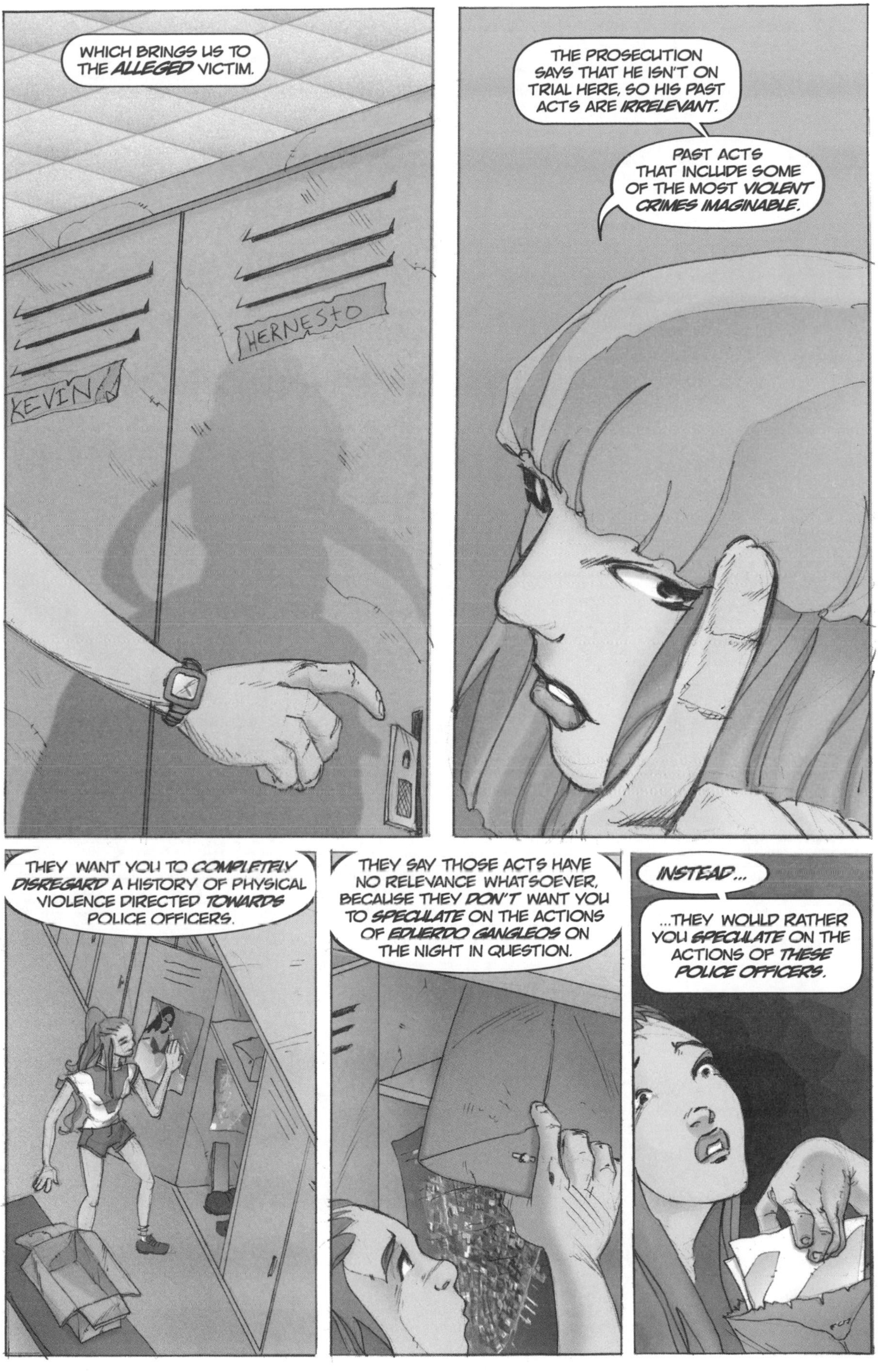
WHICH BRINGS US TO THE ALLEGED VICTIM.
HERNESTO
KEVIN
THE PROSECUTION SAYS THAT HE ISN'T ON TRIAL HERE, SO HIS PAST ACTS ARE IRRELEVANT.
PAST ACTS THAT INCLUDE SOME OF THE MOST VIOLENT CRIMES IMAGINABLE.
THEY WANT YOU TO COMPLETELY DISREGARD A HISTORY OF PHYSICAL VIOLENCE DIRECTED TOWARDS POLICE OFFICERS.
THEY SAY THOSE ACTS HAVE NO RELEVANCE WHATSOEVER, BECAUSE THEY DON'T WANT YOU TO SPECULATE ON THE ACTIONS OF EDUERDO GANGLEOS ON THE NIGHT IN QUESTION.
INSTEAD...
...THEY WOULD RATHER YOU SPECULATE ON THE ACTIONS OF THESE POLICE OFFICERS.

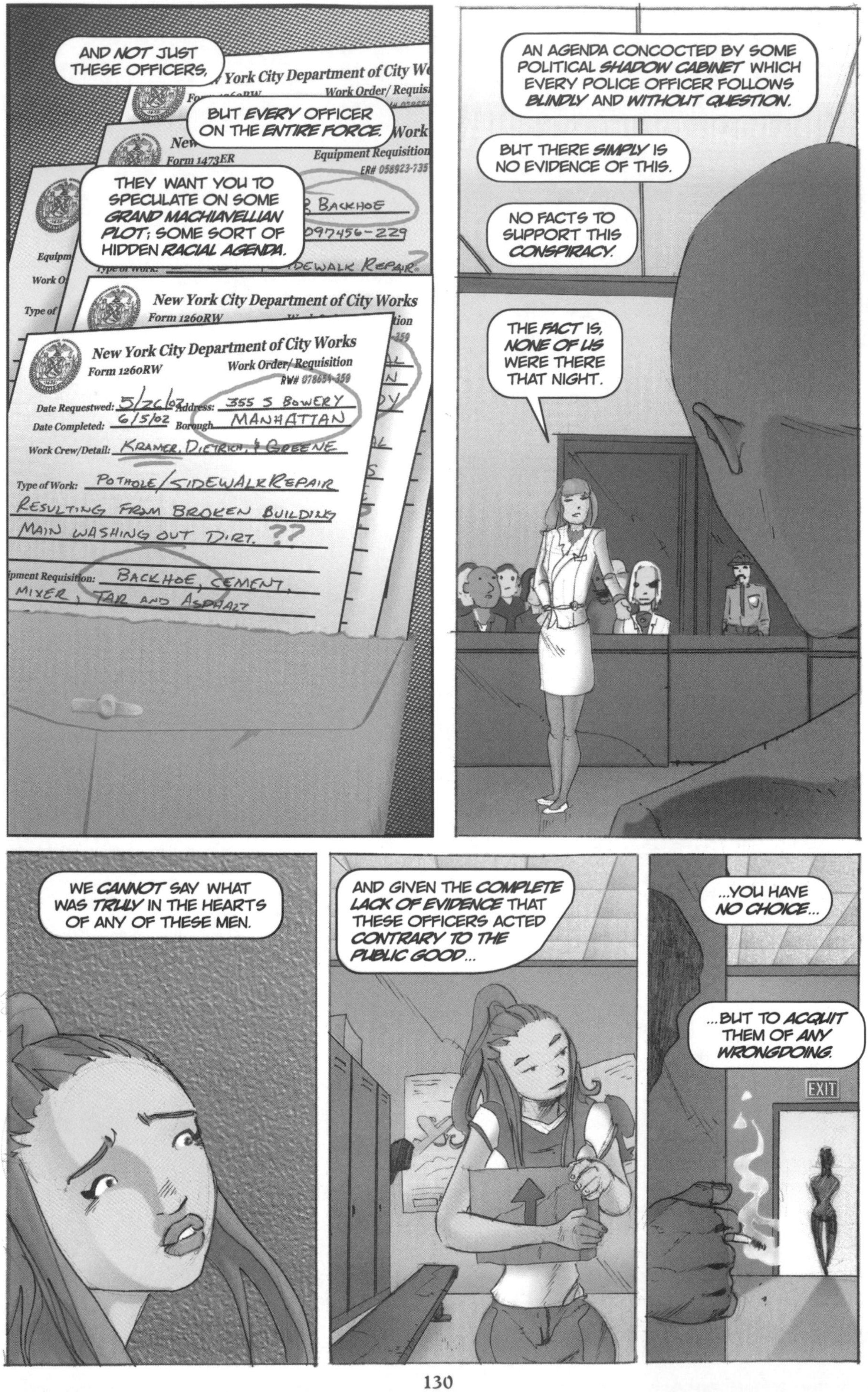
AND NOT JUST THESE OFFICERS,
BUT EVERY OFFICER ON THE ENTIRE FORCE.
THEY WANT YOU TO SPECULATE ON SOME GRAND MACHIAVELLIAN PLOT; SOME SORT OF HIDDEN RACIAL AGENDA.
New York City Department of City Works
Form 1473ER
Equipment Requisition
ER# 058923-735
New York City Department of City Works
Form 1260RW
Work Order/ Requisition
Date Requestwed: 5/26/02 Address: 355 S Bowery
Date Completed: 6/5/02 Borough MANHATTAN
Work Crew/Detail: KRAMER, DIETRICH, & GREENE
Type of Work: POTHOLE/SIDEWALK REPAIR
RESULTING FROM BROKEN BUILDING MAIN WASHING OUT DIRT. ??
Equipment Requisition: BACKHOE, CEMENT, MIXER, TAR AND ASPHALT
AN AGENDA CONCOCTED BY SOME POLITICAL SHADOW CABINET WHICH EVERY POLICE OFFICER FOLLOWS BLINDLY AND WITHOUT QUESTION.
BUT THERE SIMPLY IS NO EVIDENCE OF THIS.
NO FACTS TO SUPPORT THIS CONSPIRACY.
THE FACT IS, NONE OF US WERE THERE THAT NIGHT.
WE CANNOT SAY WHAT WAS TRULY IN THE HEARTS OF ANY OF THESE MEN.
AND GIVEN THE COMPLETE LACK OF EVIDENCE THAT THESE OFFICERS ACTED CONTRARY TO THE PUBLIC GOOD...
...YOU HAVE NO CHOICE...
...BUT TO ACQUIT THEM OF ANY WRONGDOING.
EXIT

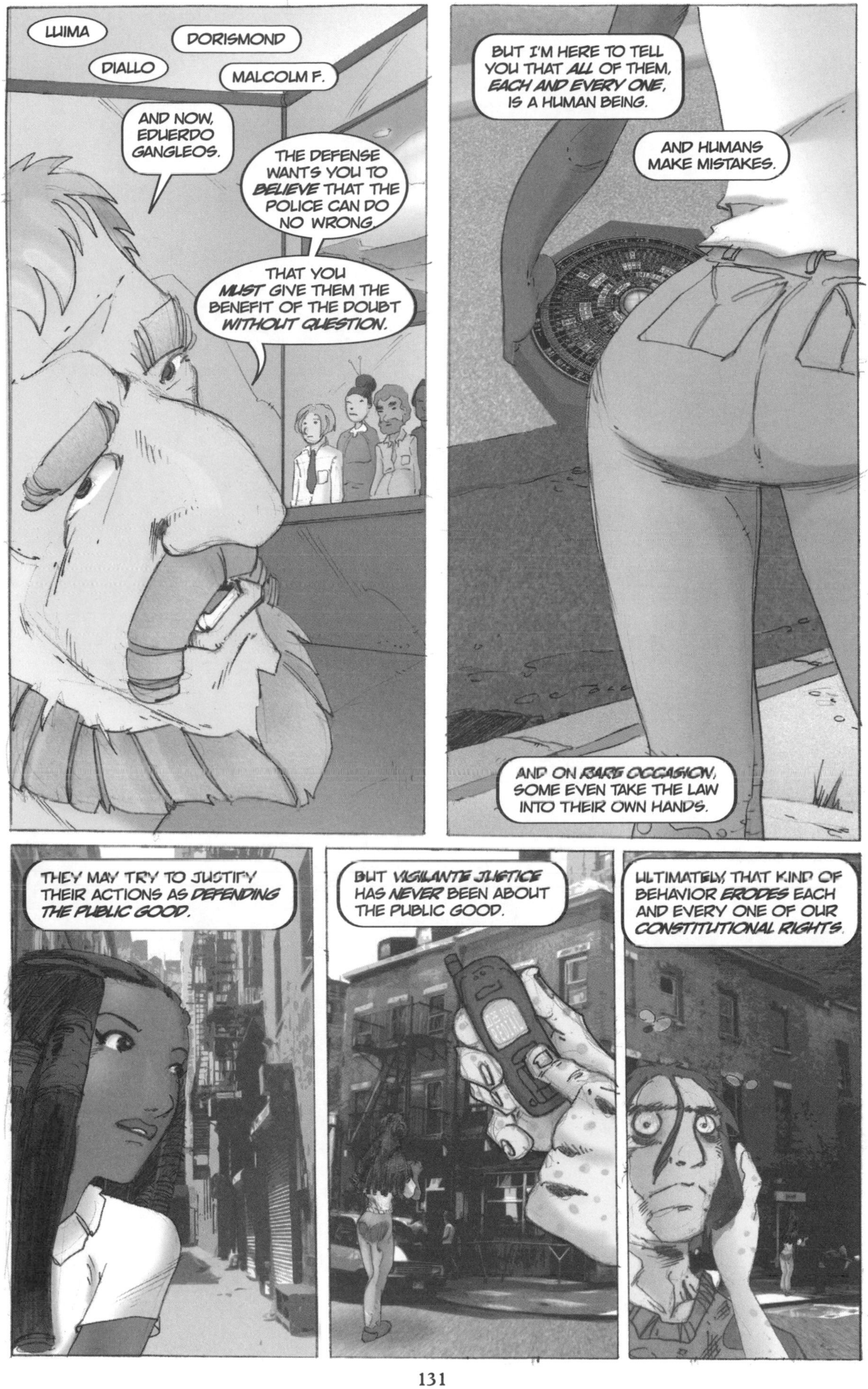
LUIMA
DORISMOND
DIALLO
MALCOLM F.
AND NOW, EDUERDO GANGLEOS.
THE DEFENSE WANTS YOU TO BELIEVE THAT THE POLICE CAN DO NO WRONG.
THAT YOU MUST GIVE THEM THE BENEFIT OF THE DOUBT WITHOUT QUESTION.
BUT I'M HERE TO TELL YOU THAT ALL OF THEM, EACH AND EVERY ONE, IS A HUMAN BEING.
AND HUMANS MAKE MISTAKES.
AND ON RARE OCCASION, SOME EVEN TAKE THE LAW INTO THEIR OWN HANDS.
THEY MAY TRY TO JUSTIFY THEIR ACTIONS AS DEFENDING THE PUBLIC GOOD.
BUT VIGILANTE JUSTICE HAS NEVER BEEN ABOUT THE PUBLIC GOOD.
ULTIMATELY, THAT KIND OF BEHAVIOR ERODES EACH AND EVERY ONE OF OUR CONSTITUTIONAL RIGHTS.

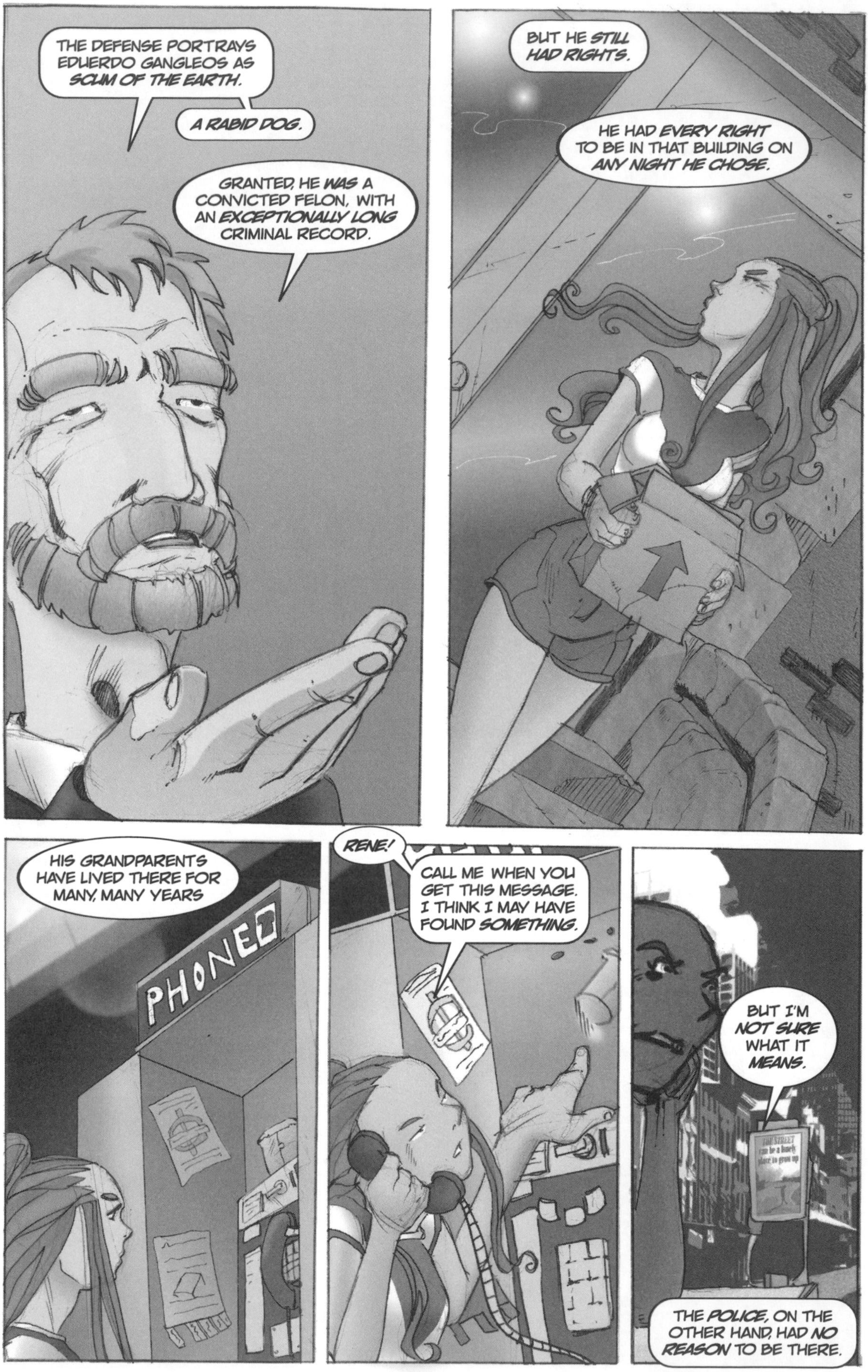
THE DEFENSE PORTRAYS EDUERDO GANGLEOS AS *SCUM OF THE EARTH.*
A RABID DOG.
GRANTED, HE *WAS* A CONVICTED FELON, WITH AN *EXCEPTIONALLY LONG* CRIMINAL RECORD.
BUT HE *STILL HAD RIGHTS.*
HE HAD *EVERY RIGHT* TO BE IN THAT BUILDING ON *ANY NIGHT HE CHOSE.*
HIS GRANDPARENTS HAVE LIVED THERE FOR MANY, MANY YEARS
PHONE
RENE!
CALL ME WHEN YOU GET THIS MESSAGE. I THINK I MAY HAVE FOUND *SOMETHING.*
BUT I'M *NOT SURE* WHAT IT *MEANS.*
THE *POLICE,* ON THE OTHER HAND, HAD *NO REASON* TO BE THERE.

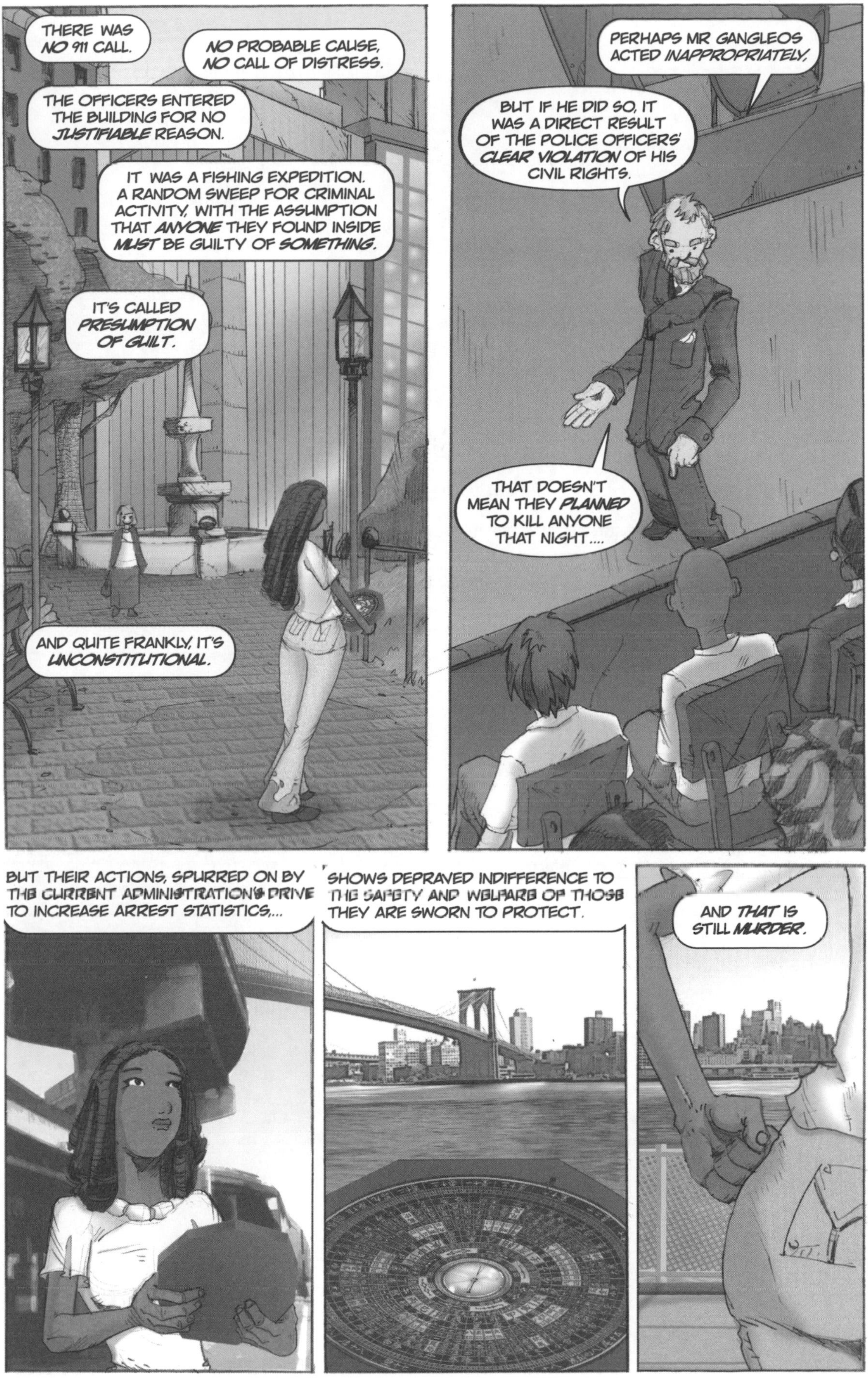
THERE WAS NO 911 CALL.
NO PROBABLE CAUSE, NO CALL OF DISTRESS.
THE OFFICERS ENTERED THE BUILDING FOR NO JUSTIFIABLE REASON.
IT WAS A FISHING EXPEDITION. A RANDOM SWEEP FOR CRIMINAL ACTIVITY, WITH THE ASSUMPTION THAT ANYONE THEY FOUND INSIDE MUST BE GUILTY OF SOMETHING.
IT'S CALLED PRESUMPTION OF GUILT.
AND QUITE FRANKLY, IT'S UNCONSTITUTIONAL.
PERHAPS MR GANGLEOS ACTED INAPPROPRIATELY,
BUT IF HE DID SO, IT WAS A DIRECT RESULT OF THE POLICE OFFICERS' CLEAR VIOLATION OF HIS CIVIL RIGHTS.
THAT DOESN'T MEAN THEY PLANNED TO KILL ANYONE THAT NIGHT....
BUT THEIR ACTIONS, SPURRED ON BY THE CURRENT ADMINISTRATION'S DRIVE TO INCREASE ARREST STATISTICS,...
SHOWS DEPRAVED INDIFFERENCE TO THE SAFETY AND WELFARE OF THOSE THEY ARE SWORN TO PROTECT.
AND THAT IS STILL MURDER.

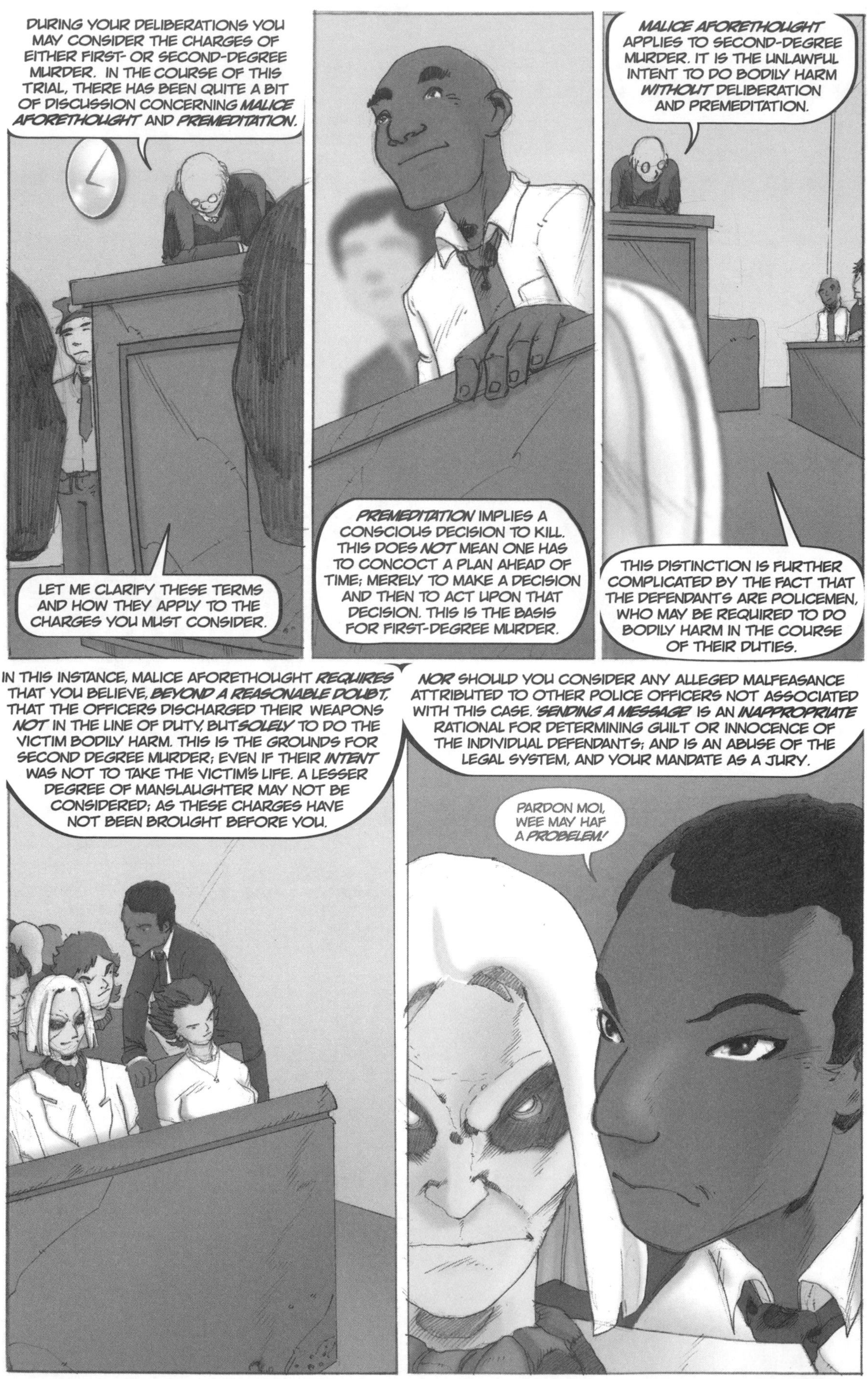
DURING YOUR DELIBERATIONS YOU MAY CONSIDER THE CHARGES OF EITHER FIRST- OR SECOND-DEGREE MURDER. IN THE COURSE OF THIS TRIAL, THERE HAS BEEN QUITE A BIT OF DISCUSSION CONCERNING *MALICE AFORETHOUGHT* AND *PREMEDITATION.*
LET ME CLARIFY THESE TERMS AND HOW THEY APPLY TO THE CHARGES YOU MUST CONSIDER.
PREMEDITATION IMPLIES A CONSCIOUS DECISION TO KILL. THIS DOES *NOT* MEAN ONE HAS TO CONCOCT A PLAN AHEAD OF TIME; MERELY TO MAKE A DECISION AND THEN TO ACT UPON THAT DECISION. THIS IS THE BASIS FOR FIRST-DEGREE MURDER.
MALICE AFORETHOUGHT APPLIES TO SECOND-DEGREE MURDER. IT IS THE UNLAWFUL INTENT TO DO BODILY HARM *WITHOUT* DELIBERATION AND PREMEDITATION.
THIS DISTINCTION IS FURTHER COMPLICATED BY THE FACT THAT THE DEFENDANTS ARE POLICEMEN, WHO MAY BE REQUIRED TO DO BODILY HARM IN THE COURSE OF THEIR DUTIES.
IN THIS INSTANCE, MALICE AFORETHOUGHT *REQUIRES* THAT YOU BELIEVE, *BEYOND A REASONABLE DOUBT,* THAT THE OFFICERS DISCHARGED THEIR WEAPONS *NOT* IN THE LINE OF DUTY, BUT *SOLELY* TO DO THE VICTIM BODILY HARM. THIS IS THE GROUNDS FOR SECOND DEGREE MURDER; EVEN IF THEIR *INTENT* WAS NOT TO TAKE THE VICTIM'S LIFE. A LESSER DEGREE OF MANSLAUGHTER MAY NOT BE CONSIDERED; AS THESE CHARGES HAVE NOT BEEN BROUGHT BEFORE YOU.
NOR SHOULD YOU CONSIDER ANY ALLEGED MALFEASANCE ATTRIBUTED TO OTHER POLICE OFFICERS NOT ASSOCIATED WITH THIS CASE. *'SENDING A MESSAGE'* IS AN *INAPPROPRIATE* RATIONAL FOR DETERMINING GUILT OR INNOCENCE OF THE INDIVIDUAL DEFENDANTS; AND IS AN ABUSE OF THE LEGAL SYSTEM, AND YOUR MANDATE AS A JURY.
PARDON MOI, WEE MAY HAF A *PROBELEM!*

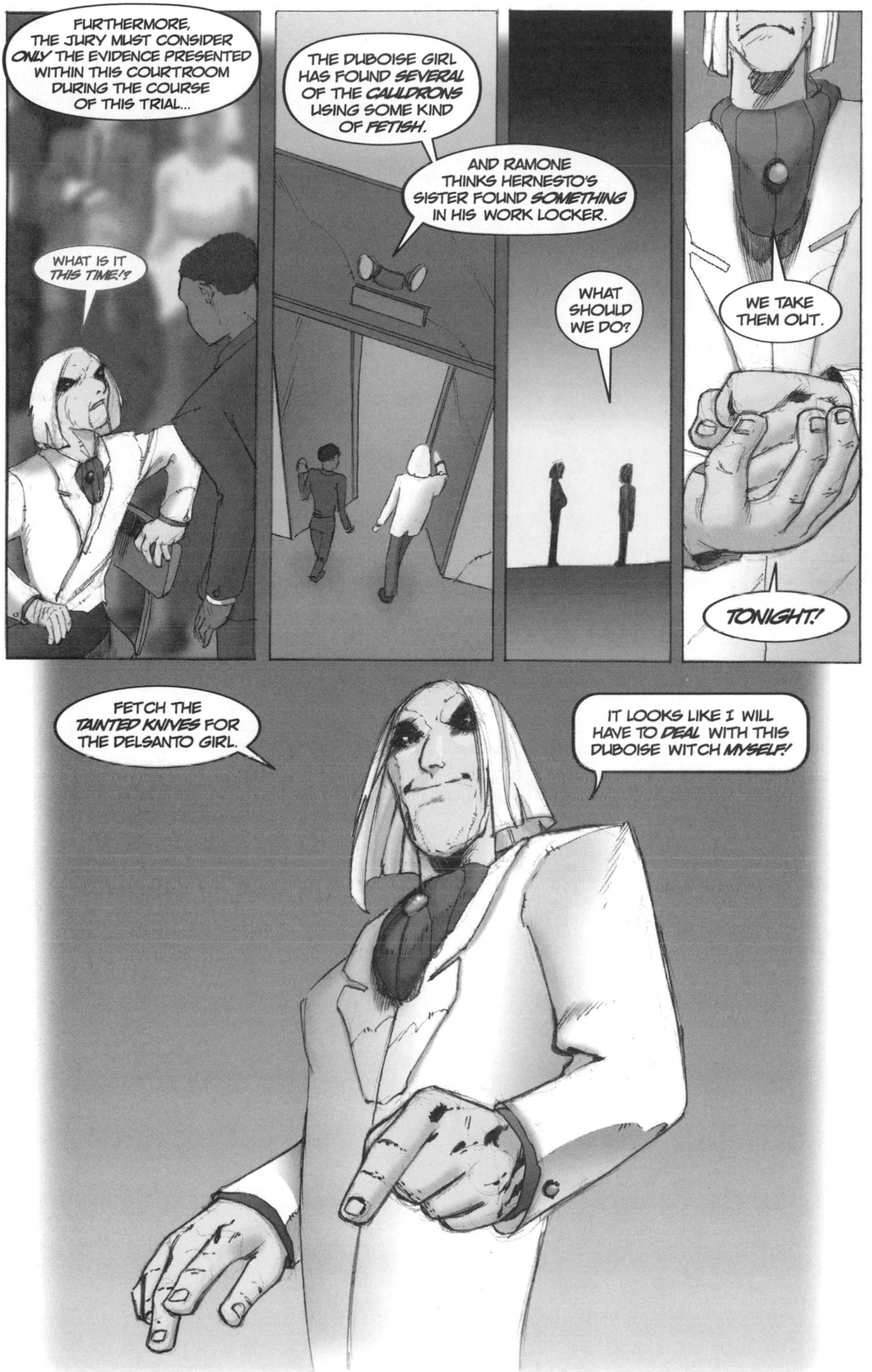
FURTHERMORE, THE JURY MUST CONSIDER ONLY THE EVIDENCE PRESENTED WITHIN THIS COURTROOM DURING THE COURSE OF THIS TRIAL...
WHAT IS IT THIS TIME!?
THE DUBOISE GIRL HAS FOUND SEVERAL OF THE CAULDRONS USING SOME KIND OF FETISH.
AND RAMONE THINKS HERNESTO'S SISTER FOUND SOMETHING IN HIS WORK LOCKER.
WHAT SHOULD WE DO?
WE TAKE THEM OUT.
TONIGHT!
FETCH THE TAINTED KNIVES FOR THE DELSANTO GIRL.
IT LOOKS LIKE I WILL HAVE TO DEAL WITH THIS DUBOISE WITCH MYSELF!

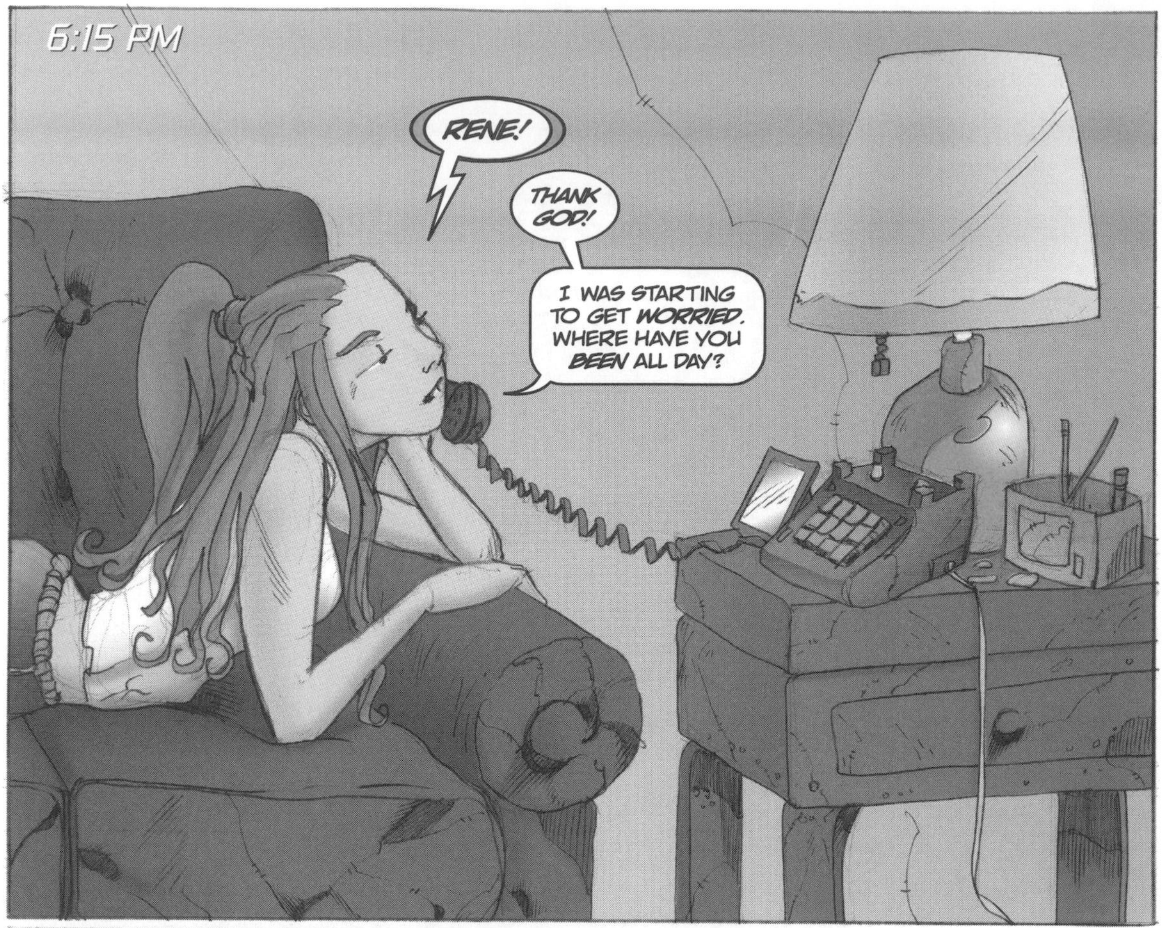
6:15 PM
RENE!
THANK GOD!
I WAS STARTING TO GET WORRIED. WHERE HAVE YOU BEEN ALL DAY?

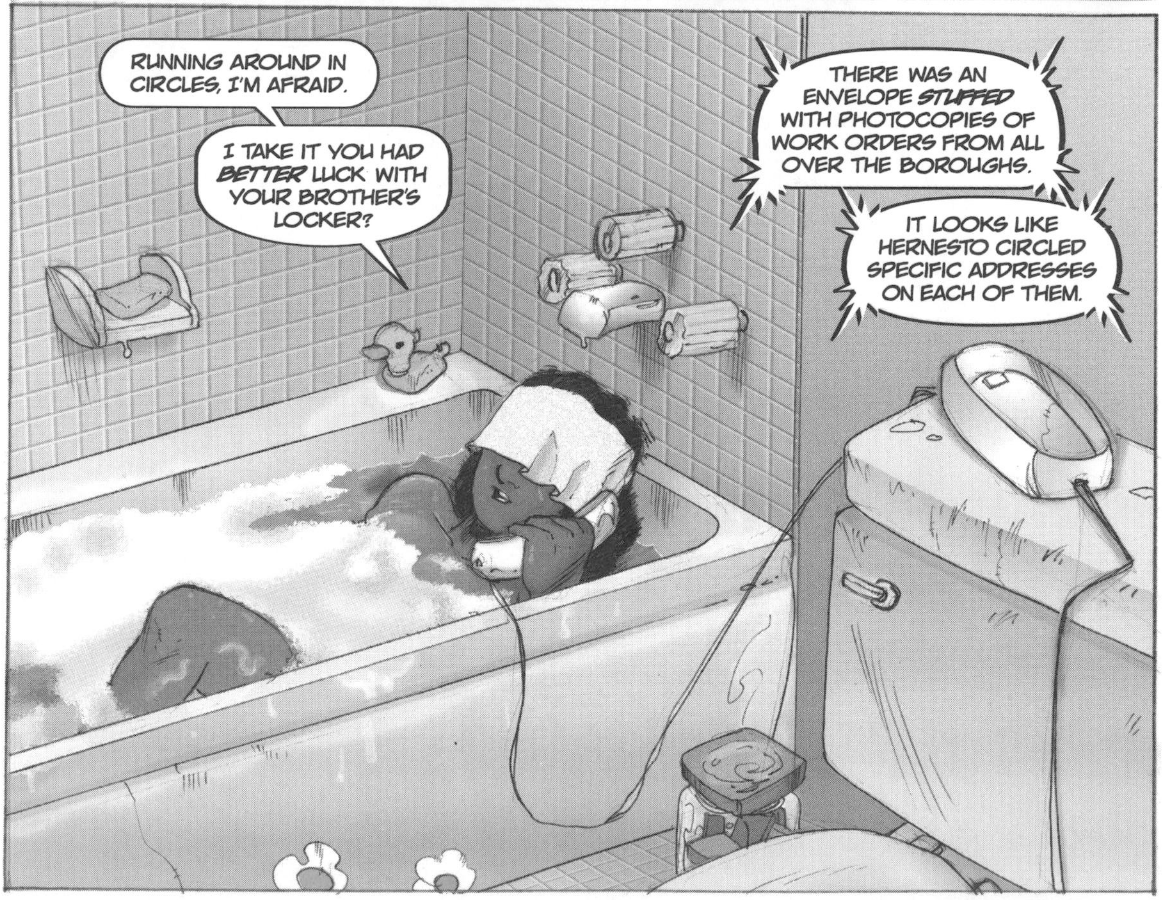
RUNNING AROUND IN CIRCLES, I'M AFRAID.
I TAKE IT YOU HAD BETTER LUCK WITH YOUR BROTHER'S LOCKER?
THERE WAS AN ENVELOPE STUFFED WITH PHOTOCOPIES OF WORK ORDERS FROM ALL OVER THE BOROUGHS.
IT LOOKS LIKE HERNESTO CIRCLED SPECIFIC ADDRESSES ON EACH OF THEM.

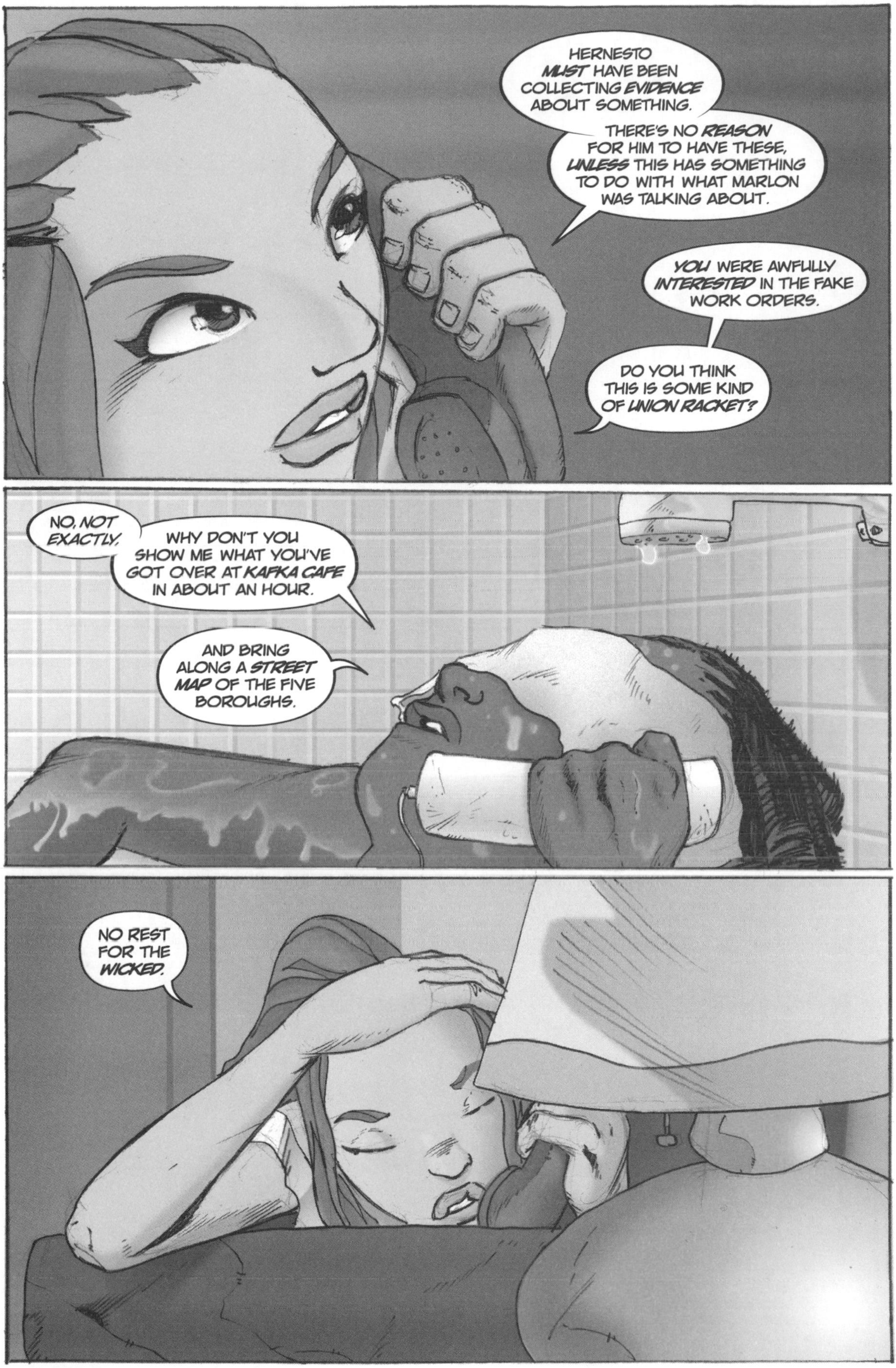
HERNESTO MUST HAVE BEEN COLLECTING EVIDENCE ABOUT SOMETHING.
THERE'S NO REASON FOR HIM TO HAVE THESE, UNLESS THIS HAS SOMETHING TO DO WITH WHAT MARLON WAS TALKING ABOUT.
YOU WERE AWFULLY INTERESTED IN THE FAKE WORK ORDERS.
DO YOU THINK THIS IS SOME KIND OF UNION RACKET?
NO, NOT EXACTLY.
WHY DON'T YOU SHOW ME WHAT YOU'VE GOT OVER AT KAFKA CAFE IN ABOUT AN HOUR.
AND BRING ALONG A STREET MAP OF THE FIVE BOROUGHS.
NO REST FOR THE WICKED.

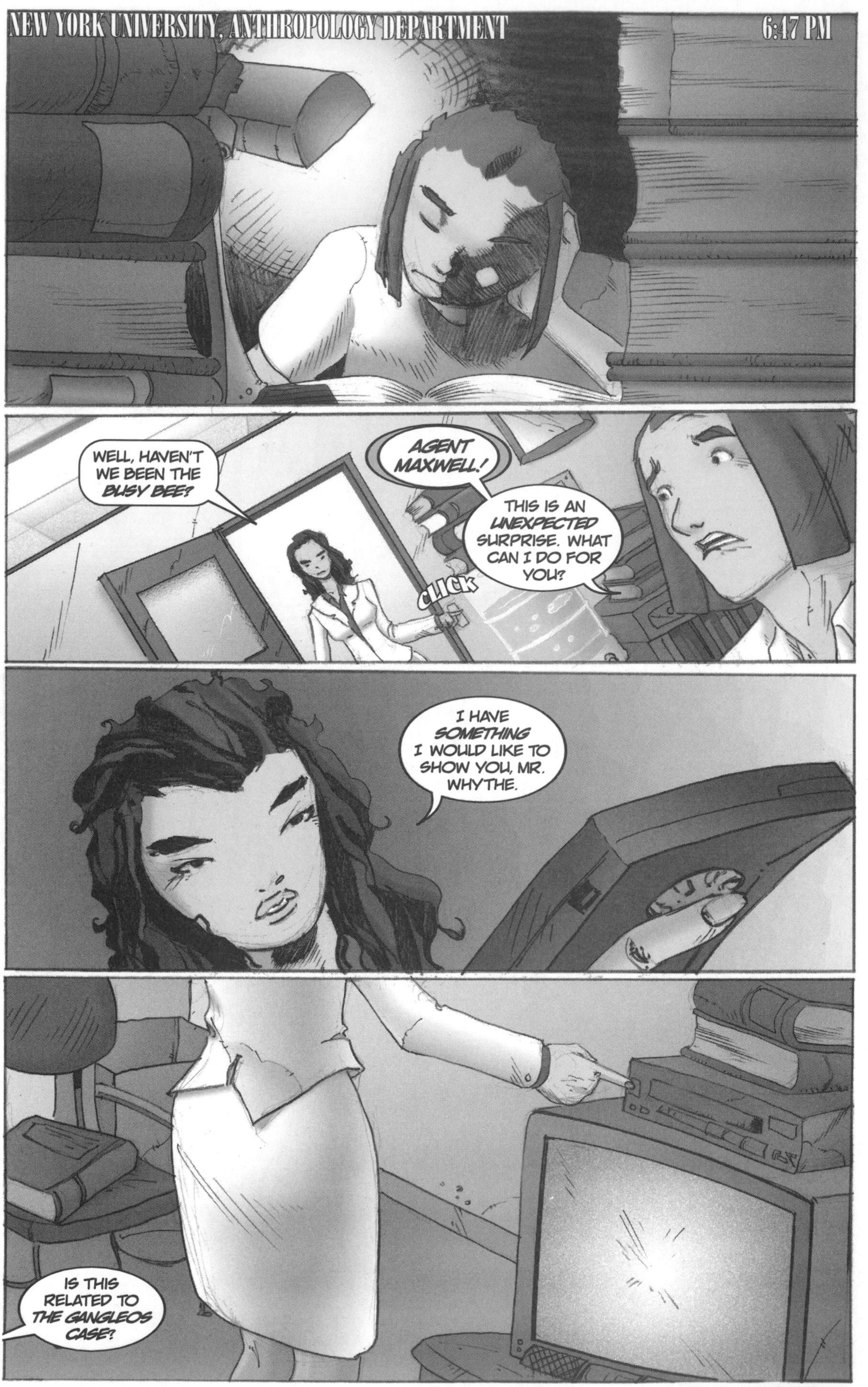
NEW YORK UNIVERSITY, ANTHROPOLOGY DEPARTMENT
6:47 PM
WELL, HAVEN'T WE BEEN THE BUSY BEE?
AGENT MAXWELL!
THIS IS AN UNEXPECTED SURPRISE. WHAT CAN I DO FOR YOU?
CLICK
I HAVE SOMETHING I WOULD LIKE TO SHOW YOU, MR. WHYTHE.
IS THIS RELATED TO THE GANGLEOS CASE?

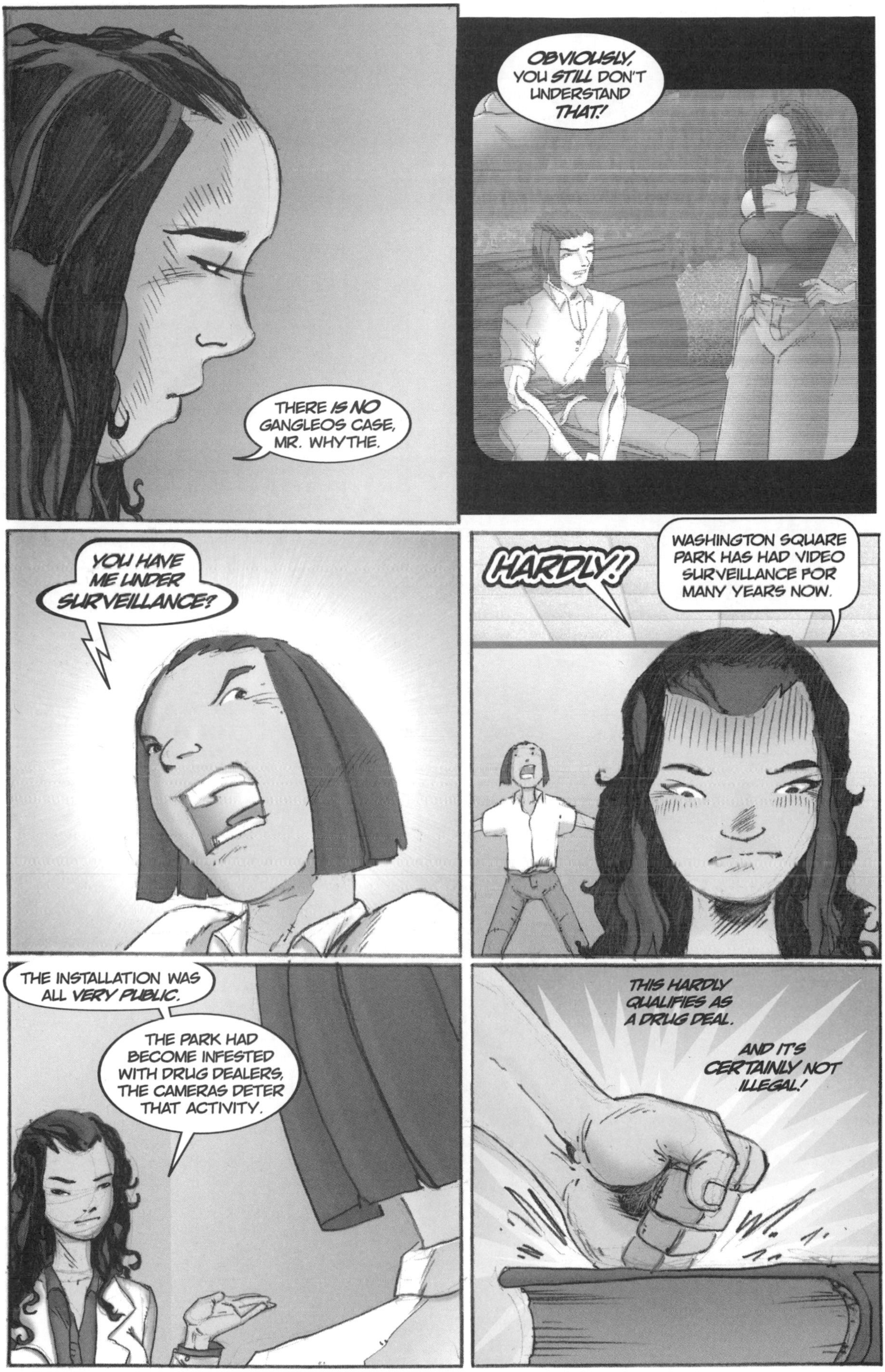
THERE IS NO GANGLEOS CASE, MR. WHYTHE.
OBVIOUSLY, YOU STILL DON'T UNDERSTAND THAT!
YOU HAVE ME UNDER SURVEILLANCE?
HARDLY!
WASHINGTON SQUARE PARK HAS HAD VIDEO SURVEILLANCE FOR MANY YEARS NOW.
THE INSTALLATION WAS ALL VERY PUBLIC.
THE PARK HAD BECOME INFESTED WITH DRUG DEALERS, THE CAMERAS DETER THAT ACTIVITY.
THIS HARDLY QUALIFIES AS A DRUG DEAL.
AND IT'S CERTAINLY NOT ILLEGAL!

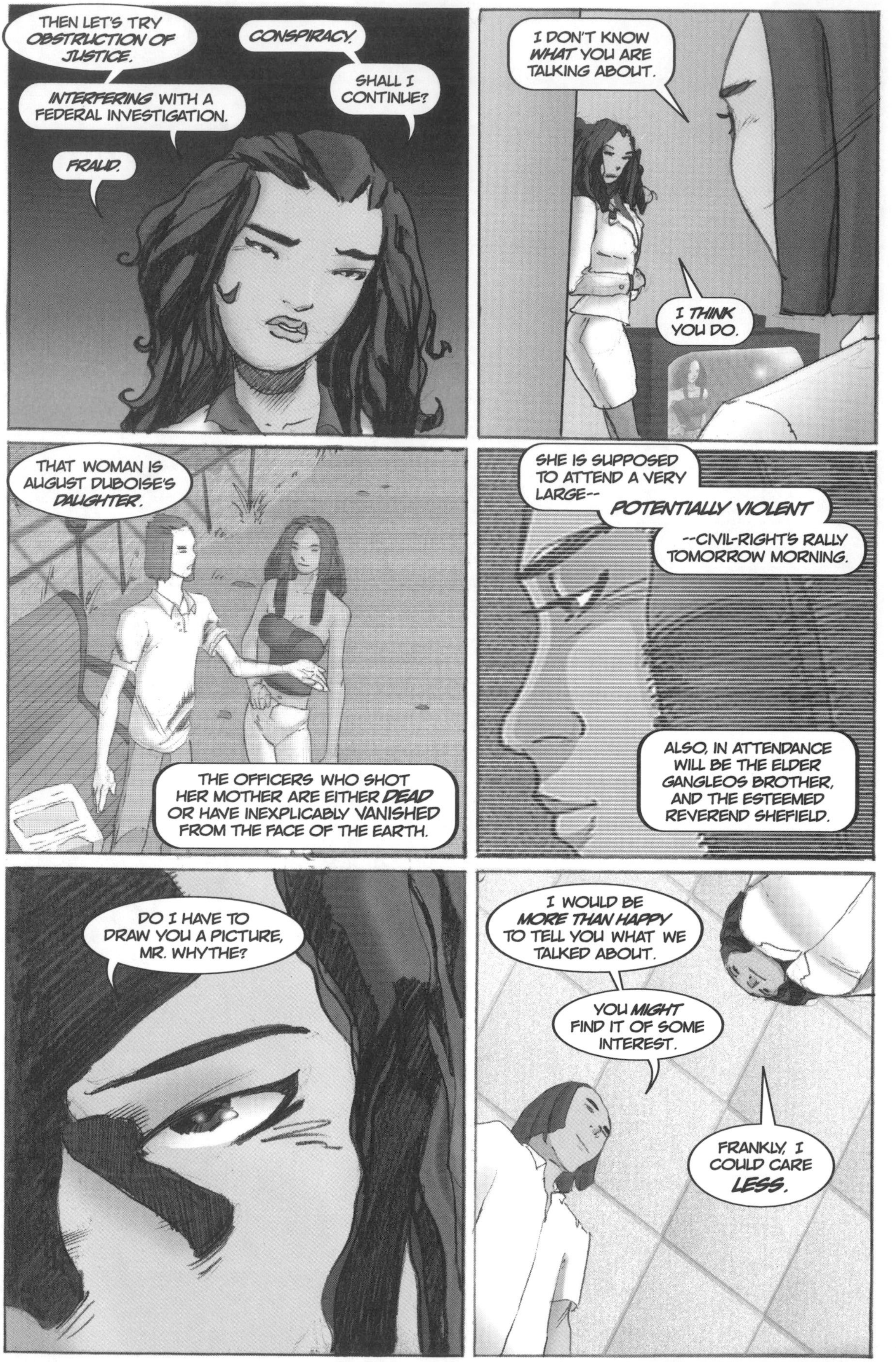

THEN LET'S TRY OBSTRUCTION OF JUSTICE.
INTERFERING WITH A FEDERAL INVESTIGATION.
FRAUD.
CONSPIRACY.
SHALL I CONTINUE?
I DON'T KNOW WHAT YOU ARE TALKING ABOUT.
I THINK YOU DO.
THAT WOMAN IS AUGUST DUBOISE'S DAUGHTER.
THE OFFICERS WHO SHOT HER MOTHER ARE EITHER DEAD OR HAVE INEXPLICABLY VANISHED FROM THE FACE OF THE EARTH.
SHE IS SUPPOSED TO ATTEND A VERY LARGE--
POTENTIALLY VIOLENT
--CIVIL-RIGHT'S RALLY TOMORROW MORNING.
ALSO, IN ATTENDANCE WILL BE THE ELDER GANGLEOS BROTHER, AND THE ESTEEMED REVEREND SHEFIELD.
DO I HAVE TO DRAW YOU A PICTURE, MR. WHYTHE?
I WOULD BE MORE THAN HAPPY TO TELL YOU WHAT WE TALKED ABOUT.
YOU MIGHT FIND IT OF SOME INTEREST.
FRANKLY, I COULD CARE LESS.

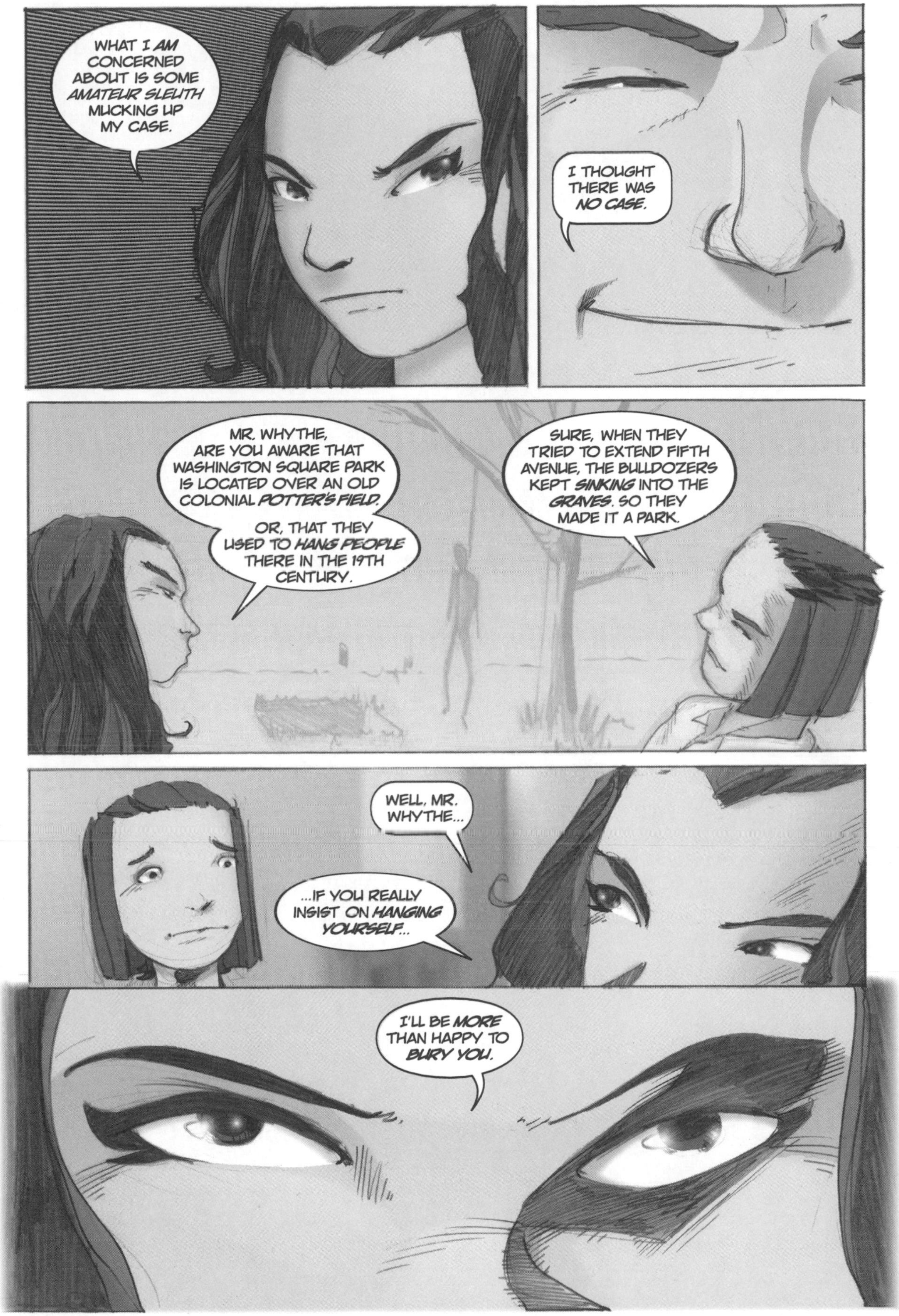
WHAT I *AM* CONCERNED ABOUT IS SOME *AMATEUR SLEUTH* MUCKING UP MY CASE.
I THOUGHT THERE WAS *NO CASE.*
MR. WHYTHE, ARE YOU AWARE THAT WASHINGTON SQUARE PARK IS LOCATED OVER AN OLD COLONIAL *POTTER'S FIELD.*
OR, THAT THEY USED TO *HANG PEOPLE* THERE IN THE 19TH CENTURY.
SURE, WHEN THEY TRIED TO EXTEND FIFTH AVENUE, THE BULLDOZERS KEPT *SINKING* INTO THE *GRAVES*. SO THEY MADE IT A PARK.
WELL, MR. WHYTHE...
...IF YOU REALLY INSIST ON *HANGING YOURSELF*...
I'LL BE *MORE* THAN HAPPY TO *BURY YOU.*

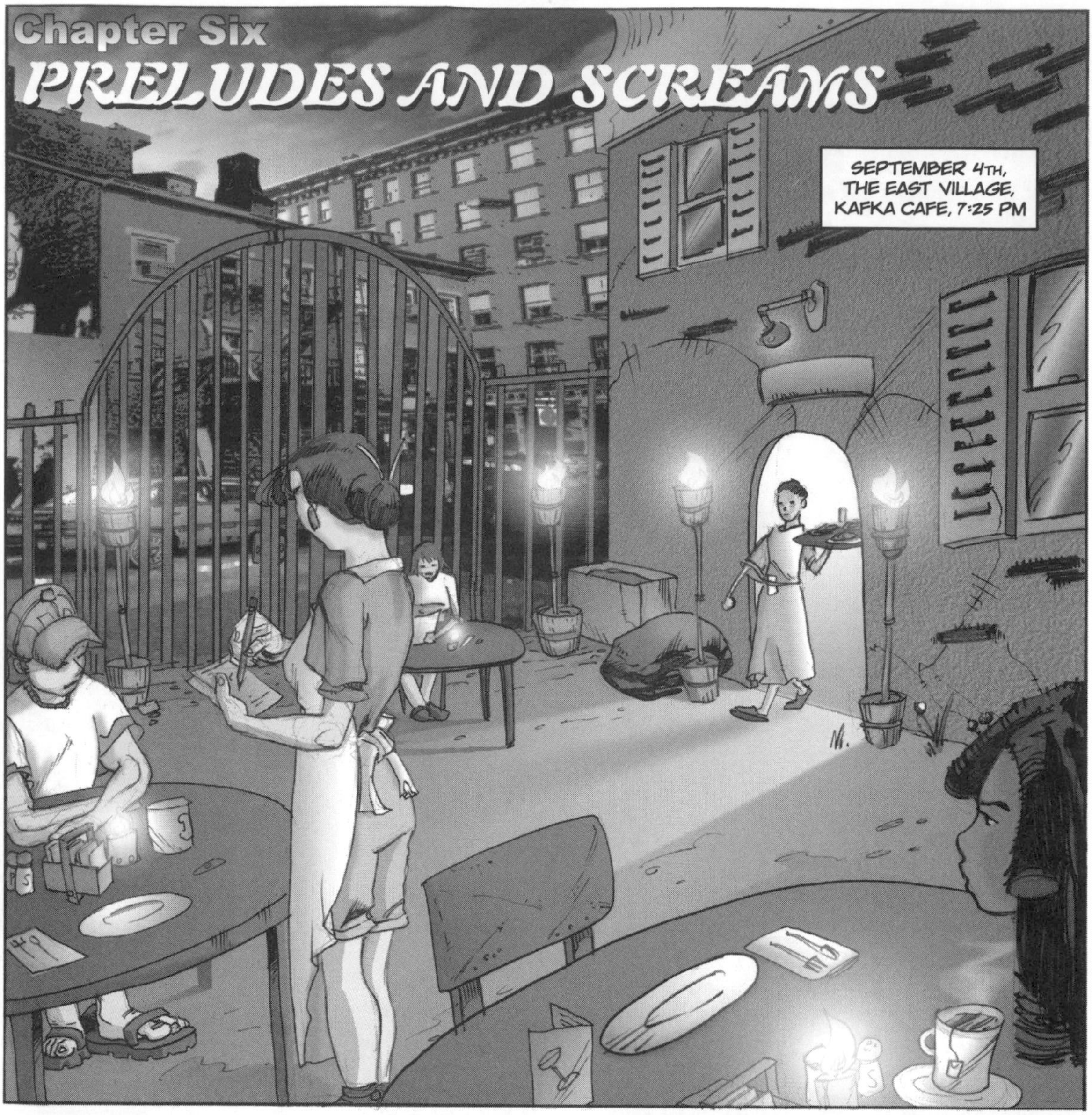
Chapter Six
PRELUDES AND SCREAMS
SEPTEMBER 4TH, THE EAST VILLAGE, KAFKA CAFE, 7:25 PM

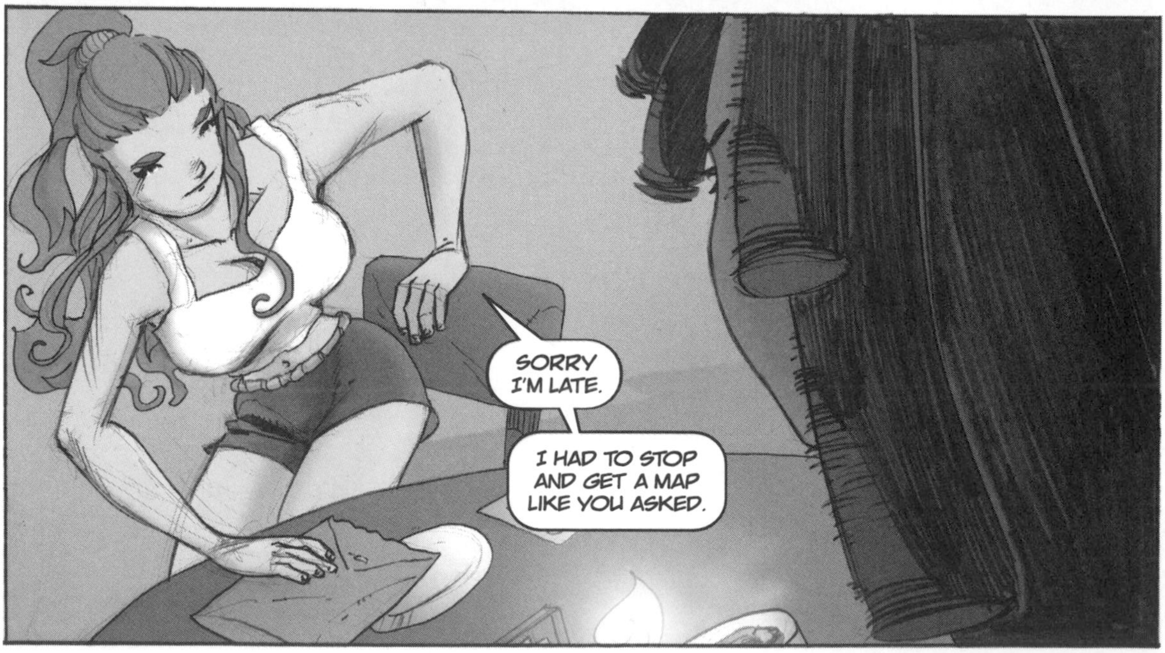
SORRY I'M LATE.
I HAD TO STOP AND GET A MAP LIKE YOU ASKED.

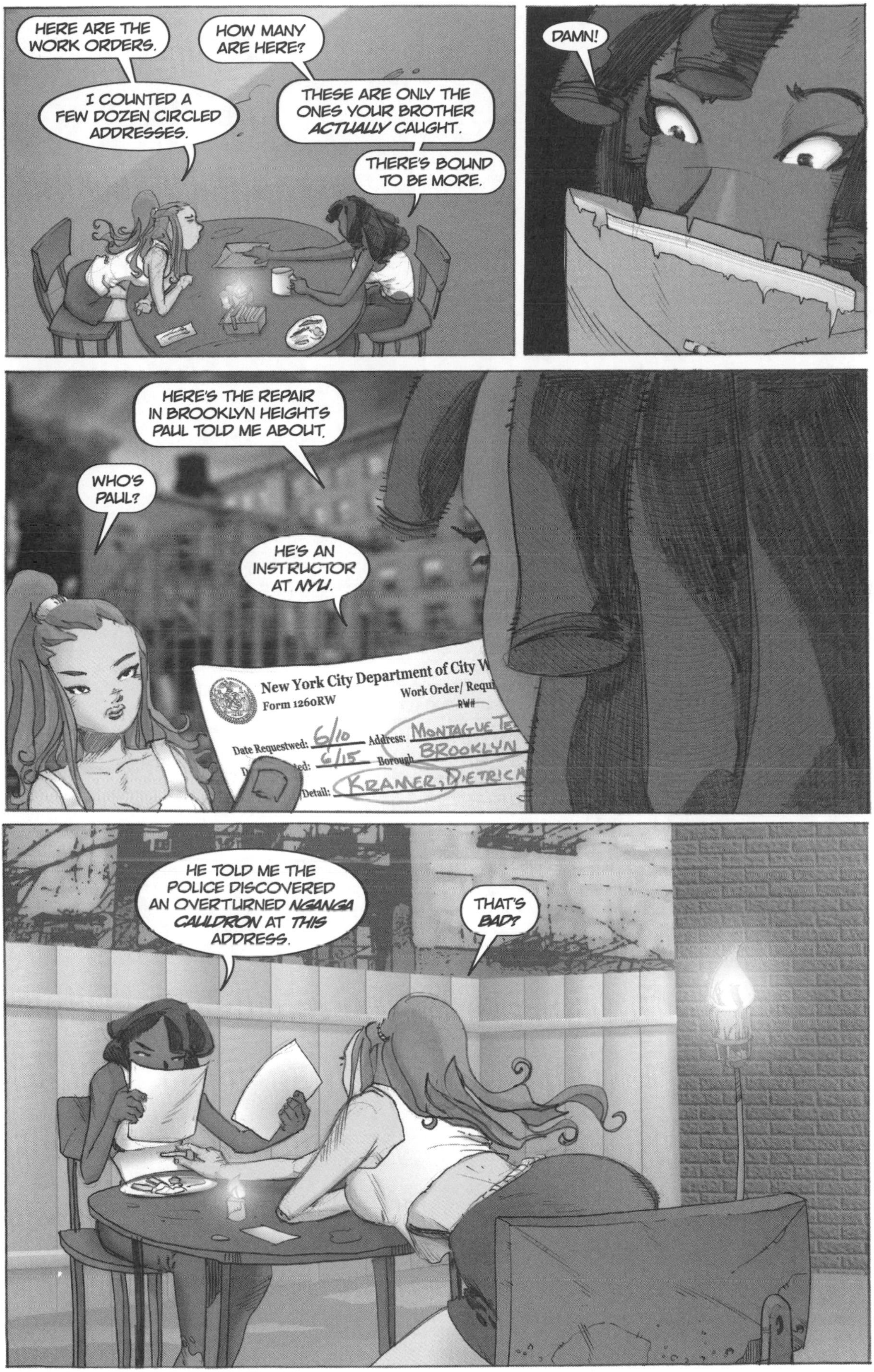

HERE ARE THE WORK ORDERS.
I COUNTED A FEW DOZEN CIRCLED ADDRESSES.
HOW MANY ARE HERE?
THESE ARE ONLY THE ONES YOUR BROTHER *ACTUALLY* CAUGHT.
THERE'S BOUND TO BE MORE.
DAMN!
HERE'S THE REPAIR IN BROOKLYN HEIGHTS PAUL TOLD ME ABOUT.
WHO'S PAUL?
HE'S AN INSTRUCTOR AT *NYU*.
New York City Department of City
Work Order/
Form 1260RW
RW#
Date Requestwed: 6/10
Address:
6/15
Borough BROOKLYN
Detail:
HE TOLD ME THE POLICE DISCOVERED AN OVERTURNED *NGANGA CAULDRON* AT *THIS* ADDRESS.
THAT'S *BAD?*

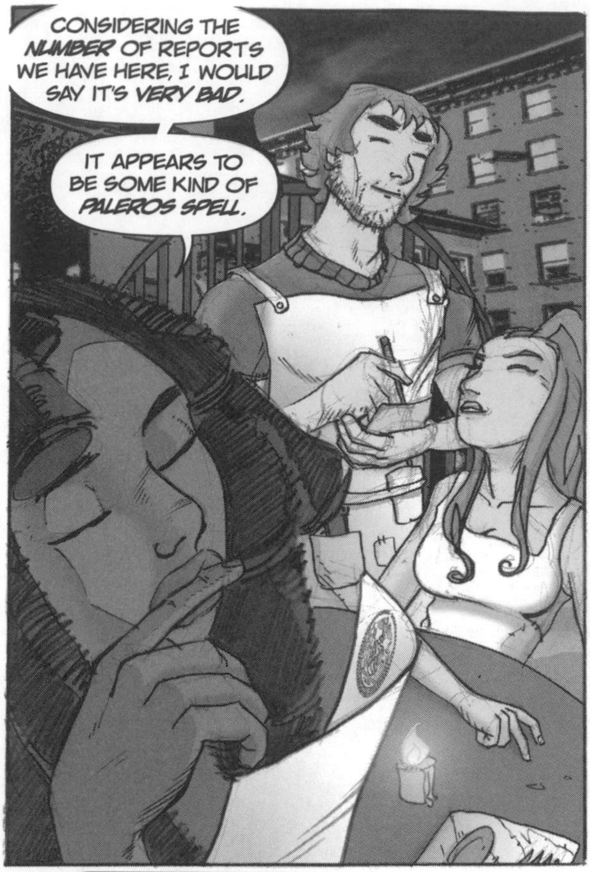
CONSIDERING THE NUMBER OF REPORTS WE HAVE HERE, I WOULD SAY IT'S VERY BAD.
IT APPEARS TO BE SOME KIND OF PALEROS SPELL.

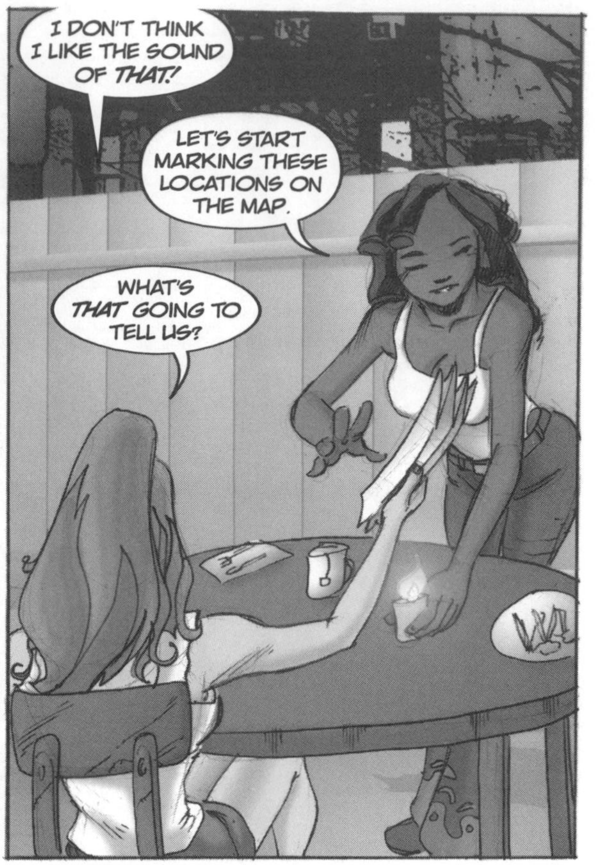
I DON'T THINK I LIKE THE SOUND OF THAT!
LET'S START MARKING THESE LOCATIONS ON THE MAP.
WHAT'S THAT GOING TO TELL US?

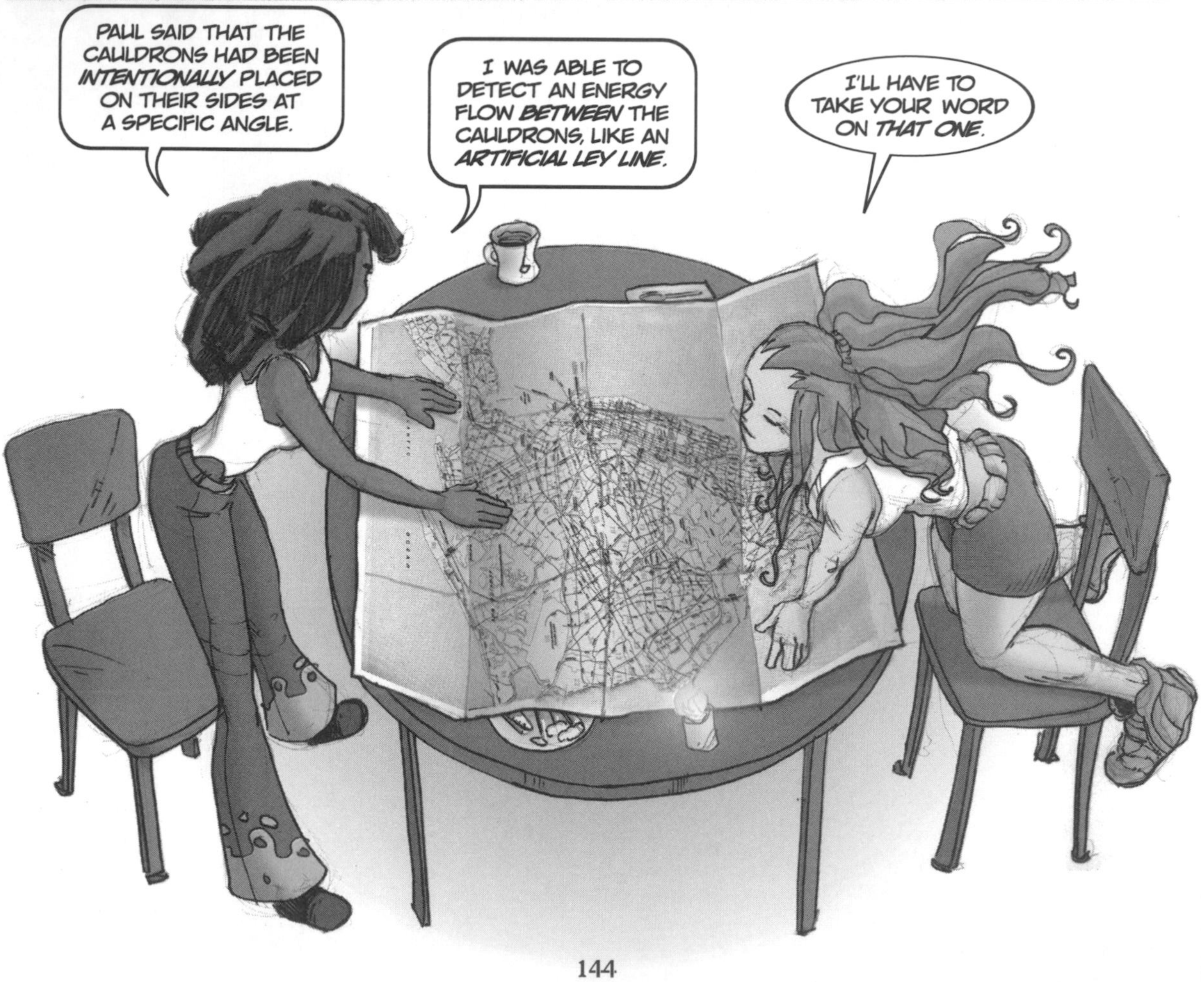
PAUL SAID THAT THE CAULDRONS HAD BEEN INTENTIONALLY PLACED ON THEIR SIDES AT A SPECIFIC ANGLE.
I WAS ABLE TO DETECT AN ENERGY FLOW BETWEEN THE CAULDRONS, LIKE AN ARTIFICIAL LEY LINE.
I'LL HAVE TO TAKE YOUR WORD ON THAT ONE.

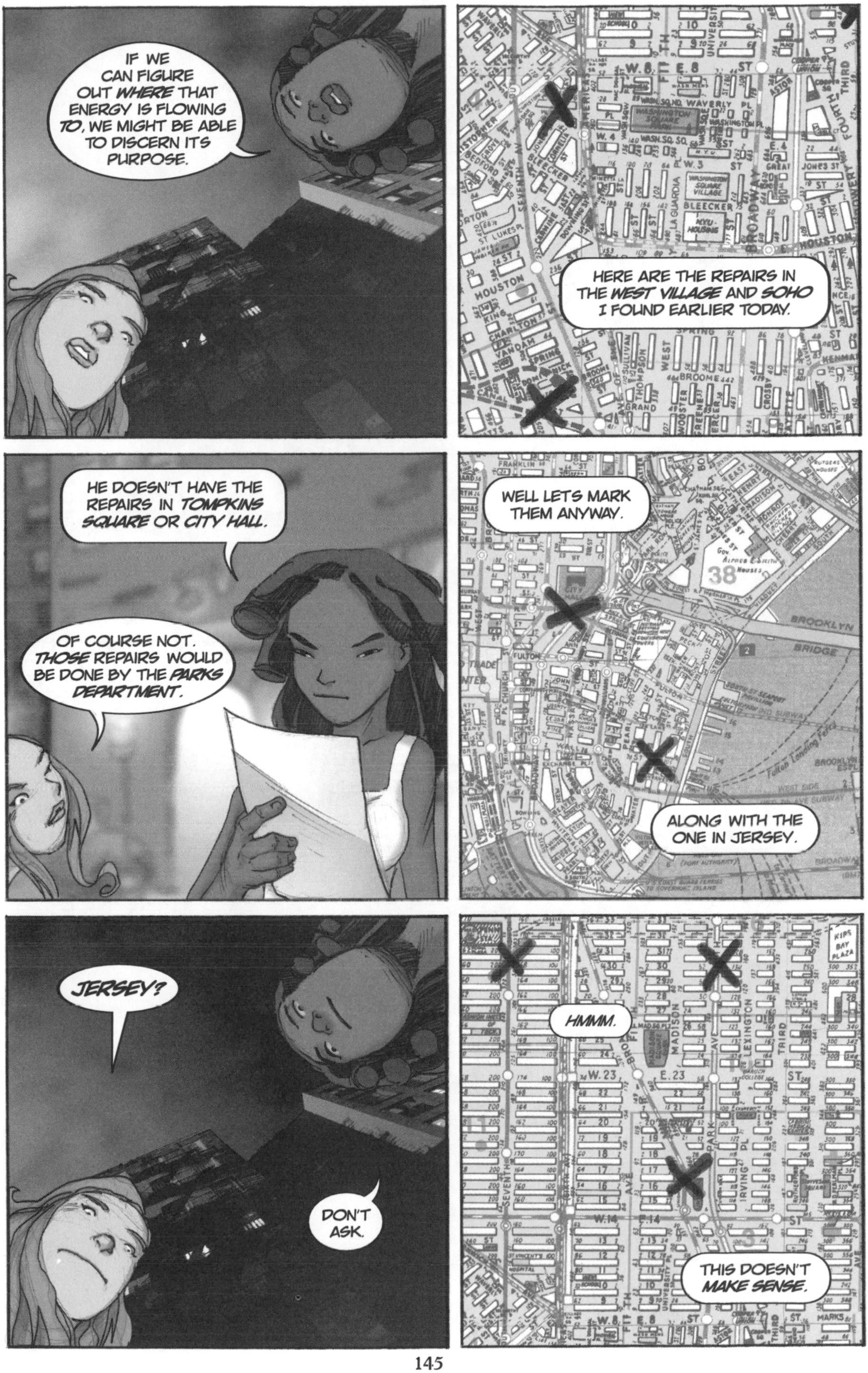
IF WE CAN FIGURE OUT WHERE THAT ENERGY IS FLOWING TO, WE MIGHT BE ABLE TO DISCERN ITS PURPOSE.
HERE ARE THE REPAIRS IN THE WEST VILLAGE AND SOHO I FOUND EARLIER TODAY.
HE DOESN'T HAVE THE REPAIRS IN TOMPKINS SQUARE OR CITY HALL.
OF COURSE NOT. THOSE REPAIRS WOULD BE DONE BY THE PARKS DEPARTMENT.
WELL LETS MARK THEM ANYWAY.
ALONG WITH THE ONE IN JERSEY.
JERSEY?
DON'T ASK.
HMMM.
THIS DOESN'T MAKE SENSE.

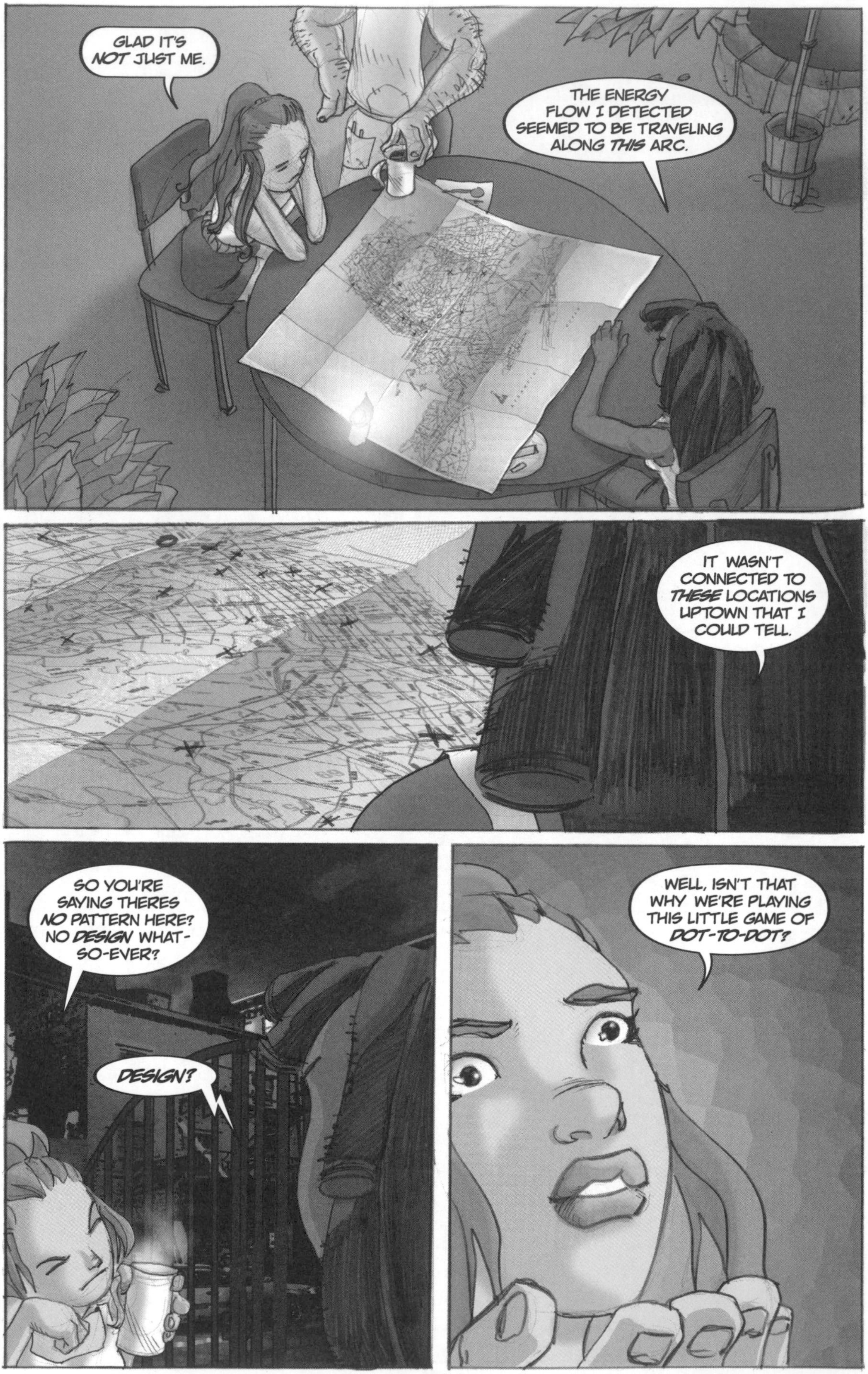
GLAD IT'S NOT JUST ME.
THE ENERGY FLOW I DETECTED SEEMED TO BE TRAVELING ALONG THIS ARC.
IT WASN'T CONNECTED TO THESE LOCATIONS UPTOWN THAT I COULD TELL.
SO YOU'RE SAYING THERES NO PATTERN HERE? NO DESIGN WHAT-SO-EVER?
DESIGN?
WELL, ISN'T THAT WHY WE'RE PLAYING THIS LITTLE GAME OF DOT-TO-DOT?

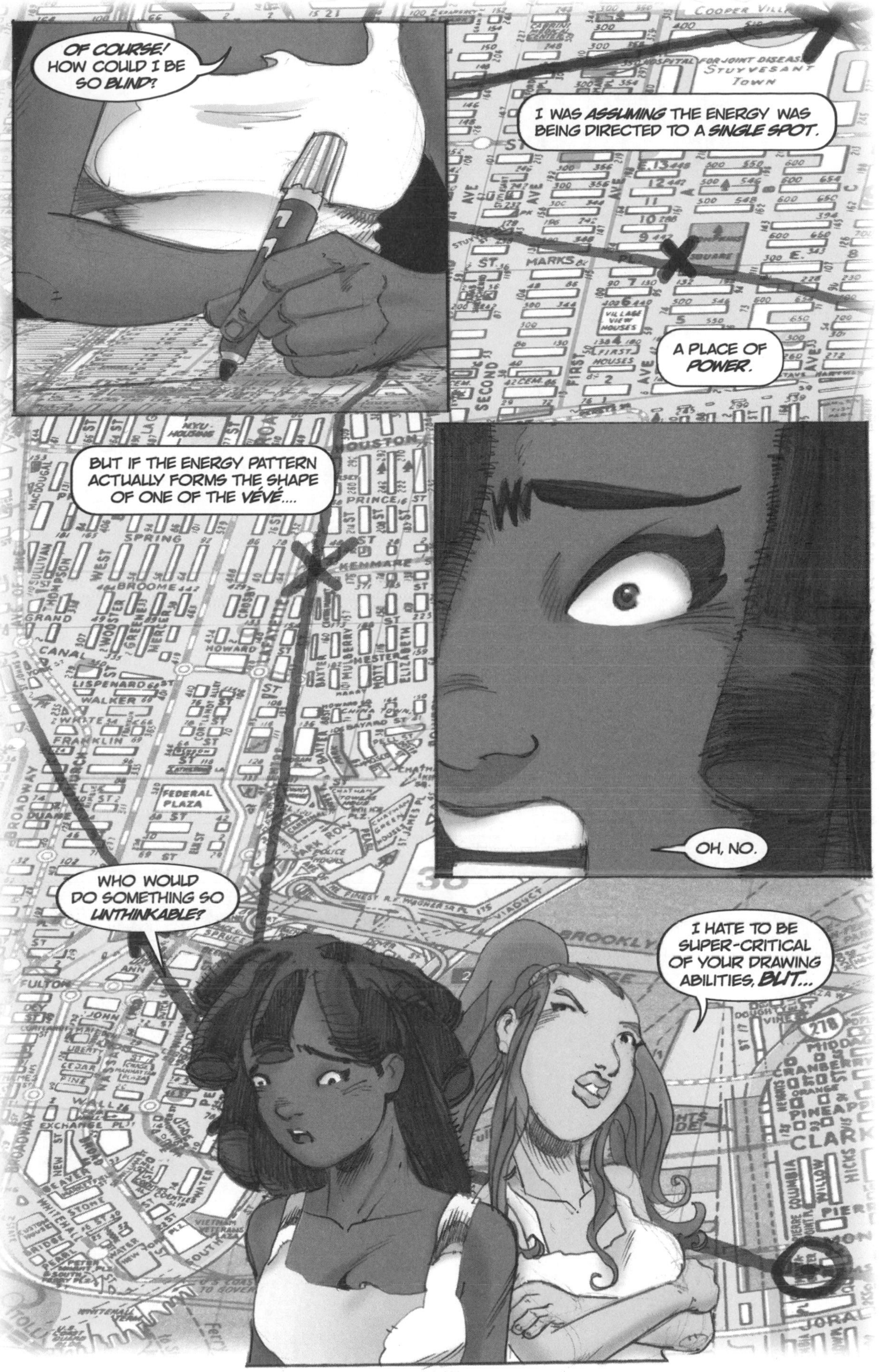
OF COURSE! HOW COULD I BE SO BLIND?
I WAS ASSUMING THE ENERGY WAS BEING DIRECTED TO A SINGLE SPOT.
A PLACE OF POWER.
BUT IF THE ENERGY PATTERN ACTUALLY FORMS THE SHAPE OF ONE OF THE VÉVÉ....
OH, NO.
WHO WOULD DO SOMETHING SO UNTHINKABLE?
I HATE TO BE SUPER-CRITICAL OF YOUR DRAWING ABILITIES, BUT...

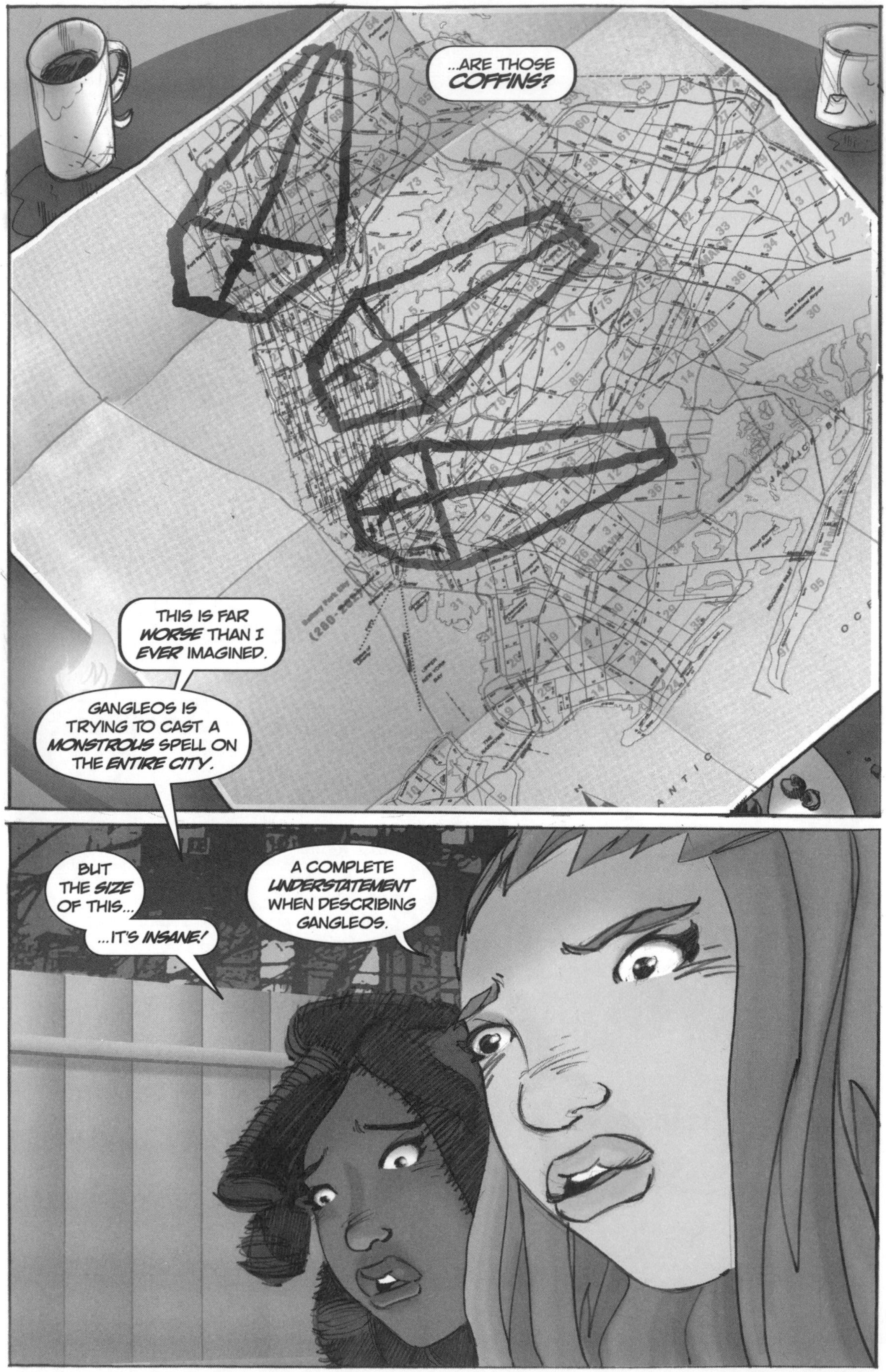
...ARE THOSE *COFFINS?*
THIS IS FAR *WORSE* THAN I *EVER* IMAGINED.
GANGLEOS IS TRYING TO CAST A *MONSTROUS* SPELL ON THE *ENTIRE CITY*.
BUT THE *SIZE* OF THIS...
...IT'S *INSANE!*
A COMPLETE *UNDERSTATEMENT* WHEN DESCRIBING GANGLEOS.

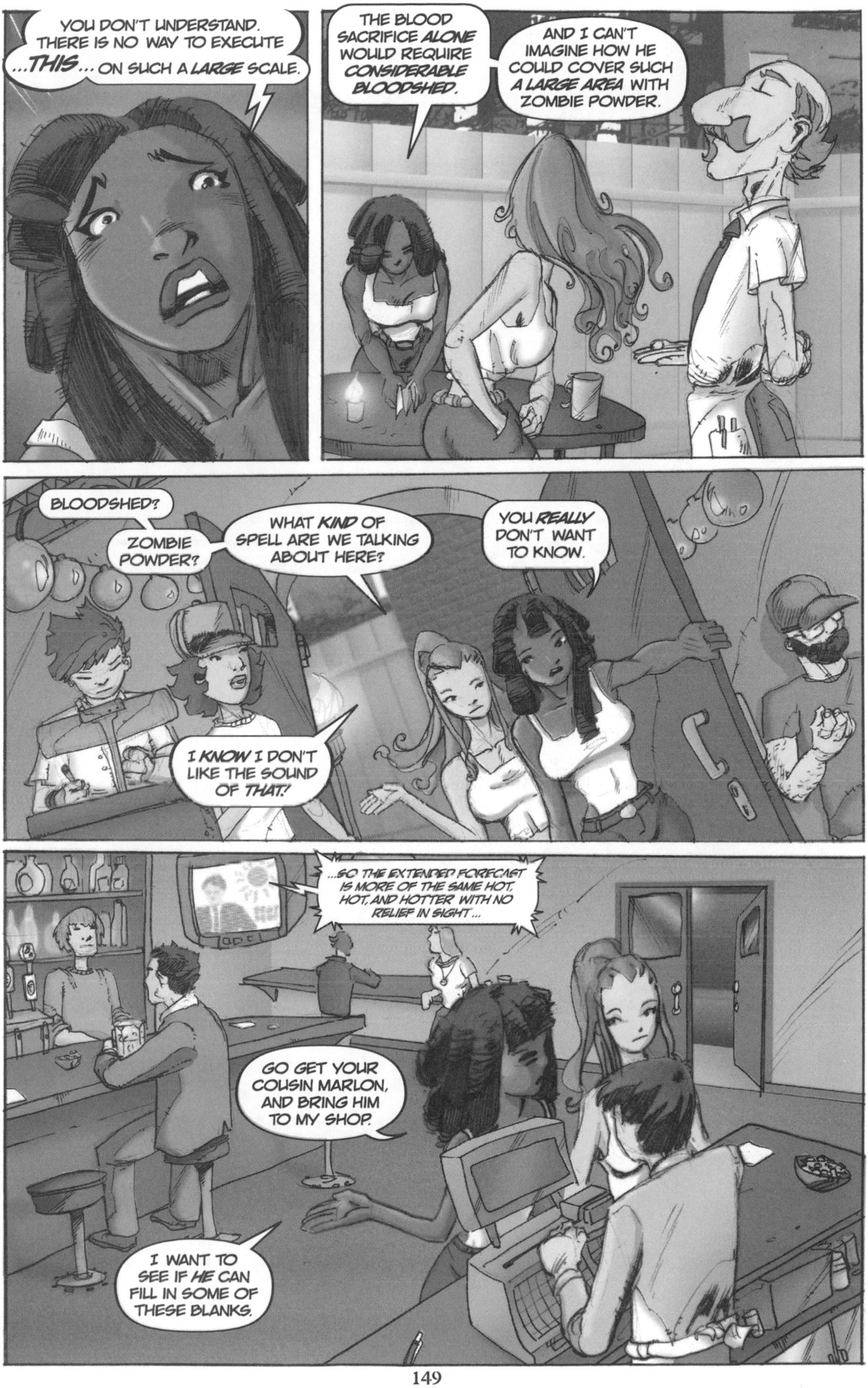

YOU DON'T UNDERSTAND. THERE IS NO WAY TO EXECUTE ...THIS... ON SUCH A LARGE SCALE.
THE BLOOD SACRIFICE ALONE WOULD REQUIRE CONSIDERABLE BLOODSHED.
AND I CAN'T IMAGINE HOW HE COULD COVER SUCH A LARGE AREA WITH ZOMBIE POWDER.
BLOODSHED?
ZOMBIE POWDER?
WHAT KIND OF SPELL ARE WE TALKING ABOUT HERE?
YOU REALLY DON'T WANT TO KNOW.
I KNOW I DON'T LIKE THE SOUND OF THAT!
...SO THE EXTENDED FORECAST IS MORE OF THE SAME HOT, HOT, AND HOTTER WITH NO RELIEF IN SIGHT...
GO GET YOUR COUSIN MARLON, AND BRING HIM TO MY SHOP.
I WANT TO SEE IF HE CAN FILL IN SOME OF THESE BLANKS.

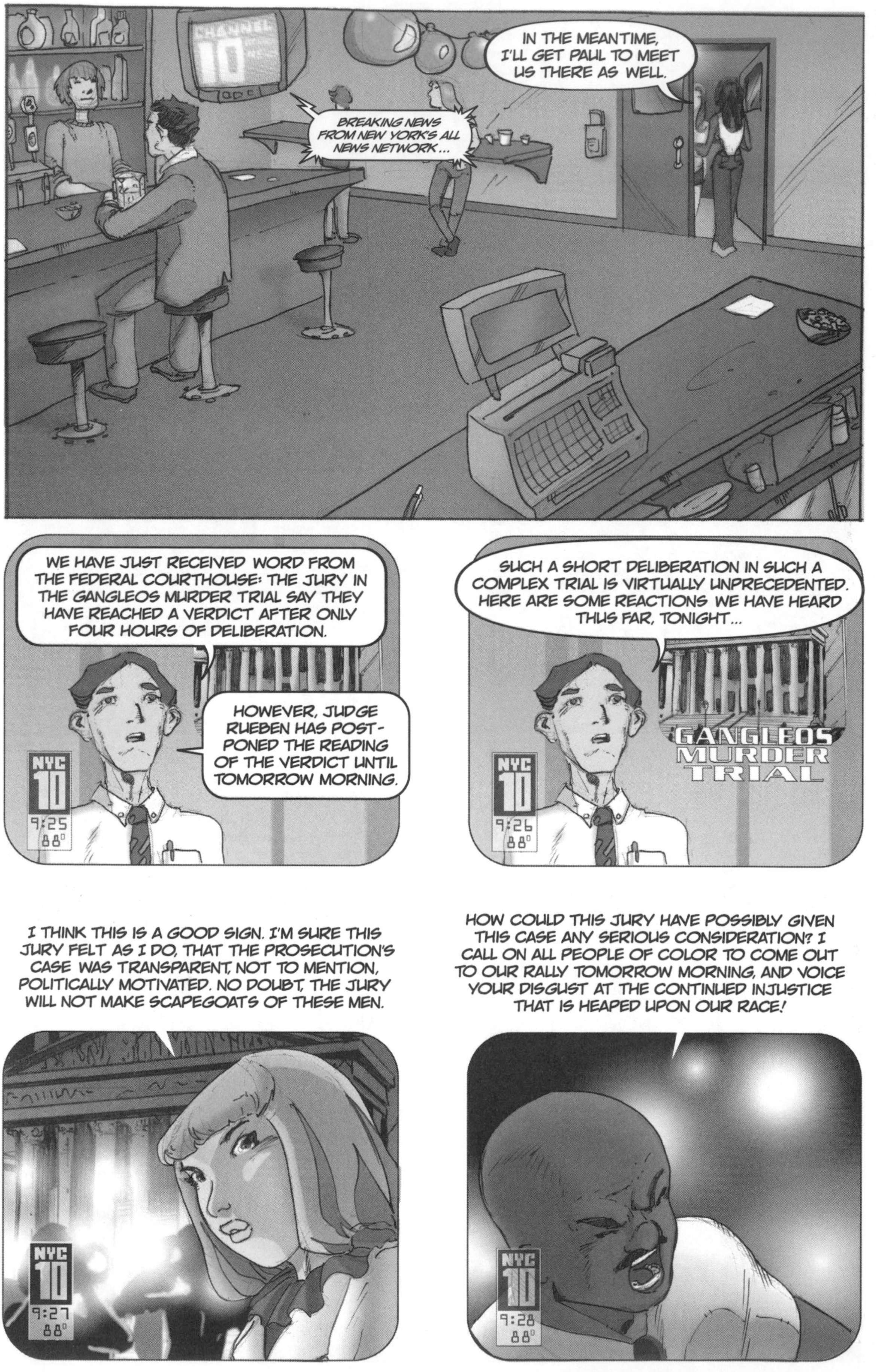
IN THE MEANTIME, I'LL GET PAUL TO MEET US THERE AS WELL.
BREAKING NEWS FROM NEW YORK'S ALL NEWS NETWORK...
WE HAVE JUST RECEIVED WORD FROM THE FEDERAL COURTHOUSE: THE JURY IN THE GANGLEOS MURDER TRIAL SAY THEY HAVE REACHED A VERDICT AFTER ONLY FOUR HOURS OF DELIBERATION.
HOWEVER, JUDGE RUEBEN HAS POST-PONED THE READING OF THE VERDICT UNTIL TOMORROW MORNING.
NYC 10 9:25 88°
SUCH A SHORT DELIBERATION IN SUCH A COMPLEX TRIAL IS VIRTUALLY UNPRECEDENTED. HERE ARE SOME REACTIONS WE HAVE HEARD THUS FAR, TONIGHT...
GANGLEOS MURDER TRIAL
NYC 10 9:26 88°
I THINK THIS IS A GOOD SIGN. I'M SURE THIS JURY FELT AS I DO, THAT THE PROSECUTION'S CASE WAS TRANSPARENT, NOT TO MENTION, POLITICALLY MOTIVATED. NO DOUBT, THE JURY WILL NOT MAKE SCAPEGOATS OF THESE MEN.
NYC 10 9:27 88°
HOW COULD THIS JURY HAVE POSSIBLY GIVEN THIS CASE ANY SERIOUS CONSIDERATION? I CALL ON ALL PEOPLE OF COLOR TO COME OUT TO OUR RALLY TOMORROW MORNING, AND VOICE YOUR DISGUST AT THE CONTINUED INJUSTICE THAT IS HEAPED UPON OUR RACE!
NYC 10 9:28 88°

CONSIDERING THE ACCUSATIONS THAT HAVE BEEN BANDIED ABOUT TONIGHT, WE ARE SUSPENDING THE ASSEMBLY PERMIT GRANTED TO REVEREND SHEFIELD, SO AS TO AVOID ANY FURTHER ESCALATION OF TENSIONS.

ANYONE WHO ASSEMBLES UNLAWFULLY *WILL BE INCARCERATED.*

BONEHEAD!

THAT'S A SURE WAY TO GET THE ENTIRE CITY OUT THERE MARCHING WITH SHEFIELD.

BRiiiANG

HELLO?

PAUL!

THIS IS RENE.

I NEED YOU TO COME OVER TO MY SHOP RIGHT AWAY.

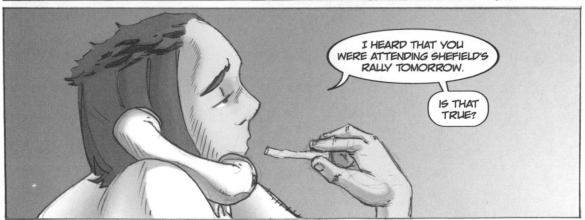

I HEARD THAT YOU WERE ATTENDING SHEFIELD'S RALLY TOMORROW.

IS THAT TRUE?

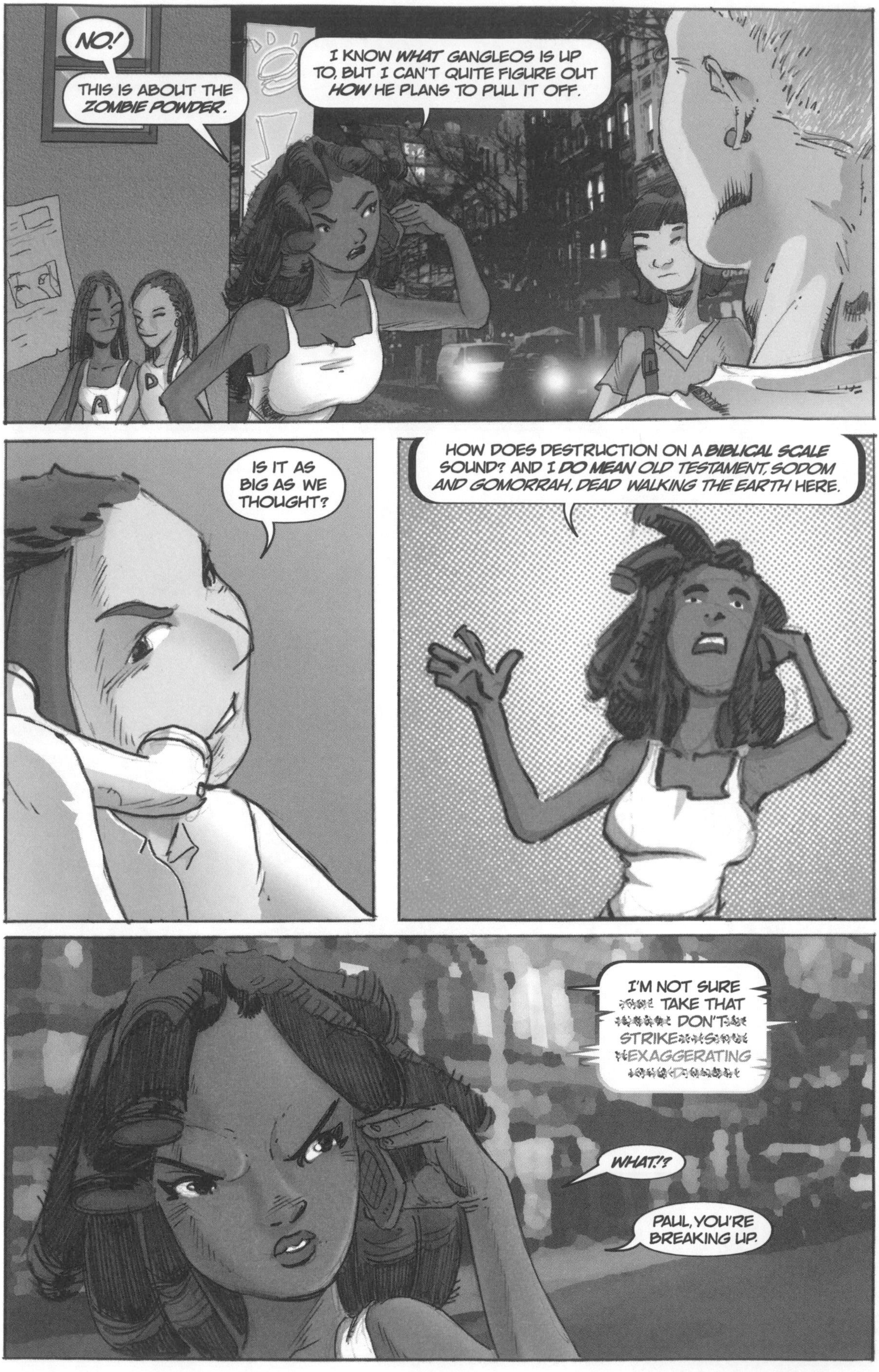
NO!
THIS IS ABOUT THE ZOMBIE POWDER.
I KNOW WHAT GANGLEOS IS UP TO, BUT I CAN'T QUITE FIGURE OUT HOW HE PLANS TO PULL IT OFF.
IS IT AS BIG AS WE THOUGHT?
HOW DOES DESTRUCTION ON A BIBLICAL SCALE SOUND? AND I DO MEAN OLD TESTAMENT, SODOM AND GOMORRAH, DEAD WALKING THE EARTH HERE.
I'M NOT SURE
TAKE THAT
DON'T
STRIKE
EXAGGERATING
WHAT!?
PAUL, YOU'RE BREAKING UP.

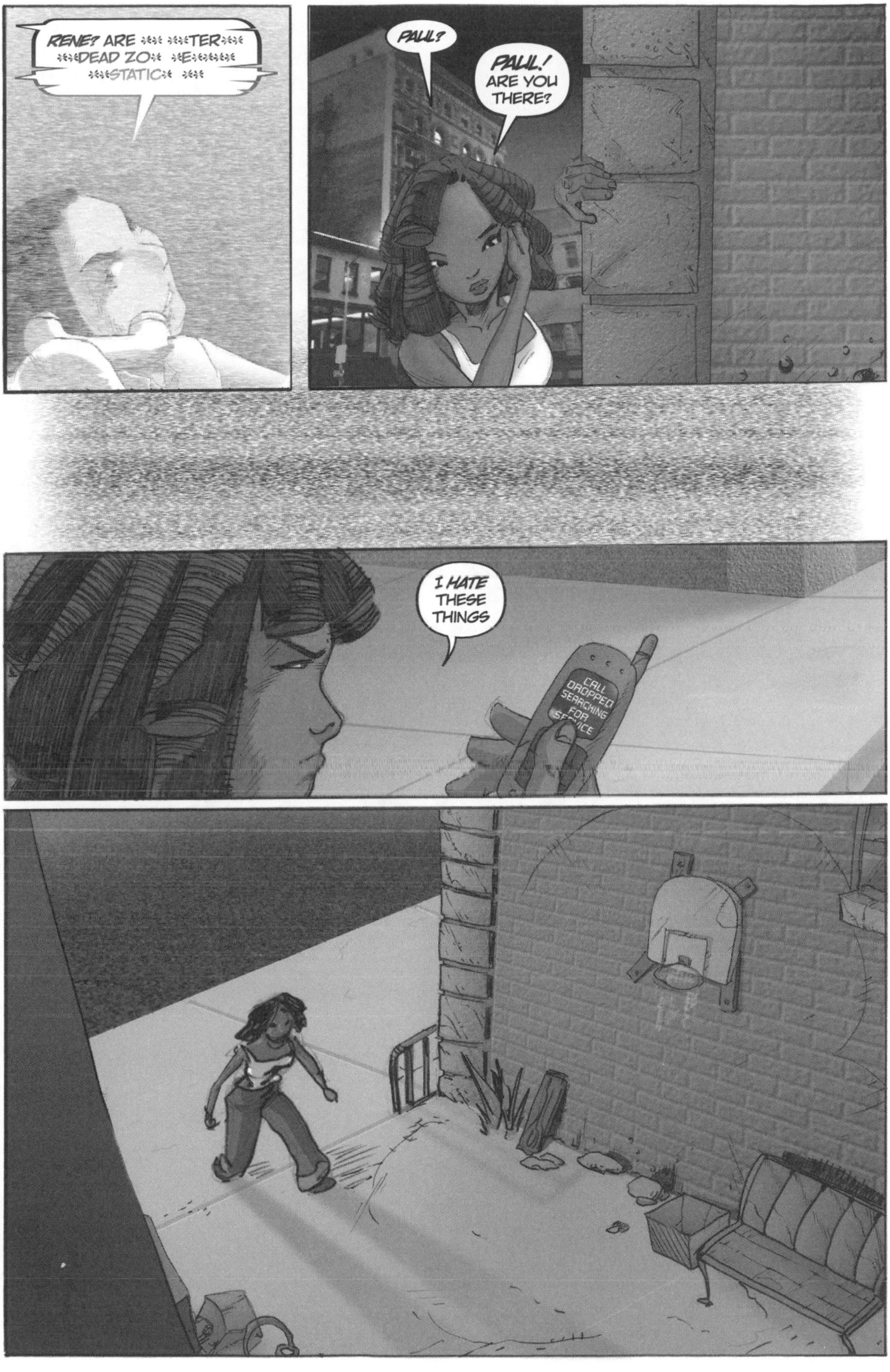
RENE? ARE ⁂ ⁂TER ⁂DEAD ZO⁂ ⁂E⁂ ⁂STATIC⁂ ⁂
PAUL?
PAUL! ARE YOU THERE?
I HATE THESE THINGS
CALL DROPPED SEARCHING FOR SERVICE

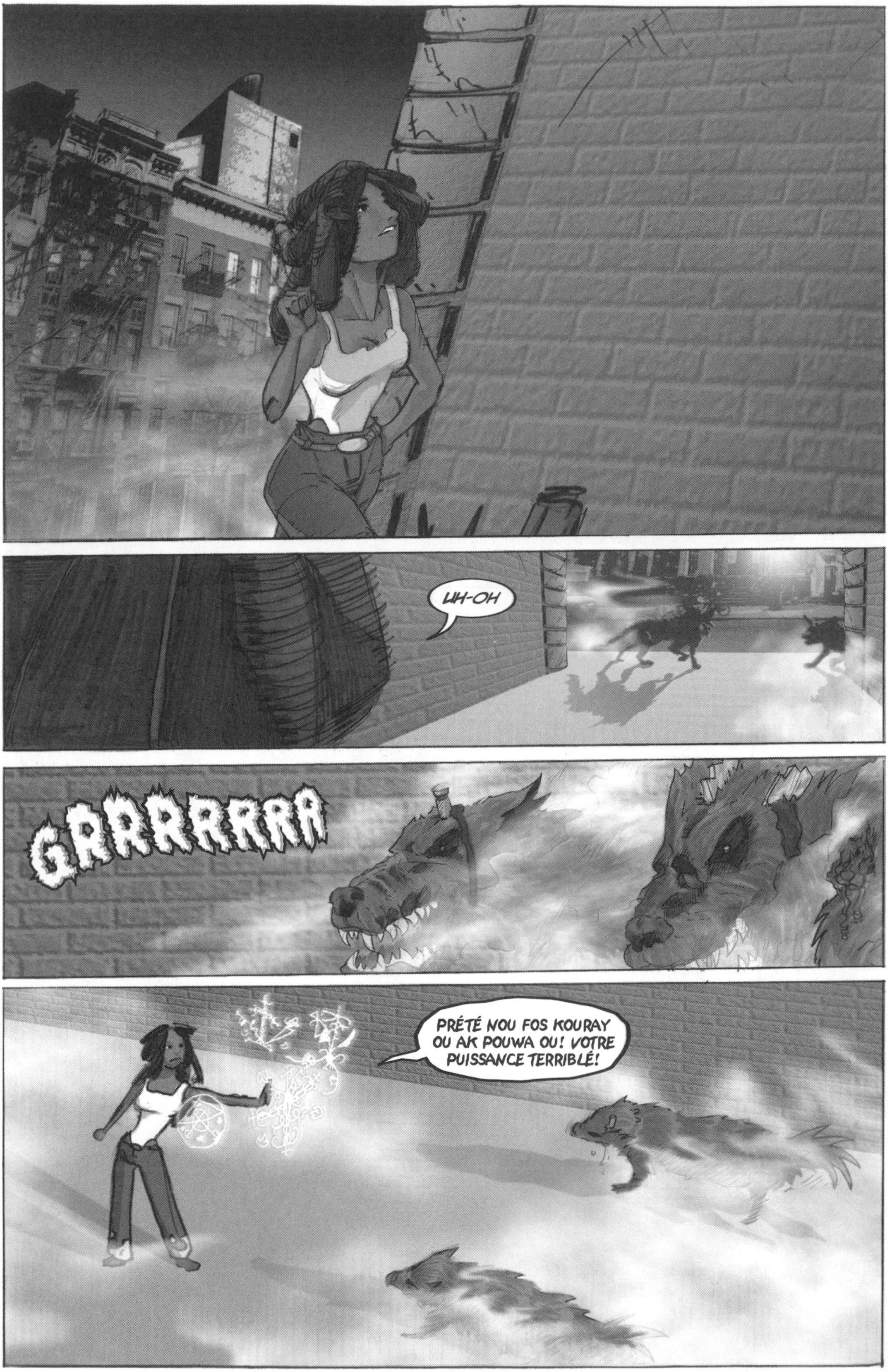
UH-OH
GARRRRRA
PRÉTÉ NOU FOS KOURAY OU AK POUWA OU! VOTRE PUISSANCE TERRIBLÉ!

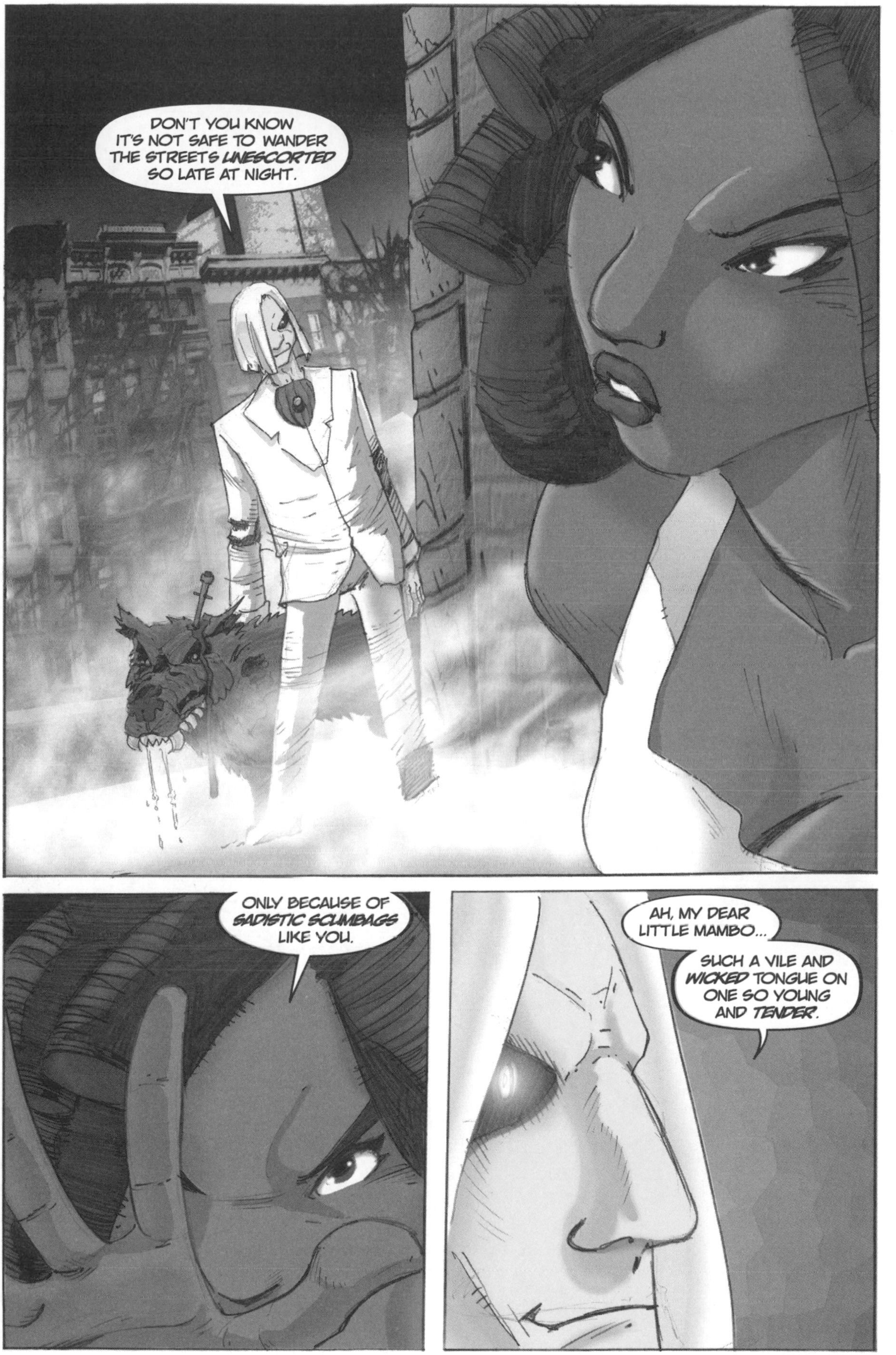
DON'T YOU KNOW IT'S NOT SAFE TO WANDER THE STREETS *UNESCORTED* SO LATE AT NIGHT.
ONLY BECAUSE OF *SADISTIC SCUMBAGS* LIKE YOU.
AH, MY DEAR LITTLE MAMBO...
SUCH A VILE AND *WICKED* TONGUE ON ONE SO YOUNG AND *TENDER*.

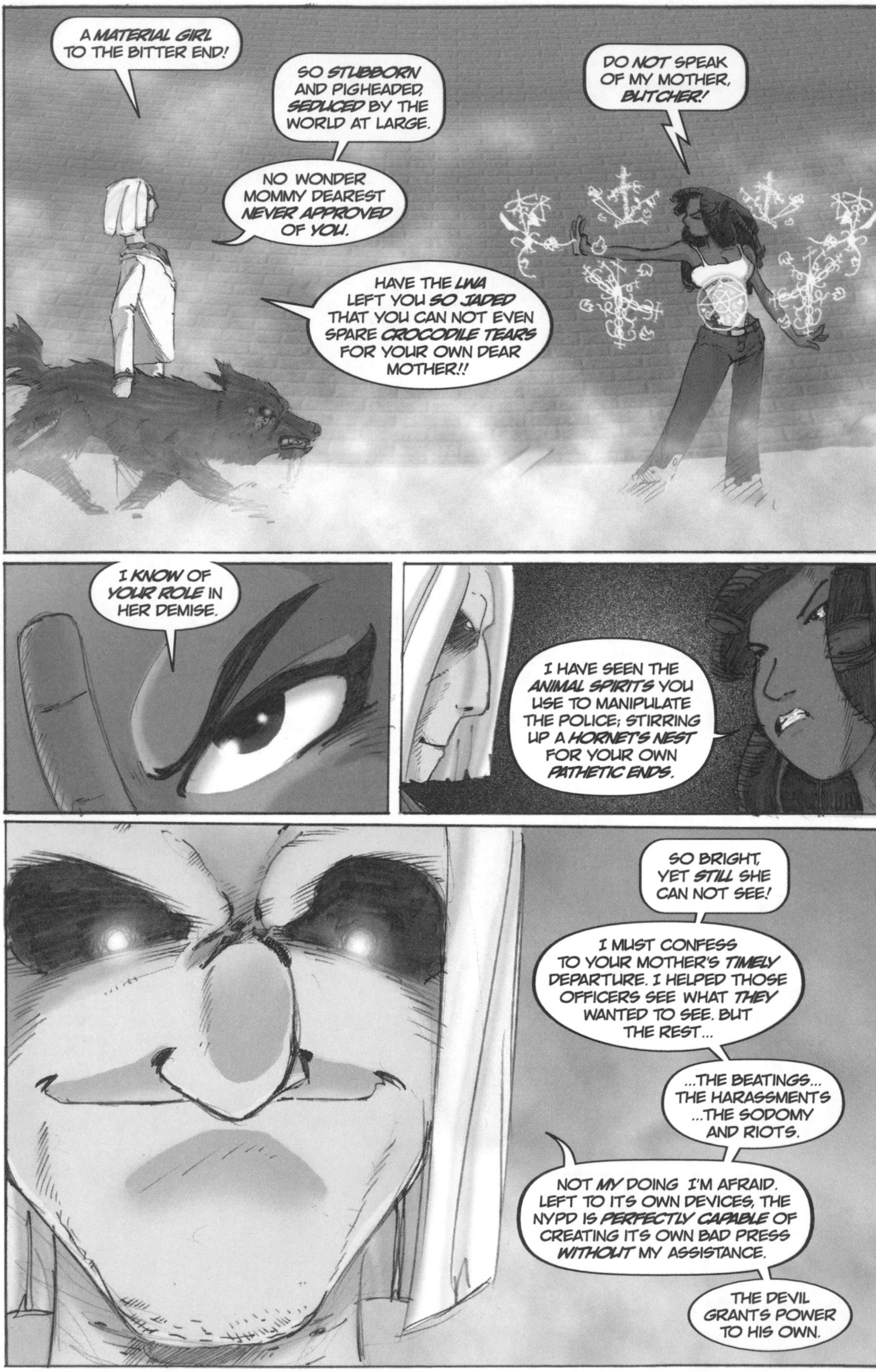
A MATERIAL GIRL TO THE BITTER END!
SO STUBBORN AND PIGHEADED, SEDUCED BY THE WORLD AT LARGE.
NO WONDER MOMMY DEAREST NEVER APPROVED OF YOU.
DO NOT SPEAK OF MY MOTHER, BUTCHER!
HAVE THE LWA LEFT YOU SO JADED THAT YOU CAN NOT EVEN SPARE CROCODILE TEARS FOR YOUR OWN DEAR MOTHER!!
I KNOW OF YOUR ROLE IN HER DEMISE.
I HAVE SEEN THE ANIMAL SPIRITS YOU USE TO MANIPULATE THE POLICE; STIRRING UP A HORNET'S NEST FOR YOUR OWN PATHETIC ENDS.
SO BRIGHT, YET STILL SHE CAN NOT SEE!
I MUST CONFESS TO YOUR MOTHER'S TIMELY DEPARTURE. I HELPED THOSE OFFICERS SEE WHAT THEY WANTED TO SEE. BUT THE REST...
...THE BEATINGS... THE HARASSMENTS ...THE SODOMY AND RIOTS.
NOT MY DOING I'M AFRAID. LEFT TO ITS OWN DEVICES, THE NYPD IS PERFECTLY CAPABLE OF CREATING ITS OWN BAD PRESS WITHOUT MY ASSISTANCE.
THE DEVIL GRANTS POWER TO HIS OWN.

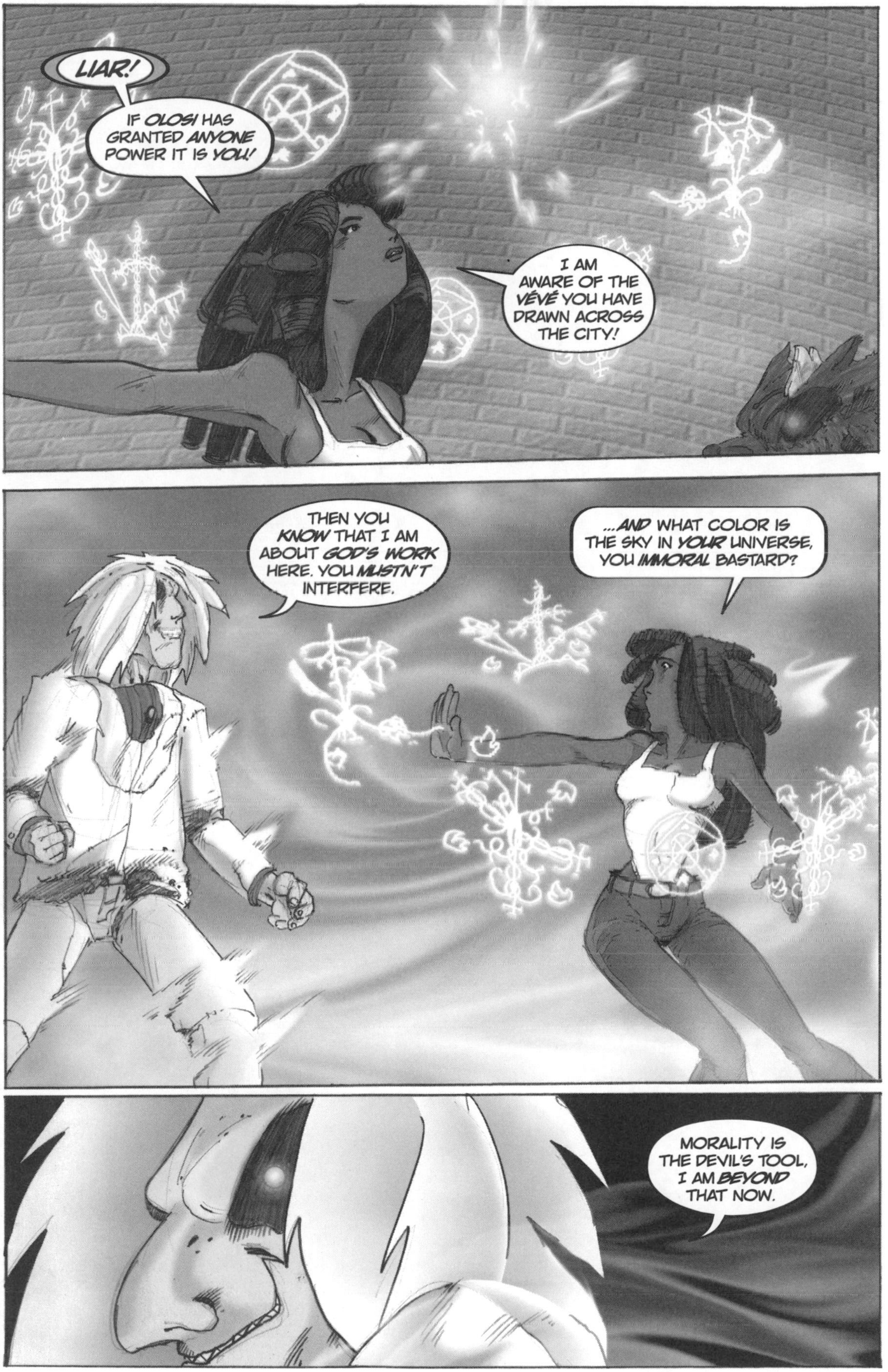
LIAR!
IF OLOSI HAS GRANTED ANYONE POWER IT IS YOU!
I AM AWARE OF THE VÉVÉ YOU HAVE DRAWN ACROSS THE CITY!
THEN YOU KNOW THAT I AM ABOUT GOD'S WORK HERE. YOU MUSTN'T INTERFERE.
...AND WHAT COLOR IS THE SKY IN YOUR UNIVERSE, YOU IMMORAL BASTARD?
MORALITY IS THE DEVIL'S TOOL, I AM BEYOND THAT NOW.

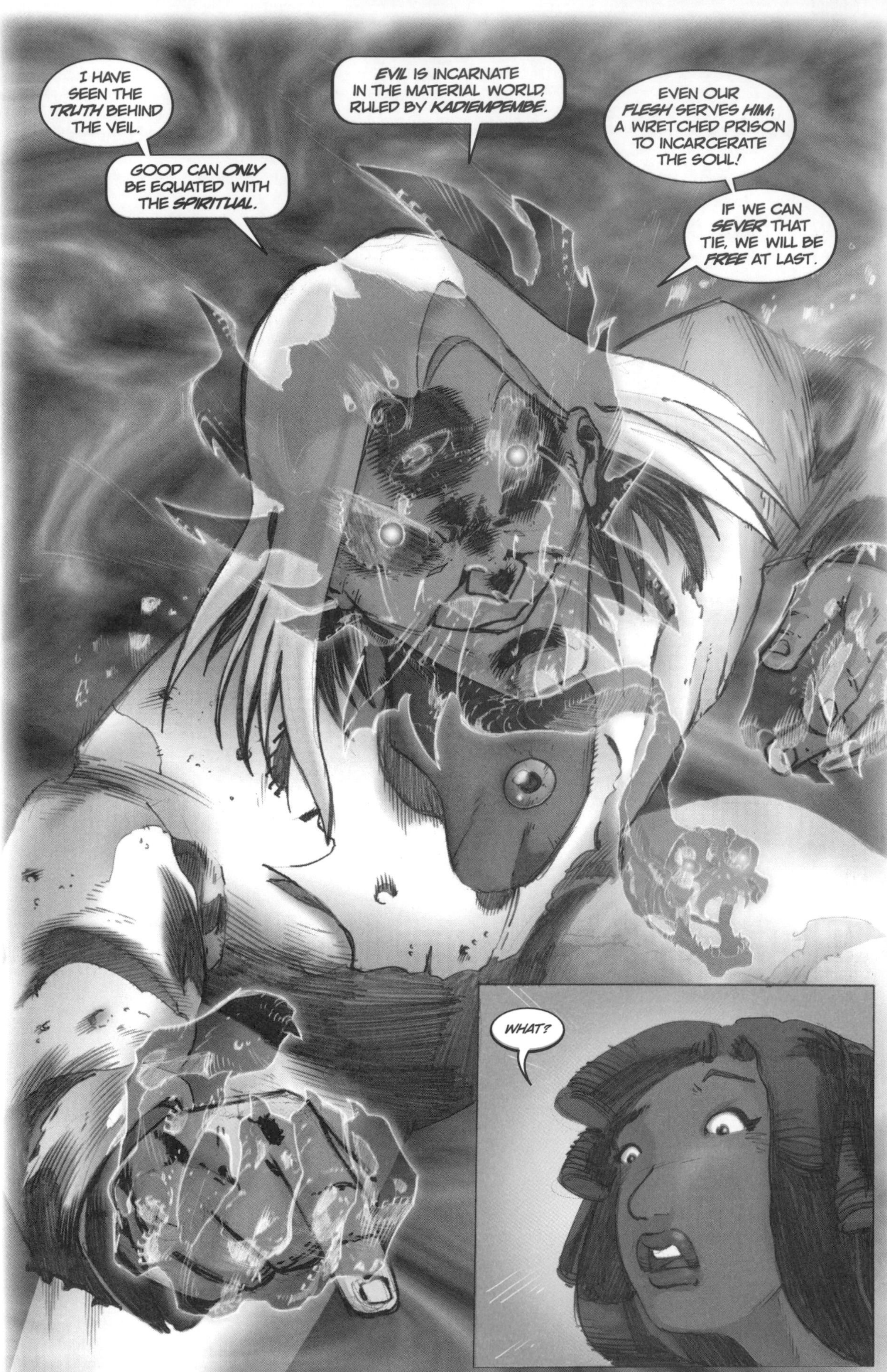
I HAVE SEEN THE TRUTH BEHIND THE VEIL.
GOOD CAN ONLY BE EQUATED WITH THE SPIRITUAL.
EVIL IS INCARNATE IN THE MATERIAL WORLD, RULED BY KADIEMPEMBE.
EVEN OUR FLESH SERVES HIM; A WRETCHED PRISON TO INCARCERATE THE SOUL!
IF WE CAN SEVER THAT TIE, WE WILL BE FREE AT LAST.
WHAT?

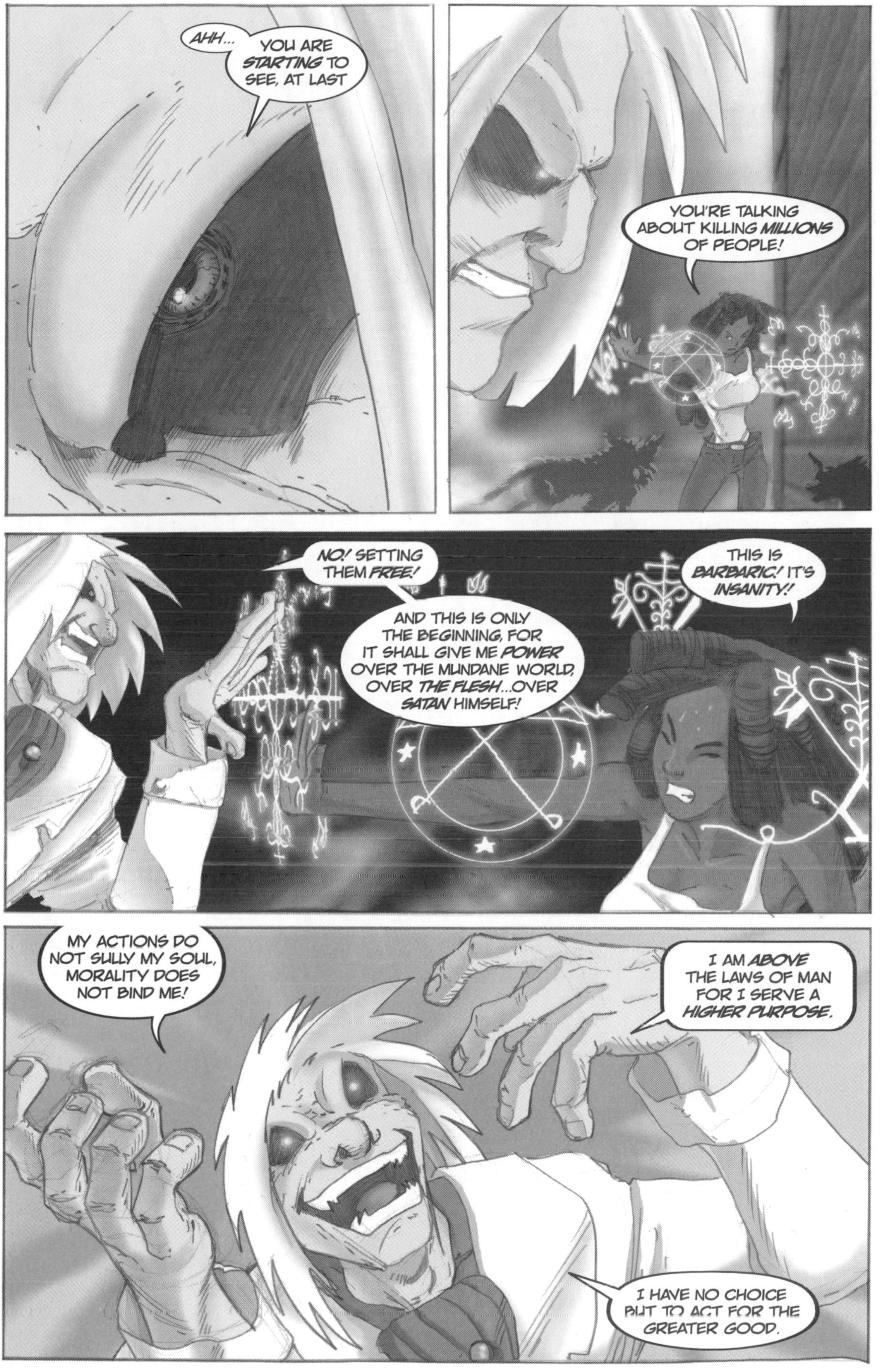
AHH...
YOU ARE STARTING TO SEE, AT LAST
YOU'RE TALKING ABOUT KILLING MILLIONS OF PEOPLE!
NO! SETTING THEM FREE!
AND THIS IS ONLY THE BEGINNING, FOR IT SHALL GIVE ME POWER OVER THE MUNDANE WORLD, OVER THE FLESH...OVER SATAN HIMSELF!
THIS IS BARBARIC! IT'S INSANITY!
MY ACTIONS DO NOT SULLY MY SOUL, MORALITY DOES NOT BIND ME!
I AM ABOVE THE LAWS OF MAN FOR I SERVE A HIGHER PURPOSE.
I HAVE NO CHOICE BUT TO ACT FOR THE GREATER GOOD.

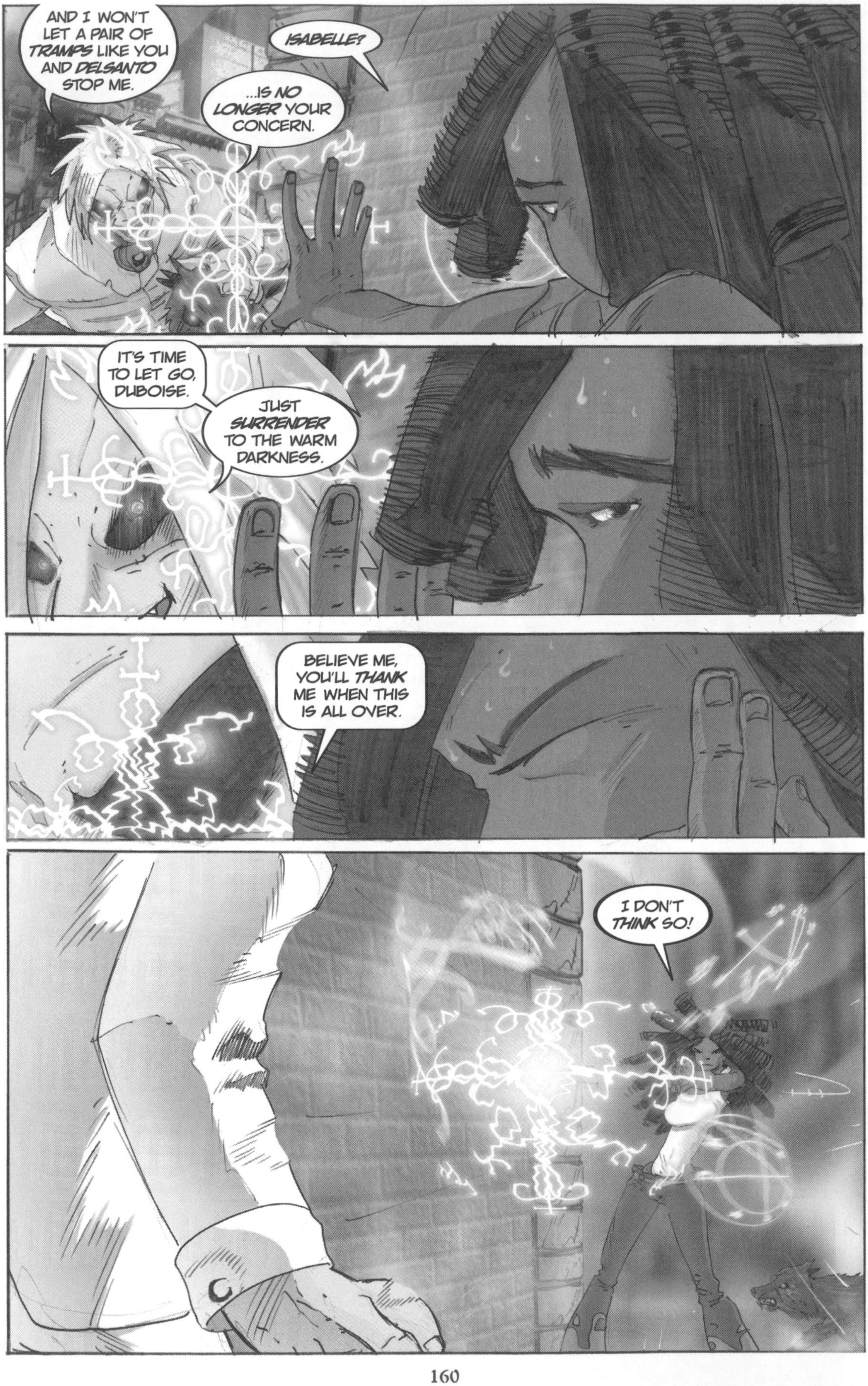
AND I WON'T LET A PAIR OF TRAMPS LIKE YOU AND DELSANTO STOP ME.
ISABELLE?
...IS NO LONGER YOUR CONCERN.
IT'S TIME TO LET GO, DUBOISE.
JUST SURRENDER TO THE WARM DARKNESS.
BELIEVE ME, YOU'LL THANK ME WHEN THIS IS ALL OVER.
I DON'T THINK SO!

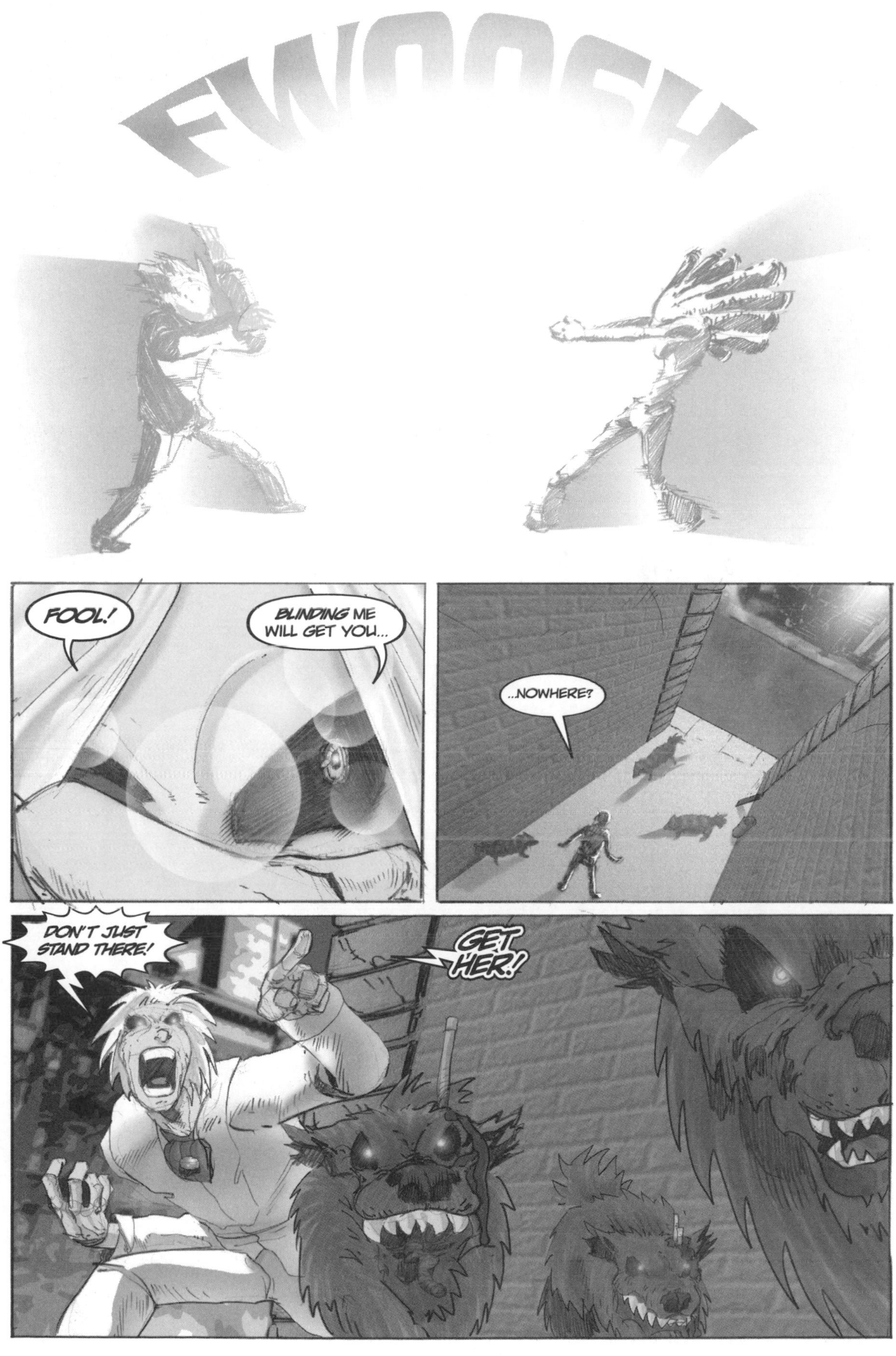
FWOOSH
FOOL!
BLINDING ME WILL GET YOU...
...NOWHERE?
DON'T JUST STAND THERE!
GET HER!

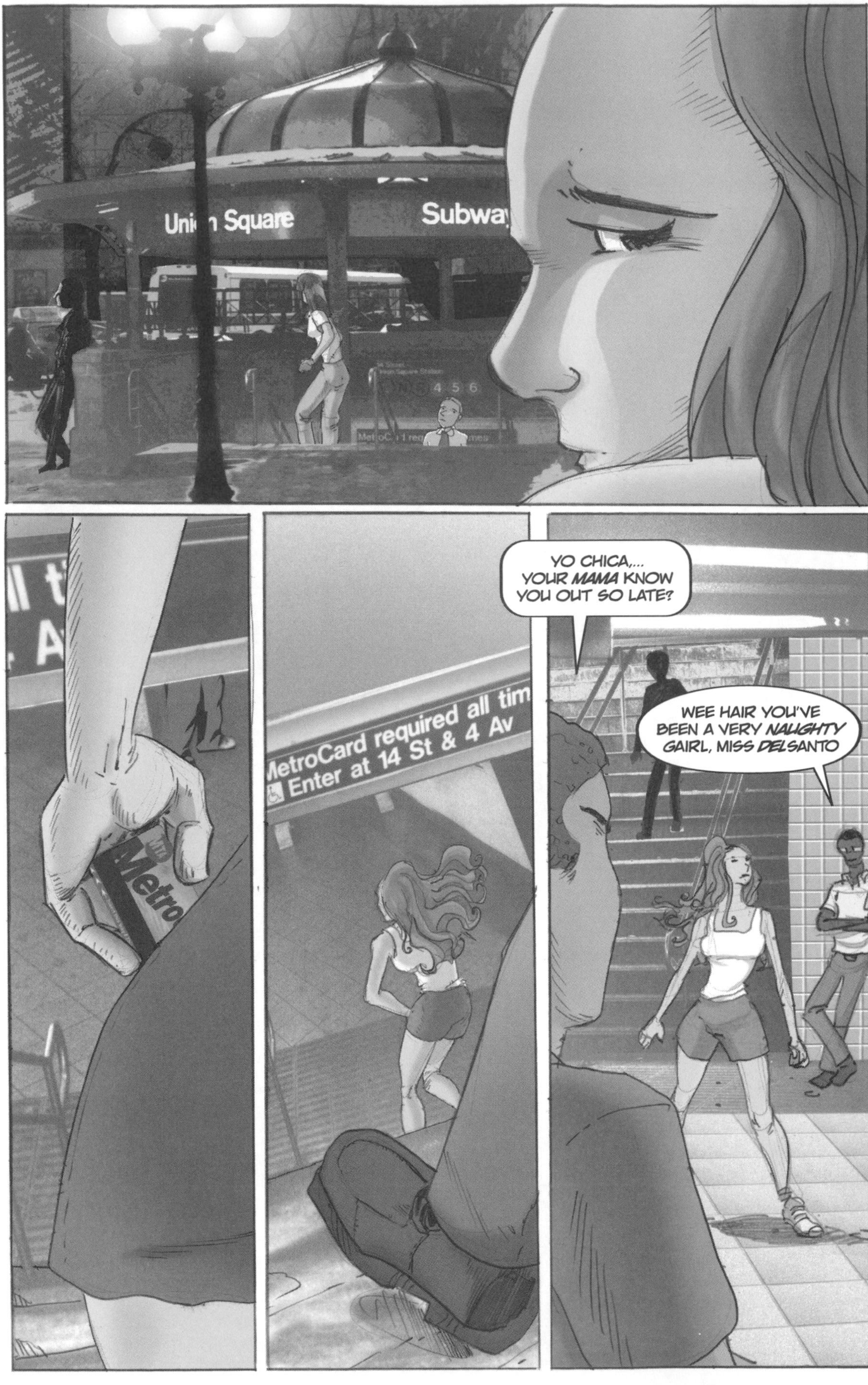
Union Square
Subway
MetroCard required all tim
Enter at 14 St & 4 Av
YO CHICA,... YOUR MAMA KNOW YOU OUT SO LATE?
WEE HAIR YOU'VE BEEN A VERY NAUGHTY GAIRL, MISS DELSANTO

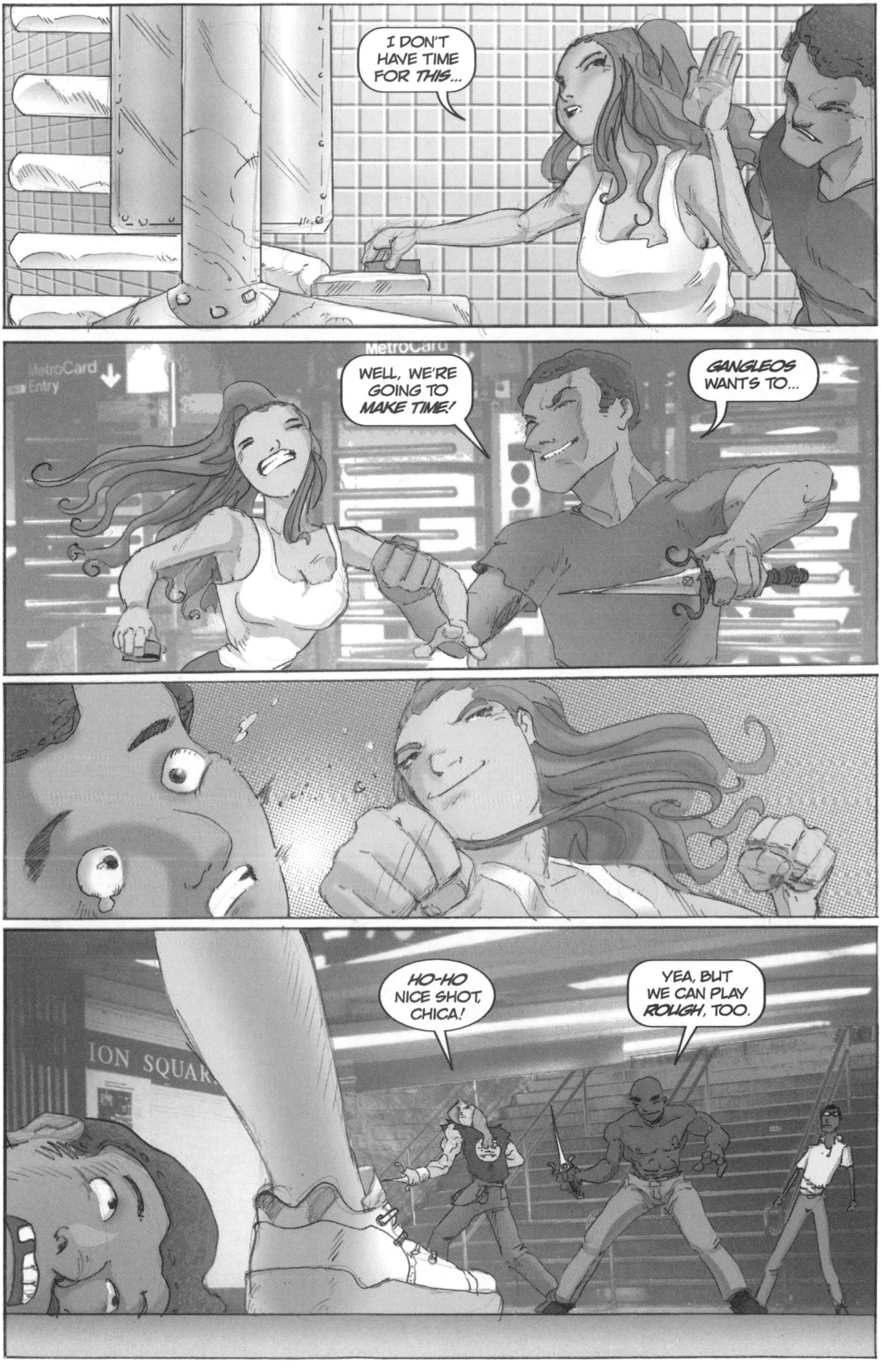
I DON'T HAVE TIME FOR *THIS*...
WELL, WE'RE GOING TO *MAKE TIME!*
GANGLEOS WANTS TO...
MetroCard
MetroCard Entry
HO-HO NICE SHOT, CHICA!
YEA, BUT WE CAN PLAY *ROUGH*, TOO.
ION SQUAR

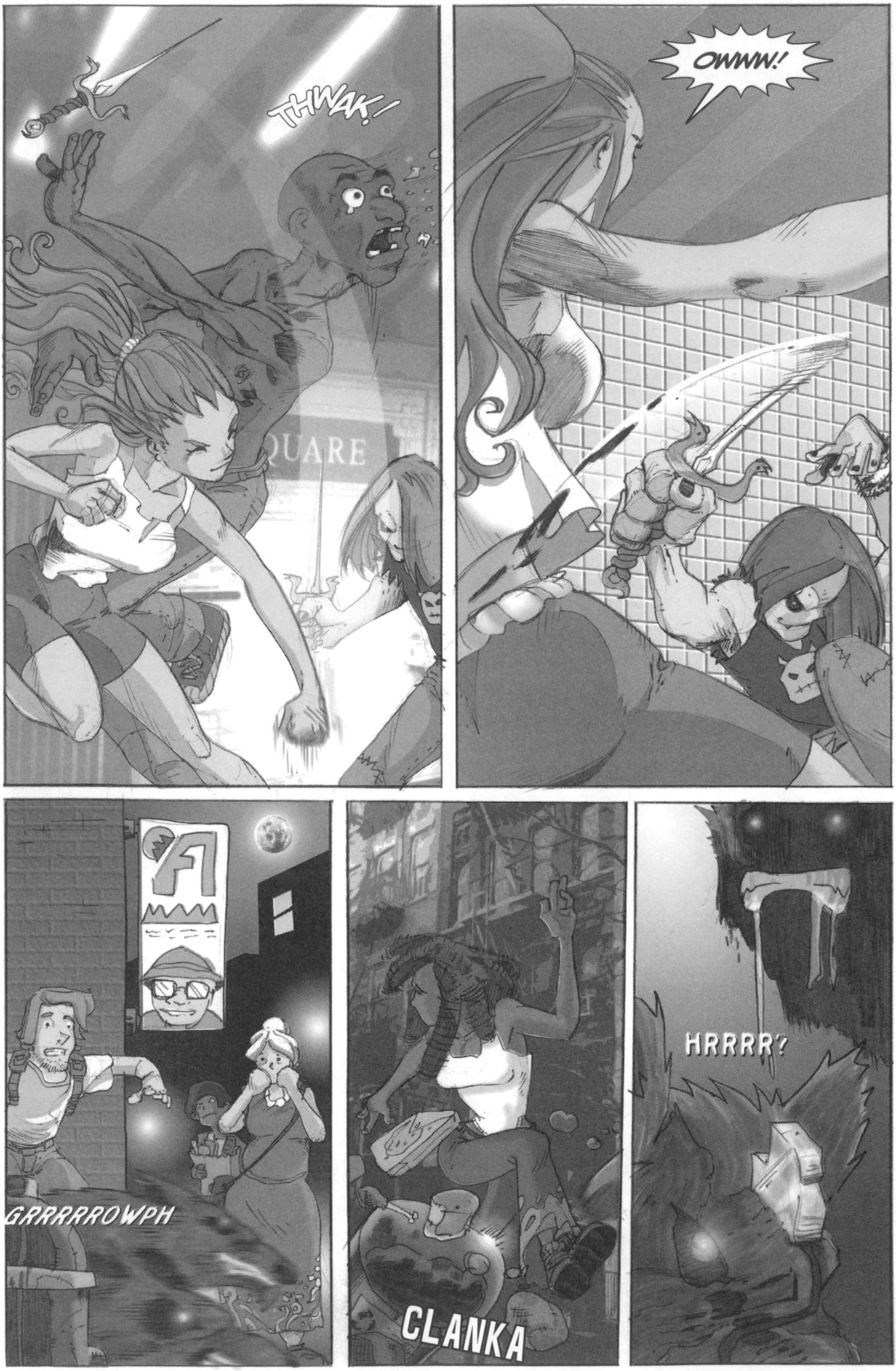
THWAK!
QUARE
OWWW!
GRRRRROWPH
CLANKA
HRRRR?

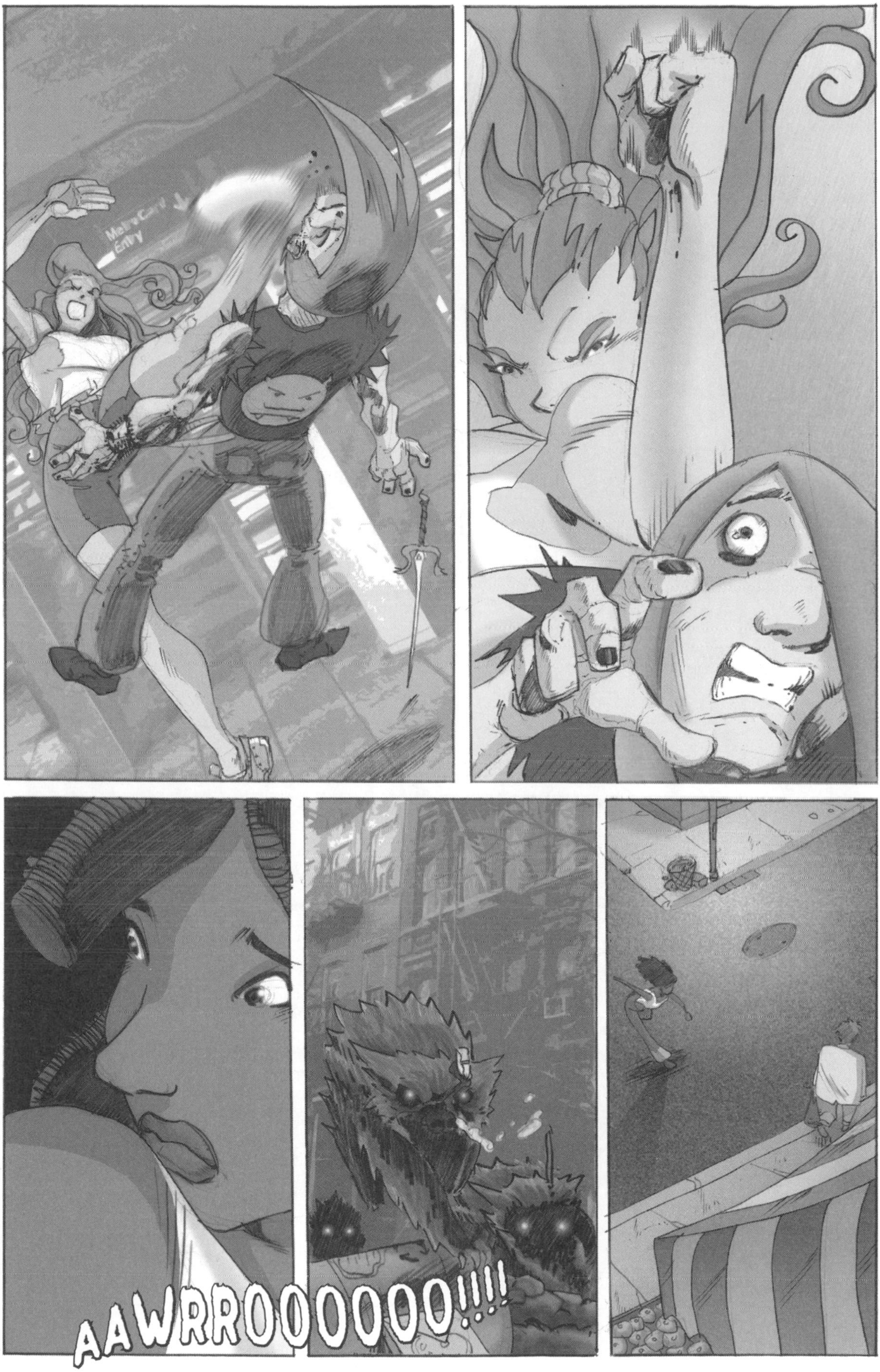
AAWRROOOOOO!!!!

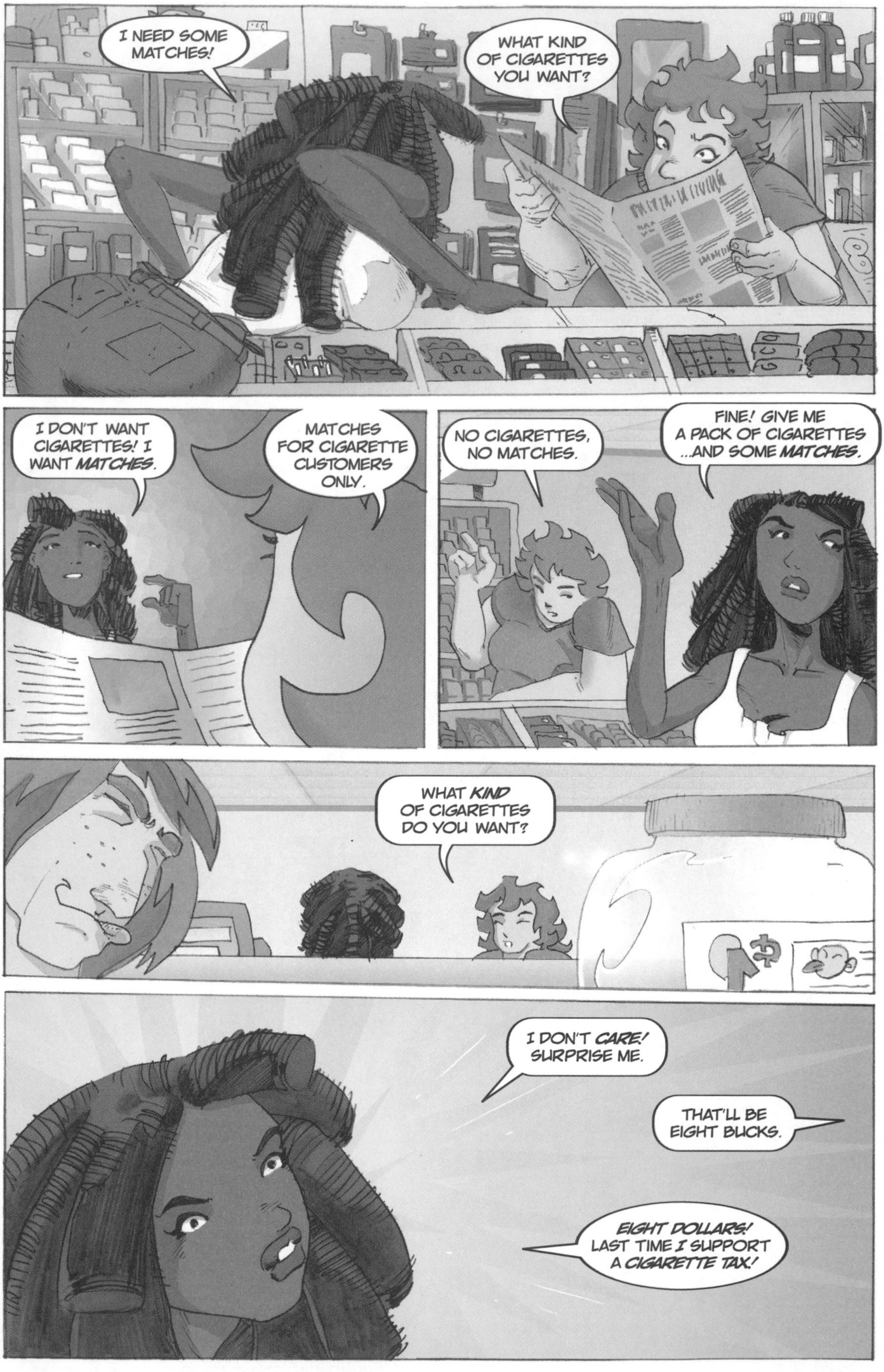
I NEED SOME MATCHES!
WHAT KIND OF CIGARETTES YOU WANT?
I DON'T WANT CIGARETTES! I WANT MATCHES.
MATCHES FOR CIGARETTE CUSTOMERS ONLY.
NO CIGARETTES, NO MATCHES.
FINE! GIVE ME A PACK OF CIGARETTES ...AND SOME MATCHES.
WHAT KIND OF CIGARETTES DO YOU WANT?
I DON'T CARE! SURPRISE ME.
THAT'LL BE EIGHT BUCKS.
EIGHT DOLLARS! LAST TIME I SUPPORT A CIGARETTE TAX!

YOU GOT I.D.?

WHAT?

MUST BE 18 TO BUY CIGARETTES

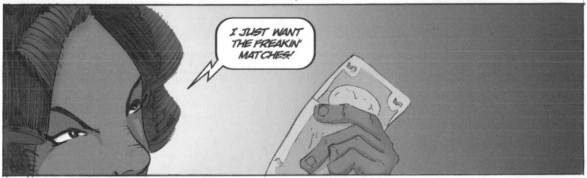

I JUST WANT THE FREAKIN' MATCHES!

DON'T YOU *RAISE YOUR VOICE* TO ME YOUNG LADY!

THIS IS *MY SHOP!*

HOW MUCH FOR THE MATCHES? ...*PLEASE!*

EIGHT DOLLARS.

FINE! HERE YOU GO.

HEY! YOU FORGOT YOUR CIGARETTES.

WHAT'S YOUR HURRY?

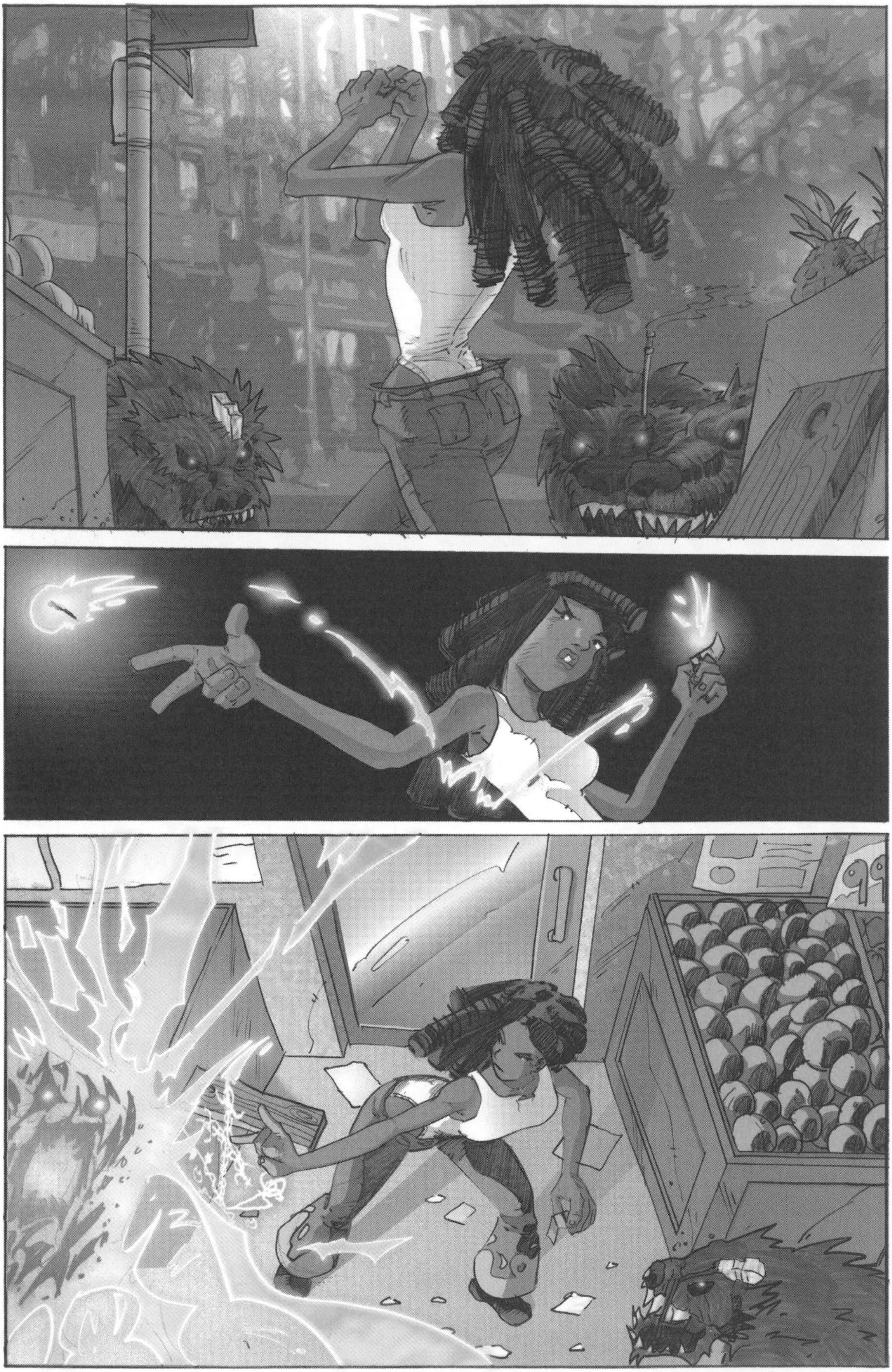

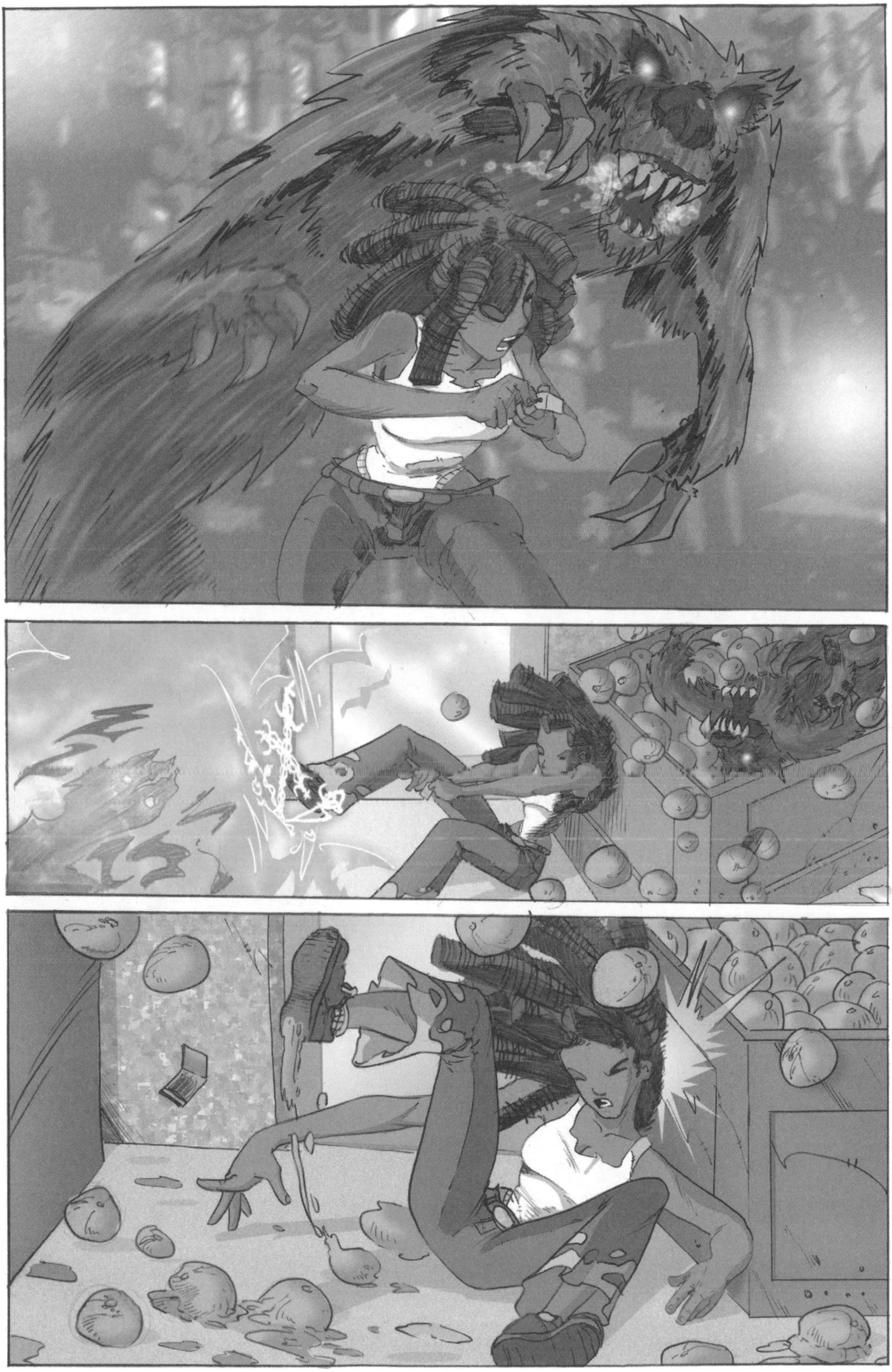

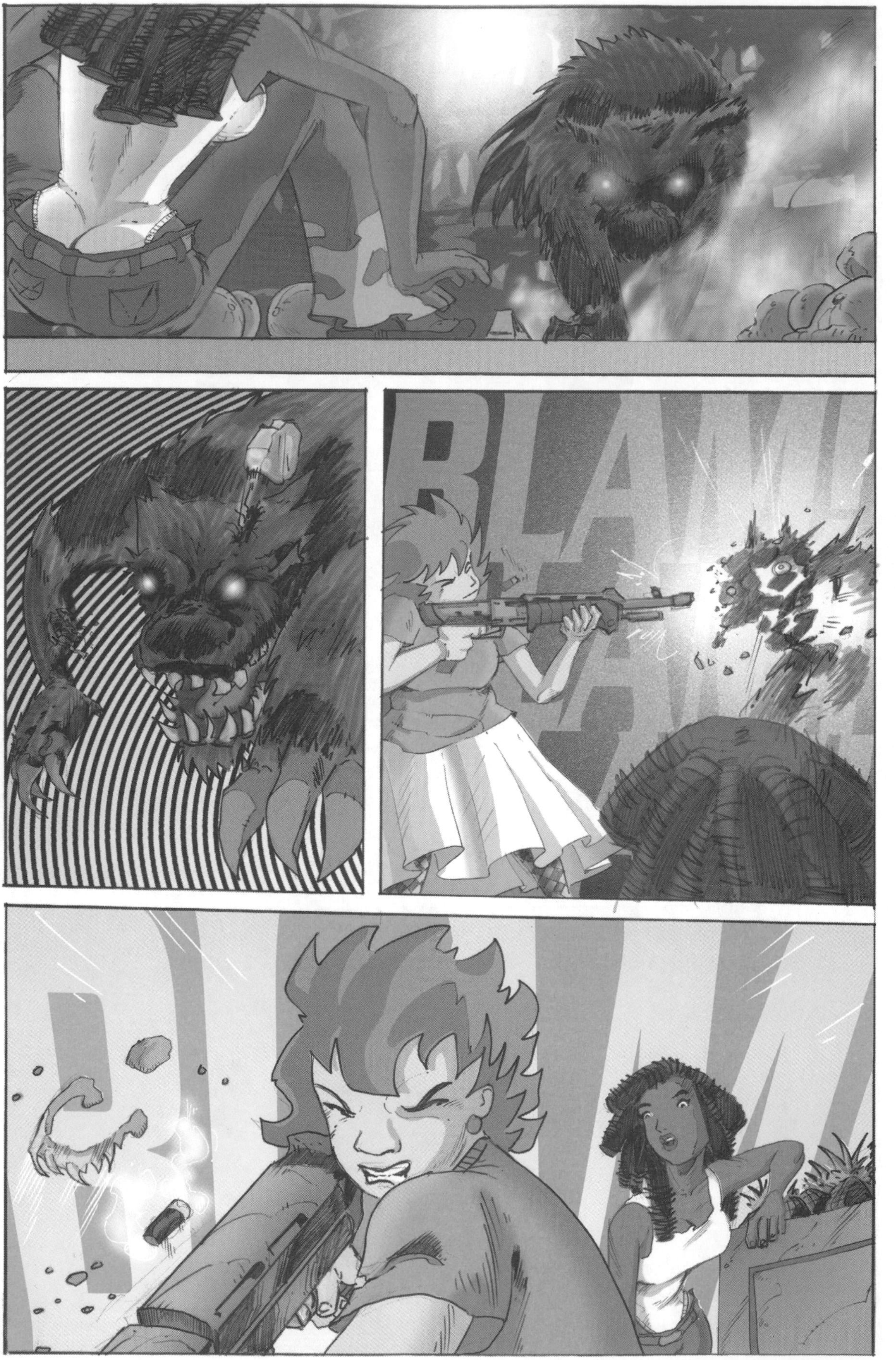

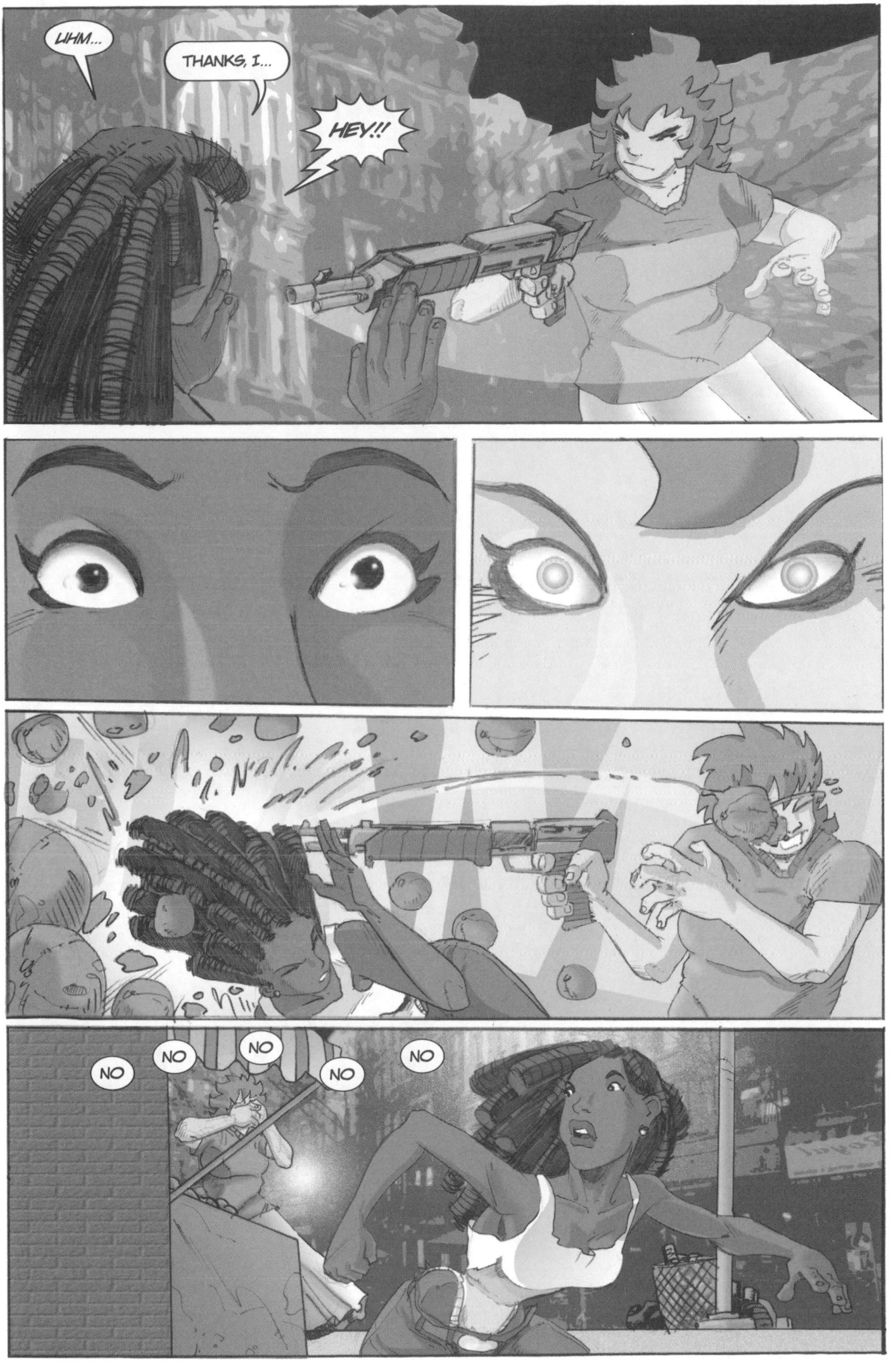
UHM...
THANKS, I...
HEY!!
NO
NO
NO
NO
NO

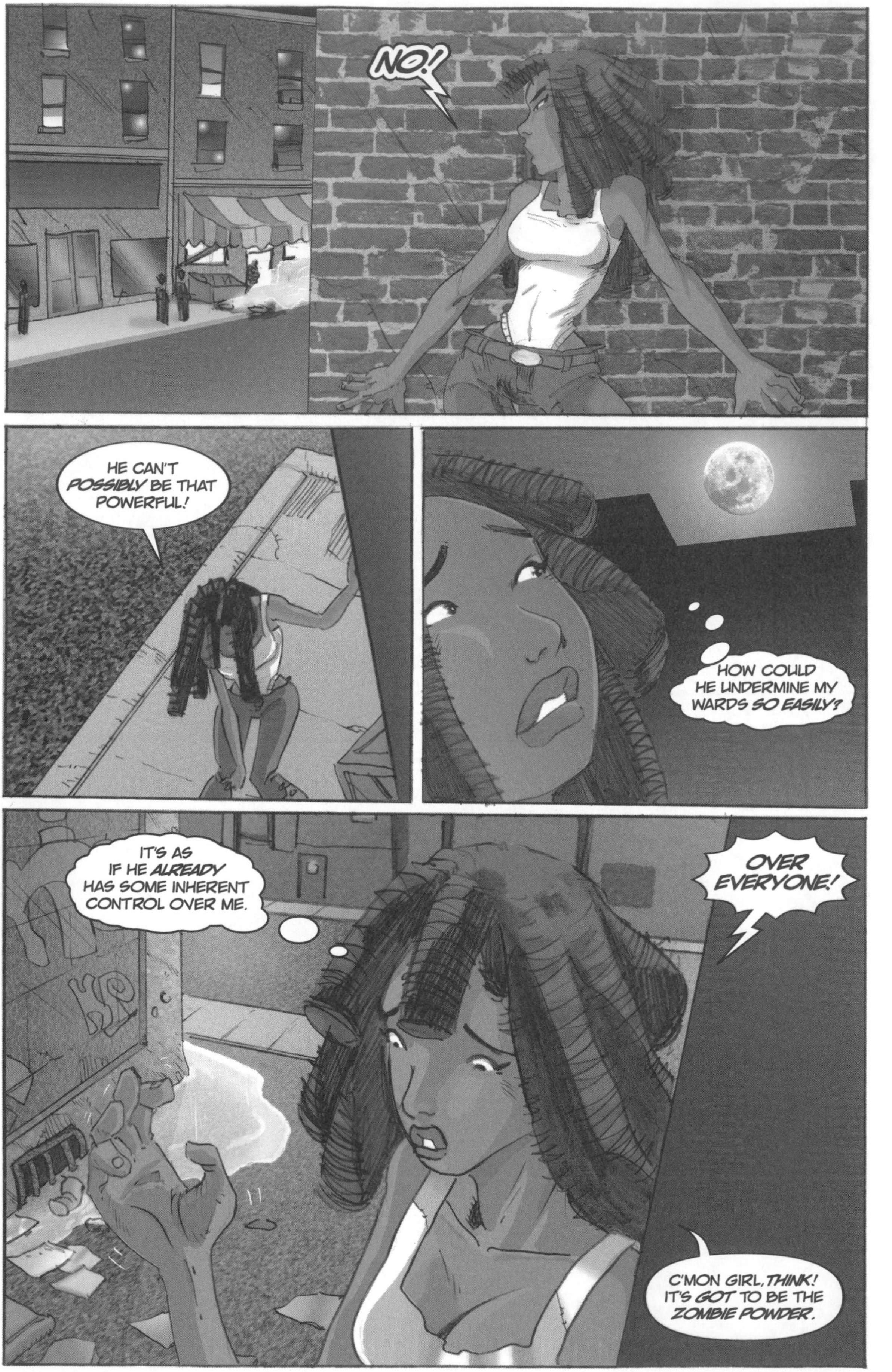
NO!
HE CAN'T *POSSIBLY* BE THAT POWERFUL!
HOW COULD HE UNDERMINE MY WARDS *SO EASILY?*
IT'S AS IF HE *ALREADY* HAS SOME INHERENT CONTROL OVER ME.
OVER EVERYONE!
C'MON GIRL, *THINK!* IT'S *GOT* TO BE THE *ZOMBIE POWDER*.

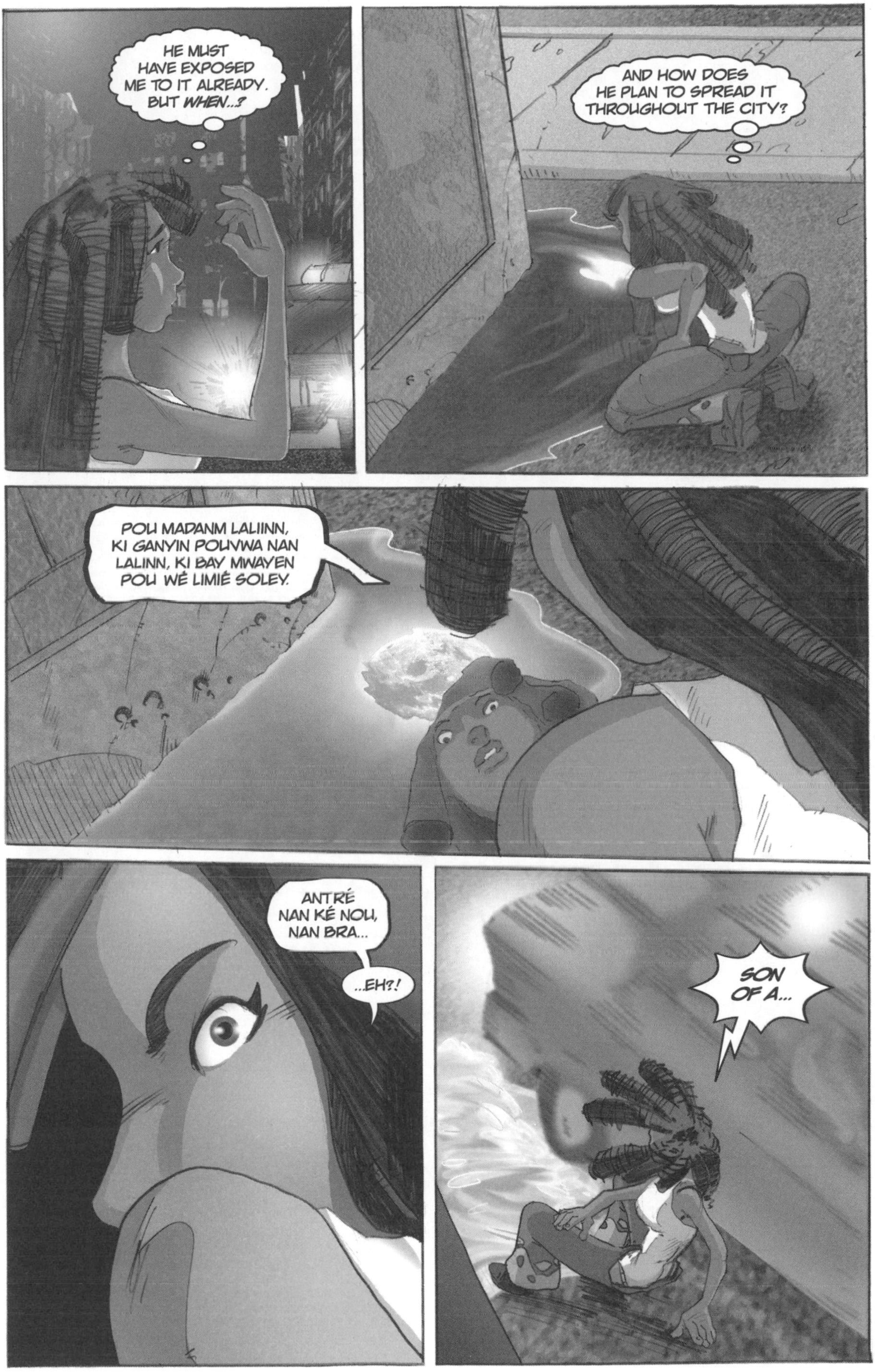
HE MUST HAVE EXPOSED ME TO IT ALREADY. BUT WHEN...?
AND HOW DOES HE PLAN TO SPREAD IT THROUGHOUT THE CITY?
POU MADANM LALIINN, KI GANYIN POUVWA NAN LALINN, KI BAY MWAYEN POU WÈ LIMIÈ SOLEY.
ANTRÉ NAN KÉ NOU, NAN BRA...
...EH?!
SON OF A...

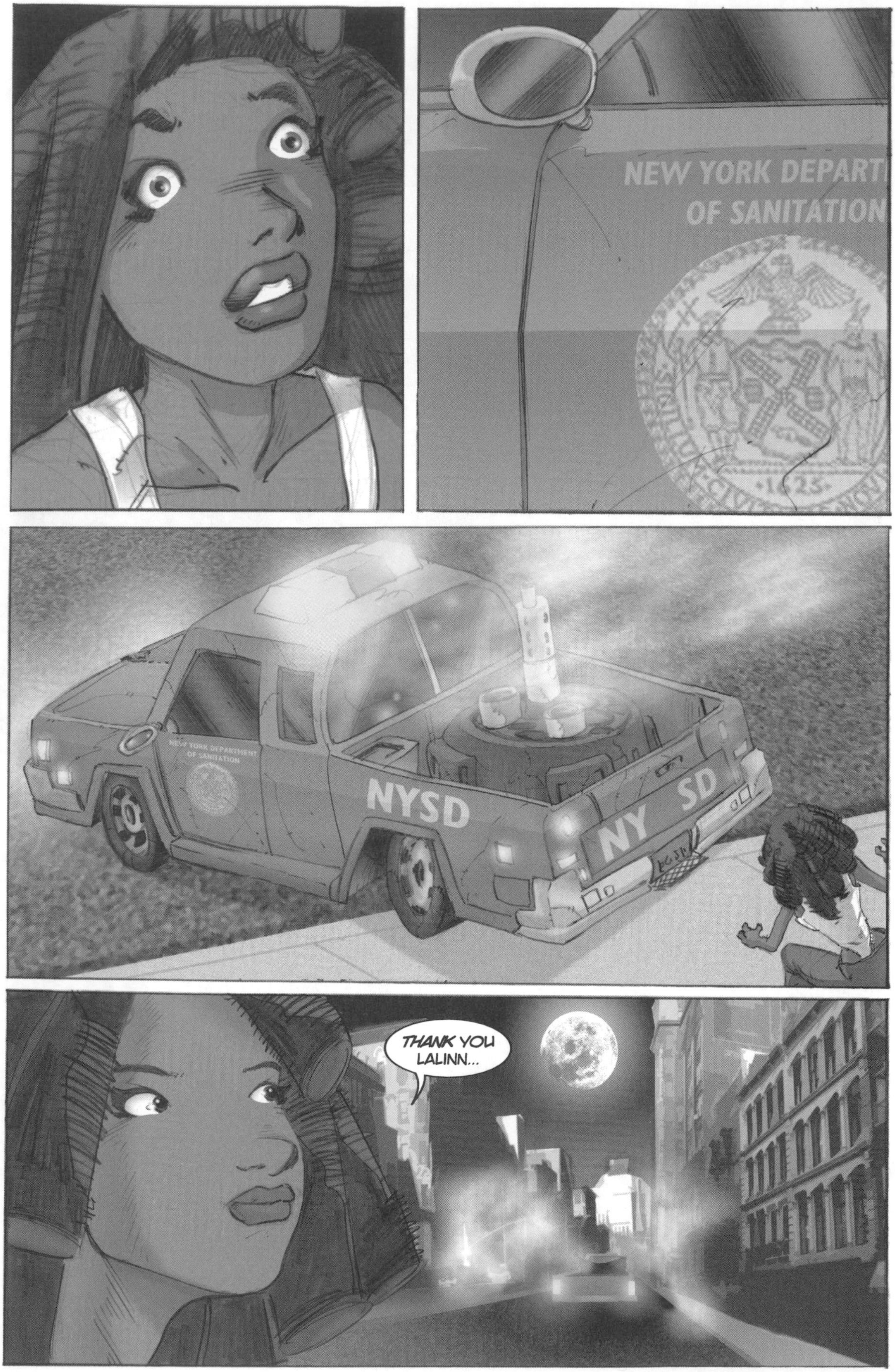
NEW YORK DEPARTMENT OF SANITATION
NEW YORK DEPARTMENT OF SANITATION
NYSD
NY SD
THANK YOU LALINN...

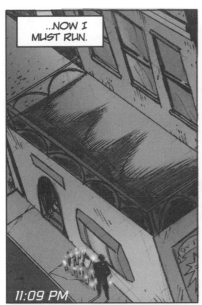

...NOW I MUST RUN.

11:09 PM

WHERE ARE YOU?

NOBODY'S HOME, COLLEGE BOY...

...BUT LET ME SHOW YOU WHERE THEY'RE AT!

HEY!

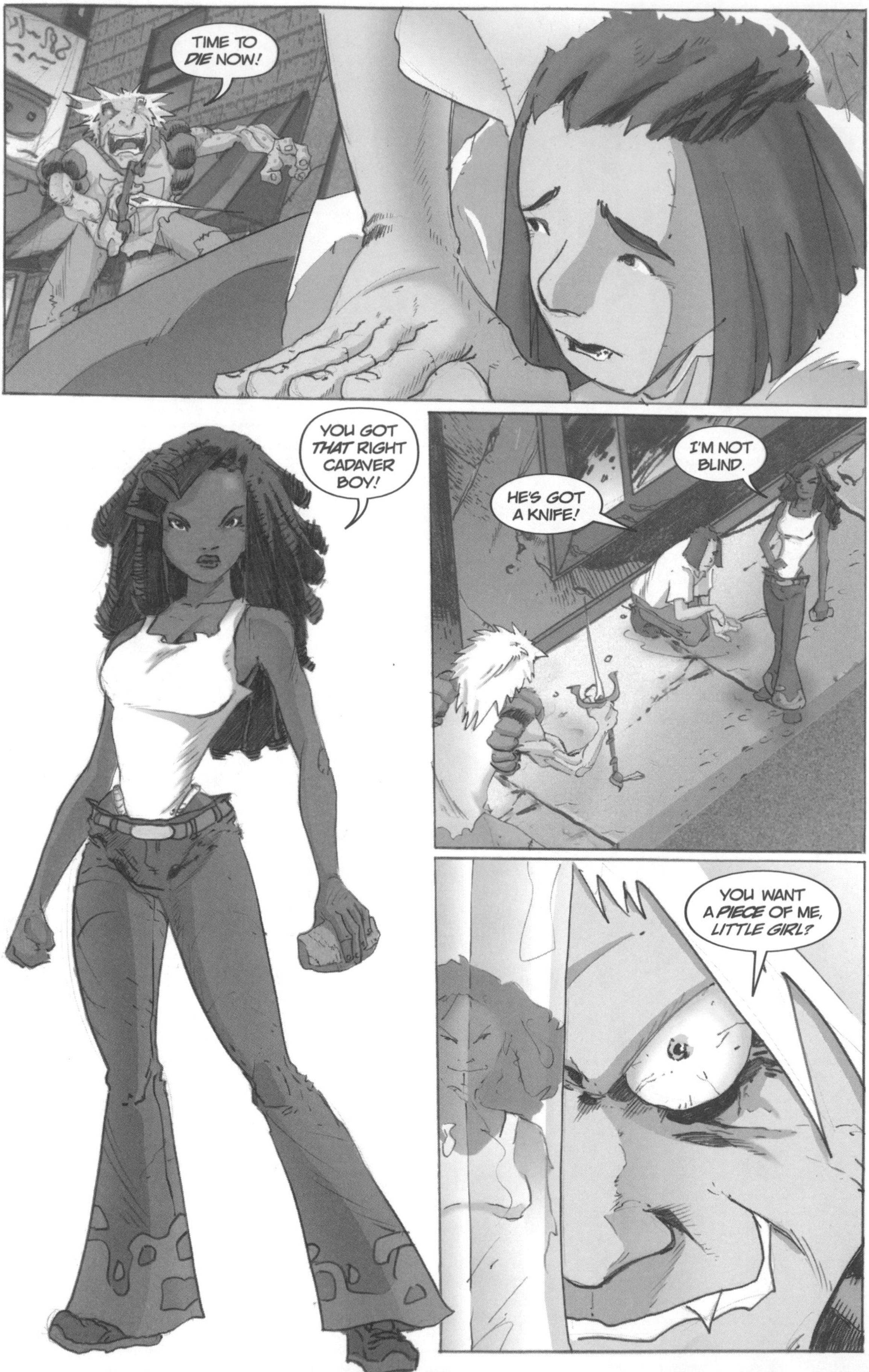
TIME TO DIE NOW!
YOU GOT THAT RIGHT CADAVER BOY!
HE'S GOT A KNIFE!
I'M NOT BLIND.
YOU WANT A PIECE OF ME, LITTLE GIRL?

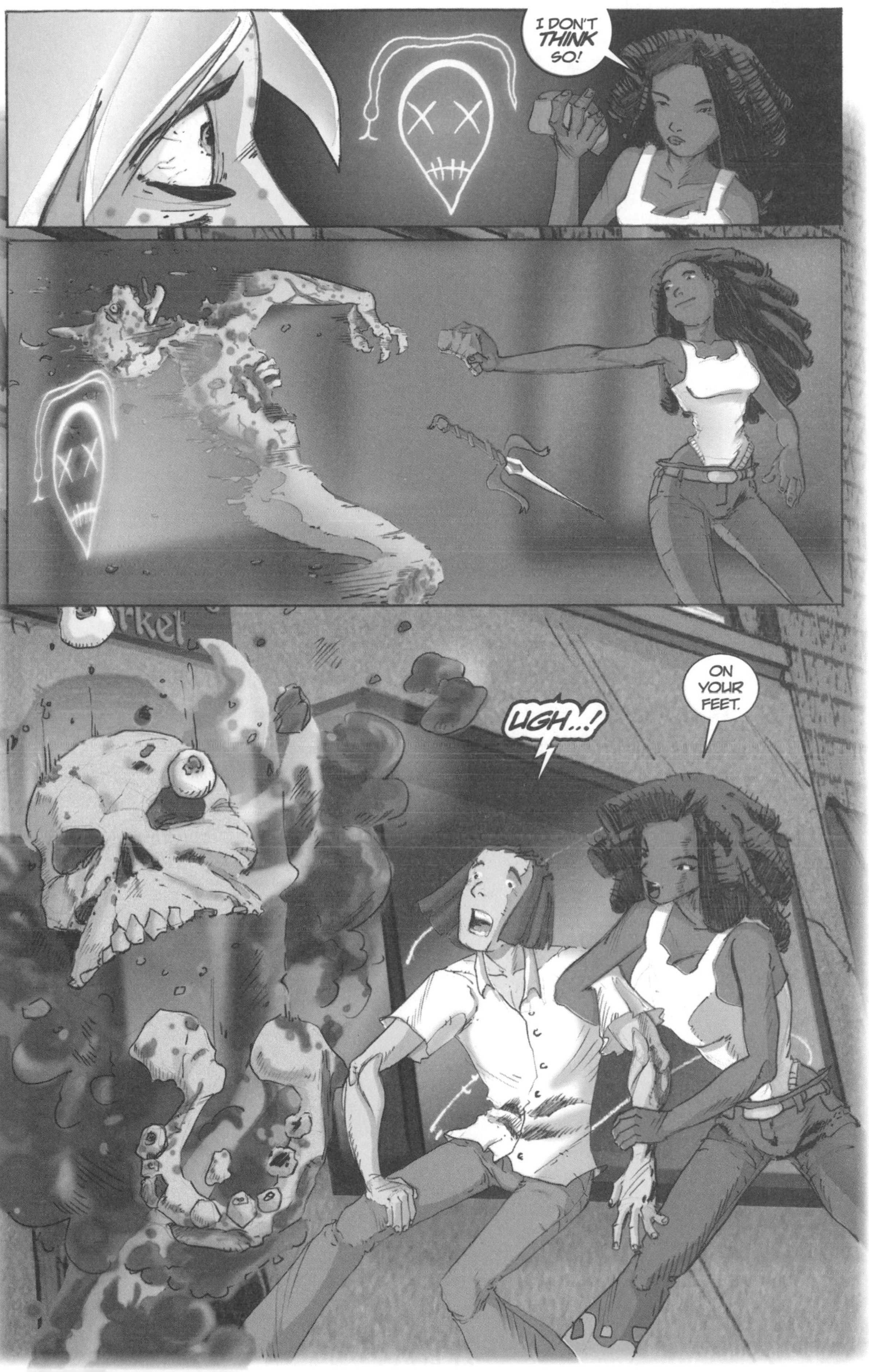
I DON'T THINK SO!
ON YOUR FEET.
UGH...!

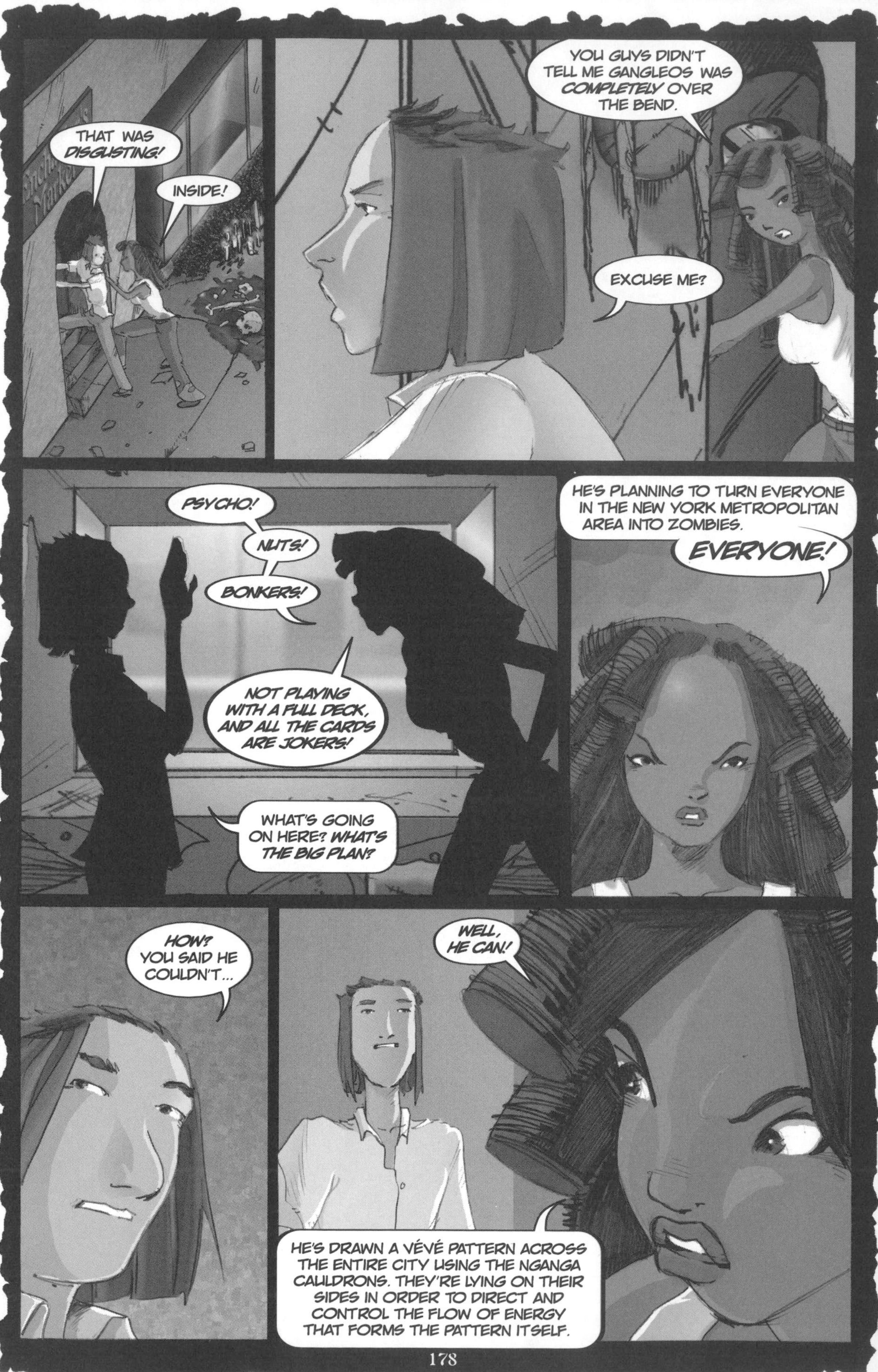

THAT WAS DISGUSTING!
INSIDE!
YOU GUYS DIDN'T TELL ME GANGLEOS WAS COMPLETELY OVER THE BEND.
EXCUSE ME?
PSYCHO!
NUTS!
BONKERS!
NOT PLAYING WITH A FULL DECK, AND ALL THE CARDS ARE JOKERS!
WHAT'S GOING ON HERE? WHAT'S THE BIG PLAN?
HE'S PLANNING TO TURN EVERYONE IN THE NEW YORK METROPOLITAN AREA INTO ZOMBIES.
EVERYONE!
HOW? YOU SAID HE COULDN'T...
WELL, HE CAN!
HE'S DRAWN A VÉVÉ PATTERN ACROSS THE ENTIRE CITY USING THE NGANGA CAULDRONS. THEY'RE LYING ON THEIR SIDES IN ORDER TO DIRECT AND CONTROL THE FLOW OF ENERGY THAT FORMS THE PATTERN ITSELF.

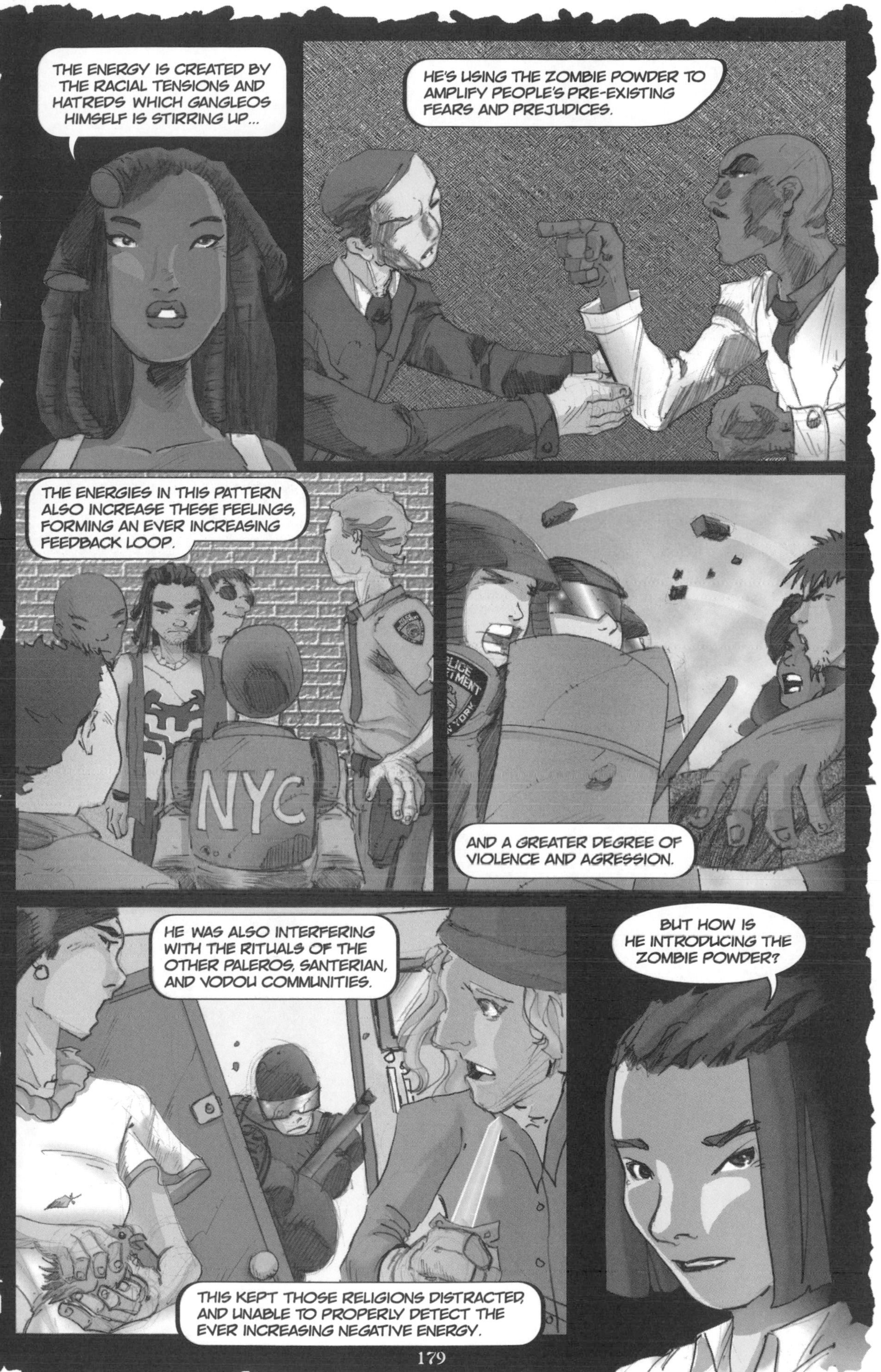
THE ENERGY IS CREATED BY THE RACIAL TENSIONS AND HATREDS WHICH GANGLEOS HIMSELF IS STIRRING UP...
HE'S USING THE ZOMBIE POWDER TO AMPLIFY PEOPLE'S PRE-EXISTING FEARS AND PREJUDICES.
THE ENERGIES IN THIS PATTERN ALSO INCREASE THESE FEELINGS, FORMING AN EVER INCREASING FEEDBACK LOOP.
NYC
AND A GREATER DEGREE OF VIOLENCE AND AGRESSION.
HE WAS ALSO INTERFERING WITH THE RITUALS OF THE OTHER PALEROS, SANTERIAN, AND VODOU COMMUNITIES.
THIS KEPT THOSE RELIGIONS DISTRACTED AND UNABLE TO PROPERLY DETECT THE EVER INCREASING NEGATIVE ENERGY.
BUT HOW IS HE INTRODUCING THE ZOMBIE POWDER?

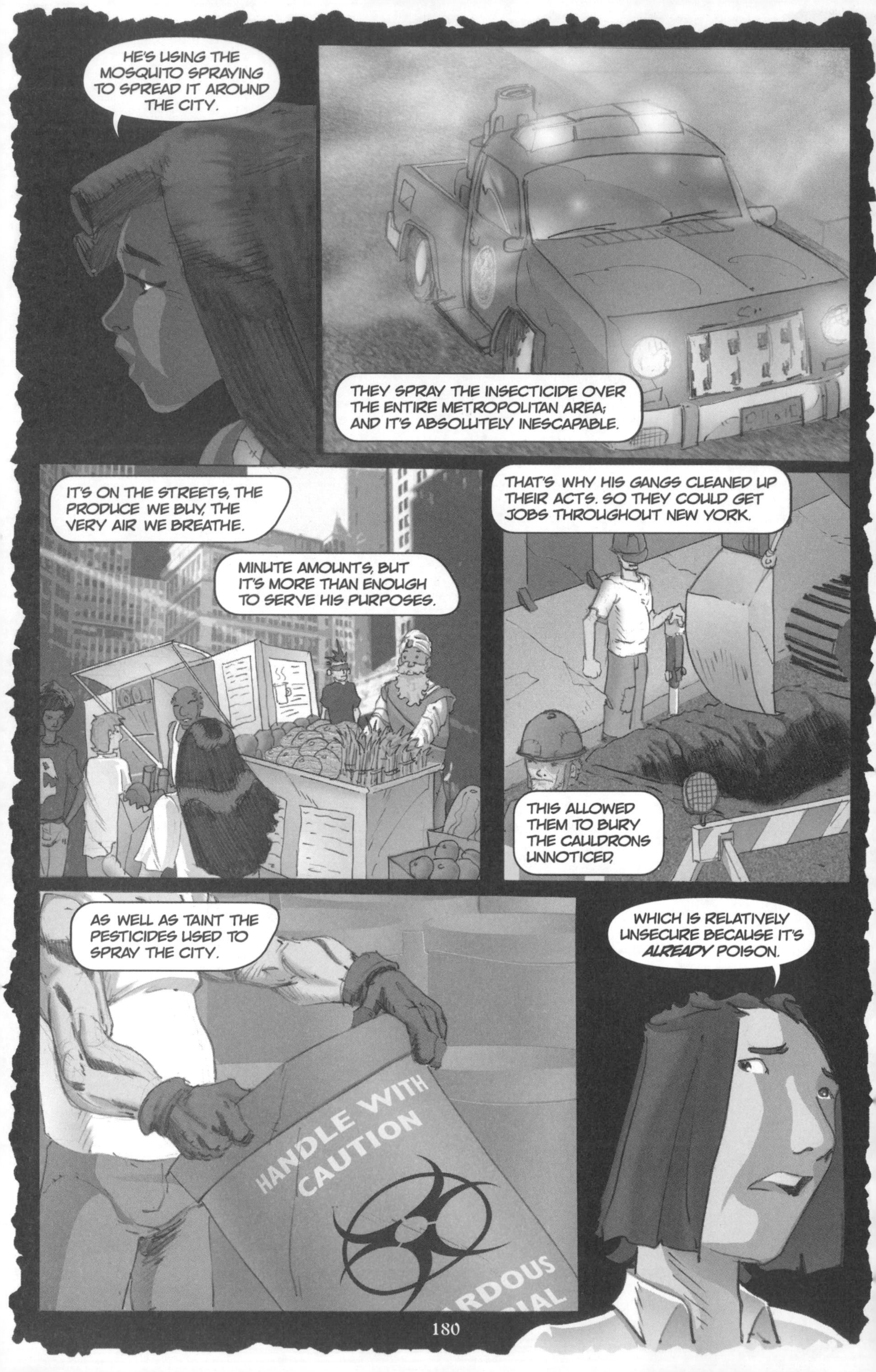
HE'S USING THE MOSQUITO SPRAYING TO SPREAD IT AROUND THE CITY.
THEY SPRAY THE INSECTICIDE OVER THE ENTIRE METROPOLITAN AREA; AND IT'S ABSOLUTELY INESCAPABLE.
IT'S ON THE STREETS, THE PRODUCE WE BUY, THE VERY AIR WE BREATHE.
MINUTE AMOUNTS, BUT IT'S MORE THAN ENOUGH TO SERVE HIS PURPOSES.
THAT'S WHY HIS GANGS CLEANED UP THEIR ACTS. SO THEY COULD GET JOBS THROUGHOUT NEW YORK.
THIS ALLOWED THEM TO BURY THE CAULDRONS UNNOTICED,
AS WELL AS TAINT THE PESTICIDES USED TO SPRAY THE CITY.
WHICH IS RELATIVELY UNSECURE BECAUSE IT'S *ALREADY* POISON.
HANDLE WITH CAUTION

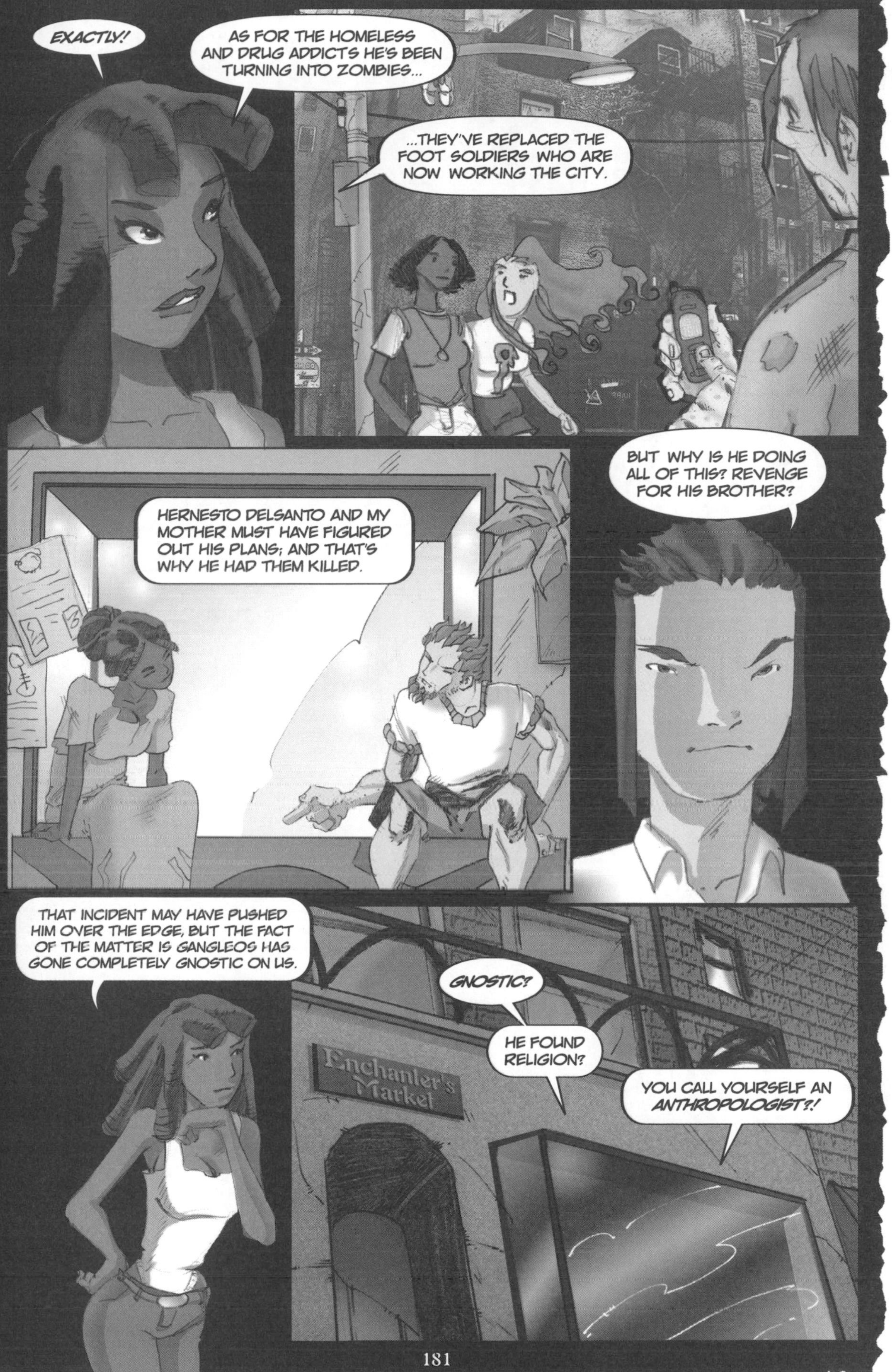
EXACTLY!
AS FOR THE HOMELESS AND DRUG ADDICTS HE'S BEEN TURNING INTO ZOMBIES...
...THEY'VE REPLACED THE FOOT SOLDIERS WHO ARE NOW WORKING THE CITY.
HERNESTO DELSANTO AND MY MOTHER MUST HAVE FIGURED OUT HIS PLANS; AND THAT'S WHY HE HAD THEM KILLED.
BUT WHY IS HE DOING ALL OF THIS? REVENGE FOR HIS BROTHER?
THAT INCIDENT MAY HAVE PUSHED HIM OVER THE EDGE, BUT THE FACT OF THE MATTER IS GANGLEOS HAS GONE COMPLETELY GNOSTIC ON US.
GNOSTIC?
HE FOUND RELIGION?
Enchanter's Market
YOU CALL YOURSELF AN ANTHROPOLOGIST?!

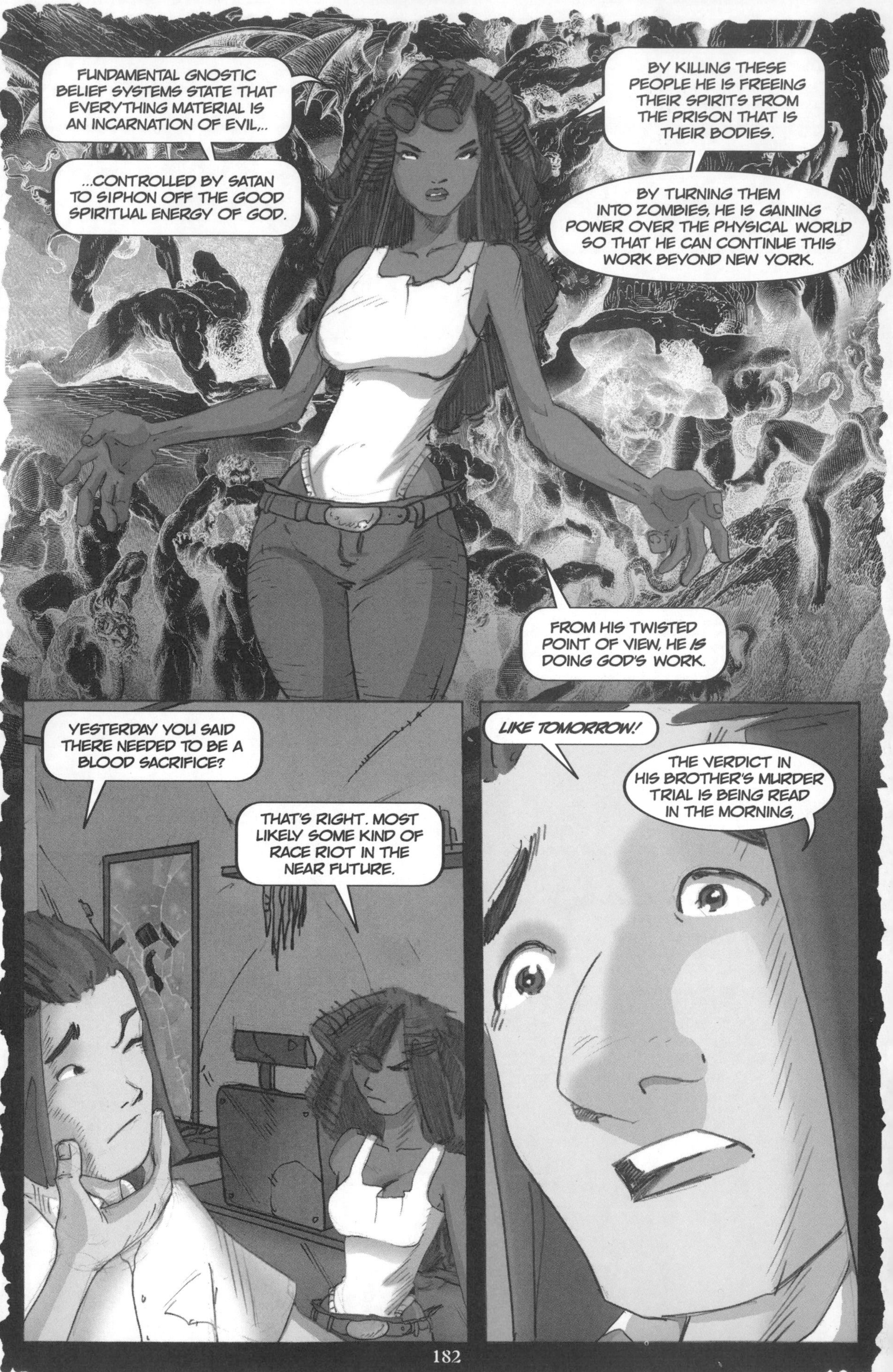

FUNDAMENTAL GNOSTIC BELIEF SYSTEMS STATE THAT EVERYTHING MATERIAL IS AN INCARNATION OF EVIL...
...CONTROLLED BY SATAN TO SIPHON OFF THE GOOD SPIRITUAL ENERGY OF GOD.
BY KILLING THESE PEOPLE HE IS FREEING THEIR SPIRITS FROM THE PRISON THAT IS THEIR BODIES.
BY TURNING THEM INTO ZOMBIES, HE IS GAINING POWER OVER THE PHYSICAL WORLD SO THAT HE CAN CONTINUE THIS WORK BEYOND NEW YORK.
FROM HIS TWISTED POINT OF VIEW, HE *IS* DOING GOD'S WORK.
YESTERDAY YOU SAID THERE NEEDED TO BE A BLOOD SACRIFICE?
THAT'S RIGHT. MOST LIKELY SOME KIND OF RACE RIOT IN THE NEAR FUTURE.
LIKE TOMORROW!
THE VERDICT IN HIS BROTHER'S MURDER TRIAL IS BEING READ IN THE MORNING,

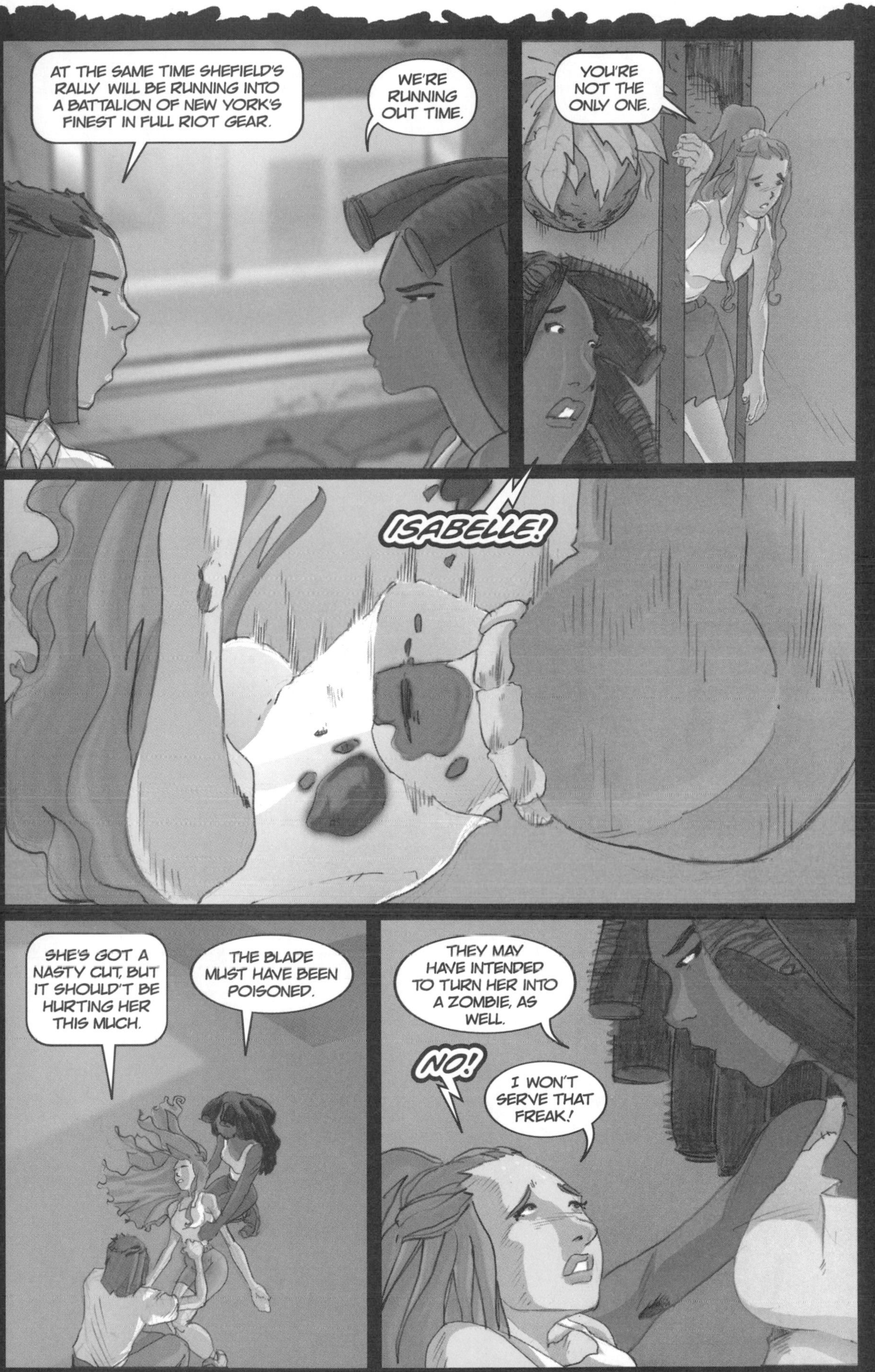
AT THE SAME TIME SHEFIELD'S RALLY WILL BE RUNNING INTO A BATTALION OF NEW YORK'S FINEST IN FULL RIOT GEAR.
WE'RE RUNNING OUT TIME.
YOU'RE NOT THE ONLY ONE.
ISABELLE!
SHE'S GOT A NASTY CUT, BUT IT SHOULD'T BE HURTING HER THIS MUCH.
THE BLADE MUST HAVE BEEN POISONED.
THEY MAY HAVE INTENDED TO TURN HER INTO A ZOMBIE, AS WELL.
NO!
I WON'T SERVE THAT FREAK!

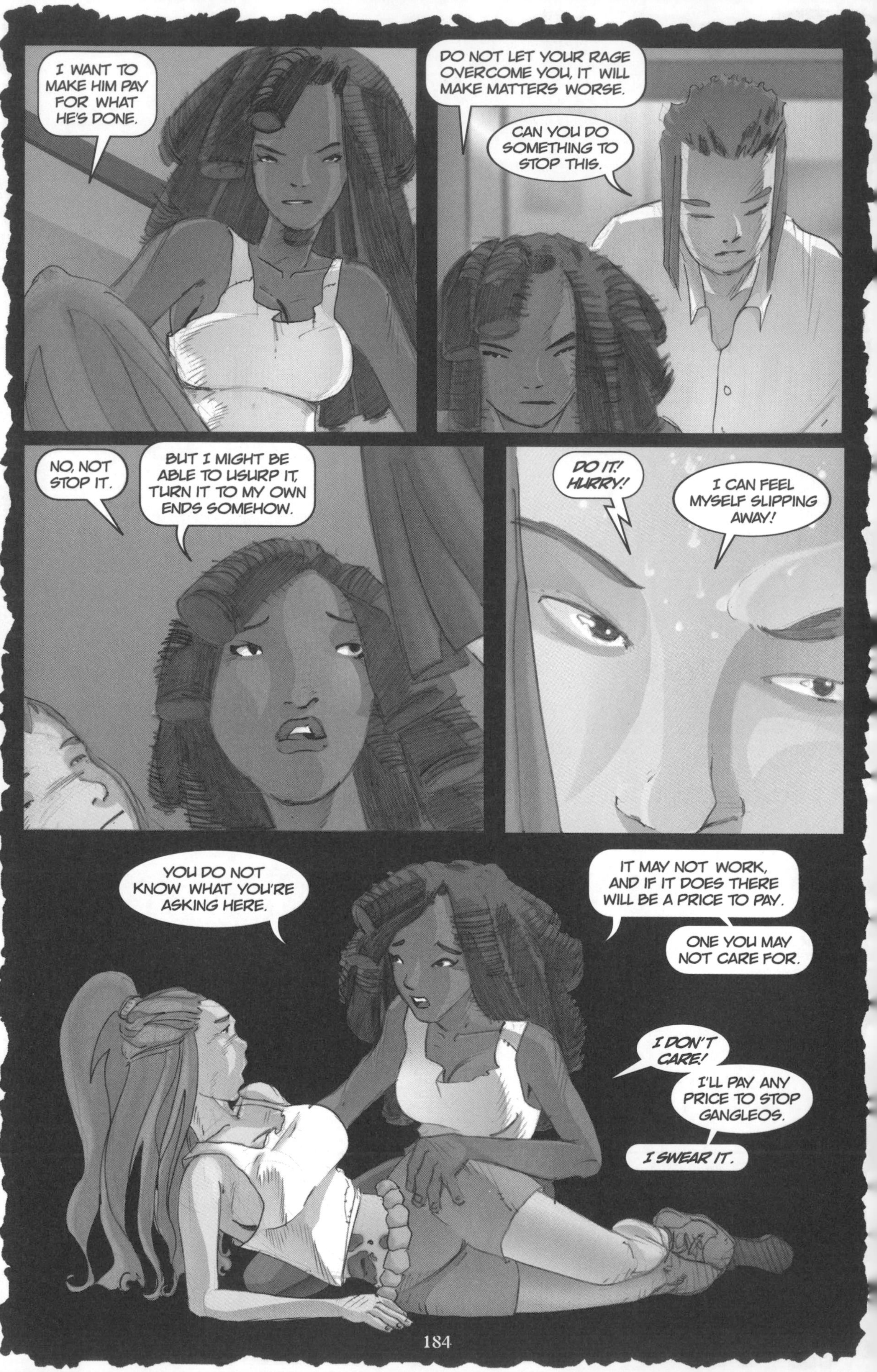
I WANT TO MAKE HIM PAY FOR WHAT HE'S DONE.
DO NOT LET YOUR RAGE OVERCOME YOU, IT WILL MAKE MATTERS WORSE.
CAN YOU DO SOMETHING TO STOP THIS.
NO, NOT STOP IT.
BUT I MIGHT BE ABLE TO USURP IT, TURN IT TO MY OWN ENDS SOMEHOW.
DO IT! HURRY!
I CAN FEEL MYSELF SLIPPING AWAY!
YOU DO NOT KNOW WHAT YOU'RE ASKING HERE.
IT MAY NOT WORK, AND IF IT DOES THERE WILL BE A PRICE TO PAY.
ONE YOU MAY NOT CARE FOR.
I DON'T CARE!
I'LL PAY ANY PRICE TO STOP GANGLEOS.
I SWEAR IT.

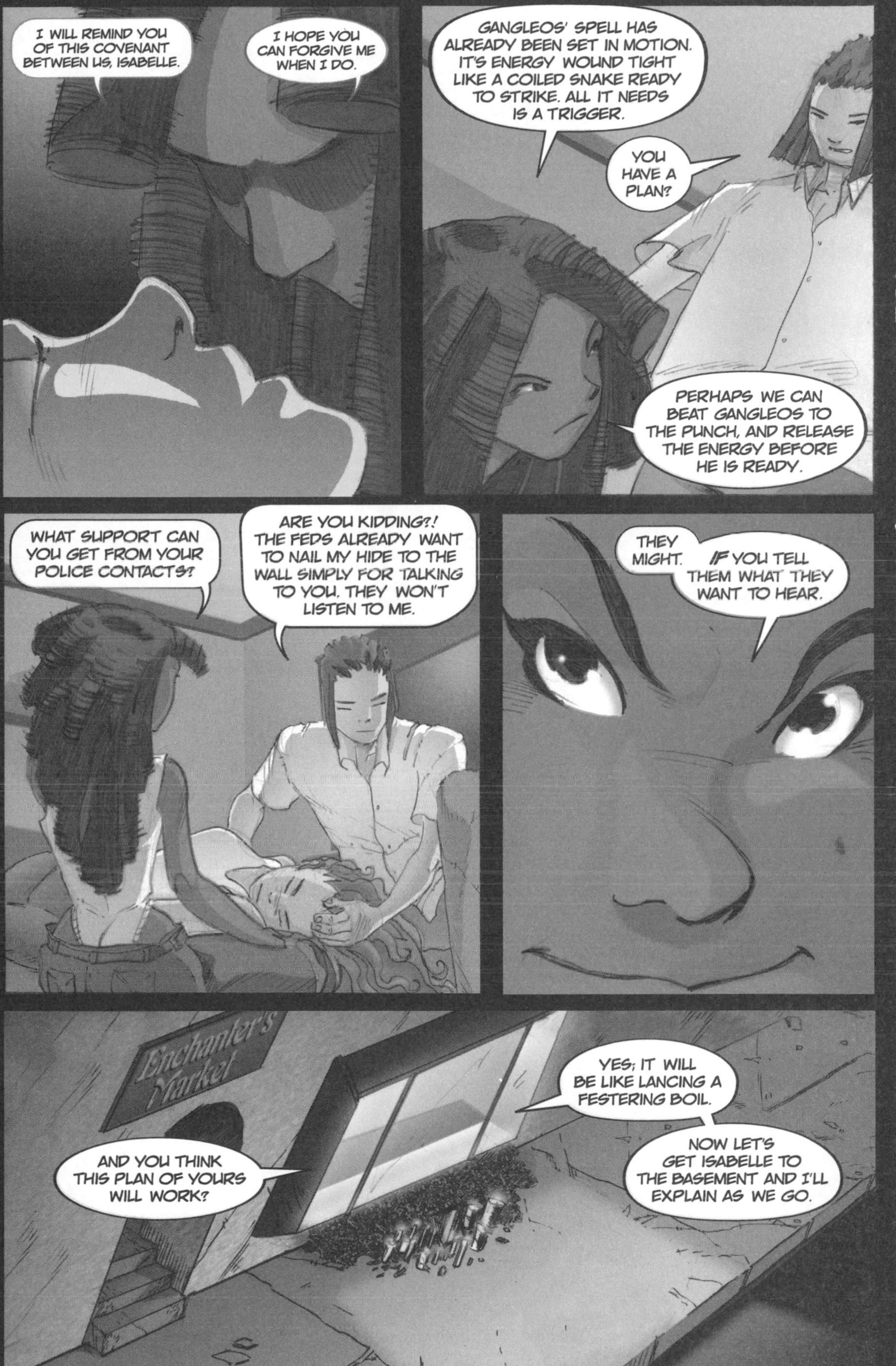
I WILL REMIND YOU OF THIS COVENANT BETWEEN US, ISABELLE.
I HOPE YOU CAN FORGIVE ME WHEN I DO.
GANGLEOS' SPELL HAS ALREADY BEEN SET IN MOTION. IT'S ENERGY WOUND TIGHT LIKE A COILED SNAKE READY TO STRIKE. ALL IT NEEDS IS A TRIGGER.
YOU HAVE A PLAN?
PERHAPS WE CAN BEAT GANGLEOS TO THE PUNCH, AND RELEASE THE ENERGY BEFORE HE IS READY.
WHAT SUPPORT CAN YOU GET FROM YOUR POLICE CONTACTS?
ARE YOU KIDDING?! THE FEDS ALREADY WANT TO NAIL MY HIDE TO THE WALL SIMPLY FOR TALKING TO YOU. THEY WON'T LISTEN TO ME.
THEY MIGHT.
IF YOU TELL THEM WHAT THEY WANT TO HEAR.
Enchanter's Market
AND YOU THINK THIS PLAN OF YOURS WILL WORK?
YES; IT WILL BE LIKE LANCING A FESTERING BOIL.
NOW LET'S GET ISABELLE TO THE BASEMENT AND I'LL EXPLAIN AS WE GO.

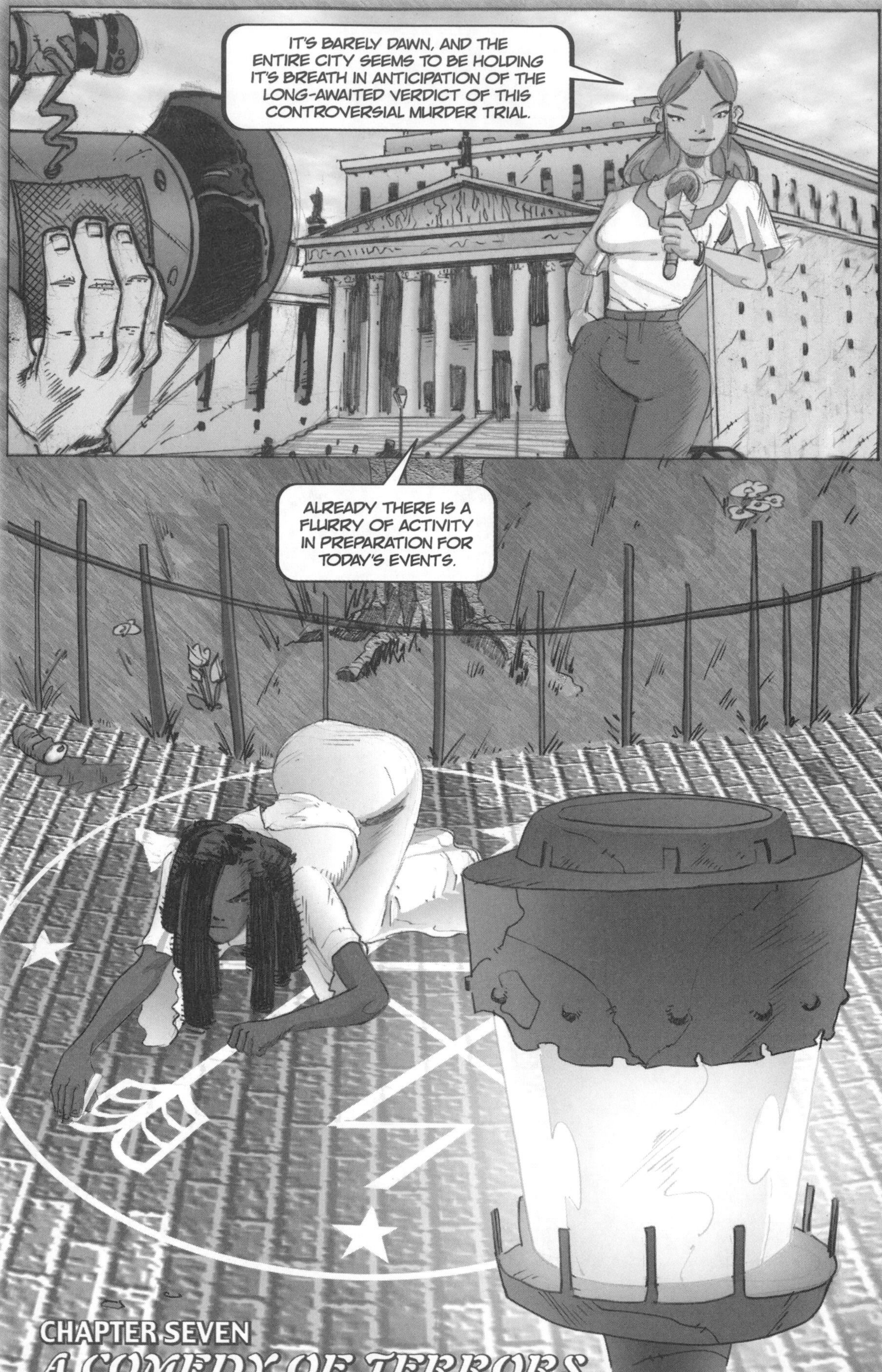
IT'S BARELY DAWN, AND THE ENTIRE CITY SEEMS TO BE HOLDING IT'S BREATH IN ANTICIPATION OF THE LONG-AWAITED VERDICT OF THIS CONTROVERSIAL MURDER TRIAL.
ALREADY THERE IS A FLURRY OF ACTIVITY IN PREPARATION FOR TODAY'S EVENTS.
CHAPTER SEVEN
A COMEDY OF TERRORS

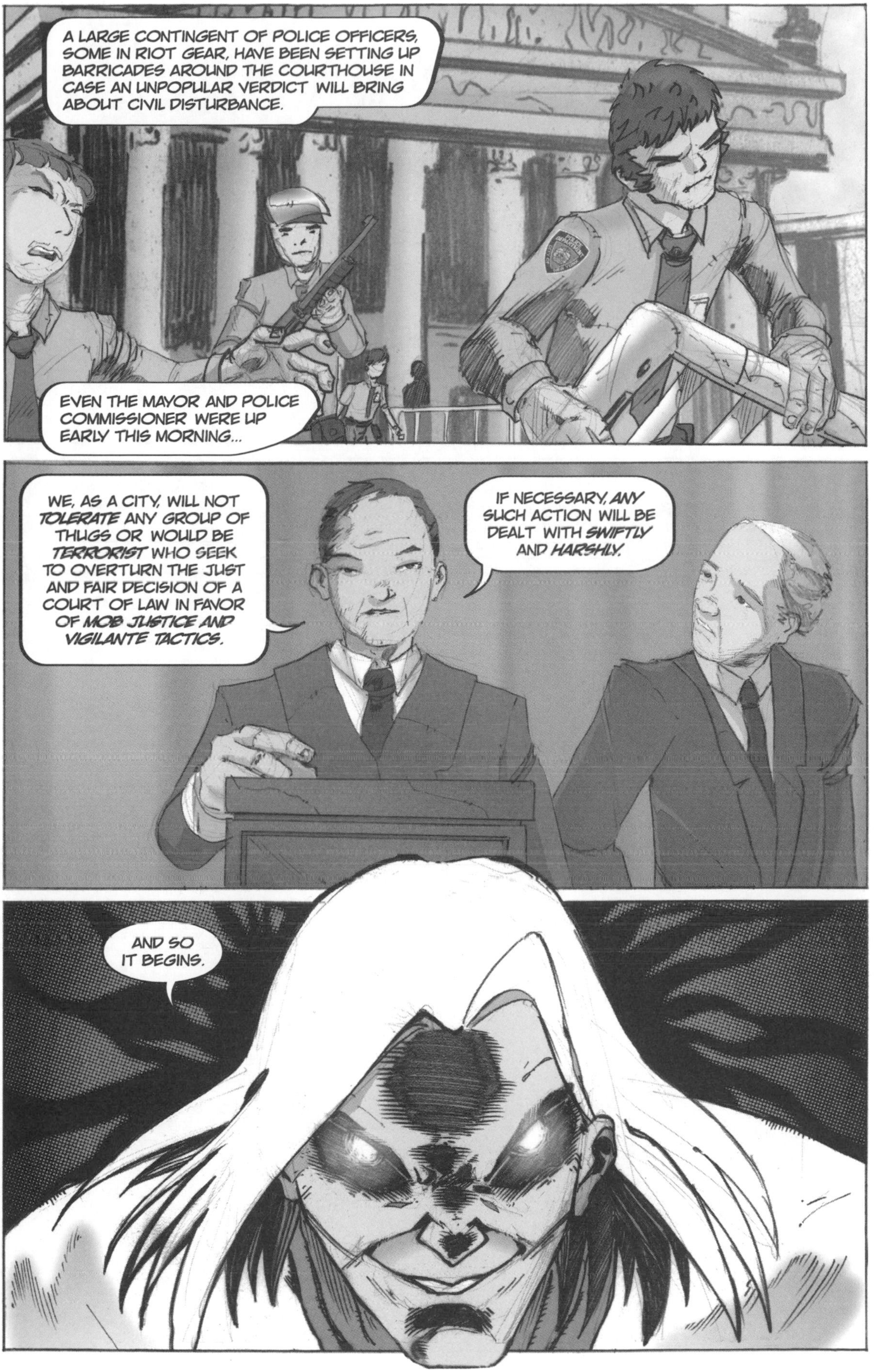
A LARGE CONTINGENT OF POLICE OFFICERS, SOME IN RIOT GEAR, HAVE BEEN SETTING UP BARRICADES AROUND THE COURTHOUSE IN CASE AN UNPOPULAR VERDICT WILL BRING ABOUT CIVIL DISTURBANCE.
EVEN THE MAYOR AND POLICE COMMISSIONER WERE UP EARLY THIS MORNING...
WE, AS A CITY, WILL NOT *TOLERATE* ANY GROUP OF THUGS OR WOULD BE *TERRORIST* WHO SEEK TO OVERTURN THE JUST AND FAIR DECISION OF A COURT OF LAW IN FAVOR OF *MOB JUSTICE AND VIGILANTE TACTICS*.
IF NECESSARY, *ANY* SUCH ACTION WILL BE DEALT WITH *SWIFTLY* AND *HARSHLY*.
AND SO IT BEGINS.

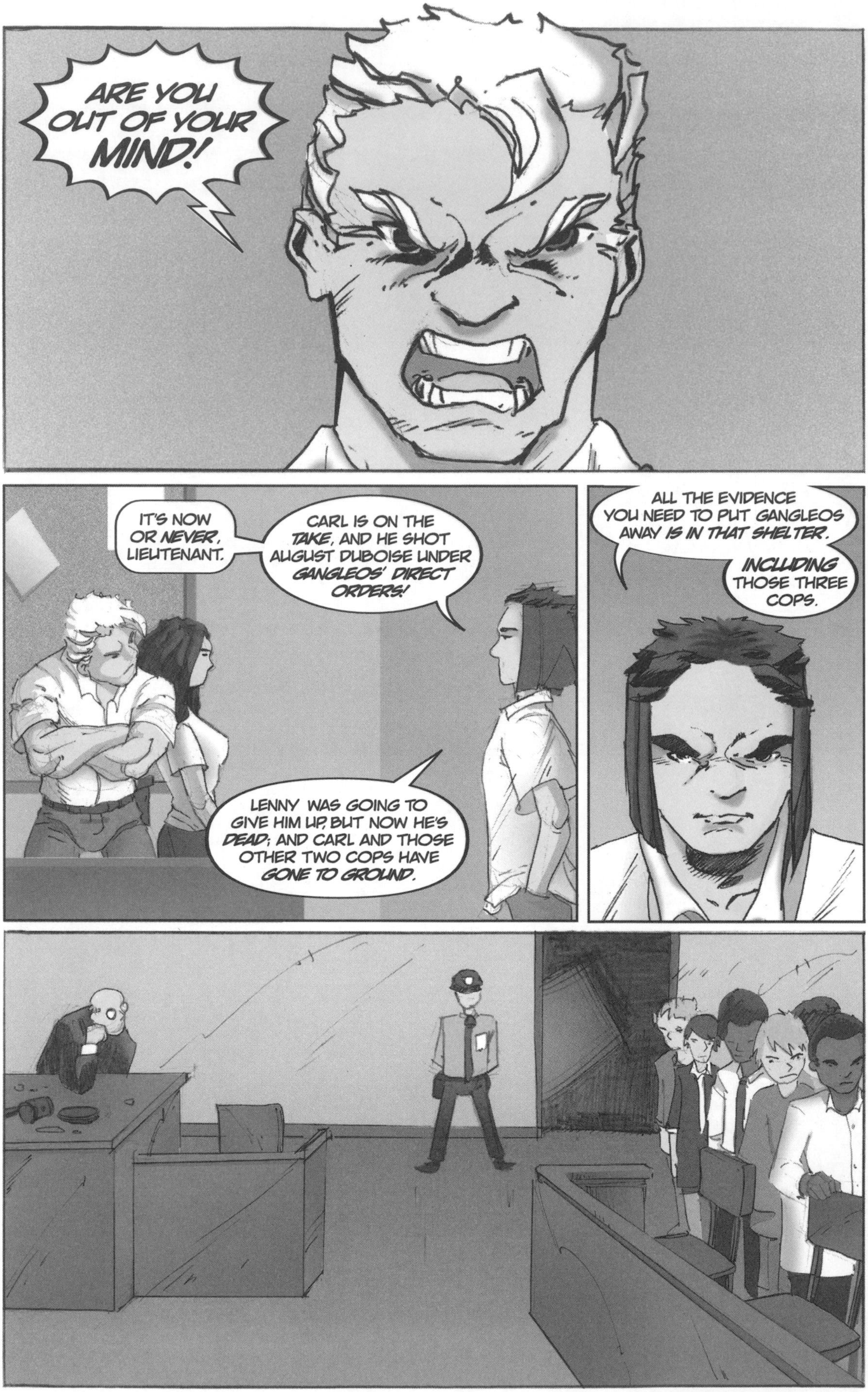
ARE YOU OUT OF YOUR MIND!
IT'S NOW OR NEVER, LIEUTENANT.
CARL IS ON THE TAKE, AND HE SHOT AUGUST DUBOISE UNDER GANGLEOS' DIRECT ORDERS!
LENNY WAS GOING TO GIVE HIM UP, BUT NOW HE'S DEAD; AND CARL AND THOSE OTHER TWO COPS HAVE GONE TO GROUND.
ALL THE EVIDENCE YOU NEED TO PUT GANGLEOS AWAY IS IN THAT SHELTER.
INCLUDING THOSE THREE COPS.

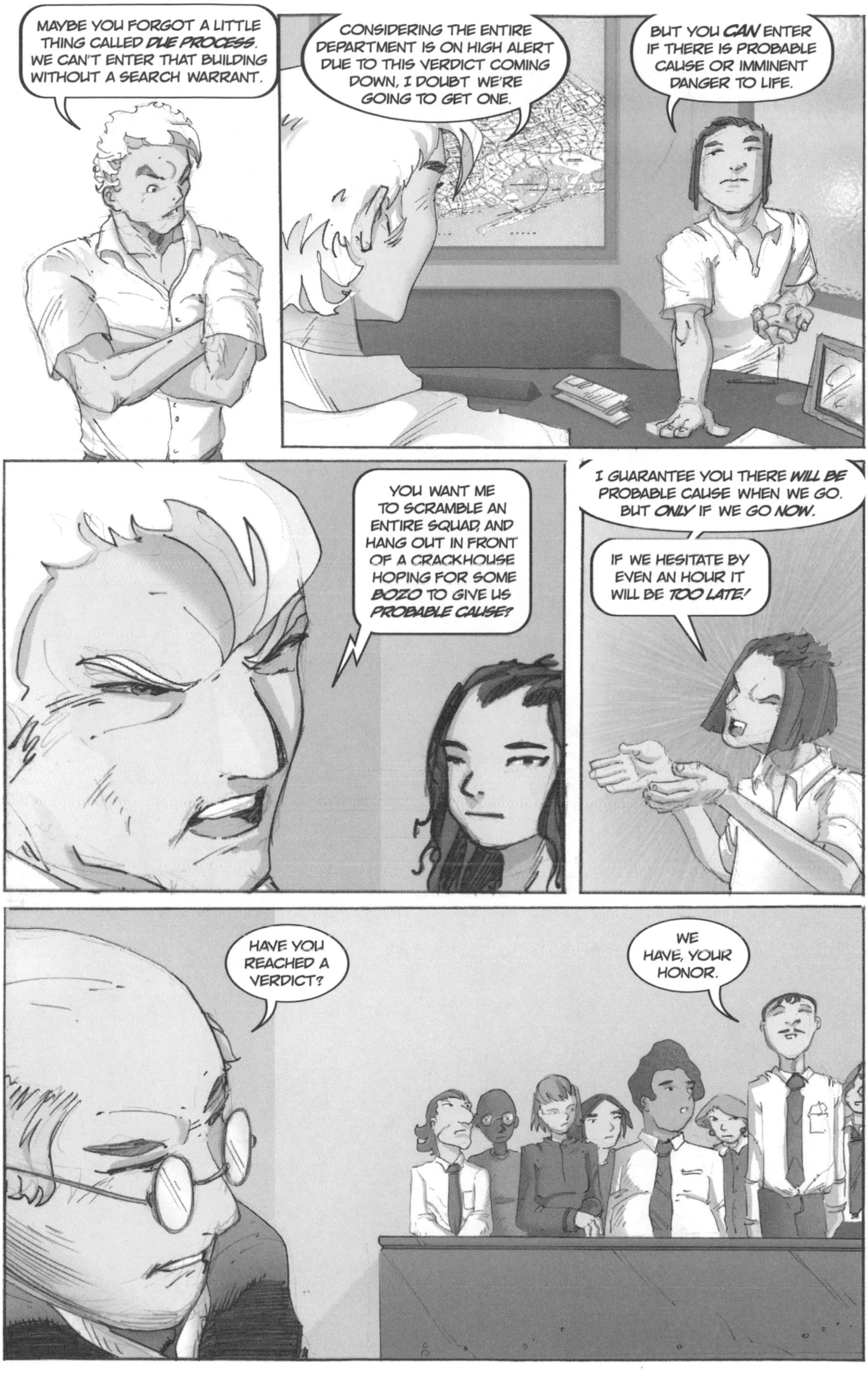
MAYBE YOU FORGOT A LITTLE THING CALLED DUE PROCESS. WE CAN'T ENTER THAT BUILDING WITHOUT A SEARCH WARRANT.
CONSIDERING THE ENTIRE DEPARTMENT IS ON HIGH ALERT DUE TO THIS VERDICT COMING DOWN, I DOUBT WE'RE GOING TO GET ONE.
BUT YOU CAN ENTER IF THERE IS PROBABLE CAUSE OR IMMINENT DANGER TO LIFE.
YOU WANT ME TO SCRAMBLE AN ENTIRE SQUAD, AND HANG OUT IN FRONT OF A CRACKHOUSE HOPING FOR SOME BOZO TO GIVE US PROBABLE CAUSE?
I GUARANTEE YOU THERE WILL BE PROBABLE CAUSE WHEN WE GO. BUT ONLY IF WE GO NOW.
IF WE HESITATE BY EVEN AN HOUR IT WILL BE TOO LATE!
HAVE YOU REACHED A VERDICT?
WE HAVE, YOUR HONOR.

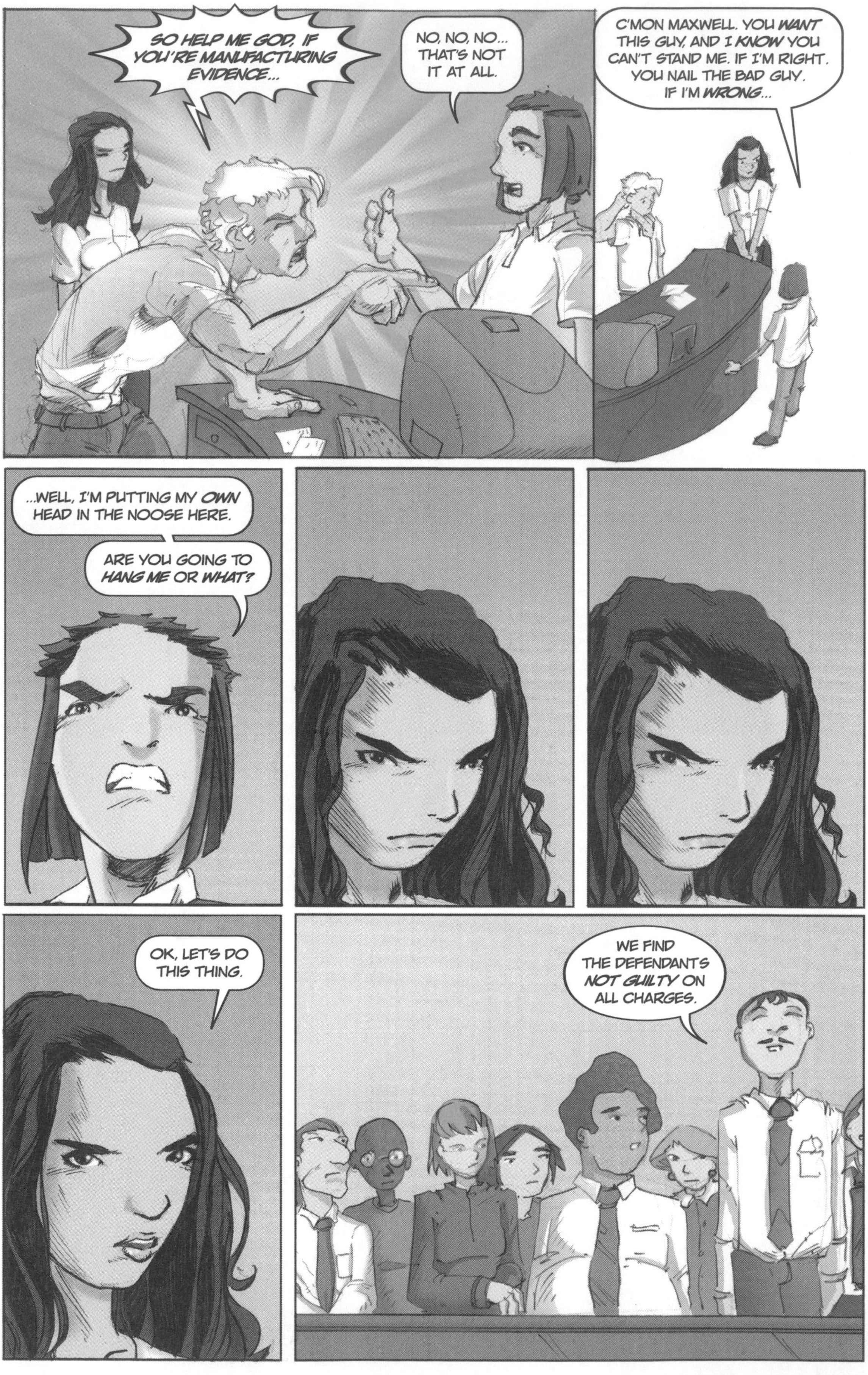
SO HELP ME GOD, IF YOU'RE MANUFACTURING EVIDENCE...
NO, NO, NO... THAT'S NOT IT AT ALL.
C'MON MAXWELL. YOU WANT THIS GUY, AND I KNOW YOU CAN'T STAND ME. IF I'M RIGHT, YOU NAIL THE BAD GUY. IF I'M WRONG...
...WELL, I'M PUTTING MY OWN HEAD IN THE NOOSE HERE.
ARE YOU GOING TO HANG ME OR WHAT?
OK, LET'S DO THIS THING.
WE FIND THE DEFENDANTS NOT GUILTY ON ALL CHARGES.

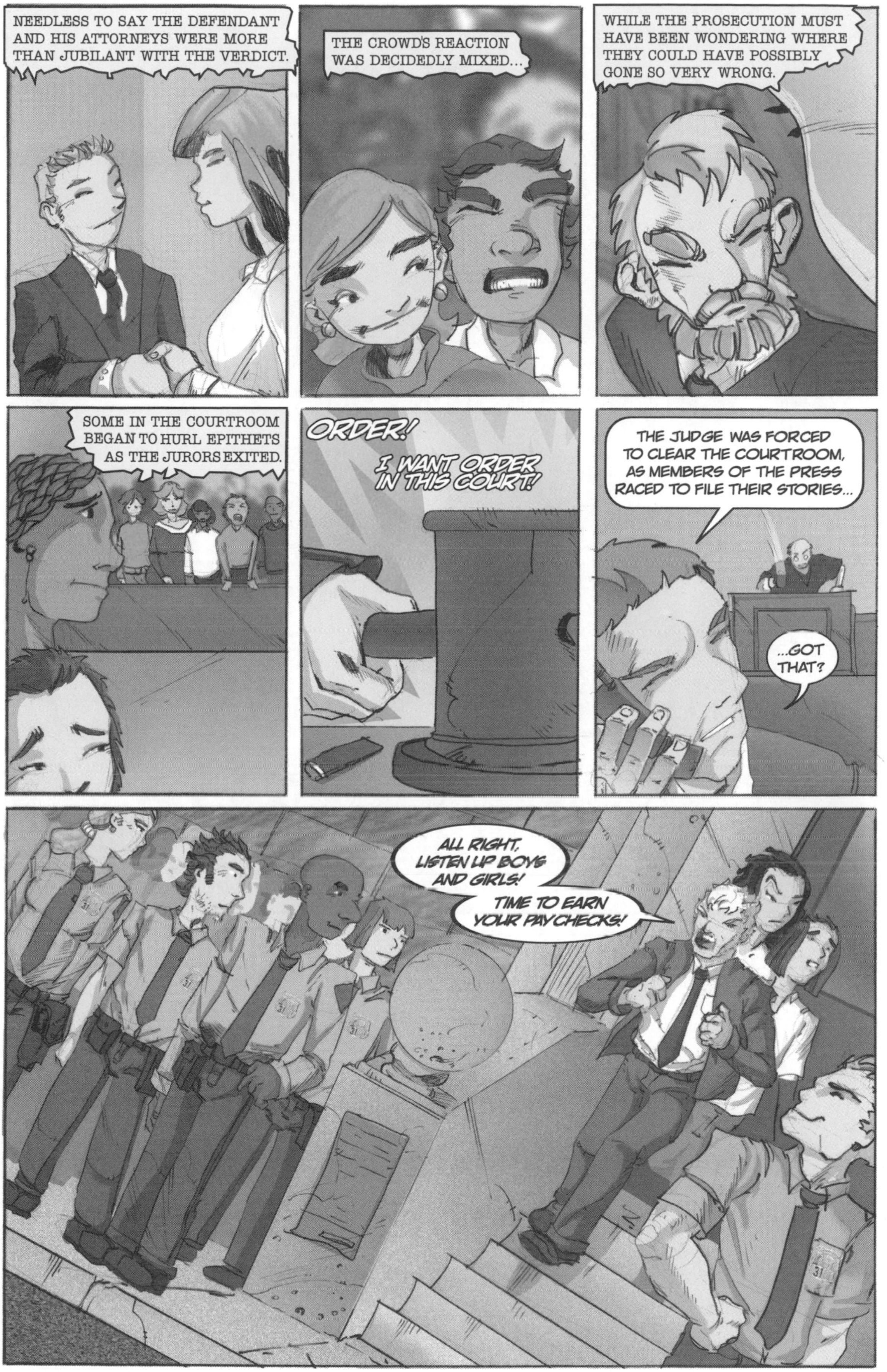
NEEDLESS TO SAY THE DEFENDANT AND HIS ATTORNEYS WERE MORE THAN JUBILANT WITH THE VERDICT.
THE CROWD'S REACTION WAS DECIDEDLY MIXED...
WHILE THE PROSECUTION MUST HAVE BEEN WONDERING WHERE THEY COULD HAVE POSSIBLY GONE SO VERY WRONG.
SOME IN THE COURTROOM BEGAN TO HURL EPITHETS AS THE JURORS EXITED.
ORDER!
I WANT ORDER IN THIS COURT!
THE JUDGE WAS FORCED TO CLEAR THE COURTROOM, AS MEMBERS OF THE PRESS RACED TO FILE THEIR STORIES...
...GOT THAT?
ALL RIGHT, LISTEN UP BOYS AND GIRLS!
TIME TO EARN YOUR PAYCHECKS!

NOT GUILTY!?

NOW WE SEE THE JUSTICE OF COMPASSIONATE CONSERVATISM,

COMPASSION FOR *JUST US* CONSERVATIVES!

AND TO ADD INSULT TO INJURY THEY SEEK TO STRIP US OF OUR CONSTITUTIONAL RIGHT TO SPEAK OUT AGAINST THIS ATROCITY,

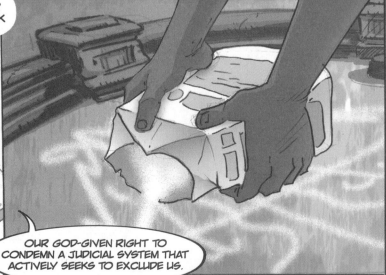

OUR GOD-GIVEN RIGHT TO CONDEMN A JUDICIAL SYSTEM THAT ACTIVELY SEEKS TO EXCLUDE US.

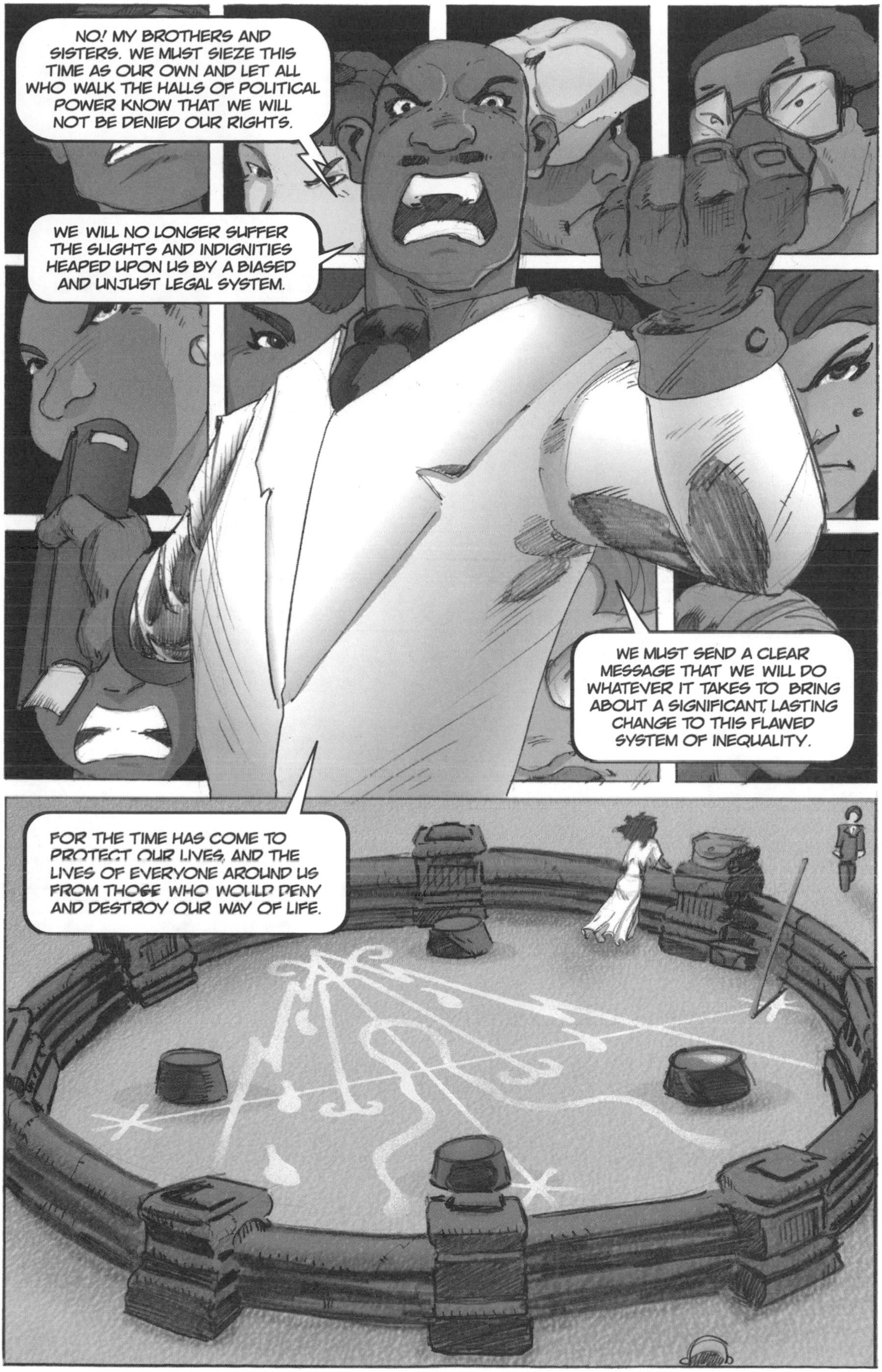
NO! MY BROTHERS AND SISTERS. WE MUST SIEZE THIS TIME AS OUR OWN AND LET ALL WHO WALK THE HALLS OF POLITICAL POWER KNOW THAT WE WILL NOT BE DENIED OUR RIGHTS.
WE WILL NO LONGER SUFFER THE SLIGHTS AND INDIGNITIES HEAPED UPON US BY A BIASED AND UNJUST LEGAL SYSTEM.
WE MUST SEND A CLEAR MESSAGE THAT WE WILL DO WHATEVER IT TAKES TO BRING ABOUT A SIGNIFICANT, LASTING CHANGE TO THIS FLAWED SYSTEM OF INEQUALITY.
FOR THE TIME HAS COME TO PROTECT OUR LIVES, AND THE LIVES OF EVERYONE AROUND US FROM THOSE WHO WOULD DENY AND DESTROY OUR WAY OF LIFE.

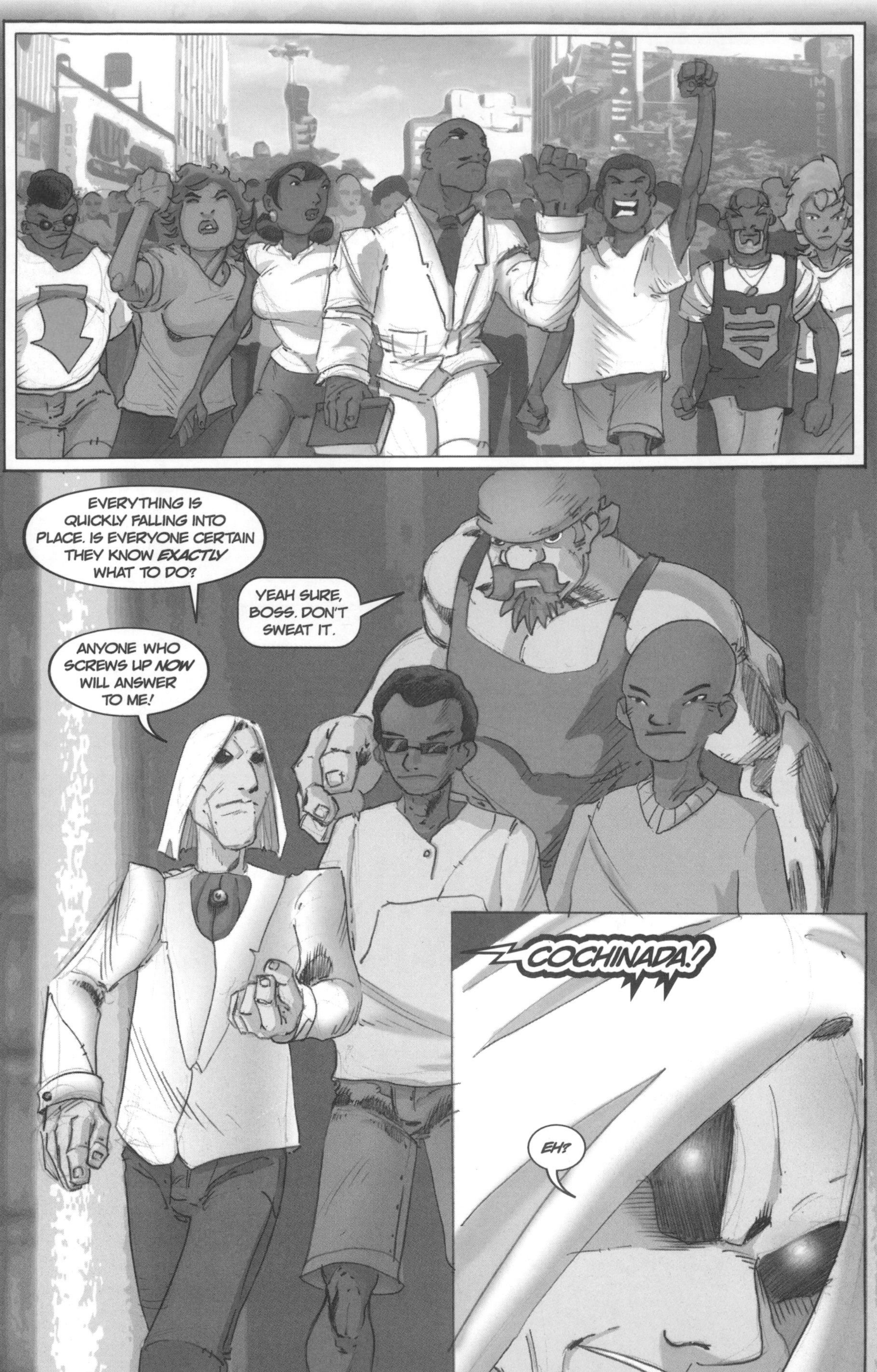
EVERYTHING IS QUICKLY FALLING INTO PLACE. IS EVERYONE CERTAIN THEY KNOW *EXACTLY* WHAT TO DO?
YEAH SURE, BOSS. DON'T SWEAT IT.
ANYONE WHO SCREWS UP *NOW* WILL ANSWER TO ME!
COCHINADA!
EH?

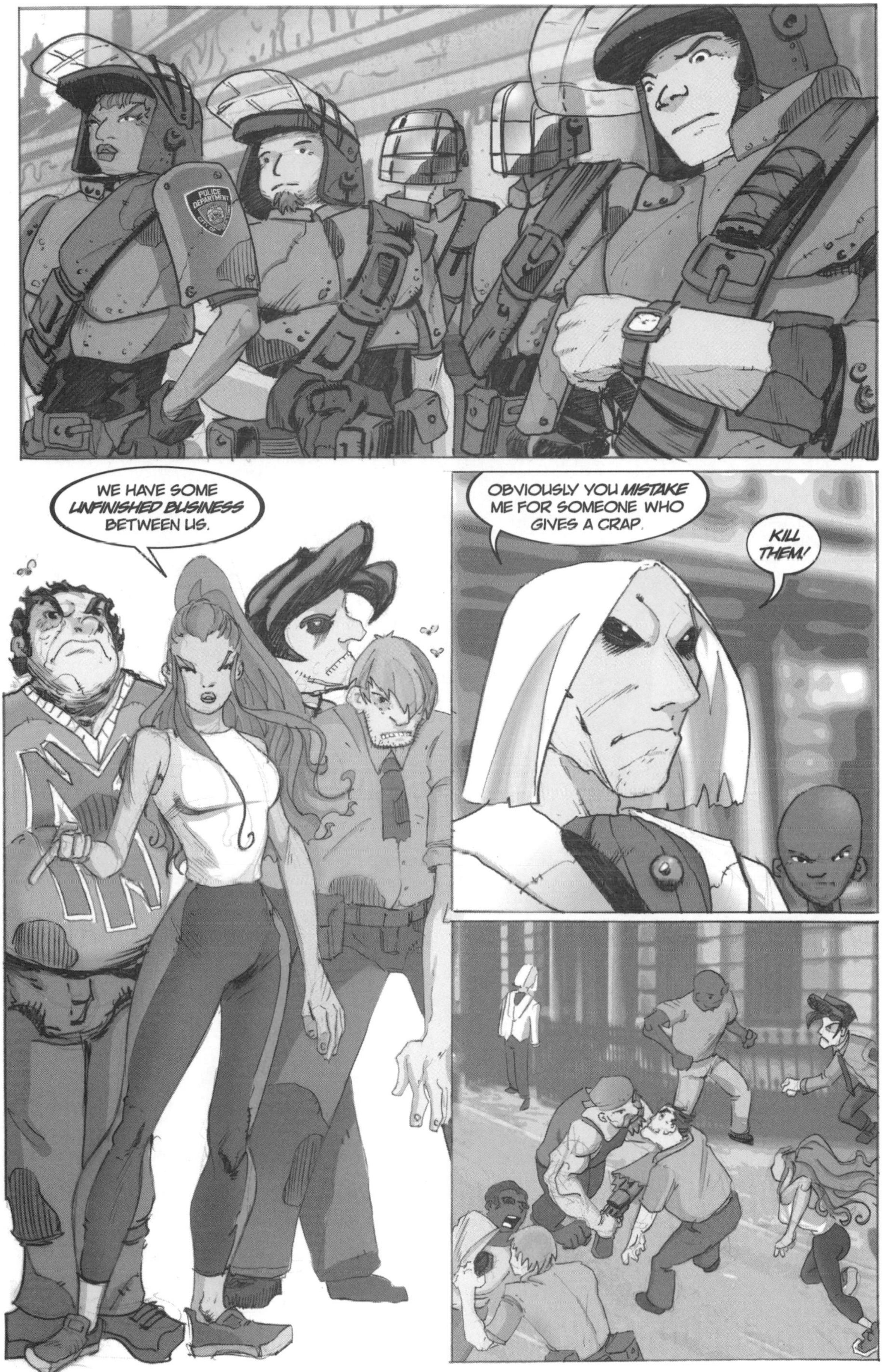
WE HAVE SOME UNFINISHED BUSINESS BETWEEN US.
OBVIOUSLY YOU MISTAKE ME FOR SOMEONE WHO GIVES A CRAP.
KILL THEM!

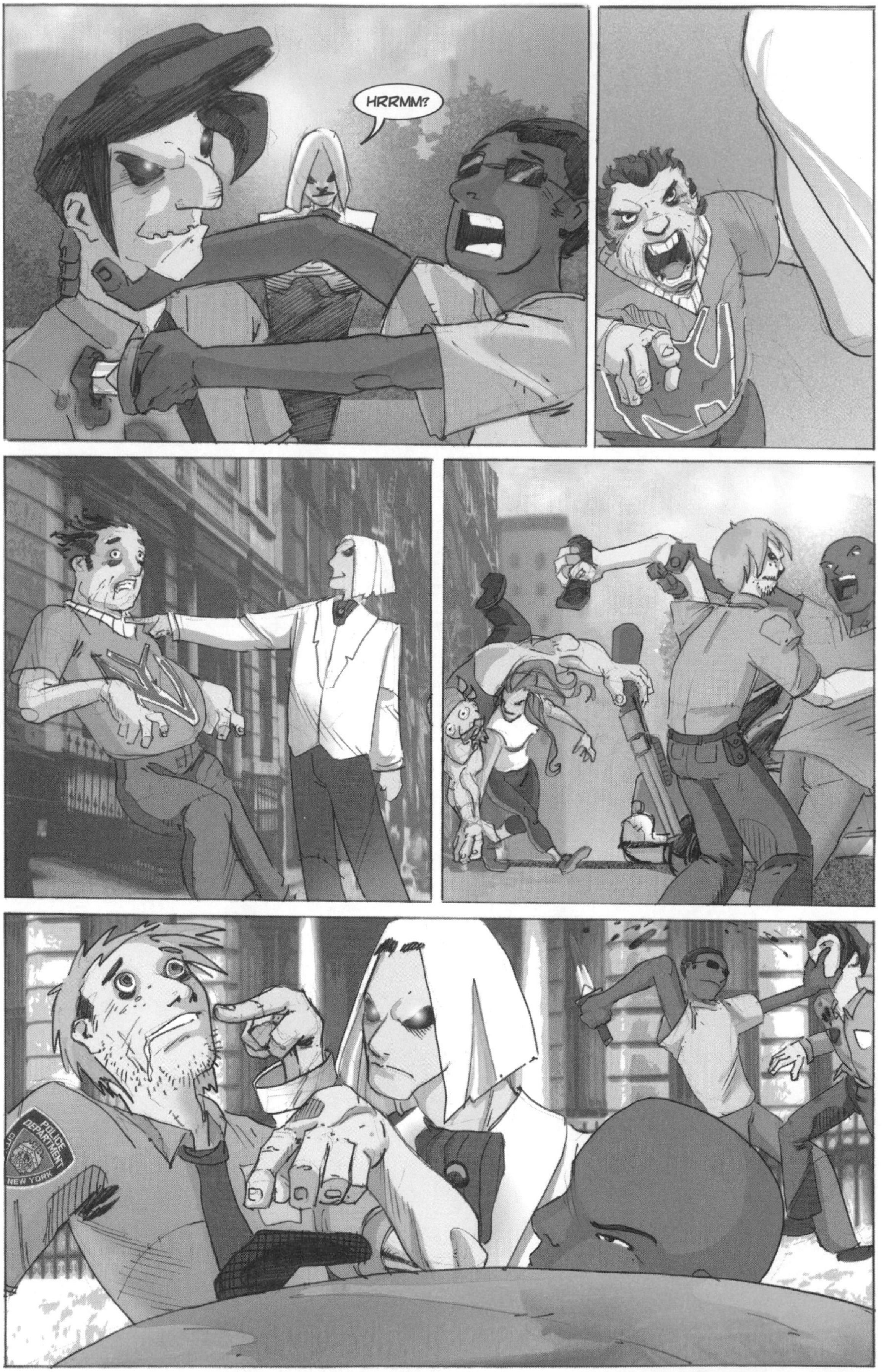
HRRMM?
POLICE DEPARTMENT
NEW YORK

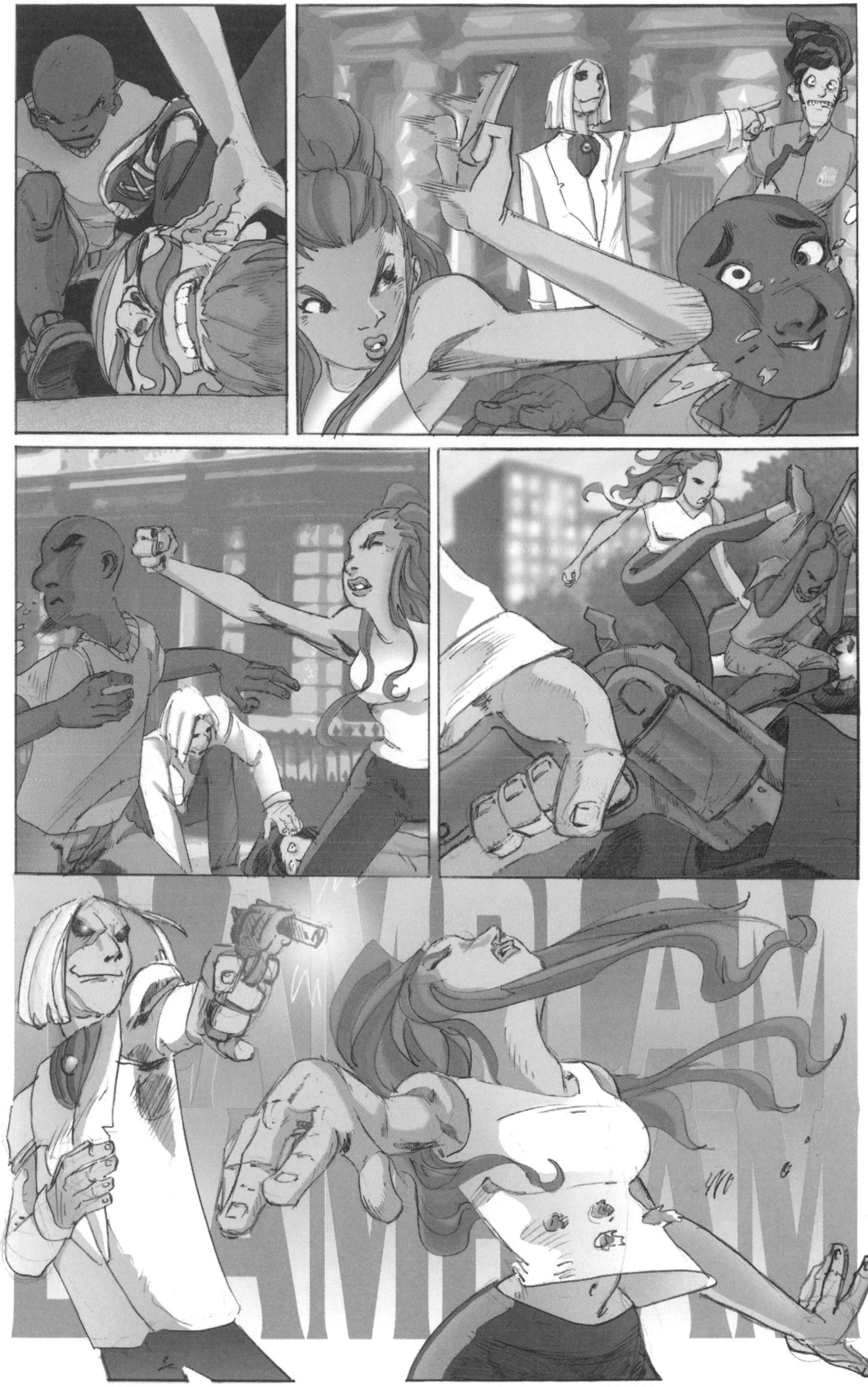

WE'VE WASTED ENOUGH TIME WITH THIS *PERRA*, LET'S BE ON OUR WAY.

JUST LIKE A MAN...

...*FIRE OFF* A COUPLE ROUNDS AND *RUN* LIKE A DOG.

WELL, *WELL!* IT LOOKS LIKE YOU DIED LAST NIGHT *AFTER ALL*...

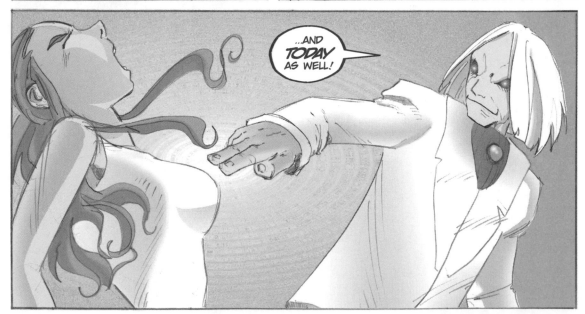

...AND *TODAY* AS WELL!

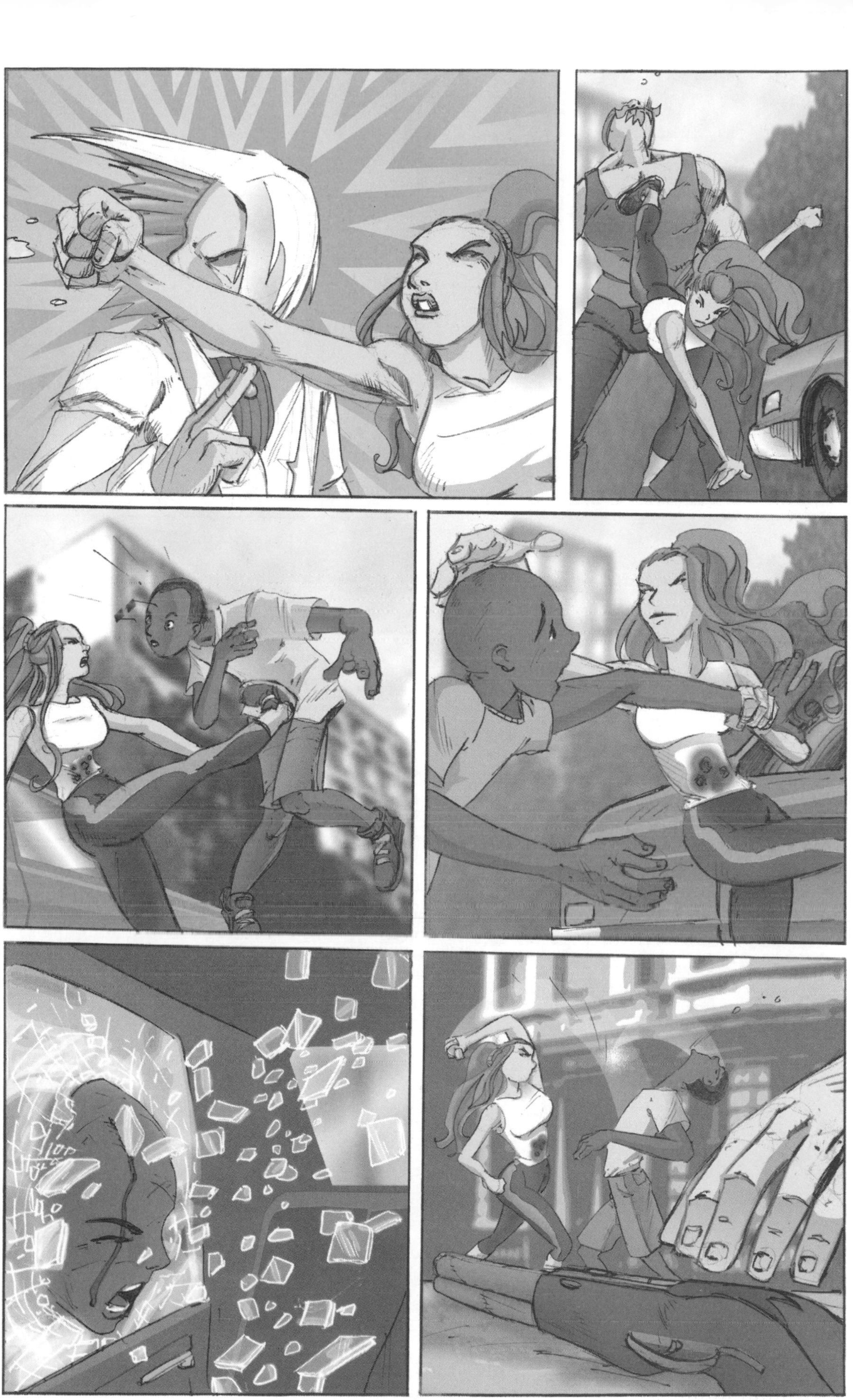

BOOM!!

I DON'T KNOW WHAT *KIND OF ZOMBIE* YOU ARE...

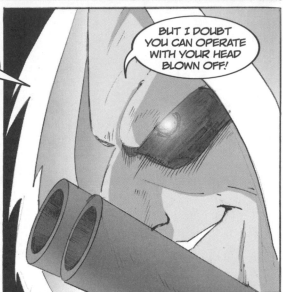

BUT I DOUBT YOU CAN OPERATE WITH YOUR HEAD BLOWN OFF!

KA-BLOOM!!

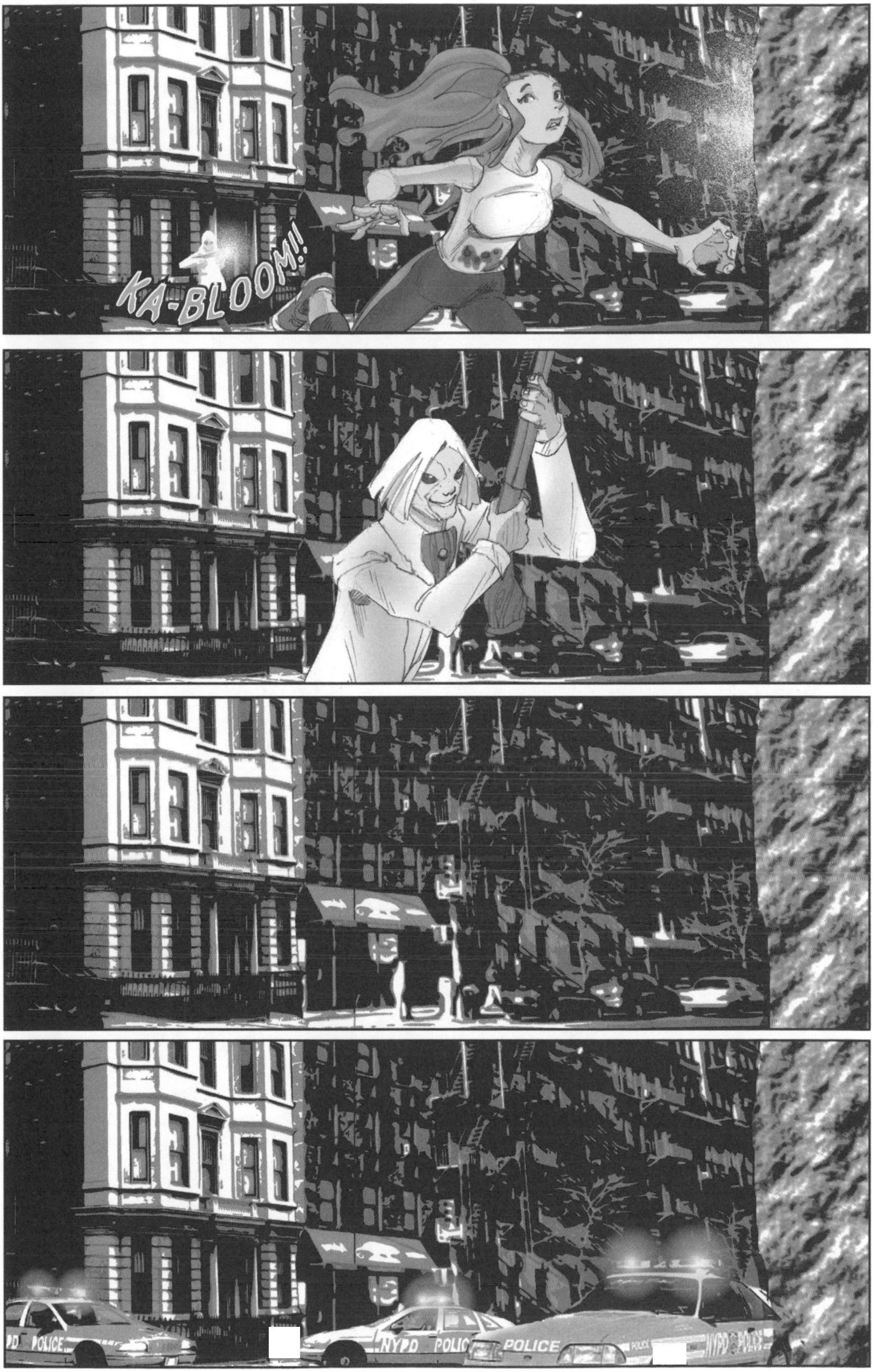
KA-BLOOM!!
POLICE
NYPD POLIC
POLICE
NYPD

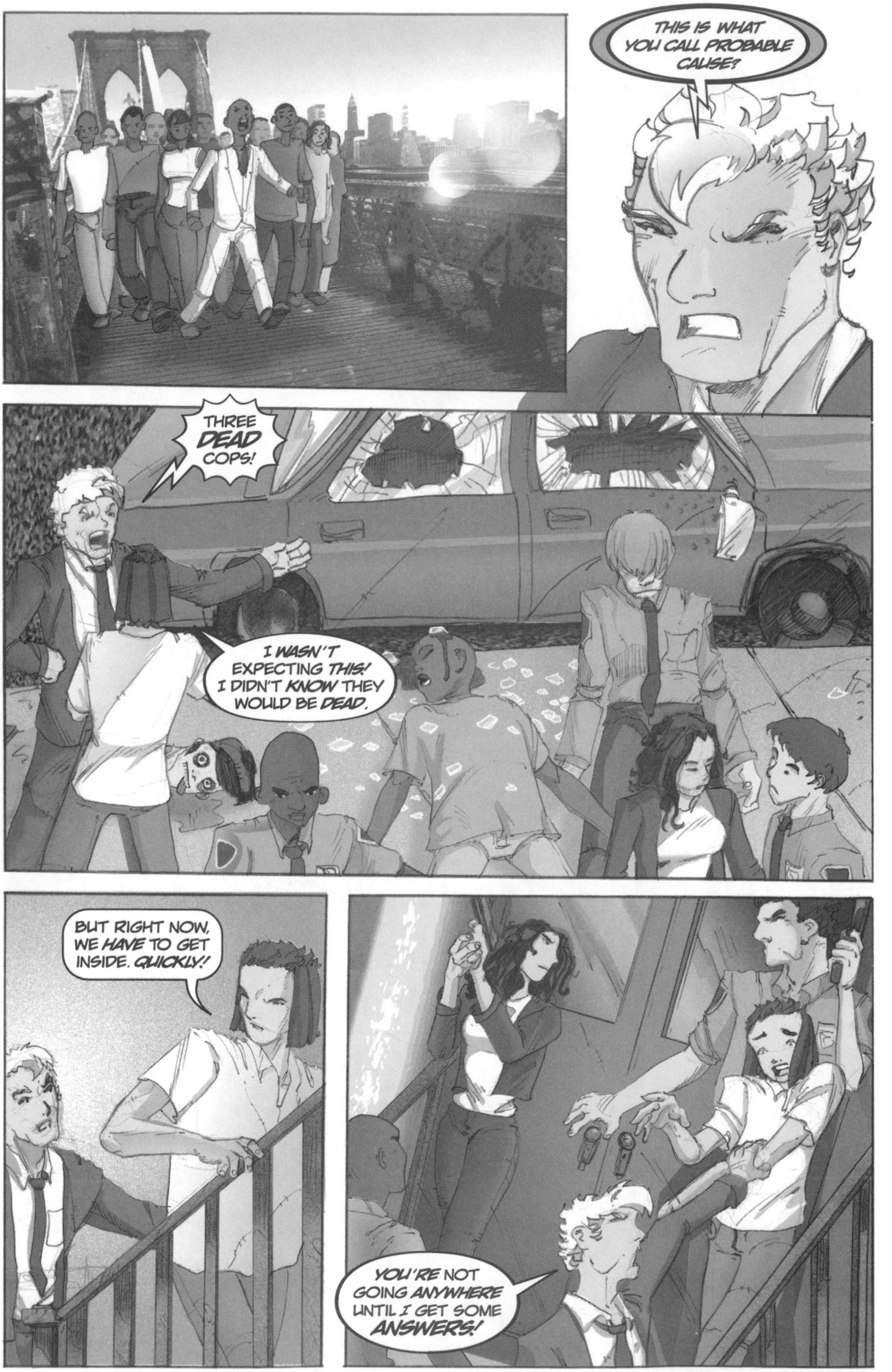
THIS IS WHAT YOU CALL PROBABLE CAUSE?
THREE DEAD COPS!
I WASN'T EXPECTING THIS! I DIDN'T KNOW THEY WOULD BE DEAD.
BUT RIGHT NOW, WE HAVE TO GET INSIDE. QUICKLY!
YOU'RE NOT GOING ANYWHERE UNTIL I GET SOME ANSWERS!

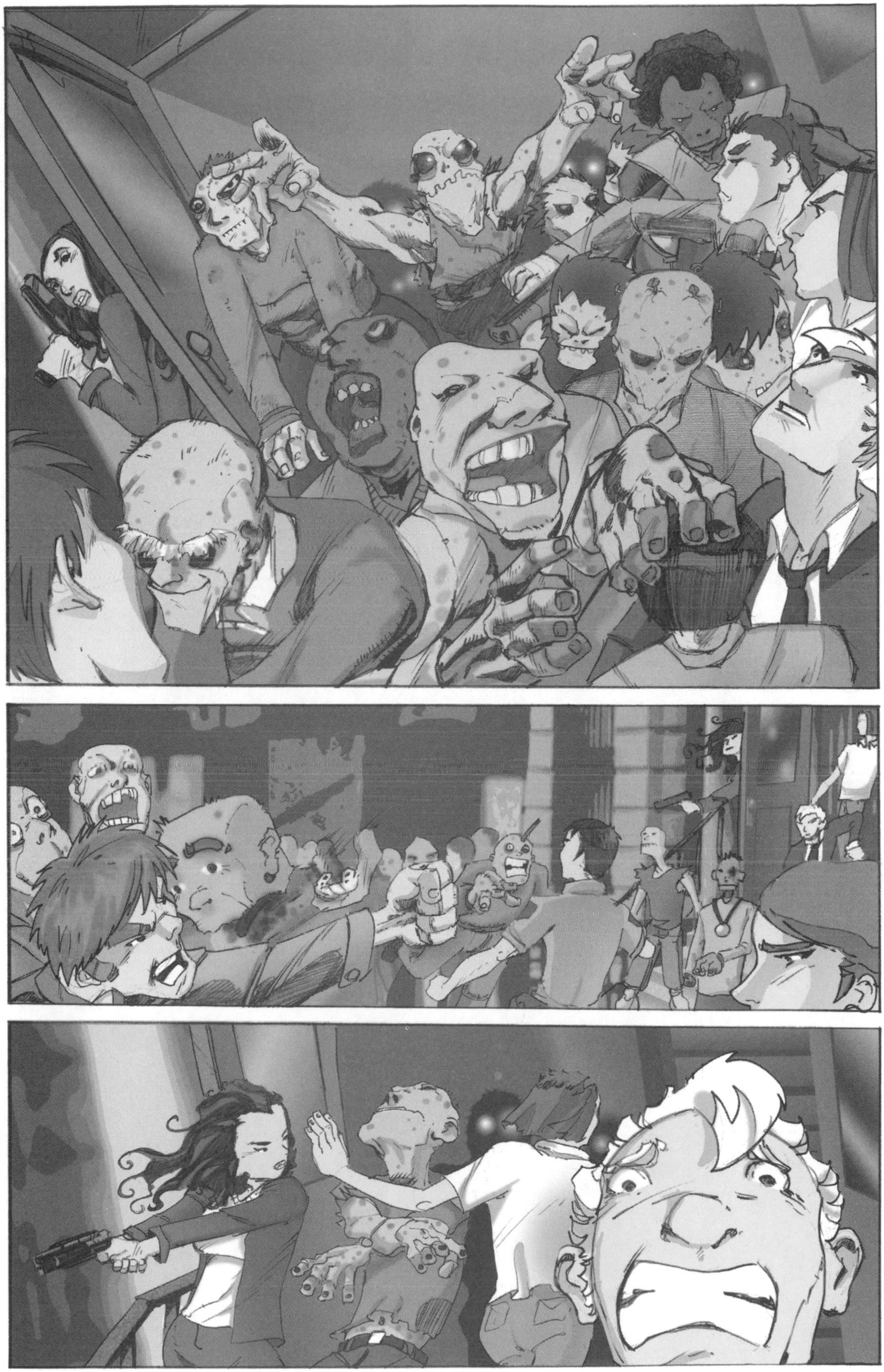

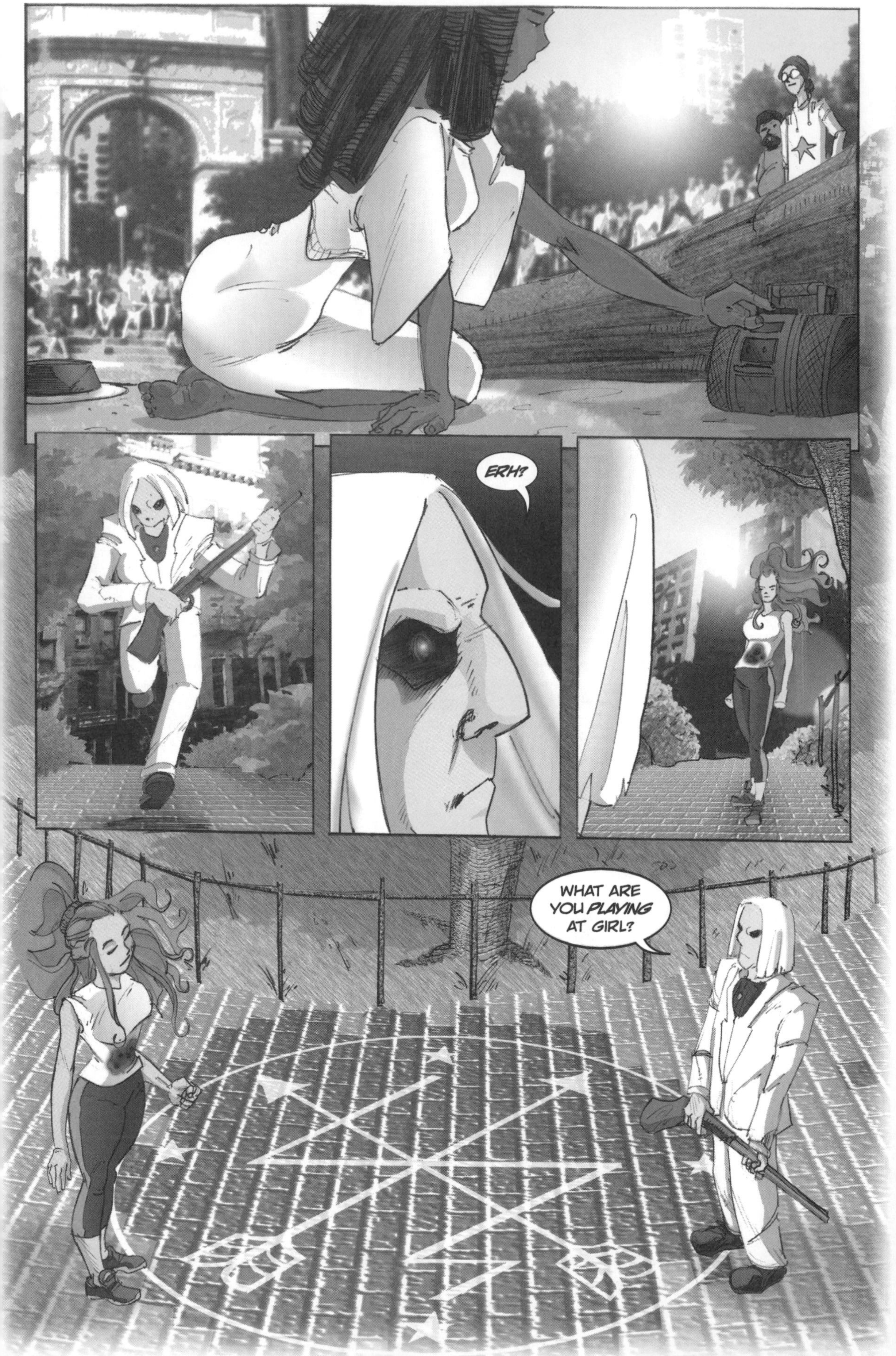
ERH?
WHAT ARE YOU PLAYING AT GIRL?

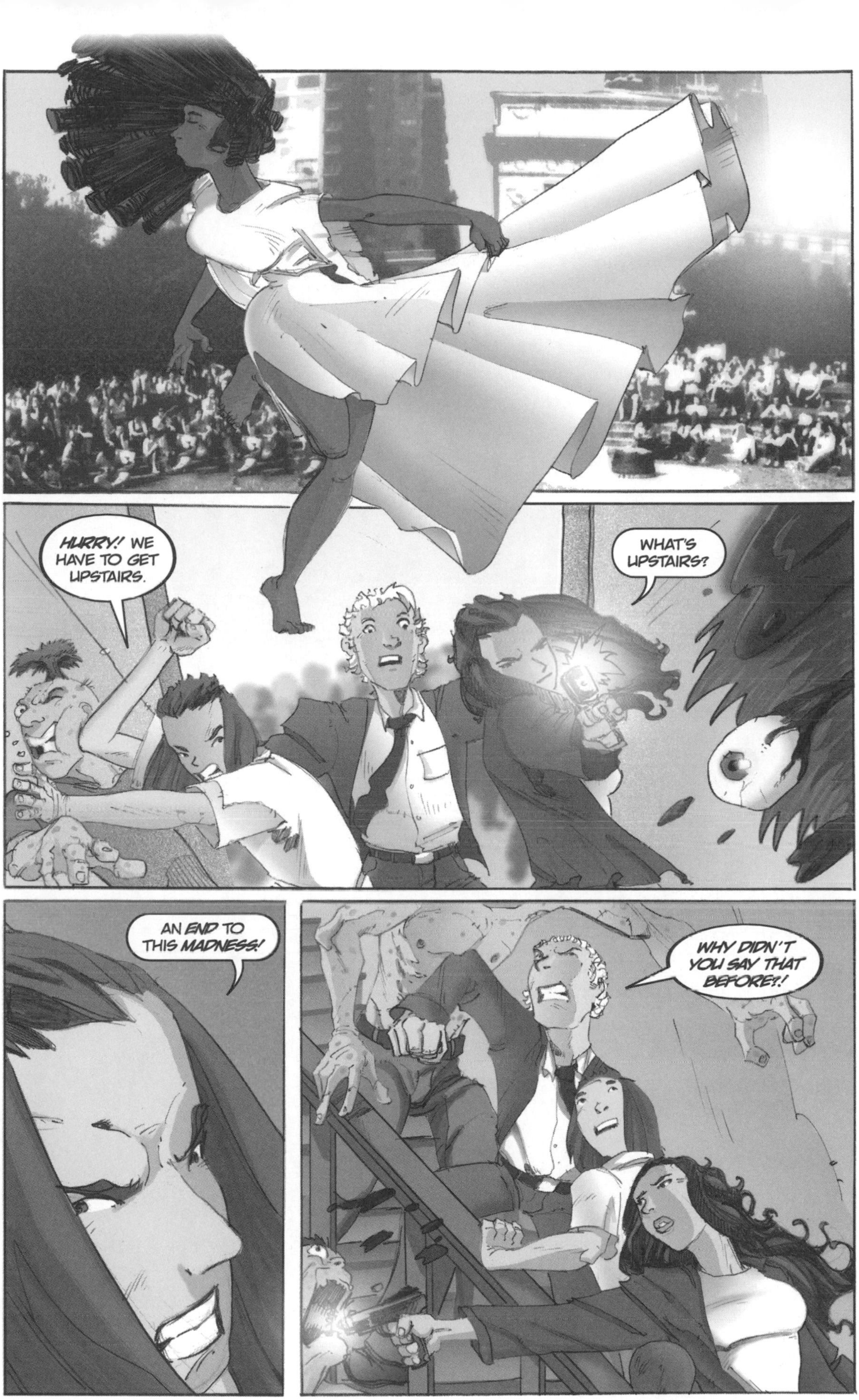
HURRY! WE HAVE TO GET UPSTAIRS.
WHAT'S UPSTAIRS?
AN END TO THIS MADNESS!
WHY DIDN'T YOU SAY THAT BEFORE?!

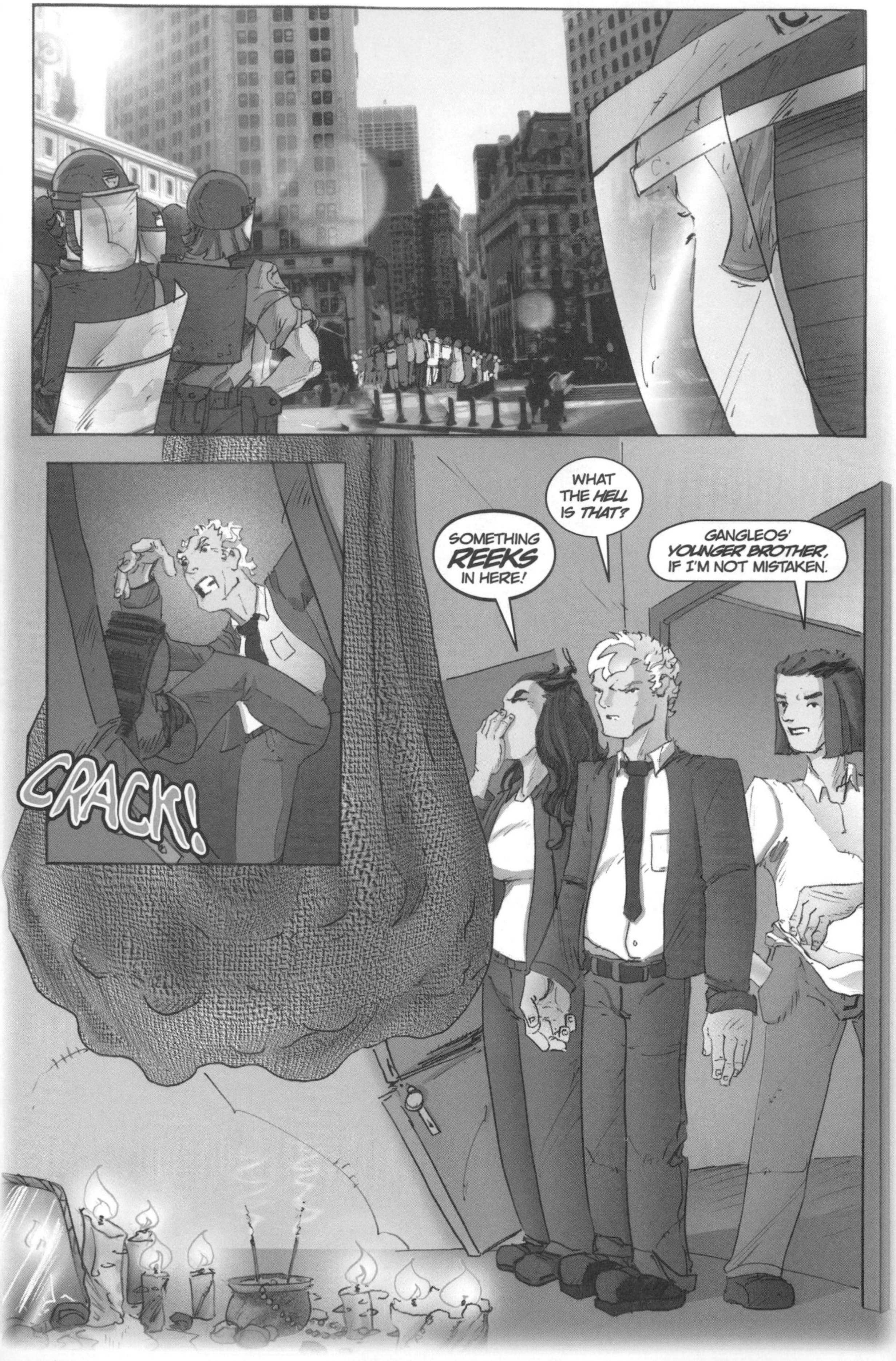
CRACK!
SOMETHING REEKS IN HERE!
WHAT THE HELL IS THAT?
GANGLEOS' YOUNGER BROTHER, IF I'M NOT MISTAKEN.

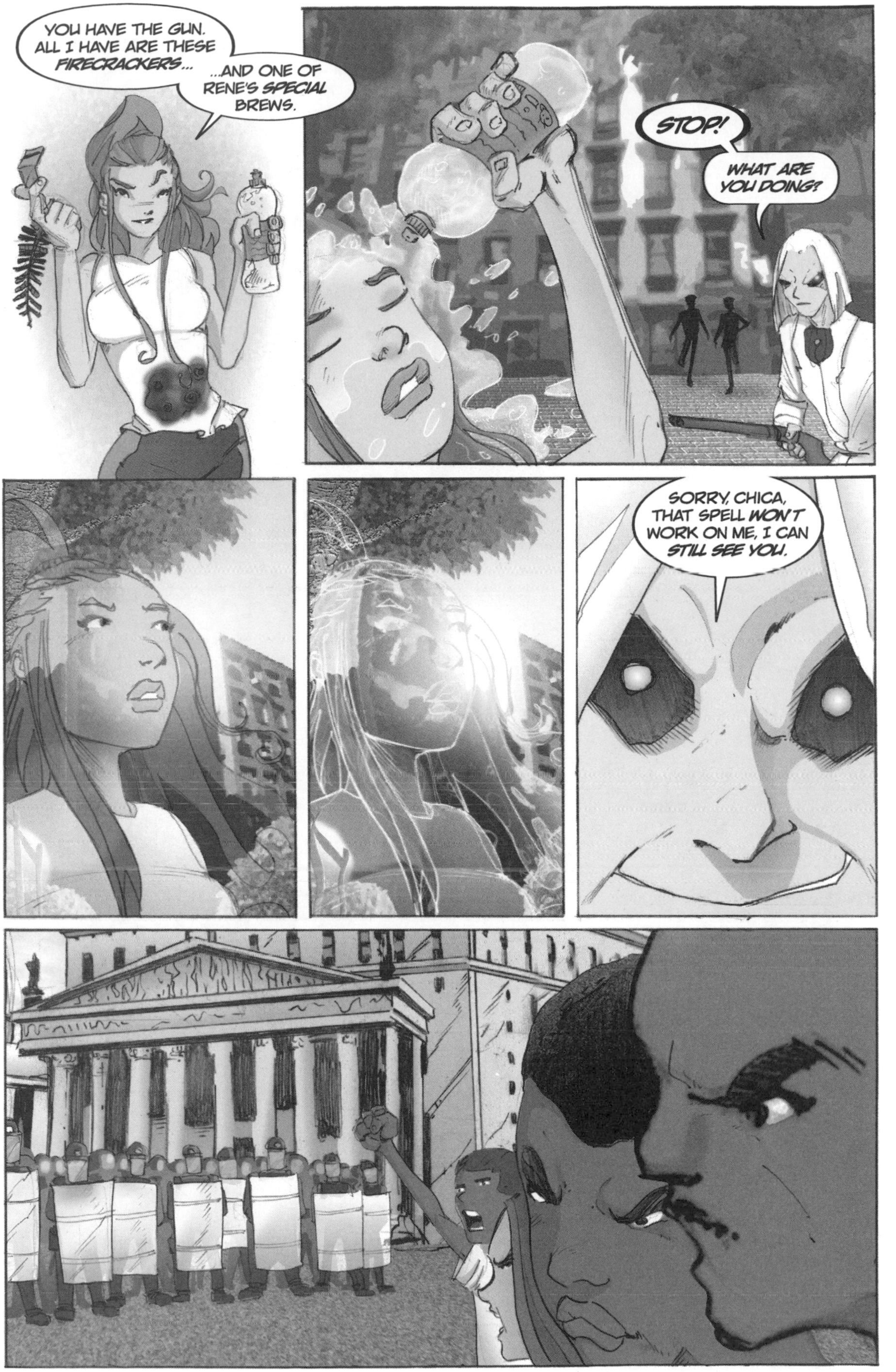
YOU HAVE THE GUN. ALL I HAVE ARE THESE FIRECRACKERS...
...AND ONE OF RENE'S SPECIAL BREWS.
STOP!
WHAT ARE YOU DOING?
SORRY, CHICA, THAT SPELL WON'T WORK ON ME, I CAN STILL SEE YOU.

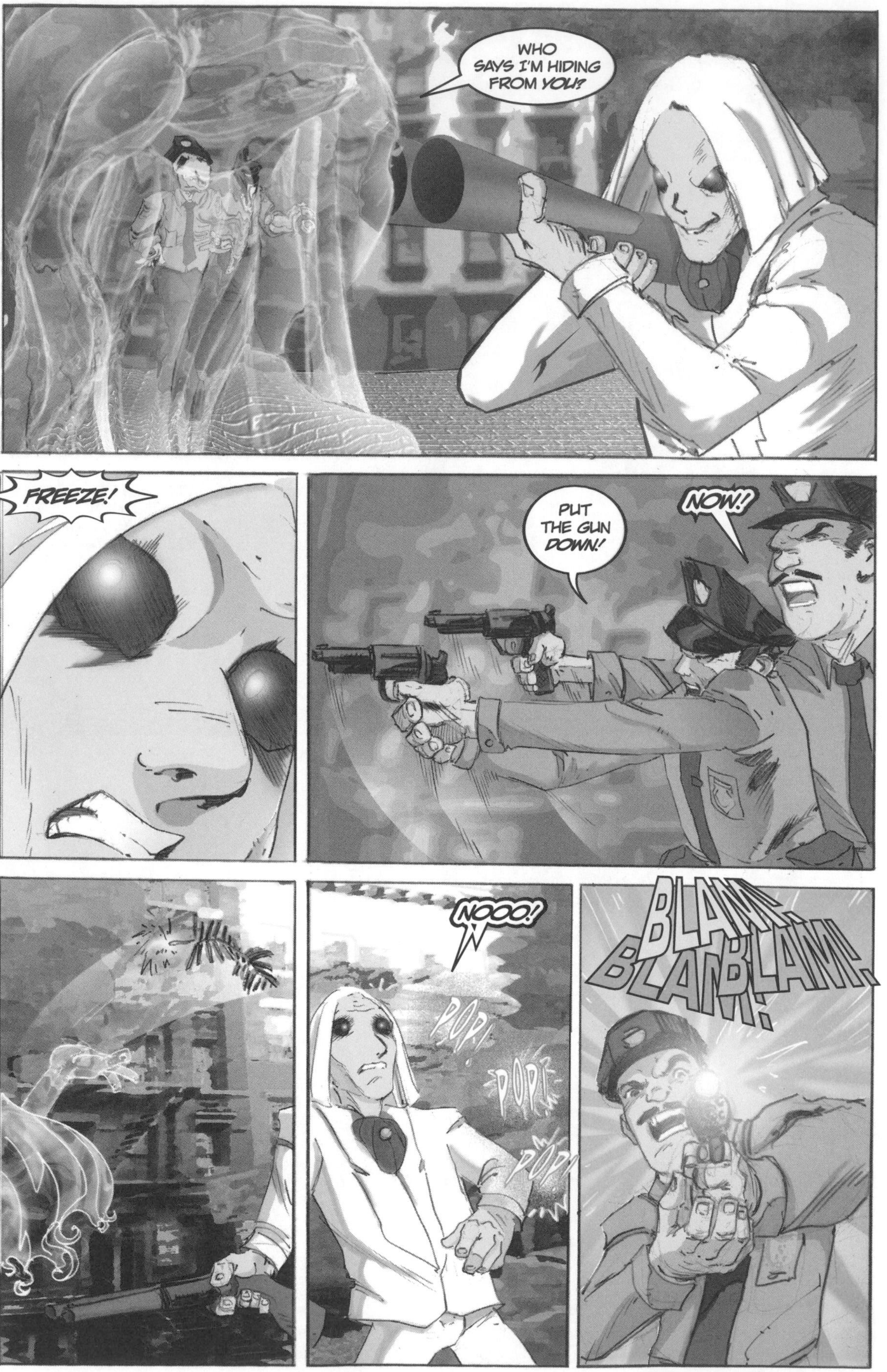
WHO SAYS I'M HIDING FROM YOU?
FREEZE!
PUT THE GUN DOWN!
NOW!
NOOO!
POP!
POP!
POP!
BLAM! BLAM! BLAM!

I BAPTIZE THEE IN THE NAME OF THE FATHER...

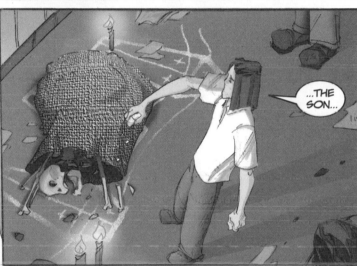

...THE SON...

...AND THE HOLY SPIRIT.

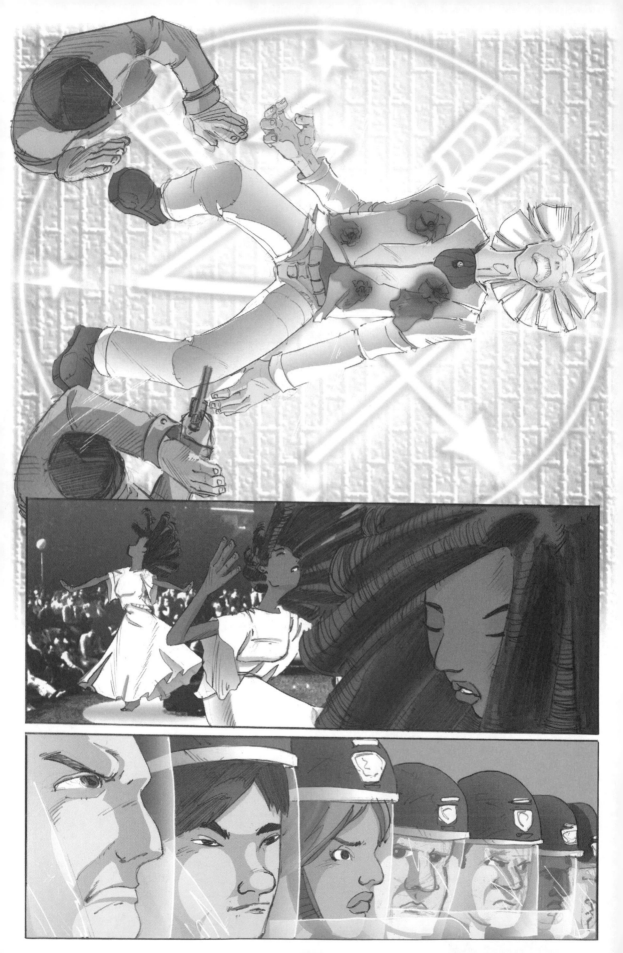

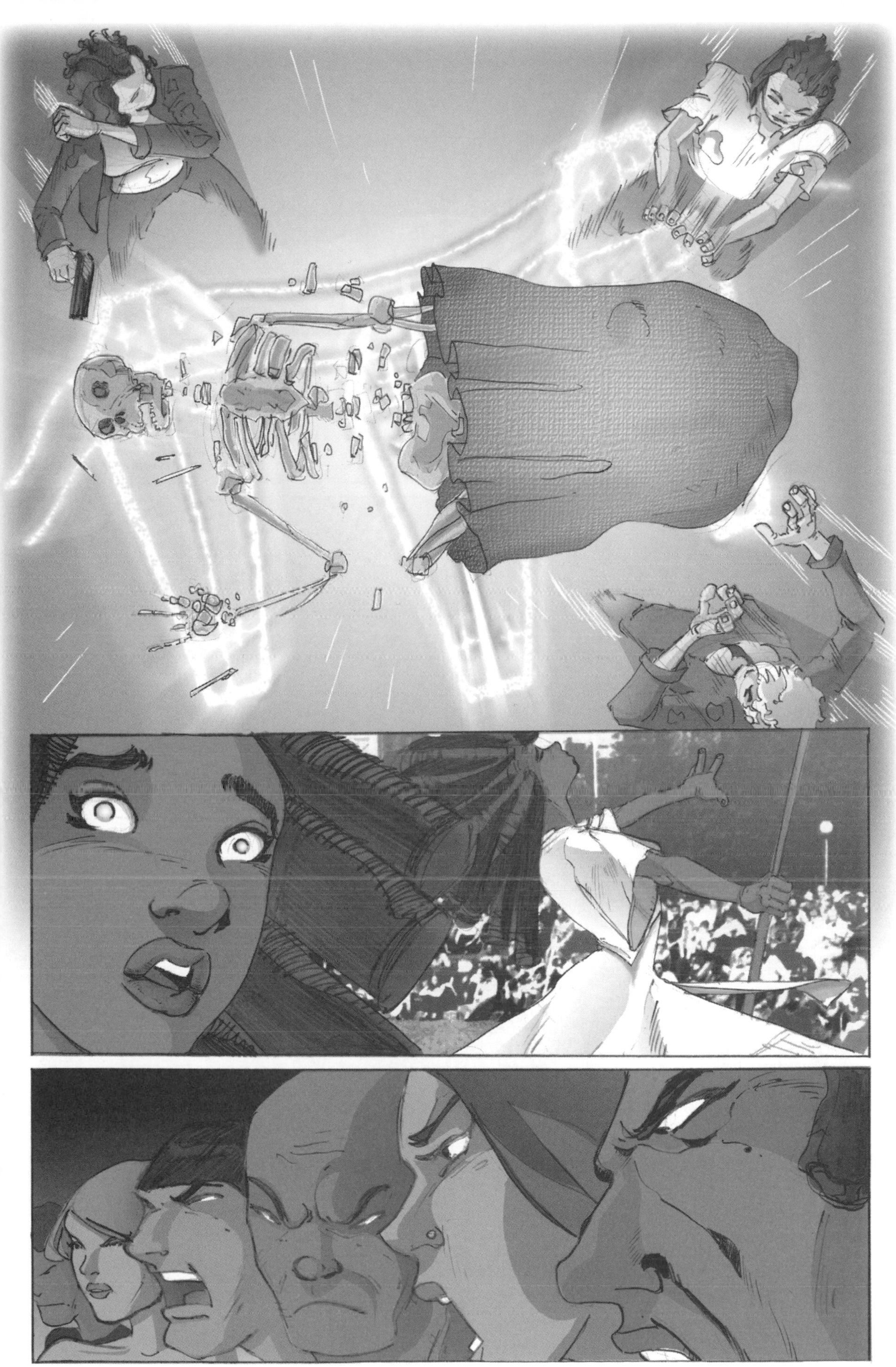

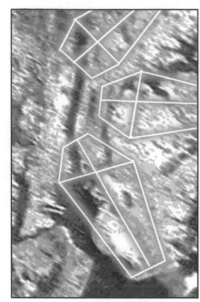
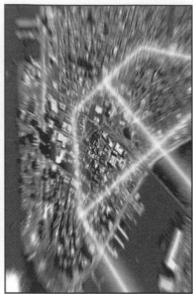
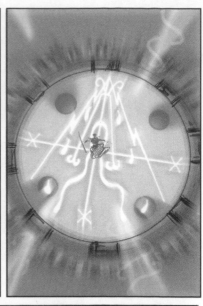

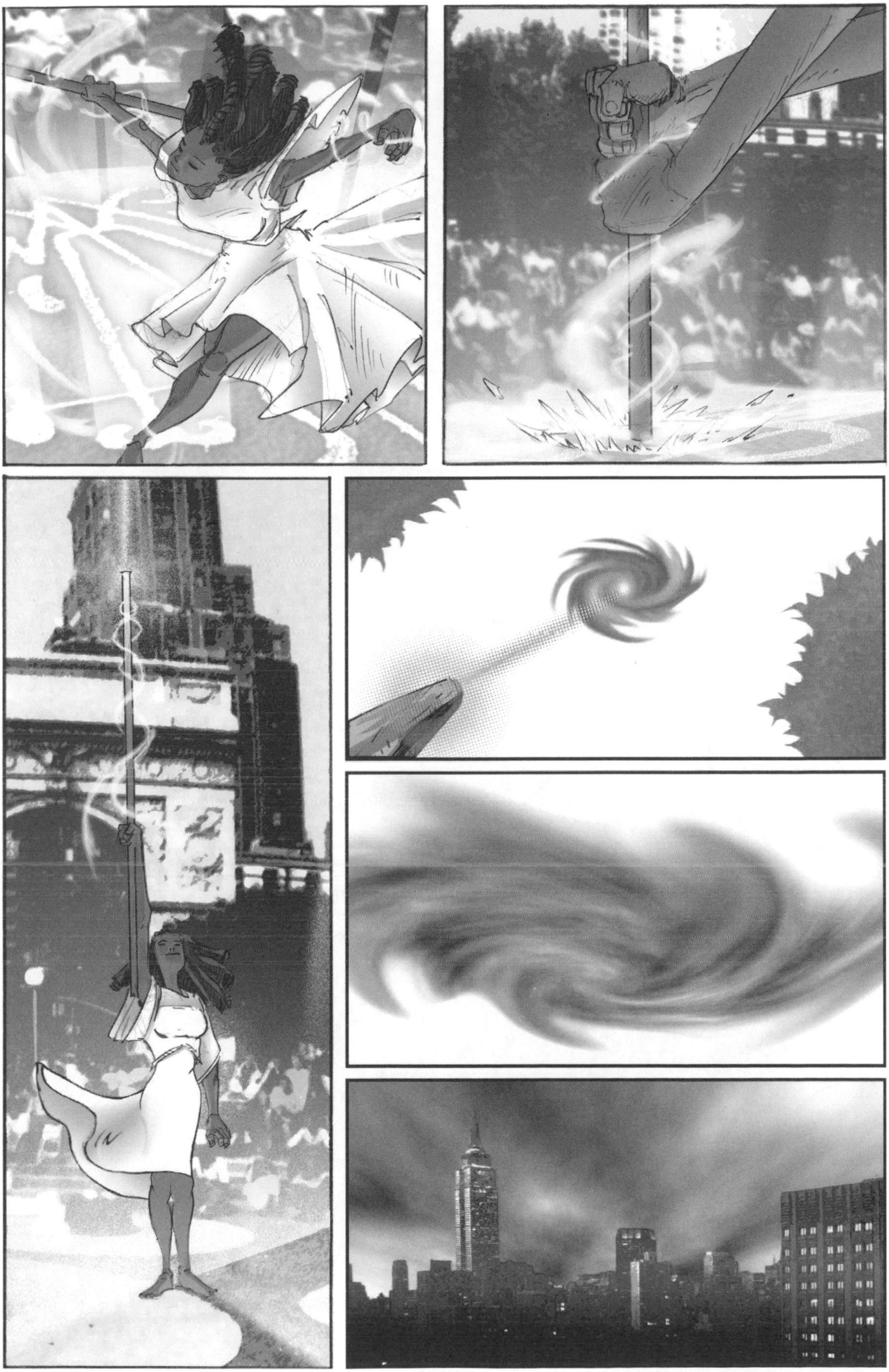

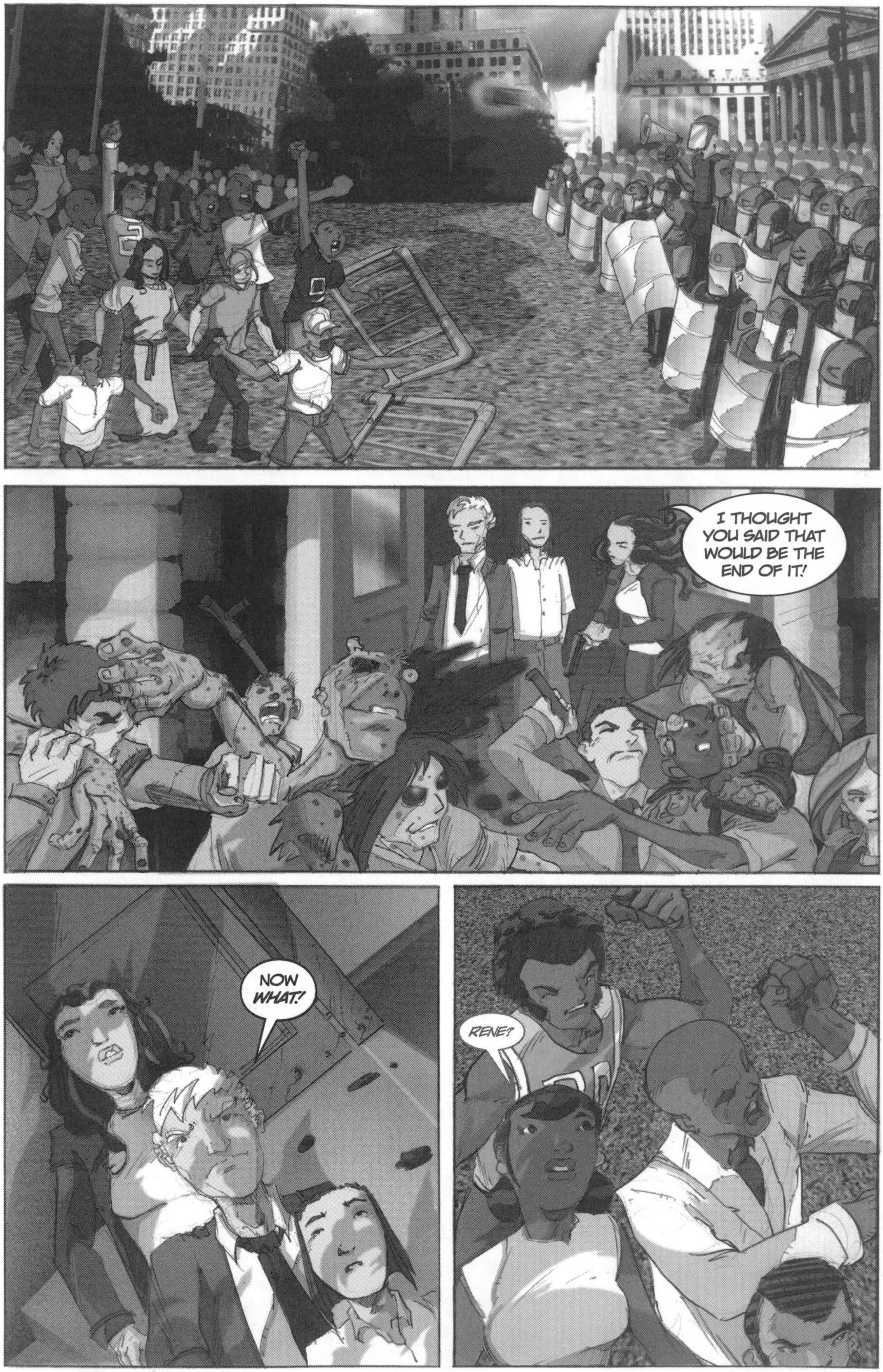
I THOUGHT YOU SAID THAT WOULD BE THE END OF IT!
NOW WHAT!
RENE?

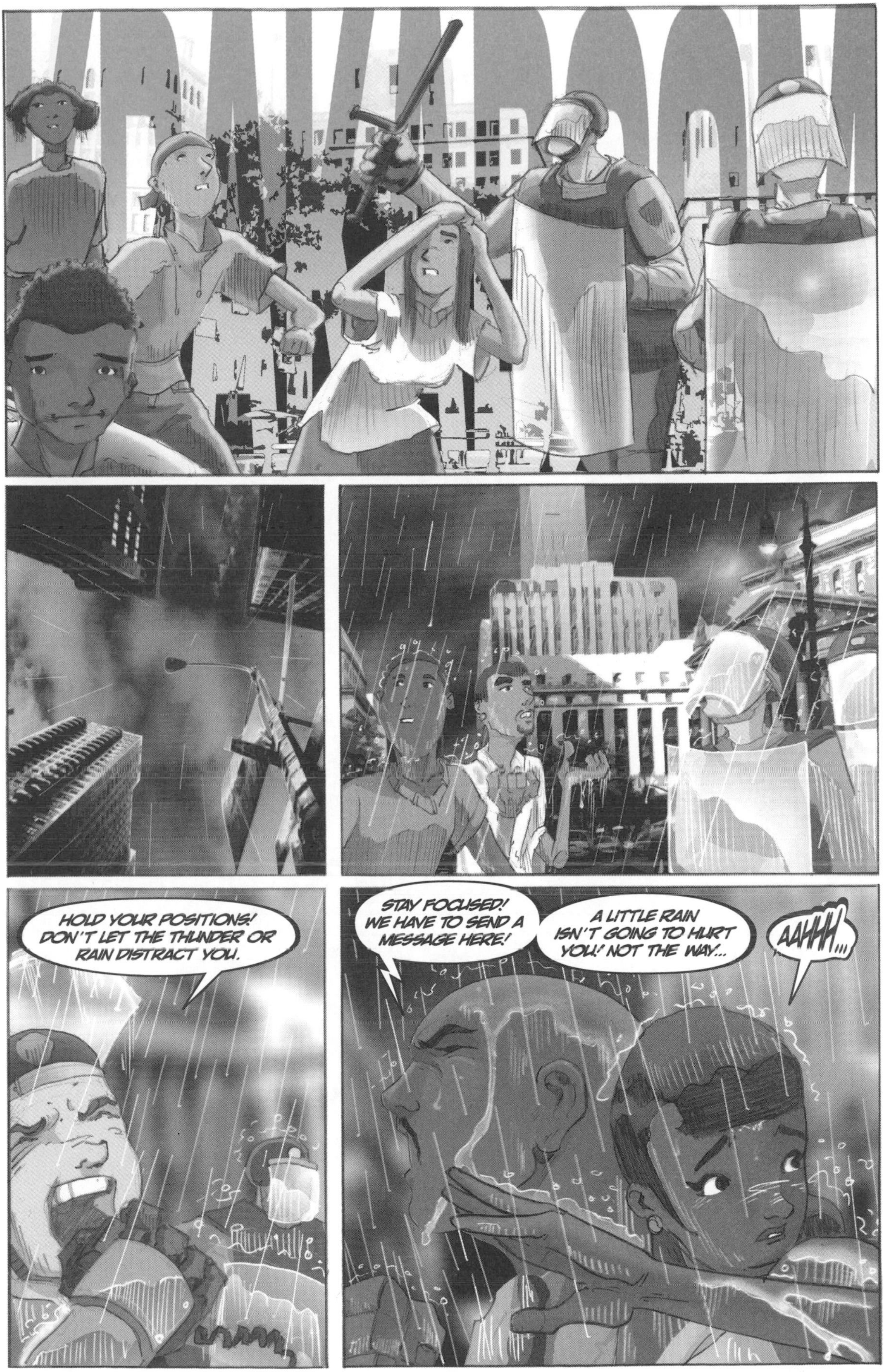
HOLD YOUR POSITIONS! DON'T LET THE THUNDER OR RAIN DISTRACT YOU.
STAY FOCUSED! WE HAVE TO SEND A MESSAGE HERE!
A LITTLE RAIN ISN'T GOING TO HURT YOU! NOT THE WAY...
AAHHH...

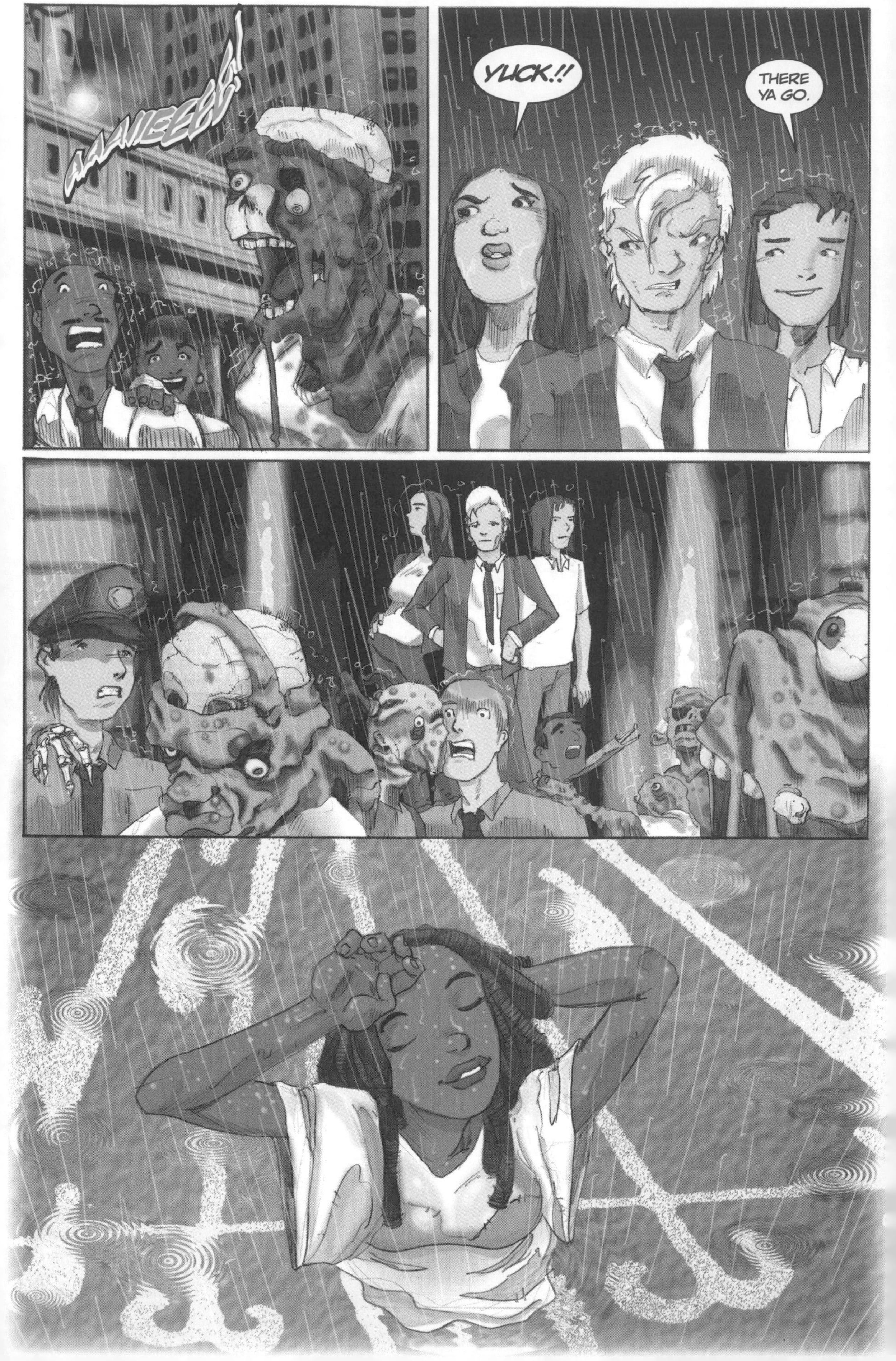
AAAIIEEEE!
YUCK.!!
THERE YA GO.

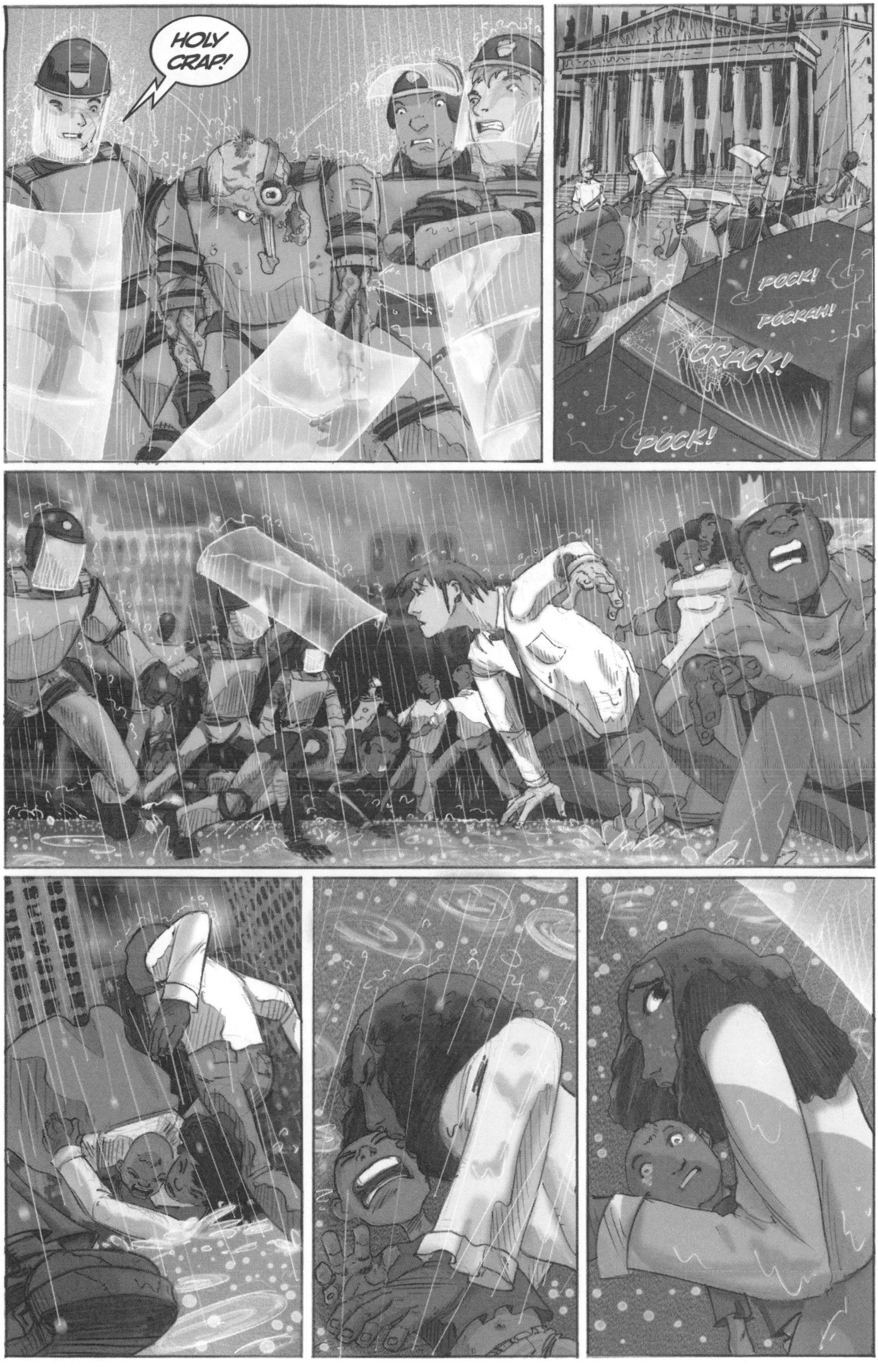
HOLY CRAP!
POCK!
POCKAH!
CRACK!
POCK!

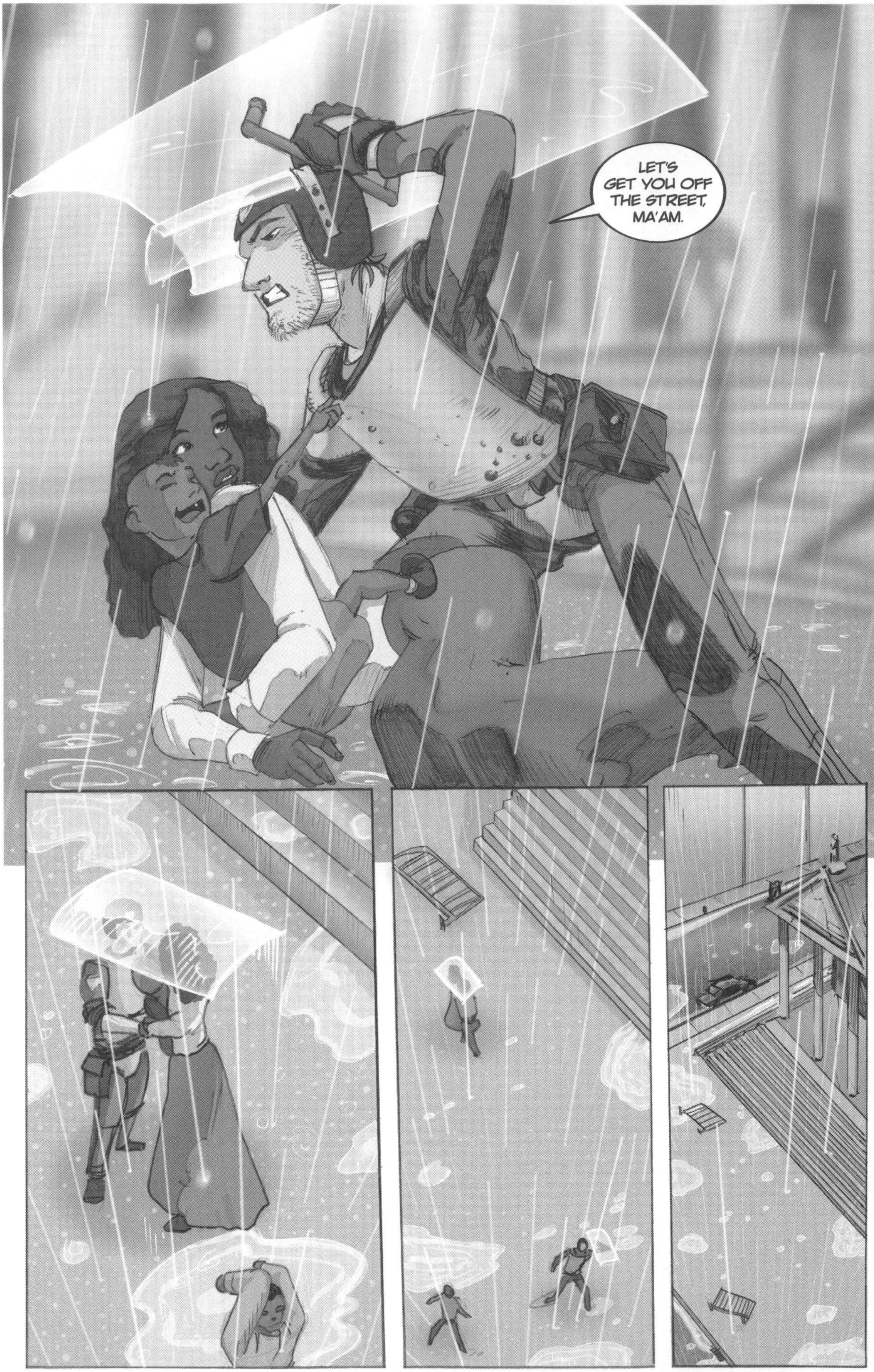
LET'S GET YOU OFF THE STREET, MA'AM.

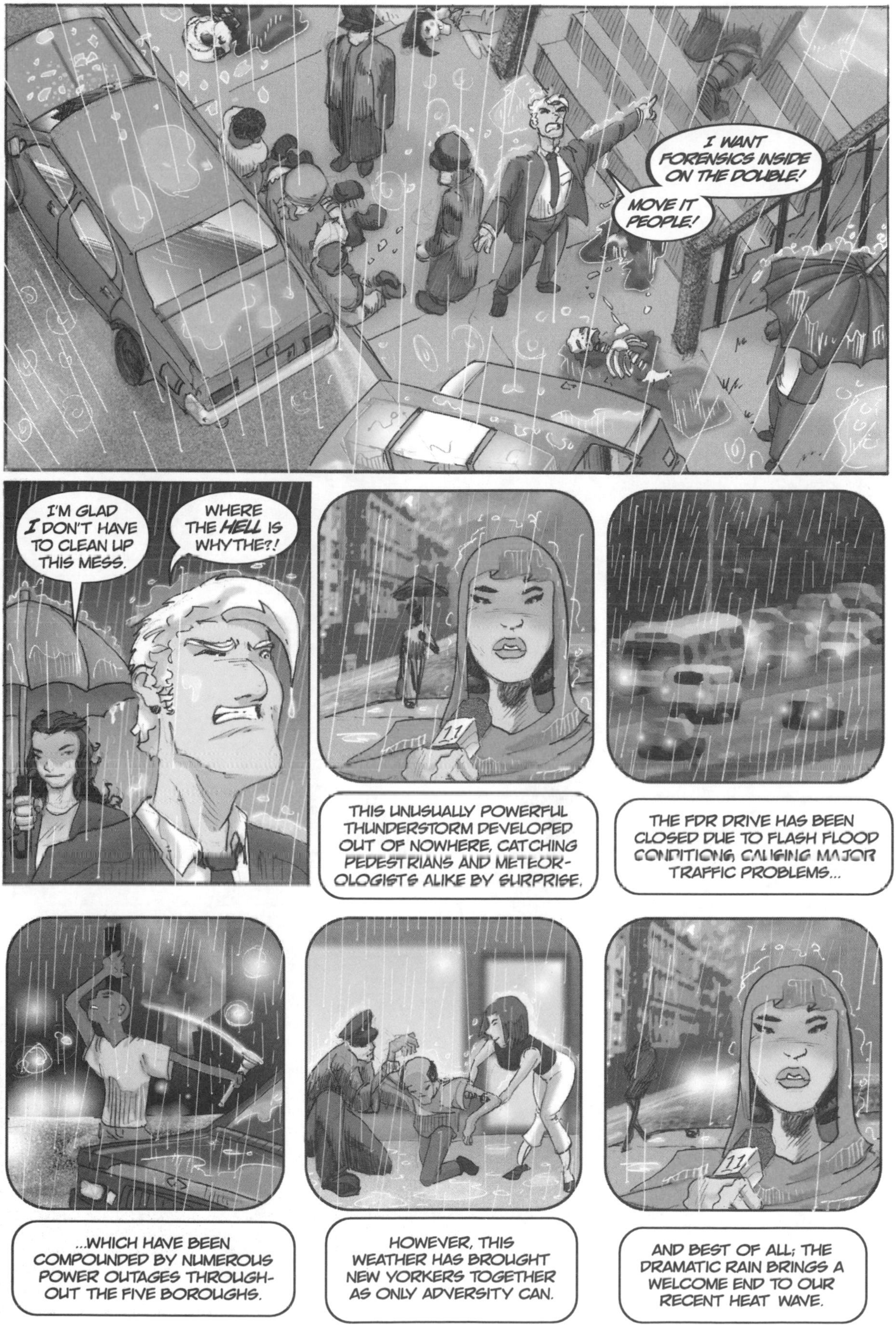
I WANT FORENSICS INSIDE ON THE DOUBLE!
MOVE IT PEOPLE!
I'M GLAD I DON'T HAVE TO CLEAN UP THIS MESS.
WHERE THE HELL IS WHYTHE?!
THIS UNUSUALLY POWERFUL THUNDERSTORM DEVELOPED OUT OF NOWHERE, CATCHING PEDESTRIANS AND METEOROLOGISTS ALIKE BY SURPRISE.
THE FDR DRIVE HAS BEEN CLOSED DUE TO FLASH FLOOD CONDITIONS, CAUSING MAJOR TRAFFIC PROBLEMS...
...WHICH HAVE BEEN COMPOUNDED BY NUMEROUS POWER OUTAGES THROUGHOUT THE FIVE BOROUGHS.
HOWEVER, THIS WEATHER HAS BROUGHT NEW YORKERS TOGETHER AS ONLY ADVERSITY CAN.
AND BEST OF ALL; THE DRAMATIC RAIN BRINGS A WELCOME END TO OUR RECENT HEAT WAVE.

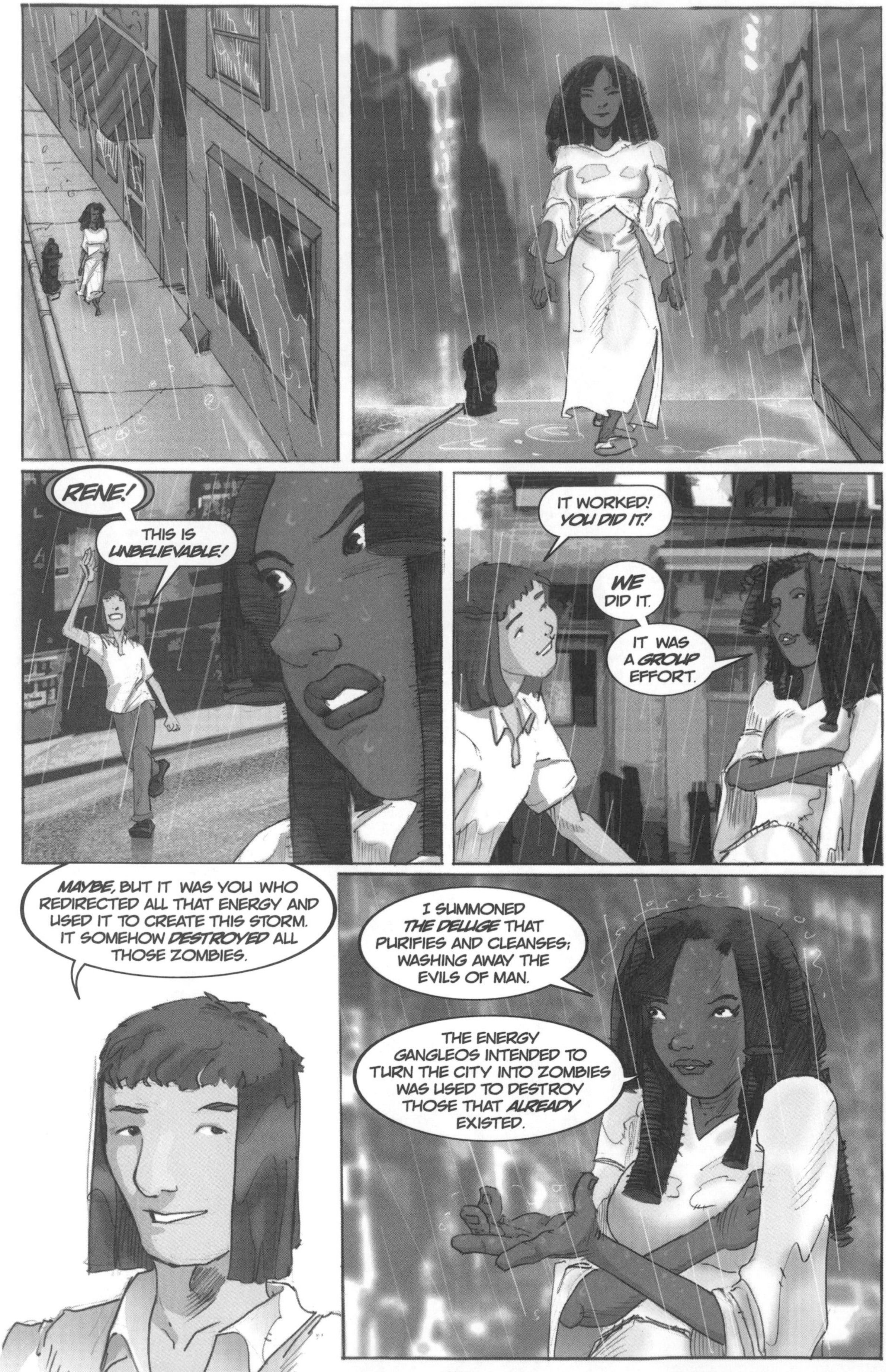
RENE!
THIS IS UNBELIEVABLE!
IT WORKED! YOU DID IT!
WE DID IT.
IT WAS A GROUP EFFORT.
MAYBE, BUT IT WAS YOU WHO REDIRECTED ALL THAT ENERGY AND USED IT TO CREATE THIS STORM. IT SOMEHOW DESTROYED ALL THOSE ZOMBIES.
I SUMMONED THE DELUGE THAT PURIFIES AND CLEANSES; WASHING AWAY THE EVILS OF MAN.
THE ENERGY GANGLEOS INTENDED TO TURN THE CITY INTO ZOMBIES WAS USED TO DESTROY THOSE THAT ALREADY EXISTED.

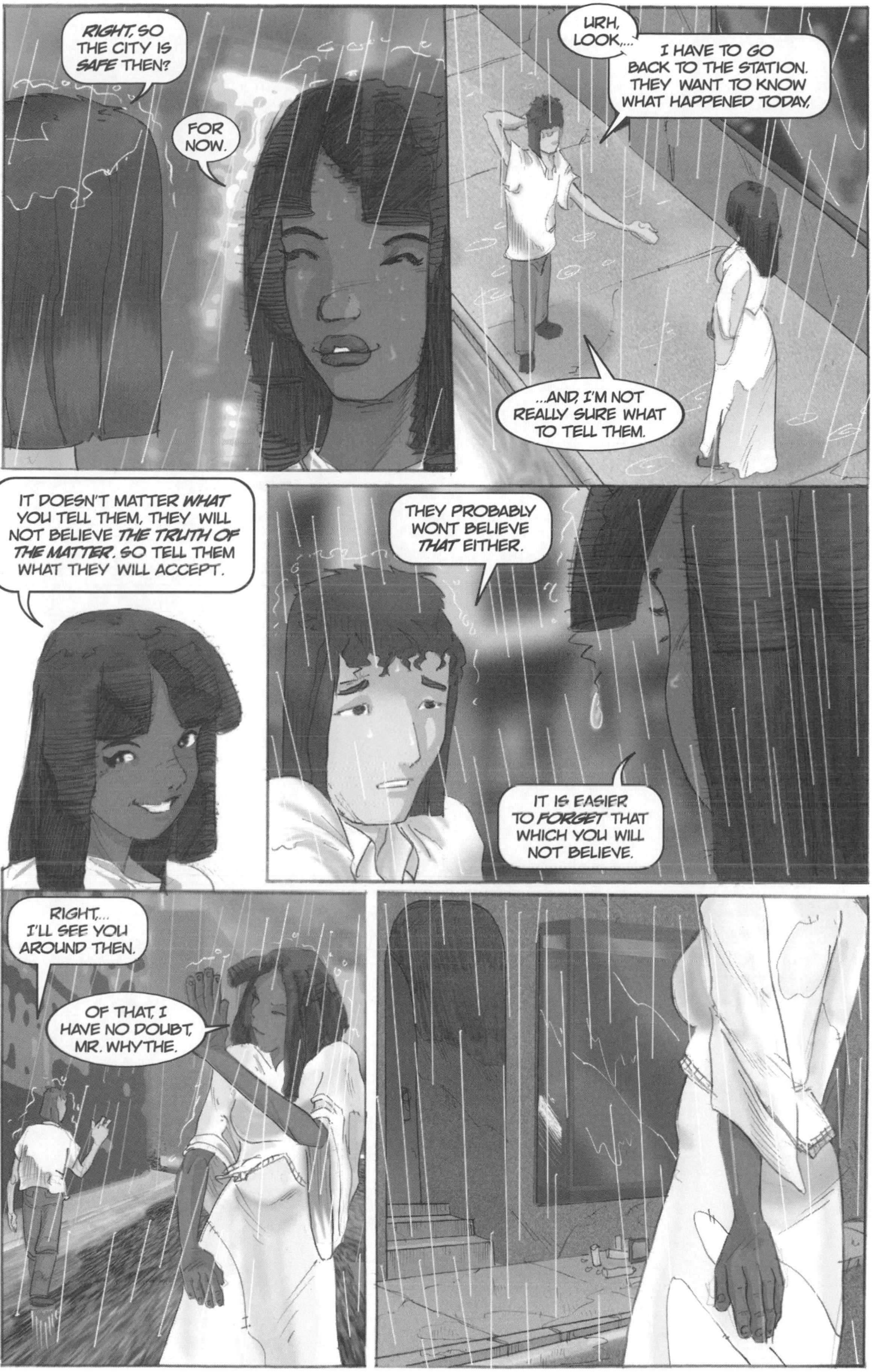
RIGHT, SO THE CITY IS SAFE THEN?
FOR NOW.
URH, LOOK,...
I HAVE TO GO BACK TO THE STATION. THEY WANT TO KNOW WHAT HAPPENED TODAY,
...AND, I'M NOT REALLY SURE WHAT TO TELL THEM.
IT DOESN'T MATTER WHAT YOU TELL THEM, THEY WILL NOT BELIEVE THE TRUTH OF THE MATTER, SO TELL THEM WHAT THEY WILL ACCEPT.
THEY PROBABLY WONT BELIEVE THAT EITHER.
IT IS EASIER TO FORGET THAT WHICH YOU WILL NOT BELIEVE.
RIGHT,... I'LL SEE YOU AROUND THEN.
OF THAT, I HAVE NO DOUBT, MR. WHYTHE.

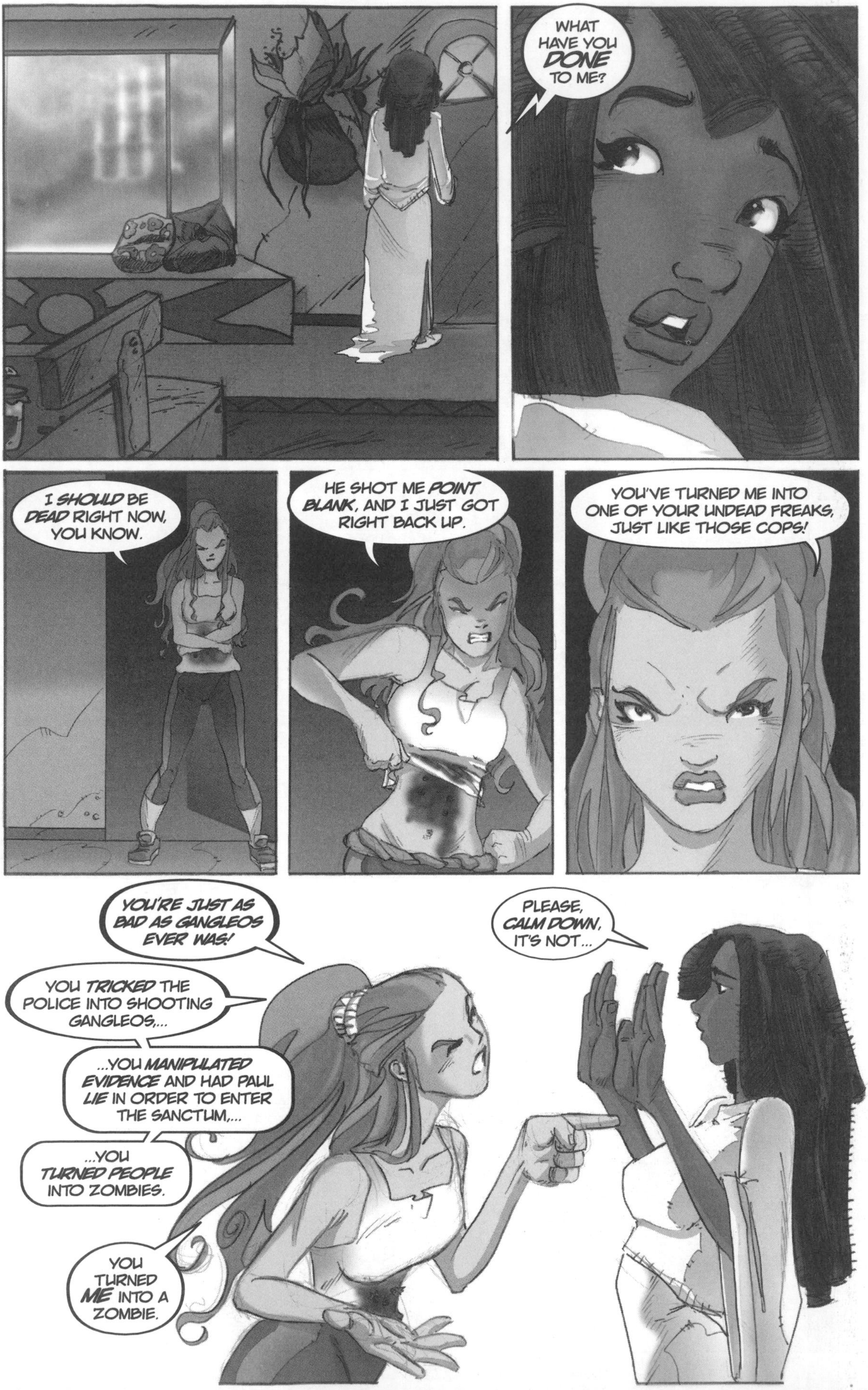
WHAT HAVE YOU DONE TO ME?
I SHOULD BE DEAD RIGHT NOW, YOU KNOW.
HE SHOT ME POINT BLANK, AND I JUST GOT RIGHT BACK UP.
YOU'VE TURNED ME INTO ONE OF YOUR UNDEAD FREAKS, JUST LIKE THOSE COPS!
YOU'RE JUST AS BAD AS GANGLEOS EVER WAS!
PLEASE, CALM DOWN, IT'S NOT...
YOU TRICKED THE POLICE INTO SHOOTING GANGLEOS,...
...YOU MANIPULATED EVIDENCE AND HAD PAUL LIE IN ORDER TO ENTER THE SANCTUM,...
...YOU TURNED PEOPLE INTO ZOMBIES.
YOU TURNED ME INTO A ZOMBIE.

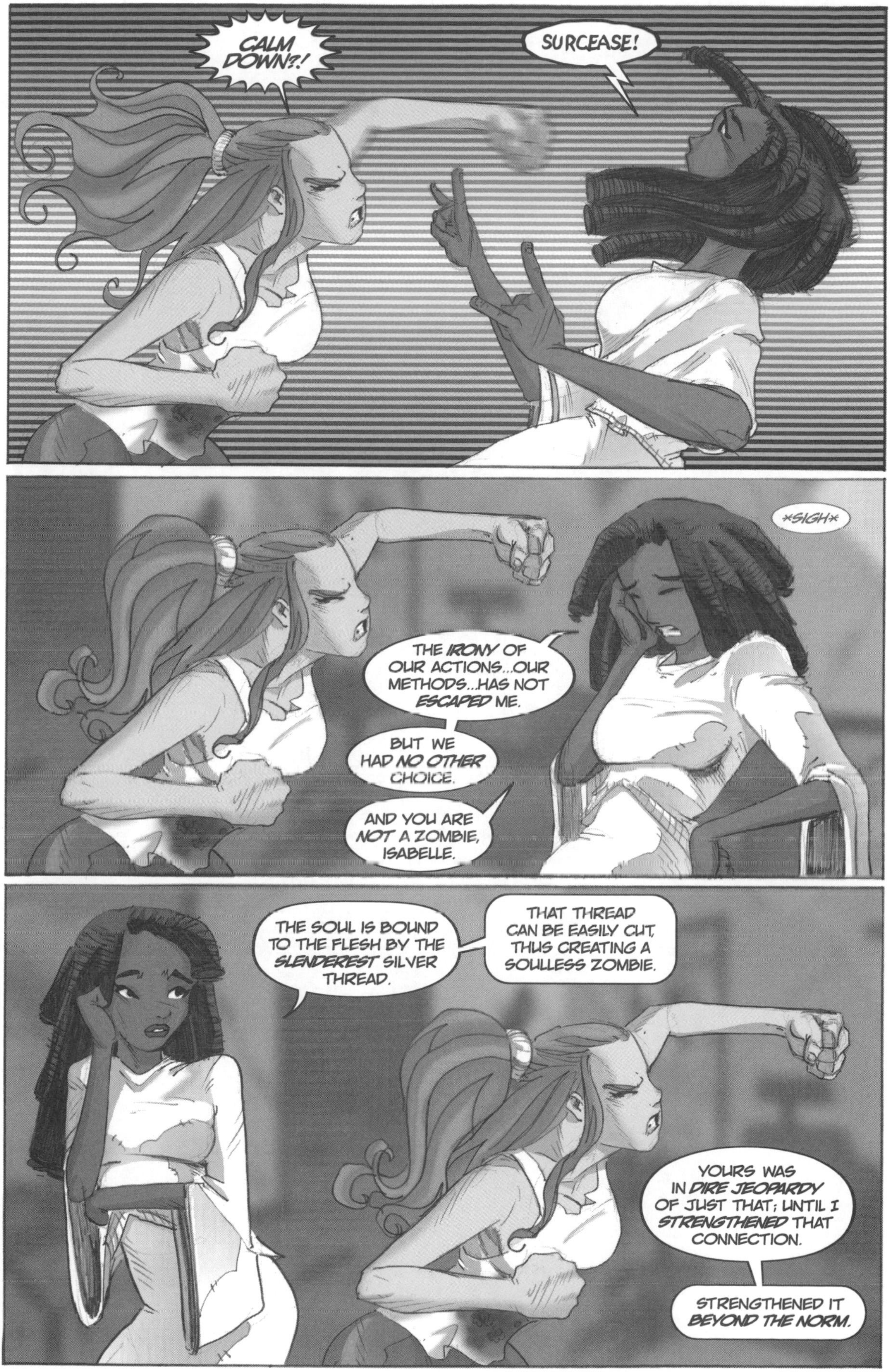
CALM DOWN?!
SURCEASE!
SIGH
THE IRONY OF OUR ACTIONS...OUR METHODS...HAS NOT ESCAPED ME.
BUT WE HAD NO OTHER CHOICE.
AND YOU ARE NOT A ZOMBIE, ISABELLE.
THE SOUL IS BOUND TO THE FLESH BY THE SLENDEREST SILVER THREAD.
THAT THREAD CAN BE EASILY CUT, THUS CREATING A SOULLESS ZOMBIE.
YOURS WAS IN DIRE JEOPARDY OF JUST THAT; UNTIL I STRENGTHENED THAT CONNECTION.
STRENGTHENED IT BEYOND THE NORM.

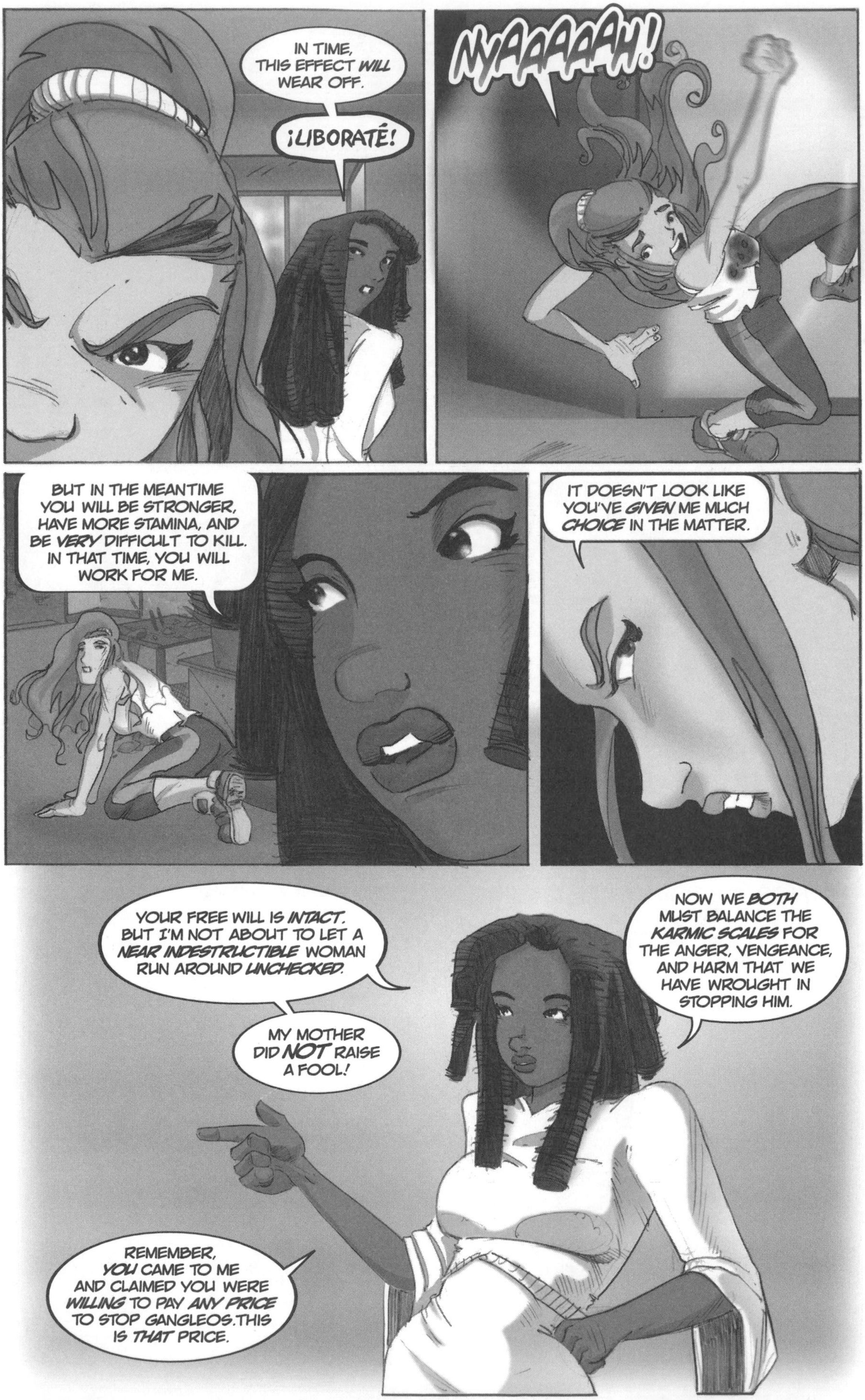
IN TIME, THIS EFFECT WILL WEAR OFF.
¡LIBORATÉ!
NYAAAAAH!
BUT IN THE MEANTIME YOU WILL BE STRONGER, HAVE MORE STAMINA, AND BE VERY DIFFICULT TO KILL. IN THAT TIME, YOU WILL WORK FOR ME.
IT DOESN'T LOOK LIKE YOU'VE GIVEN ME MUCH CHOICE IN THE MATTER.
YOUR FREE WILL IS INTACT. BUT I'M NOT ABOUT TO LET A NEAR INDESTRUCTIBLE WOMAN RUN AROUND UNCHECKED.
MY MOTHER DID NOT RAISE A FOOL!
NOW WE BOTH MUST BALANCE THE KARMIC SCALES FOR THE ANGER, VENGEANCE, AND HARM THAT WE HAVE WROUGHT IN STOPPING HIM.
REMEMBER, YOU CAME TO ME AND CLAIMED YOU WERE WILLING TO PAY ANY PRICE TO STOP GANGLEOS.THIS IS THAT PRICE.

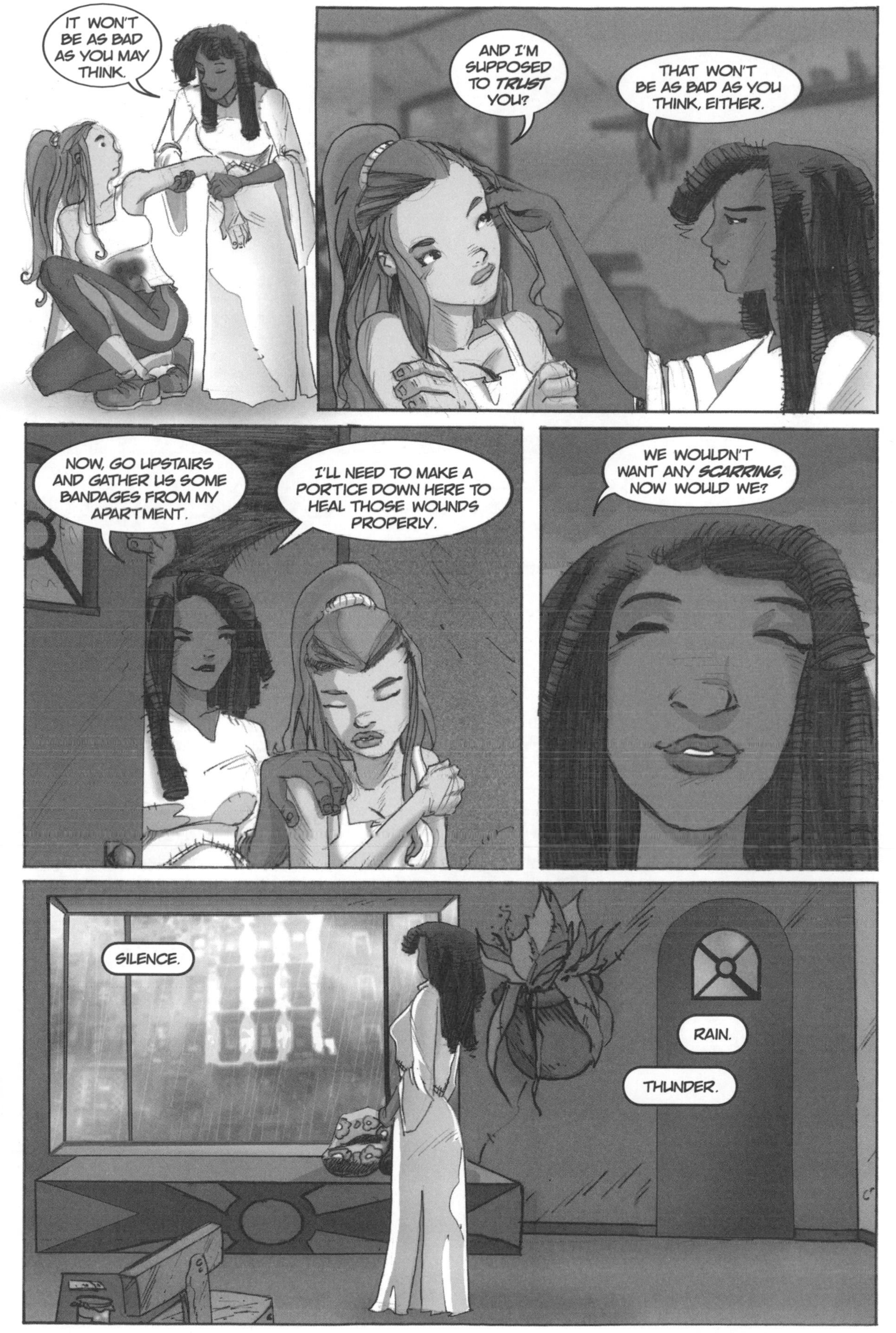
IT WON'T BE AS BAD AS YOU MAY THINK.
AND I'M SUPPOSED TO TRUST YOU?
THAT WON'T BE AS BAD AS YOU THINK, EITHER.
NOW, GO UPSTAIRS AND GATHER US SOME BANDAGES FROM MY APARTMENT.
I'LL NEED TO MAKE A PORTICE DOWN HERE TO HEAL THOSE WOUNDS PROPERLY.
WE WOULDN'T WANT ANY SCARRING, NOW WOULD WE?
SILENCE.
RAIN.
THUNDER.

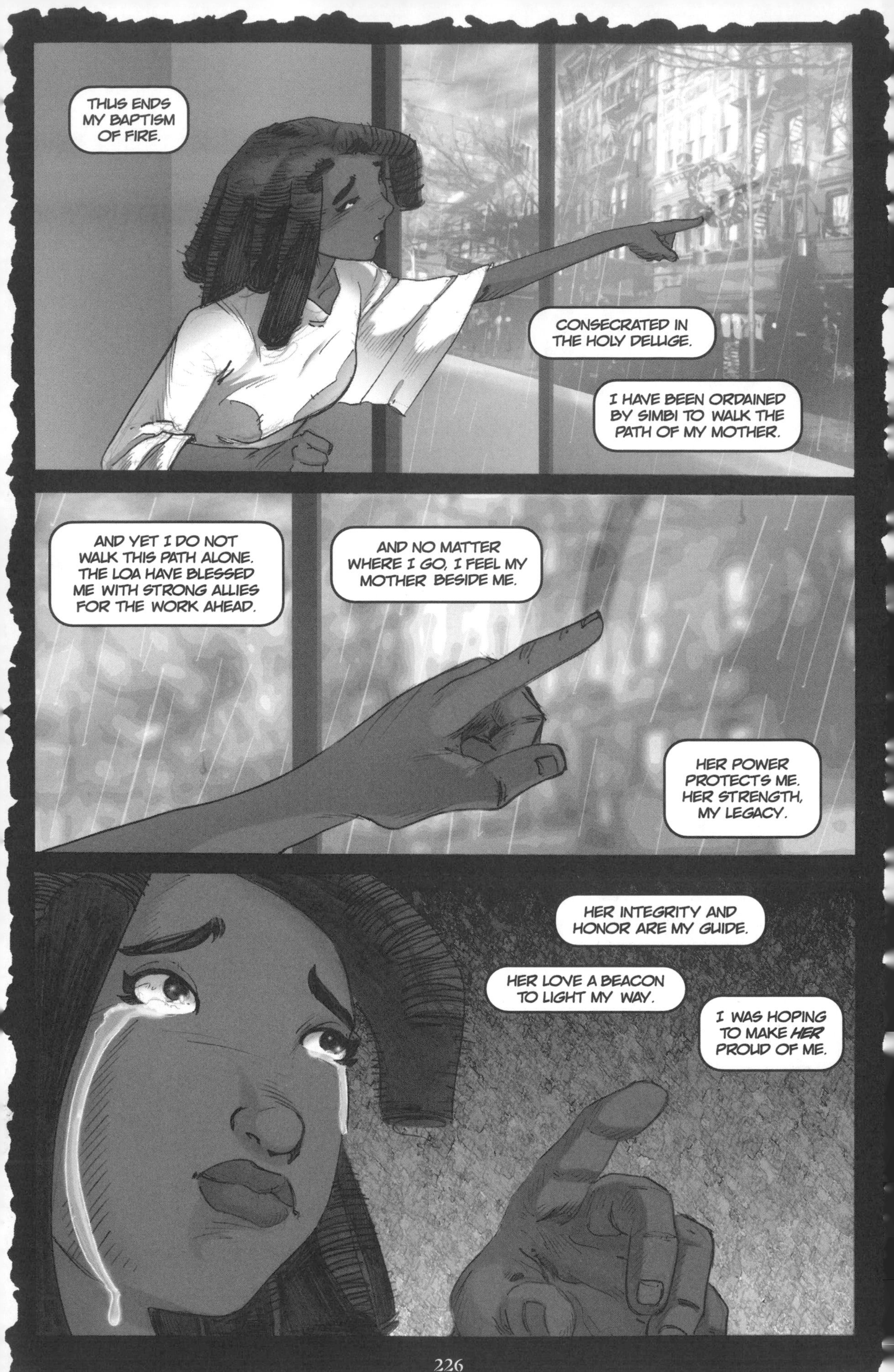
THUS ENDS MY BAPTISM OF FIRE.
CONSECRATED IN THE HOLY DELUGE.
I HAVE BEEN ORDAINED BY SIMBI TO WALK THE PATH OF MY MOTHER.
AND YET I DO NOT WALK THIS PATH ALONE. THE LOA HAVE BLESSED ME WITH STRONG ALLIES FOR THE WORK AHEAD.
AND NO MATTER WHERE I GO, I FEEL MY MOTHER BESIDE ME.
HER POWER PROTECTS ME. HER STRENGTH, MY LEGACY.
HER INTEGRITY AND HONOR ARE MY GUIDE.
HER LOVE A BEACON TO LIGHT MY WAY.
I WAS HOPING TO MAKE *HER* PROUD OF ME.

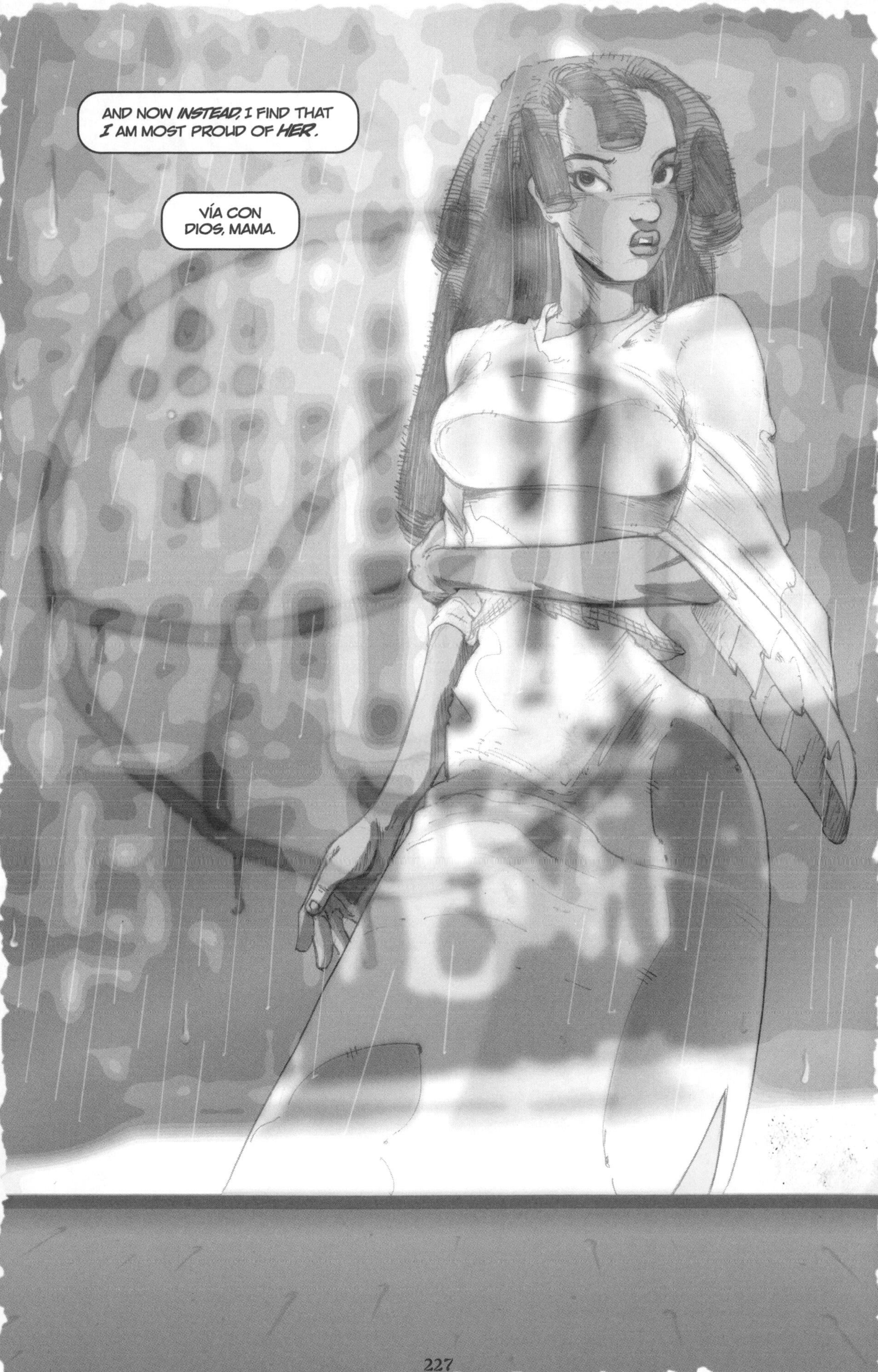
AND NOW *INSTEAD*, I FIND THAT *I* AM MOST PROUD OF ***HER***.
VÍA CON DIOS, MAMA.

Afterword

Truth is stranger than fiction.

On August 28, 2000, the *New York Post* greeted New Yorkers with a huge front-page headline: BLACK MAGIC WOMAN. Inside the paper devoted a two-page spread to the story of the NYPD's gruesome discovery of a variety of human remains in a Manhattan apartment. They found, among other things, a fully developed baby floating in a jar of formaldehyde, along with a wide assortment of religious paraphernalia. The former tenants were practitioners of Palo Mayombe—the cuban cousin of Santeria.[1]

Two months earlier *The Village Voice* reports that the father of a police officer on trial for brutally torturing a Haitian prisoner, carries "a handful of lavender rocks and holy water" as protection against Vodou retribution.

The same article also links both the mayor and police commissioner being diagnosed with colon cancer less than a month apart, as well as the unexpected collapse of the mayor's Senate bid, with a Vodou curse. [2]

You can't make this stuff up.

I never intended to write an afterward to *The Festering Season*, hoping that the book would speak for itself. In light of recent events, I have found myself repeatedly defending its content and subject matter. These events (which I will speak of later), have enlightened me as to how oblivious the rest of the country is to the police state that was New York City throughout the '90s.

Despite being set in the present, this book is a reaction to the political policies of Mayor Rudolph Giuliani's administration, and the police procedures that were a result. Despite his sudden international hero status, Giuliani has a local reputation for being an extremely divisive mayor who never hesitated from trampling his constituents's constitutional and civil rights. A man who has said on television on at least two occasions that "art is not protected under the First Amendment." And when asked what he has done for the black community replied, according to the Reverend Al Sharpton, "You're still alive aren't you?" The latter is most chilling when juxtaposed with the shooting deaths of three innocent black men by police officers in less than a year.

Now let me make it perfectly clear: I have no problem with police *officers*. Anyone who straps on a gun to protect the community for less pay than a McDonald's cashier deserves a great deal of respect. However, the NYPD's *procedures* were extremely politicized, and the police were under constant pressure to 'be more proactive,' and increase the number of arrests[3], despite a dramatic fall in the crime rate.

Keep in mind: at best, arrest statistics should mirror crime rates. People aren't supposed to be arrested unless they have (allegedly) committed a crime. And yet, in New York City during the '90s, arrests were at historically high levels when crime rates were at historical lows.

This was attributed to proactive police procedures. Procedures that included housing sweeps, in which the police would go through apartment buildings arresting anyone they found in the hallways (including in many instances, residents and guests) and charging them with criminal trespass. This gave the police the opportunity to see if these people were wanted or suspected of any other crimes. If they had no prior arrests, they were given the "opportunity" to plead guilty to the lesser crime of loitering, and be released immediately (while giving up the right to sue for false arrest).[4] Or they could spend days or even weeks sitting in a cell on Rikers Island awaiting a bail hearing. And given the state of overcrowded prisons, there's no guarantee you wouldn't be sharing a cell with a convicted rapist/murderer currently on trial for shanking his last cellmate at Sing Sing.

This is why I laugh when people use the expression 'If your innocent, you have nothing to be afraid of' as an argument for sacrificing civil rights to further the war against drugs/crime/terrorism/anarchy/un-American activities. It was this environment of presumption of guilt that inspired me to write this book.

For those of you unfamiliar with the events that transpired in New York during this time, the descriptions of inappropriate police behavior described in this book are based on actual events; with the sole exception of the three bewitched police officers coming to take Rene for a ride at the end of Chapter Three.

The death of Rene's mother is loosely based on the death of Amadou Diallo, who was gunned down in 1999 at his front door in a hail of 41 bullets fired by four police officers who mistook his billfold for a gun. Just prior to this incident, these four officers had spent several hours stopping and frisking every individual black man they found on the street that night[5] looking for a rapist/murderer whose only description was "a black male of unknown age, height, and build."

The death of Eduerdo Gangleos is loosely based on the death of Malcolm Fergeson, who was suing the police for harassment and false arrest when he was killed. During a housing sweep of an apartment building, Malcolm F.— as activists began to refer to him—was shot in the back of the head at close range while running UP a flight of stairs into a cul-de-sac of a building he was allegedly intimately familiar with, "in an attempt to escape police"[6]

Paul's tale of the security guard on pages 104-105, and the riot that ensues at August's funeral (pages 34-37) are based on the death of Patrick Dorismond. A 30-year-old security guard, and applicant to the police academy,

Dorismond was randomly approached by four undercover officers wanting to purchase drugs. When Dorismond told them to "F* off," the police officers picked a fight with him. [3,7] The end result was that the four officers shot the unarmed Dorismond "in self defense." When Dorismond's family requested there be NO police presence at the funeral, the police showed up in riot gear; arresting mourners, onlookers, and press alike. [8]

The story of the Ivy League interns from page 102 was only marginally reported in the New York media. I first heard about it from ABC affiliate Channel 7 news when the interns sued the NYPD for federal civil-rights violations. *The Village Voice* mentioned it only in passing in an article on racial profiling. [5]

The Puerto Rican Day Parade in the summer of 2000 was the basis of the incident cited on page 103, which was videotaped by many participants—and widely reported by every local newspaper and television station—involved a large group of men who were groping women and trying to pull their clothes off. Despite multiple complaints to police officers at the parade, the police took no action, citing, after the fact, fear of bad publicity. Some arrests were made in the following weeks as a result of the videotapes *after* a major public outcry. The best spin that Giuliani could come up with was to ban the sale of alcohol at street fairs, despite the fact that the incident took place at a parade where no food or alcohol was sold.

Other items of factual interest from *The Festering Season* include the actions of Rene's landlord, which is based on the actions of multiple landlords to force long-time rent-controlled tenants out of their homes in order to attract more profitable renters.

Or the fact that Washington Square Park is under constant police video surveillance as a "crime deterrent." This is odd in that most residents are unaware of this surveillance. This begs the question, how can *covert* surveillance deter crime? One protester was promptly arrested when he began handing out flyers and hanging signs informing people their every move and action within the public park was being videotaped. He was charged with littering. [9]

The NYPD Cult Task Force does in fact exist, but they do not have any problems with Vodou or Santeria as these are legitimate and widely practiced religions in New York City. These religions do have problems obtaining permits to sacrifice live animals from the ASPCA and New York Health Department, because they have neither a centralized location of worship, nor a recognized organized infrastructure. As a result raids to prevent sacrifices are not unheard of. [10]

Another important inspiration for this book was the first summer of mosquito spraying in 1999 to combat the West Nile Virus, which is particularly harmful to the very young, the elderly, and those with compromised immune systems. After several virus-related deaths, the city, and surrounding counties and states, began a massive spraying effort that covered the entire metropolitan area with the insecticide Malathion. When the press and public posed questions concerning the health risks involved, the city said the federal government had assured them that it posed no safety issues to humans. The federal government immediately came out and said this was untrue. They said Malathion was the most effective insecticide for mosquitos, but that it did pose a health threat, especially to the very young, the elderly, and those with compromised immune systems.

The Festering Season after 9/11

The events of September 11, 2001, demonstrated what it means to be a hero, to serve and protect. The New York and Port Authority police, court officers, fire department, and even Mayor Giuliani himself, were all at their best, going above and beyond what was expected. For a short, shining moment the entire city set aside politics and prejudice and pulled together as a community. It is this moment that all other actions and activities will be compared.

If there is one thing I would like everyone to know, is that the script for this book was completed a full year before the events of September 11. The art was nearly halfway complete as of that date. Given that fact, the undertones of a religious fanatic launching a low-tech biological attack in order to wipe out the city is eerily disconcerting, even to myself, the writer.

Despite a small amount of criticism about portraying the NYPD in a bad light, and the insensitivity of depicting a biochemical attack, I decided NOT to make any major changes to the script. I did however make a few minor changes to reflect the current political landscape. Hernesto's nosiness is now a result of the attorney general's call to be more vigilant.

Originally there was a small statement concerning the Giuliani administration's attempt to criminalize homelessness. That has now transformed into an observation on the failure of his highly touted workfare program, which artificially created menial labor city jobs for the unemployed. These jobs evaporated shortly after the massive city deficit and national recession that was a result of the attack.[11]

However, any concerns I had over the tone of the book, and the criticism of political policies and police procedures have now evaporated. It didn't take long for Rudy to fall back into old habits. He caused an uproar when he contemplated ways to overturn term limits so he could seize the mayoralty for a third term (even though a poll showed an overwhelming majority of New Yorkers were this action). And upon leaving office, he sequestered all of his administration's and cabinet member's official documents in a privately owned, heavily guarded storage facility. A direct violation of state law governing public documents, as well as 300 years of city tradition.

The police too have come under close scrutiny. One Police Plaza has once again embraced procedures that police departments across the country have rejected and openly criticized as ethnic profiling.[12] And officers have even openly videotaped legally authorized political demonstrations in violation of state law.[13]

Now the threats to ALL of our constitutional and civil rights comes not from City Hall, but the federal government itself. With the passing of the USA Patriot Act, the Bush administration has raised the assumption of guilt to an all new level, where even the execution of our First Amendment constitutional right to freedom of expression may be construed as an "un-American activity;"[14] and the government can label you as a potential terrorist sympathizer because of the books you buy and read.[15]

But don't worry; if you're innocent, you have nothing to fear. *Right?*

Footnotes

1: **New York Post**, August 28, 2000; *"Black-Magic Woman: Cops Haunted by the Baby in the Jar"* by Laura Italiano and Maria Mavave; pages 4-5

2: **The Village Voice**, June 20, 2000; *"Police Brutality and Voodoo Justice: Rudy, Race, and Religion in the Wake of Louima and Dorismond"* by Peter Noel; pages 51-54

3: **The Village Voice**, April 18, 2000; *"Are We in a Police State?: Nervous Cops Pull Triggers"* by Nat Hentoff; page 42

4: **The Village Voice**, March 14, 2000; *"Giuliani Justice: Arresting the Innocent"* by Nat Hentoff; page 38

5: **The Village Voice**, March 21, 2000; "Portraits in Racial Profiling" by Peter Noel, Pages 46-51

6: **The Village Voice**, February 22, 2000; *"Malcolm F's Struggle"* by Peter Noel pages 46-48

7: **The Village Voice**, April 11, 2000; *"Who Will Indict the Lawbreaking Mayor?: When Cops Act to Create Crimes"* by Nat Hentoff page 41

8: **The Village Voice**, April, 2000; *"Mourning Rush: Cops Bring Tension to the Dorismond Funeral"* by Leslie George

9: **The Village Voice**, April 3, 2001; "Shutter Bugged: New York's Hidden Cameras are Watching" by Geoffrey Gray, page 35

10: **Santeria: The Religion** by Migene Gonzales-Wippler; pages 152-154; ©1999 Llewellyn Publications

11: **The Village Voice**, February 19, 2002; *"Rich Man, Poor People"* by Sharon Lerner, page 47

12: **The Village Voice**, December 11, 2001; *"NYPD Won't Say No: Police Here Adopt Ethnic Profiling Their Western Counterparts Reject"* by Chisun Lee, page 29

13: **The Village Voice**, February 19, 2002; *"Spies in Blue: NY Cops Pushed Legal Limits in WEF Protests"* by Esther Kaplan, page 29

14: **The Village Voice**, February 19, 2002; *"J. Edgar Hoover Lives!: FBI knocking at Your Door"* by Nat Hentoff, page 37

15: **The Village Voice**, March 5, 2002; *"Big John Wants Your Reading List: Has the Attorney General Been Reading Franz Kafka?"* by Nat Hentoff, page 27

Requiem

Kevin 'Stickman' Tinsley has worked in comics and publishing for the past 15 years. An expert in prepress and desktop publishing, Tinsley's professional mantra is: "Any job worth doing well, is worth doing yourself." This sentiment, which he encourages in others, is evident in his first book, **Digital Prepress for Comic Books**. "I believe American comics are on the cusp of a significant and lasting change for the better" says Stickman. "Of course I've believed that for the last two decades; so one of these years I'm bound to be right!"

Tim Smith 3 was born in East Cleveland, and currently lives in New York City, where he has worked for such companies as Marvel Comics to Deutsche Inc., as well as numerous websites, and independent publishing companies. Madly addicted to video games and comics, Tim rarely sleeps, but when he does, is not seen for days. Tim dedicates his work on this book to: Momma and Poppa Smith; my twin sisters Devon and Ashley; all my family, especially Beady, Janet, and Eleanor; Sylvia, the ever loving wife; my friends; to the memory of Shrimati Sitadevi and Shri Bhagwandas C. Rupani; and a special dedication to the life of Diana Garret, you are loved and will be missed.

Deborah S. Creighton is an online editor for a major newspaper in New York. She wanted her name first in this list, but the egomanical Stickman refused. See if you can find her in the book (hint, check page 59). She's the editor of **Digital Prepress for Comic Books.**

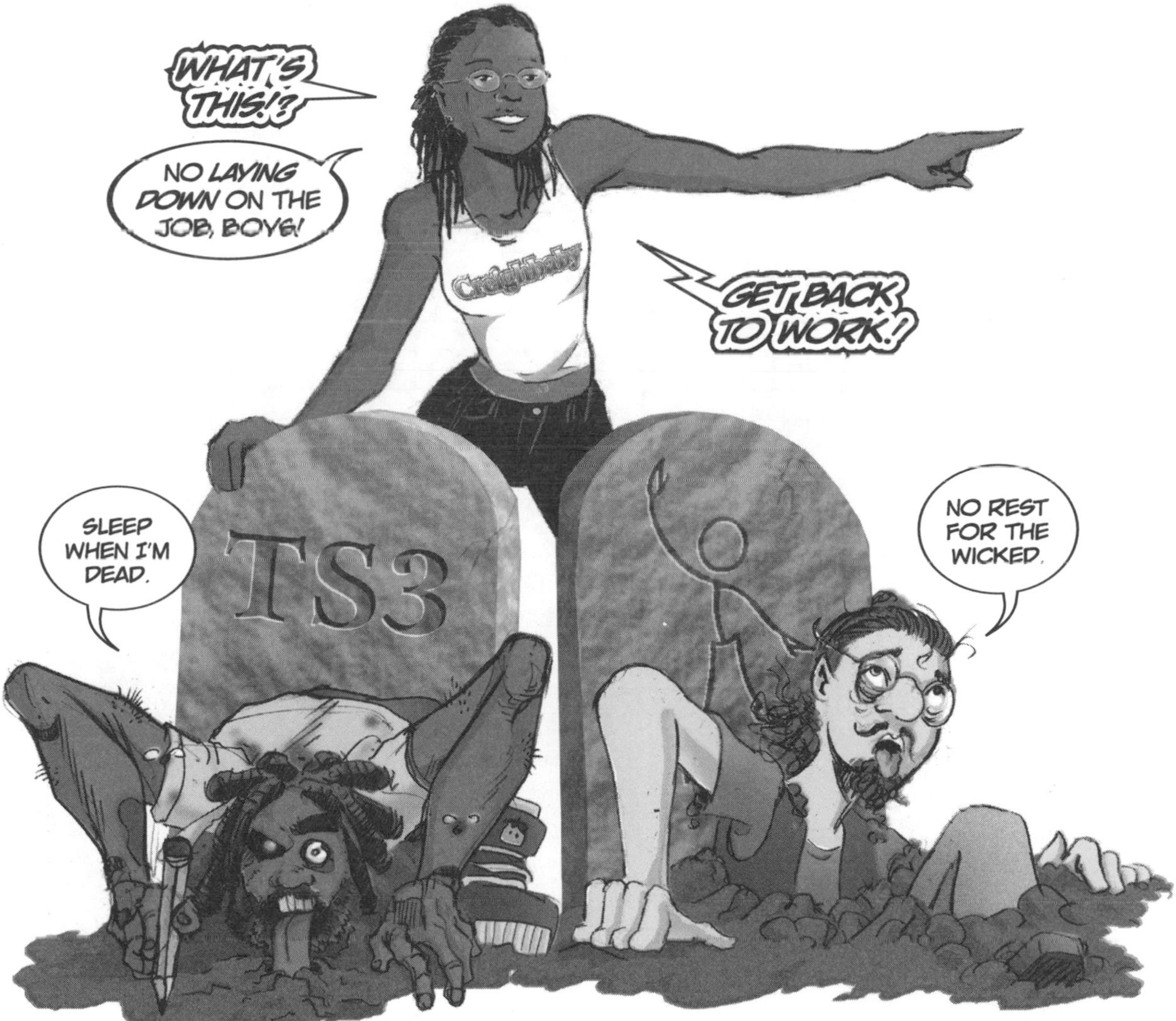
WHAT'S THIS!?
NO LAYING DOWN ON THE JOB, BOYS!
GET BACK TO WORK!
SLEEP WHEN I'M DEAD.
NO REST FOR THE WICKED.
TS3

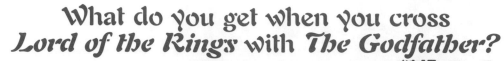

What do you get when you cross *Lord of the Rings* with *The Godfather?*

STONEHAVEN™

Milk Cartons & Dog Biscuits™

Dan Parsons has come to Stonehaven seeking his runaway daughter, Melody. When the police seem unable to assist him, he is forced to seek out the aid of a private investigator; a half elf by the name of Victor Jardine. They quickly stumble upon a fresh lead, and come to realize that Melody's life is in immediate danger from those she believes to be friends.

Meanwhile, Tong enforcer Meili Mau must contend with micro-management and power plays from the uppermost echelon of the crime family; as she is ordered to hunt down an anthropamorphic killer stalking the streets of Chinatown *before* the police find it.

Fate and circumstance make for strange bedfellows as these apparent random events crash together in the stunning climax.

234

The *Stonehaven* series is an adventure drama set in a modern day fantasy realm where elves, and dwarves, and ogres live side by side with humans in one of the largest cities in the world. The series of graphic novels feature an ensemble cast and an unusual meld of genres and stories.

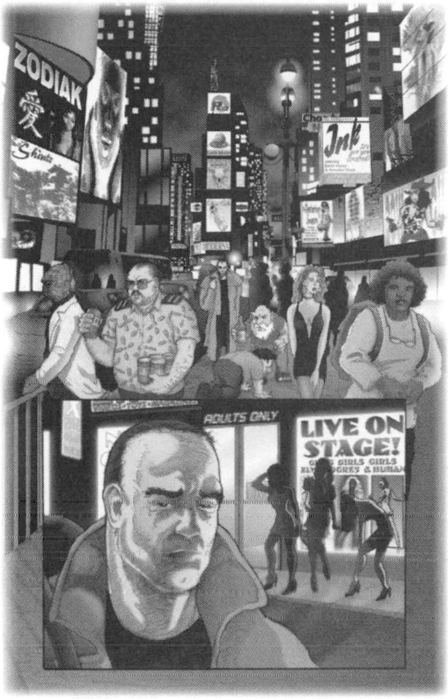
ZODIAK
ADULTS ONLY
LIVE ON STAGE!

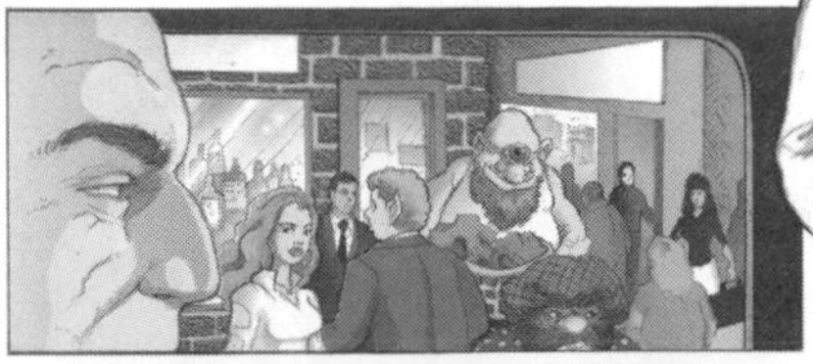

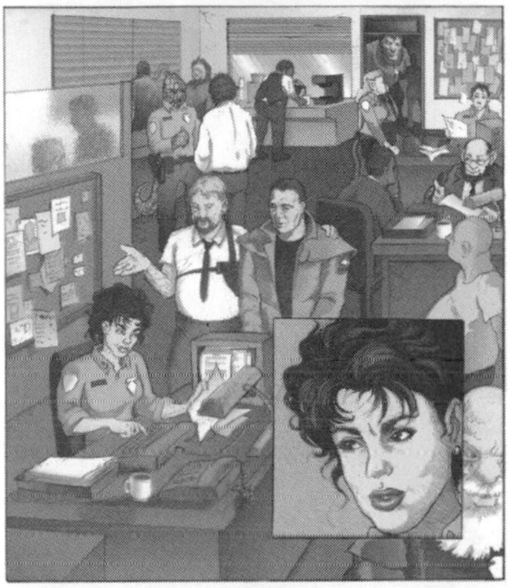

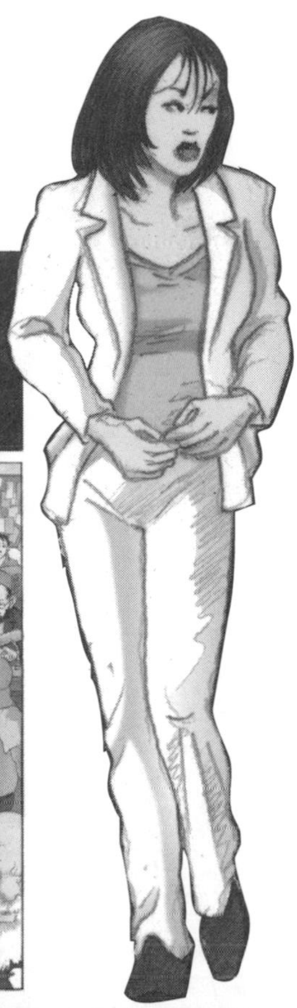

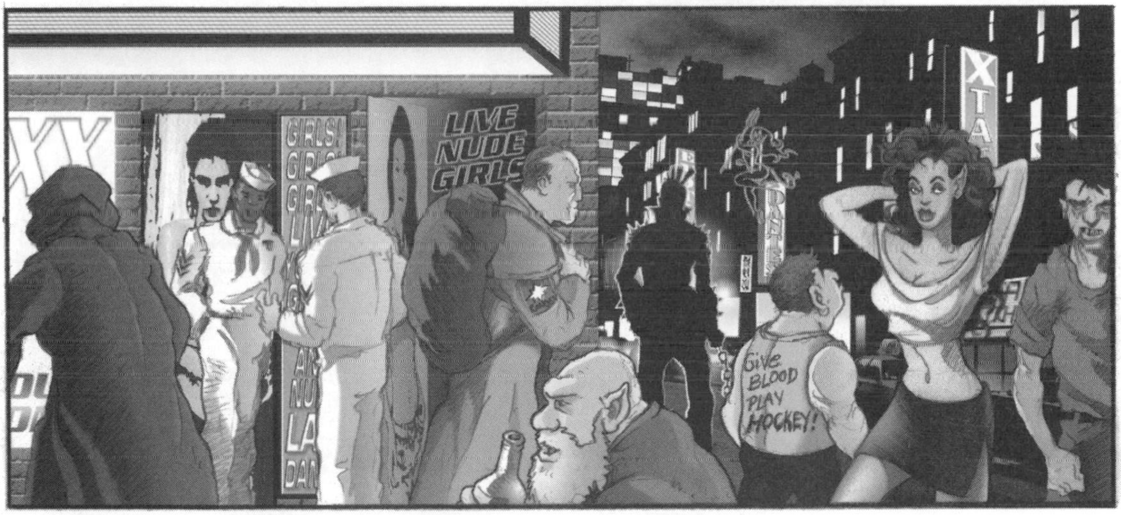
LIVE NUDE GIRLS
GIVE BLOOD PLAY HOCKEY!

A 216-page graphic novel spectacularly rendered in duotone color. Available in bookstores nationwide in paperback and hardcover editions. Brought to you by:

STICKMAN GRAPHICS

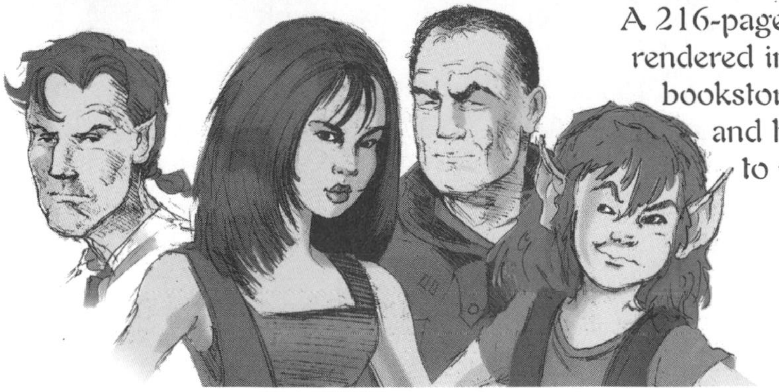

STONEHAVEN™
Subterranean Hearts™

Nheserteri Solistara Rieca, a magic student at the Stonehaven University, is in desperate need of a summer job. With the help of an advisor, she gains employment at Dwarkin Exterminators, which has recently lost one of their own magic users. As Teri becomes aquainted with the job and her new co-workers, she never suspects the destiny that awaits her in the bowels of the city.

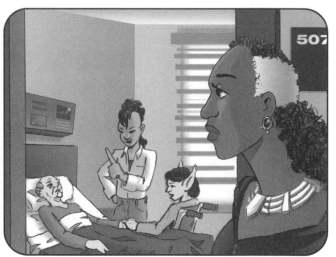

Victor Jardine has troubles of his own. The search for a missing grandfather has led to a series of mysterious disappearances in and around the subways and sewers of Stonehaven. And the little brother of Victor's new girlfriend may hold a vital key to the puzzle...if he can only keep Meili Mau from killing the boy first!

For more detailed information for this and all of our books, visit our website at *www.stickmangraphics.com*.

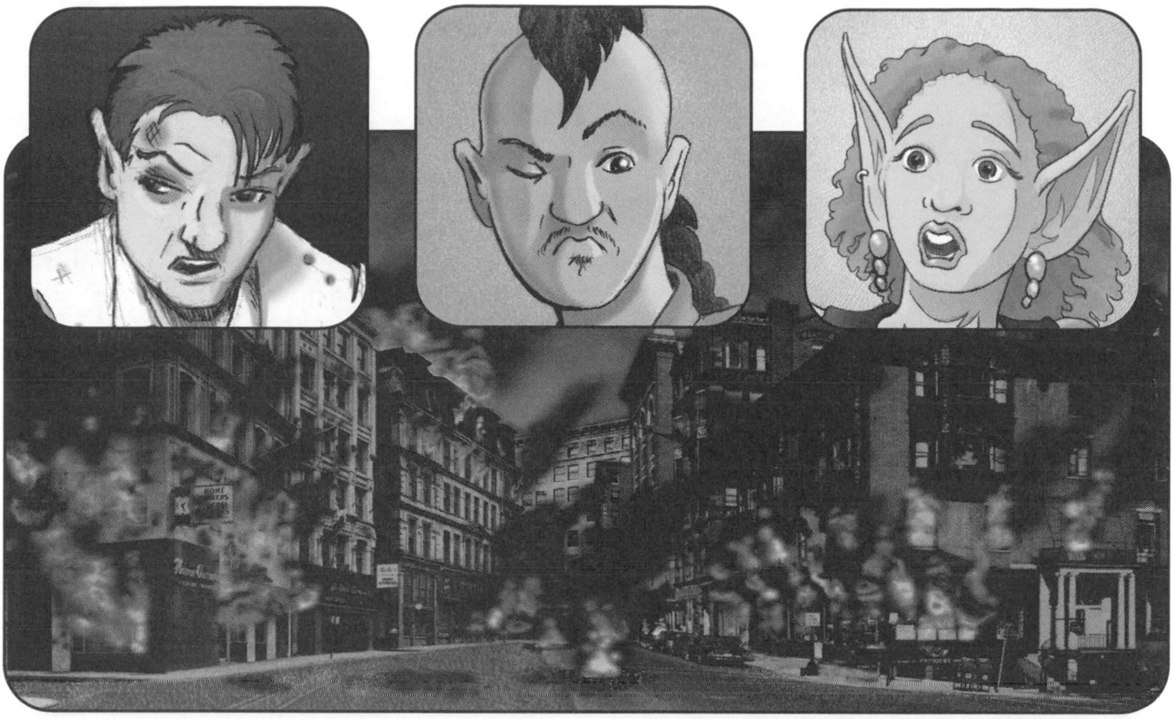

Both parties are soon to learn that danger lurks for all beneath the streets of Stonehaven as a battle of will, endurance, and magic brings about a disastrous climax which will have repurcussions for all who survive.

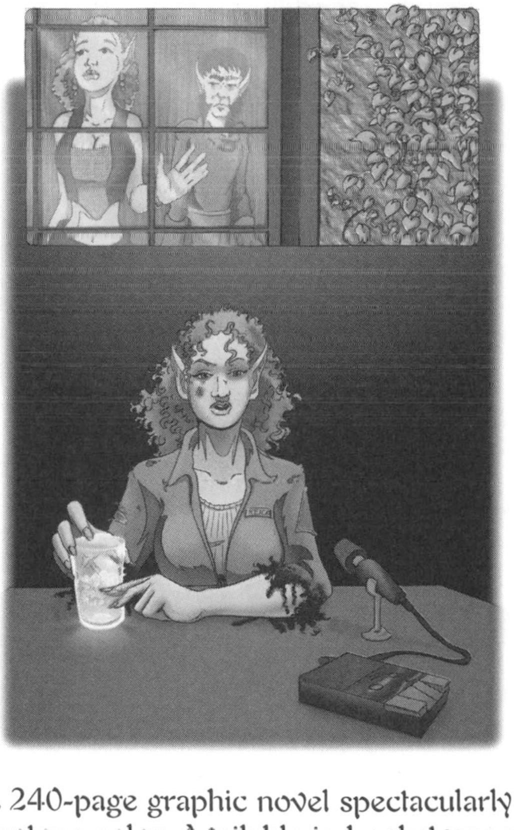

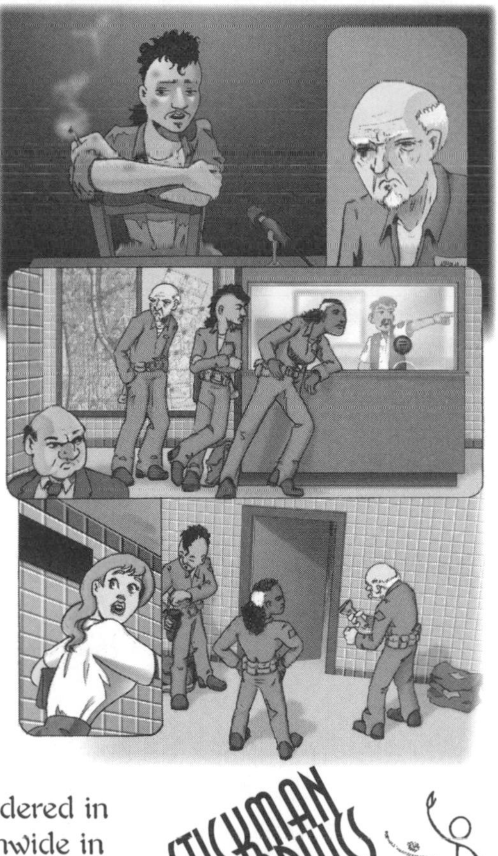

A 240-page graphic novel spectacularly rendered in duotone color. Available in bookstores nationwide in paperback and hardcover editions. Brought to you by:

STICKMAN GRAPHICS

THE DEFINITIVE DESKTOP PRODUCTION GUIDE FOR COMIC BOOK PUBLISHING!

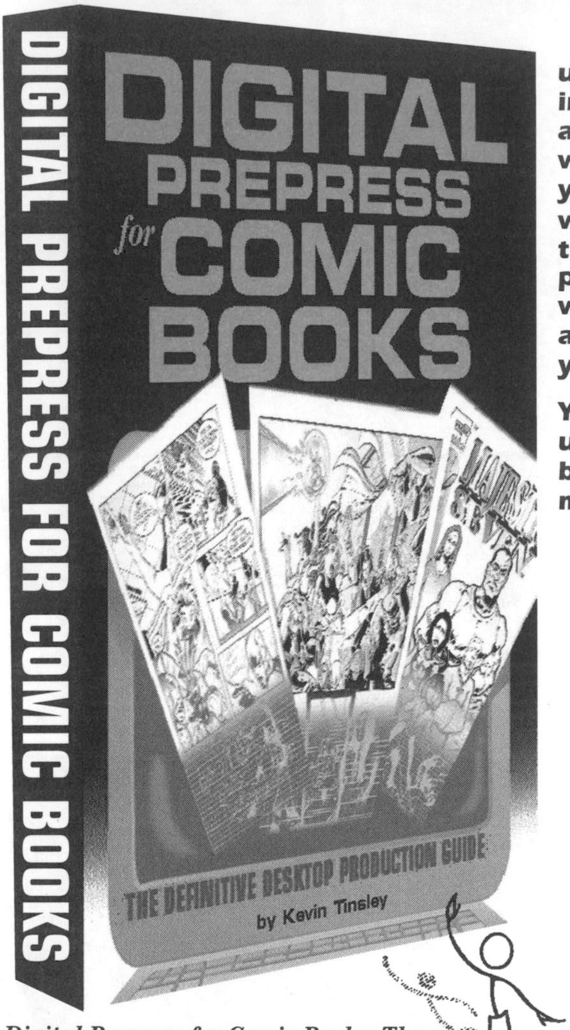
DIGITAL PREPRESS FOR COMIC BOOKS
DIGITAL PREPRESS for COMIC BOOKS
THE DEFINITIVE DESKTOP PRODUCTION GUIDE
by Kevin Tinsley

Digital Prepress for Comic Books: The Definitive Desktop Production Guide
by Kevin Tinsley $36.95 US $54.95 CAN
ISBN 0-9675423-0-8 LCCN 99-091203

On sale nationwide in all major book stores and comic shoppes located near you! Also available at major online book sellers.

This book is the ultimate reference used by professionals throughout the industry. With over 300 illustrations, and detailed instructions, this manual will provide the answers and solutions you will need to know to get your artwork off of the drawing board and into the hands of a printer. Whether you are planning to publish your own comic, or want to provide the best reproducible art possible, this item is a must have for your professional library.

You will learn the computer procedures used by virtually every major comic book companies production department. Including:

- Scanning. Learn how to make the best possible scan of line art, and look out for potential trouble spots in the inking process.
- Separations. Find out what printers look for in computer coloring, and how to achieve accurate printable colors.
- Lettering. Take all the guesswork out of properly positioned, digital lettering.
- Trapping. The secrets of solving mis-registration in multiple applications are revealed.
- Covers. Everything you need to know about stripping logos into art work and applying special effects for dynamic eye-catching covers.

'*Digital Prepress* is the best desktop production guide for comics around.' *-The Book Reader*

'Recommended for anyone working in comics!'
"★★★★" *-Computer Publishing Magazine*

'This is an extraordinarily helpful introduction for anyone planning to print a magazine.' *-Comics Buyer's Guide*

'An excellent guide to any comic book professional .... It is a must have book.' *-Comics Corner*

For more detailed information, and complete review,
visit our website at **www.stickmangraphics.com** and order online.